PROPAGANDA AND MASS PERSUASION

A Historical Encyclopedia,
1500 to the Present

PROPAGANDA AND MASS PERSUASION

A Historical Encyclopedia,

1500 to the Present

Nicholas J. Cull
David Culbert
David Welch

.

A B C  C L I O

Santa Barbara, California   ·   Denver, Colorado   ·   Oxford, England

Library of Congress Cataloging-in-Publication Data
Cull, Nicholas John.
  Propaganda and mass persuasion : a historical encyclopedia, 1500 to the present / Nicholas J. Cull, David Culbert, David Welch.
    p.   cm.
  Includes bibliographical references and index.
  ISBN 1-57607-820-5 (hardcover : alk. paper)—ISBN 1-57607-434-X (e-book)
    1. Propaganda—Encyclopedias.   2. Propaganda—History.   I. Culbert, David Holbrook.   II. Welch, David, 1950–   III. Title.

HM1231.C85   2003
303.3'75—dc21

2003009513

07   06   05   04   03   10 9 8 7 6 5 4 3 2 1

This book is also available on the World Wide Web as an eBook. Visit abc-clio.com for details.

ABC-CLIO, Inc.
130 Cremona Drive, P.O. Box 1911
Santa Barbara, California 93116-1911
This book is printed on acid-free paper.

Manufactured in the United States of America

For Philip M. Taylor

CONTRIBUTORS

Stephen Badsey
Lecturer in History
Department of War Studies
Royal Military Academy
Sandhurst, UK

David Birmingham
Professor Emeritus of History
University of Kent at Canterbury, UK

Livia Bornigia
Lecturer in Communications
University of St. Thomas
Houston, TX, United States

Susan Carruthers
Associate Professor of History
Rutgers University
Newark, NJ, United States

Steven Casey
Lecturer in International History
London School of Economics, UK

Dan Caspi
Professor of Communication
Ben-Gurion University of the Negev, Israel

Luisa Cigognetti
Chief of Audio-Visual Department
Instituto Ferruccio Parri
Bologna, Italy

Robert Cole
Professor of History

Utah State University
Logan, UT, United States

Brian Collins
Department of History
Louisiana State University
Baton Rouge, LA, United States

Mark Connelly
Lecturer in History
University of Kent at Canterbury, UK

Daniel Cooper
Humanities Programme
University of Leicester, UK

Patrick Day
Senior Lecturer
Department of Policy, Cultural and Social
    Studies in Education
University of Waikato, New Zealand

David Ellwood
Professore Associato
Insegna di Storia delle Relazioni
    Internazionalli
University of Bologna, Italy

Karsten Fledelius
Lektor
Institute for Film Media Studies
University of Copenhagen, Denmark

Karen M. Ford
Lecturer in Political Theory

Department of Government
University of Manchester, UK

Dina Iordanova
Reader in the History of Film
Department of History of Art
University of Leicester, UK

Samantha Jones
Humanities Programme
University of Leicester, UK

Mark Kristmanson
Centre for American Studies
University of Leicester, UK

Fred Krome
Adjunct Professor of Judaic Studies
University of Cincinnati
Cincinnati, OH, United States

Barak Kushner
Assistant Professor of Eastern Asian Studies
Davidson College
Davidson, NC, United States

Daniel Leab
Professor of History
Seton Hall University
South Orange, NJ, United States

James A. Leith
Professor Emeritus of History
Queens University
Kingston, Ontario, Canada

Luke McKernan
Head of Information
British Universities Film and Video
   Council
London, UK

Bryan Mann
Department of History
University of Leicester, UK

Rana Mitter
Lecturer in Chinese History
Oxford University, UK

Tara S. Nair
Entrepreneurship Development Institute of
   India
Ahmedabad, India

Nicholas Pronay
Professor Emeritus
Institute of Communications Studies
University of Leeds, UK

Graham Roberts
Senior Lecturer in Communication Arts
Institute of Communications Studies
University of Leeds, UK

Richard Robinson
Reader Emeritus
School of History
University of Birmingham, UK

Rainer Rother
Head of Film Department
Deutsches Historisches Museum
Berlin, Germany

Pierre Sorlin
Professor Emeritus of Sociology of
   Audiovisual Media
University of Paris III, France

Todd Swift
Poet and Visiting Lecturer
Budapest University (ELTE), Hungary

Elizabeth Tacey
Humanities Programme
University of Leicester, UK

Philip M. Taylor
Professor of International Communications
Institute of Communications Studies
University of Leeds, UK

James Vaughan
Lecturer in International History
Department of International Politics
University of Wales
Aberystwyth, UK

CONTENTS

PROPAGANDA AND MASS PERSUASION
A Historical Encyclopedia, 1500 to the Present

PREFACE

This book is designed to provide an accessible survey of the history of propaganda from 1500 to the present. After a historical introduction by David Welch outlining the development of propaganda, the encyclopedia presents more than 250 entries. These include geographic entries examining a country such as Britain or Portugal or—where the propaganda history is either less clearly delineated along national lines or the scholarship to date in English is more limited—a region such as Scandinavia or Latin America. We have tried to be as geographically comprehensive as possible. Case-study entries present events or movements, from abolitionism to Zionism. Technique entries deal with a particular method, such as posters, portraiture, or music; film and radio entries both have multiple subdivisions, reflecting the special role of these media in twentieth-century propaganda. Concept entries define and explain terms used by and about propagandists: black propaganda, brainwashing, and so forth. The long entry "Propaganda, Definitions of" offers multiple definitions of the term.

This encyclopedia includes entries devoted to individuals connected with propaganda, from Martin Luther to Osama bin Laden, as well as entries for some of the key institutions of propaganda—such as the Office of War Information (OWI) in the United States during World War II—and some of the best-known documents and artifacts of propaganda (such as the film *Casablanca* and the novel *Uncle Tom's Cabin*). Each entry contains suggestions for further reading, which generally also served as the chief sources for quotations and factual or other details within the entry. Most propaganda agencies—for example, the CIA or the BBC—are better known by their initials than their full names and are therefore listed that way.

This book could not have been written without the help of many people. The most important has been Bob Neville, our editor at ABC-CLIO in Oxford, without whom the project would surely have lost momentum. We are also grateful to editors at ABC-CLIO in Denver, Susan McRory, who did much to bring this volume to completion speedily and efficiently, and to Scott Horst, who worked hard to ensure a high standard of illustrations for this volume. Books that were helpful in delimiting the scope of this work include Robert Cole's *Propaganda in Twentieth Century War and Politics: An Annotated Bibliography* (London: Scarecrow, 1996). As with all such projects, this work has required the support of our families. Nick Cull is particularly grateful to his late grandfather, Bernard O'Callaghan, whose influence on this volume is especially apparent in the entries for "British Empire," "Internationale," and "Zinoviev Letter."

This book has, of course, relied on the expertise of a team of international contributors. The editors are grateful not only to the colleagues and friends who have submitted entries for this volume but also to those who used their specialized knowledge to check entries written by others. Special mention should be made of Dr. Mark Cornwall, Prof. Donald Denoon, Dr. Selim Deringel, Leen Engelen, Dr. Elizabeth Fox, Dr. Ewa Mazierska, Dr. José Ortiz Garza, and Prof. James Schwoch, whose suggestions were much appreciated. Three colleagues at the University of Leicester, Stuart Ball, Phillip Lindley, and Aubrey Newman, have also been of great help. The original idea for this volume came from Professors Nicholas Pronay and Philip M. Taylor of the Institute of Communication Studies at the University of Leeds. Phil Taylor's work is frequently cited in the entries that follow, and in recognition of his unique contribution to the field of propaganda history, the editors affectionately dedicate this book to him.

Nicholas J. Cull
David Culbert
David Welch

INTRODUCTION:
PROPAGANDA IN HISTORICAL PERSPECTIVE

The following quotation serves as a good starting point: "Propaganda is a much maligned and often misunderstood word. The layman uses it to mean something inferior or even despicable. The word propaganda always has a bitter after taste." It is singularly appropriate that these words should have been spoken by Joseph Goebbels in March 1933, immediately after being appointed to head the Ministry of Popular Enlightenment and Propaganda in Hitler's first government. It is arguable that it was in this role that Goebbels was to do more than most to ensure and perpetuate this bitter "after taste." Goebbels continued: "But if you examine propaganda's most secret causes, you will come to different conclusions: then there will be no more doubting that the propagandist must be the man with the greatest knowledge of souls. I cannot convince a single person of the necessity of something unless I get to know the soul of that person, unless I understand how to pluck the string in the harp of his soul that must be made to sound" (Welch 2002, 26). It is supremely ironic that Goebbels should set himself the mission of rescuing propaganda from such misconceptions.

Propaganda was not "invented" by Goebbels, although it is largely as a result of Nazi propaganda that the term has come to have such pejorative associations. The word "propaganda" continues to imply something sinister; synonyms for propaganda frequently include "lies," "deceit," and "brainwashing." In recent years unfavorable comparisons have been made with spin doctors and the manner in which they (allegedly) control the image of politicians and refract the political agenda to simplistic sound bites. Thus, a widely held belief suggests that propaganda is a cancer on the body politic that manipulates our thoughts and actions and should be avoided at all costs.

Is this really the case? If so, should we avoid the word? It is my contention that such assumptions should be challenged and that propaganda in and of itself is not necessarily evil. The ancient Greeks, for example, regarded persuasion as a form of rhetoric and recognized that logic and reason were necessary to communicate ideas successfully. Throughout history those who govern have always attempted to influence the way in which the governed viewed the world. If propaganda is to be a useful concept, it first has to be divested of its pejorative connotations. Propaganda is not simply what the other group does while one's own group concentrates on disseminating information or generating publicity. Modern dictatorships have never felt the need to shun the word as have democracies. Accordingly, the Nazis had a Ministry of Popular Enlightenment and Propaganda and the Soviets a Propaganda Committee of the Communist Party, whereas the British had a Ministry of Information and the Americans an Office of War Information.

Although the scale on which propaganda is practiced has increased dramatically in the twentieth century, the origin of the word can be traced back to the Reformation, when the spiritual and ecclesiastical unity of Europe was shattered and the medieval Roman Catholic Church lost its hold on the northern countries. During the ensuing struggle between the forces of Protestantism and those of the Counter-Reformation, the Roman Catholic Church found itself faced with the problem of maintaining and strengthening its hold in the non-Catholic countries. Pope Gregory XIII established a commission of cardinals charged with spreading Catholicism and regulating ecclesiastical affairs in heathen lands. A generation later, in 1622, when the Thirty Years' War (1618–1648) had broken out, Pope Gregory XV made this commission permanent as the Sacra Congregatio de Propaganda Fide (Congregation for the Propagation of the Faith) charged with the management of foreign missions and financed by a "ring tax" assessed upon each newly appointed cardinal. Within a few years, in 1627, this charge took the form of the College of Propaganda (Collegium Urbanum), which was established to educate young priests who were to undertake such missions. The first propaganda institute was therefore simply a body charged with improving the dissemination of a group of religious dogmas. The word "propaganda" soon came to be applied to any organization set up for the purpose of spreading a doctrine; then it was applied to the doctrine itself; and lastly to the methods employed in effectuating the dissemination.

From the seventeenth to the twentieth centuries we hear comparatively little about propaganda. The term had only a limited use and, though pejorative, was largely unfamiliar. During England's Puritan Revolution, propaganda by pamphlet and newsletter became a regular adjunct to military action, Oliver Cromwell's army being concerned nearly as much with the spread of religious and political doctrines as it was with victory in the field. Its employ-

ment increased steadily throughout the eighteenth and nineteenth centuries, particularly during times of ideological struggle, as in the American and French Revolutions (for example, the Girondists distributed broadsheets among the enemy troops offering them rewards for desertion). From the end of the Napoleonic Wars to the outbreak of World War I in 1914, western Europe remained at peace and there were few occasions where propaganda on a national scale was called for. Historically propaganda was associated with periods of stress and turmoil during which violent controversy over doctrine accompanied the use of force.

Between 1914 and 1918 the wholesale use of propaganda as an organized weapon of modern warfare transformed it into something more sinister. One of the most significant lessons to be learned from the experience of World War I was that public opinion could no longer be ignored as a determining factor in the formulation of government policies. Unlike previous wars, this was the first "total war" in which entire nations rather than just professional armies were locked in mortal combat. The war served to increase the level of popular interest and participation in the affairs of the state. The gap between the soldier at the front and the civilian at home was narrowed substantially in that the full resources of the state—military, economic, and psychological—had to be mobilized. In a state of total war, which required civilians to participate in the war effort, morale came to be recognized as a significant military factor, and propaganda slowly emerged as the principal instrument of control over public opinion and an essential weapon in the national arsenal, culminating in the establishment in Britain of the Ministry of Information in 1917 under Lord Beaverbrook and a separate Enemy Propaganda Department at Crewe House under Lord Northcliffe. By means of strict censorship and tightly controlled propaganda campaigns, the press, films, leaflets, and posters were all utilized in a coordinated fashion (arguably for the first time) in order to disseminate officially approved themes.

Despite major tensions, Britain's wartime consensus generally held up under the exigencies of war. One explanation for this was the skillful use by the government of propaganda and censorship. After the war, however, a deep mistrust developed on the part of ordinary citizens, who realized that conditions at the front had been deliberately obscured by patriotic slogans and "atrocity propaganda" consisting of obscene stereotypes of the enemy and their dastardly deeds. The populace also felt cheated that its sacrifices had not resulted in the promised homes and a land "fit for heroes." Propaganda was associated with lies and falsehood. Even politicians were sensitive to these criticisms; as a result, the Ministry of Information was immediately disbanded. The British government regarded propaganda as politically dangerous and even morally unacceptable in peacetime. It was, as one official wrote in the 1920s, "a good word gone wrong—debauched by the late Lord Northcliffe." The impact of propaganda on political behavior was so profound that during World War II, when the government attempted to "educate" the populace regarding the existence of Nazi concentration camps, it was not immediately believed since the information was suspected of being more "propaganda."

The experience of Britain's propaganda effort provided the defeated Germans with a fertile source of counterpropaganda directed at the postwar peace treaties and the ignominy of the Weimar Republic. Writing in *Mein Kampf,* Hitler noted: "In the year 1915, the enemy started his propaganda among our soldiers. From 1916 it steadily became more intensive, and at the beginning of 1918, it had swollen into a storm cloud. One could now see the effects of this gradual seduction. Our soldiers learned to think the way the enemy wanted them to think." By maintaining that the German army had not been defeated in the field of battle but rather had been forced to submit due to the disintegration of morale

from within, which had been accelerated by skillful British propaganda, Hitler (like other right-wing politicians and military groups) was providing historical legitimacy for the "stab-in-the-back" theory. Regardless of the actual role played by British (or Soviet) propaganda in helping to bring Germany to its knees, it was generally accepted that Britain's wartime experiment was the ideal blueprint according to which other governments would subsequently model their own propaganda apparatus. According to Hitler (again writing in *Mein Kampf),* "Germany had failed to recognise propaganda as a weapon of the first order, whereas the British has [sic] employed it with great skill and ingenious deliberation." Convinced of the essential role of propaganda for any movement determined to assume power, Hitler saw propaganda as a vehicle of political salesmanship in a mass market; it was no surprise that the Ministry of Propaganda was the first to be established when the Nazis assumed power in 1933.

The function of propaganda, Hitler argued, was to focus the attention of the masses on certain facts, processes, and necessities "whose significance is thus for the first time placed within their field of vision." Accordingly, propaganda for the masses had to be simple and concentrate on as few points as possible, which had to be repeated many times, with an emphasis on such emotional elements as love and hatred. Through the continuity and sustained uniformity of its application, Hitler concluded that propaganda would lead to results "almost beyond our understanding." Unlike the Bolsheviks, however, the Nazis did not distinguish between agitation and propaganda. In Soviet Russia agitation was concerned with influencing the masses through ideas and slogans, while propaganda served to spread the communist ideology of Marxism-Leninism. The distinction dates back to Georgi Plekhanov's celebrated 1892 definition: "A propagandist presents *many* ideas to one or a few persons; an agitator presents *only one* or *a few* ideas, but presents them to a *whole* mass of people" (emphapsis added). The Nazis, on the other hand, regarded propaganda not merely as an instrument for reaching the party elite but as a means of persuading and indoctrinating all Germans.

If the two world wars demonstrated the power of propaganda, the post-1945 period witnessed the widespread utilization of the lessons drawn from the wartime experience within the overall context of the "communications revolution." Political scientists and sociologists theorized about the nature of man and modern society—particularly in light of the rise of totalitarian police states. Individuals were viewed as undifferentiated and malleable, while an apocalyptic vision of mass society emphasized the alienation of work, the collapse of religion and family ties, and a general decline of moral values. Culture was reduced to the lowest common denominator for mass consumption, with the masses generally seen as politically apathetic yet prone to ideological fanaticism, vulnerable to manipulation through the media and the increasing sophistication of propagandists. Accordingly, propaganda was viewed as a "magic bullet" or "hypodermic needle" by means of which opinions and behavior could easily be controlled.

This bleak view was challenged by a number of American social scientists, such as Harold Lasswell (1902–1978) and Walter Lippmann (1899–1974), who argued that within the context of an atomized mass society propaganda was a mechanism for engineering public opinion and consent and thus acted as a means of social control (which Lasswell referred to as the "new hammer and anvil of social solidarity" [1927, 221]). In 1965 the French sociologist Jacques Ellul (1912–1996) took this a stage further and suggested that the technological society has conditioned people to a "need for propaganda." In his view propaganda is most effective when it reinforces previously held opinions and beliefs. The "hypodermic needle" theory has largely been replaced by a more complex "multistep" model that acknowl-

edges the influence of the mass media yet also recognizes that individuals seek out opinion leaders within their own social class and gender. Most writers today agree that propaganda confirms rather than converts—or at least is more effective when the message is in line with existing opinions and beliefs of most consumers. Writing in 1936, Aldous Huxley observed that "the propagandist is a man [who] canalizes an already existing stream; in a land where there is no water, he digs in vain" (*Harper's* 174 [1936]: 39). This shift in emphasis underscores a number of common misconceptions connected with the study of propaganda. There is a widely held belief that propaganda implies nothing more than the art of persuasion, which serves only to change attitudes and ideas. This is undoubtedly one of its aims, but it is usually a limited and subordinate one. More often propaganda is concerned with sharpening and focusing existing trends and beliefs. A second basic misconception is the belief that propaganda consists only of lies and falsehood. In fact, it operates on several levels of truth—from the outright lie to the half-truth to the truth taken out of context. (Officials in the British Ministry of Information during World War II referred to this as the "whole truth, nothing but the truth—and as near as possible the truth!") Many writers on the subject see propaganda as essentially appeasing the irrational instincts of man—and this is true to a certain extent—but because our attitudes and behavior are also the product of rational decisions, propaganda must appeal to the rational elements in human nature as well. The preoccupation with the former ignores the basic fact that propaganda is ethically neutral, that is, it may be good or bad. In all political systems policy must be explained, the public must be convinced of the efficacy of governmental decisions (or at least remain quiescent), and rational discussion is not always the most useful means of achieving this, particularly in the age of mass society. More recently, for example, the British public has been reminded on more than one occasion of the "Dunkirk" and "Falkland" spirit; it has been asked to consider "who governs Britain"; it has been assured that the rate of inflation can be "reduced at a stroke"; and it has been guaranteed that taxes will not be raised "under this government" and that the "pound in your pocket" has not—and will not—decrease in value. Therefore, in any body politic propaganda is not, as is often supposed, a malignant growth but rather an essential part of the whole political process.

Since the onset of total war, governments have sought to come to terms with the mass media, to control and harness them—particularly in times of crisis—and to ensure that they acted in the national interest as often as possible. Given rapidly evolving technology, definitions of propaganda have also undergone changes. Propaganda has meant different things at different times, although the scale on which it has been practiced clearly increased in the twentieth century. What are the characteristic features of propaganda and how can it be defined? Propaganda—I am here deliberately excluding purely religious or commercial propaganda in the form of advertising—is a distinct political activity that can be distinguished from cognate activities like information and education. The distinction between them lies in the purpose of the instigator. Put simply, propaganda is the dissemination of ideas intended to convince people to think and act in a particular way and for a particular persuasive purpose. Although propaganda can be unconscious, I am concerned here with conscious, deliberate attempts to employ the techniques of persuasion to attain specific goals. Propaganda can be defined as the deliberate attempt to influence public opinion through the transmission of ideas and values for a specific persuasive purpose that has been consciously devised to serve the self-interest of the propagandist, either directly or indirectly. Whereas information presents its audience with a straightforward statement of facts, propaganda packages those facts in order to elicit a certain response. Whereas education—at least in what

I take to be the liberal notion of education—teaches us how to think in order to enable us to make up our own minds, propaganda dictates what one should think. Information and education are concerned with broadening our perspectives and opening our minds, whereas propaganda strives to narrow them and (preferably) to close our minds. The distinction, in short, lies in the ultimate purpose or goal of each.

The importance of propaganda in the politics of the twentieth century should not be underestimated. The most obvious reason for the increasing prominence given to propaganda and its assumed power over opinion is the broadening base of politics, which has dramatically transformed the nature of political participation. Of course, the means of communication have correspondingly increased, and the growth of education and technological advances in mass communication have all proved contributory factors. We are now witnessing the explosion of information superhighways and digital data networks. Legitimate concerns have been expressed about the nature of media proprietorship and access, and the extent to which information flows freely (Noam Chomsky's "manufacture of consent"). Propagandists have been forced to respond to these changes by reassessing their audience and using whatever methods they consider most effective.

In the war to "liberate" Kosovo, both sides in the conflict understood the importance of manipulating real-time news to their own advantage. Moreover, for the first time in a war, the Internet was exploited to disseminate propaganda. Having declared war on Serbia (or, more accurately, on Slobodan Milosevic, who has been described as "a new Hitler"), NATO sought to justify its war aims by stressing the humanitarian aspect of its aerial bombing campaign and the accuracy of its weapons. Jamie Shea, the NATO spokesman, insisted that "our cause is just." Milosevic also revealed that he was capable of using the media for propaganda purposes. By allowing the BBC and CNN to continue to broadcast from Belgrade, he hoped to fragment Western opinion with nightly stories of "innocent" civilians killed by NATO air strikes. Since the most effective propaganda is that which can be verified, NATO was placed on the defensive in the propaganda war by having to confirm the accuracy of Serbian claims. Although NATO's military strategy was ultimately vindicated, the Balkan wars of the 1990s reinforced the centrality of propaganda to war. The use of propaganda by both sides in the Kosovo conflict—especially the Internet—highlights the forces of change between the pre–Cold War era and the current globalized information environment. The centrality of propaganda was hammered home once more by the terrorist attacks against the United States on 11 September 2001, which were planned for their media impact as acts of propaganda by deed. Propaganda subsequently became a major feature of the "war on terrorism" that followed.

Propaganda can also be limited in its effects: recent research has forced us to reexamine earlier simplistic assumptions by looking at "resistance" or "immunity" to propaganda. In the short term propaganda may carry its audience on a wave of fervor, like the one that followed the outbreak of war in 1914, the dispatch of a task force to the South Atlantic in 1982, or the launching of Operation Desert Storm in 1991. In the long term, however, propaganda becomes less effective because the audience has both the time and opportunity to question its underlying assumptions. As Goebbels remarked, "Propaganda becomes ineffective the moment we are aware of it" (Welch 2002). Here we come to the crux of the matter. Communication between human beings relies on a mixture of reason and emotion for its effect: if propaganda is too rational, it could become boring; if it is too emotional or strident, it might become transparent and ludicrous. Like other forms of human interaction, propaganda has to strike the right balance. When we speak of propaganda, we

think of the media as conventionally conceived—radio, television, film, the press, and so forth—but propaganda as an agent of reinforcement is not confined to these. Few would deny that the presence of Hitler's face on the stamps and coins of the Third Reich was an example of propaganda, though many might be surprised at the suggestion that the same judgment might be applied to the British monarch's visage. Postage stamps and coins are but two examples of the wider application of propaganda. Censorship has been described as the antithesis of propaganda and its necessary adjunct, but the role of commemoration in reinforcement propaganda is often overlooked. What better way of reinforcing the present and determining the future than by commemorating the glories of the past? History has indeed proved to be an invaluable source of propaganda. It is no coincidence that London has its Waterloo Station and Paris its Gare d'Austerlitz. We need to think of propaganda in much broader terms: wherever public opinion is deemed important, someone will attempt to influence it. Propaganda can therefore manifest itself in the form of a building, a flag, a coin, or even a government-mandated health warning on a pack of cigarettes. Goebbels maintained that "in propaganda, as in love, anything is permissible which is successful" (Welch 2002).

Propaganda may be overt or covert, black or white, truthful or mendacious, serious or humorous, rational or emotional. Propagandists assess the context and the audience and use whatever methods and means they consider most appropriate and effective. If we can widen our terms of reference and divest propaganda of its pejorative associations, its significance as an intrinsic part of the political process in the twentieth century will be revealed. One contemporary writer has even suggested that we need more propaganda, not less, to influence opinions and stimulate active participation in the democratic process. As E. H. Carr reminded us in 1939, "Power over opinion is therefore not less essential for political purposes than military and economic power, and has always been closely associated with them. The art of persuasion has always been a necessary part of the equipment of a political leader" (Carr 1946, 132).

David Welch

References: Carr, E. H. *The Twenty Years' Crisis, 1919–1939: An Introduction to the Study of International Relations.* New York: Harper & Row, 1946; Lasswell, Harold. *Propaganda Technique in the World War.* New York: Knopf, 1927; Welch, David. *The Third Reich: Politics and Propaganda.* 2d ed. New York: Routledge, 2002.

PROPAGANDA AND MASS PERSUASION

A Historical Encyclopedia,
1500 to the Present

A

Abolitionism/Antislavery Movement

The international campaign against slavery produced such eloquent leaders as William Wilberforce in Britain and Frederick Douglass in the United States, as well as enduringly powerful works of art with a political purpose, including Harriet Beecher Stowe's (1811–1896) novel *Uncle Tom's Cabin* (1852) and J. M. W. Turner's (1775–1851) painting *The Slave Ship* (1840).

The origin of the antislavery movement can be traced to Britain—where the importation of slaves stood at odds with both Christianity and the traditional liberty of British subjects—and France—where the idea of liberty took hold in the writings of thinkers like Jean-Jacques Rousseau (1712–1778). Eloquent abolitionists included the former slave Olaudah Equiano (1745–1797), whose autobiography entitled *The Interesting Narrative of the Life of Olaudah Equiano or Gustavas Vassa, the African . . . Written by Himself* was published in London in 1789. British antislavery activists included the member of Parliament William Wilberforce (1759–1833) and writer Thomas Clarkson (1760–1846). Clarkson collected a wealth of data on the nature of the slave trade, including diagrams showing how slaves were packed into

ships to maximize cargo space. In 1807 the British Parliament abolished the slave trade, and in 1833 it moved to abolish slavery throughout the British Empire. The British movement remained active, ensuring that the law was applied and campaigning against slavery in other parts of the world. British antislavers helped fund abolitionism in the United States.

The foundations of American antislavery were laid by the evangelical religious revivals of the early nineteenth century, which stressed the need to morally cleanse American life. Advocates of abolition as a Christian imperative included the free-born African American David Walker (c. 1796–1830), who was best known for his 1829 *Appeal to the Colored Citizens of the World,* which called upon black people in the United States and beyond to collectively resist their oppression. The Quaker campaigner Benjamin Lundy (1789–1839) founded the abolitionist journals *Philanthropist* (1819) and *Genius of Universal Emancipation* (1821). Coeditor of the latter journal beginning in 1829, William Lloyd Garrison (1805–1879) went on to become the preeminent abolitionist. Garrison founded his own newspaper, *The Liberator,* and launched the New England Anti-Slavery Society in 1831 and the American Anti-Slavery

Society in 1833. Other important figures included Arthur Tappan (1786–1865) and his brother Lewis Tappan (1788–1873). The abolitionists' views terrified the slaveholders of the American South, who engineered "gag rules" to block discussion of the issue in Congress. Defenders of the slave system included Senator John C. Calhoun (1782–1850) of South Carolina. Calhoun's arguments included the notion that slavery was part of the divine plan for the world. Proslavers also pointed to the danger of abolitionists inciting slave rebellions such as the 1831 uprising led by Nat Turner (1800–1831). The effective Southern defenses of gagging and physical attacks on antislavers proved powerful propaganda for the abolitionist cause in the North. Emotive events included the murder of the abolitionist printer and preacher Elijah Lovejoy (1808–1837).

By the late 1830s abolitionism had become a large and diverse movement and a conduit for religious and regional feeling. The movement recruited many women. Powerful abolitionist speakers included former African American slaves like Sojourner Truth (1797–1883) and Frederick Douglass (c. 1817–1895). Some abolitionist propaganda material included stories selected for their sensational value, stressing the violence and sexual abuse within slavery. Stowe's *Uncle Tom's Cabin* was a relatively late addition to the abolitionist arsenal but proved an influential best-seller both in the United States and overseas. The most significant opponent of slavery among the nonslaveholding whites of the South was Hinton Rowan Helper (1829–1909). His book *The Impending Crisis of the South* (1859) was widely distributed by the Republican Party during the election campaign of 1860.

Antislavery sentiments produced a variety of potential policy solutions. Some abolitionists became involved in political action through the Republican Party, arguing that the West should be developed as "Free Soil." In Illinois the debate over this issue solidified the reputation of Abraham Lincoln (1809–1865). In 1856 an attempt to hold a plebiscite in Kansas to determine whether the territory should be free or slave ended in violence. Antagonists included John Brown (1800–1859), who mixed the religious rhetoric of a stump revivalist with a belief in the power of direct action to inspire or lay "restraining fear" on others. Brown's actions included involvement in the murder of five proslavers alongside Pottawatomie Creek in Kansas. In 1859 Brown launched what he hoped would be the decisive inspirational event, namely, a raid on the federal arsenal at Harpers Ferry (in present-day West Virginia). He intended to sweep across the South, arming slaves as he went. Although his plan was foiled, his trial and execution became propaganda in their own right. In his final statement Brown prophesied endless bloodshed over the issue of slavery and claimed for himself the status of a martyr, which he retained in the iconography of the Union side during the Civil War.

The abolitionists remained active during the American Civil War. Although the issue of slavery had precipitated the war, it seemed plausible that the Union might be rebuilt based on a compromise rather than complete abolition. The abolitionists campaigned hard to link the Union cause to complete emancipation and were rewarded by Lincoln's Emancipation Proclamation of 1863, which freed the slaves in Confederate territory. In 1865, following the war's end, the Thirteenth Amendment made abolition part of the U.S. Constitution.

The antislavery struggles continued in Brazil (where slavery was only abolished in 1888), the Ottoman Empire, and elsewhere in Africa and Asia. Major international declarations against slavery include the Brussels Act of 1890, the International Slavery Convention of 1926, and clauses of the United Nations Declaration of Human Rights of 1948. At the start of the twenty-first century slavery remains a major concern for the United Nations and human rights activists, with antislavery issues overlapping with the problem of human trafficking associated with illegal migration.

Nicholas J. Cull

See also Britain (Eighteenth Century); Civil War (United States); Garrison, William Lloyd; Lincoln, Abraham; *Narrative of the Life of Frederick Douglass . . .; Uncle Tom's Cabin;* United States

References: Azevedo, Celia M. *Abolitionism in the United States and Brazil: A Comparative Perspective.* New York: Garland, 1995; Davis, David Brion. *The Problem of Slavery in Western Culture.* New York: Oxford University Press, 1988; Jeffrey, Julie Roy. *The Great Silent Army of Abolitionism: Ordinary Women in the Antislavery Movement.* Chapel Hill: University of North Carolina Press, 1998; Oldfield, J. R. *Popular Politics and British Anti-Slavery: The Mobilisation of Public Opinion against the Slave Trade, 1787–1807.* Manchester: Manchester University Press, 1995; Quarles, Benjamin. *Black Abolitionists.* New York: Oxford University Press, 1969; Thomas, Hugh. *The Slave Trade: The Story of the Atlantic Slave Trade, 1440–1870.* London: Picador, 1997.

Abortion

Abortion remains a major issue in political propaganda in the United States today. "Abortions will not let you forget," wrote Gwendolyn Brooks (1917–) in her poem "A Street in Bronzeville" (1945). "You remember the children you got that you did not get." *The New Penguin English Dictionary* (2000) defines abortion as "the induced expulsion of a foetus for the purpose of terminating a pregnancy." As such, there is nothing new about terminating an unwanted pregnancy, and Gwendolyn Brooks intended to shock her white readers by reminding them that among poor blacks abortion was something all too familiar. Only in the nineteenth century was abortion criminalized thanks to the efforts of Anthony Comstock (1844–1915). In 1873 the U.S. Congress passed an Act for the Suppression of Trade in, and Circulation of Obscene Literature and Articles for Immoral Use, which was intended to improve the morals of all Americans. Comstock

persuaded Congress to include information about abortion as one of the items forbidden by legislation.

Margaret Sanger (1879–1966) dealt with the problem from another angle, namely, birth control. A progressive reformer, Sanger saw firsthand the death of a poor working woman who could not afford to have another child and whose husband refused to use a condom. The U.S. Supreme Court dealt with contraception in *Griswold v. Connecticut* (1973). Justice William O. Douglas (1898–1980), writing for the majority, upheld a couple's right to contraception (including information about contraception) in a piece of convoluted reasoning: "Specific guarantees have penumbras, formed by emanations from those guarantees that help give them life and substance." In other words, the right to privacy was now guaranteed by the Court, and contraception was one of those rights.

The Court turned to abortion in *Roe v. Wade* (1973), one of the most contested rulings it ever made. Jane Roe—actually Norma McCorvey (1947–)—got pregnant and had an abortion. This was illegal in Texas, where she was a resident. The divided Court made abortion legal, in effect guaranteeing abortion on demand for any woman in the United States, claiming that the right to privacy was guaranteed by the due process clause of the Fourteenth Amendment. Legal scholars debated whether the Court had reached a verdict based on flawed reasoning. The Court's line of reasoning suggested that abortion was strictly gender-specific: it was women who got pregnant. The right to abortion should therefore be protected by the equal protection clause under the Fourteenth Amendment, which makes it unconstitutional to treat some citizens differently than others. There is much to recommend this line of reasoning.

The Court's decision was bitterly contested by many on religious grounds. The result was a substantial "right to life" movement, promoted by many religious faiths besides the Roman Catholic Church. "Right

Freedom of/from Choice Planned Parenthood poster, depicting Supreme Court justices, by Robbie Conal. (Henry Diltz/Corbis)

to life" zealots have defended the idea of murdering doctors who do abortions. Abortion clinics, once found in most large American cities, were picketed to prevent pregnant women from entering. An anti–Ku Klux Klan law from the 1870s was invoked to force such protestors to stay away from abortion clinics.

Critics of *Roe v. Wade,* and there are many, feel the Court moved too rapidly on a divisive topic; local government should first have discussed the issues, giving those with religious differences ample time to voice their views. Instead, the Court rushed into an area of public policy where there was much confusion, forcing a feminist decision that pleased some but infuriated others. The result is continuing conflict. In recent presidential campaigns, candidates have been careful to say as little about abortion rights as possible; promises to overturn *Roe* have had little result so far. Americans are deeply divided over abortion, and this division shows no sign

of ending. Feminists continue to insist that abortion is part of the move to make America equal for male and female. Opponents insist that that life begins at the point of conception and that after that moment the termination of any pregnancy is murder. The Roman Catholic Church in particular insists that the trimester plan permitting abortions in the first three months of pregnancy but not later—the plan enunciated in *Roe*—is simply legalized murder. The result is a decision that mirrors the notorious statement of Andrew Jackson regarding Justice John Marshall's ruling on behalf of the Cherokee Nation: "Mr. Marshall has made his decision; now let him enforce it." Abortion attracts propagandists on both sides of the issue—gruesome photographs of fetuses versus lurid accounts of botched illegal abortions. Abortion is heavily politicized; its connection with the emancipation of women is obscured; its religious opponents are ascendant. She who is without proper voice is the poor teenage girl who has just become pregnant and does not know what to do.

David Culbert

See also Elections (United States); Friedan, Betty; Religion

References: Faux, Marian. *Roe v. Wade.* New York: Mentor, 1992; Hull, N. E. H., and Peter Charles Hoffer, *Roe v. Wade: The Abortion Rights Controversy in American History.* Lawrence: University Press of Kansas, 2001; Garrow, David. *Liberty and Sexuality: The Right to Privacy and the Making of Roe v. Wade.* New York: Penguin, 1994.

ADL (Anti-Defamation League of B'nai B'rith)

American-based civil rights organization dedicated to fighting anti-Semitic propaganda. The Anti-Defamation League was founded in 1913 by Chicago lawyer Sigmund Livingston (1872–1946) under the auspices the Independent Order of B'nai B'rith. Livingston defined its mission as follows: "To stop, by appeals to reason and conscience, and if necessary, by appeals to law, the defamation of the Jewish people . . . to secure justice and fair treatment to all citizens alike . . . put an end forever to unjust and unfair discrimination against and ridicule of any sect or body of citizens." Early campaigns included a mass mailing to all American newspaper editors urging them not to use anti-Semitic language. Livingston himself wrote pamphlets denouncing the notorious anti-Semitic forgery *Protocols of the Elders of Zion.* The ADL was involved in general antiracist and civil rights work and played an important role in the 1950s and 1960s. On occasion the ADL has been involved in propaganda within the United States relating to international issues affecting Jews. In the late 1960s the ADL sought to combat anti-Israeli/pro-Arab propaganda with a radio program called "Dateline Israel" to present ordinary life in the country. In the 1980s the ADL championed the cause of the so-called Refuseniks—Jewish Russians unable to leave the Soviet Union; this became one of the most visible anti-Soviet propa-

ganda campaigns on the "home front" in Ronald Reagan's so called Second Cold War. The ADL's current campaigns include ensuring the continued separation of church and state and contesting Holocaust denial and anti-Semitism at the extremes of both black and white American politics. The ADL has been particularly effective at exposing anti-Semitic propaganda on the Internet.

Nicholas J. Cull

See also Anti-Semitism; Civil Rights Movement; Holocaust Denial; *Protocols of the Elders of Zion;* United States (Progressive Era)

References: Cohen, Oscar, and Stanley Wexler, eds. *"Not the Work of a Day": Anti-Defamation League of B'nai B'rith Oral Memoirs.* New York: [Anti-Defamation] League, 1987; Moore, Deborah Dash. *B'nai B'rith and the Challenge of Ethnic Leadership.* Albany: SUNY Press, 1981; Snyder, Jill Donnie, and Eric K. Goodman. *Friend of the Court, 1947–1982: The Anti-Defamation League of B'nai B'rith.* New York: [Anti-Defamation] League, 1983.

Advertising

Modern advertising is a product of the late nineteenth century and reflects the changes that took place in the economy and the revolutionary transformations that occurred in the communications field. In response to the Industrial Revolution, advertising's early development was linked to that of the mass-circulation newspapers. American and European newspapers prior to the nineteenth century had published short, factual, paid advertisements that occasionally contained a persuasive element. In the main, however, they tended to be what we would now term "classified" advertising intended to inform potential customers of the availability of goods and services.

In the final two decades of the nineteenth century the situation changed as a result of the emergence of mass-circulation newspapers and magazines, both of which depended upon advertising revenue. The small factual notices were replaced by larger advertisements intended to stand out from the printed page. This fundamental change in the physical appearance of advertisements—large print, pictures, and even some color—reflected a substantial shift in intention: the main purpose of advertising was now to persuade the purchaser to buy goods and services rather than simply to provide information.

In the 1880s brand names were first used as a means of distinguishing products that were more or less identical. Brand-name advertising tried to persuade the public to associate a particular brand with quality and other desirable attributes. Slogans and catchphrases became ubiquitous. Perhaps the most famous early example of an advertising slogan that created a popular awareness of a product was "Good Morning! Have you used Pears' Soap?" The slogan became part of everyday language in Britain and served to distinguish Pears soap from its competitors.

The period 1890–1914 witnessed the development of fully fledged advertising agencies. Large-scale advertising campaigns were launched that coordinated newspaper and magazine advertisements with outdoor poster advertisements and shopfront displays. With mass production came mass consumption and the need for mass persuasion. For example, the total annual volume of advertising in the United States expanded rapidly from $682 million in 1914 to $1.409 billion in 1919 and $2.987 billion in 1929.

World War I marked another watershed in the development of modern advertising. Following the experiences of wartime propaganda and the imperative need to manipulate public opinion in the first total war, "psychological advertising" was introduced in the interwar period, heavily influenced by the new field of behavioral psychology, which claimed that consumers were best reached through emotional appeals rather than reason. It is no coincidence that during the interwar period fascist states also based their propaganda along these lines. Both Hitler and Mussolini saw propaganda as a vehicle of political salesmanship in a mass market. The masses were viewed as malleable and corrupt, swayed not by their brains but by their emotions. Accord-

ingly, propaganda for the masses had to be simple, focusing on as few points as possible, which then had to be repeated many times, concentrating on such emotional elements as love and hatred. One of the ramifications of mass society and psychological advertising—especially in the United States—was that advertisements moved away from the product and increasingly focused more on the consumer in an attempt to convince the masses that conspicuous consumption was essential for their well-being.

Although American advertisers continued to exploit the printed word, beginning in the late 1920s they were able to exploit the new medium of radio, which had gained nationwide coverage with the creation of broadcasting networks. In 1928 the American Tobacco Company illustrated the power of this new medium when it increased sales of Lucky Strike cigarettes by 47 percent in two months after embarking on a concerted radio advertising campaign. By the 1930s, as its audience expanded, radio advertising became more sophisticated, with radio "personalities" emerging as both entertainers and salespeople. Women in particular were targeted since they tended to be at home most of the day; radio advertisements combined an emphasis on progress with appeals to traditional values of domesticity. As advertising revenue increased, radio networks now interwove advertisements into the entertainment schedules. By 1930 advertising provided almost 100 percent of the revenue for radio programs in the United States. (This would later be the case for television.) Whereas American advertising in the 1920s and 1930s (in contrast to European advertising) appealed to middle-class values, even outside the United States advertisers gradually began to identify the masses as "consumers" rather than "citizens."

American advertisers lent their talents to national propaganda by cooperating with the Office of War Information during World War II. After the war, advertisers formed the Advertising Council, which sponsored a number of patriotic propaganda campaigns, the most famous being the "Freedom Train" exhibition, which traveled throughout the United States between 1947 and 1950, and the "People's Capitalism" exhibition, which toured the world under the auspices of the United States Information Agency (USIA) during the mid-1950s. Senior advertising executives who subsequently moved into state propaganda included William Benton (1900–1973), founder of Benton and Bowles, who pioneered U.S. postwar propaganda overseas in his capacity as assistant secretary of state for public affairs from 1945 to 1947.

After World War II assumptions about the power of advertising were informed by a new liberal critique of society. Particularly influential in the 1950s and 1960s were the economist John Kenneth Galbraith (1908–) and the historian David M. Potter (1910–1971), both of whom questioned the immense influence that advertising wielded in American society. Liberal critics argued that not only did advertising raise the price of products (since manufacturers passed on the cost of advertising to the consumer) but it also operated against rational consumer choice and the efficient use of resources. The manipulative influence of advertisements created false needs by persuading consumers to buy products that they did not need. In the 1960s Marxist writers like Herbert Marcuse (1898–1979) also made a distinction between real and false needs and condemned the burgeoning advertising industry for instilling illusory attractions of consumerism as a capitalist mechanism for controlling the working class. In the late 1960s and 1970s these liberal and Marxist critiques were themselves questioned by scholars, who argued that advertising was not as powerful as was previously assumed. Such conclusions, replacing earlier assumptions about the all-powerful impact of the media on mass attitudes and values, are confirmed by recent scholarship devoted to the history of the mass media. A newer, more sophisticated

model emphasizes the complexity of this relationship and the need to understand advertising—and media influence in general—as a product of the interaction with broader cultural factors.

David Welch

See also Freedom Train; Thatcher, Margaret; United States; USIA; World War I; World War II (United States)
References: Boorstin, Daniel J. *The Image.* New York: Vintage, 1961; Marchand, Roland. *Advertising the American Dream: Making Way for Modernity.* Berkeley: University of California Press, 1986; Pope, Daniel. *The Making of Modern Advertising.* New York: Basic Books, 1983; Schudson, Michael. *Advertising: The Uneasy Persuasion.* New York: Basic Books, 1984.

Africa

The African continent has witnessed the following uses of propaganda: spread religion; support imperialism; rally support for world wars and the Cold War; support white minority regimes; and support decolonization and nation building. Today propaganda is routinely used to bolster the one-party rule that characterizes many states in the region, the most notorious contemporary exponent being President Robert Mugabe of Zimbabwe (1912–).

The African continent can be divided into two distinct regions: North Africa, with its Arabic-speaking Islamic heritage, and sub-Saharan Africa. Islam has also played an important role in much of West Africa. The entire continent was profoundly affected by imperialism. Only Liberia and Ethiopia survived the nineteenth century unconquered. Colonialism remains a major issue in African propaganda as an explanation of African poverty. Southern Africa retains a substantial white presence, especially in South Africa.

Propaganda about Africa began in ancient times with legends about the savage lands beyond civilization. Europeans of the twelfth century imagined a lost Christian kingdom beyond the realm of Islam ruled by Prester John. Such ideas conditioned European reactions to sub-Saharan Africa during the Renaissance. After accepting Africans as profoundly "other," it was only a short step to accepting their enslavement to provide the labor force for the conquest of the New World. One of the earliest examples of African propaganda is the antislavery autobiography written by former slave Olaudah Equiano (1745–1797) entitled *The Interesting Narrative of the Life of Olaudah Equiano or Gustavas Vassa, the African . . . Written by Himself,* which was published in London in 1789.

Traditional African societies developed complex systems of political communication. Successful exponents could accomplish considerable feats of mobilization, as was demonstrated by Shaka (c. 1787–1828), who founded the Zulu nation in the early 1800s, and his nephew Cetewayo, or Cetshwayo (c. 1836–1884), who scored early successes against the British in the Anglo-Zulu War (1879). Traditionally the power of the leader was combined with religious ritual—typically involving dance—to form a cohesive whole. The potent mix of religion (especially Islam) and politics seen in places like Somalia is not a modern phenomenon. Usuman dan Fodio (1754–1817) conquered an Islamic kingdom known as the Sokoto caliphate in Nigeria in the early nineteenth century. Around the same time a Sudanese leader called Seku Amadu built a kingdom across the Sahara. His propaganda included reference to a forged prophecy that a man named Amadu would become the final caliph. Later in the century Muhammad Ahmad established a theocratic state in the Sudan as the Mahdi (1844–1885). Dubbed "the Mad Mahdi" by the British press, he was defeated by a military campaign led by General Horatio Herbert Kitchener (1850–1916). For their part, Europeans justified their imperialistic designs on the African continent in religious terms. Christian missionaries like explorer David Livingstone (1813–1873) led the way. Christianity did not necessarily breed passive acceptance of Western rule. In Nyasaland (now Malawi) a Baptist minister named John Chilembwe (c. 1860–1915) led an anticolonial revolt in 1915.

European imperialism rested on propaganda both at home and in the African colony. European education emphasized the inferiority of Africans and the superiority of the white race, whose destiny was to rule Africa. In this view Africa became the "Dark Continent" needing white enlightenment. Western tools of communication such as photography, mapmaking and, in due course, cinematography were all used wittingly or unwittingly to elevate the white and denigrate the black. Novelists whose fictions perpetuated stereotypes of Africa include H. Rider Haggard (1856–1925), author of *King Solomon's Mines* (1885). African subjects were a favorite of the early French documentarians. Later filmmakers—such as the postwar French ethnographic filmmaker Jean Rouch (1917–)—have sought to combat the stereotypes of the past, although their subjective medium created distortions of its own. Since the 1970s African filmmakers have increasingly represented themselves in dynamic films of their own, such as the successful Senegalese director Ousmane Sembene (1923–).

For the European powers of the later nineteenth century, the conquest of colonies in Africa was a form of propaganda by deed, displaying the virility and prowess of the nation concerned. These colonial prophets included Cecil Rhodes (1853–1902). Latecomers to the imperialist game, like Italy and Germany, scrambled to catch up as colonialism became a vital component of domestic political propaganda and international rivalry. Successive waves of European colonization brought competing notions of imperialism. In South Africa tension between the British and the previous wave of white settlers on the continent, known as Afrikaners, sparked the Anglo-Boer War of 1899–1902—complete with modern atrocities and corresponding propaganda.

Opposition to colonialism created a common ground for the otherwise disparate peoples of the African continent. The early years of the twentieth century saw the development of a Pan-African movement. Key spokespersons included the Jamaican-born activist Marcus Garvey (1887–1940), who attempted to link people of African descent in the New World and the Old through his Universal Negro Improvement Association. Later in the century such leaders included the great African American intellectual W. E. B. Du Bois (1868–1963), who embraced Pan-Africanism late in life, following his disillusionment with the prospects for reform in the United States. Other influential anticolonial writers included Frantz Fanon (1925–1961).

Africa played a role in events leading up to World War II. When Benito Mussolini (1883–1945) attempted to conquer Abyssinia (Ethiopia) in 1935, that country and its emperor, Haile Selassie (1891–1975), became a cause célèbre. International support came only in the form of words. During World War II North Africa became a major theater, witnessing the battlefield use of psychological warfare by the Allies with mixed results. The Anglo-American compromise with the Vichy French in North Africa weakened Allied moral claims. Britain's successful military campaign against the German general Erwin Rommel (1891–1944) was captured in one the most successful documentaries on the war, Roy Boulting and David MacDonald's *Desert Victory* (1943); the American side of the story was told in Frank Capra's *Tunisian Victory* (1944). In sub-Saharan Africa the British used various propaganda methods, including film, to convince Africans to serve in the war effort. In contemporary terms, they sought to "re-brand" colonialism by presenting a "New Empire" of interracial cooperation. Such an approach helped the presentation of the British case in the generally anti-imperialist United States. The content of wartime Allied propaganda in general, with its emphasis on self-determination and opposition to Hitlerian racism, meant that imperialism—new or old—would be difficult to sustain in the postwar world.

The aftermath of World War II brought profound changes to sub-Saharan Africa. The postwar decline of the old European powers opened the way to decolonization, while the Cold War between the Soviet Union and the United States presented rival agendas for modernization. With the United States and the USSR locked in a nuclear stalemate, Africa and the developing world became the battlefield for the Cold War by proxy. Both power blocs pumped propaganda into the region and competed with aid packages, student exchanges, or prestigious projects like the Peace Corps. Cuba became heavily involved in Angola. Following the Sino-Soviet split in the early 1960s, Africa became a three-way ideological battleground as the Chinese sought to export Maoism. African leaders, for their part, have become adept at manipulating world powers to suit their own ends and have made much use of the United Nations as a forum for their aspirations.

Postwar sub-Saharan politics were dominated by the emergence of a number of charismatic male leaders with Pan-African beliefs, who led their nations to independence, including Jomo Kenyatta (c. 1889–1978) in Kenya, Kwame Nkrumah (1909–1972) in the Gold Coast, and Julius Nyerere (c. 1922–1999) in Tanganyika. Propaganda played an important part in the nation building of the 1960s, when emerging countries sought to create new identities to supersede tribal and religious differences, thereby developing a modern nation within the boundaries imposed by colonialism. New names were necessary, so the Gold Coast became Ghana, Tanganyika and Zanzibar became Tanzania, Nyasaland became Malawi, Congo became Zaire, and so forth. The new nations faced many problems as debts accumulated and secessionist violence flared, with Congo and Nigeria suffering acutely.

By the late 1960s many of the newly independent countries had slipped into military one-party dictatorships, which leaned even more heavily on the cult of personality and control of the media. The most notorious examples of African dictatorship included Idi Amin (1925–) in Uganda and "Emperor" Bokassa (1921–1996) in the Central African Republic. The dictators presented themselves as clients of the world powers. In Zaire (now the Democratic Republic of the Congo) Joseph Mobutu (1930–1997) worked closely with the Americans, while in Ethiopia Mengistu Haile Mariam (1937–) used rhetoric suggesting an alliance with the Soviet Union.

The tide of independence and majority rule encountered resistance in French Algeria, Portuguese Angola, and British Rhodesia, where politicians like Ian Smith (1919–) played to the prejudices of their white minority supporters. The most notorious rearguard action against decolonization was that fought in South Africa. In 1910, as part of the settlement of the Anglo-Boer War, the British established the Union of South Africa as a single country that included the former Boer lands of the Transvaal and the Orange Free State. Afrikaners played an important part in defining the national culture in this new country. Jan Christian Smuts (1870–1950), who served as prime minister from 1919 to 1924 and again from 1939 to 1948, managed to reconcile Afrikaner heritage with loyalty to Britain and a moderate treatment of the black African majority. J. B. M. Hertzog (1866–1942), prime minister from 1924 to 1939 and leader of the National Party (founded in 1912) adopted a more extreme position and championed a revival of Afrikaner culture. The centenary of the Boer "Great Trek" away from British influence, which occurred in 1938, became a rallying point for racist politics. Emotive events included a reenactment of the trek. Key propagandists for a policy of racial segregation from black Africans (known as apartheid) included Daniel Malan (1874–1959), editor of the newspaper *Die Burger* and Hertzog's successor as leader of the National Party. The party assumed power in 1948 as a result of antiblack scare tactics, with Malan as prime minister. The National Party introduced a shamelessly racist political system that utilized "passbooks" to control the movement of blacks. In 1961 South Africa left the British Commonwealth and became a republic.

Opposition to apartheid sprang from such groups as the African National Congress (ANC), founded in 1912, among whose leaders was Nelson Mandela (1918–). Other opposition voices included the novelist Alan Paton (1903–1988), author of *Cry, the Beloved Country* (1948), which was made into a film in 1951 and also served as the basis for the 1959 Broadway hit *Lost in the Stars* by composer Kurt Weill (1900–1950) and playwright Maxwell Anderson (1888–1959). The ANC smuggled poster and newspaper propaganda into South Africa from neighboring countries and broadcast over what was called Freedom Radio. Like the civil rights leaders in the United States, the anti-apartheid movement was able to publicize white atrocities, including the Sharpeville massacre of March 1960, in which seventy protestors died, and the numerous deaths connected with the Soweto protests of 1976. International tactics included an economic boycott of South African products and a sports-related boycott of South African teams. Among the voices preaching nonviolence was Anglican bishop Desmond Tutu (1931–), who won the Nobel Peace Prize in 1984.

The white South African government responded to the challenge of the anti-apartheid movement with their own counter-propaganda, including radio and television broadcasts calculated to strengthen tribal feeling and divide the black community. The campaign included an international dimension emphasizing South Africa's role as a regional bastion of anticommunism and emphasizing the elements of violence in ANC activities. Strict censorship prevented coverage of the ANC's campaign in the white media within South Africa. Liberal journalists who resisted this tactic included Donald Woods (1933–2001). Black leaders were "banned," jailed, and—in the case of Steve Biko (1946–1977)—murdered.

Beginning in 1989 the government of F. W. De Klerk (1936–) accepted the inevitable and embraced reform. Nelson Mandela, released from jail in 1990, became president following multiracial elections in 1994; he did much to foster what he called "the rainbow nation." Thabo Mbeki, who succeeded him in 1999, proved less adept. Mandela's South Africa demonstrated considerable skill in addressing the heritage of apartheid through the operation of the Truth and Reconciliation Commission (1996–1998), chaired by Tutu, which defused opposition propaganda by revealing the atrocities committed under apartheid without resorting to reprisals or divisive trials.

In the 1980s and 1990s international bodies such as the World Health Organization (WHO) sought to use modern mass communications in Africa to prevent the spread of AIDS, among other causes; foreign-based broadcasters such as the Voice of America and the BBC have also played a part in AIDS education. Western media coverage of African events has tended to focus on disasters rather than daily occurrences and more recent success stories such as that of Eritrea, thereby perpetuating stereotypes.

In the 1990s Africa provided an object lesson in the power of the media. American TV news coverage of events in Somalia first necessitated U.S. intervention and then—when the TV images turned horrific—forced a withdrawal. In Rwanda, where the conflict between Hutu and Tutsi tribes was not favored with Western media coverage, Hutu extremists used radio broadcasts to spread tales of atrocities in order to inspire genocide. The end of the millennium saw an attempt to turn the media to Africa's advantage with the Jubilee 2000 campaign, which demanded the remission of African debts by Western nations.

Nicholas J. Cull

See also Abolitionism/Antislavery Movement; Anglo-Boer War; Arab World; British Empire; Caribbean; China; Garvey, Marcus; Portugal; Radio (International); United Nations

References: Davidson, Basil. *Modern Africa: A Social and Political History.* London: Longman, 1994; Diawara, Manthia. *African Cinema: Politics and Culture.* Bloomington: Indiana University Press, 1992; Hachten, William A., and Anthony C. Giffard. *The Press and Apartheid: Repression and Propaganda in South Africa.* Madison: University of Wisconsin Press, 1984; Morris, Kate. *British Techniques of Public Relations and Propaganda for Mobilizing East and Central Africa during World War II.* Lewiston, NY: Edwin Mellen, 2000; Thomson, Oliver. *Easily Led: A History of Propaganda.* Stroud, UK: Sutton, 1999; Ungar, Sanford. *Africa: The People and the Politics of an Emerging Continent.* New York: Simon and Schuster, 1989.

Albania
See Balkans

All Quiet on the Western Front (Im Westen Nichts Neues) (1928/1930)

Both the novel by Erich Maria Remarque (1898–1970), first published in German in 1929, and its Universal Studios film adaptation of 1930 directed by Lewis Milestone (1895–1980) are potent examples of propaganda for peace. Both presented a devastating picture of World War I from the point of view of a small group of German soldiers. They join the army fresh out of school, fired by the patriotic speeches of their teacher, but soon learn the harsh realities of trench warfare. The narrative exposes the futility of a war that, the characters eventually realize, is being fought to serve the interests of a few kings and arms manufacturers. The novel and film both exposed the powerful effect of war propaganda on European societies in 1914 and themselves became propaganda for the peace movement of the 1930s on both sides of the Atlantic. In Germany the film and novel were equally condemned and banned by Joseph Goebbels (1897–1945). In the United States the film suffered at the hands of the censors, who were concerned by the level of violence and a scene showing sexual contact between the soldiers and a French women. In 1939 Universal released a bastardized version of the film containing an anti-Nazi commentary designed to fit the new propaganda needs of World War II.

Nicholas J. Cull

See also Film (Feature); Germany; Goebbels, Joseph; Novel; Peace and Antiwar Movements (1500–1945); World War I

References: Kelly, Andrew. *Cinema and the Great War.* London: Routledge, 1997; Kelly, Andrew. *Filming "All Quiet on the Western Front": Brutal Cutting, Stupid Censors, Bigoted Politicos.* London: I. B. Tauris, 1998.

Anglo-Boer War (1899–1902)

Alternatively known as the Second Boer War and the South African War, the Anglo-Boer War employed new mass styles of wartime propaganda in response to recent developments in media technology and the politics of mass society of the late nineteenth century. The war was fought by the British Empire against the two Dutch-speaking republics of the Orange Free State and the South African Republic (formerly the Transvaal Republic). Given the disparity of strength, the defeat and annexation of the two "Boer" (Dutch for "farmer") republics was inevitable. But early British defeats, followed by difficulties and brutalities in ending the war, earned the Boers considerable sympathy in Europe and the United States, bolstered by a pro-Boer propaganda campaign. This included the issue of British farm burnings and of "concentration camps." The first war fought by the British since the Crimean War (1854–56) against an enemy with access to British and foreign news sources, it was covered by war correspondents on an unprecedented scale, raising important issues regarding censorship and control. The war also saw the widespread use of photography and marked the important early use of the cine-camera.

The chief motives for the war were ideological imperialism and a desire to control the newly discovered goldfields of the South African Republic. Sir Alfred Milner (1854–1925), high commissioner for South Africa, largely engineered the outbreak of war, this despite the reluctance of both sides to fight. Among Milner's methods was the manipulation of the press both in South Africa and in Great Britain. Cecil Rhodes (1853–1902), chairman of the De Beers diamond enterprise, was also heavily associated with manipulating the press in South Africa. British critics of the war ("pro-Boers") argued that popular and political assent to the war had been artificially contrived, foreshadowing an important twentieth-century propaganda debate.

In 1895 a close associate of Rhodes named Leander Starr "Dr. Jim" Jameson (1853–1917) launched the so-called Jameson Raid to provoke an uprising in the South African Republic. In 1897 the latter appointed Dr. Willem Leyds of Brussels to serve as its ambassador-at-large to Europe. Leyds organized propaganda events throughout the war, notably through the use of cartoons and other visual media. Since these were not linked to any coherent political initiative, they were merely an irritation to the British government, which was nevertheless shocked at the extent and virulence of European scorn.

The war began in October 1899. The three early British defeats during "Black Week" (which occurred in December) were more important for their political and propagandistic impact than as military losses. After the occupation and annexation of the republics had been completed by July 1900, the remaining Boers changed to guerrilla tactics, requiring the British to hunt them down. In order to deprive the Boers of supplies, the British resorted to burning farmsteads and villages, placing women and children into concentration camps (separate for white and black families). The term "concentration camp" was an old one, although it had recently gained notoriety in the Spanish-American War of 1898 when it was applied to the prison camps on Cuba. At first the British camps resulted in widespread deaths due chiefly to poor organization in handling outbreaks of disease. But by the war's end (May 1902) the British were actually turning people away from the camps. Boer propaganda exploited both the British burning of farmsteads and the countless deaths from disease in the concentration camps, as revealed through a British newspaper campaign chiefly conducted by Emily Hobhouse (1860–1926). By extension, the German government's decision in the 1930s to name its Nazi detention camps for political prisoners "concentration camps" (which were unlike the British camps in nature) was meant both to reflect their unpleasant nature and to serve as a propaganda ploy against the British. The persistent belief that the British invented the concentration camp has been the war's most enduring propaganda issue.

Whereas previous British colonial wars had been covered by a handful of reporters, the Boer War involved about two hundred journalists at its height. The improvising of new forms of accreditation and censorship laid the foundations for much greater control of the press in subsequent wars occurring during the twentieth century. With few exceptions, the British also blocked reportage from the Boer side by controlling telegraph communications from South Africa. In general, the British press was willing to cooperate, the recent mass-circulation daily and illustrated weekly newspapers in particular benefiting from the war. British senior military commanders—notably Field Marshal Lord (Frederick Sleigh) Roberts (1832–1914), who served as commander-in-chief in South Africa in 1900—established a system of rewards and punishments that allowed them to exercise virtual control over the war's reportage.

The use of lightweight cameras, in particular the introduction of the Pocket Kodak in 1897, meant that this war, like the Spanish-American War, was well photographed from all sides. An early form of the cine-camera called the "Biograph" was used by W. K-L. Dickson (1860–1935) in 1899–1900 to film events from the British side. Fictional films of the war were also made in Great Britain and the United States. Coinciding with such developments as the 1896 creation of Britain's first mass-circulation newspaper (*Daily Mail*), the 1898 Imperial penny post, and the establishment by 1899 of a worldwide British telegraph cable system meant that the Boer War was reported and propagandized in a new way.

How the majority of the British working class responded to the Anglo-Boer War, the last in a series of imperial wars of expansion, remains unclear. Certainly, working-class culture was saturated with the propaganda of empire at almost every level, from trinkets to pageants. But it is difficult to prove whether the war met with popular approval in Britain, or even with much popular awareness.

Stephen Badsey

See also Africa; Britain; British Empire; Crimean War; Spanish-American War

References: Dickson, W. K-L. *The Biograph in Battle*. London: Flicks Books, 1995; Gooch, John, ed. *The Boer War: Direction, Experience and Image*. London: Frank Cass, 2000. Greenwall, Ryno. *Artists and Illustrators of the Anglo-Boer War.* Cape Town: Fernwood, 1992; Mackenzie, John M. *Propaganda and Empire*. Manchester: Manchester University Press, 1986; Pakenham, Thomas. *The Boer War*. London: Macdonald, 1979.

Anti-Semitism

Hatred of Jews has been a perennial theme of propaganda in the West since 1500. Anti-Semitism has its roots in the Christian world of the Middle Ages, when Jews were a convenient "other" against whom a Christian "self" could be defined. The race politics of the Christian Gospels, crafted to blame Jews rather than Romans for the death of Jesus, remained a stumbling block in Jewish-Christian relations. Church doctrine vilified Jews for their failure to recognize the divinity of Christ and iconography associated the image of the Jew with that of Satan. Negative stereotypes of Jews were perpetuated outside the church at all levels of society by Christians suspicious of a different culture in their

Professor Dr:
von Leers:

KRAFTE

hinter Roosevelt

Dust jacket of a book published in Munich in 1937,
Kraefte hinter Roosevelt *(The Power behind Roosevelt).*
The jacket includes a photomontage of American Jews,
including New York City Mayor Fiorello La Guardia (whose
mother was Jewish), seen licking his fingers, behind
Roosevelt; in the background the stars of the American flag
have become Jewish stars. (Courtesy of David Culbert)

midst. Medieval legends told of Jews sacrific-ing Christian infants as part of their religion and blamed them for spreading the plague by poisoning wells. Christian Europe relied on Jews to fill the necessary (but taboo) role of lending money for profit, but this merely opened a further avenue for racial hatred. The stereotype of the greedy Jewish money-lender was used to justify the periodic expul-sion of Jewish communities across Europe—especially when the king was indebted to the Jew. As non-Christians, Jews became a major target of the Spanish Inquisition. Despite progress during the eighteenth century, the nineteenth saw a resurgence of anti-Semitic propaganda, which was all the more virulent as a result of mass communication. The drive

to escape Anti-Semitic prejudice and violence became a major impetus to Jewish migration to the New World and to the development of Zionism. In France a Jewish army officer named Alfred Dreyfus (1859–1935) was wrongly accused of spying simply because he was Jewish. In Russia the tsar's secret police circulated a fake document, *The Protocols of the Elders of Zion* (1903), which revived sto-ries of a rabbinical conspiracy to take over the world.

Anti-Semitism provided a succinct, all-en-compassing explanation for the social up-heaval that resulted from the Russian Revo-lution and World War I. It married the socialist rhetoric of class warfare with the ethnic chauvinism of nationalism. Anti-Se-mitic nationalist parties flourished across eastern and central Europe. Anti-Semitism was a favorite theme of the rising German mob politician Adolf Hitler and was at the heart of his book *Mein Kampf* (1925). Hitler blamed the Jews for both bolshevism and global capitalism. After 1933 Hitler's Nazi state institutionalized anti-Semitism. The ideas of anti-Semitic academics like Alfred Rosenberg (1893–1946) were taught in schools and figured in state-sponsored films like *Jud Süss* (1940). Such propaganda laid the foundations for the murder of approxi-mately six million European Jews during World War II. Europe, however, had no mo-nopoly on anti-Semitism. In the United States industrialist Henry Ford (1836–1947) distributed anti-Semitic propaganda, and claims of Jewish conspiracy surfaced in the sermons of the charismatic radio broadcaster Father Charles Coughlin (1891–1971). The psychological appeal of anti-Semitism was strong enough for the doctrines to survive the revelation of the Nazi Holocaust. Allu-sions to Jewish world conspiracies continue to figure in the rhetoric of extreme Arab na-tionalists and American neofascists, and anti-Semitic rhetoric can also be found in ex-tremist politics across eastern Europe and Russia. The leading U.S. organization dedi-cated to exposing and refuting anti-Semitism (counterpropaganda) is the Anti-Defamation League of B'nai B'rith (ADL).

Nicholas J. Cull

See also ADL; Herzl, Theodor; Holocaust Denial; *"J'Accuse"; Jud Süss;* Labor / Antilabor; *Mein Kampf; Protocols of the Elders of Zion;* World War II (Germany); Zionism

References: Cohn, Norman. *Warrant for Genocide: The Myth of the Jewish World-Conspiracy and the "Protocols of the Elders of Zion."* London: Eyre and Spottiswoode, 1967; Morais, Vamberto. *A Short History of Anti-Semitism.* New York: Norton, 1976.

Arab World

Opposition to imperialism and Israel have been the two central themes of modern propaganda in the Arab world. The region has seen the birth of Arab nationalism along with the development of the cult of the leader, the manipulation of Islamic principles, and ultimately terrorism. As totalitarian or semitotalitarian regimes, most governmental actions in the Arab world have a propaganda dimension.

Between 1872 and World War I three currents of thought emerged in Egypt in response to the increasing challenges of the West: Pan-Islamism, Egyptian nationalism, and Arab nationalism. The first two were direct responses to the political and military threats of the West, while the last was fostered by Lebanese and Syrian intellectuals residing in Cairo who believed that the only possible defense against the West was a union of all Muslim countries. Prominent theologians like Mohammed Abduh (1848–1905) insisted that "the community of believers was the basic political unit, an indivisible whole whose separation into national or regional units was unnatural" (Lorenz 1990, 4). Although later contested by both Egyptian and Arab nationalists, this view represents the core belief of fundamentalist groups such as the Muslim Brotherhood and Al Qaeda.

When the British invaded Egypt in 1882, a surge of Egyptian nationalism spread throughout the population, aided by Lord Cromer's (1841–1917) belief that since Britain was contributing heavily to the Egyptian economy, it should be allowed to have a pervasive influence in the running of its government. The Anglo-Egyptian Treaty of 1936 represented a major step toward Egyptian independence. Nevertheless, the treaty was met with fierce opposition by the student body, which insisted upon complete Egyptian self-governance. Among these students was Gamal Abdel Nasser (1918–1970), the future ruler of Egypt.

During World War II Britain invoked Article 8 of the Anglo-Egyptian Treaty, which stated that in case of war Britain could reoccupy the country. At the conclusion of the war, Egyptian public opinion held that Britain should leave Egypt and accept its union with Sudan as compensation for Egypt's help during the conflict. When the British refused to comply, the Free Officers' Organization seized power, exiled King Farouk (1920–1965), and put General Muhammad Neguib (1901–1984) and, later, Nasser in charge. With Nasser politics shifted from Egyptian nationalism to the creation of Arab nationalism.

Anti-imperialist sentiments were pervasive in other Arab countries. Iraq declared its independence from Britain after the 1920 League of Nations Mandate expired in 1932. During the 1930s Iraqi Pan-Arabism turned increasingly anti-Western, reflecting the people's desire to be independent and self-governed. Libya did not become independent from Italy until 1951. At the time of the Suez crisis in 1956, Algeria was still under French control. Syria became the strongest advocate of Arab nationalism, with Egypt's Nasser as the undisputed leader of the movement. Saudi Arabia had been ruled by the Sa'ud family since 1932. Although it was later obliged to show moderation in its media treatment of the West due to its relationship with the United States, the Saudi ruling family always advocated conservative Islamic values—in particular the teachings of Muhammad ibn Abd al-Wahab (1703–1791), who had urged his followers to wage holy war against non-Arab Ottoman rule. Wahhabism remains the core of Saudi ideology.

Egypt's initial involvement with Arab politics was motivated by the need to guarantee support for other Arab states, particularly Syria and Palestine, but by 1937 Egyptian delegates at a Pan-Arab conference in Syria had expressed serious concern over the creation of an Israeli state, affirming that it would have constituted a great threat both to Egypt and its neighboring countries. The next year Egypt's primary position in the Middle East was confirmed when 2,500 people came to Cairo for the World Inter-Parliamentary Congress of Arab and Muslim Countries for the Defense of Palestine. Additionally, in 1944 Egypt established the League of Sovereign States, which remained in Cairo until the Camp David peace accord with Israel in 1979 and Egypt's expulsion from the league.

By 1954 Nasser had undisputed control of Egypt and had gained considerable international prestige as the father of Arab nationalism. In his *Philosophy of the Revolution* Nasser admitted that the notion of a unified Arab consciousness developed as a result of the Palestinian dilemma and imperialism. Opposition to the Baghdad Pact of 1955, the Suez Crisis of 1956, and the nationalization of the Suez Canal also motivated the Egyptian leader. Nasser's inflamed rhetoric on this occasion made him a hero in the minds of the Arab masses. He told them that the Suez Canal was "our canal . . . How could it be otherwise when it was dug at the cost of 120,000 Egyptian lives?"

Nasser consolidated his power as a cult leader through the use of the mass media. He understood that radio was the only medium that could reach people in remote areas. Television was not yet accessible to the masses and rampant illiteracy hindered the effectiveness of the press. Nasser expanded radio diffusion, put Radio Cairo under his direct control, and operated it through a board of seven members and one chairman.

The Voice of the Arabs radio station was introduced on 4 July 1953 to "expound the viewpoints of the Arab nation, reflect the hopes and fears of the Arab countries . . . unite the Arabs and mobilize their forces to achieve Arab unity." Initially it broadcast for half an hour each day, but by 1962 it had expanded to fifteen hours a day, and by the 1970s it continued almost twenty-four hours a day. Directed at the entire Arab world, the station was significant in creating mass public opinion. During the 1954 Algerian revolt against French colonialism, for example, the station allowed spokesmen for Algerian independence to express their views on the air. Some programs were created especially for certain countries, such as Israel, Iraq, and Sudan. Ahmed Said, a trusted friend of Nasser, headed the radio station. Said was described as a "Goebbels-like figure who refused to allow contradiction, who conceived every single program, even music, in political terms, and censored everything himself" (Hale 1975, 72). Radio was used to instill patriotism, nationalistic feelings of Arab unity, and anti-Israeli sentiments. Between 1 January 1952 and 31 December 1959 such phrases as "the Arab nation from the Atlantic Ocean to the Arab Gulf," "Arab Egypt," "the Arab people of Egypt," and "Arab solidarity" replaced earlier phrases such as "sons of the Nile Valley," "the Egyptian people," and "Egyptian territory." A program entitled "The Enemies of God" discredited Nasser's opponents. His personality cult was bolstered by religious elements and was used to discredit imperialist forces supporting Israel.

Part of the anti-Israeli propaganda made use of *The Protocols of the Elders of Zion*. Nasser often publicly referred to this work and frequently recommended it as a reputable source of information about the Jewish race. In 1968 a special edition was published and translated into Arabic by Nasser's brother. Innumerable copies were disseminated for propaganda purposes; Arabs who did not read foreign languages remained ignorant of the questionable authenticity of the material.

Nasser aided other friendly Arab countries in developing their own broadcasting potential through professional courses and the establishment of the Institute for Radio Training (1957), which was later done for television. Starting in 1953, the Egyptian Radio Corporation also sent trained technicians to Saudi Arabia, Libya, Kuwait, and Syria to provide assistance in the setting up of radio and television facilities. The rest of the Arab world could now more easily receive Nasser's message.

Anti-imperialism was also used by Nasser to divert attention from the failures of the regime. After the creation of the State of Israel in 1948, Nasser repeatedly affirmed that Egypt's military failures stemmed from Israel's alliance with the Western world. Nasser also attacked Arab leaders who did not share his views, calling them traitors to the cause. Until his sudden death in 1970, Nasser successfully maintained the image of a United Arab Republic. He established himself as the sole leader of the Arab nationalist movement and irritated the West with Egypt's steady stream of radio propaganda.

The countries that opposed Nasser tried to counter his propaganda by using strong verbal accusations. Radio Jordan described him as dictatorial, oppressive, and in charge of a police state. In June 1958 Radio Baghdad claimed that "hundreds of good politicians and honest men are in the prisons of Egypt" (Dawisha 1976, 172). Clandestine stations were also broadcasting anti-Nasser messages from various parts of the world. Some of these stations used Egyptian expatriates. Abdul-Fath, the former owner of the Wafdist newspaper *Al-Misri,* was hired by the French government to broadcast counterpropaganda from a clandestine station called the Voice of Egypt. This counterpropaganda did not succeed, perhaps because Nasser's status had already reached epic proportions and the power of Egyptian radio far exceeded that of any of its opponents. Moreover, the Egyptian media effectively denounced these stations

and alerted the public that imperialist countries sponsored them.

Palestinian refugees had been displaced from their homeland since the creation of Israel in 1948. Although the Arab states responded indignantly, talks of unity did not extend to an offer to absorb the large number of refugees who had been uprooted from their homes. The end result was the creation of 53 refugee camps by the United Nations Relief Works Agency, where 750,000 refugees lived in abysmal conditions. Jordan incorporated about 450,000 refugees after annexing the West Bank, and 160,000 refugees remained in Israel.

Resentment and discontent in the refugee camps led to the creation of the first underground Palestinian liberation groups. Not having access to the mass media, these groups relied on word of mouth, pamphlets, and speeches for their propaganda. Egypt's repeated military failures against Israel accelerated the creation of the first official Palestinian political group, the Harakat al-Tahrir al-Filasteni, or al-Fatah (Palestinian National Liberation Movement). Al-Fatah propagandized by spreading the notion that the dream of Arab unity had failed and that harsher measures should therefore be taken against Israel and its supporters. Guerrilla warfare and terrorism were introduced as the most effective means to harm Israel. Nasser countered the growing influence of al-Fatah by officially sponsoring the creation of the Palestinian Liberation Organization (PLO) in 1964. Located in Jordan, its army was dispersed among Egypt, Syria, and Iraq.

The PLO proved to be too moderate for the most extreme elements of al-Fatah. Supported by Syria, which wanted to show its independence from Egypt, al-Fatah settled on Syrian and Jordanian grounds, launching guerrilla attacks against Israel and recruiting fighters from the ever-increasing number of refugees living on the West Bank. In 1968 Yassir Arafat (1929–) emerged as the PLO leader. Thereafter the PLO increased terrorist attacks inside Israel and continued guerrilla warfare, thereby hoping to gain Western attention. Extremist groups within the Palestinian movement concentrated on international terrorism as a form of propaganda that would finally propel the Palestinian cause into the spotlight; these groups included the Popular Front for the Liberation of Palestine, founded by George Habash (1925–) and the Popular Democratic Front for the Liberation of Palestine, founded by Nayef Hawatmeh (1937–). Some of the best-known terrorist attacks included the kidnapping and death of eleven Israeli athletes during the 1972 Munich Olympic Games and several plane hijackings of the early 1970s.

Nasser's sudden death led to Anwar Sadat (1918–1981) being declared Egypt's new leader at a time when the political situation in the Middle East was extremely tense. Egypt had been the only country to pose a serious military threat to Israel. After the 1973 war, however, Sadat's postwar policy favored a well-defined peace with Israel. This policy was based on compelling economic reasons: the economic strains of Egypt's growing population; the cost of maintaining a big army; and the necessity of repaying the armaments mainly provided by Russia. Sadat was forced to use propaganda domestically and abroad to establish closer ties with the West, eventually achieving a peace agreement with Israel. In so doing he alienated his country from the rest of the Arab world, which considered Sadat's actions an act of betrayal pure and simple.

One of the first political moves in the "de-Nasserization" of Egypt was the liberation of all of Nasser's political prisoners. This gave Sadat a favorable image both at home and abroad. The mass media was used to achieve the same objectives. President Sadat viewed the media as a tool to shape public opinion in the interest of the government. For instance, editors of the weekly paper *Al-Musawwar,* which supported the views of many former political prisoners, discredited Nasser's image: "[T]he façade was magnificent, de-stroying capitalism, feudalism, and exploitation . . . but the application was a completely different thing . . . It did not contain any of the qualities of the façade." During Nasser's regime, journalists critical of the government were imprisoned; under Sadat they simply lost their jobs. Notable is the case of Muhammad Hassanai Haykal. A close personal friend of Nasser, he had founded the Al-Ahram publishing house. Initially he was allowed to maintain his position, but when he began to openly criticize Sadat's actions during the 1973 war, the president had him removed from his position. In the end, he could only publish books outside of Egypt. In Sadat's own words, "If freedom of the press is sacred, Egypt is more sacred and I am not prepared to relinquish any of her rights" (Rugh 1979, 48).

The U.S. government saw the Camp David peace accord as an opportunity to reestablish influence in the Middle East. The U.S. role was of paramount importance for Egypt's and Israel's propaganda, not only because of its economic and political clout but also because it represented a kind of alibi for Sadat and Israeli Prime Minister Menachem Begin (1913–1992), who were both facing strong internal opposition. In other words, the role of the United States as a mediator made both leaders appear unwilling participants in the peace talks, which was essential if they were both to maintain favorable domestic public opinion. Furthermore, a peace treaty between Egypt and Israel would have represented an important achievement of the Carter administration and valuable propaganda for President Jimmy Carter's (1924–) reelection campaign. After the assassination of President Sadat in 1981, President Hosni Mubarak (1928–) continued to honor the Camp David peace accord, simultaneously reaching out to the rest of the Arab world.

Section IIIb of the Camp David peace accord called for the creation of a Palestinian homeland in the Gaza Strip and the West Bank, rendering these territories inviolable. Palestinian propaganda had focused on this objective since the first terrorist acts of the early 1970s. However, this part of the accord was never implemented. Israel was unwilling to renounce the conquered lands of the West Bank and the Gaza Strip. The failure to create a Palestinian homeland had far-reaching consequences. Because of its intrinsic weakness based on its history, geographic location, and population demographics, Lebanon became the natural target for the Palestinian settlements and the PLO's military and terror offensives against Israel. This was countered by Israeli reprisals, culminating in the partial military invasion of southern Lebanon by the Israeli army in 1982. Syria responded by invading the Bekaa Valley to counterbalance the Israeli occupation of the Golan Heights. The Palestinian National Liberation Front was dispersed among a few friendly countries, such as Yemen, Syria, and Tunisia. The Palestinian people were once again refugees.

King Hussein of Jordan (1935–1999) opposed extreme terrorist attacks like those perpetrated by al-Fatah in the 1970s, but he wanted to recover the lost West Bank territories even if it meant allowing the turbulent Palestinians to settle in his country. Eventually the PLO was recognized by the United Nations as the only legitimate representative of the Palestinian people, and an Arab summit meeting in Morocco approved the PLO as the government-in-exile for Palestinians. Before the West Bank was finally handed over to the Palestinians, Israelis believed that the refugees should live in the neighboring Arab states. Israeli propaganda stressed that the Arab countries were responsible for keeping Palestinians in refugee camps, which were used as the main training camps for Palestinian guerrilla fighters. Israel emphasized that the refugee camps were not even supported by the Arab states but rather by the United Nations. More recently some Palestinians have been allowed to return to the West Bank, but most refugees still live in refugee camps.

The Palestinian dilemma has been used by the Arab states to justify their own political agendas. After the death of Nasser and Egypt's perceived betrayal as a result of the Camp David accord, Libyan leader Muammar al-Qaddafi (1942–) attempted to assume the role of primary crusader for Arab unity, Palestinian freedom, and independence from Western hegemony. Libyan propaganda focused on the cult of the leader. Qaddafi's *Third Way Ideology,* published in the *Green Book,* described Islam as the answer to the world's problems and identified himself as the new spiritual leader of the revolution. At the same time, Qaddafi sanctioned the creation of terrorist training camps on Libyan soil and produced strong anti-Western messages by means of the mass media. Libyan propaganda was not successful in the West because Qaddafi had seriously discredited himself by supporting terrorist activities against the United States and Israel. Moreover, Arab countries such as Egypt, Saudi Arabia, and Iraq countered Qaddafi's propaganda with their own, condemning the Libyan leader's extreme religious statements as radical and heretical.

Iraq's Saddam Hussein (1937–) manipulated the West into silently supporting his invasion of Iran by playing on America's fear of the surge of Islamic fundamentalism in Iran under the Ayatollah Khomeini (1900–1989). He also used the mass media in a totalitarian way to foster a personality cult, stressing modernization and deemphasizing religion. Both radio and television stations were subsumed under the Iraqi Broadcasting and Television Establishment, which was directly linked to the Ministry of Culture and Information. Radio programs were broadcast in Arabic, Kurdish, Syriac, and Turkoman, as well as English, French, German, Russian, and other languages. Newspapers remain under government control and are subject to censorship. Article 26 of the Iraqi constitution calls for "freedom of publication within the limits of the law." Therefore, the print press is monitored by the Ministry of Guidance, while the Ministry of Culture and Information retains sole authority to import and distribute news from the foreign press. Despite Hussein's totalitarian regime, Iraq's relationship with the United States did not deteriorate until 1990, when Iraq invaded Kuwait.

In the last decade, peace negotiations in the Middle East have repeatedly failed. The Gulf War reversed Iraq's relations with the United States and turned the Arab state into an open supporter of extremist groups. Resentment against the living conditions of Palestinian refugees remains a common source of anger against the West and Israel. While Saudi Arabia and Egypt have maintained closer ties with the United States, countries like Syria, Libya, and Iraq have openly condemned Western foreign policy and continue to support terrorist activity. The attacks against the United States on 11 September 2001 demonstrated a new level of terrorist warfare that employed the international media to the fullest extent. Extremist leader Osama bin Laden (1957–) successfully captured the attention of the Western world. Al Qaeda propaganda focuses on justice for the Palestinian cause, the imposition of distorted Islamic values for all Arab nations, and the removal of American army bases from the Holy Land. While many Middle Eastern countries have condemned the extremist actions of Al Qaeda and have shown support to the United States, bin Laden's reputation has reached cult status among some Arabs, who see him as the hero of the resistance against Western domination.

Livia Bornigia

See also Anti-Semitism; Cold War in the Middle East; Gulf War; Hussein, Saddam; Iran; Israel; Laden, Osama bin; Ottoman Empire/Turkey; *Protocols of the Elders of Zion;* Religion; Suez Crisis; Terrorism; Terrorism, War on; United Nations

References: Baker, William. *Egypt's Uncertain Revolution under Nasser and Sadat.* Cambridge, MA: Harvard University Press, 1978; Chapin Metz, Helen. *Iraq: A Country Study.* Washington, DC: Library of Congress Federal Research Division, 1988. Dawisha, Adeed I. *Egypt in the Arab World.* London: Macmillan, 1976; Dekmejian, R. H. *Egypt under Nasir: A Study in Political Dynamics.* Albany: State University of the New York Press, 1971; Gilman, Sander L. *Anti-Semitism in Times of Crisis.* New York: New York University Press, 1991; Hale, Julian. *Radio Power: Propaganda and International Broadcasting.* Philadelphia: Temple University Press, 1975; Hateem, M. Abdel-Kader. *Information and the Arab Cause.* London: Longman, 1974; Kiernan, Thomas. *The Arabs.* London: Abacus, 1982; Lorenz, Joseph P. *Egypt and the Arabs: Foreign Policy and the Search for National Identity.* San Francisco: Westview, 1990; Mansfield, Peter. *The Arabs.* New York: Penguin, 1985; Rugh, William A. *The Arab Press: News Media and Political Process in the Arab World.* New York: Syracuse University Press, 1979; Said, Edward S. *Covering Islam.* New York: Pantheon, 1981; Stephens, Robert. *Nasser: A Political Biography.* New York: Simon and Schuster, 1971.

Architecture

Although architecture may not come to mind immediately when speaking of propaganda, it is an indisputable fact that it has served ancient rulers, religious movements, Renaissance princes and republics, early European rulers, the great monarchs of the seventeenth and eighteenth centuries, and modern republican, revolutionary, and totalitarian regimes. Recently modern corporations have built impressive headquarters to strengthen their images.

Architecture can serve an ideological purpose in three basic ways: it can impress, accommodate, and serve the masses. First, architecture can impress messages on the public mind. It can do this through the style, size, placement, and decoration of public buildings. In the eighteenth century many architects viewed architecture as a type of visual language that could speak to the onlooker. They spoke of giving various structures "un caractère," that is, an appearance that would proclaim the purpose of the building. For instance, the designer would use Corinthian columns on a palace or a pleasure house but not on a courthouse or a jail. Etruscan columns were better suited for edifices with serious purpose. Such public buildings could convey their importance through sheer size. To catch the public eye they could be placed in conspicuous sites along the banks of rivers, at the ends of broad avenues, the intersection of principal streets, or on one side of a public square. Moreover, one could convey messages about such buildings by decorating them with statues of rulers or leaders, allegorical figures, and symbols, or by appending pithy inscriptions.

Second, architecture can accommodate large numbers of people for religious or political ceremonies. The Greeks built impressive theaters and amphitheaters where citizens could come together. Some scholars have argued that Roman theaters, arenas, circuses, and hippodromes were at the center of public life and strengthened allegiance to the regime in power. In the Middle Ages large churches provided meeting places for the populace, where the faithful could participate in rituals, listen to religious music, and receive their priests' homilies. Some large religious edifices built in the twelfth or thirteenth centuries, such as Chartres Cathedral in France, could also accommodate pilgrims who had come to see the sacred spring or the Black Virgin in the crypt. On occasion these large spaces also served nonreligious functions, such as communal meetings.

Third, political regimes have attempted to prove that they have the interests of the public at heart by building useful facilities for the populace. Roman rulers built highways, aqueducts, fountains, and baths for their citizens. Popes continued to support such projects during the early modern period, in addition to palaces and châteaux to house their retinue and proclaim their power. Monarchs in the sixteenth, seventeenth, and eighteenth centuries likewise built roads, public squares, fountains, canals, and hospitals. French revolutionary leaders called for the construction of public baths, lavatories, fountains, schools, theaters, arenas, and courthouses. In the twentieth century the Nazis built the autobahn (expressway), youth retreats, and art galleries, while the Soviet Union promoted communal apartment buildings, workers'

cultural centers, airports, and dams. Today's corporations sponsor sports arenas, covering every available space with logos and advertisements proclaiming their sponsorship. High-profile buildings can also be prime targets, as was demonstrated by the terrorist attacks in the United States on 11 September 2001.

James A. Leith

See also Germany; Memorials and Monuments; Ottoman Empire/Turkey; Revolution, French; Russia; Southeast Asia
References: Kopp, Anatole. *Town and Revolution: Soviet Architecture and Urban Planning, 1917–1935.* New York: Braziller, 1970; Leith, James A. *Space and Revolution: Projects for Monuments, Squares, and Public Buildings in France, 1789–1799.* Montreal: McGill-Queen's University Press, 1991; Mâle, Emile. *The Gothic Image: Religious Art in France of the Thirteenth Century.* New York: Harper, 1958; Taylor, Robert R. *The Word in Stone: The Role of Architecture in National Socialist Ideology.* Berkeley: University of California Press, 1974.

Argentina
See Latin America

Art

The use of images and symbols as a tool for the dissemination of social, political, or religious ideas is a traditional facet of the visual arts. All artistic production is necessarily representative of its creator and its time and consequently holds some propaganda value. The most common use of art as a propaganda tool is through the manipulation of narrative art and graphic symbols to alter the viewer's opinion. This function of art has been extensively used in modern times to engender support for ideologies and political regimes, but it dates back to Egyptian and other ancient civilizations.

The intimate relationship between artistic production and the state underlies the persuasive element of fine art. Egyptian, Roman, and medieval rulers all used art to support their regimes; similarly, the despots of Renaissance Italian states and the early modern monarchies of Western Europe saw art and architecture as a means to bolster their rule. Art communicated the self-confidence of the rising nations of the seventeenth century, such as the Netherlands. The state deployment of art in eighteenth-century Europe is best seen in the work of Jacques-Louis David (1748–1825), whose *Oath of the Horatii* (1785) can be seen as an intensely dramatic affirmation of patriotism. Similarly, David's depiction of the death of Marat endowed that revolutionary leader with the status of an icon. David's later depictions of Napoleon are a prime example of art as propaganda intended to mythologize and glorify a regime. Many of the forms established in doing this were resurrected throughout the nineteenth century, such as in Eugene Delacroix's (1798–1863) *Liberty Leading the People* (1830).

The Napoleonic Wars were a popular subject for history painting and narrative art. By this time the very nature of the subject matter was calculated to elicit a nationalist response. In Spain, Goya's *Third of May 1808* (1814) became the supreme expression of Spanish Nationalism. Art became a central element in nationalism across nineteenth-century Europe.

The British taste for narrative art was pervasive throughout the nineteenth century. Celebratory art glorified imperialism, endorsing Britain's claim to a God-given right to rule over colonial nations. This narrative impulse also lent itself to social and moral commentary; a tradition of satire flourished alongside more academic subjects, as in the work of William Hogarth (1697–1764) and James Gillray (1757–1815). In France this social content of art established itself through works such as *Raft of the Medusa* (1819) by Théodore Géricault (1791–1824), a polemic against the Bourbon restoration and readable as political allegory. Géricault's artistic legacy can be seen in realism and social realist art.

In the twentieth century the rise of the avant-garde led to the breakdown of academic hierarchy. Such work, created outside formal social structures, loosened the hold of history painting, although its principles, particularly as a strong tool for propaganda, are still evident in Picasso's *Guernica* (1937) and the output of the socialist-inspired Mexican Muralists. The avant-garde rested on the idea of the autonomy of the artist; hence this mode of art would be challenged by the restrictions on art production imposed by mid-twentieth-century dictatorships. The strict regulation of the art world under various totalitarian regimes was unprecedented in the annals of art history and represented the high point of the appropriation of art as propaganda.

In Nazi Germany the state sponsored both high and low art. The Nazis imposed strict controls on all aspects of culture. Artistic style and subject matter alike had to reflect the idealized values of the *volk* (people). This contrasts with Fascist Italy, which saw some crossover between official art and modernism. The tenets of a "German Art" were displayed in the famous exhibition "Blut und Boden" (Blood and Soil) of 1935, which promoted the depiction of idyllic scenes and heroic individuals in monumental poses. Portrayals of the workers themselves were generally subordinated to displays of heavy industry, and unemployment was never shown. Posters, an immediate form of communication ideally suited to the government's aim, played an important role in wartime propaganda. Artists creating opposition propaganda included John Heartfield (1891–1968), whose photomontages satirized Nazi policy.

In the USSR art figured in Soviet "Agitprop" (Agitational Propaganda). The most famous example of Agitprop art was Vladimir Tatlin's (1895–1953) Monument to the Third Communist International, a response to Lenin's call for monumental propaganda. Agitprop was all-embracing in society: even candy wrappers were used in this way. The dynamic tradition of Russian modernist art gave way to a dreary academic style glorifying the party, the state, or workers. Only political posters remained a vibrant and modern aesthetic medium.

In Mexico, Diego Rivera (1866–1957) considered mural painting a powerful form of propaganda and switched from his earlier Cubist style, winning international acclaim. His compatriots David Alfaro Siqueiros (1894–1974) and José Clemente Orozco (1883–1949) also received such praise. These artists eventually moved to the United States, where they won commissions and introduced a new political dimension into American art. Orozco completed a mural cycle in Dartmouth College (1932) depicting Western imperialism and twentieth-century industrialization. Siqueiros completed both *Tropical America* and *Portrait of Present Day Mexico* in Los Angeles. Rivera created the most famous mural of the group for Henry Ford, *Detroit Industry* (1933), which presented a radical representation of labor and technology. A Rivera mural in Rockefeller Center in New York drew criticism because it included a portrait of Lenin; as a result the mural was destroyed.

The effect of the muralists on the American art scene was immense, especially in New York: the center of social realist art. Social realism in the United States was wholly different from the form seen in Soviet Russia. Artists such as Ben Shahn (1898–1969) and Phillip Evergood (1901–1973) took inspiration from labor unrest and racial discrimination. U.S. government responses to the Great Depression included the commissioning of art by the Works Progress Administration Federal Arts Projects (WPA-FAP). Famous (and controversial) works included the murals in the Coit Tower in San Francisco, with their apparent Communist subtext.

The Cold War had major implications for art, emphasizing the polarity between the free Western model of high-cultured, formalist, and abstract art against the Soviet model, which was figurative and restrictive. The CIA and other U.S. organizations subsidized and promoted U.S. abstract expressionist artists overseas as symbols of the creative freedom enjoyed within the U.S. system. Ironically many of these artists had been associated with the political left, and their abstract style was a conscious rejection of politics in art. Their role in the cultural Cold War was a case of art being appropriated as propaganda as opposed to the conscious construction of art as propaganda. Propaganda art found more fertile ground in criticizing the U.S. government during the Vietnam conflict through works such as the famous Art Workers Coalition piece *Q. And Babies? A. And Babies* (1970), which commented on the horror of the My Lai incident. The postmodern period has seen the marginalization of politicized art, although totalitarian art lives on in places like Iraq, China, and North Korea.

Daniel Cooper

See also CIA; David, Jacques-Louis; France; Germany; Goya; *Guernica;* Mexico; Portraiture; Postage Stamps; Posters; Revolution, French; Russia; Spain

References: Ades, Dawn. *Art and Power: Europe under the Dictators 1930–45.* London: South Bank Centre, 1995; Doss, Erika Lee. *Benton, Pollock, and the Politics of Modernism: From Regionalism to Abstract Expressionism.* Chicago: University of Chicago Press, 1991; Lee, Anthony W. *Painting On the Left: Diego Rivera, Radical Politics, and San Francisco's Public Murals.* Berkeley: University of California Press, 1999; Pearson, Nicholas M. *The State and the Visual Arts: A Discussion of State Intervention in the Visual Arts in Britain, 1760–1981.* Milton Keynes, UK: Open University Press, 1982; Petropoulos, Jonathan. *Art as Politics in the Third Reich.* Chapel Hill: University of North Carolina Press, 1996; Rosenblum, Robert. *Art of the Nineteenth Century: Painting and Sculpture.* London: Thames and Hudson, 1984.

Atrocity Propaganda

Atrocity stories are a time-honored technique of propagandists, particularly in war propaganda. It is with the Crusades that the study of atrocity propaganda in wartime began. Pope Urban II (c. 1035–1099), in a sermon given at Clermont in 1095, justified the war against Islam by claiming that the

This atrocious image—the execution of a Chinese farmer by a Communist soldier—was circulated by the U.S. government overseas in the 1950s. (National Archives)

enemy had ravaged the churches of God in the Eastern provinces, circumcised Christian men, violated women, and carried out the most unspeakable torture before killing them. Urban's sermon succeeded in mobilizing popular enthusiasm for the People's Crusade.

Powerful representations of martyrdom can be found in the sixteenth-century engravings in the *Book of Martyrs* (1556) by John Foxe (1516–1587), which depicted Catholic atrocities in graphic detail. In 1571 the Convocation of Canterbury decreed that the book was to be placed, together with the Bishop's Bible of 1568, in the house of every bishop, dean, and archdeacon. In the preface to the first edition Foxe claimed that he wished to reach "every man" and the "simple people." In many ways the horrifically graphic portrayal of torture can be seen as the fore-

runner to the type of atrocity propaganda that one finds in the twentieth century. As religious propaganda the message disseminated by the engravings influenced anti-Catholic sentiments for generations and provoked bitter reprisals.

During World War I atrocity propaganda was employed on a global scale. Unlike previous wars, the Great War was the first total war in which whole nations and not just professional armies were locked in mortal combat. This and subsequent modern wars required propaganda to (1) mobilize hatred against the enemy; (2) convince the population of the justness of one's own cause; (3) enlist the active support and cooperation of neutral countries; and (4) strengthen the support of one's allies. Having sought to pin war guilt on the enemy, the next step is to make the enemy appear savage, barbaric, and inhumane. All the belligerents in World War I employed atrocity propaganda, and as a result stereotypes emerged that had been largely developed in the period leading up to the outbreak of war. The Germans referred to the British as the "perfidious Albion" and provided accounts of the Allied use of dum-dum bullets, mutilation, and brutality, as well as the use of "savages" from Africa and Asia to fight civilized peoples. The Germans also referred to the British naval blockade as an "atrocity." Britain, however, is justifiably regarded as deploying atrocity propaganda with more intensity and more skill than most. Tales of the spike-helmeted German "Hun" cutting off the hands of children, boiling corpses to make soap, crucifying prisoners of war, and using priests as clappers in cathedral bells were widely believed by the British public, particularly after the Bryce Commission, which had been established to look into these claims, concluded that many were true. Both the British stereotype of the Hun and the French image of the *Boche* provided a platform for Allied propaganda to launch a moral offensive against a society founded upon militaristic values, thereby bringing home to its own populations the unimaginable consequences of defeat. Atrocity propaganda therefore played a major role in the wave of patriotism that enveloped Europe in the early stages of World War I.

In the years immediately following the conflict, various investigations, particularly in France and Britain, suggested that much of atrocity propaganda was false. As a result, atrocity propaganda was never used on the same scale in World War II. The British took the view that Nazism itself was an atrocity. In fact, much of British propaganda in World War II was characterized by the use of humor to deflate the enemy. The Nazis, however, had no such reservations and used atrocity propaganda whenever it was deemed appropriate. It was used extensively in Nazi anti-Bolshevik campaigns. Perhaps the most famous propaganda coup was the revelation of the Katyn

massacre in 1943. Its repercussions led to the breaking off of diplomatic relations between the Soviet Union and the Polish government-in-exile. On 13 April German radio announced the discovery of a mass grave in the Katyn Forest near Smolensk, where Polish officers had been methodically killed. Both the press and the newsreels carried lurid accounts of the manner in which the Poles were slain, charging that Jewish officers of the Red Army were responsible for the murders. A documentary film entitled *Im Wald von Katyn* (In the Forest of Katyn) was also compiled and shown in all the major movie theaters in Germany and occupied Europe. There was a further tragic consequence of the atrocity stories of World War I. The discrediting of wartime propaganda and the revelations that few, if any, of the atrocity stories had been true led to a widespread disinclination on the part of the British and American public during World War II to believe real atrocity stories of extermination camps when they began to emerge from Nazi Germany.

In the post-1945 world, atrocity propaganda continued to figure prominently in all major modern wars, from Korea to Kosovo. In the Gulf War, for example, Western journalists focused on the *Anfal*—the Iraqi extermination of ethnic Kurds. Ethnic cleansing, as well as the atrocities that occur as a result of such polices, were strongly featured in the reporting of the Kosovo conflict. Both Albanians and Serbs employed atrocity stories to whip up xenophobic emotions—the surest method of eliciting from the masses savage patriotism that places the blame for every political folly or military action upon the head of the enemy.

David Welch

See also Austrian Empire; The Big Lie; Bryce Report; Fakes; Goya; Gulf War; Ireland; Latin America; Netherlands, Belgium, and Luxembourg; Ottoman Empire/Turkey; Poland; Raemakers, Louis; Reformation and Counter-Reformation; Scandinavia; World War I; World War II (United States)
References: Ponsonby, Arthur. *Falsehood in War-Time: Containing an Assortment of Lies Circulated*

throughout the Nations during the Great War. London: G. Allen and Unwin, 1928; Read, James Morgan. *Atrocity Propaganda, 1914–18.* New Haven, CT: Yale University Press, 1941; Roetter, Charles. *Psychological Warfare.* London: Batsford, 1974; Welch, David. *The Third Reich: Politics and Propaganda.* London: Routledge, 2002.

Australia

Australia, a continent and the world's largest island, supports a population of 19 million living in an area just under 3 million square miles. Two thirds of the entire country's population live in a few urban areas of the southeast, making Australia one of the most urbanized countries on the planet. Why Australia has so few people and how those people got there are questions that have fueled longstanding debates about the Australian national character, which in turn have given rise to pervasive national myths, all of which are of interest to the student of propaganda. More recently there is an increasing recognition that there is more to Australian national identity than gauging the degree of English or American cultural domination. Australia had an Aboriginal population long before the first English settlers arrived. In sum, questions of national identity have affected official and unofficial propaganda in the twentieth century.

Australia's eastern coast was first charted by Captain James Cook (1728–1779) in 1770. Britain made Australia a penal colony, permanently exiling convicted criminals in this "empty" land. Although the policy of permanent exile ended in 1809, the remainder of the nineteenth century saw a steady influx of colonists, mostly but not entirely from Britain. In January 1901 the six Australian colonies were renamed states as part of the establishment of the Commonwealth of Australia, an entity still connected by more than sentiment to the British crown. Australia's Commonwealth identity was shaped by three concerns: immigration; the growth of a labor movement; and the need to develop a sense of loyalty to a federal (as opposed to a local)

Australia. The Immigration Restriction Act of 1902 required that immigrants possess fluency in a European language, a rule designed to keep the Chinese from entering the country. This whites-only exclusionist (racist) policy remained in force until the 1960s, helping to keep Australian identity tied to London, as well as preventing the population from growing too rapidly.

Film came early to Australia. In 1896 a Lumière representative filmed the Melbourne Cup race. A year later one newsreel contained footage of Aboriginals. In 1901 Sir William Baldwin Spencer began to film Aboriginals in central Australia. On Boxing Day (26 December) 1906 *The Story of the Kelly Gang,* a sixty six minute tale of Australia's famous bandit Ned Kelly (1855–1880)—considered the world's first feature film—premiered in Melbourne Town Hall. The original advertising cannot be accused of understatement: "The greatest, most thrilling and sensational moving picture ever taken!" Australian film flourished until the coming of sound in the late 1920s. That, plus the Great Depression, meant that for the next forty years going to the movies meant going to watch American and British movies.

In World War I more than three hundred thousand Australians fought in the Middle East and on the Western Front, of which nearly sixty thousand died. This extraordinary sacrifice is captured in the name "Gallipoli," the scene of enormous Australian losses (as well as New Zealand and British) in an ill-fated effort to conquer Constantinople from the sea in an attempt to take the Ottoman Empire out of the war. The effective Turkish resistance was organized by Mustafa Kemal (1881–1938), though both sides suffered three hundred thousand casualties apiece. The experience became foundational for Australian national identity, and its cultural meaning is well captured by the Australian feature film *Gallipoli* (1981), directed by Peter Weir (1944–). Some consider *Gallipoli* one of the greatest antiwar films of all time, but one can also view Weir as using the past to justify an Australian foreign policy of isolationism and pandering to Republican, antimonarchist sentiments.

World War II presents its own set of problems for the student of propaganda in Australia in the form of collaboration with the enemy. In 1943 the Imperial Japanese Army Secret Service and Australian servicemen made a film revealing the pleasant conditions in which prisoners of war were living while under Japanese supervision. The film, *Calling Australia!* (1943), was meant to soften up Australian public opinion and to make a forthcoming invasion of Australia as painless as possible. No invasion took place and the film was forgotten, only to be rediscovered in 1969. The film reveals Australian POWs and Dutch internees on Java frolicking at a country club, a scene remote from reality, though the Australians are easily identifiable. Geoffrey Barnes made a fine documentary about the ethics of collaboration entitled *Calling Australia! Prisoners of Propaganda* (1987). Another instance of collaboration, this time involving radio, is the story of Maj. Charles Hughes Cousens (1903–1966), a popular broadcaster for Radio 20B (Sydney). Cousens was captured during the fall of Singapore. When his Japanese captors learned of his credentials, they forced him to broadcast from Tokyo. Radio Tokyo (short-wave) carried Cousens's first broadcast in August 1942; he worked closely with the infamous "Tokyo Rose" and went to San Francisco in 1949 to testify on her behalf. In 1945 Cousens was charged with treason, but his case never came to trial because the attorney general of New South Wales did not feel the evidence warranted an indictment, though the army felt otherwise. Cousens was not court-martialed, but he was stripped of his commission, effectively branding him a traitor. That Australians of a certain age continue to debate Cousens's guilt indicates how sensitive some veterans are to the behavior of one who, instead of making some futile heroic gesture, did what he was told.

Sometimes doing what one is told has other consequences. Australia's willingness to confront its Aboriginal past is a troubling issue for a country that for so long ignored this part of its national cultural identity. For example, thousands of Aboriginal children were forcibly taken from their own families as part of a government policy, a process legitimized by federal and church-run institutions set up to house these so-called orphans. A 1997 Human Rights and Equal Opportunity Commission report provided detailed evidence of a policy seemingly intended to force white values on Aboriginal children. Phillip Noyce (1950–) has directed *Rabbit-Proof Fence* (2002), a film that asks Australians to confront a subject traditionally considered taboo by the Australian film industry. Noyce addressed the propaganda content of his subject in an interview: "I could feel in the wind that white Australia wanted a vehicle— whether it was a movie, whether it was a book, or whatever—that got beyond the slogans and allowed them to come to terms with the history of race relations in this country" (*Christian Science Monitor*, 20 February 2002, 7). As Australia becomes a multiracial society, it is important for all of its citizens to recognize the social costs of imposing white societal values on the original Aboriginal inhabitants. This will inevitably downgrade traditional national stereotypes of the shearer, the digger, and the farmer—all pioneers who occupy uncharted wilderness in the traditional national narrative.

Australia's media history is synonymous with two Murdochs, father and son: Sir Keith Murdoch (1885–1952) and his son, Keith Rupert Murdoch (1931–), the latter being one of the world's most powerful media operatives. The father was an overseas correspondent during the Gallipoli campaign of 1915 and compiled detailed information about the incompetence of British commander Sir Ian Hamilton (1853–1947), which he brought with him to Marseilles, where he transmitted his accusations in the form of a report to his own prime minister in Australia, concluding with the observation that Hamilton was committing "murder through incapacity." When Sir Keith's report was reprinted as a Cabinet paper in London, the result was the recall in disgrace of Hamilton. For the rest of his life Sir Keith was an authentic Australian hero, the war correspondent who got the Aussies out of Gallipoli. Sir Keith became the chief executive of the *Melbourne Herald* newspaper group and the founder of the first powerful newspaper empire in Australia, one given to promoting conservative political values. Sir Keith's son, Rupert, inherited a reduced media empire in 1952; indeed, Rupert can truthfully claim to be a self-made man, starting with the *Adelaide News,* a small paper left to him by his father. In 1960 Murdoch purchased the dying *Sydney Paper,* turning it into the largest-selling newspaper in Australia thanks to a racy tabloid style and aggressive promotion. In 1964 he started *The Australian,* a national newspaper for a more serious audience. After that Murdoch moved the center of his media operations to London. In time Murdoch owned two television stations in Australia and became deeply involved in global media with satellite television. Since 1960 it would be wrong to say that Murdoch's primary focus has been Australian media, but nobody thinking of Australian media today could possibly ignore Murdoch's powerful presence. Broadcasting is regulated by the Australian Broadcasting Authority. National broadcasting is in the hands of the Australian Broadcasting Corporation (ABC). A special broadcasting service offers radio and television programming in sixty languages, mostly to small numbers of viewers. In 1997, 99 percent of all homes in Australia had television. There are fifty daily newspapers. Regarding the content of the Australian media, *Americanization and Australia* (1998), a book edited by two Australian academics, states the matter bluntly. Philip Bell's essay on television makes an important point: "What is strange about *Crocodile Dundee* and *The Castle* and recent television schedules generally, is the seamless, invisible (or seldom noticed) transitions between the vernacular populism of local programs and the very different accents, narratives, acting styles and *mise-en-scene* of the American-produced 'shows' which are regularly broadcast following local productions. *Melrose Place, L.A. Law* or *The X-Files* do not merely offer glamourized and hyper-dramatized 'worlds apart'; they seem not to address audiences as national or local subjects at all. Theirs is, by contrast, the televisual itself, making no specific demands on the viewer to identity as 'Australian,' but not as 'American' either." One might deem this an insidious sort of cultural propaganda; one wonders if such nuances might escape the attention of the inattentive viewer. It seems likely, however, that future discussions about the Americanization of Australian culture a result of propaganda—is to be found in such careful discussions of the televisual self.

David Culbert

See also Murdoch, Rupert; New Zealand; Pacific/Oceania; World War I

References: Bell, Philip, and Roger Bell, eds. *Americanization and Australia.* Sydney: University of New South Wales Press, 1998; Bertrand, Ina, ed. *Cinema in Australia: A Documentary History.* Kensington: New South Wales Press, 1989; Chapman, Ivan. *Tokyo Calling: The Charles Cousens Case.* Sydney: Hale & Iremonger, 1990; Goldman, Wendy. *The Murdoch Mission: The Digital Transformation of a Media Empire.* New York: John Wiley, 2002; More, Elizabeth, and Glen Lowis, eds. *Australian Communications Technology and Policy: A Reader.* Sydney: Australian Communication Association, 1988.

Austrian Empire

The vast Austrian Empire (today's Austria, Hungary, Czech Republic, and Slovakia) sought to maintain itself through propaganda, which played a part in its fragmentation and figured centrally in the histories of the nations that came into being in the old Habsburg provinces. At the start of the early modern period Emperor Maximilian (1495–1519) used his power as a patron of the arts to enhance his position. Court artists included Albrecht Dürer (1471–1528). Favorite depictions of the emperor stressed his virtue as a Christian knight. Habsburg propaganda reached its apogee during the rule of Maximilian's grandson Charles V (1500–1558). Painters such as Titian (c. 1488–1576) portrayed Charles V as a Roman emperor, while the house of Habsburg adopted Hercules as a mascot, reproducing that image on their currency. Emperor Rudolf II (1552–1612) combined his patronage of the arts and sciences (from his court in Prague) with an attempt to extend Catholicism. In Hungary his policies led to a revolt. The court trumpeted its victories and slandered its enemies—most famously the Turks, whose atrocities both real and imagined were widely depicted in woodcuts. The Habsburgs became the key force in maintaining a Catholic mission against the Turks.

The developing print culture of the seventeenth century was controlled by state censors and produced a steady stream of propaganda, including atrocity stories during the Thirty Years' War. In the eighteenth century the favored method of Austrian court propaganda was extravagant architecture. The architect Johann Bernhard Fischer von Erlach (1656–1723) rebuilt Vienna as a baroque celebration of Habsburg power. Emperor Joseph II (1741–1790) relaxed the censorship laws but emerged unscathed from the so-called *Broschurenflut* (flood of leaflets) that followed. The great challenge to Habsburg power occurred during the Napoleonic Wars, with their awakening of national sensibilities across the Austrian Empire. The Austrian state made some attempt to appeal to Czech nationalism in their own propaganda—to little effect. Austria, under the leadership of Prince Metternich (1773–1859), resisted nationalist impulses through rigid conservative politics and censorship.

The historian Miroslav Hroch has identified a common pattern in the nationalist revivals that swept across Europe in the nineteenth century, seeing a progression from an academic phase, through a cultural awakening, to full-fledged political activity. This model elevates the role of the propagandist to the fore as cultural activists across the region promoted what they saw as the distinctiveness of their particular group. Each national group had its prophets of nationalism. In the Czech lands (Bohemia, Moravia, and Silesia) Frantisek Palacky (1798–1876) led the way by writing a multivolume history of Bohemia and organizing the first Pan-Slav Congress in Prague in 1848. This united and influenced Slavic peoples across the entire region, inspiring Czechs, Poles, Slovaks, Slovenes, and Croats and Serbs living under Ottoman rule. The Pan-Slav movement used music, costume, flags, and epic history to foster a sense of self (as distinct from the "warlike" Germans or Turks). The movement rallied support in western Europe. The key Hungarian voices of the same period included the poet Sandor Petofi (1823–1849); Baron Jozsef Eotvos (1813–1871), who attacked Austrian corruption in his novel *The Village Notary* (1844–1846); and the lawyer Lajos Kossuth (1802–1894), an able orator who fermented opposition to Austrian rule in the journal *Pesti Hirlap* (Pesti News).

In 1848, inspired by the February revolution in France, the "irresistible force" of nationalism clashed with the "immovable object," namely, Metternich. As Hungarians, Italians, Galician Poles, and Czechs all rose up against Austrian rule, Metternich fled into exile. The Hungarians forced Austria to put an end to censorship and to create a new constitution. The new policy unleashes a flood of propaganda in the form of pamphlets strewn across the empire. In 1849 Hungary declared its complete independence. As the revolutionary movements foundered, the Austrians reasserted their power in the person of politicians such as Prince Felix zu Schwarzenberg (1800–1852) and his successor, Alexander Bach (1813–1893), who pursued renewed policies of centralization, censorship, and Germanization. Kossuth fled Hungary yet continued to campaign from his place of exile, with the lost cause of 1848 swiftly becoming a romantic propaganda story in its own right. Austrian rule in Hungary continued to inspire resistance; well-known examples include the satirical writing of Count Istvan Szechenyi (1791–1860). In 1867 Vienna agreed to an *Ausgleich* (compromise), with Hungary accepting its half of the dual Austro-Hungarian crown.

In the later nineteenth century Pan-Slavism became a major force in Russian politics. Slavophile authors such as historian and editor Mikhail Pogodin (1800–1875) used the cause to justify Russian imperialist ambitions. Russia sponsored a second Pan-Slav conference in 1867. Pan-Slav propaganda inflamed Russian opinion to such an extent that it made any compromise with Austria over issues such as the fate of Serbia all but impossible. In August 1914, when Austria moved against Serbia, the Russians felt compelled to rally to Serbia's defense, precipitating World War I.

Austrian-Hungarian propaganda during the Great War included the "Red Book" of 1915, which detailed Serbian and Montenegrin atrocities. Stories included the castration of prisoners of war and an account of the roasting of a pro-Austrian civilian. In the neutral United States the Austrian embassy attempted to encourage strikes among munitions workers, the discovery of the plan becoming propaganda for the Allied cause. In contrast, the government believed that its tactical deployment of "Front Propaganda" against the Russians in 1917 (in conjunction with Germany) paid dividends and aided the Russian Revolution. Austria attempted a similar campaign against the Italian army (1917–1918), but Italy rallied successfully. The British role in directing Allied propaganda against Austria-Hungary (such as dropping leaflets revealing troop positions) was exaggerated somewhat after the war. Recent research has revealed that the campaign remained largely in Italian hands and has questioned the degree to which "Allied propaganda" hastened Austria's collapse, as the British claimed after the war. The best evidence suggests that Allied arguments

acted as a catalyst in existing internal political developments. The state's "Enemy Propaganda Defense" work launched among the armed forces in 1918 could do little to reverse matters.

One of the most effective propaganda campaigns of World War I was that waged by Thomas Masaryk (1850–1937) on behalf of his dream of a Czechoslovak state. A philosophy professor, Masaryk had campaigned for reform while under Austrian rule as a member of parliament in Vienna. He spent the war promoting the Czech cause among the Allies. He raised a Czechoslovak legion and persuaded the Allies that his country should be given independence in the postwar world. Even before the end of the war, the Allies had recognized Czechoslovakia as a fellow Allied power. U.S. President Woodrow Wilson (1876–1924) appealed to both the Allied and Central Powers for a peace based on self-determination. The 1918 armistice, largely based on Wilson's terms, had massive implications for the national aspirations of the subject peoples of Austria-Hungary.

The postwar settlement (the treaties of Saint-Germain in 1919 and Trianon in 1920) established "successor states" across the Austrian and Ottoman imperial lands. These new states sought to establish cohesive identities through policies emphasizing cultural coherence over centrifugal tendencies. Perhaps the clearest example of this was the "Kingdom of the Serbs, Croats, and Slovenes," created between 1917 and 1918 from the Habsburg provinces of Croatia, Slovenia, Bosnia, and Herzegovina and the prewar kingdoms of Serbia and Montenegro. As part of this attempt to forge a common identity, in 1929 the state acquired its new name of Yugoslavia.

In Hungary a short-lived Marxist government of Bela Kun (1886–1937) gave way to the nationalist rule of Miklos Horthy (1868–1957). Themes in state propaganda included the formerly Hungarian lands (and the million-plus Hungarians) that lay outside the borders drawn up in 1920. In Czechoslovakia Thomas Masaryk worked hard to establish a liberal and democratic state and tried to promote this new identity through the educational system, a national flag and anthem, and so forth. Although Czechoslovakia had the most liberal press in the region, the state was challenged by ethnic propaganda from the periphery, most ominously by the Germans of the Sudetenland, who, under the leadership of Konrad Henlein (1898–1945), called for Adolf Hitler to liberate them from Czech oppression.

During the interwar period Austria witnessed extremes of both the right and the left. In 1927 paramilitary forces—the monarchist Heimwehr (home guard) and Marxist Schutzbund (protection group)—exchanged slogans and battled on the streets of Vienna. An increasing number of Austrians fell under the spell of the Pan-German propaganda emanating from the Austrian-born dictator in Berlin. Key themes in this propaganda included the injustice of the postwar settlement forbidding a German-Austrian Anschluss and the alleged responsibility of Jews for the economic misfortunes of the country. Though the Austrian state survived an attempted Nazi coup in 1934, in March 1938 Hitler moved troops into Austria and forced the Anschluss. Hitler then acquired the Sudetenland as a result of the Munich Conference of September 1938, and in March 1939 he seized the rest of Czechoslovakia, setting Europe on the path to war.

During World War II Nazi propaganda worked hard to divide and rule the nations of eastern Europe, exploiting preexisting anti-Semitism. They proved particularly successful in Yugoslavia, where they bolstered Croat nationalism. Ancient hatreds soon subsumed Yugoslav national feeling. Hungary took advantage of the war to recover its "lost territory" and joined the Axis. Propaganda campaigns directed at the region during the war included broadcasts by the BBC, including an unsuccessful campaign to prevent the deportation of Hungarian Jews. The war ended with much of the region under Soviet occupation.

After World War II Austria (which had both U.S. and Soviet zones) underwent a process of de-Nazification through attendant propaganda programs. Although lacking full sovereignty until 1955, the country effectively "relaunched the national image" with a highly effective campaign of public diplomacy. With embassy-sponsored cultural programs and tourist-related publicity Austria converted itself from the homeland of Hitler into a realm of chocolate cake, Mozart, and prancing white horses.

The Soviet influence prevailed as first Yugoslavia and then Hungary and Czechoslovakia became Communist states. Soviet propaganda attempted to revive the Pan-Slav rhetoric of the nineteenth century to justify its domination of Eastern Europe. Each national state maintained a tight control on its mass media. Symbolically the chief newspaper in Czechoslovakia was named *Rudé Právo* (Red Truth). After the death of Stalin in 1953, Hungary introduced a more liberal media regime. Political liberalization followed swiftly, prompting the Soviet invasion of Hungary in 1956. Many Hungarians fought back in an anti-Soviet uprising. One controversy relating to the latter concerned the precise role of U.S.-sponsored Radio Free Europe in encouraging an armed uprising against Soviet forces. Some Hungarians later claimed that the American radio station had encouraged the move by promising military support. Media liberalization was also an early sign of the so-called Prague Spring in Czechoslovakia in 1968, associated with the moderate administration of Alexander Dubcek (1921–1992). Again the USSR crushed free expression with tanks.

In Czechoslovakia during the 1970s, as elsewhere in the region, opposition material circulated clandestinely. This genre was known as samizdat. Leading opposition voices included the dramatist Vaclav Havel (1936–), leader of the Charter 77 dissident group. Havel endured both imprisonment and the banning of his plays but remained a staunch advocate of reform. By

1989 opposition rallies had reached such a scale that the regime had no alternative but to negotiate and share power. In the so-called Velvet Revolution Havel became president of Czechoslovakia (1990–1992) and returned after the separation from Slovakia to become president of the Czech Republic.

In Hungary a reform-minded moderate named Karoly Grosz (1930–1996) came to power in 1988 and presided over a relatively smooth dismantling of the Communist state. Grosz had a sound understanding of the mass media, having risen from printer to newspaper editor, and subsequently held a number of senior positions in the Hungarian Socialist Worker's Party propaganda apparatus, becoming its head in 1974. The liberalization of Hungarian television reached across the border to Romania and hastened the fall of the regime of Nicolae Ceausescu (1918–1989).

Post-Communist Eastern Europe supports a lively media culture even though issues of delineation between the media and the state are still moot. Regional propaganda issues include the rise of the radical right, which is visible in its most extreme form in Austria, where in 1999 Jörg Haider (1950–) used anti-immigrant rhetoric to achieve electoral gains for the extreme right-wing Austrian Freedom Party. In early 2000 Haider resigned as party leader to facilitate a less controversial participation in coalition government.

Nicholas J. Cull

See also Balkans; Cultural Propaganda; Funerals; Herzl, Theodor; Hitler, Adolf; Italy; Northcliffe, Lord; Ottoman Empire/Turkey; Poland; Reformation and Counter-Reformation; Religion; Russia; Spain; World War I; Zionism

References: Cornwall, Mark. *The Undermining of Austria-Hungary.* London: Macmillan, 2000; Hroch, Miroslav. *Social Preconditions of National Revival in Europe.* Cambridge: Cambridge University Press, 1985; Milland, Gabriel. "The BBC Hungarian Service and the Final Solution in Hungary." *Historical Journal of Film, Radio and Television* 18 (August 1998): 353–374. Roper, Hugh Trevor, *Princes and Artists: Patronage and Ideology in Four Habsburg Courts, 1517–1633.* London: Thames and Hudson, 1976; Tanner, Marie. *The Last Descendant of Aeneas: The Hapsburgs and the Mythic Image of the Emperor.* New Haven, CT: Yale University Press, 1992.

B

Balkans

Most of the Balkan countries—Albania, Bulgaria, Greece, Romania, and the nations that made up the former Yugoslavia—were part of the Ottoman Empire. The region has experienced great religious diversity, including: Orthodox, Catholic, and Protestant Christianity; Islam; and the pagan Manichean heresy of the Bogomils in Bosnia. National identity developed through resistance to the Ottomans in the eighteenth century and grew stronger in the nineteenth century as the countries of the region gradually won their independence. This centuries-long process involved debates, struggles for religious emancipation, international diplomacy, and wars and uprisings. The first and second Serbian uprisings (1804 and 1815) began the process.

In 1832 Greece became the first to gain independence. Many of the Serbian, Bulgarian, and Romanian intellectuals were educated in newly independent Greece. Romantic nationalism spread from Greece throughout the region. Gradually, however, the diverse cultural communities began to distinguish themselves from the Greeks and nationalist anti-Greek propaganda developed. Bulgaria became independent in 1878, as did Serbia (formally recognized in 1882),

while Macedonia remained part of the Ottoman Empire until 1913. Orthodox Christianity also played a key role in national self-definition. Over the course of the nineteenth and twentieth centuries national churches across the region secured independence within Orthodox Christianity. The process had begun in 1833 with the Greek Orthodox Church. The Bulgarian Orthodox Church was independent as of 1870. The process continued in the interwar years with the Turkish (1921) and Albanian (1929) Orthodox Churches.

Literary texts defined national identities throughout the Balkans. Vuk Karadzic (1787–1864), the patriarch of the Serbian literary language, was responsible not only for the first Serbian grammar, dictionary, and translation of the Bible but also for a host of works that laid the groundwork for Serbian nationalism. The Albanian national movement (*rilindja*) is often linked to the name of national poet Naim Frasheri (1846–1900). Most Balkan anti-Ottoman propaganda revolved around epics of resistance to Ottoman conquest such as the battle of Kosovo in 1389. Nationalists stressed the cruelty of Ottoman rule and praised the heroism of those who preserved language and religion under the Ottoman yoke. Historians asserted the past pre-Ottoman glory of their respective nations and typically claimed a territory for their nation that covered most of the peninsula. Such claims became a basic premise of almost all national mythologies in the region and fueled ongoing territorial disputes. Various Balkan movements favored some form of federation of Balkan nationalities. Advocates included members of the Croat-led Illyrian movement, which began in the early nineteenth century, and Stefan Stambolov (1854–1895), prime minister of Bulgaria from 1887 to 1894.

Around the turn of the century nationalist propagandists turned their attention from the waning Ottomans to Europe's Great Powers, who were ruthlessly and incompetently redrawing the map of the region. Various treaties redefined territories, sometimes dividing a country in half and triggering a strong nationalist drive toward unification (as in Bulgaria), sometimes denying territory to a group struggling for independence (as in Macedonia, which was divided between Greece, Serbia, and Bulgaria). Propaganda against Western intervention has figured in the region ever since. The newly liberated countries were not satisfied with the borders assigned to them; claims against neighbors led to the two Balkan wars (1912–1913), both of which were marked by realignments and fierce propaganda against whoever might be the Balkan enemy of the day. Serbian resentment over Austria-Hungary's annexation of Bosnia provided the spark that triggered World War I in 1914.

The settlement reached at the end of the war established Romania and the Kingdom of Serbs, Croats, and Slovenes (which also included Montenegro, Bosnia-Herzegovina, and parts of Macedonia). Later the latter developed into a federation of republics, assuming the name of Yugoslavia in 1929. Despite efforts to achieve internal cohesion, nationalist tensions (often fueled by fears of Serbian domination) undermined this supranationalism. Balkan propaganda frequently focused on the monarchy. Liberals in the region denounced the monarchists as creatures of foreign influence who cared little for the interests of the respective nations, such as Greece or Bulgaria. Pro-monarchists argued that a constitutional monarchy was the best guarantee of a democratic system. Absurd extremes of monarchism include the career of Zog I (Ahmed Bey Zogu) (1895–1961) of Albania, a commoner who appointed himself king after having been elected prime minister a few years earlier.

The challenges to the interwar order began as early as 1923 with a coup in Bulgaria. In the 1930s profascist governments came to power in most countries and engaged in fascist propaganda. World War II saw the joint conquest of Yugoslavia by German, Italian, Hungarian, and Bulgarian forces. Serbia was occupied and partitioned. Macedonia was placed under Bulgarian occupation, while Italy created an Albanian puppet monarchy comprising Albania, Kosovo, and part of Montenegro. In 1941 the Nazis installed the Ustasha regime of Ante Pavelic (1889–1959) in Croatia, which soon launched a massive genocide of Jews, Gypsies (Roma), and Serbs. The pro-Nazi regime of General Ion Antonescu (1882–1946) in Romania also "cleansed" the Jewish population. The action was not unprecedented. At one time or another countries in the Balkan region have carried out programs aimed at assimilating, expelling, or (in extreme cases) destroying their respective minorities, most often targeting groups found scattered across the region (mostly Roma and Jews). Whichever national group happens to be in the minority—Turks and Pomaks in Bulgaria, Slav Macedonians in Greece, Hungarians in Romania, Albanians in Yugoslavia—has been seen as an extension of its respective kin nation and has become a target for allegations of conspiracies.

In Yugoslavia the anti-Nazi resistance was carried out by Communist partisans, led by Josip Broz Tito (1892–1980), and nationalist-minded Chetniks, led by Draza Mihajlovic (1893–1946). Here and elsewhere in the region underground Communist propaganda accompanied resistance. Yugoslav publications included *Borba, Hammer and Sickle, Komunist,* and *Proleter.* At the end of the war the Balkans lay within the Soviet sphere of influence and the partisan movements moved to establish Communist governments. Pro-Stalinist regimes were installed throughout most Balkan countries by 1948 and lasted until the mid-1950s. Some relaxation followed Stalin's death, but censorship and Communist propaganda remained, including personality cults around Vulko Chervenkov (1900–1980) in Bulgaria, Enver Hoxha (1908–1985) in Albania, and Nicolae Ceausescu (1918–1989) in Romania.

Religious clashes have long fueled propaganda in the Balkans. The clergy of the region have acted as censors and sought to control the minds of their congregations, but during the Communist period atheistic propaganda was equally strong. In 1967 Enver Hoxha officially declared Albania an atheist country after eliminating all religious institutions. Hoxha's decision was justified by rhetorical reference to the national enlightenment poet Vaso Pasha (1825–1892) who had written in *Oh, My Albania* (1880): "Don't look at churches and mosques; the religion of Albanians is Albanianism." Along with its suppression of other religious practices, Bulgaria banned the legacy of the original religious thinker Petar Dunov (1864–1945), leader of the so-called White Fraternity, a sun-worshiping religion combining elements of paganism, Christianity, and Eastern religions.

In 1949 Yugoslav leader Tito split from Stalin and launched his own brand of independent communism, which appeared to be more liberal and less dependent on propaganda. Tito still exercised tight control over the media and the artistic output of writers and filmmakers by means of a personality cult. Other key figures in postwar Yugoslav politics and propaganda included the philosopher Milovan Djilas (1911–1995), the economist Edvard Kardelj (1910–1979), and Aleksandar Rankovic (1909–1983), head of the secret police. Djilas gradually grew disillusioned and, after publishing a critical study of state socialism entitled *The New Class* (1957), became a dissident and a victim of censorship. In the 1960s dissident Marxist intellectuals gathered around the journal *Praxis.* Internal tensions between the Yugoslav republics included a secessionist drive in Croatia (1968). Tito played a key role in international politics through his involvement with the nonaligned movement, seeking to balance the Cold War superpowers.

In Albania, Enver Hoxha, like Tito, also dissented from Soviet communism. During the 1960s both Hoxha and—quite independently—the Romanian leader Nicolae Ceausescu looked to China as an alternative model. The Chinese alliances did not last long, but they provided a fresh theme in the preexisting anti-Chinese propaganda in other countries of the Soviet sphere.

Since the 1950s national film industries across the region have produced propagandist epics glorifying their respective nation's past, such as the numerous Albanian films about the national hero Gjergj Kastroiti Skenderbeg (1405–1468). Balkan directors in this mold include the Romanian Sergio Nicholaescu (1930–), director of *Dacii* (1967), and the Bulgarian Lyudmil Staikov (1937–), director of *Time of Violence* (1988). In Yugoslavia directors like Branko Marjanovic (1909–1955) and Veljko Buljaic (1928–) made partisan sagas, but the so-called Black Wave film directors, including Zelimir Zilnik (1942–) and Dusan Makavejev (1932–), critically subverted communist ideology.

The supranationalist approach to the Yugoslav federation gradually eroded, and by the time of Tito's death in 1980 it was no longer a viable proposition. The disintegration of the country had slowly started from within. When the political and cultural elites abandoned the federal project, they created the conditions for the collapse of the Yugoslav state. Novelist Dobrica Cosic (1921–) advanced a notion of Serbian victimhood in the early 1960s and was punished for his nationalism. In the 1980s, however, Cosic returned to the spotlight as one of the intellectuals (which also included members of the *Praxis* group) behind the notorious 1986 Memorandum of the Serbian Academy of Sciences, which provided a blueprint for Serbian nationalism. Serbian and other nationalisms filled the gap left by the failing creed of communism. This provided a welcome opportunity for ambitious and ruthless officials, such as the Serb Slobodan Milosevic (1941–) and the Croat Franjo Tudjman (1922–1999). After 1987, with nationalism rising, the Yugoslav split became inevitable.

With the advent of glasnost in the Soviet Union, dissident intellectuals in Bulgaria and Romania began openly questioning the moral premises of communism and calling for a reconsideration of the official interpretation of the past. Bulgaria lived through an internal party coup in 1989, and thereafter full-fledged anti-Communist propaganda became commonplace. In Romania a coup led to the downfall of Ceausescu, which ended with the speedy "trial" and execution of the dictator. The Romanian "revolution" of 1989 is now believed to have been a well-orchestrated media spectacle, in which television was used to exaggerate the dangers confronting the revolutionaries.

In Yugoslavia growing nationalism defined the politics of all constituent republics, most of which declared their independence in 1991–1992. This act was followed by several wars of Yugoslav succession: Slovenia's speedy secession was followed by the bloody but short war for Croat independence and the lengthy Bosnian war (1992–1995). The crisis continued, with mounting pressure, in Kosovo (1998–1999) and Macedonia (2000–2001). Attempts to maintain Pan-Yugoslav media outlets (like the television station Yutel) were abandoned in the early 1990s. The Slovenian weekly *Mladina* was an important source of early criticism against the central government. Vocal nationalist groups took control of key media outlets and produced nationalist propaganda and hate speeches. The leading Serbian newspaper,

Politika, which had supported Milosevic in the 1980s, and the RTS-Belgrade radio station both became government mouthpieces. Through selective hiring and other forms of control Tudjman's government in Croatia forced media outlets to stay in line, but newspapers like *Slobodna Dalmacija* or the Split-based *Feral Tribune* still raised independent critical voices. The Bosnian media took sides along ethnic lines and became mouthpieces for nationalist propaganda. Antinationalist forces attempted to counterbalance the nationalist hysteria, the best known of which include the independent Belgrade radio station Studio B and the Serbian magazine *Vreme.* Conditions for free speech gradually deteriorated in Serbia, with the most serious crackdown against the media occurring during the NATO bombing of Belgrade in 1999.

All sides involved in the conflicts in the former Yugoslavia deployed propaganda. Alongside real violence wildly exaggerated reports of various abuses and atrocities also circulated. Both the Serbian and the Muslim side claimed that during the Bosnian war their babies had been thrown as food to zoo animals. Propagandists misrepresented enemy dead as members of their own ethnic group or, with respect to civilian massacres, claimed that the other side had killed its own people for propaganda purposes (as with the Sarajevo breadline massacre of 1992 or the Racak massacre of 1999). All parties used documentary and feature film propaganda, the best known controversy surrounding the award-winning film *Underground* (1995), directed by Emir Kusturica (1954–), which was viewed by some as serving a Serb agenda.

As usual in the Balkans, the United States and Western European countries were involved early on. Their public rhetoric was aimed at proclaiming their own innocence, claiming Western superiority over the Balkan barbarity as reason for the "just war" involving the bombing of Serbia over Kosovo. On occasion Western forces shut down Balkan media outlets, seizing the transmitter of the Banja Luka radio station in

1997 and bombing the RTS-Belgrade station in 1999. The post-Communist power vacuum of the 1990s saw a revival of promonarchist tendencies in Albania, Romania, and Serbia. In Bulgaria in July 2001 former child-monarch Simeon II (1937–), who had been exiled in 1949, returned as Simeon Borisov Sakskoburggotski and won a landslide victory as prime minister.

Dina Iordanova

See also Bosnian Crisis and War; Greece; Kosovo Crisis and War; Ottoman Empire/Turkey; Russia

References: Glenny, Misha. *The Balkans, 1804–1999: Nationalism, War and the Great Powers.* London: Granta, 1999; Mazower, Mark. *The Balkans.* London: Weidenfeld and Nicholson, 2000; Robinson, Gertrude. *Tito's Maverick Media: The Politics of Mass Communication in Yugoslavia.* Urbana: University of Illinois Press, 1977; Thompson, Mark. *Forging War: The Media in Serbia, Croatia and Bosnia-Herzegovina.* Luton, UK: Luton University Press, 1999; Wachtel, Andrew. *Making a Nation, Breaking a Nation: Literature and Cultural Politics in Yugoslavia.* Stanford, CA: Stanford University Press, 1998.

Battleship Potemkin (1926)

This film, directed by Sergei Eisenstein (1898–1948) for the state film studio Goskino, represents the pinnacle of Soviet film propaganda. The film presents a fictionalized account of a key event in the revolution of 1905, namely, the mutiny aboard the battleship *Potemkin* while at anchor off the Crimean port of Odessa. It set a new standard in filmmaking technique. *Potemkin* is best known for a sequence in which tsarist soldiers massacre sympathetic civilians on the Odessa steps. To bring this sequence to life Eisenstein makes excellent use of montage, or "American editing"—involving a rapid sequence of multiple images to stir the audience—pioneered in American films like *The Birth of a Nation* (1915). Eisenstein shows ranks of boots advancing relentlessly down the steps, transforming the tsarist soldiers into an impersonal machine, while showing the faces of

their victims. Humanity is only present on one side in this version of the event. He selects emotive details, including the death of a mother, whose fall sends her baby carriage rolling down the steps. The film was not especially popular in Russia, where audiences seemed more interested in escapist Hollywood films like *Robin Hood* (1922), but it was an important piece of propaganda overseas, where, despite Western censorship, it won sympathy for the Soviet Union.

Nicholas J. Cull

See also *The Birth of a Nation;* Eisenstein, Sergei; Film (Documentary); Film (Feature); Russia

References: Barna, Ion. *Eisenstein.* London: Secker and Warburg, 1973; Marshall, Herbert, ed. *The "Battleship Potemkin": The Greatest Film Ever Made.* New York: Avon, 1978; Taylor, Richard. *The Battleship Potemkin.* London: I. B. Tauris, 2000; Taylor, Richard, ed. *S. M. Eisenstein: Writings, 1922–1934.* Bloomington: Indiana University Press, 1988.

BBC (British Broadcasting Corporation)

Britain's national broadcasting organization has served as the propaganda arm of the British government overseas—and occasionally at home as well. The BBC was chartered in 1926 as a public body to succeed the radio manufacturers' own creation, the British Broadcasting Company, which was founded in 1922. John Reith (1889–1971), its first director general, believed that the BBC had a duty to educate. The corporation's bias was socially conservative, which was hardly surprising when one realizes its controlling board was top-heavy with establishment figures. During the General Strike of 1926 its airwaves were commandeered to powerful effect by the government.

In 1932 the corporation branched out and became an external arm of the British government's cultural propaganda, inaugurating an English-language Empire Service to promote imperial cohesion. An Arabic service followed in 1938 to counter the dictatorial powers ruling the Middle East. Broadcasts were funded and guided by the Foreign Office. During the buildup leading up to and throughout World War II BBC external services multiplied to include a plethora of languages, broadcasting to Allied, enemy, and neutral territories alike. The BBC sought to gain a reputation for credibility as a news service. This contrasted with the totalitarian approach to propaganda and ensured that when the British really needed to lie, it was likely to be believed. At home the BBC was an essential instrument of domestic wartime propaganda and helped maintain both morale and political cohesion. Successful broadcasters included Prime Minister Winston Churchill (1874–1965) and writer J. B. Priestley (1894–1984), who used the BBC to advance ideas of the war as an opportunity for social reform.

After the war, the BBC's foreign-language services were regrouped into the World Service and played a major role in Cold War propaganda aimed at the Communist network. It is a testament to its potency that broadcasts were frequently jammed in the Eastern bloc. At home the BBC was slow to become a prime forum for political debate. Since 1944 the BBC had been forced to wait two weeks before carrying political comment on an issue being debated in Parliament. This rule withered following the Suez Crisis of 1956. Subsequently BBC programming became an essential forum for the propaganda duels of British politics.

British governments have occasionally sought to control the output of the BBC for propaganda reasons. Coverage of the "troubles" in Northern Ireland proved particularly controversial. In 1985 Margaret Thatcher (1925–) attempted to quash the documentary *At the Edge of Union;* broadcast journalists protested with a one-day strike. Self-censorship has proved more effective, as in the suppression of the 1965 film *The War Game.* BBC programs have played a part in raising public consciousness on particular issues, the best known example being the 1966 docudrama *Cathy Come Home* dealing with homelessness.

During the 1990s the BBC became a major player in international satellite news. The export of BBC news and feature programs remains a major element in British cultural projection overseas.

Nicholas J. Cull

See also Britain; British Empire; Cold War; Falklands/Malvinas War; Ireland; Psychological Warfare; Radio (Domestic); Radio (International); Reith, Lord John; Suez Crisis; Television; Thatcher, Margaret; *The War Game*

References: Briggs, Asa. *The BBC: The First Fifty Years.* Oxford: Oxford University Press, 1985; Negrine, Ralph. *Television and the Press since 1945.* Manchester: Manchester University Press, 1998; Nelson, Michael. *War of the Black Heavens: The Battles of Western Broadcasting in the Cold War.* London: Brassey's, 1997; Walker, Andrew. *A Skyful of Freedom.* London: BBC, 1992.

Beaverbrook, Max (1879–1964)

William Maxwell Aitken, the first Baron Beaverbrook, became synonymous with British propaganda when, in 1918, he became Britain's wartime minister of information. Born in Canada, Beaverbrook made his fortune in business, moved to Britain, and entered politics. His tenure as minister brought a cohesion and direction to British propaganda policy that had been lacking earlier in the war. In 1919 he focused his energies on the newspaper business, buying the *Daily Express* and building it into the most read daily newspaper in the world. Beaverbrook's flair for propaganda was soon in evidence at the paper, which he used to campaign for a variety of causes, including the famous Empire Free Trade crusade, which he began in 1929. During World War II he played a valued role as Churchill's minister of aircraft production (1940–1941) and minister of supply (1941–1942); in both jobs he made full use of propaganda to engage the public in that aspect of the war effort.

Nicholas J. Cull

See also Britain; British Empire; Canada; Churchill, Winston; Intelligence; World War I; World War II (Britain)

References: Chisholm, Anne, and Michael Davie Taylor. *Beaverbrook: A Life.* London: Hutchinson, 1992; Taylor, A. J. P. *Beaverbrook: A Biography.* New York: Simon and Schuster, 1972.

Belgium

See Netherlands, Belgium, and Luxembourg

The Big Lie

From atrocity stories against the Saracens during the Crusades to stories of babies being used in the manufacture of soap during World War I, the "big lie" or falsehood has always been part of the propagandist's stock-in-trade. The big lie can be defined as the intentional distortion of the truth, especially for political purposes.

The pejorative associations with the term "propaganda" brings into focus the relationship between propaganda and truth—or the accuracy of facts. A generally held view is that propaganda is synonymous with lies and that lies or falsehood are necessary for propaganda to be effective. Adolf Hitler (1889–1945) believed implicitly in the big lie, claiming that propaganda for the masses had to be simple and target the lowest level of intelligence. Hitler believed that the bigger the lie, the greater its chance of being believed. Writing in *Mein Kampf,* he claimed that "the great mass of people will more easily fall victim to a big lie than to a small one." Joseph Goebbels (1897–1945), the Nazi propaganda minister (who was often referred to in Allied propaganda as the "Big Liar") took a different view, claiming that propaganda should be as accurate as possible. Similarly, in the early part of the twentieth century Lenin (1870–1924) proclaimed that "in propaganda, truth pays off," and this dictum has largely been accepted by propagandists.

It is true that after World War I propaganda was widely associated with lies and falsehood. In Arthur Ponsonby's (1900–1982) influential book *Falsehood in Wartime,* which reflected public opinion at the time,

the author wrote that "when war is declared truth is the first victim . . . Falsehood is the most useful weapon in case of war." As a result of the innumerable lies, deliberate or otherwise, that were disseminated and believed during World War I, propaganda was inexorably associated with falsehood and was viewed by many as something to be ashamed of. In the immediate years following the end of the Great War, the Allies in particular quickly disbanded agencies that had been established for propaganda purposes. Other, less democratically inclined nations such as Bolshevik Russia, Fascist Italy, and Nazi Germany viewed propaganda in a radically different light and used the new communications technologies as a means of manipulating mass opinion. Partly as an antidote to the widespread use made of propaganda by authoritarian regimes, in the interwar period British government officials even considered banishing the word from the diplomatic vocabulary, the implication being that whereas fascist regimes resorted to lies, democracies told the truth.

This is not to suggest that propaganda does not use the big lie. Propagandists will continue to invent stories about adversaries, falsify statistics, and "create" news. From the propagandist's point of view, lies must only be told about unverifiable facts. For example, in World War I the German admiralty continued to exaggerate the successes achieved by German U-boats even after they had reached their peak of effectiveness. They could do this only because it was relatively safe to disseminate such news without fear of contradiction. If, however, the public always associates propaganda with lies, then the propaganda will never be believed and, as such, becomes counterproductive.

To explain this contradiction French sociologist Jacques Ellul (1912–1994) has made a distinction between a fact and intentions or interpretations, that is, between material and moral elements. According to Ellul, the truth that pays off is in the realm of facts. The necessary falsehoods, which also pay off, are in the realm of intentions and interpretations. In the light of Lenin's dictum, the dissemination of false news can create its own problems. Propagandists have discovered that it is better to reveal bad news oneself than to wait until it is revealed by the enemy.

It is now generally considered a major stipulation of propaganda manuals that, with the exception of harmful and unbelievable truths, wherever possible the truth should be told. When Sir John Reith (1889–1971) was appointed minister of information in 1940, he laid down two of the MoI's fundamental axioms for the balance of the war, namely, that "news is the shocktroops of propaganda" and that propaganda should tell "the truth, nothing but the truth and, as near as possible, the whole truth." In its manual, Supreme Headquarters Allied Expedition Force (SHAEF) recommends that "when there is no compelling reason to suppress a fact, tell it. Aside from consideration of military security, the only reason to suppress a piece of news is if it is unbelievable . . . When the listener catches you in a lie, your power diminishes . . . For this reason, never tell a lie which can be discovered."

This has to be qualified by the recognition that the public cannot accept an undiluted diet of bad news. One of the skills of the propagandist is the manner in which "facts" are presented. The publication of a "true" fact is not in itself dangerous. However, if it would be dangerous to make it public, the propagandist prefers to hide it, to say nothing rather than to lie. Silence is therefore one method of preventing known facts from appearing in the public domain. It has been estimated that approximately one-fifth of all press directives given by Goebbels during the war were orders to remain silent concerning various events. Silence on a particular issue or event—even when the facts are known—becomes a means of preventing the knowledge of facts by modifying the context. This propaganda technique, known as selection, leads to an effective distortion of reality and in the process becomes yet another example of the "big lie."

David Welch

See also Fakes; Goebbels, Joseph; Hitler, Adolf; Lenin, Vladimir Ilyich; MoI; Rumor; World War I; World War II (Germany)
References: Ellul, Jacques. *Propaganda: The Formation of Men's Minds.* New York: Vintage, 1965; Ponsonby, Arthur. *Falsehood in Wartime: Propaganda Lies of the First World War.* Sudbury, UK: Bloomfield, 1991; Welch, David. *The Third Reich: Politics and Propaganda.* London, Routledge, 2002.

The Birth of a Nation (1915)

Produced and directed by D. W. Griffith (1875–1948), this was the first Hollywood motion picture to demonstrate the persuasive power of the epic feature film. Unfortunately, being an adaptation of the racist historical novel *The Clansman* (1905) by Thomas Dixon Jr. (1864–1946), it served the cause of white supremacy. *The Birth of a Nation* told the story of two American families and their experience of the Civil War and its aftermath. In Griffith's hands black Americans were reduced to happy, loyal slaves or deranged rapists desperate for white women. He did much to advance a new stereotype of the "mulatto," mixed-race Americans who were particularly dangerous since they possessed both the supposed superior intelligence of the white race and a desire to better their position. The film advanced the erroneous idea that the Civil War had ended with the South being ruled by a dictatorship of black people. Its climax showed a "heroic" charge by the Ku Klux Klan to restore white Southerners to power. Although inscribing the stereotypes of racism for a new generation of Americans, it also provided a rallying point for African Americans. The forerunners of the civil rights movement organized opposition to screenings of the film, eventually restricting its circulation in some parts of the United States. Griffith's film became a model for combining entertainment and propaganda filmmaking. Students of his technique included the Soviet filmmaker Sergei Eisenstein (1898–1948).

Nicholas J. Cull

See also Civil War, United States; Film (Feature);
NAACP; United States

References: Cripps, Thomas. *Slow Fade to Black:
The Negro in American Film, 1900–1942.* New
York: Oxford University Press, 1977; Schickel,
Richard. *D. W. Griffith: An American Life.* New
York: Simon and Schuster, 1984.

BIS (British Information Services)

This British overseas information agency,
eventually housed within the Foreign Office,
is best known for its campaigns in the United
States. BIS was founded in 1941 as part of a
consolidation of the various British information offices working in the United States to
combat American neutrality. The word "service" was borrowed from the existing British
Press Service (BPS), which was founded in
New York the previous year. The word "service" had been selected by British ambassador
Lord Lothian (1882–1940) as an alternative
to the terms "propaganda" (taboo since
World War I) and "relations," which Lothian
felt had been debased by both commerce and
U.S. government overuse.

BIS played an important role in smoothing
Anglo-American relations during the war
years and thereafter. Branches in other locations followed, and BIS offices became an important mechanism of overt British propaganda during the Cold War. Between 1952
and 1954 the whole system of British publicity overseas—including BIS, the British
Council, and the BBC World Service—was
scrutinized by the Drogheda inquiry but
managed to survive. As John Dumbrell has
noted, BIS offices in the United States played
a significant role in the 1970s and 1980s, promoting Britain's view of the conflict in
Northern Ireland. Activities included the distribution of specially produced television
segments on the crisis.

Nicholas J. Cull

See also Britain; Ireland; MoI; Public Diplomacy;
World War II (Britain); World War II (United
States)

References: Cull, Nicholas J. *Selling War: British
Propaganda and American Neutrality in World War*

Two. New York: Oxford University Press, 1995;
Dumbrell, John. *A Special Relationship: Anglo-
American Relations in the Cold War and After.*
Basingstoke, UK: Macmillan, 2001; Taylor,
Philip M. *British Propaganda in the Twentieth
Century: Selling Democracy.* Edinburgh:
Edinburgh University Press, 1999.

Black Propaganda

The source of propaganda is likely to be an
institution, organization, group, or individual. Sometimes there is complete openness
about the source of the propaganda, while on
other occasions it is necessary to conceal the
source's identity in order to achieve certain
objectives. "Black" propaganda (sometimes
referred to as "covert" propaganda) tries to
conceal its own identity by purporting to
emanate from someone or somewhere other
than the true source. In black propaganda not
only is there deliberate distortion but the
identity of the source is usually concealed or
inaccurate. When the identity is concealed,
the task of the analyst is a demanding one. It
is quite difficult to detect black propaganda
until after all the facts are known.

During the early phase of World War II the
Nazis operated at least three radio stations
that sought to give the impression that they
were broadcasting somewhere in Britain. One
of the stations was called Radio Free Caledonia and claimed to be the voice of Scottish nationalism; another referred to itself as the
Workers' Challenge Station and disseminated
unorthodox left-wing views; a third, the New
British Broadcasting Station, provided news
bulletins and comments in the style of the
BBC but with a concealed pro-German bias.
None of these stations reached large audiences and they only broadcast for a few hours
a day. The aim of this black propaganda was to
undermine the morale of the British people—particularly during the Battle of Britain.
The Nazis used similar techniques on French
soldiers serving on the Maginot Line between
1939 and 1940. Radio broadcasts from
Stuttgart were fronted by a Frenchman
named Paul Ferdonnet, who pretended to

broadcast from within France. Ferdonnet's broadcasts were designed to weaken the French soldiers' morale by comparing the poor conditions of the ordinary foot soldiers in the Maginot Line with the luxurious lifestyle of French officers enjoying the delights of Paris. Ferdonnet also described in lurid detail the behavior of British soldiers billeted in French towns who, because they earned higher pay than their French counterparts, were seducing French women. French soldiers listened to Ferdonnet's broadcasts not necessarily because they were deceived by the "black" nature of the broadcasts but more often because they were simply more entertaining than official French broadcasts.

Later in the war the British (who sometimes conflated black propaganda with political warfare) set up their own black radio station, which claimed to be an official German radio station run by German soldiers for those on the western front. At the same time leaflets in the form of newspapers were dropped over the German lines purporting to originate from nonexistent German resistance organizations. In addition, fake ration cards and other ingenious devices were also employed.

Black propaganda, by definition, seeks to deceive and encompasses all types of deception—from leaflets, posters, and postage stamps to radio and television stations and now even the Internet. This type of propaganda consequently receives the most attention when it is revealed. The success or failure of such propaganda largely depends on the receiver's willingness to accept the authenticity of the source and the content of the message. For black propaganda to achieve its aims, great care has to be taken to place the message—and the manner in which it is disseminated—within the social, political, and cultural experiences of the target audience.

One of the most successful examples of black propaganda was Radio Free Hungary, which began broadcasting after the unsuccessful Hungarian uprising of 1956. The radio station called for intervention from the United States and graphically detailed Soviet atrocities. In fact, Radio Free Hungary was a KGB operation designed to embarrass the United States by showing that the latter could not be relied upon to help smaller countries opposing Soviet communism. Radio Free Hungary was even able to deceive the U.S. Central Intelligence Agency, which did not recognize the source until after it had stopped operating. In 1982, during the Falklands/Malvinas War, a BBC-fronted program began broadcasting under the guise of an Argentinian radio station. The British government invoked an obscure clause in the BBC charter that allowed the government to requisition the BBC transmitters in time of crisis. One of the programs broadcast was called "Ascension Alice," in which a sexy female announcer attempted to undermine the morale of the troops stationed in the Falklands. For example, the announcer (Alice) would claim that the Argentine president had stated on a television program that he was prepared to sacrifice forty thousand men to defend the Falklands. The radio station also played sentimental Argentinian ballads in an attempt to divert the soldier's attention to loved ones back home. It even played classics like "Under Pressure" by the rock group Queen. Ascension Alice also broadcast a fictitious request program from Argentinian mothers who made emotional appeals to their sons to look after themselves and return home safely. Following the end of the conflict, the British government was criticized for compromising the BBC's reputation for objective and accurate reporting. The British government, for its part, felt that the propaganda war justified such draconian measures provided the source of the radio station remained concealed.

Black propaganda was reported to be part of the responsibility of the Office of Strategic Influence (OSI), a body established at the Pentagon during the War on Terrorism in 2001. In early 2002 the White

House proposed retaining this office as a component of the broader U.S. psychological war on terrorism.

David Welch

See also BBC; CIA; Crossman, Richard; Falklands/Malvinas War; Gray Propaganda; Psychological Warfare; Radio (International); Rumor; Terrorism, War on; White Propaganda; World War II (Britain); World War II (United States)

References: Delmer, Sefton. *Black Boomerang.* London: Secker and Warburg, 1962; Howe, Ellic. *The Black Game.* London: Michael Joseph, 1980; Jowett, Garth, and Victoria O'Donnell. *Propaganda and Persuasion.* London: Sage, 1992.

British Prime Minister Tony Blair addresses the United Nations. (United Nations)

Blair, Tony (1953–)

Media-savvy British Labour politician and prime minister since 1997, Anthony Charles Lynton Blair was born in Edinburgh, Scotland, and grew up in the northeast of England. After graduating from Oxford University, he worked as a lawyer in London. He won the parliamentary seat of Sedgefield (also in the northeast) in 1983. He rose through the Labour Party ranks during the long period of opposition to the Thatcher government. His briefs included that of spokesman on Treasury matters, especially trade and consumer affairs. In 1988 he joined the shadow cabinet as shadow minister for energy; in 1989 he moved to the employment brief, where he shifted the Labour Party away from its traditional policy of backing union "closed shops" in the workplace.

Beginning in 1983, under the leadership of Neil Kinnock (1941–), the Labour Party supplemented internal reform by adopting the sophisticated media approach of the British Conservatives and various American political parties. Rising politicians like Blair received coaching from media consultants, while media insiders like film producer David Puttnam (1941–) made party election broadcasts. The Labour Party took the red rose as its logo. The key figure in this transformation was Peter Mandelson (1953–), scion

of an old Labour political family and former producer for London Weekend Television, who served as the party's director of campaigns and communications from 1985 to 1990.

In 1992 the Labour Party suffered a surprise defeat in the general election. Blair, a close associate of Mandelson, moved to the fore as a key acolyte of the new leader, John Smith (1938–1994), holding the post of shadow home secretary. Blair soon became known for his pledge to be "tough on crime, tough on the causes of crime." Following Smith's death, Blair (with Mandelson's help) won election to the party leadership. He and Mandelson worked to "re-brand" the party as "New Labour." Participants at a 1995 party conference voted to drop its commitment to nationalization as expressed in "Clause IV" of the party constitution. No less significantly, Blair also visited the media mogul Rupert Murdoch (1931–), whose tabloid newspaper *The Sun,* which had hitherto opposed Labour in elections, now changed sides. New Labour fought an energetic campaign, placing particular emphasis on appealing to the younger voter. Labour also pointed to a succession of corruption ("sleaze") scandals involving the Conservative Party, though analysts found that hard policy issues of health and education were more important factors in voters' decision making. Blair's campaign song was the upbeat "Things Can Only Get

Better." His party won with a stunning majority. Early policy successes included the conclusion of the Good Friday agreement in Northern Ireland in 1998.

Blair proved both a formidable speaker and an excellent judge of the national mood. He, rather than the royal family, led the national response to the death of Diana, princess of Wales, in August 1997. In office, however, Blair's news-management tactics became a major topic of debate. Together with the charge of cronyism, this became a staple of anti-Blair propaganda. Critics suggested that after being in the opposition for so long, the Labour Party now lived in a perpetual state of campaigning, employing a "rapid-response unit" to ensure that each opposition story could be matched and refuted before it could cause damage. Blair's government greatly expanded the practice of employing "special advisers" (popularly known as spin doctors) to manage the news. The key figure in Labour's news management was a former *Daily Mirror* journalist named Alistair Campbell (1957–), who had been Blair's press adviser and spokesman since 1994. Critics charged that Campbell acted as de facto deputy prime minister. He and such other special advisers as Charlie Whelan at the Treasury became notorious for "briefing against" colleagues, that is, leaking stories to the press suggesting that the prime minister was displeased; casualties included Northern Ireland minister Mo Mowlam (1949–). Other issues involving image included the need for the Labour Party to appear pristine—having attacked the Conservatives for "sleaze." Here, ironically, casualties included Peter Mandelson, who (apparently at Campbell's insistence) was obliged to resign on two separate occasions (1998 and 2001), once for receiving a favor and once for allegedly giving one.

In 2001 the Labour Party fought and won a second substantial general election majority. However, that autumn the charge of "spin doctoring" reemerged following the revelation that Jo Moore, an adviser to transport secretary Stephen Byers, had reacted to the 11 September terrorist attacks in the United States by sending an e-mail pointing out that it was a "very good day" to "bury" bad news. Both Moore and Byers resigned in 2002. Tony Blair had always been active on the world's stage, but during the War on Terrorism he became a key figure in the propaganda strategy of the international alliance, traveling widely and stressing that the Western powers respected the Islamic religion.

Nicholas J. Cull

See also Britain; Elections (Britain); Exhibitions and World's Fairs; Funerals; Gulf War (2003); Kosovo Crisis and War; Murdoch, Rupert; Terrorism, War on; Thatcher, Margaret

References: Jones, Nicholas. *Sultans of Spin: The Media and the New Labour Government.* London: Orion, 2000; Macintyre, Donald. *Mandelson and the Making of New Labour.* London: HarperCollins, 2000; Rentoul, John. *Tony Blair: Prime Minister.* Boston: Little, Brown, 2001.

Bosnian Crisis and War (1992–1995)

Events surrounding this central episode in the disintegration of the Federal Republic of Yugoslavia were largely determined by the relative success of competing propaganda strategies. Militarily weak compared to its enemies, the survival of the Bosnian state depended on the extent to which it could attract outside support through diplomatic and propaganda means. The Bosnian government successfully won over members of the international press—particularly those from the United States—who were based in its capital city Sarajevo. The resulting disagreement in strategy between the United States and the European powers frustrated attempts at peace. United Nations forces deployed to Bosnia (United Nations Protection Force, or UNPROFOR) mounted a poorly funded and largely ineffectual propaganda campaign. The war was notable for the speed with which television reporting transformed local incidents in Bosnia into major international issues. A cease-fire in November 1995 led to the deployment of IFOR (Implementation Force), a NATO-based military force with a much stronger military posture and better-organized propaganda, which resulted in a peace settlement.

From 1987 onward, Serbia, under Slobodan Milosevic (1941–), sought to eliminate the privileges of the other states of post-Communist Yugoslavia under the 1974 constitution, precipitating the disintegration of the federation. In 1991 Slovenia seceded from Yugoslavia relatively peacefully, followed by Croatia. The sticking point was multiethnic Bosnia-Hercegovina, with significant Croat and Serb populations as well as the dominant Bosnian Muslims. Although Bosnia's secession in April 1992 was recognized by the United States and the European Community (EC; later the European Union, or EU), it was still subject to a United Nations arms embargo against all of Yugoslavia, introduced in September 1991. The result was a complex and highly factional civil war, at first involving Croats, Muslims, and Serbs. All sides habitually used brutal methods that constituted war crimes, particularly "ethnic cleansing" by means of force and intimidation. With access to established national and international media, and using essentially Communist methods, all sides also utilized extensive propaganda and disinformation strategies. This made it very difficult for the outside world to follow events, and some basic facts about the war continue to be disputed.

The propaganda war began before the fighting, during the winter of 1991–1992, with inflammatory hate propaganda broadcast by television and other media by all sides as a preliminary salvo. Western observers were first surprised and then deeply pessimistic about the success of such propaganda, seeing it as an example of media meant to evoke deeply rooted psychological and cultural responses. According to UN officials, all sides habitually generated artificial crises (such as shelling their own people) in order to promote their own cause internationally through the media. The Bosnian government strategy was most successful in projecting itself as the victim of aggression, obtaining outside support—including smuggled armaments—on a large scale. A controversial mortar attack on a Sarajevo market in February 1994, ostensibly by Bosnian Serbs, led to the UN demand that certain Bosnian towns be designated as "safe areas." Members of the international (chiefly U.S.) press in Sarajevo also sided with the Bosnian position against that of UNPROFOR, demanding direct American intervention in the war.

UNPROFOR, which included ground troops from EC countries but not from the United States, was organized and deployed to Yugoslavia shortly before the Bosnian War began. UNPROFOR's structure and objectives were based on traditional UN peacekeeping operations, in which lightly armed UN forces oversaw tense but peaceful situations. Its official mandate was to protect food convoys to beleaguered areas in order to prevent starvation, while maintaining strict impartiality. In addition to being inadequately funded and subject to obstruction by belligerent forces, UNPROFOR propaganda was based on the traditional UN idea of the primacy of truth, which was wholly inappropriate under the circumstances. As the war progressed and the United States became more interventionist on the Bosnian side, the Serbs came to see UNPROFOR as hostile.

In propaganda terms the Bosnian War was the largest and most typical of the postmodern wars of the 1990s. Global television coverage, in particular, effectively eliminated the distinction between local and international events, as well as between military operations and propaganda. The war was characterized by mutual recriminations by UNPROFOR and members of the international press regarding their respective stances. It revealed serious shortcomings in the ability of the United Nations to conduct such operations, including major weaknesses in UN media and information policy. The United States and EC countries seriously underestimated the sophistication of the propaganda campaigns mounted by the various belligerent camps. The ability of a small country like Bosnia to influence Western opinion and the consequent demonizing of the Serbs were also matters of concern to some observers. International reporting of the crisis and war nevertheless confirmed that national contexts and agendas frequently predominated over facts.

The resolution of the conflict came in the summer of 1995 when U.S. aircraft (acting under the North Atlantic Treaty Organization, or NATO) carried out attacks against Bosnian Serb forces. The Bosnian Serb response was to take UN ground troops hostage—a vivid propaganda image broadcast around the world—and to overrun some of the Bosnian safe areas, including Srebenica. In the autumn of 1995 American-trained Croat forces, supported by U.S. bombing raids as part of Operation Deliberate Force, inflicted a decisive defeat against the Bosnian Serbs. This resulted in a compromise peace in November, known as the Dayton Accords, and the deployment of IFOR (consisting of American, British, and French troops) to police a cease-fire agreement according to which Bosnia remained essentially intact. NATO commentators pointed out that IFOR combined a good information organization with considerable armed force and the mandate to use it—all of which UNPROFOR lacked. This appeared to support the common Western military position that propaganda directed at a potential enemy was only effective when backed by force or the threat of force. The lasting effect of the war in propaganda terms was to establish a frame of reference for most Westerners in which the Serbs were demonized.

Stephen Badsey

See also Kosovo Crisis and War
References: Badsey, Stephen, ed. *The Media and International Security.* London: Frank Cass, 2000; Combelles Siegel, Pascale. *Target Bosnia.* Washington, DC: C4ISR Cooperative Research Program (CCRP), Department of Defense, 1998; Gow, James. *Triumph of the Lack of Will.* London: Hurst, 1996; Gow, James, Richard Paterson, and Alison Preston, eds. *Bosnia by Television.* London: BFI Press, 1996; Ripley, Tim. *Operation Deliberate Force.* London: Centre for Defence and International Security Studies (CDISS), 1999; Simms, Brendan. *Unfinest Hour: Britain and the Destruction of Bosnia.* London: Allen Lane, 2001; Thompson, Mark. *Forging War.* Luton: University of Luton Press, 1999.

Bracken, Brendan (1910–1958)

Bracken, Britain's minister of information during most of World War II, was born in Ireland. He worked in British journalism in the 1920s, and in 1928 became managing director of the *Economist.* Entering Parliament in 1929 as a Conservative, he became a trusted ally of Winston Churchill (1874–1965)—so close that he was widely rumored to be his illegitimate son—and in 1941 succeeded Alfred Duff Cooper (1890–1954) at the Ministry of Information (MoI). Bracken's close relationship with the prime minister gave him the necessary political leverage to make the MoI a force to be reckoned with in Whitehall, and the ministry prospered under his tenure. By the end of the war he had lost his political touch. During the 1945 election campaign he made the notorious blunder of smearing the Labour Party as totalitarian. Churchill attempted this in his "Gestapo Broadcast" of June 1945, which caused widespread offense at the expense of Conservative electoral fortunes. His ministry (and initials) provided the inspiration for "Big Brother" and the Ministry of Truth in George Orwell's (1903–1950) celebrated novel *Nineteen Eighty-four* (1949).

Nicholas J. Cull

See also Britain; Elections (Britain); Churchill, Winston; MoI; Orwell, George; Wick, Charles Z.; World War II (Britain)
References: Boyle, Andrew. *"Poor, Dear Brendan": The Quest for Brendan Bracken.* London: Hutchinson, 1974; Cockett, Richard, ed. *My Dear Max: The Letters of Brendan Bracken to Lord Beaverbrook, 1925–1958.* London: Historians' Press, 1990.

Brainwashing

Brainwashing, a term favored in popular culture but treated with skepticism in academic literature, denotes the complete erasure of an individual's thought patterns after a process of mental reprogramming. In many instances the precise mechanics of this repatterning remain unclear but often include hypnosis, psychotropic drug treatments, physical torture, subliminal suggestion, and rote indoctrination. The outcome of such processes is the production of a brainwashed subject, stripped of autonomy and demonstrating robotic obedience to the brainwasher's instructions and unquestioning adherence to the latter's ideological precepts.

For fifty years notions of brainwashing have shaped the popular understanding of how individual or group behavior can be manipulated to produce total conformity. The term continues to be widely used, particularly in relation to how cult movements and/or fundamentalist religious sects indoctrinate their adherents. In 2001, for example, the participation of John Lindh, a young American, in Al Qaeda, was widely explained in the U.S. news media—and by his mother—as the result of brainwashing. The term was first coined in 1950 by Edward Hunter, an American journalist whose exposé of techniques employed in the People's Republic of China to produce the "new Communist man" was printed in the *Miami News*. Hunter, who claimed that the term "brainwashing" was a transliteration of the Chinese term *hsi nao* ("wash brain"), wrote a book on the subject entitled *Brainwashing in Red China* (1951).

Hunter's account of the ways in which Chinese Communists harnessed peer pressure to compel individuals to engage in public "self-criticism" might have remained a matter of purely esoteric interest to Western audiences had it not been for the capture of several thousand UN prisoners of war (POWs) by North Korean and Chinese forces during the Korean War. Soon media reports began to appear in the U.S. press suggesting that U.S. POWs were being brainwashed by their Communist captors. When, in May 1952, two American airforce men corroborated Chinese propaganda claims that U.S.

forces had engaged in germ and bacteriological warfare in Korea, many Americans believed that brainwashing explained their "confessions" and other "anti-imperialist" propaganda broadcasts that followed. Such alarmism was heightened at the end of the war when twenty-one U.S. POWs refused repatriation to the United States in favor of a new life in Communist China—a decision so perverse, in the opinion of many Americans, that it could only have been the result of brainwashing. As one contemporary commentator skeptically noted, in popular accounts "nothing less than a combination of the theories of Dr I. P. Pavlov and the wiles of Dr Fu Manchu would produce such results."

Popular representations of brainwashing, notably John Frankenheimer's feature film *The Manchurian Candidate* (1962), have perpetuated a belief that Communists possessed techniques to erase and repattern human thought processes, and that these owed a good deal to Pavlov's work on the conditioned reflex. However, more measured social scientific studies—based on debriefings of U.S. POWs returning by ship from Korea in 1953—cast an altogether different light on the behavior to which these men had been subjected. Psychologists such as Edgar Schein (1928–) and Albert D. Biderman (1923–) sought to debunk brainwashing by suggesting that instead of having successfully implanted new beliefs, the Chinese Communists were expert in manipulating "social milieu." In other words, in the closed conditions of POW camps they were able to extract high levels of compliant behavior from prisoners without having to reorient their fundamental belief structures.

These social scientific studies described the ways in which Chinese camp commandants encouraged "collaboration" by destroying old hierarchies and encouraging new allegiances. To this end, they offered rewards to "progressives" who appeared amenable to indoctrination and punished "reactionaries" who stubbornly resisted. Violence and the threat of brutality were thus never far from the surface of camp life. Given the scarcity of food, its rationing and deployment as a reward loomed large in the incentive structure; prisoners' access to mail was similarly controlled as a further inducement to comply. Manipulation of the social environment and group dynamics was accompanied by rote ideological instruction, which included lectures on Marxist and Maoist precepts and the insistence that prisoners engage in "self-criticism," first by repeatedly rewriting their life stories with a new class consciousness and then by publicly recanting their old allegiances. Under such coercive conditions, high levels of collaboration were only to be expected. Whereas those who clung to brainwashing as an explanation imagined that the Chinese had successfully instilled Communist beliefs in the prisoners, behaviorists stressed that the vast majority of POWs merely "went along" with their captors to the extent necessary to survive camp life, without shifting their convictions toward Communism. In fact, most American prisoners resisted ideological instruction; this was so apparent to their captors that the Chinese abandoned formal "training" months before the end of the war. As for the twenty-one prisoners who refused repatriation—seemingly the epitome of the brainwashed POW—most were less confirmed Communists than men who, having engaged in more serious acts of collaboration, feared being court-martialed upon their return to the United States.

These measured findings, however, made much less of an impression on the popular imagination than lurid accounts of brainwashing, and the concept's utility to Cold War anti-Communist propaganda is abundantly clear. Seemingly unpersuaded by the findings of social scientific studies, the U.S. Central Intelligence Agency (CIA) continued its own search to produce robotic, mind-warped individuals, clandestinely financing psychiatric experimentation on unwitting patients, who were subjected to extreme forms of drug and electromagnetic shock treatment under a program known as MK Ultra. Thus,

while brainwashing has given rise to many scenarios that properly belong in the realm of science fiction, fantasies of total control over the mind have, in some cases, been matched—if not exceeded—by experiments enacted on human subjects in the name of a Cold War victory.

Susan Carruthers

See also China; CIA; Cold War; Korean War; Prisoners of War; Terrorism, War on

References: Biderman, Albert. *March to Calumny: The Story of American POWs in the Korean War.* New York: Macmillan, 1963; Hunter, Edward. *Brainwashing.* New York: Farrar, Straus & Cudahy, 1956;———. *Brainwashing in Red China.* New York: Vanguard, 1951; Lifton, Robert. *Thought Reform and the Psychology of Totalism: A Study of "Brainwashing" in China.* London: Victor Gollancz, 1961; Marks, John. *The Search for the "Manchurian Candidate."* New York: Norton, 1979; Schein, Edgar. *Coercive Persuasion: A Socio-Psychological Analysis of the "Brainwashing" of American Civilian Prisoners by the Chinese Communists.* New York: Norton, 1961; Winn, Denise. *The Manipulated Mind: Brainwashing, Conditioning and Indoctrination.* London: Octagon, 1982.

Brazil
See Latin America

Britain
Propaganda and persuasion occupy a central place in the workings of the British system of government. The priority given to consensus arrived at through debate and persuasion differentiated the political development of England from the early modern period onward.

During the fifteenth century England took a path toward the development of the nation-state that differed from the majority of Continental states. While Continental kings subjugated their respective parliaments, estates general, and diets by advancing notions of absolute monarchy, in England between 1309 and 1485 the barons, allying themselves with the gentry, resisted and at times bloodily disposed of kings who attempted to do the same. Instead of fading, the Parliament developed procedurally into an ever more effective institution for limiting royal power and for developing consensus among what could increasingly be called the political class. England emerged from the Middle Ages as a parliamentary monarchy. This divergence from the systems of government of most of the Continent was made final and irreversible in the seventeenth century by Parliament's call for the execution of Charles I (1600–1649) and the deposition of James II (1633–1701), the last two English kings who sought to go the Continental way.

Parliamentary monarchy led to a characteristic "debating society" view of the process of government. Currents in the English Civil War suggested that if the landed classes fell to fighting among themselves, they might be replaced by those below them. Hence Parliament awarded the highest priority to consensus, above such other objectives as speed of decision making, expertise, or even social justice. Earlier and to a greater extent than in most countries in postfeudal Europe, the arts of political persuasion thus became an integral part of the English system of government. From the sixteenth century onward techniques of political persuasion developed parallel with the development of the English system of government itself. With the incorporation of Wales and Ireland in the sixteenth century and the linking up with Scotland in the seventeenth century, it became possible to talk about a "British" approach to persuasion in the modern state.

Around 1500 England, like the rest of Europe, embraced printing and the theater as new media for communication, art, and propaganda. In time the English variant became distinctive. Henry VIII (1491–1547) used personal display, costume, pageantry, and precisely choreographed court etiquette to project the majesty of the monarch in much the same way as Francis I (1494–1597) of France. Although Elizabeth I (1533–1603) continued to employ these techniques with panache, the further development of such forms of symbolic propaganda that projected an image of the monarch as the embodiment of the state did not take place in England. By the second half of the seventeenth century a striking contrast was apparent between the godlike image of France's Louis XIV (1638–1715) as the "Sun King" and England's Charles II (1661–1700) as the "Merry Monarch," a human being who shared his subjects' appetites and situations and dressed in casual attire.

English propaganda developed in verbal rather than symbolic forms. Written media, political poems, manifestos, tracts, and treatises were already emerging in the fifteenth century; over the centuries they developed into what was probably the world's largest body of political pamphleteering. The three characteristic core techniques of the British approach to political persuasion initially took the form of written persuasion: (a) factuality—persuasion by means of the manipulation of facts rather than an emotive appeal use of literary or rhetorical devices; (b) pragmatic argumentation—the case being built up as a compelling accumulation of specific "facts" rather than as a deduction from an a priori principle or an authority, with current facts illustrations; and (c) presentation in the form of a judicial style often employing a legalistic manner, incorporating some of the facts and contentions of the other side and using the "on the one hand/on the other hand" style of persuasion. These characteristics of style and approach to political propaganda in the written medium naturally presupposed the existence of a regular forum of debate into which information and views are fed and also that the debate would be conducted among practical laymen interested in politics rather than learned academicians. In other words, it presupposed something like Parliament at the heart of the political framework.

In the spoken medium, too, the characteristically British rhetorical devices reflected—and still reflect—the central assumption of an ongoing debate on practical issues among practical people interested in politics, with the objective of coming up with a workable consensus for the time being. The characteristic elements of British political oratory—the "throwaway line," self-deprecation, understatement, the use of a chairperson to whom the speaker defers, concentration on practical details or consequences, and humorous rather than adversarial references to opponents—are designed to defuse rather than inflame, to particularize rather than generalize, and to decrease rather than magnify the positional distance between the speaker and the listener. Grand oratory from first principles, charismatic addresses by the leader, the use of inspirational imagery, or theatrical staging are not typically part of the spoken forms of British—especially English—political persuasion except in rare formal contexts or special circumstances such as wartime. "Heckling" (allowing members of the audience to interrupt) and the skillful manipulation—indeed, incorporation—of such interruptions into a speech is a characteristic device of British political oratory.

Britain also has a great tradition of religious oratory largely independent of its political oratory (which is not the case in the United States) despite some intermingling between the two approaches during the English Civil War. Even then, the participatory debating framework—in Parliament or among soldiers, such as the Putney Debates (1647)—rather than the inspirational "mass meeting" soon became the norm. Secular political movements that tried to introduce religious techniques, such as the early socialists before and the fascists after World War I, always found themselves swimming against the tide.

In accordance with the perception that consensus matters most, as early as the eighteenth century the ability to persuade in public became the prime criterion and the most essential professional skill—rather than those of the courtier, the administrator, or the technocrat—for obtaining political office in Britain. The employment of professional persuaders to assist office seekers also developed early. Governments and politicians—in or out of office either as individuals or collective groups, such as political parties—have employed propagandists since the reign of Elizabeth I. Since leading political figures were expected to function as public persuaders, this was typically a covert rather than overt role. Consensus was perceived as the balance in the public's mind between the ideas, information, and arguments it received over time from various sources—the more outwardly independent the better. Professional propagandists have typically been used in Britain to quietly "feed" those ideas, views, and bits of information that their employers wish to promote as the main ingredients from which public opinion crystallizes. Fine distinctions between "publicity" and "propaganda," overt and covert, and constant debates about consensual rules concerning their use or avoidance have also been a characteristic feature. Professional orators first appeared in the nineteenth century, but this gave way to the use of professionals behind the scenes, with politicians themselves doing the actual presentation.

Ever since the reign of Elizabeth I, the general perception that it is a proper function of government—albeit often necessarily a secret one—to shape public opinion naturally led to concern with what was being communicated through the great verbal medium of the theater. The Lord Chamberlain's Office for the censorship of the stage, established in 1545 and given a statutory basis in 1737, became the longest continuously operating organization for the censorship of the stage in Europe. Combining censorship with sponsorship of the stage in various forms resulted in perhaps the most effective political control of this medium. It was only relinquished in 1968 when the theater ceased to be a medium of consequence for the public at large, its place being taken by television.

Equally effective was the harnessing of the technology of wireless broadcasting to promote consensus through the creation of the "public service broadcasting" concept, and a unique institutional framework for it, to act as "the integrator for democracy," in the words of John Reith (1889–1971), the first director general of the BBC. The application to film of the concepts and rules for controlling the theater through the creation of the British Board of Film Censorship proved less effective in the end. Political messages relayed through British films were indeed effectively controlled; foreign films with strongly contrarian messages were kept off the public screens or allowed to appear only with the strongest of those messages removed or toned down. British film production was also kept alive through various forms of financial support in the face of the overwhelming strength of Hollywood. In terms of negative propaganda, the exclusion of messages liable to undermine fundamental elements of the dominant ideology has made British cinema screens among the most tightly controlled in Europe. However, the proportion of British feature films to American could not be maintained at a sufficiently high ratio to achieve the positive propaganda potential that British politicians also saw in film. The application to the medium of film of the three core techniques of the British approach to political persuasion (ultimately reinforced by state funding) did produce the documentary genre, which represents the principal British contribution to the art of the moving image and propaganda.

It was no accident that Britain emerged from the world wars as a pioneer of external propaganda, psychological warfare, and "cultural diplomacy." Britain regarded persuasion as the central factor in the working of the state for three hundred years and thus had a pool of expertise to draw on when needed. "Propaganda with facts" remains the characteristic British approach to external propaganda both in wartime and in peacetime, for this was merely the application to external political persuasion of the recipe that proved so effective in domestic politics.

A preference for affecting the balance of information and public views by quietly feeding into the flow of ideas desired information rather than excluding undesirable news through censorship (except as a last resort) has also been a consistent characteristic, as is the preference for doing both from behind the scenes rather than through formal and overt state organs. Ministries of Information, state censorship bodies, and the like are only formally set up in Britain during wartime. Governments have preferred close and sophisticated relations with the press, which is perceived as a partner in evolving consensus. From the beginning of the modern period, the British system of government gave primacy to the generation of a practical consensus among the "political nation"—the group or groups effectively involved in government at the time—over not only coercion but also almost anything else in politics. It thus places persuasion and propaganda at the heart of the working of the state. This led to the development of both a set of characteristic core techniques and frameworks for maintaining a free but not unregulated flow of ideas. Britain was thus exceptionally well placed when liberal-democratic ideals replaced absolutism in Europe. Its "debating society" approach permitted a gradual widening of the membership of the "political nation" within the constitutional framework rather than requiring its replacement. The centrality of persuasion in its political system secured for Britain a greater degree of stability, continuity, and ideological cohesion than have alternative approaches to the development of the postfeudal European nation state and its subsequent transformation into democracies.

Nicholas Pronay

See also Anglo-Boer War; Art; BBC; BIS; Blair, Tony; Britain (Eighteenth Century); British Empire; Churchill, Winston; Civil War, English; Crimean War; Elections (Britain); Falklands/Malvinas War; Film (Newsreels); Grierson, John; IRD; Ireland; John Bull; Milton, John; MoI; Psychological Warfare; PWE; Shakespeare, William; Sport; Thatcher, Margaret; Women's Movement: Precursors; Women's Movement: First Wave/Suffrage; Women's Movement: Second

Wave/Feminism; World War I; World War II
(Britain)

References: Anglo, Sydney. *Spectacle, Pageantry and Early Tudor Policy.* Oxford: Oxford University Press, 1969; Downie, J. A. *Robert Harley and the Press: Propaganda and Public Opinion in the Age of Swift and Defoe.* Cambridge: Cambridge University Press, 1979; Harris, Tim. *London Crowds in the Reign of Charles II: Propaganda and Politics from the Restoration to the Exclusion Crisis.* Cambridge: Cambridge University Press, 1987; Koss, Stephen R. "The Rise and Fall of the Political Press in Britain." In *Propaganda, Politics and Film, 1918–1945.* Ed. Nicholas Pronay and D. W. Spring. London: Macmillan, 1982.

Britain (Eighteenth Century)

The eighteenth century represented the formative period in the development of the press and political propaganda in Britain and its American colonies, which also saw the use of propaganda to define and perpetuate ideas of British national identity. The overwhelming power of the Whig aristocracy (attributed to a complex machinery of patronage and exclusion) would appear to have left little need for manipulation of mass public opinion. However, while only a small percentage of the population was entitled to vote (historians estimate 25 percent of adult males in 1714 and decreasing thereafter), regular appeals to the public for support from both government and opposition are a testament to the perceived influence of public opinion. These appeals were targeted not only at independent members of Parliament and the electorate "out-of-doors" but also extended to members of the wider literate community, who were arbitrarily excluded from voting but wielded sufficient influence through petitions and street demonstrations (which often turned into riots) to occasion reversals of policy and changes of ministry.

Political propaganda used print as its primary medium, which included newspapers, almanacs, periodicals, cartoons, engravings, pamphlets, and broadsides. The lapse of the Licensing Act in 1695 not only ended pre-publication censorship but also permitted the development of printing in provincial centers, while the improvement of road and water transportation enabled London-based (and Edinburgh-based) newspapers to reach a provincial audience with national news. Three triweekly newspapers appeared in London in 1695. By the end of the century London had thirteen daily and ten triweekly newspapers competing with over fifty provincial weeklies. Annual sales of newspapers reached seventeen million by 1793. Through coffeehouses and taverns a single issue could reach a readership of thousands.

The reign of Queen Anne (1702–1714) saw an unprecedented rise in the political use of print media, notoriously associated with London's Grub Street. The first daily newspaper appeared in 1702. By 1714 there were seven dailies and numerous triweekly and biweekly papers. Richard Steele's (1672–1729) *Tatler,* Joseph Addison's (1672–1719) *Spectator,* and Daniel Defoe's (1660–1731) *Review* collectively provided a forum for discussion of political issues and gossip. The frequent elections mandated by the 1694 Triennial Act engendered fierce competition for public support, driving both the Whig and Tory parties to create complex organizations involved in the production and dissemination of propaganda.

Political activity centered on taverns and coffeehouses, such as the Cocoa Tree in London, the headquarters for Tories. Newspapers and broadsides advertised meetings and circulated addresses and petitions. Local constituency organizations such as the Steadfast Society in Bristol and the Royston Club in Hertfordshire disseminated material and supplied events to be reported, such as printing "instructions to MPs." The production and quality of political pamphlets burgeoned with every political and religious crisis, as both Tories and Whigs employed the satirical skills of such literary talents as Alexander Pope (1688–1744), Jonathan Swift (1667–1745), and Defoe.

As a leader of the Tory opposition, Robert Harley (1661–1724) recognized the potential of press propaganda. While in office (1710–1714) he developed a complex organization that produced and distributed favorable material and hampered the opposition press. When Robert Walpole (1676–1745) took office, he adopted some of Harley's techniques in reaction to the success of the opposition press of the 1720s. Between 1731 and 1741 Walpole spent over fifty thousand pounds on the production and distribution of newspapers and pamphlets, using treasury funds to bankroll the *London Journal, Daily Courant* and *Daily Gazetteer.* He also promoted the ministerial interest and circulated thousands of free copies of pamphlets and newspapers through the post office. For example, in 1741, 10,800 copies of the *Daily Gazetteer* were sent to the post office for dispersal, with clerks given explicit instructions not to circulate antiministerial papers such as the *Craftsman,* the *London Evening Post,* and the *Champion.*

Walpole's measures were insufficient to combat the great popularity of opposition propaganda, disseminated through constituency clubs and personal networks. The Tories, who were excluded from office by their association with Jacobitism, combined with Country Whigs to oppose Walpole's monopoly of power. Both John Trenchard (1662–1723) and Thomas Gordon's (d. 1750) *Independent Whig* and Bolingbroke's (1678–1751) *Craftsman* (1727–1736) appealed to a country or commonwealth ideology in denouncing the overweening power of the executive and the corruption of the constitution. The so-called Robinocracy, as well as Walpole's neglect of many famous writers, led to some of the best examples of pamphleteering wit and political satire, such as Pope's *Dunciad* (1728), John Gay's (1685–1732) *Beggar's Opera,* and the engravings of William Hogarth (1697–1764).

Popular politics also employed a variety of nonprint media. Patriotic songs such as "Rule Britannia" and "God Save the Queen" competed with satirical (and often bawdy) songs of opposition. The production of printed car-

toons flourished. They grew increasingly bold in their satirical portrayal of political personalities, thanks to the brilliance of artists like James Gillray (1757–1815) and Isaac Cruikshank (1764–1811). The production of political memorabilia, snuffboxes, mugs, and medals also focused on the graphic representation of the associated cause. Frequently ritual and celebration united classes in street demonstrations and popular protests.

Without the Licensing Act, authorities were able to prosecute printers and authors under seditious libel. Parliamentary privilege prohibited the reporting of parliamentary process. Newspapers published unauthorized and often inaccurate division lists of key commons votes, and monthly periodicals—such as the *Political State* after 1711 and *Gentleman's Magazine* beginning in 1731—published accounts of debates during parliamentary recess. This was explicitly prohibited in 1738. By the 1760s a number of newspapers had resumed publishing regular reports of debates, particularly John Almon's (1737–1805) *London Evening Post* and William Woodfall's (1746–1803) *Morning Chronicle.* The government did not prosecute the printers and conceded the ban in 1771.

Political opposition focused on popular issues or causes, such as support for John Wilkes (1727–1797), the rebellion of the American colonists, Protestant toleration, and antislavery, resulting in a huge array of political pamphlets and newspaper letters. For example, the *Letters of Junius* (1767–1772) focused on liberty of the press, American grievances, and corruption in government. A number of opposition groups developed a radical organization—using the traditional political forms of petition and address, reproduced in newspapers and handbills—calling for extraparliamentary mobilization of public opinion in support of a variety of issues. A loose coalition of radical reformers developed campaigns for Protestant tolerance and parliamentary reform, such as the Feather's Tavern Petition (1772), John Wilkes's Middlesex agitation (1768–

1774), Christopher Wyvill's (1740–1822) Yorkshire Association (1779–1785), and the antislavery campaign (1783–1791). Harry (H. T.) Dickinson has argued that while "the exploitation of the power of the press and the skilful dissemination of propaganda were copied from earlier campaigns against the Court," the country opposition sought only electoral endorsement of its policies, whereas "the radicals wanted the people, even those without the vote, to exert a powerful influence over Parliament." The same methods of organization and dissemination were adopted by populist movements such as the Protestant Association, organized by Lord Gordon (1751–1793), whose protest in 1780 against Catholic emancipation resulted in the most violent rioting of the period.

Buoyed by the success of the American Revolution, radicals argued for the formation of "a great national association," proposed by James Burgh (1714–1775) in his *Political Disquisitions* (1774–1775). The Society of the Supporters of the Bill of Rights (1769), the Society for Constitutional Information (1780), the London Corresponding Society, and the Friends of the People published petitions and addresses, circulated political pamphlets, and organized public readings, opening a forum for political debate to the literate artisan and rural working class. The reformers greeted both the centenary of the Glorious Revolution and the outbreak of revolution in France as expressions of the constitutional principles they wished to restore. In *Reflections on the Revolution in France* (1791) Edmund Burke (1729–1797) rejected this argument, portraying the reformers as dangerous revolutionaries, thus initiating an unprecedented pamphlet war. Hundred of replies to Burke were published and sold cheaply or circulated free of charge by radical societies—including Mary Wollstonecraft's (1759–1797) *Vindication of the Rights of Woman* (1792), James Mackintosh's (1765–1832) *Vindicae Gallicae* (1791) and, most famously, Thomas Paine's (1737–1809) *Rights of Man*—and met with responses from supporters such

as Hannah More (1745–1833). The literary furor was matched by street demonstrations, the planting of liberty trees, and the mocking of the king's birthday celebrations.

The outbreak of war with France in 1793 provided the justification for the suppression of the radical movement. Extremist pamphlets were proscribed and a number of printers prosecuted for seditious libel. Thomas Muir (1765–1799) and six other members of the Friends of the People were sentenced to transportation for the dissemination of radical works. The Treason and Sedition Bill (1796) and the outlawing of radical societies in 1799 effectively killed the parliamentary reform movement. Patriotic propaganda was also used to denounce radical ideas, disseminated through Church and King associations, such as John Reeves's Association for Preserving Liberty and Property against Republicans and Levellers and the Goldsmiths Hall Association in Edinburgh.

Following the Act of Union in 1707, the dissemination of news from Westminster and military campaigns abroad was an important component in the forging of a British identity united by Protestantism, commerce, and empire. Linda Colley has shown that this new identity, subjoining to rather than supplanting former national and local identities, was created by a propaganda of Protestantism, commerce, and war. The production of affordable editions of Protestant texts, such as *Pilgrim's Progress* (1678–1684) by John Bunyan (1628–1688) and John Foxe's (1516–1587) *Book of Martyrs* (1563), and the celebration of Britain's Protestant history in almanacs and public ceremonies reinforced the perceived connection between true religion and the prosperity and liberty unique to Britain.

Karen M. Ford

See also Abolitionism/Antislavery Movement; Britain; Censorship; Defoe, Daniel; Ireland; John Bull; Livingston, William; Paine, Thomas; Portraiture; Revolution, American, and War of Independence; Revolution, French; Wilkes, John

References: Black, Jeremy, ed. *Britain in the Age of Walpole*. London: Macmillan, 1984; Colley,

Linda. *Britons: Forging the Nation, 1707–1837.* London: Yale University Press, 1992; Dickinson, H. T. *Liberty and Property : Political Ideology in Eighteenth-Century Britain.* London: Weidenfeld and Nicolson, 1977;———. *The Politics of the People in Eighteenth-Century Britain.* London: Macmillan, 1994; Holmes, Geoffrey, and Daniel Szechi. *The Age of Oligarchy: Pre-Industrial Britain, 1722–1783.* London: Longman, 1993; Plumb, J. H. *England in the Eighteenth Century, 1714–1815.* Harmondsworth, UK: Penguin, 1950.

British Broadcasting Corporation

See BBC

British Empire

The British Empire of the nineteenth and twentieth centuries was inspired by and, in turn, sustained through a variety of propaganda. The bulk of this was produced privately and included much commercial material, from songs and celebration knickknacks to vast quantities of juvenile literature. As John MacKenzie notes in *Propaganda and Empire* (1984), "A wide variety of nongovernmental agencies discovered that imperial propaganda was also profitable."

The British Empire was built by trade and the need for naval bases to protect that trade. Missionary societies strengthened the cultural dimension, propagating Christianity in Africa and the Pacific. These diverse efforts were not supported by a major ideological drive until the years following the Indian Mutiny of 1858, when, with India under direct rule, Britain consolidated its imperial possessions worldwide. Architects of this process included Prime Minister Benjamin Disraeli (1804–1881), who in 1876 took the crucial step of making the queen empress of India, thus overlaying the empire and the monarchy as institutions. From the 1870s to World War I imperial propaganda flourished. Official manifestations included the Imperial Institute in London, which encouraged the study of subject peoples, and numerous exhi-

bitions, beginning with the Great Exhibition of 1851. Private groups dedicated to promoting the empire included the Royal Colonial Institute and the British Empire League. The image of Queen Victoria became ubiquitous in various printed forms and in numerous statues erected to celebrate her golden and diamond jubilees. The church promoted the empire through its missionary societies and by encouraging popular admiration for Christian heroes of the empire like Charles George Gordon of Khartoum (1833–1885). Starting in 1904 the British celebrated Empire Day—an obvious focal point for imperial propaganda—established as the result of a campaign by Sir Joseph Chamberlain (1836–1914). Artistic figures caught up in imperial themes included the composer Edward Elgar (1857–1934) and the poet and novelist Rudyard Kipling (1865–1936).

Ideas of empire flourished in British popular culture, where ordinary Britons seized on the opportunity to participate in an empire "on which the sun never sets" and which privileged the whiteness of their skin regardless of the emptiness of their pockets. Products as diverse as soap and coffee were festooned with images relating to empire. Stars of the imperial music hall stage included Gilbert Hastings Farrell (The Great) Macdermott (1845–1901), who performed the famous "Jingo Song" (1878), written by G. W. Hunt (c. 1829–1904), which ran: "We don't want to fight, but, by jingo if we do, / We've got the ships, we've got the men, we've got the money too." It gave the world the term "jingoism," for unquestioning patriotism. Songs celebrating the imperial armed forces included "Soldiers of the Queen" (1881) by Leslie Stuart (1864–1924).

The empire proved a particularly potent subject in propaganda aimed at children, from the rhetoric of the Boy Scouts movement, founded in 1908 by Robert Baden-Powell (1857–1941), to the colorful trading cards placed in cigarette and tea packets that charted heroes, flags, and uniforms of the empire. Boys' literature such as the novels of

G. A. Henty (1832–1902) or journals such as the *Boy's Own Paper* (1879–1967) or *The Boy's Friend* (1895–1927) presented stories of imperial adventure and propagated the stoical ethic of duty and self-sacrifice. In school, history textbooks taught that the empire was national destiny, while poetry lessons meant memorization of works like "Vitai Lampada" by Sir Henry Newbolt (1862–1938), with its implicit comparison of cricket and war and the famous refrain: "Play up! Play up! and play the game!" Such lessons conditioned British youth for the sacrifices of World War I.

In the aftermath of the war the British government sought to encourage imperial solidarity as part of its strategy for recovery. Events included the Empire Exhibition at Wembley (1924–1925). The Beaverbrook press launched an Empire Crusade. In 1926 the government established the Empire Marketing Board (EMB) under Sir Stephen Tallents (1884–1958) to promote imperial products. Propaganda included leaflets, newspaper advertisements and, most significantly, the EMB film unit under John Grierson (1898–1972), which pioneered documentary filmmaking in Britain but closed in 1933. Tallents went on to direct public relations for the General Post Office and the British Broadcasting Corporation (BBC). His book *The Projection of England* (1932) laid the foundation for much of Britain's later cultural propaganda efforts. The BBC also sought to reach out to the empire with its Empire Service, launched in 1932. The conception of empire developed significantly at this time as a result of the Statute of Westminster (1931), which recognized the dominions (Australia, New Zealand, South Africa, and Canada) as independent and equal within the Commonwealth of Nations. During World War II the empire became a central theme in British propaganda in the United States, largely because of American hostility to the institution. Prime Minister Winston Churchill (1874–1965) was emphatic in his support for the empire and intended to retain it at war's end, broadcasting his opinions to this effect.

With the wave of decolonization that followed World War II, the notion of a commonwealth rapidly superseded that of empire. The commonwealth received a substantial boost with the coronation in 1953 of Elizabeth II (1926–), but Churchill's promised New Elizabethan age did not materialize. Interest in the commonwealth rapidly diminished. Despite the end of empire, imperial attitudes toward race and national destiny lived on in British culture and emerged periodically in the latter part of the twentieth century in matters involving immigration policy and, most spectacularly, during the Falklands/Malvinas War of 1982.

Nicholas J. Cull

See also Africa; Australia; BBC; Beaverbrook, Max; Canada; Caribbean; Churchill, Winston; Exhibitions and World's Fairs; Falklands/Malvinas War; Grierson, John; Indian Subcontinent; New Zealand; Pacific/Oceania; Sport; World War I; World War II (Britain)

References: Brewer, Susan. *To Win the Peace: British Propaganda in the United States during World War II.* Ithaca, NY: Cornell University Press, 1997; MacKenzie, John. *Propaganda and Empire: The Manipulation of British Public Opinion, 1880–1960.* Manchester: Manchester University Press, 1984; MacKenzie, John, ed. *Imperialism and Popular Culture.* Manchester: Manchester University Press, 1984; Said, Edward W. *Culture and Imperialism.* New York: Knopf, 1994; Taylor, Philip M. *The Projection of Britain: British Overseas Publicity and Propaganda, 1919–1939.* Cambridge: Cambridge University Press, 1981.

Bryce Report (1915)

This report represents a prime example of the atrocity propaganda deployed by Britain during World War I. More properly known as the *Report of the Committee on Alleged German Outrages,* the Bryce Report consisted of a 360-page compendium of evidence that the German army had brutalized Belgian and French civilians, mostly in the form of depositions collected from refugees. The depositions told of numerous cases of rape, child murder, and mutilation. Lord Bryce (1838–1922), who had chaired the official committee that collected the evidence, wrote an introduction to the report urging readers to believe its contents. His involvement heightened the report's impact, especially in the United States, where Bryce had served as a much-respected British ambassador until 1913. After the war none of the stories contained in the report could be substantiated. The report was seen as just another British attempt to trick the United States into joining the war.

Nicholas J. Cull

See also Atrocity Propaganda; Britain; Fakes; World War I

References: Ponsonby, Arthur. *Falsehood in War-Time: Containing an Assortment of Lies Circulated throughout the Nations during the Great War.* Sudbury UK: Bloomfield, 1991; Sanders, Michael, and Philip M. Taylor. *British Propaganda during the First World War.* London: Macmillan, 1982.

Bulgaria

See Balkans

C

Canada

The high period of Canadian propaganda, beginning with World War II and ending with the October Crisis in 1970, is a narrative of "whiteness." As with Robert Rauschenberg's all-white paintings of the early 1950s, one might say that the "only image was the shadow cast by the spectator." Despite its light shadings, Canadian propaganda was no less notable. Indeed, if propaganda's efficacy is often inversely proportional to its stridency, then the precise difference between Canada's air of neutrality and its actual close ties to Western censorship, intelligence, and propaganda circuits is worthy of attention.

Propaganda played a role in the nation's earlier periods. During the colonial era, from the early 1600s to the end of the nineteenth century, Canada's aboriginal peoples were targeted by religious "propaganda" in its original sense of propagating conversion to Christianity. Simultaneously with their dispossession and depletion by Europeans, stereotypical representations of aboriginals as virtuous "noble savages" gave way to fearful pictorial and print "propaganda" (in its secular, modern sense) portraying bloodthirsty warriors capable of satanic cruelty.

Throughout the international conflicts of the eighteenth century, British North America proved to be a fertile ground for propaganda, rumor, and deception. Reversing one's snowshoes was a handy ruse to confound pursuers, but early propaganda efforts extended to concerted print and rumor campaigns too. Thus, American revolutionaries fomented anti-British feeling among French Montrealers during the Revolutionary War.

Between the Act of Confederation that established the Canadian nation in 1867 and the outbreak of World War II in 1939, the federal government used propaganda on an ad hoc basis in accordance with imperial purposes and increasingly also to achieve sovereign national ends. Propagandists were heartily employed both to sway Canadians one way toward "reciprocity" in trade with America or the other toward "imperial preference" and exclusive trade with British Empire countries.

The Canadian government's responses to the Métis minority's uprisings in Manitoba's Red River region in effect sanctioned propaganda demonizing their charismatic leader Louis Riel (1844–1885) in English-Canadian public opinion. Riel's trial and execution in Regina in 1885 and the displacement of the Métis from their land accentuated French-English divisions in eastern Canada and helped secure a place in the next century for the hastily assembled North-West Mounted Police.

World War I had a profound impact on the development of Canadian propaganda and public attitudes toward government information generally. Domestic propaganda sought to neutralize the true horrors of the western front in order to maintain public support for the war. Not surprisingly, recruitment posters and press accounts emphasized camaraderie and glory rather than casualties and battlefield conditions. Mounting recruitment difficulties eventually culminated in a full-scale conscription crisis that opened a wide rift between English and French Canadians, not to mention many Canadians of "recent European origin." Large numbers of the latter were consigned to internment camps.

Max Aitken (1879–1964) emerged from small-town New Brunswick to become the Fleet Street press baron Lord Beaverbrook. As Canada's official "War Eye Witness" in France, Aitken tirelessly fostered the impression that Canadian valor alone carried forward the war aims. To the government's chagrin, Aitken's new standards of professionalism in Western propaganda were being achieved at some cost to Britain's prestige. Aitken's recruitment to lead the main British propaganda effort marked a new threshold in centralized government control of wartime information. Ever sensitive to archival retention and historical memory, Aitken's initiatives left a vivid legacy of the Great War, not least through the paintings of his official war artists.

Immediately following the war, the 1919 Winnipeg General Strike provoked an outpouring of nativist and antilabor propaganda at the behest of commercial interests, with tacit government support. Thirty thousand strikers brought the city to a standstill, but they were effectively isolated as "Bolshevists" and "alien scum" by the mainstream media and a "Citizens' Committee of 1,000." Mounted police crushed the strikers on "Bloody Saturday," helping to radicalize many foreign-language presses and, in turn, occasioning the growth of police and military translation and censorship bureaus.

The Special Branch of the Royal Canadian Mounted Police (RCMP) cultivated its own propaganda capability through its relations with journalists and its infiltration of Canada's left-wing and foreign-language presses. The minuscule Communist Party of Canada produced thundering propaganda whose main effect was to expose more moderate and broader-based "Popular Front" elements to decisive counterattack from the right. During the 1920s and 1930s the police frequently harassed the Communist Party and a successful agitprop play, *Eight Men Speak,* lashed out against the imprisonment and assault of party leader Tim Buck (1891–1973). In 1937 Quebec premier Maurice Duplessis (1890–1959) passed notorious "Padlock Laws" authorizing police closure and padlocking of any establishment suspected of promoting Communist propaganda.

Canada's high point of propaganda began in 1940 when John Grierson's (1898–1972) National Film Board (NFB) produced *Peoples of Canada* to celebrate Canadian tolerance of ethnic difference. This new theme played well in a Europe torn asunder by interethnic strife. The NFB's *Canada Carries On* and *The World in Action* series of newsreels became a staple of mass-media wartime information, but it was the new multiculturalist theme that best coincided with the 1941 Atlantic Charter and with Britain's new "internationalist" theme deemphasizing its imperialist past. In Ottawa a "Nationalities Branch" was instituted in 1943 to prepare and distribute propaganda articles for the foreign-language press in Canada.

Clandestine British "black propaganda" activities in Canada during World War II included Camp X, a clandestine training facility for the British Special Operations Executive (SOE), created without the knowledge of Prime Minister Mackenzie King (1874–1950). Camp X also served as the "Hydra" transmitter site for British Security Coordination (BSC). Hundreds of Canadians, including many women, were recruited by the BSC for operations in New York and elsewhere. In 1945 a well-disguised secret service operation produced the defection in Ottawa of cipher clerk Igor Gouzenko, whose information exposed Soviet spy rings operating in Canada and the United States. American columnist Drew Pearson (1897–1969) made Canada the eye of an international propaganda storm when he published Gouzenko's revelations in 1946. The Gouzenko Affair became a defining event that enmeshed Canada in the Anglo-American alliance at the onset of the Cold War.

By the end of World War II Canada had developed a remarkable propaganda capacity in the mass media. The NFB had grown in size and professionalism, and its films were staples in Canadian movie theaters and in prisoner-of-war camps at home and abroad. The domestic radio service of the Canadian Broadcasting Corporation (CBC) had honed its ability to shape public opinion, and by 1945 it had launched a full-scale program of short-wave radio propaganda through its International Service. From studios in Montreal linked to powerful transmitters in Sackville, the International Service broadcast across the Atlantic in a growing repertoire of European languages. In conjunction with the larger Voice of America and the BBC World Service, Canadian radio propagandists were fully prepared to enjoin the Cold War's "Battle of the Antennas." Canadian radio propagandists already regarded themselves as the "whitest" of these three services and they nurtured this credibility as a distinctively Canadian subtlety of persuasion.

With the formalization of various security arrangements at the end of World War II came a new bureaucracy for propaganda. An interdepartmental Psychological Warfare Committee supervised Canada's propaganda agencies and established their Cold War policy orientation. In the Department of External Affairs, Defense Liaison II (DLII) was the group most concerned with these matters, and purges of supposed leftists through RCMP security screenings in the late 1940s and early 1950s eliminated dissent in the

NFB and the CBC services. Afterward DLII found it necessary to soften the hectoring anti-Soviet tone of the NFB's *Freedom Speaks* series.

Gouzenko's successful books kept Toronto ghostwriters busy, and a 1948 Hollywood film based on his story (*The Iron Curtain*) brought North American audiences face to face with the insidious Communist enemy. Former BSC chief Sir William Stephenson (1896–1989) amplified aspects of the Gouzenko case and other intelligence exploits during World War II. The best-selling "Intrepid" books about the Winnipeg-born millionaire were themselves a masterful genre of propaganda aimed at self-aggrandizement, the blurring of fact and fiction, and the hardening of public opinion against the Soviet Union. From the left came a series of propaganda ripostes such as the anti-McCarthyist radio satire *The Investigator* (1954) by Reuben Ship (1915–1975) and Paul Robeson's (1898–1976) five heroic Peace Arch Concerts on the U.S.-Canadian border (1952–1956).

As Quebec nationalism gathered force during the postwar "Quiet Revolution," Canadian propaganda took a new turn. Despite its international image as a model police force, the RCMP employed highly aggressive "black propaganda" and disinformation tactics in order to disrupt Quebec's sovereignty movement during the 1960s and 1970s. When the 1970 October Crisis came to a head with kidnappings of a Quebec cabinet minister and a British diplomat, Prime Minister Pierre Trudeau (1919–2001) declared martial law, called in the military, and placed hundreds of suspects in detention. A decade later the MacDonald Royal Commission investigated the RCMP and censured the Mounties for clandestine infiltration and sabotage of legitimate political organizations. Subsequent research has revealed that the RCMP had, in fact, developed sophisticated capabilities in "black propaganda" and strategic deception. In 1983 a new standalone civilian agency, the Canadian Security and Intelligence Service, was established to take over various RCMP activities.

National unity remained a central tenet of Canadian domestic propaganda throughout the surges of Quebec nationalism that culminated in a hairline victory for federalists in a 1995 referendum. The Péquiste campaign adopted a catchy "flower power" motif that nearly carried their elderly and crotchety male leaders to victory. On the federalist side, a mass campaign that rushed Canadian flags and buses packed with anglophone Ontarians to Montreal had little impact. In fact, the decisive propaganda battle had been fought over the years in every facet of Quebec society—English signs, school curricula, university courses, map layouts—through advertising campaigns.

The crisis at Oka, Quebec, in 1990 brought yet another turn in Canada's propaganda story. Mohawks objecting to the expansion of a golf course on disputed land adjacent to their Kanesatake reserve gained world attention through a well-orchestrated propaganda campaign that portrayed their occupation of the disputed land in the starkest terms. Mohawk "Warriors" first faced an ill-prepared and impatient provincial police contingent until a police officer was shot. An implacable and media-conscious military force then moved in and thereafter both sides manipulated media images and practiced deception techniques to pressure the other side to end the standoff. Eventually the military prevailed, but not before the Mohawks had created a cause célèbre that tarnished Canada's international reputation.

Perhaps the uneasiness that underscores Canadian attitudes toward propaganda is symptomatic of Canada's fitful progress as a nation whose sovereign interests gradually and only partially were distinguished from those of Britain and the United States. During the Gulf War and in the more recent War on Terrorism, the carefully cultivated Canadian "air of neutrality"—as symbolized by Lester Pearson's (1897–1972) Nobel Peace Prize following the Suez Crisis and the peacekeeping duties undertaken by Canadians around the world—has been replaced by a perhaps truer image of Canada as a faithful Anglo-American ally.

Mark Kristmanson

See also Beaverbrook, Max; British Empire; Cold War; Cultural Propaganda; Exhibitions and World's Fairs; Grierson, John; Intelligence; Radio (International); World War I; World War II (Britain)

References: Evans, Gary. *In the National Interest: A Chronicle of the National Film Board of Canada from 1949 to 1989.* Toronto: University of Toronto Press, 1991; Gouzenko, Igor. *This Was My Choice.* Toronto: J. M. Dent, 1948; Keshen, Jeffrey A. *Propaganda and Censorship During Canada's Great War.* Edmonton: University of Alberta Press, 1996; Kristmanson, Mark. *Plateaus of Freedom: Nationality, Culture and State Security in Canada, 1940–1960.* Oxford: Oxford University Press, 2002; MacDonald, Bill. *The True Intrepid: Sir William Stephenson and the Unknown Agents.* Surrey, BC: Timberholme, 1998; McLoughlin, Michael. *Last Stop Paris: The Assassination of Mario Bachand and the Death of the FLQ.* Toronto: Viking, 1998; Scher, Len, ed. *The Un-Canadians: True Stories of the Blacklist Era.* Toronto: Lester, 1992; Siegel, Arthur. *Radio Canada International: History and Development.* Oakville, Ont.: Mosaic, 1996; Stafford, David. *Camp X.* Toronto: Lester & Orpen Dennys, 1986; Trigger, Bruce G. *Natives and Newcomers: Canada's "Heroic" Age Reconsidered.* Kingston: McGill-Queen's University Press, 1985; Whitaker, Reg, and Gary Marcuse. *Cold War Canada: The Making of a National Insecurity State, 1945–1957.* Toronto: University of Toronto Press, 1994; York, Geoffrey, and Loreen Pindera. *People of the Pines: The Warriors and the Legacy of Oka.* Toronto: Little, Brown, 1992.

Capa, Robert (1913–1954)

Capa was a Hungarian-born photojournalist (his real name was Endre Friedmann) whose images of the Spanish Civil War became classics of photographic propaganda first for the cause of the Spanish Republic and then against war in general. Expelled from Hungary because of his left-wing student politics, Friedman studied journalism in Berlin and got his break photographing Leon Trotsky (1879–1940) while on a visit to Denmark in 1932. During the early months of the Spanish Civil War he invented the name Robert Capa for an imaginary American journalist whom he planned to make the source of his photographs from the front. Although his subterfuge was later exposed, the name stuck and he changed his own name accordingly. Capa photographed combat and civilian suffering in Spain beginning in 1935. Using a small Leica 35mm camera to get into the midst of the action, he covered the war in China in 1938, World War II (including the D-day landings), the early struggles of Israel, and French Indochina, where he was killed by a land mine. Capa was unafraid to use his photographs to show the suffering and nobility of people with whom he identified. His most famous image—depicting the death of a Loyalist militiaman near Cerro Muriano (Córdoba front), ca. 5 September 1939—shows a soldier, apparently just struck by a bullet, falling back with his arms outstretched. It was the subject of controversy, as some scholars have suggested that the subject is only training and not engaged in active combat. Subsequent investigators have validated its authenticity. The image became well known in the 1960s as a peace poster bearing the word "Why?"

Nicholas J. Cull

See also Civil War, Spanish; Peace and Antiwar Movements (1945–); Photography
References: Capa, Robert. *Photographs.* New York: Aperture, 1996; Whelan, Richard. *Robert Capa.* New York: Knopf, 1985.

Capra, Frank (1897–1991)

Capra was an American feature filmmaker who successfully turned his hand to propaganda films during World War II. Born in Italy, he moved to the United States as a child. During the 1930s he established a reputation as one of Hollywood's foremost directors, winning Academy Awards for films like *It Happened One Night* (1934). During World War II he accepted a commission as a major in the Army Signal Corps and agreed to make a series of seven orientation documentaries for the U.S. Army under the title

Why We Fight. These were supplemented by films in the *Know Your Ally* and *Know Your Enemy* series and a one-shot film called *The Negro Soldier* designed to combat racism in the army. Capra oversaw the writing and production of these films, which reflected the same commitment to "American values" of community and the common man as his prewar films. The impact of these films on audiences at the time is questionable since most were not available for distribution until relatively late in the conflict. After the war Capra returned to commercial filmmaking, though his career never quite reached its prewar heights.

Nicholas J. Cull

See also Film (Documentary); Why We Fight; World War II (United States)
References: Carney, Raymond. *American Vision: The Films of Frank Capra.* Cambridge: Cambridge University Press, 1986; McBride, Joseph. *Frank Capra: The Catastrophe of Success.* London: Faber and Faber, 1992.

Caribbean

This region has suffered from stereotypes and experienced the propaganda of imperialism and the Cold War, but it has also produced campaigns and campaigners of its own. Its propaganda history parallels that of both Latin America (with which it overlaps through such Spanish Caribbean islands as Cuba) and the Pacific/Oceania. The Caribbean (named after the Carib Indians) was the first point of contact between Europeans and the "New World." Following the voyages of Christopher Columbus (1451–1506), the region saw a wave of both religiously driven missionary activity and propaganda about the inhabitants that stressed their savagery and cannibalism (a word also derived from Carib). The plantation slavery system followed. The Caribbean reflected a shifting map of colonial control with Spain, France, and Britain as the chief players. Holland also had possessions, and Denmark maintained the Virgin Islands as a royal colony until the United States purchased them at the end of the nineteenth century.

As in Latin America, the ideas of the French Revolution had a major impact. In 1791 Toussaint L'Ouverture (1744–1803), a former slave, led a rebellion on the island of Haiti. His name ("the Opening") derived from a battlefield exploit involving the opening of a breach in enemy lines. By 1801 he had conquered the neighboring colony of Santo Domingo, but in 1802 Napoleon's forces suppressed his rebellion and imprisoned him in France, where he died. Haiti, however, remained independent. Toussaint L'Ouverture became an enduring symbol of liberty and black leadership. Celebrations of his life include poems by William Wordsworth (1770–1850) in England and Alphonse de Lamartine (1790–1869) in France, as well as a biography and play by the Trinidadian socialist writer C. L. R. James (1901–1989).

After figuring in the movement against slavery (which was abolished in the British Empire in 1833), the region was the scene of anticolonial activities, especially in the Spanish Caribbean. Among the leaders was José Martí (1853–1895), poet, essayist, and campaigner for Cuban independence, whose works include *Nuestra América* (1891). Martí spent most of his adult life in exile working on newspapers in Latin America and the United States. He died in one of the first engagements of the Cuban rebellion he had worked to ferment. Like Toussaint L'Ouverture, Martí became a major reference point for later generations, most notably Fidel Castro (1927–).

In the twentieth century the British and French Caribbean experienced the propaganda implicit in their respective educational systems. The U.S. cultural and military presence in the region increased, and the rulers of independent countries of the region looked to propaganda to undergird their regimes. The most successful Caribbean propagandist of the 1920s was the Jamaican-born Marcus Garvey, who launched a transnational Universal Negro Improvement Association from the United States. The movement attracted over eleven million members among people of African descent in the United States, Central America, West Africa, and the Caribbean. It included a major theological component that insisted that God is black and invoked Africa as the true homeland. The nationalist agenda of the Garvey movement in Jamaica was taken up in the 1930s by the Rastafarian faith, which looked to the Ethiopian king Haile Selassie (formerly Ras Tafari) (1891–1975) as the messiah. Campaigners for labor rights in Jamaica included Alexander Bustamante (1884–1977), a powerful speaker and able union organizer, who began work in the 1930s. After spending 1941–1942 in jail, he founded the Jamaica Labour Party. Bustamante was knighted by the queen of England in 1955. Following independence in 1962, he served as Jamaica's first prime minister until 1967. The French island of Martinique was the birthplace of philosopher Frantz Fanon (1925–1961), who became a leading Pan-Africanist and anticolonial voice in the late 1950s.

The Spanish Caribbean saw the equivalents of the European totalitarians, including Rafael Trujillo (1891–1961), dictator of the Dominican Republic, and Fulgencio Batista y Zaldívar (1901–1973) in Cuba. Their regimes were built upon personality cults and were characterized by censorship (and murder) of opponents. The most extravagant dictator in the region was François "Papa Doc" Duvalier (1907–1971), a former doctor and health minister, who seized power in 1957 with the support of the army. He ruled by means of terror campaigns, carried out by his notorious secret police (Tonton Macoutes). Their name ("bogeymen" in Haitian Creole) was designed to intimidate, as were their ubiquitous dark glasses, but the image was backed up with torture and summary execution. Duvalier's propaganda leaned heavily on voodoo, which he practiced. Duvalier identified himself with the terrifying voodoo spirit Baron Samedi, the bringer of death. Denunciations of his regime included the novel *The Comedians* (1966) by the English writer Graham Greene (1904–1991). When Papa Doc died in 1971, rule passed to "Baby Doc," his nineteen-year-old son Jean-Claude (1951–), who attempted to improve Haiti's international image. He did enough to earn developmental and military aid from the United States but fell from power in 1986.

The chief figure in the Cold War Caribbean is, of course, Fidel Castro. Following the Cuban revolution of 1959, Castro's Cuba became an epicenter of Communist propaganda in the region. The United States responded to the threat of revolution by backing anti-Communist regimes. Beyond this, the United States intervened in 1965 to end a civil war in the Dominican Republic. The episode saw the strategic use of psychological warfare, and the United States felt sufficiently encouraged by the results to amend its campaign in Vietnam accordingly. The other major U.S. intervention in the Caribbean occurred in 1983 on the island of Grenada. In 1974 Grenada had achieved full independence from Britain with Eric Gairy (1922–1997) as prime minister (an eccentric interested in UFOs). In 1979 the left-wing New Jewel movement led by Maurice Bishop (1944–1983) seized power in a bloodless coup and began a defiantly anti-U.S. radio propaganda campaign. U.S. president Ronald Reagan portrayed Grenada as being a foothold for the Soviet Union in America's backyard and emphasized (and—it later emerged—exaggerated) Cuban involvement on the island. When, in October 1983, Bishop died in an internal power struggle, the United States mounted Operation Urgent Fury to overthrow the New Jewel regime. The intervention was, in many ways, propaganda through performance. Still suffering from the aftermath of Vietnam, the United States needed to project a sense of military force. The operation featured tight control of the media along the lines of the British management of the Falklands/Malvinas War of the previous year.

The later 1980s saw the emergence of the charismatic Haitian Catholic priest Jean-Bertrand Aristide (1953–). Aristide followed the regional tradition of liberation theology, which called upon the church to combat earthly injustice. In 1990 he ran for president on behalf of the Fanmi Lavalas left-wing coalition. He won, only to be driven from the country by a military coup a few months later. The U.S. government had mixed feelings about his rule and his potential return. He was the victim of a rumor campaign in Washington, D.C., attacking his sanity. Despite this, he served a second term as president-in-exile. In 1994 the Clinton administration intervened in Haiti to restore him to power, deploying both military and psychological warfare to do so. Aristide was advised not to run for president in 1995 and stepped down (he also left the priesthood and married). In February 2001 he won a fourth term in office.

In the second half of the twentieth century, Caribbean musical forms, such as calypso and Jamaican reggae, which had been used for political expression and satire, became well known outside the region. Bob Marley (1945–1981), the best-known exponent of reggae, infused his music with a strong antiracist and Rastafarian-related liberation message. By the end of the century, the chief propaganda effort of most Caribbean governments occurred in the field of tourism, some of which was coordinated by the Caribbean Community and Common Market (CARICOM), an organization founded in 1973. Public health and development issues remained significant. Other common activities included a joint declaration with the small nations of the Pacific and elsewhere of its nuclear-free status and the 1994 UN conference on small islands, held on Barbados.

Nicholas J. Cull

See also British Empire; Castro, Fidel; Latin America; Reagan, Ronald; Spanish-American War

References: Bark, Dennis L., ed. *The Red Orchestra: Instruments of Soviet Policy in Latin America and the Caribbean.* Palo Alto: Hoover Institution Press, 1986; Beck, Robert J. *The Grenada Invasion: Politics, Law and Foreign Policy*

Decision Making. Boulder, CO: Westview, 1993;
Bethell, Leslie, ed. *The Cambridge History of
Latin America.* Vol. 7, *Latin America Since 1930:
Mexico, Central America and the Caribbean.*
Cambridge: Cambridge University Press,
1990; Ferguson, James. *Papa Doc–Baby Doc:
Haiti and the Duvaliers.* Oxford: Blackwell,
1987; James, C. L. R. *The Black Jacobins:
Toussaint L'Ouverture and the San Domingo
Revolution.* London: Penguin, 2001; Martí,
José. *Inside the Monster: Writings on the United
States and American Imperialism.* Ed. Philip S.
Foner. London: Monthly Review Press, 1975;
Parry, J. H., and P. M. Sherlock. *A Short History
of the West Indies.* London: Macmillan, 1971;
Turton, Peter. *José Martí: Architect of Cuba's
Freedom.* London: Zed, 1986.

Cartoons

As Aldous Huxley remarked in *Point Counter
Point* (1928), "Parodies and caricatures are the
most penetrating of criticisms." Cartoons are
among the most powerful weapons in the propagandist's arsenal, though some would argue
that the political cartoon more often gives
pleasure to the already persuaded than discomfort to the subject in question. The term
"cartoon" comes from the Italian *cartone,* or
pasteboard, and originally referred to an
artist's preparatory sketches, such as Raphael's
cartoons for the figures of the Sistine Chapel.
The modern political cartoon, a satirical
drawing commenting on public—and usually
political—matters, is an English contribution.
William Hogarth (1697–1764), for example,
preached against the dangers of gin. His "Gin
Street" indicates the curse of gin in a way no
viewer can ignore. As David Low notes in his
book about British cartoonists, Hogarth's "was
not the art of the rapier, but of the tank." Exposing the foibles of the English monarchy was
a particular concern of the Scotsman James
Gillray (1756–1815), who managed to enrage
the king but did not put an end to the excesses
he so enthusiastically exposed.

In France the work of Honoré Daumier
(1808–1879) continues to be admired. He
frequently belittled the pretensions of the
pretentious. Many a lawyer has winced at
Daumier's image of the grand and rich
lawyer telling the poor widow whose case he
has just lost: "But at least you had the honor
of my having represented you." Thomas Nast
(1840–1902), the greatest American cartoonist, was born in Germany but came to America at age six. Nast created full-page engravings for *Harper's Weekly,* whose circulation of
three hundred thousand made it the closest
thing in nineteenth-century America to a national newspaper. Nast created the symbols
of the Republican (elephant) and Democratic
(donkey) parties.

The greatest English cartoonist of the
twentieth century is David Low (1891–
1963), who was born in New Zealand. Low
created the figure of Colonel Blimp in 1934
to describe a certain type of superannuated
political thinking. Blimp was the subject of a
fine British feature film entitled *The Life and
Death of Colonel Blimp* (1943). Surely Low's
greatest cartoon is "Rendezvous," published
in the *London Evening Standard* on 20 September 1939. It shows Hitler tipping his hat to
Stalin, who returns the gesture, with both
figures in midair above a generic dead body.
Hitler says: "The scum of the earth, I believe."
Stalin's response is: "The bloody assassin of
the workers, I presume." This cartoon, which
Low claims is the bitterest he ever drew, is an
iconic commentary on the cynicism of the
surprise Nazi-Soviet Non-Aggression Pact of
23 August 1939, making the invasion of
Poland virtually inevitable.

In twentieth-century America, Herbert
Block (1909–2001), or Herblock, the longtime cartoonist for the *Washington Post,* had
enormous impact during the heyday of
Joseph McCarthy (1909–1957), the junior
senator from Wisconsin for whom Herblock
claims he coined the term "McCarthyism."
Herblock depicts McCarthy as swarthy and
ill-kempt; the senator was often shown carrying a bloody hatchet. (Herblock was not a
man to use gentle imagery; he, too, preferred
the tank to the rapier.) Herblock denounced
the anti-Communist actions of Richard
Nixon in numerous cartoons. A memorable

A political cartoon entitled "Peace Creeps," put out by the American Nazi Party, Arlington, Virginia, 1962. Those protesting the atomic bomb are shown as stereotypical peacenik hippies, Jews, and black protesters: "Sit-ins Yes!! Fall-out No!!" (Courtesy of David Culbert)

example shows a welcoming committee awaiting the arrival of Nixon, who is to give a speech. The caption reads: "Oh here he comes now." Nixon is seen climbing out of the sewer—a clear reference to Nixon's preference for the smear or below-the-belt tactics in his quest to expose Democrats as crypto-Communists in the early 1950s. Nixon was so offended by his cartoon image that he forbade delivery of the paper to his home, publicly insisting that it would upset his children. Herblock was back in top form only in the second term of Nixon's presidency, when the Watergate scandal led to a series of cartoons that powerfully attacked Nixon's credibility, including the memorable comment: "I am not a crook."

The political cartoon can also include the technique of photomontage, though the purist might insist that the medium of pho-tography is fundamentally different from that of the cartoonist, who uses pen and ink. The German John Heartfield (1891–1968) was born Helmut Herzfeld, anglicizing his name during World War I to indicate his opposition to the German war effort. Heartfield made a series of covers for the socialist publication *Arbeiter-Illustrierte Zeitung* (AIZ), many of which have become icons of anti-Hitler sentiment. For example, in the German elections of April 1932, when Hitler proclaimed that "Millions Stand Behind Me," Heartfield made it seem that the millions represented the contribution of German big business by adroitly manipulating a standard Hitler photograph and adding a stream of coins.

The political cartoon is alive and well in the twenty-first century. However, the earlier era's assumption that the cartoonist should possess the skills of the illustrator is no longer the case. Many cartoonists today make it clear that traditional drawing skills are no hard-and-fast requirement for the cartoonist. The politicians of every country continue to provide ample targets for the cartoonist and the student of propaganda.

David Culbert

See also McCarthy, Joseph R.; Mexico; Nast, Thomas; Nixon, Richard; Raemakers, Louis
References: Block, Herbert. *The Herbert Block Book.* Boston: Beacon, 1952; Keller, Morton. *The Art and Politics of Thomas Nast.* New York: Oxford, 1975; Low, David. *British Cartoonists, Caricaturists and Comic Artists.* London: William Collins, 1942; Pachnicke, Peter, and Klaus Honnef. *John Heartfield.* Cologne: DuMont, 1991; Seymour-Ure, Colin, and Jim Schoff. *David Low.* London: Secker and Warburg, 1985.

Casablanca (1942)

Directed by Michael Curtiz (1886–1962) for Warner Brothers, *Casablanca* is one of the best examples of feature film propaganda from World War II. Warner had a long tradition of using its films to comment on issues in the news, and *Casablanca* was planned in 1941 as exactly such a film. It was filmed at a time when the U.S. government urged all Hollywood producers to ask, when selecting their projects, "Will this picture help to win the war?" Its propaganda value was manifold. On one level it provided an escape into a world of glamour, international intrigue, and melodrama. The film contained many politically useful stereotypes: heroic Allies, comic Italian Fascists, and dangerous, fanatical Germans. Moreover, the story met the requirements of homefront propaganda, highlighting the need for Americans to sacrifice personal interests to the greater national goal of victory. The story concerns Rick (Humphrey Bogart [1899–1957]), a cynical American bar owner living in wartime Morocco, who encounters Laszlo, a European resistance leader on the run from the Nazis. Rick is forced to choose between his public duty to help the anti-Fascist cause, and his private love for

Laszlo's wife (Ingrid Bergman [1915–1982]). He embraces the path of action and self-sacrifice. In one particularly emotive moment, the issue of the war is encapsulated in the musical duel between German soldiers, bellowing "Watch on the Rhine," and the French and Allied café patrons who drown them out with the "Marseillaise." The scene was reputedly so moving at the time of shooting that members of the film crew, with tears in their eyes, joined in the singing.

Nicholas J. Cull

See also Film (Feature); "La Marseillaise"; United States; World War II (United States)
References: Doherty, Thomas. *Projections of War: Hollywood, American Culture, and World War II.* New York: Columbia University Press, 1993; Koppes, Clayton R., and Gregory D. Black. *Hollywood Goes to War: How Politics, Profits, and Propaganda Shaped World War II Movies.* New York: Free Press, 1987.

Castro, Fidel (1926–)

Cuban revolutionary and Communist leader and one of the best-known propagandists of the later twentieth century, Castro was born and raised in Oriente province. He grew up with a keen appreciation for the history of revolution in Cuba. His early heroes included the poet, patriot, and martyr José Martí (1853–1895). He studied law and by the early 1950s had joined the struggle against the island's dictator Fulgencio Batista y Zaldívar (1901–1973). On 26 July 1953 Castro took part in a failed raid on Moncada barracks. He was arrested and put on trial. However, he turned the situation to his advantage by making a dramatic speech in which he declared: "History will absolve me," denouncing Batista, and rallying his country to liberalism. The speech laid the foundation for Castro's reputation. In 1955 Batista released Castro from jail as part of an amnesty agreement. Castro traveled to Mexico, where, in collaboration with the Argentinian-born Ernesto "Che" Guevara (1928–1967), he organized the 26 July movement. In 1956 Castro and eleven others (including Guevara)

Cuban Premier Fidel Castro addresses the UN General Assembly during his first visit to the United States in nineteen years, 12 October 1979. (Bettmann/Corbis)

landed in Cuba and commenced a guerrilla rebellion against Batista, an action that captured the popular imagination. In 1959 Batista's government fell and Castro established himself as premier.

Soon after seizing power, Castro began a program of agricultural reform that brought him into direct conflict with U.S. corporate plantation owners. Castro also used anti-American rhetoric to rally his population. By 1961 he had formally aligned himself with the Soviet Union and declared himself a Marxist. In so doing Castro embarked on a propaganda duel with the United States that would outlast the century. The initial U.S. response—the abortive attempt to invade Cuba with an army of exiles at the Bay of Pigs—helped to bolster Castro's reputation, both in his own country and around the world, as a man prepared to defy the United States.

Castro established himself at the center of a totalitarian media apparatus, which in-

cluded a rigidly ideological state education system, state-run film and broadcasting, control of the state newspaper, *Granma,* and Prensa Latina, the largest news agency in the developing world. Castro censored opponents and jailed writers who clashed with the regime. He nurtured a personality cult, establishing himself as the personification of his country and his ideology. Castro became famous for long speeches—some lasting more than nine hours. He conveyed a sense of assuredness in his use of Marxist rhetoric and appropriated the mantle of José Martí, a mixture that proved enduringly persuasive on both television and radio.

Overseas Castro sponsored revolutionary movements around Latin America, the Caribbean, and in West Africa, deploying arms, advisers, and propaganda. Diplomatic manifestations of this policy included Castro's sponsorship of the Organization of Solidarity with the Peoples of Africa, Asia, and

Latin America, and his chairmanship (since 1979) of the Non-Aligned Movement. Castro's activities remained of major concern to the United States and served as a justification for U.S. counterpropaganda and military intervention in the region (as it had in the Dominican Republic in 1965). In 1983 the United States launched a major propaganda initiative against Castro in the form of a radio station staffed by Cuban exiles (administered by USIA). It challenged Castro's claim to the heritage of the Cuban struggle for independence by adopting the name Radio Martí. A television equivalent followed in 1990, although the effect of both was limited by jamming. In the 1990s issues in the propaganda war between Castro and the United States have included the U.S. trade boycott of Cuba and the fate of a child named Elian Gonzalez. In 1999 Elian attempted to flee Cuba with his mother, who died at sea. His family in Florida attempted to retain him, but the U.S. government was obliged to return the child to his father in Cuba in the summer of 2000. Castro exploited Elian's reunion with his father as propaganda for his regime.

Nicholas J. Cull

See also Caribbean; Cold War; Kennedy, John F.; Latin America; Radio (International); Reagan, Ronald; Russia; United Nations; Wick, Charles Z.

References: Perez, Louis A., Jr. *Cuba: Between Reform and Revolution.* New York: Oxford University Press, 1988; Rice, Donald E. *The Rhetorical Uses of the Authorizing Figure: Fidel Castro and José Martí.* New York: Praeger, 1992; Ruiz, Ramon. *Cuba: The Making of a Revolution.* New York: Norton, 1970; Szulc, Tad. *Fidel: A Critical Portrait.* New York: Morrow, 1986.

Censorship

Censorship is the process of suppressing the circulation of information or opinions offensive to the values of those representing the censor. It has been referred to as a negative form of propaganda. Without some form of censorship propaganda—in the strictest sense of the word—would be difficult to imagine. Censorship and propaganda remain two sides of the same coin, both involving the manipulation of opinion. Censorship is of little value unless it selectively blends fact and opinion in order to deceive its intended audience. In this respect, the propagandist must work closely with the censor. In wartime censorship chiefly affects the supply of news; in peacetime it impacts the expression of opinion.

Censorship can take two forms: (1) the selection of information to support a particular viewpoint or (2) the deliberate manipulation or doctoring of information to create an impression different from the one originally intended. The first type of censorship can be traced back to the Middle Ages, with the most obvious example being ecclesiastical censorship, whereby the only channel for the dissemination of news and opinion was by word of mouth, particularly from the pulpit. Censorship took the form of the suppression of heresy. The best know example of this is the *Index Librorum Prohibitorium,* dating from the sixteenth century, which represents one of the oldest forms of book censorship whereby all works considered pernicious to Roman Catholics were censored. An example of the second type of censorship through doctored information is Bismarck's (1815–1898) famous Ems telegram of 1870, which led directly to the Franco-Prussian War.

In wartime governments establish censorship to prevent the enemy from acquiring sensitive information and also to bolster the morale of its soldiers and citizens. The Great War of 1914–1918 was the first modern war in which all the belligerents deployed the twin weapons of censorship and propaganda to rigidly control public opinion. Most nations considered it vital, from the point of view of national security, to control the means of communication. Of all the means available, none was more highly regarded than the press. Such was the pervasiveness of official censorship and propaganda that a huge gap was manufactured between those fighting the war and the civilian home front that supported them. In

U.S. war poster, 1943, "Let's Censor Our Conversation about the War." Every combatant used similar appeals. (Corbis)

Germany the justification for tight censorship was the upholding of the *Burgfrieden* (political truce) and the fear that newspapers might publish sensitive military information. There was little to support this fear, for the only wire service in Germany was the "official" Wolff Telegraph Bureau (WTB), which, at the outbreak of war, became the German newspaper's sole source of official war news, with all sensitive material first being cleared by the German Foreign Office.

In Britain, under the Defence of the Realm Act (DORA), such a severe system of censorship was created that it continues to have implications for British society to this day. Technically all press censorship was voluntary; editors were entitled to submit for advance consideration any material that was likely to violate DORA. The press bureau was to provide official war news and the war correspondents were expected to publish its communiqués without comment. The willingness of the newspaper proprietors to accept self-censorship and their cooperation in disseminating propaganda ultimately undermined public trust in the press. British war correspondents identified with the armies in the field and largely shielded the government and the military leadership from public criticism by withholding accounts of military setbacks and focusing on the camaraderie of life in the trenches. Once the Americans had entered the war, they set up their own propaganda organization, the Committee on Public Information (CPI), with responsibility for censorship.

During the interwar period the growing popularity of the commercial film industry attracted increasing censorship. There was a widespread fear, both in the United States and elsewhere, that film's persuasive power might be used for harmful ends. The dominance of Hollywood ensured that controversies surrounding the content of movies shaped the kinds of films the rest of the world saw. From 1934 until the 1950s the Production Code, backed by the Production Code Administration (PCA), heavily influenced the content of American films.

In the opening phase of World War II Britain attempted to repeat the experience—and mistakes—of World War I, where censorship and propaganda had been conducted separately. Once again censorship was to be on a "voluntary" basis. Beginning in January 1940, when Sir John Reith (1889–1971) became its head, the Ministry of Information (MoI) began to assert itself, insisting that "news is the shocktroops of propaganda" and that propaganda should tell "the truth, nothing but the truth and, as near as possible, the whole truth." By 1941 the system was operating so effectively that most observers were unaware that a sophisticated form of precensorship was in force—even within the BBC. This explains why Britain's wartime propaganda gained its reputation for telling the truth when, in fact, the whole truth could not be told.

The Falklands/Malvinas War (1982) revealed how much the British had learned from the their experience in the propaganda war against the Irish Republican Army (IRA) in Northern Ireland and also from the American experience in Vietnam. During the war the British government established near total control of information flowing out of the war zone. British media management during the war provided a model for American military-media relations in subsequent conflicts—notably Grenada (1983) and Panama (1989). Since 1982 wars in the Gulf, Bosnia, Kosovo, and Afghanistan have been reported on a global scale, with extensive and virtually instantaneous coverage guaranteeing huge audiences. Nevertheless, a key feature in all these wars is the continued use of censorship by means of restrictive media management.

David Welch

See also BBC; Britain; Caribbean; China; Film (Newsreels); Film (Nazi Germany); Germany; Gulf War; Falklands/Malvinas War; Ireland; MoI; Orwell, George; Radio (International); Russia; Scandinavia; United States; Vietnam War; Wilkes, John; World War I; World War II (Britain); World War II (United States)

References: Carruthers, Susan L. *The Media at War: Communication and Conflict in the Twentieth*

Century. Basingstoke, UK: Macmillan, 2000; Levy, Leonard. *Emergence of a Free Press.* New York: Oxford University Press, 1985; Pratkanis, Anthony, and Elliot Aronson. *Age of Propaganda: The Everyday Use and Abuse of Persuasion.* New York: W. H. Freeman, 1991; Welch, David. *Germany, Propaganda and Total War, 1914–18.* New Brunswick, NJ: Rutgers University Press, 2000.

Central Intelligence Agency

See CIA

Chile

See Latin America

China

Propaganda is central to the operation of the Chinese system of government. Aspects of propaganda—in particular the formalization of imagery and language—can be traced back to the earliest period of Chinese history, but propaganda has been most effective in the twentieth century thanks to the mass media and a powerful authoritarian government.

The earliest surviving texts on governance in China pay great attention to the need for rulers to control and formalize language to secure their authority. Confucius (c. 551–479 B.C.E.), the most influential philosopher of early China, noted that the "rectification of names" was crucial to the establishment of stable government. The most important source for Confucius's thoughts are *The Analects,* a series of dialogues that he is claimed to have held with various disciples, in which he argued for the importance of virtue and moral authority as a means of creating a stable state. Other works believed to have been edited by Confucius, along with the writings of his student, Mencius (c. 371–289 B.C.E.), form part of a canon formalized in the twelfth century. Confucian thought was supplemented by vast numbers of commentaries, which gave rise to various schools of Confucianism. Over the centuries Confucian thought hardened into a doctrine of state governance that stressed the importance of hierarchy; it was made the basis of the examinations qualifying candidates for the state bureaucracy. Confucianism has remained a powerful resource for Chinese rulers even into the present era.

Before the age of mass media, the sharing of religious rituals was one of the most important ways in which state propaganda could be transmitted among the population at large. The state could promote cults of gods based on dead heroes who had served the state, which would then be filtered down to temples at the nonelite level. Even at the elite level, the late imperial period, under the ethnically Manchu Qing dynasty (1644–1911), saw an increasing use of state propaganda to legitimate the rule of the Manchus in the face of loyalism to the overthrown Ming dynasty. The Kangxi emperor, who ruled from 1661 to 1722, issued a sixteen-point "Sacred Edict" in 1670 that justified his reign in terms of Confucian orthodoxy, thereby successfully challenging Chinese officials to follow that same orthodoxy and serve him. His successor, the Yongzheng emperor, who ruled from 1723 to 1735, expanded on the edict, training scholars in its precepts so that they could go to towns and villages to educate ordinary Chinese citizens about its requirements, thereby ensuring that success in the civil service examinations was based not only on a knowledge of the edicts but also the emperor's comments on them.

The late nineteenth century saw the Qing dynasty become unstable due to a combination of economic crisis, internal rebellion, and the impact of Western imperialism. During this period Western social and cultural ideas—often transmitted through Japan—were influential among Chinese elites. Among those ideas was that of the public sphere separate from the state, and of associated institutions, such as newspapers. The most politically influential newspaper of the period was *Shibao* (Times), written by a group of Chinese intellectuals, of whom the

Chinese poster from the Cultural Revolution of the 1960s promoting the resettlement of educated urban youth in rural areas. (Stefan Landsberger/Hangzhou Fine Arts Group)

most notable was the reformer Liang Qichao (1873–1929). *Shibao,* published from 1904 to 1939, served as a forum for debates on constitutional reform in China, which influenced the newly emerging urban middle class, particularly in major cities such as Shanghai. Much of the vocabulary of modernity was also popularized through *Shibao* and other publications by Liang, paving the way for the introduction of ideological thought (nationalism, communism, anarchism, etc.) in the following century.

The 1911 revolution ended China's imperial system, and a republic was established. The Republican period (1911–1949) was marked by great instability, with no central government and a China divided up among warring militaristic leaders. This was followed by a decade of uneasy unity, under Nationalist leader Chiang Kai-shek (1887–

1975), which was swiftly undermined by the war with Japan (1937–1945). Some of the militaristic leaders—such as the northeasterner Zhang Zuolin (1875–1928), who controlled much of northern China in the early 1920s—had little interest in legitimating their rule by any means other than force. However, when Chiang Kai-shek established a Nationalist government at Nanjing in 1928, he used propaganda to characterize his authority (which in reality was fairly fragile) as firm and part of a wider project of nation-building, which had been started by his predecessor Sun Yat-sen (1866–1925). The most notable of his propaganda exercises was the New Life Movement of the 1930s, which took ideas from Confucianism and European fascism. Its goal was to control the daily behavior of ordinary Chinese citizens (for instance, encouraging them not to spit in public) as a means of instilling wider respect for the Nationalist nation-building project. The other major propaganda exercise under Chiang was the anti-Communist campaign. After Chiang turned against the Chinese Communists, who had been part of a united front with the Nationalists until 1927, the official press and media were encouraged to portray the small areas under Communist control in the 1930s as hotbeds of lawlessness and even sexual degeneracy ("property in common, wives in common" was a common gloss on the Communists at the time) in order to instill fear in the population at large. Communists were almost always referred to in official sources as "bandits." This language was swiftly toned down after 1937, when a second united front was established against the Japanese.

The Japanese invasion of Chinese territory, starting with the occupation of the northeast (Manchuria) in 1931, created a new language and imagery of resistance, which became increasingly powerful throughout the 1930s and the war years. Manchurian exiles from the Japanese occupation used their positions on well-known periodicals such as *Shenghuo zhoukan* (Life Weekly)—which may have reached 1.5 million readers—to write about atrocities in occupied Manchuria, helping to stimulate an urban protest movement against Chiang Kai-shek's policy of appeasement of the Japanese. The imagery of resistance permeated popular fiction of the period as well; in one 1933 best-seller all the characters joined the anti-Japanese resistance. In Manchuria itself, meanwhile, Japanese-sponsored propaganda exercises—such as new schoolbooks and the Concordia Association, a pressure group created to stimulate Sino-Japanese cooperation in the occupied zone—countered the arguments of anti-Japanese nationalism.

During the Sino-Japanese War, writers and artists used their powers graphically to portray the nature of the Japanese invasion. Newspaper reporters such as Fan Changjiang (1909–1970) and Lu Yi (1911–) reported from the front lines for the first time in history. Their reports, an important element in the stimulation of nationalist sentiment in China, used a combination of realistic reporting and standardized imagery to portray valiant Chinese fighters combating vicious Japanese invaders. Cartoonists also contributed to this imagery; the stark images of Feng Zikai (1898–1975) remain among the best-known cartoons from the war period. Street theater was also used to present anti-Japanese propaganda to the illiterate masses. The Nationalist government in exile in Chongqing established film studios to produce patriotic epics. The use of mass propaganda techniques during the war gave the Chinese Communists an invaluable platform to develop propaganda for such other policies as land reform. The collaborationist government set up in Japanese-occupied China, under the former Nationalist politician Wang Jingwei (1883–1944), also used propaganda posters and reports—in this case to portray Japanese-dominated rule as being the best bulwark against Communism.

The Nationalist government was exiled from the mainland in 1949 after losing the civil war against the Communists. The People's Republic of China was established, and was dominated by Mao Zedong (1893–1976), the chairman of the Communist Party, until his death. After 1949, the public sphere, which had existed tenuously under the Nationalists, no longer functioned. The press and broadcasting were taken over by the state. Mao's China was notable for the constant use of mass campaigns to legitimate the state and its rulers' policies. It was the first Chinese government successfully to make use of modern mass propaganda techniques, adapting them to the needs of a country, which had a largely rural and illiterate population. The most notable campaigns included: Resist America, Aid Korea (1950), Anti–Hu Feng (1955), Hundred Flowers (1957), Anti-Rightist (1957), Great Leap Forward (1958–1961), Socialist Education (1963–1964), and the Cultural Revolution (1966–1976).

Mao Zedong was the guiding spirit behind these campaigns; although the methods used in them were similar, his motivations differed in each case. Mao's propaganda techniques had been developed during the years when the Communists were fighting for power. The Rectification Movement of 1942, launched at the party's wartime base in Yan'an, in northwest China, marked a turning point for him. "Rectification" impressed on all Communist cadres—and, by extension, on nonparty members over whom they had control—that "Mao Zedong Thought" was the cornerstone of Chinese Communist ideology. Candidates for party membership were forced to imbibe Mao's writings and were subjected to stringent tests. The groundwork was thus laid for the cult of personality around Mao, which became most notable during the Cultural Revolution of the 1960s. The Communists set up a state propaganda apparatus that used both the mass media (press, radio, and film) and group meetings to transmit the leadership's line. Language grew in importance during this period, with the use of correct phrasing becoming as significant—often more so—than actions in keeping step with the party's demands.

Propaganda campaigns in Mao's China usually took some easily identifiable target as their starting point, but they frequently had a hidden agenda involving factional struggles within the Communist leadership. A 1955 national campaign attacked the writer Hu Feng, who had expressed doubts as to the usefulness of Marxism as an arbiter of aesthetic quality. Conveniently, the campaign coincided with problems involving the collectivization of Chinese agriculture; the anti-Hu activities diverted attention from the failings of Communist economic policy. Similarly, Mao sparked off the Cultural Revolution in 1966 in part because he felt that he had been sidelined by other members of the Politburo. However, Mao's campaigns also encapsulated his broader concerns and fears, in particular his fear that the party would become ossified and bureaucratic. The use of mass campaigns, he felt, would keep both the party and the people alert against a lessening of revolutionary zeal. Specific examples were used to galvanize all the campaigns. For example, in 1963, as part of the Socialist Education campaign, Lei Feng, a soldier whose diary was alleged to have been found posthumously, was touted by the party as a model citizen; his diary—almost certainly concocted by party propagandists—is filled with praise of Mao and accounts of Lei Feng's efforts to inspire revolutionary zeal among his comrades. Also prominent by 1963 was *Quotations from Chairman Mao* (the "Little Red Book"), a compilation by the defense minister Lin Biao of statements and observations from Mao's writings. The contents were studied intensively by millions of soldiers, giving Mao iconic status. The book received an even wider readership during 1966–1969—the most intense phase of the Cultural Revolution—when Mao ordered the country's youth to "bombard the headquarters" and overthrow the existing structures of party power. Styling themselves "Red Guards," Chinese youths used quotations from Mao to justify their actions, including the elimination of "demons and ghosts," which included intellectuals, high party officials, and anyone who had had contact with foreigners.

The death of Mao Zedong in 1976 ushered in an interregnum period, followed by the ascendancy of Deng Xiaoping (1904–1997) as paramount leader starting in 1978. Deng's primary concern was to make good the social and economic losses of the Cultural Revolution while continuing to maintain the Communist Party's legitimacy—and he regarded Mao's cult of personality as one of the major obstacles to achieving those goals. The regimes of Deng and his successor, Jiang Zemin (1926–), have consciously steered away from building up personality cults of the leader. Furthermore, popular disillusionment with the great mass campaigns of the Mao era have meant that propaganda campaigns against such perceived problems as "spiritual pollution" and "bourgeois liberalization" have been less fervent than in the past. A partial exception was the campaign to inspire patriotism following the 1989 student-worker protests in Chinese cities, which resulted in the killings of protestors in Tian'anmen Square in Beijing. In the 1990s propaganda took on new tasks, in particular the creation of a brand of nationalism based on traditional Chinese culture and on recent history not directly related to the Communist Party, such as the war against Japan. One of the goals behind the nationalist campaign was to encourage reunification with Taiwan, which remains one of the last unfulfilled goals of the Communist Party. While propaganda remains a constant in Chinese everyday life thanks to the powerful control the state continues to exercise over the media, publishing, and education, censorship has lessened. The appearance of new media, such as the Internet, has provided alternative forums for nonstate views, though these are also subject to strict controls when they go beyond the bounds of what the government considers permissible.

Rana Mitter

See also Brainwashing; Counterinsurgency; Japan; Korea; Korean War; Mao Zedong; Murdoch, Rupert; Olympics; Postage Stamps; Posters; Prisoners of War; *Quotations from Chairman Mao;* RFE/RL

References: Hung, Chang-tai. *War and Popular Culture: Resistance in Modern China, 1937–1945.* Berkeley: University of California Press, 1994; Judge, Joan. *Print and Politics:"Shibao"and the Culture of Reform in Late Qing China.* Stanford, CA: Stanford University Press, 1996; Lewis, Mark Edward. *Writing and Authority in Early China.* Albany: SUNY Press, 1999; Schoenhals, Michael. *Doing Things with Words in Chinese Politics: Five Studies.* Berkeley: Institute of East Asian Studies, University of California, 1992; Schram, Stuart. *The Thought of Mao Tse-tung.* Cambridge: Cambridge University Press, 1989.

Chomsky, Noam (1928–)

Political dissident and professor of linguistics at Massachusetts Institute of Technology (MIT), Noam Chomsky is famous for his critique of the nature of modern media proprietorship and access and the extent to which information flows freely. The phrase "manufacture of consent," introduced during the interwar period by Walter Lippmann, is now largely associated with Chomsky's critique of the relationship between propaganda and public opinion in the United States.

In 1988, Chomsky (together with coauthor Edward Herman) provided a propaganda model intended to analyze what he claimed was the systematic bias of the American media that "manufactured" consent. The model referred to five significant factors: (1) the concentration of ownership in the hands of a few large corporations with the aim of maximizing profits rather than informing; (2) the increasing dependence on advertising for revenue; (3) the dependence of the media on government, corporate, and specialist sources for information; (4) a preoccupation with negative events; and (5) media anti-Communism. According to Chomsky, dominant government and corporate groups have been allowed unrivaled access to the media and have successfully marginalized dissenting voices in the process. As a result there is no difference between the official agenda and the media agenda. These powerful controlling groups manufacture consent by disseminating bland and mendacious propaganda intended to fool the people about the forces that govern them.

Chomsky has been criticized in recent years for adopting the theory of a top-down conspiracy driven by cynical elites that underestimates the integrity of journalists and the possibility that those who aspire to shape mass opinion can be responsive as well as manipulative.

David Welch

See also Introduction; Television (News); United States

References: Chomsky, Noam, and Edward S. Herman. *Manufacturing Consent: The Political Economy and the Mass Media.* New York: Pantheon, 1988; Herman, Edward S. *Beyond Hypocrisy: Decoding the News in an Age of Propaganda.* Boston: South End Press, 1992;

Taylor, Philip M. *Munitions of the Mind. A History of Propaganda from the Ancient World to the Present Day.* Manchester, UK: Manchester University Press, 1995.

Churchill, Winston (1874–1965)

British Conservative politician and prime minister from 1940 to 1945 and again from 1951 to 1955, Winston Churchill holds an anomalous position in the history of propaganda. Although in some ways he was the consummate propagandist, Churchill dismissed the importance of propaganda in modern war and politics, preferring deeds.

As the son of the politician Randolph Churchill (1849–1895), Winston seemed fated for politics from an early age. After a series of adventures during war service as a correspondent in South Africa, he entered Parliament in 1900. He left the Conservative Party to join the Liberals and quickly rose to prominence. During World War I he was First Lord of the Admiralty. During this period he learned the trick of holding back bad news until he had a piece of good news to counteract it. This approach to news management served him well during World War II.

During the General Strike of 1926 it was Churchill (then chancellor of the Exchequer) who directed government propaganda. He took over the BBC to give the government a monopoly on broadcast news and edited a special newspaper called *The National Gazette.* Churchill was a talented writer, and when his belief in empire pushed him into the political wilderness, he boosted his income with much journalism and historical writing. In the 1930s he warned against the rising danger of Hitler and Mussolini. He also gained experience as a broadcaster and was one of the few British speakers who could command a radio audience in the United States during the interwar period. When war came, Prime Minister Neville Chamberlain (1869–1940) brought Churchill back into the cabinet as First Lord of the Admiralty. Churchill's reputation as a longstanding advocate of preparedness for war ensured that when Chamberlain resigned in the spring of 1940, it was Churchill who became prime minister and formed a coalition government.

Churchill's greatest achievements as a wartime propagandist were his radio broadcasts to Britain during the summer of 1940. His words expressed the defiant spirit of the country and did much to rally public confidence following the fall of France: "We will fight them on the beaches; we will fight them in the fields and on the landing grounds, and we will never surrender" (4 June 1940, House of Commons), and "if the British Empire and its Commonwealth lasts for a thousand years men will still say, 'This was their finest hour'" (broadcast 18 June 1940). His rhetoric favored old-fashioned, short words and echoed the classics of English literature. His tribute to the airmen of the Battle of Britain on 20 August 1940—"Never in the field of human conflict, has so much been owed by so many to so few"—echoed the words Shakespeare gave to Henry the Fifth: "We few, we happy few, we band of brothers." Churchill's broadcasts were relayed to the then neutral United States, doing much to stimulate American sympathy for the British cause. Churchill's bulldog appearance was a gift to photographers and cartoonists, and he played to this by adopting a characteristic "V" for victory hand gesture. The "V" for victory was first used not by Churchill but as graffiti by the Belgian resistance, encouraged afterward by a BBC radio campaign.

Despite his talent as a speaker, Churchill trusted the broader administration of British propaganda to his friend Brendan Bracken (1901–1958), taking little interest in the day-to-day running of campaigns. He insisted that the best propaganda was one of action and sought to impress the world with deeds rather than words. He was reluctant to attend press conferences or meet journalists. To the chagrin of such American allies as President Franklin D. Roosevelt (1882–1945), he was also slow to define British war aims, speaking only in terms of fighting for "victory . . . for

"LET US GO FORWARD TOGETHER"

British poster from 1940 featuring wartime prime minister and skilled propagandist Winston Churchill (Hulton-Deutsch Collection / CORBIS)

without victory there can be no survival." Roosevelt eventually obtained Churchill's commitment to a set of liberal aims contained in the Atlantic Charter of August 1941, which provided a framework for closer American involvement in the war and prepared the way for the postwar United Nations. Churchill's vociferous attachment to the British Empire meant that he was considered a propaganda liability in some quarters. Japanese propaganda made much use of Churchill's remark that he "did not become the King's First Minister to preside over the break-up of the British Empire." Churchill's broadcasts continued throughout the war; by 1943 public-opinion experts had concluded that the British public considered him something of a windbag. Wanting more than Churchill's old world of empire, returning soldiers elected Clement Attlee (1883–1967) and a Labour government to office in 1945.

Out of office, Churchill remained a major voice on the world stage. In March 1946, in a speech in Fulton, Missouri, Churchill took a stand against the Soviet Union, proclaiming that an "Iron Curtain" had fallen across Europe. The speech became a landmark in the developing Cold War between East and West. Looking back on the war at the end of his life, he commented that "the British people were the lion . . . I just provided the roar." His influence persists in rhetorical styles throughout the English-speaking world and in the continued use of the victory sign, which was ubiquitous in the streets of Eastern Europe when the Berlin Wall fell in 1989.

Nicholas J. Cull

See also BBC; Beaverbrook, Max; Bracken, Brendan; Britain; British Empire; Cold War; Elections (Britain); Funerals; Garvey, Marcus; MoI; Netherlands, Belgium, and Luxembourg; Portugal; Reith, Lord John; Scandinavia; Shakespeare, William; Thatcher, Margaret; United Nations; World War II (Britain)
References: Addison, Paul. *Churchill of the Home Front.* London: Jonathan Cape, 1992; Cull, Nicholas J. *Selling War: British Propaganda and American Neutrality in World War Two.* New York: Oxford University Press, 1995; Gilbert, Martin. *Winston S. Churchill.* Vols. 5–8. London: Heinemann, 1977–1988.

CIA (Central Intelligence Agency)

The CIA is the spy agency of the United States and, like the Office of Strategic Services (OSS), its wartime predecessor agency, is a sometime practitioner of covert propaganda. President Harry Truman (1884–1972) founded the CIA in 1947 as part of a rearming effort by the United States in anticipation of the Cold War. The CIA's first director, Allan Dulles (1893–1969), had no doubt of the value of propaganda and involved the agency in all manner of propaganda activity. At its most basic, the CIA subsidized the propaganda of anti-Communists. This was used effectively in the Italian election of 1948. The agency secretly sustained the short-wave radio stations Radio Free Europe (RFE) and Radio Liberty (RL) and, most famously, founded and sustained the Congress for Cultural Freedom, a group of European intellectuals promoting anti-Communist ideas, based first in Berlin and then in Paris. The CIA also secretly funded the British magazine *Encounter* and actively funded and promoted the abstract expressionist art movement as an example of creative freedom in the West. In the mid-1960s a series of newspaper investigations exposed the scale of CIA involvement in secret propaganda and forced the agency to abandon much of this activity. In the 1970s the CIA covertly funded the Chilean newspaper *El Mercurio* to the tune of $1.65 billion to attack that country's president, Salvador Allende (1908–1973). The CIA was also heavily involved in much propaganda connected to the U.S. role in Central America in the 1980s.

Nicholas J. Cull

See also Art; Brainwashing; Cold War; Cultural Propaganda; Disinformation; Intelligence; Latin America; Orwell, George; Radio (International); RFE/RL; Sukarno; United States

References: Saunders, Frances Stonor. *Who Paid the Piper? The CIA and the Cultural Cold War.* London: Granta, 1999; Soley, Lawrence C. *Radio Warfare: OSS and CIA Subversive Propaganda.* New York: Praeger, 1989.

Civil Defense

Fear of technological and military developments have prompted civil and emergency planning boards to use propaganda to educate the public. Civil defense propaganda was a particularly significant part of the British government's output during World War II, also figuring in Cold War propaganda on both sides of the Atlantic. Civil defense propaganda has been used to draw populations closer to their government by emphasizing shared risks and responsibilities.

In World War I German air raids over London resulted in mass panic, stampedes for shelter, and even assaults on uniformed Royal Air Corps officers for failing to prevent the bombing. The impact was sufficient in 1924 for the British government to create a subcommittee of the Committee of Imperial Defense to look into the question of Air Raid Precautions (ARP). The newsreel footage of the blitzkrieg of Spanish towns in the 1930s during the Spanish Civil War revealed the vulnerability of European cities to such attacks. Based on the pessimistic predictions of the Ministry of Health and the Air Staff, a plan was developed in the 1930s to ensure that lines of communication and supply channels remained open, as well as to give the government the authority to control the civilian population by force if, as was predicted, mass panic should ensue.

Shortly after Hitler's invasion of Austria in March 1938, the home secretary, Sir Samuel Hoare (1880–1959), broadcast an appeal to the nation requesting millions of volunteers for civil defense. After the Munich Pact, a massive publicity drive took place to recruit ARP wardens and personnel for other services. Posters appeared throughout the country and a booklet describing how to protect homes against air raids was delivered to every household. This was backed up by a further propaganda campaign on the use of gas masks and the need to black out windows. Perhaps the most successful publicity campaign in 1940 was that leading to the formation of the Local Defence Volunteers (LDV), later renamed the Home Guard and nicknamed "Dad's Army" because most recruits were men too old to fight in the regular armed forces.

Prenuclear plans differ most significantly from their descendants in terms of the level of provision by the government to individual households. Civil defense activities created a politically useful sense of participation in the war effort. Ministry of Information (MoI) films and leaflets frequently used depictions of civil defense activities to boost morale at home and impress opinion overseas, as in Harry Watt and Humphrey Jennings's documentary *London Can Take It* (1940) or Jennings's memorial to the courage of London's firefighters entitled *Fires Were Started* (1942).

The Cold War resulted in an escalating nuclear arms race. In Britain it provided the basis for the reemergence of an official civil defense organization, the Civil Defence Corps (CDC) through the provision of the 1948 Civil Defence Act. The Atlee government decided to launch a major recruitment campaign to be coordinated by the Central Office of Information (COI) by means of a nationwide publicity campaign bearing the slogan "You can't be certain. You can be prepared." Posters and film were used in the campaign, including a Crown Film Unit production entitled *The Waking Point* (1951), which targeted the social conscience and attempted to expose the global communist threat to democratic life.

In the United States, fear of communism, spy mania, and the knowledge that the Soviet Union now possessed a nuclear capability led to increased spending on nuclear armaments and a number of propaganda campaigns to inform the American public of what precautions could be taken in the event of a Soviet nuclear attack. The Federal Civil Defense Administration (FCDA) produced posters, pamphlets, and a number of short films for television and movie theaters. The new medium of television proved particularly receptive. The most famous example in this genre was the cartoon series *Duck and Cover,* which featured "Bert the Turtle," who informed movie theater audiences how they should react during an atomic explosion. In the early 1960s the FCDA produced another film series entitled *Home in the Middle,* which was intended to reassure the public that the Defense Department was continuing research in the area of civil defense and to encourage citizens to educate themselves. By continuing to emphasize the danger of a Soviet nuclear attack, civil defense propaganda was also used to justify increased defense spending.

By 1960, with the popularity of the CDC in decline, the British government launched a new campaign combining a massive recruitment drive with a nuclear-information program. The campaign took advantage of all available media, beginning with a four-week intensive press campaign in the national press. A forty-page booklet for public speakers was published, providing detailed guidance on the presentation of the civil defense case to various pressure groups. The Thatcher election victory in 1979 added a further layer to the debate over civil defense and nuclear policy by associating neoliberal government plans with a strong nuclear stance. The 1980s marked the first time that civil defense came under concerted attack from critics, forcing governments on both sides of the Atlantic to offer organized counterarguments to specific accusations. Though civil defense had been involved with propaganda from the beginning, this was the first time it became the subject of a propaganda battle. President Ronald Reagan's (1911–) "Star Wars" initiative shifted the debate on civil defense away from the participatory role of ordinary citizens to state provision in space. Satirizing civil defense propaganda became a regular tactic of the antinuclear movement in the 1980s.

David Welch

See also Cold War; *London Can Take It;* Peace and Antiwar Movements (1945–)

References: *20th-Century Defence in Great Britain: An Introductory Guide.* London: CBA, 1996; Bosset, Leo. *Cool Words: Cold War.* Washington, DC: American University Press, 1995; MacLaine, Ian. *Ministry of Morale: Home Front Morale and the Ministry of Information in World War II.* London: Unwin, 1979; McEnaney, Laura. *Civil Defense Begins at Home: Militarization Meets Everyday Life in the Fifties.* Princeton, NJ: Princeton University Press, 2000; Schwartz, William, and Charles Derber. *The Nuclear Seduction.* Berkeley: University of California Press, 1989.

Civil Rights Movement (1955–1968)

The civil rights movement encompassed a social, political, and legal struggle to gain equal rights for African Americans in the 1950s and 1960s. The battle was primarily a challenge to the system of laws and customs—collectively known as segregation—enforced by whites to control and separate blacks. The movement grew in strength first through the power of the spoken word and later through worldwide publicity created by often violent confrontations. Propaganda not only played a crucial role in organizing black resistance and nationalizing racial issues but also created a political context. First, wartime propaganda had affirmed the U.S. government's commitment to liberty and opposition to the racism of Hitler. The federal government now had important strategic reasons to respond to the protestors: not to do so would have left the United States vulnerable to propaganda attack from the Soviet Union, which emphasized racial inequity in the United States in its propaganda to Third World nations.

Black civil rights organizations, such as the National Association for the Advancement of Colored People (NAACP) and the Southern Christian Leadership Conference (SCLC) aimed their propaganda at both black and liberal white communities. This dual strategy had two aims: encouraging blacks to undertake direct action and gaining white sympathy, which, in turn, would exert pressure for political reform. The power of speech was the most effective and powerful method of propaganda used by such organizations. Martin Luther King Jr. (1929–1968), a young Baptist minister and president of SCLC, came to personify the movement and became its spokesman, delivering inspirational and eloquent sermons. The power of his preaching lay in his simplicity and his religious zeal. King's speeches and protests attracted an audience of thousands and ensured that the movement received full media attention, including live televised debates and documentaries.

The exact dates of the civil rights movement are still a subject of disagreement. The movement clearly grew out of the age-old traditions of the black church as a focus for community activity, and the institutional foundations laid in the Progressive Era, most importantly the founding of the NAACP in 1910. The modern era is often regarded as having begun with the Montgomery, Alabama, bus boycott on 1 December 1955. The boycott followed the arrest of Rosa Parks (1913–), a local NAACP member who refused to give up her seat to a white person. By November 1956 a federal court outlawed segregated buses in Montgomery and the boycott ended in triumph and became an inspiration for all African Americans. The boycott attracted wide participation through the encouragement of the church. Ministers provided the institutional strength needed for a community-wide protest and infused the entire movement with religious idealism and fervor. They were the ideal means through which the movement could reach every black family and coordinate protests since they were also experienced in the art of delivering speeches and held respected positions within local communities. By highlighting white prejudice and appealing to the Bible (which stressed the equality of all

A poster showing Black Panther leaders Bobby Seale and Huey P. Newton, the latter heavily armed in a theatrical touch. (Library of Congress)

before God), the Constitution, the Declaration of Independence, and the American dream, ministers convinced their congregations to resist oppression through nonviolent activities such as sit-ins, boycotts, and protest marches.

Much of the success of the civil rights movement can be attributed to the rise of Martin Luther King. He was able to inspire the participation of thousands of blacks while also securing the support of many liberal whites, particularly in the north. A highly educated minister, he was the perfect symbol for the black community and preached a moderate, nonviolent approach. King used his growing notoriety to his advantage, providing the movement with much-needed publicity. In 1963 in Birmingham, Alabama, King purposefully used children to front his protest march in the knowledge that the cameras would report the violent outbursts of the local police. Images of small children being sprayed by high-pressure hoses and attacked by dogs were condemned on television and reached a worldwide audience.

Two years later images of peaceful protesters being brutally clubbed by white police appeared as headline news on "Bloody Sunday." The contrast between King's call for humanity and equality through peaceful activities and the violent behavior of Southern law officials was accentuated by television coverage. King became the camera-friendly face of the controversial struggle and regularly appeared on live television debates and talk shows. Just months after Birmingham, in August 1963, well over 10 million TV viewers watched King address 250,000 black and white protesters during the March on Washington.

While factual television—such as the NBC White Paper documentary *Sit In*—depicted rural poverty, segregation, and civil rights protests, television's entertainment programs grew overwhelmingly white to avoid controversy. News magazines aimed at middle-class whites fully embraced the struggle. *Newsweek* was the most supportive of the civil rights movement, effectively using public-opinion polls to highlight sympathetic attitudes and revealing appalling conditions within America. *U.S. News and World Report* espoused a conservative ideology and sympathized with whites.

In the mid-1960s media attention grew increasingly hostile as the movement became more radical and King's popularity waned. King's northern campaigns against crime and poverty were largely unsuccessful, and his opposition to the Vietnam War eroded much of the support he had gained from white liberals and the government. A long-term white propaganda strategy associated King with communism. Increasingly disillusioned by the slowness of gains through nonviolent tactics, young campaigners turned to the more radical civil rights protesters, such as the Student Non-Violent Coordinating Committee (SNCC) and the Black Panthers, inspired by Malcolm X (1925–1965). The media was quick to report how black separatism and "black power" had supplanted moderate demands: the song "We Shall Overcome," which once dominated protest marches, was re-placed by chants of "Burn, Baby, Burn" and "I'm Black and I'm Proud." For many young blacks the posters, songs, and sermons of black nationalism offered them new hope and a distinctive identity of which they could be proud. Both Malcolm X and Martin Luther King became martyrs in 1965 and 1968, respectively. While some cite King's death as marking the end of the civil rights era, others point to the passage of the Voting Rights Act of 1965—with some arguing that it is still continuing. Overseas movements inspired by the civil rights movement include the Catholic Civil Rights Movement in Northern Ireland.

Samantha Jones

See also Garvey, Marcus; King, Martin Luther, Jr.; Malcolm X; Memorials and Monuments; NAACP; United States

References: Cook, Robin. *Sweet Land of Liberty? The African-American Struggle for Civil Rights in the Twentieth Century.* London: Longman, 1998; Dudziak, Mary L. *Cold War Civil Rights: Race and the Image of American Democracy.* Princeton, NJ: Princeton University Press, 2000; Fairclough, Adam. *The Civil Rights Movement in America, 1941–1988.* London: Macmillan, 1995; Salmond, John A. *My Mind Set on Freedom: A History of the Civil Rights Movement, 1954–1968.* Chicago: Ivan R. Dee, 1997.

Civil War, English (1642–1649)

As with any conflict, propaganda played a part in the English Civil War, fought between the forces loyal to King Charles I (1600–1649) and parliamentary forces commanded by Oliver Cromwell (1599–1658). Propaganda during the war took the new and revolutionary format of "newsbooks," weekly fragments of news consisting of from eight to sixteen pages. They were cheap to produce and looked it, with uneven type printed on cheap paper. On 29 November 1641 the first newsbook reached the streets of London and announced the innovative nature of its contents with a rather plain title: *The Heads of Severall Proceedings in this Present Parliament, from the 22 of November, to the 29, 1641.* This title signaled two important changes. First, by providing a time span, it signified that future issues would follow. Second, it was reporting current domestic news. Previously the printing of domestic news in England had been strictly prohibited. There was a widespread belief among government officials that too much information—a "liberty of discourse"—would demystify and undermine its authority.

Newsbooks had existed much earlier in England, but they only printed news pertaining to continental Europe. However, with the Scottish and Irish rebellions (1639 and 1641, respectively) and the subsequent political turmoil, the mechanisms of governmental censorship broke down. Printing was closely controlled by the Court of High Commission, the Star Chamber, and the Stationer's Company in conjunction with the king and the archbishop of Canterbury. But in 1640 the Long Parliament impeached Archbishop William Laud (1573–1645) and imprisoned him in the Tower of London in 1641. Later that same year the Long Parliament abolished the Star Chamber and the Court of High Commission and rescinded the privileges of the Stationer's Company. The printers of London took advantage of the uncertain political situation to print and sell as much as they dared. The result was an explosion of quickly composed and cheaply printed newsbooks that began to flood the streets of London. Between 1640 and the Restoration of 1660, over thirty thousand different publications were printed in London. Their impact was widespread; at a penny each for the cheapest, they appealed to the less literate and less educated, sowing sedition and spreading untruths among the masses.

Each side in the war had its own propaganda outlets, but at the beginning of the turmoil newsbooks were involved in printing the proceedings of Parliament and tended to be on the side of the Parliamentarians, reporting events in detail when it favored its faction's reputation and ignoring events when they detracted from it. Even if some of the early newsbooks tried impartially to report on events, they served to drive a wedge between the king and Parliament. By distributing information about the conflicts in both houses, newsbooks spawned debates and encouraged readers to take sides. Although not the only printers, Marchamont Nedham (1620–1678) and Sir John Berkenhead (1616–1679) emerged as the main publishers on opposing sides of the conflict. Nedham's newsbooks—*Mercurius Britanicus, Politicus,* and *Publick Intelligencer*—put forth the Parliamentarian position. Nedham favored Parliament, attacked the Lords (who joined the king in Oxford), insulted Queen Henrietta Maria (1609–1669), and accused Charles I of becoming a Catholic.

The king was initially reluctant to use propaganda and newsbooks, perhaps because he distrusted appeals to the public when he felt he ruled through divine right. He soon set up his own propaganda machine, which was based at Oriel College, Oxford, and headed by Sir John Berkenhead. Berkenhead's journal *Mercurius Aulicus* numbered 118 editions despite constant harassment and Royalist defeats. Printed with a Sunday dateline to annoy the Puritans, it was regularly smuggled into London and served to raise Royalist morale by attacking Parliament and Oliver Cromwell. Even as the king's cause became more hopeless, the journal continued to turn skirmishes into great battles and stalemates into Royalist victories. Printing was not simply limited to these two men. Numerous other Royalist and Parliamentarian newsbooks were produced, as well as newsbooks representing the Quakers and the radical social politics of the Levellers and Diggers.

Both Lords and Commons attempted to regain control over the presses—with little success. In 1643 Parliament reinvested the Stationer's Company with its previously held "search and seizure" powers to root out the source of these disorderly printers. In protest, John Milton (1608–1674) published his famous plea for a free press entitled *Areopagitica, A Speech for the Liberty of Unlicensed Printing* (1644), yet the problem still continued. Additional decrees to control printing were to follow in 1647 and 1649, which imposed a forty-shilling fine on anyone carrying or mailing seditious books or pamphlets. This was again renewed in 1652, but warfare and propaganda through newsbooks continued. Real control of the presses and wartime propaganda didn't return till the Restoration, when printing was again controlled by royal prerogative and a new professionalism emerged in journalism, leaving the propaganda of the Civil War years behind.

During these years, almost every printer in the land spent some time in jail trying to keep on the "right" side of the constantly changing boundaries. However, the authorities couldn't control the press and its propagandistic writings, which, whether actively or passively, shaped the public sphere of debate by providing information to the masses and provinces about the workings of government. They forced people to take sides on issues and drove a wedge between the king and Parliament, determining the course of the Civil War.

Perhaps the defining act of propaganda occurred at the end of the war. On 30 January 1649 Parliament executed Charles I, but the king's performance on the scaffold left a lasting impression on witnesses. The book *Eikon Basilike* (1649) developed this image of the king as a martyr to political principle, and arguably became the most influential propaganda work of the English revolution. Milton wrote *Eikonoklastes* in order to counteract the influence of this work. Despite such attempts to justify their regicide, Parliament could not compete with the image of the king facing death with dignity and his skillful manipulation of the power of monarchy. A mere eleven years later his son, Charles II (1630–1685), had regained the throne by public acclaim.

Bryan Mann

See also Britain; Funerals; Ireland; Milton, John; Religion

References: Corns, Thomas N. *Uncloistered Virtue: English Political Literature, 1640–1660.* Oxford: Oxford University Press, 1992; Feather, John. *A History of British Publishing.* London: Croom Helm, 1988; Raymond, Joad. *Making the News: An Anthology of Newsbooks of Revolutionary England, 1641–1660.* Moreton-in-Marsh, UK: Windrush Press, 1993; Raymond, Joad, ed. *News, Newspapers and Society in Early Modern Britain.* London: Frank Cass, 1999; Zaret, David. *Origins of Democratic Culture: Printing, Petitions and the Public Sphere in Early Modern England.* Princeton, NJ: Princeton University Press, 2000.

Civil War, Spanish (1936–1939)

The Spanish Civil War of 1936–1939 was an ideological conflict and, as such, saw extensive use of propaganda. Domestically the war involved a clash between a traditional order of the Catholic Church (represented by the army under General Francisco Franco [1892–1975]) and a more popular conception of public life (represented by the forces of the Republican government in Madrid). Abroad it was seen as a confrontation between fascism and democracy. The attitude of an international community that had the power to send aid and volunteers or ignore the war was so important that each camp resorted to written and audiovisual propaganda on a massive scale. The press and film companies were also intent on providing as much information as possible. Seldom have so many images of a domestic conflict been published internationally. Foreign journalists whose images played a part in forming opinion during and after the war include the photographer Robert Capa (1913–1954) and the writers George Orwell (1903–1950) and Ernest Hemingway (1899–1961). The war also spurred artist Pablo Picasso (1881–1973) to paint *Guernica* (1937), his famous protest against the bombing of civilians. Images of the war lived on long after the end of the conflict and became enduring icons of antiwar propaganda.

When Franco's military rebellion against the Republican government broke out in July 1936, freelance photographers rushed to take pictures, and most film companies sent crews to the Iberian peninsula. During the first weeks of the conflict the government was too busy preparing counterattacks to care about propaganda. The only organization able to film and distribute movies was the Anarchist Federation, which emphasized popular participation and voluntary enlistment of the masses. Very soon the Soviet Union, which backed the Madrid government, sent two of its best filmmakers to Spain. Traveling across the country and working close to the front lines between August 1936 and July 1937, they shot more than 18,000 meters (about 60,000 feet) of film. The Soviet cameramen introduced a cinematic style that was more factual than the Anarchist approach. They helped the Madrid government produce its own documentaries and newsreels. Franco's rebels, on the other hand, were on their guard against reporters who, in their view, would only circulate biased information. Cameramen and journalists were forbidden to communicate news other than that supplied by headquarters. There was thus little that could be filmed: parades, troops in the streets, and, in the Navarra region, the enthusiastic enlistment of volunteers amid much religious display. The Italians sent by Mussolini to fight on Franco's side opened an information office, which took and diffused powerful pictures. Under the Italian influence, Franco's rebels set up a propaganda section whose documentaries could compete with the Republican ones.

In the summer of 1936 the world was anxious to hear news from Spain. The first illustrated papers or newsreels left a deep impact on public opinion, "freezing" an image of each camp that remained largely unchanged up to the victory by Franco in March 1939. In order to illustrate the liberation of the Spanish proletariat, the Anarchists took pictures of mobs destroying religious symbols, of armed women urging men to fight, and of volunteers rushing to the front. These pictures established an image of the Republican side as full of enthusiasm but uncoordinated

and anti-Catholic. Conversely, pictures taken in Franco's camp stressed order and respect for the church. Drawing on these images, many contemporary accounts of the war reduced the conflict to the symbolic words "order" and "anarchy."

After Franco failed to take Madrid, it became plain that the conflict would last much longer. Unable to maintain a permanent crew in Spain, most newsreel companies often purchased their material from the Soviets, whose prices were attractive. Cut and reedited, this raw material frequently lost its original meaning. The Francoists were especially good at recycling pictures taken by the Republicans—for example, using shots of Madrid bombed by the Italians as if they had been taken in a city bombed by the Republicans. Today no film of the war can be taken at face value. In their broader propaganda both sides insisted on their military might and the certainty of their victory. The dominant theme in Republican propaganda was the martyrdom of a population deprived of freedom, humiliated, and forced into exile. In nationalist propaganda the aim was general reconciliation in an attempt to reconstruct eternal Spain. Paradoxically, both sides rarely set out their political program. The Republicans made little reference to social reforms and were extremely careful not to criticize those Spaniards who had aligned with the nationalists or to defame the Catholic Church. The nationalists attacked the "Communists and atheists" who led the republic but took care to distinguish between the population and their leaders.

However different the two camps may have been, their messages were characterized by extreme simplicity. Neither side left room for political debate. Their infinitely repeated images in print and news documentary left a profound impression on those who received them, but the impact was not necessarily what their authors intended. In Britain images of the air bombing of towns like Guernica were read as a testament to the power of the bomber and an argument against war rather than a justification for aid to the Spanish republic. In the longer term the Spanish conflict resulted in previously unknown forms of ideological communication, the radicalized confrontation between two visions of the world giving rise to a new language of propaganda. The level of propaganda foreshadowed that of World War II, but the visual and verbal language of the Spanish Civil War anticipated the beginning of the Cold War, where the ideological conflict again pitted the Reds against the imperialist powers.

Luisa Cigognetti and Pierre Sorlin

See also Capa, Robert; Film (Newsreels); *Guernica;* Orwell, George; Spain

References: Aldgate, Anthony. *Cinema and History: British Newsreels and the Spanish Civil War.* London: Scholar Press, 1979; Brothuru, Caroline. *War and Photography: A Cultural History.* London: Routledge, 1997; Higginbotham, Vincent. *Spanish Film under Franco.* Austin: University of Texas Press, 1988; Valleau, Marjorie A. *The Spanish Civil War in American and European Films.* Ann Arbor: University of Michigan Press, 1982; Vernon, Kathleen M., ed. *The Spanish Civil War and the Visual Arts.* Ithaca, NY: Cornell University Center for International Studies, 1990.

Civil War, United States (1861–1865)

The war between the eleven Confederate states that seceded from the Union in the spring of 1861 and the remaining states grew out of a bitterly contested ideological battle over Southern slavery. Both sides used propaganda to raise armies, though eventually first the Confederacy and then the Union turned to conscription to compel service. On both sides propaganda came from enthusiastic citizens rather than governments. Northern activists organized such ventures as the Union League clubs (first seen in Philadelphia in 1862) or the Loyal Publication Society of New York. Songs figured on both sides, often with the same tune sung to a different text, as was the case with the early favorite "John Brown's Body." In 1862 the *Atlantic Monthly* published "Battle Hymn of the Republic," a rousing poem by the abolitionist (and, later, women's suffrage) campaigner Julia Ward Howe (1819–1910), which fitted this tune and became an enduring piece of American patriotic propaganda.

The North fought its war on the pages of the region's many newspapers and weekly magazines. Union supporters included Horace Greeley (1811–1872), editor of the *New York Tribune.* In the early months of the war Greeley presented the headline: "Forward to Richmond" (the Confederate capital), which became "On to Richmond" in other Union papers. Photographic pioneers like Mathew Brady (c. 1823–1896) recorded the conflict; although their work could only be seen in exhibitions—the American press lacked the technology to reproduce photographs—it played a considerable role in dramatizing the conflict on the home front. Much more significant in propaganda terms were the artists who worked for illustrated papers like *Harper's Weekly.* Winslow Homer (1836–1910) depicted life in the Union camp and Thomas Nast (1840–1902) produced images ranging from allegorical cartoons to powerful renderings of alleged Confederate guerrilla atrocities. Journalists traveled with the armies and sent dispatches home from the field by telegraph. The U.S. military controlled the lines and one H. E. Thayer acted as censor. For the first time Americans were able to read telegraphed news in bulk, but these dispatches were notoriously inaccurate. Edwin M. Stanton (1814–1869), the Union secretary of war, attempted to control the press, with varying degrees of success. Tactics ranged from banning correspondents from the battlefield to suspending entire newspapers. Stanton even threatened to execute a *New York Tribune* correspondent who refused to be censored. Bribery and patronage worked well. The once critical James Gordon Bennett (1795–1872) of the *New York Herald* altered his paper's position in 1862—shortly after his son had been awarded a lucrative government job as a revenue agent. Eventually Stanton wrote news himself in the form of daily war bulletins for the Associated Press wire. He routinely underplayed Union casualties and was not above planting entirely bogus stories in the Northern press to mislead the enemy.

The Confederate press, like many other aspects of Southern life, suffered from its prewar reliance on Northern supplies, in this case paper and printing machinery. Southern journals, which tended to be published weekly, organized their own Press Association of the Confederate States, with the government allowing reports to travel freely along the military telegraph on the ground that news was "good for morale." In addition to professional war correspondents like Felix Gregory de Fontaine (1834–1896), the Southern press also printed private letters from the front; though rousing, they were no accurate guide to the progress of the war, widening the gap between newspaper propaganda and battlefield reality. Although both sides had difficulty keeping soldiers in the field, discipline proved a more serious problem for the Confederacy owing to the conflict between Confederate propaganda and the needs of war. The Confederacy emphasized both states' rights and the right of a gentleman to think for himself, creating problems for the entire chain of command.

Unlike Jefferson Davis (c. 1808–1889), the uninspiring Confederate president, Abraham Lincoln (1809–1865), the eloquent Union president, proved an asset to his cause in both word and deed. By committing the Union to freeing slaves held in Confederate territory through the Emancipation Proclamation of September 1862, Lincoln transformed the Northern war effort into a crusade for more than just the reunification of the country, a cause he articulated superbly in the Gettysburg Address of November 1863 as "a new birth of Freedom."

The Union and the Confederacy both conducted propaganda campaigns in Europe, sending touring lecturers and placing articles in the press to rally support. Henry Shelton Sanford (1823–1891), the U.S. minister to Belgium, bribed journalists and even subsidized European newspapers that supported his cause. Britain became a key theater of this propaganda war, with the South arguing that Britain needed to defend its cotton supply. The Union view, aided by Lincoln's written appeal to the cotton workers of Manchester, prevailed and Britain remained neutral. The Union also conducted recruitment campaigns in Europe. Recruits in Hamburg in 1864 included the Hungarian-born Joseph Pulitzer (1847–1911), who was to play a major role in the future of American journalism.

The propaganda war between the states long outlived the military war. In the late 1860s and early 1870s this took the form of rival denunciations of conditions in prisoner-of-war camps. Alluding to war service ("waving the bloody shirt") became a notorious cliché of Republican oratory on Capitol Hill. Rival views of postwar Reconstruction compounded the issue, and by the early twentieth century it seemed that, in popular culture at least, the Southern perspective on the war had prevailed. Films such as D. W. Griffith's epic *The Birth of a Nation* (1915) perpetuated for a new generation postwar propaganda stories of the South suffering under "Negro dictatorship."

Nicholas J. Cull

See also Abolitionism/Antislavery Movement; *The Birth of a Nation;* Crimean War; Lincoln, Abraham; *Narrative of the Life of Frederick Douglass . . .;* Nast, Thomas; *Uncle Tom's Cabin;* United States

References: Andrews, J. Cutler. *The North Reports the Civil War.* Pittsburgh: University of Pittsburgh Press, 1955;———. *The South Reports the Civil War.* Princeton, NJ: Princeton University Press, 1970; McPherson, James M. *Battle Cry of Freedom: The Civil War Era.* New York: Oxford University Press, 1988; Randall, James Garfield, and David Donald. *The Civil War and Reconstruction.* Boston: Heath, 1968.

Clinton, William Jefferson (1947–)

Bill Clinton was president of the United States from 1993 to 2001. He was born in

Official presidential portrait of Bill Clinton (Library of Congress)

Hope, Arkansas, and developed his interpersonal skills at an early age. After graduating from Georgetown University in Washington, D.C., he went to Oxford, England, as a Rhodes Scholar. Next he earned a law degree from Yale. While studying there he met and married his classmate Hillary Rodham (1947–). In 1979, aged thirty-two, he was elected governor of Arkansas—the youngest U.S. governor. Clinton's persuasive skills as a public speaker, his wit, and his personal charm made him attractive to Democrats, who were looking for a charismatic presidential candidate. He defeated incumbent Republican president George Bush (1924–) in the 1992 election, aided by third-party candidate Ross Perot (1924–), who garnered nearly 20 percent of the popular vote.

Clinton worked in vain to overhaul the U.S. health care industry. He benefited from an amazing economy, in which stock market prices reached previously undreamed of heights. Clinton, however, is more likely to be remembered for taking risks rather than

for his presidential leadership. The former usually entailed sex—and the lies needed to cover up the sex. He barely survived a formal impeachment trial in the U.S. Senate as a result of an "inappropriate" relationship with a similarly inclined young White House intern named Monica Lewinsky (1973–).

Clinton's adulterous ways were established during his years as Arkansas governor. In 1991 Paula Corbin Jones (1966–) filed a sexual harassment suit, claiming that Clinton had exposed himself to her in a hotel room. In 1997 the U.S. Supreme Court unanimously agreed that the suit could go forward while Clinton was president. Meanwhile, Kenneth Starr (1946–), an independent counsel, was looking into alleged financial improprieties involving Bill and Hillary Clinton dating back to their Arkansas days. Starr soon turned to something more titillating: evidence of a sexual relationship between Bill and Monica. The affair continued apace, next to the Oval Office. Clinton lied under oath, insisting that he had not had a "sexual relationship with that woman." It soon became obvious that he had had just that when a dress Lewinsky had kept (rather than have dry-cleaned) was revealed to have dried semen on it, which DNA analysis confirmed was Clinton's. On 17 August 1998 Clinton admitted to Starr under oath that his relationship with Monica Lewinsky entailed "inappropriate conduct," and that earlier he had lied about this under oath. In December 1998 the House Judiciary Committee recommended impeachment. Clinton was charged with perjury and obstruction of justice. He was acquitted in a trial that ended on 12 February 1999. Clinton, of course, was guilty of lying under oath and doing everything possible to keep Starr from learning of his relationship with Lewinsky—both examples of criminal misconduct. The lies were solely intended to cover up a steamy sexual relationship, but not everyone felt the president should be removed from office for covering up an affair. Besides, the Starr Report, published in September 1998 and weighing in at 322 pages, disclosed every titillating detail of the affair; it was published online as well, marking the first time a major government investigation was made available in such a fashion. Many felt the institution of the presidency had been permanently damaged by Clinton's actions. Propaganda concerns for the Clinton presidency will certainly continue to center on his relationship with Monica Lewinsky. Clinton spent the final hours of his presidency issuing pardons to notorious felons, including financier Marc Rich (1934–). It remains to be seen if the president will be remembered as one senator claims: "The name Clinton has already gone into the lexicon as a synonym for an elegant and well-crafted lie."

David Culbert

See also Elections (United States)
References: Kurtz, Howard. *Spin Cycle: Inside the Clinton Propaganda Machine.* New York: Free Press, 1998; Morris, Dick. *Behind the Oval Office: Getting Reelected against the Odds.* Los Angeles: Renaissance Books, 1999.

CNN (Cable News Network)

Founded in 1980 by Atlanta-based entrepreneur Ted Turner (1938–), CNN was the runaway media success story of that decade. Adopting a "rolling news" format, CNN offered news whenever the viewer needed it. Rivals compared this to convenience food and dubbed the network "chicken noodle news." By the mid-1980s the network had developed a substantial overseas presence via satellite and led the way with electronic news-gathering techniques. This ushered in an era of real-time news in which populations and leaders alike could follow events as they happened. The downside of this approach was the perceived problem that areas not covered by CNN (such as central Africa) slipped from the political agenda. The alleged role of CNN in setting foreign-policy agendas has been dubbed the CNN effect. CNN played a major role in the Gulf War of 1991. Iraq sought to sway world opinion by allowing Peter Arnett (1934–) to broadcast from Baghdad during the bombard-

ment. CNN poses a major challenge to state-funded international broadcasters, especially now that the network has begun to broadcast in foreign languages. By the end of the last century CNN faced stiff competition from broadcasters, including BBC World, Rupert Murdoch's (1931–) Sky News, and regionally specific stations such as Al Jazeera of Qatar.

Nicholas J. Cull

See also Gulf War; Murdoch, Rupert; Satellite Communications; Television; Terrorism, War on
References: Porter, Bibb. *Ted Turner: It Ain't as Easy as It Looks: The Amazing Story of CNN.* London: Virgin, 1994; Taylor, Philip M. *Global Communications, International Affairs and the Media since 1945.* London: Routledge, 1997.

Coins

The earliest coins, from the eastern Mediterranean region, were minted in the seventh century B.C.E. However, it was the Roman Empire that first exploited the propaganda possibilities of coinage. At its height the empire covered nearly a million square miles, with a population of some 100 million. Given the numerous subject peoples, each with a different language, coinage was one of the few forms of mass communication available to indicate each person's relationship to the Roman emperor. Always uncertain about matters of legitimacy, emperors often used a coin to promote their accomplishments and virtues. Roman coinage established conventions of how to legitimize the state and ruler that have remained unchanged to this day. The obverse (front) of the coin, the side with the principal stamp or design, pictured the ruler. The reverse (back) contained some heraldic reference to the state. This was a form of visual propaganda that one could hold in one's hand: the leader is the embodiment of the state, and symbols of the state are embodied in the current ruler.

Coinage declined during the early Middle Ages; almost no gold coins were minted in Europe between 500 and 1250. Coins developed a commemorative function in the sixteenth century—particularly the large silver coin, the thaler—with enough space to permit the depiction of successful events. In Puritan England coins commemorated the beheading of Charles I (1600–1649), the legend appearing in English. When Charles II (1630–1685) returned to the throne in 1660, symbolic of his restoration was the use of Latin inscriptions rather than English. In the American colonies paper money sufficed, often with extreme anti-British content. Since the paper money was not backed up by national gold reserves, it was often worthless, giving rise to the common expression (before 1789) "not worth a continental," a reference to paper currency issued by the Continental Congress on an emergency basis.

The first paper money issued by the U.S. government occurred during the Civil War. The reverse was printed in green ink—hence the term "greenback," an expression still heard to this day. The South printed a wide variety of currencies, often issued by individual banks or cities; the drop in quality of the printing parallels the declining fortunes of the Confederacy between 1861 and 1865.

Twentieth-century German coinage and paper money also reflects the numerous changes in government, as well as the various ways of using money for propaganda purposes. A thousand-mark note from 1910 includes both the symbols of Kaiser Wilhelm II's (1859–1941) Reich and the trappings of bourgeois respectability and fiscal prudence: the Prussian eagle dominates the reverse, set between two figures draped in flowing classical gowns, symbolizing general prosperity. A large floral garland topped by a stylized bishop's miter establishes the Christian, agricultural, and industrial basis of Kaiser Wilhelm's Reich. The collapse of Germany in 1918 gave rise to literally thousands of pieces of *Notgeld,* emergency currency issued by local authorities in Germany as well as what had been the German part of the Austro-Hungarian Empire. Some were well printed, while others seemed intended but for the mo-

ment. This form of currency is a fascinating device for exploring German society in time of crisis. For example, one city where invalids in wheelchairs came to recover contains a visual pun on the obverse of its currency: "*Das Paradies der Schieber*" depicts a shady character pushing someone in a wheelchair. In German *Schieber* can mean wheelchair or pusher, as in drugs. Coinage made of light metal undermines the message of power intended by the regime. When one sees a thin, fifty-pfennig coin minted in Germany in 1941, the eagle of the thousand-year Reich, holding the swastika in its talons, sends a different message than that intended by the Nazi government. Certainly the feather-light coinage of the German Democratic Republic (East Germany) dating from the 1970s conveys something less, in economic terms, than the permanence of the so-called workers' paradise.

The Euro currency introduced in Europe in 2002 reflects the mixed signals of coinage as a tool for propaganda. The obverse of each coin is identical, but the reverse differs from country to country. This German eagle is stylized in such a way as to indicate that it has no fierce intent, having gained so much weight that it must experience difficulty becoming airborne. Euro currency is the same across Europe; not surprisingly, architectural motifs predominate, particularly images of aqueducts—visual bridges linking one country to another—a rather different image, one presumes, from what Roman engineers had in mind.

David Culbert

See also Fakes; Netherlands, Belgium, and Luxembourg; Scandinavia; Spain

References: Carson, R. A. G., *Coins: Ancient, Mediaeval & Modern.* 2d ed. London: Routledge and Kegan Paul, 1970; Grant, Michael. *Roman History from Coins.* Cambridge: Cambridge University Press, 1968; Harrigan, Peter. "Tales of a Thaler," *Saudi Aramco World* (January–February 2003), pp. 14–23.

Cold War (1945–1989)

This appellation describes the period of hostility between the Communist and capitalist countries in the years following World War II. The American journalist Walter Lippmann (1899–1974) popularized the term "Cold War" when he used it as the title of a 1947 book. Just when the Cold War began and ended remains open to question, but what is clear is that the heyday of that conflict was the decade following the cessation of combat in 1945. If, after 1955, there was an occasional hiccup—as in the early years of the Kennedy administration—during the early 1960s there was never a direct confrontation between the United States and the USSR. Their allies did become involved in direct hostilities, as in the Korean and Vietnam wars, but with rare exceptions (a plane shot down, an infiltrator executed, spies caught and punished), the only war between the two superpowers was one of propaganda, both in terms of indoctrinating their citizens and in attempting to win over nonnationals. The period of Soviet-American tension following the Russian invasion of Afghanistan in 1979 is sometimes called the "second" Cold War. Fought on various fronts, this war assumed different guises, but essentially it remained an exercise in mass persuasion.

The Communists had to propagandize not only to the world at large but also to their own populations. Domestically they did this by isolating the citizens of Communist countries. In the Communist states—whether China, Cuba, or the Soviet Union—however their citizens may have viewed the world or whatever their leaders' ultimate outlook, these governments practiced what William E. Griffith has called "the Propaganda of Dictatorship," which was utilized to present views on everything that had or might occur, as well as to effect the "transformation" of human personalities.

The United States and its allies also tried to convince their citizens that they lived in the best possible society. It may not have been as free, democratic, or egalitarian as the propaganda asserted, but it did boast free markets, limited government, the rule of law, individualism, and human rights. A system

selling these beliefs domestically was successfully in place despite the debunking efforts of its enemies at home and abroad. According to Sovietologist Frederick C. Barghoorn, the Soviet Union attempted but failed to "sap the faith of Americans in their leaders and their institutions." Soviet propaganda—and Communist propaganda generally—also tried to isolate the countries of the Third World from the influence of the United States and its allies, to present an unfavorable picture of the United States to the world in what amounted to a cultural war.

American propaganda overseas was designed to provide background to U.S. actions and attitudes. The United States established a series of official agencies, such as the United States Information Agency (USIA), which operated from 1953 to 1999. The various tools of American propaganda were coordinated first by the Psychological Strategy Board, created during the Truman administration, and later by the Operations Coordinating Board, created during the Eisenhower years. During the 1990s, as the archives were unsealed, it became clear that the Americans and, to a limited extent, the less affluent British government had followed a policy of hidden persuasion, which involved distributing "negative" covert anti-Communist propaganda by supporting ostensibly nongovernmental, independent operations.

Interestingly, despite the ultimate outcome of the Cold War, which saw the destruction of the Soviet Union, at the height of this propaganda war many Americans remained convinced that the United States was not competing successfully. Typical was the complaint, in the early 1960s, that there was not only a "missile gap" but also a "propaganda gap." For a variety of reasons, many Americans both in government and in civilian life were concerned that the "Campaign of Truth" (Truman's characterization of 1950) was not achieving its aims—but they were wrong.

During the Cold War the creators of propaganda all utilized their own interpretation of the "truth" to sell an ideological point of view to their citizens and to the world at large. The appeal was meant—as is the wont of propaganda—to stir, to legitimize, to mobilize. Despite new frames of reference, in the final analysis Cold War propaganda harked back to traditional concepts on all sides, resulting in very different interpretations of "freedom" or "security," once again proving that the propaganda that functions best is that which seems to require the least effort to convince.

The defining moments of Cold War propaganda include Joseph Stalin's (1879–1953) "Election" speech in February 1946 and Winston Churchill's (1874–1965) "Iron Curtain" speech in March 1946; President Harry Truman's (1884–1972) "Containment " speech in March 1947; Nikita Khrushchev's pledge to back Third World liberation movements in January 1961 and John F. Kennedy's rousing inaugural address that same month, in which he pledged to rise to this challenge; and, in the "second" Cold War, Ronald Reagan's (1911–) Westminster speech of 1982, in which he pledged to leave "Marxism-Leninism on the ash-heap of history."

Daniel Leab

See also BBC; Black Propaganda; Canada; Castro, Fidel; China; Churchill, Winston; CIA; Civil Defense; Cold War in the Middle East; Cultural Propaganda; Film (Feature); Freedom Train; Gray Propaganda; IRD; Kennedy, John F.; KGB; Korean War; Latin America; Mao Zedong; Marshall Plan; McCarthy, Joseph R.; Murrow, Edward R.; Nixon, Richard; Peace and Antiwar Movements (1945–); Philippines; Psychological Warfare; Radio (International); Reagan, Ronald; RFE/RL; Russia; Scandinavia; Southeast Asia; Stalin, Joseph; United Nations; USIA; Vietnam War; VOA; Wick, Charles Z.

References: Barghoorn, Frederic. *Soviet Foreign Propaganda.* Princeton, NJ: Princeton University Press, 1964; Dunham, Donald. *Kremlin Target: USA—Conquest by Propaganda.* New York: Ives Washburn, 1961; Griffith, William E. "Communist Propaganda." In *Propaganda Communication in World History.* Vol. 2, *Emergence of Public Opinion in the West.* Ed. Harold Lasswell et al. Honolulu: University of Hawaii Press, 1980; Hixson, Walter. *Parting the Curtain: Propaganda, Culture, and the Cold War, 1945–1961.* New York: St. Martins, 1998; Joyce, Walter. *The Propaganda Gap.* New York: Harper, 1963; Lashmar, Paul, and James Oliver. *Britain's Secret Propaganda War, 1948–1971.* Stroud, UK: Sutton, 1998; Saunders, Frances Stoner. *Who Paid the Piper?: The CIA and the Cultural Cold War.* London: Granta, 1999; Sorenson, Thomas. *The Word War: The Story of American Propaganda.* New York: Harper & Row, 1968.

Cold War in the Middle East (1946–1960)

During the mid-1950s the Middle East became a pivotal point within the system of cultural, political, and ideological conflict known as the Cold War. The sensitivities of newly independent governments to questions of sovereignty and nationalism made the struggle to define "imperialism" in ways that advanced the interests of one protagonist at the expense of the other perhaps the central contest of the propaganda war in the Middle East. Certainly it is no longer possible to accept the argument, promoted by Western security specialists during the 1980s, that the Soviets stole a march on the United States (handicapped by its alliances with Britain and France) in setting the ideological agenda in the developing world. It is now clear that both sides in the Cold War propaganda battle sought to depict their adversaries as imperialist, expansionist, and aggressive while proclaiming their own commitment to the principles of peaceful coexistence, nonaggression, and respect for the sovereignty of the states whose support they wished to enlist.

Soviet propagandists fostered the idea of a malevolent "Western imperialism" in terms familiar to any student of V. I. Lenin's (1870–1924) analysis of capitalism and imperialism (a task facilitated in the Middle East by the presence of British military bases and Western oil companies). The immediate objective of Soviet propaganda was, if not to replace Western with Soviet regional hegemony, at least to make life as awkward as possible for

Western strategists keen to preserve a status quo that left British and American influence predominant across the region. To that end, Moscow Radio, Soviet information workers entrusted with inserting material into Middle Eastern newspapers, and local Communist groups influenced by Moscow all sought to stimulate distrust of the Western powers. The expansion of the TASS news agency's services in the Middle East in the 1950s reflects the importance attached to the region by Soviet policymakers.

The Soviets also seized upon the Arab-Israeli dispute as a means of stirring up regional instability. In 1953 an anti-Zionist campaign was initiated that, though it had the effect of undermining Communist groups in Israel, was clearly intended to open the West to Arab charges of pro-Zionism. This strategy enjoyed limited immediate success. While it undoubtedly put Western policymakers on the defensive, U.S. and British diplomats stuck rigidly to policies of studied neutrality with regard to the Arab-Israeli conflict, with Britain in particular only too happy to score propaganda points in the Arab world through strongly worded condemnations of Israeli raids across the Jordanian and Egyptian borders.

Another serious concern for Western propagandists was the development of a strong neutralist trend in the Middle East, which posed more of a danger to Western than Soviet interests since, given the pro-Western status quo, any neutralist drift by an Arab government would mean a shift toward the Soviet Union. Since the exclusion of the Soviet Union from any position of influence in the Middle East was a fundamental tenet of U.S. strategic policy, Western propagandists launched a major antineutrality campaign in the 1950s. Pamphlets illustrating the folly of neutrality were disseminated across the region in a bid to deter Arab governments from diplomatic flirtation with the Soviet Union. Many cited historical examples (Belgium's experience at the hands of German aggression in 1914 and 1940 was a particular favorite), and some were authored by leading

intellectuals (a Bertrand Russell essay was translated and used as Arabic antineutrality propaganda by the British in 1953). Intelligence reports filed by the United States Information Agency (USIA) suggest deep concern over the neutralist and anticolonial ideas promoted by Indian propagandists (who were reported to be more active and effective than ever by the mid-1950s). In addition, the orientation of Egypt toward the nonaligned movement, together with the popular acclaim that greeted President Nasser's (1918–1970) arms deal with the Soviet bloc in September 1955 suggest that the achievements of Western propaganda campaigns against neutrality were decidedly meager.

Concerned that the Middle East was increasingly vulnerable to neutralist ideas and Soviet subversion, Western propagandists launched a series of anti-Soviet campaigns that differed little from those employed in other regions (indeed, the first three of USIA's "global themes" all dealt with anti-Soviet and anti-Communist arguments). Anti-Communist propaganda agencies such as Britain's Information Research Department (IRD) produced enormous quantities of material denouncing Communist totalitarianism and exposing the social and economic hardships of life behind the Iron Curtain. USIA organized cultural events across the Middle East designed to counter Soviet charges of U.S. philistinism. Sports teams, opera divas, and—of particular importance, given the sensitivity of American propagandists to criticisms of racial segregation in the United States—black jazz musicians all embarked on high-profile Middle East tours. Unique to anti-Communist material targeting the Middle East was the bid to mobilize Islam as a barrier against Soviet influence. Both the IRD and the USIA sought to manipulate the content of the Friday sermons of Muslim clerics; both worked to encourage activity at Al Azhar, the leading Islamic university in Cairo. Throughout the 1950s the USIA orchestrated a prominent campaign to publicize statements by Muslim intellectuals stressing the essential compatibility of Western and Islamic ideals and values. Communism was consistently denounced as a "godless creed" and the persecution of Muslim minorities within the Soviet Union provided a potent theme for Western propaganda agencies.

Nevertheless, Western propaganda struggled to make a serious impact on Muslim opinion. The view that Israel, not the Soviet Union, was the most immediate threat to Arab security left the West's Cold Warriors preaching to an audience that proved reluctant to interest itself in the dangers supposedly posed by "Red Colonialism." By the end of the 1950s, a significant section of the Arab world, with Syria and Egypt in the vanguard, had shifted markedly toward the Soviet camp, a development that, while ultimately a shallow and transient victory for the Soviets, was a clear sign of the impotence of much Western Cold War propaganda in the Middle East.

James Vaughan

See also Arab World; Cold War; IRD; Suez
    Crisis; USIA
References: Dawisha, Adeed, and Karen
    Dawisha, eds. *The Soviet Union in the Middle
    East: Policies and Perspectives.* London:
    Heinemann, 1982; Lashmar, Paul, and James
    Oliver. *Britain's Secret Propaganda War,
    1948–1977.* Stroud, UK: Sutton, 1998;
    Rawnsley, Gary, ed. *Cold-War Propaganda in the
    1950s.* Basingstoke, UK: Macmillan, 1999.

Comintern (1919–1943)

This international propaganda organization founded by the Soviet Union was the Third International, the name used by various associations formed to unite Socialist and Communist organizations throughout the world. The Third (Communist) International was formed by the Bolshevik administration in Moscow in March 1919. For Joseph Stalin (1879–1953) the Comintern was a means of increasing Soviet influence abroad and publicizing and defending shifts in Soviet policy. Stalin agreed to disband the organization in May 1943 as a goodwill gesture toward his capitalist allies. The Comintern's impact on public opinion may have been negligible. Nevertheless, its activities could prove important in terms of setting agendas for the labor movements of the West.

Graham Roberts

See also International; KGB; Revolution,
    Russian; Russia; Stalin, Joseph; Zinoviev Letter
References: Schapiro, Leonard. *The Communist
    Party of the Soviet Union.* London: Eyre and
    Spottiswoode, 1970; Tucker, Robert C. *Stalin
    in Power.* New York: Norton, 1990.

The Communist Manifesto (1848)

This groundbreaking work of Communist propaganda was published in London (in German) in 1848 by two German exiles, Friedrich Engels (1820–1895), who produced the first draft, and Karl Marx (1818–1883), who transformed it into dynamic prose. Of little impact at the time, its influence grew, and by the end of the century it had helped to inspire an international Communist movement.

The Communist Manifesto sought to chart the crimes of the system of "bourgeois property," arguing that the solution lay in the exploited working class rising up and taking control of the "means of production." For Marx and Engels this was not a possibility but a scientific inevitability. Their work sought to rally the working class by illuminating this prospect of a utopian future.

Beyond its argument and analysis, the work included some memorable phrases. In the manner of a Gothic novel, the opening statement claimed that "a spectre is haunting Europe: the spectre of Communism." At the conclusion of the work Marx and Engels proclaimed that "the proletarians have nothing to lose but their chains; they have a world to win. 'Working Men of All Countries, Unite!'"(The latter was often rendered as "Workers of the World, Unite!")

Nicholas J. Cull

See also Engels, Friedrich; International; Marx,
    Karl; Russia
References: Cowling, Mark. *The Communist
    Manifesto: New Interpretations.* Edinburgh:

University of Edinburgh Press, 1998; Engels, Friedrich, and Karl Marx. *The Communist Manifesto.* London: Verso, 1998; McLellan, David. *Karl Marx: His Life and Thought.* London: Macmillan, 1973; Raddatz, Fritz J. *Karl Marx: A Political Biography.* London: Weidenfeld and Nicolson, 1979.

Counterinsurgency

Counterinsurgency is a term applied to strategies—military, political, and psychological—employed to quell violent challenges to authority over a particular territory. In its earliest twentieth-century uses, the term tended to denote the responses of *colonial* regimes to militant resistance that espoused an anti-imperialist and/or nationalistic political program. In the 1950s and 1960s it aptly described U.S. strategy in Vietnam. Under the presidencies of John F. Kennedy and Ronald Reagan in particular, the provision of counterinsurgency training and assistance to troubled regimes in the developing world, such as Indonesia and the Philippines, formed a key plank of U.S. global strategy.

Since "insurgencies" arise from struggles over political legitimacy and territorial sovereignty, it is important to recognize that language itself forms a site of contestation between incumbents and challengers. "Counterinsurgency" is thus a designation favored by embattled regimes to denote (and legitimate) their responses to the provocation of a substate group that has resorted to violence rather than pursuing grievances through political channels. To underscore their opponents' illegitimacy even further, states often elide the terms "insurgent" and "terrorist." Thus, British colonial authorities who encountered violence in Palestine, Malaya, Kenya, and Cyprus in the early postwar period routinely termed their opponents "terrorists." For their part, these insurgents (or terrorists) prefer to describe themselves as "freedom fighters" or "guerrillas." Reversing the allocation of responsibility for violence, these characterizations stress armed uprising as a necessary response to the bankruptcy (or unavailability) of political channels in a repressive regime susceptible to change only through violent means.

The precise measures that constitute counterinsurgency strategy vary in terms of geographical settings and time. Although generalized definitions are problematic, it is possible broadly to suggest that in the interwar period rebellion against British colonial rule—whether in Ireland (the Anglo-Irish War of Independence in 1919–1921), in Palestine under the Mandate (the Arab rebellion of 1936–1938), or in the North-West Frontier province of India—tended to be met primarily with force, as was the case with unrest in French colonial territories. Counterinsurgency thus combined policing and military operations; in extra-European, imperialist settings it made considerable use of airpower as a means of quelling dissent. After 1945 counterinsurgency became more commonly associated with a strategy that combined physical repression of violence with psychological strategies to regain popular support for precarious regimes. Commentators on particular counterinsurgencies frequently differ in their estimation of the balance struck between violence, coercion, and persuasion, with some suggesting the primacy in British strategy of "minimal force," while others see only brutal repression.

Since the 1950s counterinsurgency has frequently been subsumed under the banner of "winning hearts and minds," a phrase attributed to Field Marshal Sir Gerald Templer (1898–1979) referring to the approach he pursued in Malaya against the Communist Malayan Races Liberation Army (MRLA). The phrase emphasizes the psychological and material inducements to cooperate with the colonial government that were presented to the peoples of Malaya during the "Emergency" (1948–1960). Propaganda was employed intensively and was aimed at both the insurgents and the population as a whole. Leaflets and aerial broadcasts encouraged the surrender of armed members of the MRLA, who quickly retreated to Malaya's mountainous jungle interior to pursue a guerrilla campaign against locally recruited and British armed forces. Some of those who duly gave themselves up were then recruited as psywar (psychological warfare) operatives, producing "black" propaganda that purported to emanate from Communist sources. As for the civilian population, propaganda not only encouraged Malays to reject the Communist insurgents as a foreign movement controlled by the Chinese Communist Party in Beijing but also to appreciate the benefits that British rule had provided and the quickened pace of self-government that Templer encouraged.

However, the physically coercive components of the strategy—played down by the phrase "hearts and minds"—should not be ignored. Templer's campaign also relied heavily on the construction of "New Villages," consisting of fortified encampments in rural Malaya into which the largely Chinese peasant population was forcibly "swept." Government propaganda promoted "villagization" as a progressive measure, not only securing vulnerable peasantry from Communist attack but also delivering amenities (electricity, water, health care, education) hitherto unknown to rural "squatter" populations. Templer's detractors characterized these New Villages as little better than concentration camps. Far from prioritizing the welfare of their inhabitants, critics charged that the heavily fortified villages were primarily devices to deny the Communists their bases of logistical support. High security was intended to lock in villagers (whose guilt was assumed) as much as it was intended to keep the "Communist terrorists" out.

Whether primarily through coercion, persuasion, or their judicious combination, Templer's strategy served to quell Communist insurgency. When the United States stepped up its endeavors to repel the forces of Communist nationalism in Indochina, it turned to Britain's "success" in Malaya as a model. The U.S. government drew on the expertise, in particular, of Sir Robert Thompson (1916–

1992). Although some aspects of U.S. strategy in Vietnam bear a clear resemblance to British innovations in Malaya—most notably the "Strategic Hamlets" program—the transferable lessons proved rather few. Arguably American strategists underestimated the considerable differences between Britain's position in Malaya and their own in Vietnam. In Malaya, a colonial power, British authorities were able to promise (and deliver) self-governance, capitalizing on the Chinese ethnicity of the insurgents, which set them apart from the majority Malay population and undercut the MRLA's claims to represent the nationalistic aspirations of all of Malaya's ethnic groups. In Vietnam the United States enjoyed neither formal status as a sovereign colonial power nor the same opportunities to pursue a "divide and rule" strategy. Where Britain had been able to employ military force against the MRLA (including aerial bombardment and the use of defoliants), with only minimal international press scrutiny, the same was clearly not the case in Vietnam, where press attention to the military dimensions of U.S. strategy became ever more invasive—and critical—as the war progressed.

Susan Carruthers

See also Black Propaganda; British Empire; Ireland; Philippines; Psychological Warfare; Southeast Asia; Terrorism; Vietnam; Vietnam War

References: Carruthers, Susan L. *Winning Hearts and Minds: British Governments, the Media and Colonial Counter-Insurgency, 1944–1960.* Leicester: University of Leicester Press, 1995; Mockaitis, Thomas. *British Counterinsurgency, 1919–60.* Basingstoke, UK: Macmillan, 1990; Purcell, Victor. *Malaya: Communist or Free?* London: Victor Gollancz, 1954; Schmid, A. P., and J. de Graaf. *Violence as Communication: Insurgent Terrorism and the Western News Media.* London: Sage, 1982; Stubbs, Richard. *Hearts and Minds in Guerrilla Warfare: The Malayan Emergency, 1948–60.* Oxford: Oxford University Press, 1990; Thompson, Robert. *Defeating Communist Insurgency: Experiences from Malaya and Vietnam.* London: Chatto and Windus, 1966; Townshend, Charles. *Political Violence in Ireland: Government and Resistance Since 1848.* Oxford: Clarendon Press, 1983.

CPI (Committee on Public Information)

A U.S. government propaganda agency operating both at home and abroad, CPI was founded in April 1917 to promote the national effort during World War I. Under the direction of George Creel (1876–1953)—it is sometimes known as the Creel Committee—it represented the first major U.S. government initiative in the field of propaganda. The CPI strove to avoid the extremes of private interventionist propaganda. It avoided atrocity stories in favor of building up the promise of the American system and the personal prestige of the president. In September 1917 the CPI acquired a film division to create film propaganda for the home market; by linking the distribution of CPI films to the export of Hollywood entertainment, it also gained access to foreign audiences. The CPI's Foreign Section directed propaganda to Allied, neutral, and enemy territory. It included a news service called Compub. The CPI provided propaganda support during President Woodrow Wilson's (1856–1924) antirevolutionary intervention in Russia. In 1919 the agency closed amid allegations that it had been too partisan in its presentation of Wilson.

Nicholas J. Cull

See also Creel, George; United States; World War I
References: Mock, James R., and Cedric Larson. *Words That Won the War: The Story of the Committee on Public Information.* Princeton, NJ: Princeton University Press, 1939; Vaughn, Stephen. *Holding Fast the Inner Lines: Democracy, Nationalism, and the Committee on Public Information.* Chapel Hill: University of North Carolina Press, 1980.

Creel, George (1876–1953)

An American propagandist active during World War I and a muckraking journalist, Creel was born in Blackburn, Missouri. He initially campaigned on social issues, such as child labor. Creel was first exposed to political propaganda while working on Woodrow Wilson's presidential campaign in 1916. He then shot to fame as the director of the Committee on Public Information (CPI), the official responsible for "selling" the war effort to the traditionally neutral American public. CPI activities included poster campaigns and war-bond drives. Methods used by the CPI included the "Four Minute Men," a network of volunteer speakers across the entire country who received their instructions by telegraph. In 1920 Creel published an account of his achievements and in so doing contributed to the growth of a public reaction against propaganda, which created a major obstacle for propagandists attempting to rally American support against Hitler two decades later.

Nicholas J. Cull

See also CPI; United States; World War I
References: Creel, George. *How We Advertised America: The First Telling of the Amazing Story of the Committee on Public Information.* New York: Harper, 1920; Mock, James R., and Cedric Larson. *Words That Won the War: The Story of the Committee on Public Information.* Princeton, NJ: Princeton University Press, 1939.

Crimean War (1853–1856)

Also known at the time as the "Russian War," with its main theater of action in the Crimea, it was fought—chiefly by France and Britain (from 1854) as allies of the Ottoman Empire—principally to halt the encroachment of the Russian empire into southeastern Europe, marking a watershed in European war propaganda. The war was precipitated by long-standing regional strategic issues arising from the decline of Ottoman power. But in the eyes of the European press the immediate cause was the emotive issue of the rival claims of Russia and France to be the guardian of the "Holy Places" of Palestine. Although the French effectively controlled their press through censorship and sustained popular enthusiasm for the war, Britain proved a different story. Newspaper reports of living conditions from the theater of war—relayed by steamship and telegraph, particularly those sent to the *Times* (London) by the Anglo-Irishman William Howard Russell (1821–1907), which earned him the first-ever use of the title "war correspondent"—caused a scandal in London. Russell's criticisms led the *Times* to denounce the government of Lord Aberdeen (1784–1879), playing a part in its fall and also encouraging a climate of reform after the war. This and other demonstrations of the power of the press—including descriptions of the main British hospital at Scutari, near Constantinople, by Thomas Chenery (1826–1868), also of the *Times*—forced subsequent governments to take the media and war reporting seriously. Florence Nightingale (1820–1910) also used the press to exaggerate her own role in medical reform at Scutari. At the prompting of Prince Albert (1819–1861), the British government responded by sending court photographer Roger Fenton (1819–1868) to the Crimea in 1855 as the world's first accredited war photographer.

Russell's account of the charge of the British light cavalry brigade at the Battle of Balaclava in 1854 inspired Alfred, Lord Tennyson (1809–1892) to write his poem *The Charge of the Light Brigade*. While appalled at the losses in the charge, Tennyson, like Russell, stressed the heroism and sense of duty of the men. His poem became a cornerstone of propaganda stressing the ethic of self-sacrifice and was recited in British schoolrooms for the next hundred years.

Nicholas J. Cull

See also British Empire; Civil War, United States; Ottoman Empire/Turkey; Poetry

References: The History of the "Times." Vol. 2, The Tradition Established, 1841–1884. London: Times, 1939; Hankison, Alan. Man of Wars: William Howard Russell of "The Times." London: Heinemann, 1982; Keer, Paul. The Crimean War. London: Boxtree, 1997; Lambert, Andrew. The Crimean War: British Grand Strategy against Russia, 1853–1856. Manchester: Manchester University Press, 1990; Lambert, Andrew, and Stephen Badsey. The Crimean War: The War Correspondents. Stroud, UK: Sutton, 1994.

Crossman, Richard (1907–1974)

Expert British practitioner of psychological warfare during World War II and subsequently Labour cabinet minister. A brilliant classical scholar at Oxford University, Richard Crossman seems to have developed an interest in propaganda during a visit to Germany in 1930, when he gained much insight into the working of Communist propaganda in that country. While still teaching at Oxford he became active in British Labour politics and became assistant editor of the *New Statesman* in 1938. In 1940 he joined the wartime Ministry of Economic Warfare, parent organization for the Political Warfare Executive. He masterminded British propaganda against Nazi Germany and, as assistant chief of the Psychological Warfare Division of SHAEF (Supreme Headquarters Allied Expeditionary Force), played a leading role in the Allied effort to break the German will to resist following D-day. Crossman's approach to psychological warfare emphasized the value of credibility and the reliance on the truth, particularly in such gambits as leaflets appealing for enemy troops to surrender. His views on such matters were widely circulated within NATO during the early Cold War.

Crossman's subsequent political career never really lived up to his intellectual promise, although he served in Harold Wilson's cabinet, finishing as minister of health and social security. His association with the wartime "cloak and dagger world" did not serve him well, and he was nicknamed "Dick Double-Crossman." Returning to the backbenches of Parliament, in his final years he became best known for his legal battle to publish his *Diaries of a Cabinet Minister* (1975, 1976, and 1977), whose revelations about the Wilson government proved once again that the truth could be excellent propaganda.

Nicholas J. Cull

See also Black Propaganda, Psychological Warfare, PWE, World War II (Britain).

References: Crossman, Richard, "Supplementary Essay," in Lerner, Daniel. Sykewar: Psychological Warfare against Germany, D-Day to VE-Day. New York: G. W. Stewart, 1949, pp. 323–346; Howard, Anthony. Crossman: The Pursuit of Power. London: Jonathan Cape, 1990.

Cuba

See Caribbean

Cultural Propaganda

Cultural propaganda is a long-term process intended to promote a better understanding of the nation that is sponsoring the activity. The United States refers to it as "public diplomacy," whereas Britain and France prefer to call it "cultural diplomacy" or "cultural relations." Such activity involves the dissemination of cultural products—films, magazines, radio and television programs, art exhibitions, traveling theater groups and orchestras—as well as the promotion of language teaching and a wide range of "educational" activities, such as student-exchange schemes. Over a period of time, these activities are designed to enhance the nation's image among the populations of other countries, with a view to creating goodwill and influencing the polices of their governments through the pressure of public opinion.

Following the demise of the Empire Marketing Board in 1933, the British Council was established in 1934 under Foreign Office control to promote Britain's long-term cultural relations. The model for the British Council was the successful French Alliance Française. The British Council emphasized the educational and cultural aspects of its work. Equally important, however, were pressing political considerations. The totalitarian use of propaganda, much of it directed against British interests abroad, persuaded the British government that the council should develop a response focusing on British democratic institutions and the "British way of life."

The universal appeal of American mass culture had been clear as early as the 1920s, given the enormous success of Hollywood movies, music, and other mass-produced goods. During the interwar period the American studios were producing over 75 percent of all films shown worldwide. The mass appeal of American films exerted a powerful influence on language, fashion, and consumer behavior. By World War II film had established itself as the most successful medium of mass entertainment, as well as a social force of fundamental significance.

The Cold War was perceived as a conflict between opposing ways of life. In 1948 the Smith-Mundt Act created the legal framework for a permanent overseas information program, using the media, exchange programs, and exhibitions to counter the massive disinformation campaigns launched from Moscow by the KGB to discredit the United States. Beginning in the mid-1950s, U.S. policymakers believed that cultural diplomacy would successfully complement psychological warfare and in the long term might prove more effective. During this period the export of American culture and the American way of life was heavily subsidized by the U.S. government and coordinated by the United States Information Agency (USIA). Cultural exchange programs, international trade fairs and exhibitions, and the distribution of Hollywood movies were just some of the activities designed to extract propaganda value based on the appeal of America's way of life, particularly its popular culture and material success. The Voice of America (VOA) broadcast American jazz and rock music to audiences behind the Iron Curtain, using their popularity to boost the standing of the United States. While radio remained an important weapon for waging psychological warfare against the Soviets, American authorities saw broadcasting as a means by which the United States could win hearts and minds around the world through a long-term process of cultural propaganda.

During the Cold War, the United States was also able to call upon private "philanthropic" and multinational concerns such as Coca-Cola, McDonalds, and Levis. The universal popularity of such symbols of "Americanization" testified to the success of this approach. Such "cultural imperialism" was designed to homogenize the world into a global village dominated by American values.

One of the most interesting and bold experiments in cultural propaganda was the policy of "reeducation" adopted by the Allies in different forms after the war. It represented a political experiment unique in modern history. The rationale behind Britain's policy of reeducation in the period 1945–1955 was to change the political behavior and social outlook of the German people through a fundamental restructuring of the various media. In practice this control extended beyond the press, radio, and film to include the entire educational system. The methods of presentation to be employed in the media and the cultural sphere were seen not as a means of reestablishing German culture but rather of projecting British values and the British way of life.

David Welch

See also Austrian Empire; BBC; British Empire; Canada; CIA; Cold War; Disinformation; Public Diplomacy; Shakespeare, William; USIA; VOA

References: Hixson, Walter L. *Parting the Curtain: Propaganda, Culture and the Cold War, 1945–1961.* Basingstoke, UK: Macmillan, 1997; Ninkovich, Frank A. *The Diplomacy of Ideas: U.S. Foreign Policy and Cultural Relations, 1938–1950.* Cambridge: Cambridge University Press, 1981; Taylor, Philip M. *British Propaganda in the Twentieth Century: Selling Democracy.* Edinburgh: Edinburgh University Press, 1999; Turner, Ian D., ed. *Reconstruction in Post-war Germany: British Occupation Policy and the Western Zone.* Oxford: Berg, 1989; Wagnleitner, Reinhold. *Coca-Colonization and the Cold War.* Chapel Hill: University of North Carolina Press, 1994.

Cyprus
See Greece

Czech Republic
See Austrian Empire

D

David, Jacques-Louis (1748–1825)

A French neoclassical painter active during the French Revolution, who later became court painter to Napoleon, David was born in Paris and trained in Italy. He gained fame based on a series of historical paintings—including *The Oath of the Horatii* (1784) and *The Lictors Returning the Bodies of His Sons to Brutus* (1789)—which caused a sensation by giving unprecedented life and drama to classical subjects. They also reflected an admiration for the classical civic virtues associated with the Roman Republic and hence were propaganda for a revival of republicanism. During the Revolution David recorded events in his sketchbook and painted portraits of the major figures. His best-known work was *The Dead Marat* (1793), which depicted the revolutionary leader as a martyr. David was active in revolutionary politics, sat in the Convention, and was one of the revolutionaries who voted for the execution of Louis XVI (1754–1793). David worked closely with Robespierre (1758–1794), serving as artistic director for the cycle of propagandistic festivals held to promote the new ideas of the Revolution. Under Napoleon (1769–1821) David used his skills to develop a heroic image of the emperor. Strong classical echoes resurfaced in his painting of Napoleon crossing the Alps, which pictures the emperor, with billowing cloak, astride a rearing horse, recalling Hannibal, whose name is carved on a stone at Napoleon's feet. After Napoleon's defeat, David went into exile in Brussels, where he died in 1825.

Nicholas J. Cull

See also Art; France; Napoleon; Revolution, French

References: Crow, Thomas. *Emulation: Making Artists for Revolutionary France.* New Haven, CT: Yale University Press, 1994; Lajer-Burcharth, Ewa. *Necklines: The Art of Jacques-Louis David after the Terror.* New Haven, CT: Yale University Press, 1999; Nanteuil, Luc de. *Jacques-Louis David.* New York: Abrams, 1985.

Defoe, Daniel (1660–1731)

Said by some to be the founder of British journalism, the son of a London butcher, Daniel Foe was educated at a Dissenting (that is, non-Anglican Protestant) academy in Stoke Newington. He worked as a hose factor (seller of leggings), establishing a substantial mercantile business while traveling throughout Britain. His political sympathies at this time were evident in his support for the Monmouth Rebellion (1685) and the Glorious Revolution (1688–1689). In 1692 he faced bankruptcy, subsequently taking a minor government office in 1695 and adopting the name Defoe.

Defoe's poem "The True Born Englishman" (1701) attracted royal attention for its attack on prejudice against the king's foreign birth. However, his irony in "The Shortest Way with the Dissenters" (1702), which called for the suppression of dissent, was misinterpreted as an assault on the Anglican Church. As a result Defoe was fined, pilloried, and jailed in Newgate Prison. In 1703 Robert Harley (1661–1724) recruited Defoe as a propagandist for the Tory Party and as a negotiator in the union debates with Scotland. Using treasury funds, in 1704 Defoe established a triweekly newspaper, *The Review*, and supported the Tory ministry in several antiopposition pamphlets. When Harley fell from power, Defoe again found himself in prison. After 1715 he began working for the Whig ministry.

Defoe was a prolific writer, publishing over 560 books and pamphlets. His reputation as "the Great Reporter" is based on his nonfiction, including *The Complete English Tradesman* (1726), and his numerous accounts of criminal lives. His three-volume *Tour through the Whole Island of Great Britain* (1724–1727) and *London the Most Flourishing City in the Universe* (1728) provide a vivid, firsthand survey of Britain. Pat Rogers, however, has remarked that "the truth is that Defoe possessed a wild inventive streak, a demonic imaginative power . . . he was the Great Fabricator." Defoe's imaginative talent is illustrated by his account of a journey to the moon entitled *The Consolidator* (1705) and the *New Voyage Round the World* (1724), as well as his *History of the Pirates* (1724–1728) and *Letters by a Turkish Spy* (1718). Defoe's keen observation and literary skill combined to provide an authoritative narrative that often masked his ultimate political intent. Defoe's lasting legacy is his development of the novel as a literary form in such works as *Robinson Crusoe* (1719), *Captain Singleton* (1720), *Journal of the Plague Year* (1722), *Captain Jack* (1722), *Moll Flanders* (1722), and *Roxana* (1724).

Karen M. Ford

See also Britain; Britain (Eighteenth Century); Novel

References: Black, Jeremy, ed. *Britain in the Age of Walpole*. London: Macmillan, 1984; Rogers, Pat, ed. *A Tour through the Whole Island of Great Britain*, by Daniel Defoe. Harmondsworth, UK: Penguin, 1971.

De-Nazification
See Reeducation

Denmark
See Scandinavia

Disinformation
Disinformation is a term used to describe propaganda that is usually covert and therefore considered a form of "black" propaganda. The term is derived from the Russian *dezinformatsia*, which comes from the section (known as Service A for "Active Measures") of the KGB devoted to black propaganda.

Disinformation means false, incomplete, or misleading information that is passed, fed, or confirmed to a targeted individual, group, or country. Disinformation is not merely misinformation that is erroneous. Disinformation is comprised of news stories deliberately designed to weaken opponents, which are often planted in newspapers by secret agents of a foreign country masquerading as journalists. The intention is to obscure the identity of the originator of the message in order to foster a high degree of credibility for both the message that is being planted and the apparent source that is giving it credence. The CIA and the KGB have long been attempting to discredit the other side by spreading rumors of the other country's dirty deeds. Invariably these are passed off as true and from a verifiable source. Testifying before the House of Congress in 1980, Ladislav Bittmann, former deputy chief of the Disinformation Department of the Czechoslovak Intelligence Service, claimed that Soviet intelligence services had successfully penetrated Western newspapers around the world and that a relatively high number of these secret agents were operating as journalists.

In 1985 the Soviet Union launched a concerted disinformation campaign, accusing the United States of developing the virus responsible for AIDS for use in biological warfare. Despite repeated denials, the story appeared in newspapers throughout the world and was still surfacing in British newspapers in 1987. Turkey was also targeted by this story, which urged Turkish citizens to campaign for the removal of U.S. bases in Turkey as a result of servicemen infected with AIDS. Another story planted by the KGB in the 1980s claimed that wealthy Americans were plundering children in Third World countries for "spare-parts surgery" back home.

Whereas the extent of Soviet disinformation is now well documented as a result of Soviet defectors and the end of the Cold War, the activities of the CIA remain more obscure. For many years the United States denied using disinformation, although there now exist a number of Internet sites intent on exposing CIA activities. One notorious example that came to light in 1985 involved a CIA propaganda officer named John Stockwell who admitted to fabricating a widely reported story that Cuban soldiers who had raped some girls in Angola had subsequently been caught, tried, and executed by a firing squad. Even the photograph of the "firing squad" was a fake. In 1995 the *Times* reported that American academic research centers in Moscow were front organizations for the CIA. In the 1980s a U.S. disinformation campaign charged the Sandinistas in El Salvador with drug running. The Iran-Contra hearings in 1987 revealed that for many years the CIA and the Contras were, in fact, involved in a major Central American drug-smuggling operation.

The scope of the KGB's disinformation operations in the West during the Cold War was overwhelming. One of the most complete pictures of the KGB and its operations is presented in *The Sword and the Shield: The Mitrokhin Archive* (1999), written by Vasili

Mitrokhin (1922–) and Christopher Andrew. Mitrokhin worked for thirty years in the KGB archives. Following the Soviet Union's collapse, he carried to Britain a massive secret collection of Cold War material about the KGB's activities.

According to the Mitrokhin archive, in 1971 the KGB sought to stir up racial tension in the United States. KGB chief Yuri Andropov (1914–1984) personally approved the fabrication of pamphlets full of racist propaganda purporting to emanate from the extremist Jewish Defense League (JDL) and calling for a campaign against "black mongrels," who, it was claimed, were looting Jewish businesses. At the same time, forged letters were sent to numerous black organizations providing fictitious details of atrocities committed by the JDL against blacks. Similarly, before the 1984 Los Angeles Olympics, KGB agents sent forged letters, purportedly written by the Ku Klux Klan, to the Olympic committees of the African and Asian nations.

Mitrokhin also claimed that Philip Agee— the CIA's first ideological defector, who wrote the best-selling book *Inside the Company: CIA Diary* (1975), which identified 250 agency agents and made serious allegations of CIA malpractice—was, in fact, not the author of the work but rather the KGB and its Cuban equivalent, the DGI (Directorate General of Intelligence). In 1978 Agee, again with assistance from the KGB and the DGI, began publishing the *Covert Action Information Bulletin,* which was designed to destabilize the CIA by exposing its covert activities. One of its claims, picked up and carried in the American media, was that CIA agents were behind the assassination of President Kennedy. Forged letters from Lee Harvey Oswald, dated two weeks before Kennedy was murdered, to CIA officers were passed on anonymously to groups and individuals in the United States who were susceptible to conspiracy theories.

Once the planted stories have been taken up by the mainstream media and reported as fact, invariably the United States denounces them as forgeries, allowing Moscow to claim "anti-Soviet slanders." The important point from the propaganda perspective is that *both* sides would be reported. The disinformation that journalists were fed by the KGB often contained a kernel of truth surrounded by a tissue of lies. The falsehood, however, can frequently become conventional wisdom. As Philip M. Taylor has noted, future historians will need to be wary when searching the international media of this period as primary sources for their research since such stories abounded, making it difficult if not impossible for contemporaneous readers to identify which story was real and which was a propaganda plant.

David Welch

See also CIA; Cold War; Intelligence; Olympics; Psychological Warfare; Russia; USIA

References: Agee, Philip. *Inside the Company: CIA Diary.* New York: Stonehill, 1975; Mitrokhin, Vasili, and Christopher Andrew. *The Sword and the Shield: The Mitrokhin Archive.* New York: Basic Books, 1999; Schultze, Richard H., and Roy Godson. *Dezinformatsia: Active Measures in Soviet Strategy.* Washington, DC: Brasseys, 1986.

Drugs

Illegal narcotics and legal intoxicants have been a staple of state and pressure-group propaganda since the nineteenth century, when the campaign against alcohol produced the temperance movement. By the end of the twentieth century, the U.S. government's war on drugs had brought state propaganda against the traffic in and use of drugs to the international stage.

The most sustained propaganda campaign against drugs was developed in the United States in the early years of the twentieth century in tandem with prohibition. Legal landmarks included the Harrison Narcotics Act of 1914. Drug use was variously associated with "foreign threats": newspapers associated opium with the Chinese and marijuana with Mexican immigrants. During World War I they spread stories that German spies were foisting drugs on American youth to turn them into "heroin maniacs." In 1930 the U.S. government established a Federal Bureau of Narcotics under an eager commissioner, Harry J. Anslinger (1892–1975), who served in this post until 1962. Like his similarly long-serving contemporary J. Edgar Hoover (1895–1972) of the FBI, Anslinger was a tireless campaigner and publicist for his views and his agency. He successfully lobbied for the 1937 Marijuana Tax Act, which criminalized possession and use of this drug. He also lobbied internationally for uniform antidrug laws, in particular to "protect" U.S. military personnel serving overseas during World War II. Film propaganda made by sympathetic antidrug campaigners included the notorious *Reefer Madness* (1936).

The 1960s brought the phenomenon of propagandists for drug use, most notably Timothy Leary (1920–1996) and Ken Kesey (1935–2001). Drug experiences were a key element in the counterculture of the era, which duly launched a campaign to relax America's drug laws. The Nixon administration reasserted the law with the Controlled Substances Act of 1970. In 1971 protestors demonstrated to free jazz musician and writer John Sinclair (1941–), who received a ten-year jail sentence for supplying two joints to an undercover police officer. The "ten for two" campaign included a protest song by John Lennon (1940–1980) and a benefit concert. Sinclair was released after serving three years. A drift toward liberalization came to an abrupt halt with the election of Ronald Reagan to the presidency in 1980.

President Reagan (1911–), whose family had experienced drug abuse at first hand, made drugs a major policy issue. First Lady Nancy Reagan (1923–) became the figurehead of a campaign to "just say no" to drugs. His successor, President George H. W. Bush (1924–), launched a "War on Drugs," which included a strong foreign policy component and whose message was disseminated by the United States Information Agency (USIA).

Events included the 1989 invasion of Panama to remove dictator, drug supplier, and former U.S. ally Manuel Noriega (1940–) from power. Pressure groups engaged in propaganda for drug-law reform at the end of the century included a lobby on both sides of the Atlantic to legalize marijuana for medicinal use. Recurrent problems in government antidrug campaigns include the refusal to distinguish between various classes of drugs and the loss of credibility inherent in lecturing to an audience that has experienced the substances under discussion. The issue of past student drug use was raised to embarrass Bill Clinton during the presidential election of 1992, and links between the Taliban of Afghanistan and heroin traffic surfaced in Western propaganda early in the 2001 War on Terrorism.

Nicholas J. Cull

See also Reagan, Ronald; *Reefer Madness;* Temperance; Women's Movement: First Wave/Suffrage

References: King, Rufus. *The Drug Hang-Up: America's Fifty-Year Folly.* New York: Norton, 1974; McWilliams, John C. *The Protectors: Harry J. Anslinger and the Federal Bureau of Narcotics, 1930–1962.* Newark: University of Delaware Press, 1990; Sloman, Larry "Ratso." *Reefer Madness: The History of Marijuana in America.* New York: St. Martin's, 1998.

E

Egypt

See Arab World

Eisenstein, Sergei (1898–1948)

A Soviet filmmaker best known for his recreations of revolutionary events in *Battleship Potemkin* (1926) and *October* (1927), Eisenstein was a master of what was then called "American editing," which involved pacing and communicating meaning through rapid cutting between images. Despite their subject matter, his films were widely admired in the West, where he achieved considerable influence, especially among documentary filmmakers. In 1938 he made the anti-Nazi allegory *Alexander Nevsky* about the Russian hero resisting Teutonic knights. The film was initially suppressed because of the Nazi-Soviet pact of 1939. By the end of the war Eisenstein had fallen out of favor with the Stalin regime. He died in obscurity.

Nicholas J. Cull

See also *Battleship Potemkin;* Film (Feature); Revolution, Russian; Russia

References: Barna, Ion. *Eisenstein.* London: Secker and Warburg, 1973; Taylor, Richard, ed. *S. M. Eisenstein: Selected Works, Vol. 1, 1922–1934.* Bloomington: Indiana University Press, 1988.

Elections

The purpose of propaganda may be to influence people to adopt attitudes that correspond to those of the propagandist or to engage in certain patterns of behavior (for example, joining a political party or pressure group or contributing money to a cause). In democracies elections are viewed as the legitimization of the political process whereby citizens make their voices heard. However, elections have increasingly become a vehicle for propagandists or "spin doctors" to influence the political agenda and voting behavior. Prior to World War II the press largely shaped political debate in democracies and voters tended to buy newspapers that reflected their own political views and values. Paul Lazarsfeld and his associates conducted a study during the presidential election of 1940 to determine whether mass media influenced political attitudes. To their surprise, they discovered that face-to-face discussions were a more important source of political influence than the media. However, since the 1950s the mass media has played a very important role in influencing voting behavior and now largely displaces traditional allegiances to political parties. Television, in particular, has radically reshaped politics.

Politicians have to air "sound bites" to ensure themselves limited coverage on television news, and television commercials account for a major portion of campaign budgets. The television image of candidates, and political leaders in particular, has become a determining factor in voter decision making. In a complex society where a proliferation of information exists, voters depend on the media to set the agenda for public discussion and to supply information they lack and have neither the time nor the inclination to find out. There is evidence to suggest that more and more voters are abandoning party lines and dividing their votes among candidates from different parties. This development is partly due to the "personality cult" that television has fostered and to a growing reliance on issues to simplify voting choices. These issues have largely been shaped by the media, which determine the political agenda. Politicians are then required to appear on television to "sell" their policies. The gatekeeping function of the media has become a significant factor that determines what (and who) gets into print or is televised. Shearon Lowery and Melvin DeFleur predict that mediated information may play a greater role in future elections, whereas, "reinforcement and crystallization, in the sense of cultivating prior loyalties, presumably will have a reduced role."

When the electorate thinks of recent presidents or prime ministers, it is arguable that the first thing that comes to mind is how the candidates looked on television—which can be at the expense of issues and policies. Indeed, there is evidence that the grind of daily fundraising, together with the need to project an appropriate image for the television cameras, causes talented candidates to leave politics. In a TV-dominated world, television propaganda may be turning the electorate off politics to the extent that they no longer bother to vote. Again, there is evidence to suggest that voters have become increasingly cynical of the politicians and their spin doctors during elections.

David Welch

See also Blair, Tony; Censorship; Elections (Britain); Elections (Israel); Elections (United States); Fakes; Italy; Kennedy, John F.; Opinion Polls; Poland; Reagan, Ronald; Spain; Thatcher, Margaret
References: Lazarsfeld, Paul, Bernard Berelson, and Hazel Gaudet. *The People's Choice: How the Voter Makes Up His Mind in a Presidential Election.* New York: Duell, Sloan & Pearce, 1948; Lowery, Shearon, and Melvin DeFleur. *Milestones in Mass Communication Research.* New York: Longman, 1988.

Elections (Britain)

The story of election propaganda in Britain is intimately linked to the course of political reform and technological innovation. In the eighteenth and nineteenth centuries British elections were riotous, as candidates plied electors with drink and bribes. Election propaganda ranged from speeches, cartoons, poems, and debates at the election hustings to painted signs and special pottery items. The Westminster campaign of 1784 attracted particular attention as the duchess of Devonshire, the former Lady Georgiana Spencer (1757–1806), allegedly sold kisses to butchers on behalf of Whig politician Charles Fox (1749–1806). The chaos at elections continued well into the nineteenth century, reaching a peak of disorder in the 1860s.

Electoral reform became a principal demand of the Chartists, who were named after their list of demands, the People's Charter of 1838. Chartist propaganda methods included rallies and a national petition. Further reform came in 1867, though not as a direct result of their efforts. Charles Dickens (1812–1870) drew attention to the absurdities of British elections in a memorable scene in *The Pickwick Papers* (1836–1837). The introduction of the secret ballot in 1872 and the Corrupt and Illegal Practices Act of 1883 significantly cleaned up British elections. The latter set limits on election expenditure and permitted only one election agent for each candidate; all other election workers had to be volunteers. This legislation necessitated the rapid development of constituency parties to provide volunteers.

William Ewart Gladstone (1809–1898), the politician behind the reforms of 1872 and 1883, was also the great pioneer of political campaigning. After losing office as prime minister, Gladstone rebuilt his political fortunes by campaigning for the seat of Midlothian, near Edinburgh, Scotland. The Midlothian Campaign of 1879–1880 utilized American-style whistle-stop speeches. Gladstone fought on a broad platform of nationally relevant (Liberal) ideologies rather that local issues tied to an individual candidate. The Conservative Party eventually matched this approach, and elections in Britain came to be fought in national party terms. Candidates offered up individual election statements and pledges. The first party with a formal manifesto was the Labour Party in the general election of 1906.

In the twentieth century the Conservative Party led the way in campaign innovations. Radio broadcast time was allocated equally. Conservative prime minister Stanley Baldwin (1867–1947) proved a master of the "fireside chat" technique. Baldwin also made great use of film in the general elections of 1931 and 1935, and the party apparatus included mobile screening vans. Joseph Ball (1885–1961), the party's director of publicity in the 1930s, was a former intelligence officer who resorted to dirty tricks, including placing a spy in the Labour Party's printing works. On occasion Conservative rhetoric proved self-defeating, as was the case during the general election of 1945, when Prime Minister Winston Churchill (1874–1965) made the mistake of predicting that a Labour government would use some form of "Gestapo" to force socialism on Britain. He lost.

The strict controls on political broadcasting devised in the radio era remained in the television age. Parties are allocated a fixed amount of air time for "party election broadcasts" in proportion to their share of the vote, and commercial stations cannot carry paid political advertising. Television was already

important in the election of 1959, but it proved a real advantage for the Labour Party of the 1960s under the leadership of the telegenic Harold Wilson (1916–1995). In 1964 Wilson trounced the stiff Conservative prime minister Alec Douglas-Home (1903–1995). The Labour Party slogan in that election, "Let's Go with Labour for the New Britain," curiously anticipated the party's successful slogan "New Labour, New Britain" in 1997.

The Conservative Party introduced a fresh wave of modernization in the late 1970s under the leadership of Margaret Thatcher (1925–), who employed the advertising agency Saatchi and Saatchi. In elections held during the 1980s the party introduced morning press conferences, which effectively set the agenda for the day's debates and news. By the late 1980s the key figure in Conservative propaganda was Tim Bell (1941–). The party was greatly helped by the support of the mainly Conservative tabloid press in Britain. Following the April 1992 election, the *Sun* went so far as to claim responsibility for the result by printing the following memorable headline: "It's the *Sun* wot won it."

The Labour Party, however, took steps to modernize under the influence of former television producer Peter Mandelson (1953–). The climax of the 1992 campaign suggested that there were limits to the public tolerance of American-style election razzmatazz. Labour leader Neil Kinnock (1942–) apparently damaged his fortunes by appearing overly confident at an election-eve rally in Sheffield. The Labour Party had more success with the American technique of rapid rebuttal, developing a computer database of Conservative political statements to permit almost instantaneous responses. The campaign of 1997, which resulted in a landslide victory for Tony Blair (1953–), witnessed the distribution by the Labour Party of a how-to-vote video for young voters and a ubiquitous campaign pop song entitled "Things Can Only Get Better."

Oddities of British elections include the continued use of posters. Their unveiling became favorite campaign photo opportunities, and particularly effective or controversial posters could be cross-reported as news stories in their own right. Key examples of the controversy genre included a Conservative poster in 1997 showing Tony Blair with demonic eyes and Labour posters in 2001 showing the Conservative leader as a zombie sporting a Margaret Thatcher wig. British politicians have avoided American-style presidential debates, viewing them as an unnecessary risk.

Nicholas J. Cull

See also BBC; Blair, Tony; Britain; Churchill, Winston; Elections; Thatcher, Margaret; Zinoviev Letter

References: Cockerell, Michael. *Live from Number 10: The Inside Story of Prime Ministers and Television.* London: Faber and Faber, 1988; Cockett, Richard. "The Party, Publicity and the Media," in *Conservative Century: The Conservative Party since 1900.* Ed. Anthony Seldon and Stuart Ball. Oxford: Oxford University Press, 1994; Cull, Nicholas, ed. "The Battle for Britain: Political Broadcasting and the British Election of 1997." *Historical Journal of Film, Radio and Television* 17 (October 1997); Foreman, Amanda. *Georgiana, Duchess of Devonshire.* London: HarperCollins, 1998; Hanham, H. J. *Elections and Party Management: Politics in the Time of Disraeli and Gladstone.* London: Longmans, 1959; Kavanagh, Dennis. *Election Campaigning.* Oxford: Blackwell, 1995.

Elections (Israel)

Israeli election propaganda has strikingly and dramatically reflected the shift from *representation by trustee* that characterized the founding fathers of the State of Israel to a new style of mass media–era politics largely based on *representation by delegate*. This shift has been identified with the sweeping Americanization of Israeli politics.

Several social trends and political shifts have accelerated the adoption of American-style campaigning in Israel. The size of the Israeli electorate has increased significantly: around 500,000 voters in the first elections of 1949; over 2.5 million in the tenth elections of June 1981; 3 million in 1988; about 3.5 million eligible voters in 1992; some 4 million in 1996; 4.2 million voters in 1999; and 4.7 million in the 2001 elections. First, a new generation of young leaders has emerged who possess neither the historical reputation nor the charismatic personal qualities of their predecessors. Second, the election industry has developed over the years. A few advertising firms, undoubtedly responding to increasing demand, have offered their professional services in managing political campaigns, thereby exposing the parties to professional communicators for the first time, including consultants, advisers, copywriters, public relations professionals, advertisers, and their respective staffs. Third, the adoption of certain components of U.S. electoral style raises hopes for a stable and powerful leadership.

Recent campaigns have rapidly adopted a new style of electoral politics that can be characterized by at least five main features:

1. Telepolitics: Vigorous propaganda campaigns conducted through the broadcast media, particularly television, including extensive candidate coverage. Spin doctors set up events to coincide with broadcasting lineups.
2. Consultant Involvement: Having imported the best available know-how on effective and rational campaign management, professionals isolate candidates and take control of election headquarters, shoving aside dedicated party members and campaign workers.
3. Personalization of the Political Debate: The increasing presence of experts in campaign staffs reduces public debate to a personal confrontation between candidates. The candidates and their personalities occupy center stage in the election campaign.
4. "Carnivalization": Every political event and election rally turns into a kind of gala, complete with balloons, signs, performers, singing, and dancing. Party

conventions become projects for professional producers, who freely mix entertainment and political speeches.

5. "Pollsification": The political weakness that first opened campaign headquarters to outside experts also spurs candidates to commission polls to analyze every move they make. Politicians and the media are trapped in a kind of vicious circle that benefits the poll industry: the more polls, the more findings; the more findings, the more differences among them; the more differences, the greater the uncertainty; and so on.

The new electoral propaganda style is likely to shape the quality of the political leadership, for it promotes a process of negative selection that encourages mediocre candidates possessing manipulative skills but lacking vision and leadership qualities. The mediocrity that is taking control of democracy—the *demediocracy*—is perhaps more bearable in an established Western democracy but may prove disastrous for a younger one that still faces problems of survival.

Dan Caspi

See also Elections (United States); Israel
References: Caspi, Dan. "When Americanization Fails? From Democracy to Demediocracy in Israel." *Israel Studies Bulletin* 15 (Fall 1999): 1–5; ———. "American-style Electioneering in Israel: Americanization versus Modernization." In *Politics, Media and Modern Society.* Ed. D. L. Swanson and P. Mancini. Westport, CT: Praeger, 1996; Lehman-Wilzig, S. "The 1992 Media Campaign: Toward the Americanization of Israeli Elections?" In *Israel at the Polls.* Ed. D. Elazar and S. Sandler. Lanham, MD: University Press of America, 1995; Weimann, G., and G. Wolfsfeld. "Struggles Over the Electoral Agenda: The Elections of 1996 and 1999." In *The Elections in Israel 1999.* Ed. M. Shamir and A. Arian. Jerusalem: Israel Institute for Democracy, 2000.

Elections (United States)

"Nothing," wrote Alexander Hamilton (1755–1804) in *Federalist* no. 1 (1787), "could

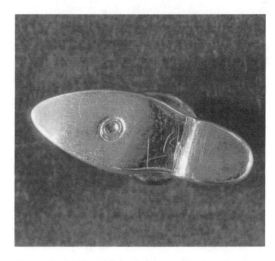

During the 1952 presidential campaign Democratic candidate Adlai Stevenson was photographed with his legs crossed, revealing a most-visible hole in the sole of his shoe. Small sterling silver lapel pins of the shoe sole became symbols of Stevenson's campaign. (Courtesy of David Culbert)

be more ill-judged than that intolerant spirit which has at all times characterized political parties." Elections in America have been transformed by revolutionary changes in transportation as well as through the advent of electronic mass media. In addition, the electoral process as one observes it today is vastly different from that imagined by the founding fathers, as indicated by the sentiment expressed by Hamilton. When George Washington (1732–1799) was elected first president of the United States in 1789, the Constitution allowed for no direct vote, fearing that the average citizen was not intelligent enough to cast a vote with proper insight. Instead, the Constitution called for an electoral college system in which each state has the same number of electoral votes as its congressional delegation (in other words, large states have more votes than smaller ones).

The system, which is regularly denounced, continues to this day. Now citizens are allowed to vote directly for their president, but they are actually only voting for a slate of electors pledged to vote for a particular candidate. The system is a testament to the fear of democracy that characterized the many lawyers who wrote the Constitution. There were no political parties before 1828, which helps explain how different campaigning techniques were in a preindustrial society. But this does not mean that voting was a sedate occupation of prosperous gentlemen. The scurrilous efforts of James Callender (?–1803)—who first raised the issue of Thomas Jefferson's (1743–1826) having fathered the children of his slave and mistress Sally Hemings (1773–1836)—appeared in Virginia newspapers during the election of 1800. Those who did not like Jefferson read such information with pleasure. The year 1828 marks the beginning of the party system in American politics, though what is today's two-party system of Democrats and Republicans did not become the norm until 1860 and, in some respects, not until the end of the Civil War in 1865.

The election of 1860 featured four candidates and was viewed as a mandate for what to do about slavery. The election of Abraham Lincoln (1809–1865) helped persuade the South to secede. Lincoln was not the first president to be photographed—Andrew Jackson (1809–1845) was photographed on his deathbed in 1845—but Lincoln's singular appearance (which gave rise to the euphemism "Lincolnesque" to describe a very homely individual) was a genuine campaign asset. The pre-electronic era is perhaps best captured in a series of public debates between Lincoln and his chief opponent, Stephen A. Douglas (1813–1861), which were heard at most by a few hundred persons. They were mostly read in newspaper accounts published with the aid of the telegraph, but they were still published by local newspapers. The vast size of America and the primitive nature of mass transportation made it impossible for any single newspaper to cover the entire country.

The election of 1876 is remembered because the candidate who lost the popular vote—Rutherford B. Hayes (1822–1893)—was able to steal the election from the candidate who should have won—Samuel B. Tilden (1814–1886). The explanation was vote fraud in three Southern states (South Carolina, Florida, and Louisiana) where federal troops were still enforcing military reconstruction: An electoral commission was set up in the House of Representatives to examine the nineteen electoral votes in dispute—votes that would, of course, have gone to the Democratic candidate since the South accepted as a given that the Republican Party was synonymous with Radical Reconstruction and the military occupation of the South. Thanks to yet more fraud, every disputed electoral vote went to the Republican candidate, and Hayes became president by a single electoral vote. The result was something that shaped electoral politics in America until the 1960s: the so-called solid South, which blamed Reconstruction on the Republican Party and voted any Democrat to office rain or shine, and no Republican, however qualified.

Ironically, progressive reform in the selection of presidential candidates helped fix the South's commitment to the Democratic Party. In 1904 Florida became the first state to institute a system of presidential primaries, in which candidates for the office of the presidency campaigned and citizens voted directly on primary day, the winner gaining that state's delegation at the national party convention. The result was to greatly extend the season of campaigning and make fundraising a major requirement for any serious candidate for president.

From the early days of the Republic, the chief political strategist for an incumbent president was the postmaster general, who did not need to spend much time arranging for slow-moving mail delivery in an era in which most bulk mailing was unknown, although many newspapers—particularly weeklies—were delivered by mail. Jim Farley (1888–1976), FDR's postmaster general, was one of the most effective strategists. The last postmaster general to occupy a cabinet post resigned in 1971; since then political strategists come from elsewhere.

The twentieth century has seen an enormous change in the style of campaigning, given the arrival of the automobile and airplane and the advent of radio and television, to say nothing of the Internet. Radio first covered a national party convention in 1924; television followed in 1940. In 1960 four one-hour national television debates heralded a new style of campaigning in which voters would decide which candidate to vote for based solely on the issues. John F. Kennedy (1917–1963) defeated Richard Nixon (1913–1994) by 115,000 votes out of 69 million cast, but television turned out to be more useful for paid political messages than as a medium for public debate. The 2000 election was also hotly contested. The question of how to count ballots in Florida left the outcome in doubt for weeks until the U.S. Supreme Court intervened in a decision that left supporters of Democratic candidate Al Gore (1946–) livid. A detailed recounting, completed months later, revealed that George W. Bush (1947–) had won in Florida, but the closeness of the popular vote nationally clearly indicated that voters saw little difference between Gore or Bush.

David Culbert

See also Civil War, United States; Clinton, William Jefferson; Elections; Kennedy, John F.; Lincoln, Abraham; Long, Huey; Nixon, Richard; Roosevelt, Franklin D.; United States
References: Farley, James A. *Behind the Ballots: The Personal History of a Politician.* New York: Harcourt, Brace, 1938; McGinniss, Joe. *The Selling of the President 1968.* New York: St. Martin's, 1969; Posner, Richard A. *Breaking the Deadlock: The 2000 Election.* Princeton, NJ: Princeton University Press, 2001; White, Theodore H. *The Making of the President 1960* [and 1964, 1968, and 1972]. New York: Atheneum, 1961 [1965, 1969, and 1973].

Elizabeth I (1533–1603)

Queen of England from 1558–1603 and a masterly manipulator of her own image, Elizabeth was the daughter of Henry VIII (1491–1547) and his ill-fated second wife, Anne Boleyn (c. 1504–1536). As a Protes-

tant, Elizabeth spent much of the early years of her reign engaged in fending off Catholic opposition, and to this end she built up the state, including both a considerable intelligence service and a cult of personality centering on herself. Elizabeth paid considerable attention to her image, distributing portraits throughout the kingdom made from officially sanctioned originals. Elizabeth also proved a formidable public speaker, most famously rallying the country against the Spanish Armada of 1588, declaring: "I know I have the body of a weak and feeble woman, but I have the heart and stomach of a king and a king of England too" (collected in Lord Somers, *A Third Collection of Scarce and Valuable Tracts* [1751]). In later years the image of Elizabeth became a staple of British patriotic propaganda. The British film *Fire over England* (1937) and the U.S. film *The Sea Hawk* (1940) used the Spanish threat as an effective allegory for British resistance against the Nazis.

Nicholas J. Cull

See also Britain; Portraiture; Reformation and Counter-Reformation
References: Cole, Mary Hill. *The Portable Queen: Elizabeth I and the Politics of Ceremony.* Amherst: University of Massachusetts Press, 1999; MacCaffrey, Wallace T. *Elizabeth I: War and Politics, 1588–1603.* Princeton, NJ: Princeton University Press, 1992; Strong, Roy. *The Cult of Elizabeth: Elizabethan Portraiture and Pageantry.* London: Thames and Hudson, 1987.

Engels, Friedrich (1820–1895)

Although born in Germany, this nineteenth-century pioneer of Communism lived most of his life in England, where his father owned a cotton factory. Engels developed his political ideas in the 1840s. Shocked by the poverty that followed in the wake of industrialization, in 1845 he published *The Condition of the Working Classes in England in 1844.* In 1844 he had met Karl Marx (1818–1883), who was to be his lifelong friend and collaborator and with whom he wrote the *Communist Manifesto* (1848). Both men took part in radical activity in the German Rhineland during the revolutions of 1848–1849, fleeing to London when the revolutions collapsed. Engels supported Marx both financially and intellectually, and following Marx's death in 1883 he arranged for the posthumous publication of his friend's remaining works. Engels was active in the formation of the Second International of 1864.

Nicholas J. Cull

See also *The Communist Manifesto;* International; "The Internationale"; Marx, Karl; Russia

References: Carver, Terrell. *Friedrich Engels: His Life and Thought.* London: Macmillan, 1989; McLellan, David. *Friedrich Engels.* New York: Viking, 1977.

Environmentalism

A belief in the need to conserve the natural environment, environmentalism developed from localized intellectual routes in the nineteenth century to become a movement of global significance by the end of the twentieth century. Its propaganda has ranged from serious literature to headline-grabbing feats of direct action. Local and national governments have sponsored antipollution propaganda and a number of politicians have sought to endorse the cause as part of their personal campaign rhetoric. Al Gore (1948–), U.S. vice president in 1993–2001 and unsuccessful presidential candidate in 2000, campaigned with a genuine commitment to environmentalism and authored *Earth in the Balance* (1992).

The foundations of environmentalism can be found in an admiration for nature that emerged from nineteenth-century romantic art and literature. In the United States the writers Henry David Thoreau (1817–1862) and Ralph Waldo Emerson (1803–1882) argued for respect for the natural world. In 1864 George Perkins Marsh (1801–1882) published the pathbreaking book *Man and Nature*—reissued in 1874 as *The Earth as Modified by Human Action*—which laid the foundations for the science of ecology. Con-

servation per se began with campaigns initiated by a lobby with an interest in hunting. George Bird Grinnell (1848–1938) campaigned for the preservation of America's wilderness as the editor of the magazine *Forest and Stream.* In 1872 he succeeded in winning protection for Yellowstone as the first U.S. national park, and in 1886 he founded the first major environmental advocacy group, the Audubon Society, named for the ornithologist and bird painter John James Audubon (1785–1851). Other key campaigners included the Scottish-born writer John Muir (1838–1914), through whose efforts California's Yosemite Valley became a national park in 1890. In 1892 Muir founded the Sierra Club, one of the key environmental advocacy groups in the United States. He also formed a strong political alliance with President Theodore Roosevelt (1858–1919). Roosevelt matched his personal eloquence on the subject of the environment (and hunting) with legislation to develop a network of national parks during his presidency (1901–1909).

In the twentieth century politicians sought to manipulate ideas about the environment for their own ends. Much environmental writing emphasized a mystical bond between the individual and the national landscape. The environment hence became a common propaganda theme in Nazi Germany, where art, rhetoric, and state-sponsored activities emphasized "blood and soil."

The environmental movement moved into a new phase in the 1950s and 1960s as concern deepened over the effect of pollution on wildlife. Key advocates included Rachel Carson (1907–1964), who addressed the problem of ocean pollution in *The Sea Around Us* (1951) and that of pesticides in *Silent Spring* (1962). The issue of respect for nature fitted in well with other countercultural currents of the era. Public demonstrations in the cause of the environment culminated in global celebrations to mark Earth Day in 1970. Government-backed campaigns included a poster and TV advertisement featuring Native American

Environmentalist John Muir, c. 1902. (Library of Congress)

actor Iron Eyes Cody (1907–1999) weeping at the sight of litter and pollution, bearing the slogan "Keep America Beautiful." The environmental movement developed in tandem with the antinuclear movement. The best known radical environmental group, Greenpeace, emerged in 1971 to protest against U.S. government nuclear tests off Alaska.

Many European countries developed "Green" parties. The most successful of these is probably the Germany Green Party (founded in 1979); by the end of the century Germany's Greens had become the nation's third party. In 1998 they became part of a coalition government together with the Social Democrats, and were rewarded when the government agreed to phase out nuclear power. Green parties also joined coalitions in France, Finland, New Zealand, and elsewhere. Britain's "first past the post" electoral system kept Greens out of Parliament, but environmental politics was still visible at the end of the century as "anti-road" protestors blocked the path of projected new roads, forcing confrontations with the police, and campaigners against genetic modification used direct action, destroying "GM" crops in the fields while symbolically dressed in biohazard protection suits.

Environmentalism has emerged as a major issue in global politics. In 1972 the United Nations held its first conference on the environment in Stockholm. Major Earth summits followed in Rio (1992) and Kyoto (1997). Countries whose politicians have made particular commitments to environmentalism include Sweden and Denmark. The island nations of the Pacific have campaigned on the issue of global warming and the associated problem of rising sea levels. In response, global corporations engaged public relations consultants to seek to identify themselves with sound environmental practice.

Nicholas J. Cull

See also Pacific/Oceania; Peace and Antiwar
Movements (1945–); Scandinavia; *Silent
Spring*

References: Fox, Stephen. *John Muir and His
Legacy: The American Conservation Movement.*
Boston: Little, Brown, 1981; Hays, Samuel P.
*Beauty, Health and Permanence: Environmental
Politics in the United States, 1955–1985.*
Cambridge: Cambridge University Press,
1987; O'Neill, Michael. *Green Parties and
Political Change in Contemporary Europe: New
Politics, Old Predicaments.* London: Ashgate,
1997; Pearce, Fred. *Green Warriors: The People
and the Politics behind the Environmental
Revolution.* London: Bodley Head, 1991; Wall,
Derek. *Green History: A Reader in Environmental
Literature, Philosophy and Politics.* London:
Routledge, 1994.

Exhibitions and World's Fairs

Ever since the huge success of the 1851
Great Exhibition in London, the idea of exhibitions and world's fairs to promote trade,
industry, art, and knowledge has become an
industry in itself. In 1928 an international
convention established the Bureau of International Expositions to organize and control
exhibitions and fairs. Exhibitions and world's
fairs have always been about far more than
the simple promotion of knowledge and
trade. They have been used to celebrate historical events, which usually meant that the
host country took the opportunity to stress
its national culture and achievements. They
have also been used to underscore a nation's
superiority over its rivals, thereby, strictly
speaking, violating the original spirit behind
the concept.

The inspiration for the Great Exhibition
was Prince Albert (1819–1861). The prince
consort was very much a man of his time, and
his idea for a celebration of the industry of
nations reflected nineteenth-century concepts of liberalism, where free trade and free
discourse would bring peace to the world.
The Crystal Palace promoted this idealism
while simultaneously celebrating Britain. As
the world's greatest industrial and imperial
power, the vast bulk of the exhibition was

given over to British and imperialist products. From the very outset exhibitions were
therefore strongly connected with national
pride and the promotion of national culture.

The British used exhibitions and fairs to
show off their empire and encourage imperial unity. The second half of the nineteenth
century witnessed a number of fairs of this
kind in Sydney (1879–1880), Melbourne
(1880–1881), Calcutta (1883–1884), London (1886), and Adelaide (1887–1888). In
1911 Sydenham, the home of the Crystal
Palace after its removal from Hyde Park, witnessed a Festival of Empire. Huge military
tattoos, reenactments of famous imperial
battles, and other entertainments all served
to stress the idea of a powerful, united empire. The culmination of these celebrations
occurred in 1924–1925 at Wembley. The
centerpiece of the exhibition was the new
Empire Stadium. King George V (1865–
1936) opened the exhibition in a lavish ceremony involving representatives from across
the far-flung empire. The exhibition drew
large crowds—proving that the appeal of
empire was much greater than has sometimes
been suggested—as did the Glasgow Festival
of Empire in 1938.

For other nations, too, trade and industrial
fairs provided an opportunity to promote national pride and culture. In 1876 Philadelphia
hosted a world exhibition, which also celebrated the centennial of the Revolution.
Chicago hosted the World's Columbian Exposition in 1893; it marked Chicago as *the*
great city of the Midwest, boosting civic
pride after having won the right to host the
fair following stiff competition from New
York. In 1905 Portland, Oregon, played host
to the Lewis and Clark Centennial and American Pacific Exposition and Oriental Fair,
proving that the United States was as much a
Pacific country as an Atlantic one. Victory in
the Spanish-American War was never far
from the surface at the 1898 Omaha Trans-
Mississippi Exposition. Strong racial messages were also imparted, for the exhibition
stressed the need for paternal control of the

People in Bolivia inspect John Glenn's Mercury space capsule, exhibited in 1962 as part of its Cold War information program by the U.S. Information Agency. (National Archives)

"degenerate" Indians. A similar spirit pervaded the famous 1904 Louisiana Purchase International Exposition, held in St. Louis, where there were numerous "anthropological exhibits." (The St. Louis Fair committee also brought the Olympics to the city.) The British imperial fairs also contained specially built villages designed to display the customs and culture of the various subject peoples.

Between 1890 and 1914 Belgium hosted a cluster of fairs and exhibitions that largely reflected the growing wealth and confidence of Belgium as an industrial and colonial power: Antwerp (1894), Brussels (1897), Liège

(1905), Brussels (1910), and Ghent (1913). The French revealed themselves to be even more infatuated by the concept. After a hugely successful fair in 1867, Paris hosted exhibitions in 1878, 1889, and 1900. The 1889 centenary of the Revolution proved to be a particularly spectacular affair, with the completion of the Eiffel Tower. The 1900 exhibition witnessed the presence of international rivalries. Britain had recently clashed with France over Africa. The Germans had wanted to host the exhibition and so were determined to outshine France, which duly occurred. Meanwhile, the Americans and the Japanese also put on strong displays, causing a certain amount of national introspection. The Paris exhibition of 1925 served as a moment of rehabilitation, giving Soviet Russia the chance to make its presence felt on the international stage. In the depths of economic depression in 1931, France seized the moment to promote its empire, holding a successful Exposition Coloniale Internationale, in which French culture and its civilizing influence on the globe were the main themes.

The most politically volatile of the Parisian exhibitions occurred in 1937. It was clear that Nazi Germany and Soviet Russia were planning to use the occasion for maximum propaganda effect. Albert Speer (1905–1981) designed an imposing German pavilion, topped by an enormous German eagle over which floated an even bigger swastika-emblazoned flag. Visitors were able to view Leni Riefenstahl's famous film *Triumph of the Will* (1935). The Soviets erected an equally big pavilion and decorated with a similarly huge hammer-and-sickle–emblazoned flag. Britain was drawn in, to a certain extent, employing Sir Edwin Lutyens (1869–1944), one of its finest architects, to design its pavilion; unfortunately, the contents of the British pavilion were rather tame by comparison. Other exhibits at the fair included Picasso's antiwar painting *Guernica* (1937). The British pulled out all the stops for a massive propaganda effort at the New York World's Fair of 1939. Aiming to win American sympathy on the eve of World War II, they stressed the common heritage of Britain and the United States, sending over the king and queen for a related visit.

The Cold War continued the theme of political rivalries, seeking propaganda opportunities through the medium of exhibitions and fairs. At the 1958 exhibition in Brussels the United States was determined to outshine the USSR. The latter was equally determined to rise to the occasion. President Eisenhower demanded huge sums to pay for the U.S. exhibits and wanted to promote the United States as an affluent and happy society. The Soviets stressed their scientific knowledge—particularly in the field of space exploration—and their allegedly superior culture. West Germany was keen to be seen as a well-balanced and hardworking society, while Britain, France, and Belgium presented the last glimmers of their imperial glory.

More recently exhibitions have returned to the tradition of celebrating important landmarks. In 1967 the Montreal Expo permitted Canada to celebrate its hundredth birthday. Vancouver seized the chance to promote itself on its centenary in 1986. In 1988 Brisbane hosted the World Expo; it was a major part of the bicentennial celebrations and was opened by the queen. Seville played host to the 1992 Columbus Quincentennial Exposition. The exhibitions—including the World's Fair in Hanover—mounted to mark the millennium proved disappointing. The Millennium Dome in London became a major political embarrassment for the government of Tony Blair (1953–).

Mark Connelly

See also British Empire; Cultural Propaganda; Freedom Train; Olympics; USIA

References: Cull, Nicholas J. "Overture to an Alliance: British Propaganda at the New York World's Fair, 1939–1940." *Journal of British Studies* 36, 3 (July 1997): 325–354; Findley, John E., and Kimberly D. Pelle. *A Historical Dictionary of World's Fairs and Expositions,*

1851–1988. Westport, CT: Greenwood, 1990; Rydell, Robert W. *All the World's a Fair: Visions of Empire at the American International Expositions, 1876–1916*. Chicago: University of Chicago Press, 1984; Rydell, Robert W., John E. Findling, and Kimberly D. Pelle. *Fair America: World's Fairs in the United States*. Washington, DC: Smithsonian Institution Press, 2000.

F

Fakes

Throughout history propagandists have resorted to the use of fake texts or visual memorabilia to elicit an emotional response from the intended audience. Usually fake propaganda is employed to create or reinforce existing prejudices against a target group. An example of this is *The Protocols of the Elders of Zion,* a scurrilous publication describing alleged Jewish plans for world domination, which remains one of the most notorious uses of a fake text for propaganda purposes.

Another example of the use of a fake for propaganda purposes involves the sinking of the *Lusitania*. On 7 May 1915 the *Lusitania* was sunk by a German U-boat without prior warning, resulting in the loss of 1,198 lives, 128 of them American. A year later a German artist named Karl X. Goetz (1875–1950) struck a medal privately to commemorate the sinking of the passenger liner, which the Germans claimed had been carrying munitions. The German medal depicted the *Lusitania* laden with guns, beneath which were the words "No Contraband." On the reverse was the motto "Business before Everything." The British Foreign Office managed to obtain a copy of the medal, photographed it, and sent copies to the United States, where it was published in the *New York Times*

on the anniversary of the sinking. This attracted so much attention that the British decided to further exploit anti-German feeling by producing a boxed replica together with an "explanatory" leaflet intended to demonstrate the bestiality of German actions against innocent women and children. Wellington House initially produced fifty thousand replicas of the *Lusitania* medal. Demand was so great that responsibility for production and distribution was handed over to Gordon Selfridge (1858–1957), the department-store entrepreneur. The replica of the medal was eventually produced in the hundreds of thousands. What was originally a private German initiative on the part of an individual artist to justify the submarine campaign to his own people became an international cause célèbre.

Although the *Lusitania* incident coincided with the publication of the Bryce Report, it did not bring America into the war. However, the British version of events generally prevailed, helped by the fake commemorative medal struck by them. The replica medal, together with the "explanatory" note, served to reinforce the stereotype of the brutal Hun that British propaganda had been trying to create. Goetz continued to treat political subjects in his work, designing coins and producing propaganda medals in Nazi Germany.

David Welch

See also Anti-Semitism; Atrocity Propaganda; Latin America; Oates, Titus; *Protocols of the Elders of Zion;* World War I; Zinoviev Letter

References: Cohn, Norman. *Warrant for Genocide: The Myth of the Jewish World-Conspiracy and the Protocols of the Elders of Zion.* London: Eyre and Spottiswoode, 1967; Sanders, Michael, and Philip M. Taylor. *British Propaganda During the First World War, 1914–18.* London: Macmillan, 1982.

Falklands/Malvinas War (1982)

Lasting from April to June 1982, this war between Argentina and Britain was fought over the Falkland Islands and South Georgia in the South Atlantic. Britain's management of the media during the war showed the application of the lessons of Vietnam and established an influential model, reflected in U.S. government practice in Grenada (1983), Panama (1989), and the Gulf War (1991). The conflict originated as a result of a crisis in the military regime of Argentina. The junta, led by General Leopoldo Galtieri (1926–2003) faced economic difficulty (600 percent inflation) and revived a long-standing territorial claim to "las Islas Malvinas" to rally his population. This claim had been a basic element in geography lessons at school and hence was widely supported. In a prime example of propaganda by deed, the Argentinean military seized the Falklands and South Georgia on the second and third of April, respectively, and waited for the British to react.

The British response included the securing of a UN resolution (502), which required the withdrawal of Argentina's troops prior to any negotiations over sovereignty, which gave Britain's response moral standing. Margaret Thatcher (1925–), utilizing World War II rhetoric, compared Galtieri to Hitler and argued that a dictator should never be appeased. She successfully rallied the support of both the British and much of the American public in sending a task force to recapture the islands.

The key organs of British propaganda on the home front were the tabloid newspapers (with the exception of the *Daily Mirror*). These papers supported the war for commercial and editorial reasons, much as the U.S. yellow press had behaved during the Spanish-American War of 1898. The most notorious of many jingoistic headlines was the "Gottcha" response of the *Sun* to the sinking of Argentina's warship *General Belgrano.* Operating under Foreign Office counsel, the BBC World Service stressed Britain's eagerness to find a peaceful solution. When the domestic BBC news attempted to open discussion of British policy early in the conflict, this effort was branded as "unpatriotic" by the Thatcher government.

The remoteness of the islands permitted an extraordinary level of British control of images of the war. Twenty-nine journalists— all British—and seven official "minders" sailed with the troops. The latter applied moral pressure for "supportive" reporting and occasionally blocked stories. One even brazenly informed a journalist: "You knew when you came you were expected to do a 1940 propaganda job." Ministry of Defense censors removed particular phrases, such as the description of British casualties as "horribly burned." Radio (and other audio) reports could be heard virtually in real time, but the television pictures were flown back by air and screened between nine and twenty-one days after the actual events had taken place (taking longer to reach London than dispatches from the Crimean War). In London the BBC attracted criticism for plugging the gaps with footage from enemy sources. The Ministry of Defense altered its usual practice of closed briefings and placed Ian McDonald, its acting head of public relations, in front of the cameras to deliver the official version of the news in an intentionally monotone voice. Closed briefings resumed as the conflict progressed. It later emerged that ministry briefings included comments and outright denials calculated to mislead the enemy, which proved controversial.

Radio propaganda also figured in war. Argentina established Radio Nacional Islas Malvinas on the facilities of the Falkland Islands Broadcasting Station (FIBS). The station broadcast a mixture of morale-boosting programs for the occupying troops and news in English for the Falkland Islanders mounted by the old staff. A television service (with plenty of soccer coverage) followed. Meanwhile the British sought to address enemy troops through a clandestine short-wave radio station called Radio Atlántico del Sur (Radio South Atlantic), based on Ascension Island. Listenership was limited since few Argentinean soldiers had short-wave radios. The Argentinean position could be heard in English on Radio Liberty, where "Miss Liberty, the Buenos Aires Belle" roundly denounced Margaret Thatcher from a studio either in Argentina or, some believed, Algeria. After the war FIBS returned with increased short- and medium-wave transmissions in conjunction with the British Forces Broadcasting Service.

In Argentina the press followed the military line. The latter portrayed the invasion as both just and successful and exaggerated both the morale and capabilities of their forces on the islands. When the promised victory evaporated with the British landings and recapture of the islands, the regime lost credibility. Argentina's counterstrategies included blaming the United States for having deserted a fellow American power, but the debacle led directly to the fall of the junta in 1983 and a return to civilian rule. In Britain the war proved a welcome political boost for Margaret Thatcher. She made the most of the victory, mounting homecoming celebrations for the forces and a victory parade. She won reelection in 1983 by a landslide due—many believed—to the "Falklands Factor."

Subsequent debates arising from the war have included allegations of British atrocities against prisoners of war (now largely disproved), mistakes that increased British casualties, and discussion of the role of the British arms industry in supplying Argentina in the first place. The conflict figured in protest songs performed by Billy Bragg (1957–). Accounts of the fighting that could be considered antiwar propaganda include the memoir *When the Fighting Is Over: A Personal Story of the Battle for Tumbledown Mountain and Its Aftermath* (1990) by wounded officer Robert Lawrence (1960–).

Nicholas J. Cull

See also Black Propaganda; Britain; Caribbean; Censorship; Latin America; Radio (International); Sport; Thatcher, Margaret; United Nations; Vietnam War

References: Cockerell, Michael. *Live from Number 10: The Inside Story of Prime Ministers and Television.* London: Faber, 1988; Freedman, Lawrence, and Virginia Gamba-Stonehouse. *Signals of War: The Falklands Conflict of 1982.* Princeton, NJ: Princeton University Press, 1991; Glasgow Media Group. *War and Peace News.* Milton Keynes: Open University Press, 1985; Morrison, D., and H. Tumbler. *Journalists at War: The Dynamics of News Reporting during the Falklands Conflict.* London: Sage, 1988; Rock, David. *Argentina, 1516–1987: From Spanish Colonization to Alfonsin.* Berkeley: University of California Press, 1989.

Fascism, Italian (1922–1943)

This Italian right-wing movement was founded by Benito Mussolini (1883–1945), who ruled Italy from 1922 to 1943. Italian Fascism relied heavily on propaganda to legitimize its rule and motivate its participants. Key areas of activity included control of the press and film and radio propaganda. Key techniques included promoting the cult of "il Duce," or the leader.

Mussolini's background as the founder of the newspaper *Populo d'Italia* in 1914 gave him a deep understanding of the importance of the press. Mussolini was adamant about preapproving interviews and articles that could be distributed only by the Agenzia Stefani. Il Duce also established a press office, which, from the mid-1920s onward, sent directives to the press and tried to exert control through financial subsidies. Journalists could retain their positions only after demonstrating loyalty to the new regime. During

World War II the *Giornale d'Italia* engaged in heavy propaganda. As the war progressed, Fascist propaganda became more pervasive in newspapers such as *Il Resto del Carlino, La Voce d'Italia, Il Secolo,* and others.

Mussolini created a mass "Fascist culture" through the use of photographs, symbols, and posters. Pictures of Il Duce launching grandiose public projects such as the "Battaglia del Grano" (Battle of the Grain), or followed by an army of blackshirts, symbol of Fascist virility, were widespread. Il Duce also favored monumental architecture, attempting to build a new Rome out of marble and concrete. As a result, Cinecittà, a Hollywood-inspired studio, and EUR, a new borough of Rome, reflected a mixture of neoclassical and futuristic architecture.

At the beginning of World War II Fascist propaganda artists used posters to depict Italy as victorious and all-powerful. As the Axis lost ground, Fascist propaganda changed direction, using images of a heroic country and a people being destroyed by ferocious monsters. They depicted Britain as a spider, with a death's head, about to trap Italy in its web; the United States and Russia were brutes, ready to bomb churches, kill children, and destroy art and culture. After Mussolini fled to the north in 1943, the last efforts of Fascist propaganda concentrated on promoting the new government and enticing young men to join Il Duce's army to fight the regime's traitors.

Despite intense efforts, Mussolini failed to control the film industry. Italian moviemakers escaped strict control and produced satires and farces that sharply contrasted with the artificial facade presented by the Fascist Party. In 1924 the Istituto Luce was created to promote images of Fascist culture. Run by Luciano de Feo, the institute produced documentaries and newsreels reflecting various achievements of the regime, such as the "Battaglia del Grano" and "Il Cammino degli Eroi," related to Italy's conquest of Ethiopia. A decree passed in 1926 made it mandatory to show a LUCE newsreel before any com-

mercial film. The institute lasted until the fall of Mussolini.

Prewar cinema was expected to help reform Italian taste and create a mass culture. In 1934 Mussolini established the Direzione Generale per la Cinematografia, headed by Luigi Freddi, which was designed to be a "form of positive, energetic encouragement aiming to encourage the spiritual and cultural growth of the Nation and the civilization." However, Italian cinematographers preferred farces and comedies, leading to the era of Italian filmmaking known as the "white telephones," named after a favorite prop. In 1941 the Direzione Generale created the slogan "Discipline, Imagination, Intelligence" to inspire filmmakers to create films that "represented for our people a weapon of faith, resistance, and serenity." Despite the regime's efforts, the film industry never fully responded to the call for propaganda, producing a total of only thirty-four propaganda films between 1930 and 1943.

In April 1924 Mussolini effected a major governmental reorganization that reflected his new commitment to the development and control of communications by consolidating the Department of Transportation, Posts, Telegraphs, and Telephones under the Ministry of Communications. In the same year, after denying Guglielmo Marconi (1874–1937) exclusive franchise over radio, Il Duce approved the formation of the first Italian broadcasting company, the Unione Radiofonica Italiana (URI). By 1927 URI was transformed into the Ente Italiana Audizioni Radiofoniche (EIAR), marking the end of Italian radio's experimental stage and its entry into the world as a mass communication medium.

Despite strict government controls in the 1920s, radio enjoyed a certain degree of freedom in the area of entertainment programming. The government created a department within the Ministry of Communications above EIAR, the Committee of Vigilance, whose aim was to supervise programming and improve technical development. Representing a wide spectrum of political, industrial, and artistic interests, its appointees were all loyal members of the Fascist Party. By 1935, on the eve of the Ethiopian war and Italy's anti-British broadcasts through Radio Bari and Radio Roma, radio was brought directly under the control of the state's Ministry of Press and Propaganda.

From 1935 to the beginning of World War II, Il Duce's desire to strengthen state control of radio was evident in the abolition of the Committee of Vigilance, which was no longer deemed fit to serve the regime's interests. In its place, with the intended goal of "simplifying" the committee, a royal decree created a four-member commission composed of two artistic experts, a technical expert, and a representative chosen by the government.

Mussolini used Radio Bari's short-wave broadcasts as an important tool to spread anti-British propaganda. Initially Radio Bari aimed primarily at establishing itself among the Arabs as a good source of news and entertainment. In 1935, however, Fascist propaganda took a drastic anti-British turn. Mussolini hoped to foster anti-Arab feelings and encourage a revolt that would divert attention from his imperialist goals, both of which proved unsuccessful. Radio Bari broadcasts, which incited Arabs to free themselves from their British oppressors, sharply contrasted with Mussolini's own repressive actions in Libya.

In 1937 the Ministry of Press and Propaganda was transformed into the Ministry of Popular Culture, whose Inspectorate for Radio Diffusion and Television was created to "coordinate all activities attributed to the ministry concerning radio diffusion and television." As the war intensified and Italy's defeats grew, audiences became increasingly skeptical of Il Duce's propaganda. Moreover, the government was concerned about foreign radio stations—especially London's BBC and Radio Moscow—broadcasting anti-Fascist propaganda. In 1935 the Ministry of Press and Propaganda had already forbidden Italians to listen to foreign radio shows, but it

wasn't until 1938 that the foreign stations became truly popular.

In 1940 the inspectorate was reorganized into three sections, one for internal affairs, one for foreign affairs, and one devoted to jamming anti-Fascist broadcasts. Starting on 23 June 1940, Italian radio broadcast primarily war information and commentaries, as well as domestic and foreign propaganda, devoting almost no airtime to entertainment. As the war progressed, it became increasingly difficult for EIAR commentators to deal with the increasing number of Italian defeats at sea and in North Africa, as well as to justify German aid. Most of these news items were either ignored or mentioned much later. Weak Italian propaganda was countered by accurate and powerful British counterpropaganda. Following landings in Italy in 1943, the Allies successfully used psychological-warfare techniques to speed up the surrender of Italian forces and to break the ideological hold of the Fascist regime.

Livia Bornigia

See also Civil War, Spanish; Hitler, Adolf; Italy; Mussolini, Benito

References: Arnold, W. V. *The Illusion of Victory: Propaganda and the Second World War.* New York: Peter Lang, 1998; MacDonald, C. "Radio Bari: Italian Wireless Propaganda in the Middle East and British Countermeasures, 1934–38." *Middle Eastern Studies* (1991): 195–207; Reeves, N. *The Power of Film Propaganda.* London: Cassell, 1999; Sassoon, D. *Contemporary Italy.* New York: Longman, 1986.

Film (Documentary)

The nonfiction documentary film dates back to the birth of cinema in 1895 and the Lumière brothers—Louis (1864–1948) and Auguste (1862–1954). The cinematograph could go virtually anywhere and did so, capturing footage of remote parts of the planet as well as everyday scenes from specific locales. Soon the subject matter turned to royal personages to give the new medium greater respectability. The feature film came to dominate filmgoing, leaving the documentary to occupy space on the program with the news-reel. The history of the documentary, then, is often—though by no means always—that of a poor country cousin.

Robert Flaherty (1884–1954) in the United States and Dziga Vertov (1896–1951) in the Soviet Union made important types of documentaries in the 1920s. Flaherty enjoyed genuine commercial success with *Nanook of the North* (1922), a film about Inuit life in the Canadian north, with charming visual touches that leave the viewer with a pleasurable feeling—not always the case with the earnest, humorless documentarian. Vertov (a pseudonym meaning "spinning top") made a monthly series of *Kinopravda* (Film Truth) based on daily events, such as a trolley being repaired or needy children being helped in a hospital. The editing was intended to emphasize meaning through juxtaposition. In Britain the father of the documentary was John Grierson (1898–1972), who remains the most eloquent propagandist of the documentary to date. Grierson was more spokesman and coordinator than filmmaker; his support made possible such memorable social documentaries as *Housing Problems* (1935) by Edgar Anstey (1907–1987) and Arthur Elton (1906–1973). In the United States Roosevelt's New Deal program presented its solution to the problems of erosion and conservation in two films by Pare Lorentz (1905–1992), *The Plow That Broke the Plains* (1936) and *The River* (1937).

In Germany the documentary took on feature-length form in the extraordinary films of Leni Riefenstahl (1902–). Her *Triumph of the Will* (1935) glorified Hitler and remains of value to every political handler assigned to make a candidate look good. Her camera team was skilled in using the camera in motion to give the feeling of action to essentially static events, such as 100,000 party faithful standing at attention, listening to a long-winded speech. Her *Olympia* (1938) remains the finest sports film of all time; the editing of the concluding high-diving sequence is one of the great moments of filmmaking. It is im-portant to remember that the documentary filmmaker need not represent the spirit of the left; many prominent documentary filmmakers have worked for the right.

World War II was a golden age for documentary film, much of it either military in subject matter or concerned with issues of peace. Frank Capra's (1897–1991) Why We Fight series explained official American war aims to soldiers and, in some cases, civilians as well. Capra's series used the techniques of compilation (the recutting of other films, often from an enemy source) in combination with a strident commentary to sell the meaning of the series title to all who would view the finished product. Some documentaries about World War II came later, most memorably Alain Resnais's *Night and Fog* (1955) about the Holocaust. Erik Barnouw's *Hiroshima-Nagasaki, August 1945* (1970) is a brilliant compilation of footage shot on location by Japanese cameramen just after the dropping of the first atomic bombs.

The late 1950s saw the rise of the documentary in a new medium—television—and the use of hand-held cameras to offer a seeming authenticity in films about social problems, what we remember as cinema verité. A striking use of such techniques is seen in Claude Lanzmann's (1938–) *Shoah* (1985), a nine-hour film about the Holocaust that nevertheless was commercially released. The advent of the mini–video camera in the 1980s permitted the filmmaker to shoot and edit the final product. Thanks to cable and satellite, inexpensive documentaries are produced today on a variety of subjects—some mundane, some highly charged exposés; some thoughtful; some not.

In the United States Ken Burns (1953–) has become the resident documentary filmmaker for the Public Broadcasting System (PBS). His miniseries *The Civil War* (1990) attracted an enormous number of viewers, and is used extensively in classrooms. His miniseries on the history of jazz was careful not to get embroiled in the more recent history of the subject, where exposing the racism of whites is just one of several controversial issues.

David Culbert

See also Capra, Frank; Film (Nazi Germany): Film (Newsreels); Grierson, John; Indonesia; *The Plow That Broke the Plains;* Riefenstahl, Leni; Russia; *Triumph of the Will;* Why We Fight

References: Barnouw, Erik. *Documentary.* 2d ed.; New York: Oxford, 1992; Cumings, Bruce. *War and Television.* New York: Verso, 1992; Nichols, Bill. *Representing Reality: Issues and Concepts in Documentary.* Bloomington: Indiana University Press, 1991; Toplin, Robert Brent, ed. *Ken Burns's "The Civil War": Historians Respond.* New York: Oxford, 1996.

Film (Feature)

The feature film is the twentieth century's great contribution to leisure-time activity, a type of entertainment that has proved popular in every country on the planet. Motion pictures may be said to have begun in 1895; soon the film turned to fictional plots, aided by the illusion of movement created by projecting a strip of film onto a screen. Early filmmakers in every country worked to improve the style and the content of what was at first escapist fare for working-class audiences. Soon films became longer, movie theaters grander, and plots and editing more sophisticated. This process occurred in every country. In the United States, by the time production facilities had moved from the East Coast to Hollywood (1915 at the latest) the feature film assumed the form it possessed in its heyday (the 1930s and 1940s), aided by the arrival of sound in 1927. Feature film is a wonderful medium for the propagandist. Every feature film—good or bad; lavish or spartan in its production values; frivolous or earnest—is loaded with cultural propaganda for the country or society that produced it. Moreover, feature films can also be overt vehicles for specific content sought by the film director, slipped in by the scriptwriter, or specifically called for by the sponsoring agency.

Notorious examples include D. W. Griffith's (1857–1948) *Birth of a Nation* (1915),

which transformed moviegoing in America. Griffith was able to charge more for this lavish, lengthy film, which called for pleasure palaces rather than dingy storefronts. The respectable sort flocked to see his brilliant achievement, with editing skills still worthy of note. But this was a film with a virulent message of racism: the South lost the Civil War and was ruined during federal military occupation (1865–1877, known as Reconstruction) because blacks were given control of a world for which they lacked the intellectual ability. Once in power, blacks turned to sex and liquor, resulting in chaos. It was the Ku Klux Klan that saved the prostrate South. This incendiary message may not have persuaded every viewer, but the film literally served as the inspiration for the revival of the Ku Klux Klan in the 1920s, a movement that eventually numbered some five million members. Anyone studying race relations in the United States in the twentieth century cannot ignore the impact of Griffith's deeply flawed masterpiece. One might seriously argue that the South lost the Civil War but won the battle for the hearts and minds of Americans in the first decades of the twentieth century thanks to this film.

Nazi Germany provides another notorious example of a feature film capable of delivering an explicit racist message within a feature film with high production values and plenty of sex and violence—the staples of escapist fare. *Jud Süss* (1940) was one of the most successful feature films produced in Nazi Germany between 1933 and 1945.

A third example of the propaganda potential of the feature film is instructive for different reasons. In Hollywood's heyday there were five major studios—Loew's (including MGM), Paramount, Twentieth Century-Fox, Warner Brothers, and RKO—all of them integrated companies that not only produced motion pictures but distributed them worldwide and owned chains of theaters where distribution of a particular studio's films were guaranteed. During World War II, after the German invasion of the Soviet Union in

1941, each of the major studios agreed to promote friendship between the United States and the Soviet Union by releasing a feature film with a Russian theme. In 1943 Warner Brothers released *Mission to Moscow,* a sort of docudrama in which Joseph Davies (1876–1958), the former ambassador to the Soviet Union, related what had happened to him while stationed in Moscow. The result was a ridiculous puff piece glorifying Stalin. It created an uproar, its silly falsifications were exposed, and it flopped at the box office.

Audience response is essential to understanding the propaganda content of the feature film, both in Hollywood's heyday and today. The propagandist is concerned with numbers of tickets sold and evidence of mass attitudes shaped or changed by a particular film. Social scientists have long known that this presumes a sort of "magic bullet," in which general attitudes on a particular question are changed by a powerful film. This is asking more than a feature film is capable of. But any feature film that attracts a large number of viewers is valuable to the student of propaganda, who wants to see how and in what ways a popular feature film suggests the general shaping of societal values. Certainly feature films can shape attitudes and dictate appropriate behavior or modes of attire—and sometimes their impact can prove even greater.

David Culbert

See also *All Quiet on the Western Front;* Australia; Balkans; *Battleship Potemkin; The Birth of a Nation;* Capra, Frank; *Casablanca;* Eisenstein, Sergei; Greece; *The Green Berets; Mission to Moscow*

References: Ellwood, David, ed. *The Movies as History: Visions of the Twentieth Century.* Stroud, UK: Sutton, 2000; Harpole, Charles, ed. *History of the American Cinema.* 10 vols. New York: Scribner's, 1990–2000; Rosenstone, Robert. *Revisioning History: Film and the Construction of a New Past.* Princeton, NJ: Princeton University Press, 1995.

Film (Nazi Germany)

Hitler (1889–1945) and Goebbels (1897–1945) shared a common interest in film. However, the film industry represented a number of structural, economic, and artistic problems for the Nazis. Indicative of the high estimation of film is the fact that the Reich Film Chamber was founded by Goebbels some months before the Reich Chamber of Culture, of which it became a part. The Nazis also regulated film finance by means of a Filmkreditbank, which assisted officially approved films. A Reich Cinema Law, introduced in February 1934, created a new "positive" censorship by which the state encouraged the production of National Socialist films.

An analysis of the different type of films produced during the Third Reich reveals a good deal about Goebbels's *Filmpolitik.* Of the 1,097 feature films produced, only about one sixth were overtly propagandistic, with direct political content. The majority of these films were *Staatsauftragsfilme* (state-commissioned films). Such films were classified as *Tendenzfilme,* that is, films that exhibited "strong National Socialist tendencies." Of the entire production of feature films, half were either love stories or comedies, and a quarter were dramatic films like crime thrillers or musicals. Yet all went through the precensorship process and all were associated with the National Socialist ideology in that they were produced and performed in accordance with the propagandistic aims of the period.

Surprisingly, little or no overall pattern to German film propaganda is discernible. A trilogy of films (*SA-Mann Brand, Hitlerjunge Quex,* and *Hans Westmar*) eulogized the *Kampfzeit* (time of struggle) and glorified the movement and its martyrs in 1933. Similarly, in 1940 three films (*Die Rothschilds, Jud Süss, Der ewige Jude* [*The Wandering Jew*]) intended to prepare the German people for the "Final Solution" appeared. The year 1941 marked the highest concentration of *Staatsauftragsfilme* produced at the bidding of the Propaganda Ministry. Goebbels's main concern was to keep the important themes of Nazi ideology constantly before the public. These films in-

Leni Riefenstahl, in an elevator used for filming crowd scenes from above, at a Nazi Party rally in Nuremberg, 1934. (Courtesy of David Culbert)

cluded *Das alte recht* (The Old Right, 1934), which justified the state's hereditary farm law; *Ich für Dich—Du für mich* (I for You—You for Me, 1934), which emphasized the importance of "blood and soil"; *Der Herrscher* (The Ruler, 1937), which provided analogies with Hitler's teachings and called for strong leadership; *Sensationsprozess Casilla* (The Sensational Trial of Casilla, 1939), a work of anti-American propaganda designed to ridicule the American way of life; and *Heimkehr* (Homecoming, 1941), which presented the sad fate of German nationals living abroad. Goebbels chose to keep prestigious film propaganda at its maximum level of effectiveness by spacing out the films—except, that is, for newsreels ("Deutsche Wochenschau"), which depended on their ability to capture the immediacy of events. Full-length documentaries such as Leni Riefenstahl's *Triumph des Willens* (Triumph of the Will, 1935) and *Olympia* (1938) were all the more effective for their comparative rarity.

This strategy illustrates Goebbels's desire to mix entertainment with propaganda. He encouraged the production of feature films that reflected the ambience of National Socialism instead of loudly proclaiming its ideology. The results of such a *Filmpolitik* were a monopolistic system of control and organization that stressed profits, increased audience attendance, and resulted in an extremely high standard of technical proficiency. In the final analysis, however, it contributed little stylistically to the history of the cinema.

David Welch

See also Germany; Goebbels, Joseph; Hitler, Adolf; *Jud Süss;* Riefenstahl, Leni; RMVP; *Triumph of the Will;* World War II (Germany)

References: Leiser, E. *Nazi Cinema.* London: Secker and Warburg, 1974; Welch, David. *Propaganda and the German Cinema, 1933–45.* London: I. B. Tauris, 2002.

Film (Newsreels)

Newsreels consisted of a diverse selection of news stories contained on a single reel of film. They were generally shown in movie theaters either weekly or semiweekly between 1908 and the late 1970s. Newsreels were silent until the late 1920s, with any message beyond purely pictorial information being relayed through titles. With the arrival of sound in the late 1920s, they assumed their most familiar form, consisting of background music and an authoritative, unseen commentator. In the era before television, they were a powerful medium for the communication (and suppression) of news in moving images, and their impact on millions of viewers was considerable.

News stories had been a staple of moving pictures since their inception in the mid-1890s, but the first attempt to bring together a selection of such news stories on a single reel occurred in France with "Pathé Fait-Divers"(1908), which subsequently became "Pathé Journal." The Pathé firm dominated world film distribution at this time; its "Animated Gazette" followed in Britain in 1910, and Pathé's "Weekly" in the United States in 1911. Many competitors emerged, with Pathé and its French rival Gaumont establishing a news presence in many territories. Newspaper interests began to add newsreels to their empires, notably William Randolph Hearst (1863–1951), the producer of "International News" and later "Hearst Metrotone News" in the United States and Lord Beaverbrook (1897–1964), onetime owner of "Pathé Gazette" in Britain. Starting in the 1930s, although the names of Pathé and Gaumont retained their presence and importance, the Hollywood studios Universal, Paramount, and Fox (owners of Movietone) controlled the major newsreels.

The newsreels became notorious for their light approach to the news. While Oscar Levant's (1906–1972) oft-quoted comment that the newsreel was "a series of catastrophes, ended by a fashion show" is unjust, the attitude of the newsreels toward the news was undeniably passive. Forced by the necessary delays of film processing and the weekly or biweekly release schedule to follow the newspapers in the supplying of news stories, the newsreels were most often content to be purveyors of moving pictures of what had already been read as news in other media. Their most insidious effect was support of the status quo. Commentators critical of the newsreels in the 1930s generally accused them of a right-wing bias, and only "Paramount News" in the United States and Britain did not shy away from controversy and a less supine attitude toward prevailing orthodoxies. The regular excuse of the newsreels was that they were an entertainment medium. There was pressure by exhibitors, who wanted nothing controversial added to the overall movie package; given the small portion of that program occupied by the newsreels, they were in no position to protest.

Direct government intervention in newsreel content first occurred with the arrival of World War I. Officialdom gradually recognized the growing popularity and power of the movies; in mid-1917 the French created an official newsreel entitled "Annales de la Guerre," closely followed by the British, who took over an existing newsreel to create the "War Office Official Topical Budget," later called the "Pictorial News (Official)" under Lord Beaverbrook's (1879–1964) Ministry of Information. Following its entry into the war, the United States followed suit with the "Official War Review," produced by George Creel's (1876–1953) Committee on War Information.

During World War II, governmental control of the newsreels was present in varying degrees in different countries. In Britain initial plans for official control through a single newsreel were fought off by the newsreel companies, but a pooling or rotation ("rota") system controlled the footage that was supplied, and all newsreels were subject to official censorship. In the United States a similar rota system was introduced, with all footage censored and processed by the war and navy departments. The U.S. government financed its own newsreel, "United Newsreel," which ran from 1942 until 1945, for overseas exhibition, taking material from the five commercial newsreels. Similarly, in Britain the Newsreel Association produced the composite "British News" for consular and British Council use, which ran from 1940 to 1967. In Germany official control was absolute. Newsreels had been used to prepare the German people for war, and in 1940 all newsreel production was reorganized under the title "Deutsche Wochenschau." Goebbels first used the newsreel to glorify early Nazi triumphs and then to present a sanitized picture of the war. Public resistance to what Nicholas Reeves has described as the "remorseless optimism" of the newsreel demonstrated the ultimate futility of offering news that ran counter to people's experience and understanding of events. Following Germany's defeat, the American and British authorities created a reeducation newsreel, "Welt im Film," for exhibition in Germany, which ran until 1950.

Newsreels in the United States and particularly in Britain enjoyed their greatest hour during World War II; they were eloquent, informative, and committed, reflecting a medium that understood that its hour had come. In the postwar years the newsreels unsuccessfully tried to combine this newfound seriousness of purpose with the entertainment values that were part of the total package that the movies offered. The concerns of the Cold War were juxtaposed with beauty pageants and horse races—both topics that the newsreels presented best. The competition presented by live television of the 1950s, together with a shrinking movie audience, spelled their end. They continued in some locations until the 1970s, often by using color to differentiate their product from television news, but they had descended to reporting trivia. In their time, however, they represented a powerful and influential medium, and the existence of extensive newsreel libraries and the use of archival footage in television documentaries ensures that the newsreels will continue to shape our view of the recent past.

Luke McKernan

See also Britain; Canada; Civil War, Spanish; Fascism, Italian; Latin America; Mussolini, Benito; Reeducation; RMVP; World War I; World War II (Britain); World War II (Germany); World War II (Russia); World War II (United States)

References: Fielding, Raymond. *The American Newsreel, 1911–1967*. Norman: University of Oklahoma Press, 1972; ———. *The March of Time, 1935–1951*. New York: Oxford University Press, 1978; Reeves, Nicholas. *The Power of Film Propaganda: Myth or Reality?* London: Cassell, 1999.

Flagg, James Montgomery (1877–1960)

Flagg, the American artist who in 1917 created the famous Uncle Sam poster ("I want you for U.S. Army"), was born in New York. By World War I he had become a popular magazine illustrator, working for such publications as *Harper's Weekly* and *Cosmopolitan,* and had gained a reputation as a man-about-town. His personal life was colorful and often scandalous. He also illustrated books of comic poems and produced satirical portraits of the famous faces of his day. With the entry of the United States into World War I in 1917, Flagg accepted work from the governor of New York and joined the Division of Pictorial Publicity, a New York–based voluntary group of artists assembled by illustrator Charles Dana Gibson (1867–1944) to create posters for the federal government. Flagg modeled his famous Uncle Sam poster on a British poster of 1914 featuring Secretary for War Lord Kitchener (1850–1916). Flagg used his own face as the model for Uncle Sam. He also created the poster bearing the caption "Tell that to the Marines," which depicted a man responding to a newspaper account of German atrocities by putting on his coat—presumably to enlist.

In addition to creating some forty-odd posters, Flagg's contributions to the war effort included work on propaganda films for the Marine Corps and the Red Cross. He also offered his services as a portrait artist free of charge to anyone who purchased a thousand-dollar Liberty Bond. After the war he thrived as a society portrait painter. In the 1930s he created Forestry Service and polio-related posters. During World War II he produced recruitment posters (including a more muscular version of his 1917 Uncle Sam), and a reelection poster for President Franklin Delano Roosevelt (1882–1945).

Nicholas J. Cull

See also CPI; Posters; Uncle Sam; World War I
References: Flagg, James Montgomery. *Roses and Buckshot*. New York: Putnam, 1946; Meyer, Susan E. *James Montgomery Flagg.* New York: Watson-Guptill, 1974; Paret, Peter, Beth Irwin Lewis, and Paul Paret. *Persuasive Images: Posters of War and Revolution*. Princeton, NJ: Princeton University Press, 1992.

France

Propaganda has been a factor in French society, religion, politics, and war since 1500. In those five centuries the role of the vox populi has grown, as have the propaganda channels and techniques that address it. The printing press entered French life in the sixteenth century. Mass-produced books, pamphlets, placards, journals, newspapers, and cartoons were all useful as propaganda tools, as were photography, film, and broadcasting in the nineteenth and twentieth centuries. Whatever the cause—religion, rebellion, absolutism, revolution, reaction, republicanism, socialism, laissez faire, democracy, fascism, or patriotism—the purpose was the same: to appeal to the crowd in support of a particular position either for or against the status quo.

Protestantism emerged in France during the reign of Francis I (1515–1547). Dissenters posted placards in Paris and across the country attacking the "abuses" of the papal mass and distributed books, tracts, and woodcuts such as "Muster of the Archers at the Popinjay" and "The Great Marmite [pot] Overturned." The church responded in kind with censorship, sermons, and bloody persecution of heretics, probably in league with the parliament of Paris but not with the crown. Even Marguerite of Navarre (1492–1549), the king's independent-minded sister, was attacked for daring to question clerical dogma. A satirical play staged at the College de Navarre depicted her as preaching heresy and tormenting all those who would not heed her. Francis and his heirs failed to resolve the religious conflict, and the "war of words" often became one of bloody mayhem as well.

The 1560s, 1570s, and 1580s were characterized by Catholic-Protestant civil war, including assassinations and massacres. Both sides appealed to the crowd through propaganda. François Hotman's (1524–1590) *Francogallia* argued that France had been enslaved by popery, while Louis Dorléans's (1542–1629) *Advertisement of the English Catholics to the French Catholics* was a call to arms to the Catholic League. In 1589 Henry IV (1553–1610) ascended the throne as a Protestant. His struggle with the league, which controlled Paris and a number of other cities, went on for years, propaganda playing a central role on both sides. Paris printers were well paid to produce material that extolled Catholicism while excoriating Protestantism and King Henry. An example was an antiheretical placard that read: "Hang and strangle them / So that death can strap them in / And dissolve them into the earth / Because they haven't wanted to live / According to the Church of Saint Peter." For the far larger illiterate population, engravings, paintings, orations from the pulpit, and street demonstrations were used to advocate the same thing.

Meanwhile, Henry's propagandists presented him to the French as a chivalric, courageous, patriotic absolute ruler who worked for the well-being of all of the people. Miniature portraits of the king were sold in the Latin Quarter in Paris to rouse Parisians for Henry and against the league. Propagandists also produced satirical pieces like "Pleasant Satire or the Efficacy of Catholicon," in which league zealots confessed their sordid motives when fed the wonder drug "Catholicon." Unable to overcome the league through propaganda or war, Henry "recanted" his Protestantism. This was his ultimate propaganda ploy. Taking communion at Notre Dame gained him recognition by all as the king of France but represented no genuine change of heart regarding religion. Paris was "worth a mass" if it fulfilled a vital political necessity.

Governments and dissidents used propaganda to promote political and social action throughout the seventeenth and eighteenth centuries. Royal governments patronized newspapers such as the *Gazette de France,* the *Journal des Savans,* and *Mémoires de Trévoux,* which reciprocated by promoting state policies. Dissidents sometimes spoke out in the theater, as in the play *La Fausse Prude,* of uncertain authorship, allegedly a satire on Madame de Maintenon, the mistress of Louis XIV (1643–1715); the state censored it immediately. Dissident propaganda was even more evident in the writings of the *philosophes.* Rousseau (1712–1778) advocated social and political improvement for the people and coined the revolutionary slogan "Liberté, égalité, fraternité." Voltaire (1694–1778) attacked the ecclesiastical establishment. Beaumarchais (1732–1799) poked fun at the privileged classes in *Le Mariage de Figaro.* Diderot (1713–1784) and the *Encyclopédie* (1751–1772) recognized the importance of propaganda in implementing change. After the early volumes set the writers on a collision course with church and state, Diderot's coeditor d'Alembert (1717–1783) resigned. In 1753 *La Grand Remonstrance,* an attack on l'ancien régime, sold twenty thousand copies in three weeks. Such material encouraged popular resentment of a government unresponsive to change and of a society in which the "haves" were indifferent to the "have nots."

In 1788, a time of national economic crisis, Louis XVI (r. 1774–1792) summoned the first Estates General in nearly two hundred years, opening the door for propaganda advocating populist change and even revolution.

Since only members of the Third Estate were elected, the opposition began circulating guides for writing "cahiers de doléances" (grievance petitions) and published the pamphlet by l'Abbé Sieyès (1748–1836), *Qu'est-ce que le Tiers Etat?* (What Is the Third Estate?). Meanwhile, in Paris speeches, pamphlets, and newspapers were stirring the poor against the regime. Revolution soon followed, beginning with the fall of the Bastille on 14 July 1789, in itself a piece of symbolic propaganda. There followed cartoons depicting revolutionary women urinating on the crowned heads of Europe and "mooning" royalist soldiers, mass rallies on the Champ de Mars to celebrate the people's victory, and extremist newspapers, such as *Le Père Duchesne* and *L'Ami du Peuple,* which encouraged mob violence and glorified revolutionary soldiers. The latter were the subject of some three thousand revolutionary songs; one of these was Rouget de L'Isle's (1760–1836) "La Marseillaise," which evolved into one of the first national anthems in history. Meanwhile, artists like Jacques-Louis David (1748–1825) illustrated the revolution and its imperial aftermath with cartoons of fallen aristocrats and heroic paintings of everyone from Danton (1759–1794) to Napoleon Bonaparte (1769–1821).

Bonaparte represented the final stage in the revolutionary process. He emerged in 1804 as Emperor Napoleon, modeling himself on Julius Caesar. Napoleon used propaganda songs, fireworks, parades, public balls, annual celebrations of his coronation, and flag ceremonies to celebrate his famous battles, while patriotic theater and the press served to glorify his reign and promote patriotism for his endless wars. He also promoted Italian and Polish nationalism as weapons against Austria and Russia and supported a general European repudiation of Britain. Construction of the Arc de Triomphe began during his reign. Patterned after the Arch of Constantine in Rome, it was an excellent example of "monument propaganda."

Propaganda played a central role in subsequent revolutions in France. In 1830 an Or-

léanist press helped Louis Philippe (1773–1850) replace Charles X (1757–1836); he appeared on a balcony of the Hôtel de Ville draped in the revolutionary tricolor flag. In 1848 an anti-Orléanist press (in which Honoré Daumier [1808–1879] caricatured the king by giving his visage the shape of a pear), public orations, and revolutionary art helped replace Louis Philippe with the Second Republic. Louis Napoleon (1808–1873), nephew of Bonaparte, used populist propaganda to create support for his overthrow of that republic and established the Second Empire. As Emperor Napoleon III he played on the heroic, Caesarian image of his uncle, which was maintained and promoted through the press, official ceremonies, Paris-based world's fairs in 1855 and 1867, and through his transformation of the city of Paris into a New Rome. (He once remarked: "I want to be a second Augustus.") However, Napoleon's failures overseas, as in Mexico, and his relations with the Austrian Empire and Prussia, gave his Caesarian propaganda an increasingly hollow ring. The anti-Napoleonic journal *Lanterne,* with a circulation of five hundred thousand, was only one example of propaganda disseminated against him in the latter part of the 1860s.

The Franco-Prussian war of 1870–1871 was partly the result of a clever piece of Prussian propaganda intended to inflame French opinion. The war ended Napoleon's reign, saw Germany annex Alsace-Lorraine, and inspired the Paris-based Commune uprising in March 1871. The Communards took control of the city and disseminated propaganda that demeaned their enemies, proclaimed their own heroism, and denounced any who attempted to betray the Commune. The government of the newly formed Third Republic spread anti-Communard propaganda across France that justified the bloody violence used in crushing the Commune in June. This included a fake photograph depicting Communards summarily executing French officers, clergy, and civilians lined up against a brick wall.

The Third Republic's propaganda sought to minimize the defeat of 1871, romanticize the French empire, and to call for *la revanche*. As reparation for its treatment of the Commune, the state built the basilica of Sacre Coeur in Paris, which bears the inscription "Gallia Paenitens" (France Penitent) on the domed ceiling. Populist General George Boulanger (1837–1891) found himself discredited by a government-inspired "whispering campaign." In the press *Les Droits de l'Homme* and *L'Humanité* called for socialism, *La Citoyenne* advocated women's rights, and the *Confédération Général du Travail* advocated trade unionism by threatening violent strikes. *Le Petit Journal* and *La Croix* blamed the political failings of the Third Republic on Jews. Posters depicted Jews as freaks, while street mobs shouted anti-Jewish slogans and the press lauded Catholic leaders. During the Dreyfus Affair, a toy gallows with a noose around the neck of Alfred Dreyfus (c. 1859–1935) and a toy-size Émile Zola (1840–1902) with removable trousers sold well. Despite this, Zola's pro-Dreyfus article "J'Accuse" had sold three hundred thousand copies. Dreyfus was tried and convicted but was eventually exonerated.

World war and extremist politics dominated France in the first half of the twentieth century. World War I opened with the populace generally favoring war with Germany. Poster and press propaganda encouraged this by promoting patriotism ("pour la Patrie"), France as the defender of democracy, public support for loans needed to pay for the war, and recovery of Alsace-Lorraine, as well as by depicting "les Boches" (slang for Germans) in the pages of *La Liberté, Le Gaulois, Le Matin, L'Echo de Paris,* and *L'Action Française* in particular as perpetrators of atrocities. Popular enthusiasm waned after the slaughter at Verdun, and pacifist propaganda began to circulate— probably secretly financed by Germany.

Film now entered the scene as a propaganda tool. The Service Photographique et Cinématographique de l'Armée oversaw newsreel filmmaking and commissioned private filmmakers to make propaganda films for public consumption. Film also was an important propaganda tool for leftists and pacifists in the 1930s, celebrated examples of which are René Clair's *A Nous la liberté* (1931), Jean Renoir's *La Marseillaise* (1938), and Abel Gance's *J'Accuse!* (1938).

World War II presented a dramatically different experience. France fell in 1940, with Germany occupying northern and western France, including Paris. The profascist Vichy state was established under the leadership of World War I icon Marshal Philippe Pétain. Vichy propaganda attacked Jews and promoted an anti-Paris view of a France returned to its rural roots. Vichy also presented the British as war criminals, Pétain as a hero, and the Germans as saviors of Europe from bolshevism. Collaborationists in occupied France published profascist newspapers, speeches, and posters. Meanwhile, the resistance put out such clandestine newspapers as *Pantagruel* and *Combat,* slipped pamphlets and tracts—some written by Jean-Paul Sartre (1904–1980) and Albert Camus (1913–1960)—into letterboxes, and wrote anti-Nazi graffiti on posters advertising German films. The BBC encouraged the French people with "Ici Londres" broadcasts of war news and speeches by Free French leaders.

Since 1945 France has experienced a shaky period of economic recovery, political crises, colonial wars in Vietnam and Algeria, the emergence of the anti-immigrant National Front, the bicentennial of the French Revolution (which met with a mixed response), and development of the European Community. Propaganda was a constant in all such developments. Examples include American economic propaganda in association with Marshall Plan aid, which was countered by French Communist propaganda claiming that Coca-Cola was part of a U.S. spy network; Charles de Gaulle (1890–1970) using radio broadcasts to undercut Secret Army Organization (OAS) opposition to ending the war in Algeria; university students temporarily paralyzing Paris through mass demonstrations against the war in Vietnam; the National Front railing against immigrants and other foreigners; farmers clogging roadways with tractors to protest the government's agricultural policies; and the government itself using the press and the broadcast media to gain public support for French involvement in the European Union. Traditional propaganda tools were supplemented first by television and then by the Internet.

Robert Cole

See also Art; Cultural Propaganda; David, Jacques-Louis; Exhibitions and World's Fairs; Film (Newsreels); "The Internationale"; "J'Accuse"; "La Marseillaise"; Marshall Plan; Mexico; Napoleon; Novel; Pacific/Oceania; Paine, Thomas; Peace and Antiwar Movements (1500–1945); Portraiture; Revolution, French; Spain; Vietnam; Women's Movement: European; World War I
References: Greengrass, Mark. *France in the Age of Henri IV: The Struggle for Stability.* London: Longman, 1984; Horne, Alistair. *The Terrible Year: The Paris Commune, 1871.* London: Macmillan, 1971; Klaits, Joseph. *Printed Propaganda under Louis XIV: Absolute Monarchy and Public Opinion.* Princeton, NJ: Princeton University Press, 1976; McMillan, James F. *Dreyfus to De Gaulle: Politics and Society in France, 1898–1969.* London: Edward Arnold, 1985; Rude, George. *The Crowd in the French Revolution.* Oxford: Oxford University Press, 1959.

Freedom Train (1947–1949)

This exhibition, mounted in a touring train, featured the key documents of American political history and toured the United States between 1947 and 1949. The Freedom Train was one of the most successful examples of patriotic propaganda, rallying American self-confidence for the Cold War. The train was the brainchild of Attorney General Tom Clark (1889–1977), who sought to encourage a reawakening of American civic virtues. Congress provided funds and additional private support came from the specially incorporated American Heritage Foundation, the railroad industry, and the Advertising Council. Powered by a red, white, and blue engine

(no. 1776), exhibition cars carried 150 documents reflecting freedom and the triumph of democracy, including Thomas Jefferson's original draft of the Declaration of Independence, key documents dating from the Civil War, a selection of historic banners, and such recent documents as the articles of surrender signed by Japan in 1945. The train's visit to the Deep South prompted controversy since Southern railroads were still racially segregated. The African American poet Langston Hughes (1902–1967) commented on this in a protest poem called "Freedom Train," which was first published in the *New Republic.* Hughes asked, "When it stops in Mississippi will it be made plain / Everybody's got the right to board the Freedom Train." As things turned out, the train skipped Birmingham, Alabama, and Memphis, Tennessee. It was featured in popular songs and comic strips and sparked imitations in Kentucky and New York relating to state government documents. The train stopped rolling in 1949 and the final display of its contents at the National Archives closed in late 1950.

Nicholas J. Cull

See also Advertising; Cold War; Exhibitions and World's Fairs; Revolution, American, and War of Independence
References: Fried, Richard M. *The Russians Are Coming! The Russians Are Coming! Pageantry and Patriotism in Cold War America.* Oxford: Oxford University Press, 1998; Lucas, Scott. *Freedom's War.* Manchester: Manchester University Press, 1999; Hughes, Langston. *Selected Poems.* New York: Knopf, 1973.

Friedan, Betty (1921–)

A feminist writer, Betty Naomi Friedan was born in Peoria, Illinois, the daughter of a Jewish furrier. Friedan graduated from Smith College in 1942, settling uneasily into the life of suburban mother, trying to find fulfillment in raising her three children. Her unease with such "domestic bliss" led to a series of articles and the 1963 best-seller, *The Feminine Mystique,* a key text in the American feminist movement. Friedan defined woman only as "husband's wife, children's mother, server of physical needs of husband, children, home, and never as person defining herself by her own actions in society." In 1966 Friedan founded the National Organization for Women (NOW), though her forceful personality was ill suited to the sharing of authority with other feminists and she eventually lost her position in the organization. Friedan worked hard to assure the passage of the Equal Rights Amendment (ERA), but on 30 June 1982 it failed to be adopted by the requisite three-quarters majority of the states. Friedan's best-seller bears a curious relationship to demographics: far from American women being forced back into the home as homemaker after 1945, by 1960 twice as many women were employed as had been in 1940; two fifths of all women over the age of sixteen held jobs. Nevertheless, Friedan's impassioned plea undoubtedly encouraged women seeking professional careers to act on their desires. Friedan, who divorced in 1969, has been featured recently in *Modern Maturity,* house organ for millions of American retirees. Today, she publicly claims to have found fulfillment in the success of her children and grandchildren.

David Culbert

See also Abortion; Women's Movement: Second-Wave/Feminism

References: Friedan, Betty. *The Feminine Mystique.* New York: Dell, 1984; Hull, N. E. H., and Peter Charles Hoffer. *Roe v. Wade: The Abortion Rights Controversy in American History.* Lawrence: University Press of Kansas, 2001.

Funerals

Rites of passage such as birth, coming-of-age, marriage, and death have been used to transmit propaganda messages. Funerals, in particular, have become associated with the dissemination of ideas and ideals, serving as reminders of individual worth while also providing common rallying points and potent symbols of nation, duty, and power. Panegyrics were often composed to accompany the funeral rites, providing summations of the qualities of the deceased. Funerals were a key part of the European monarchy. As with coronations, the funeral similarly provided the opportunity to list the titles and honors of the monarch. In this way contentious claims were often kept alive. All English monarchs, for example, were also buried as monarchs of France up until the reign of Queen Victoria (1819–1901). Possibly the most brilliant list of titles belonged to Emperor Charles V (1500–1558). At his funeral it was intoned that he was king of the Romans; emperor of the Holy Roman Empire; *semper augustus;* king of Spain, Sicily, Jerusalem, the Balearic Islands, the Canary Islands, the Indies, and the mainland on the far side of the Atlantic; archduke of Austria; duke of Burgundy, Brabant, Styria, Carinthia, Carniola, Luxembourg, Limburg, Athens, and Patras; count of Habsburg, Flanders, and Tyrol; count palatine of Burgundy, Brabant, Hainault, Pfirt, and Rousillion; landgrave of Alsace; count of Swabia; and lord of Asia and Africa. Occasionally states staged "antifunerals" to desecrate the memory of an individual. Charles II (1630–1685) ordered the exhumation of Oliver Cromwell (1599–1658) and the removal of his head, which was placed on a spike on the gatehouse of London Bridge as a warning to all who would defy the monarch. In twentieth-century Argentina Eva Perón (1919–1952) first received a lavish public funeral marked by frenzied mourning from her adoring public, followed by an "antifuneral" as her body was stolen, hidden, and buried in exile. She was granted a second state funeral in the 1970s when the body was finally returned to Argentina.

By the nineteenth century, with the growth of the modern nation-state, funerals had become important celebrations of the nation as well as the individual. In this way, famous commoners could achieve a funeral akin to those reserved for royalty. London saw three impressive state funerals in the nineteenth century, each of which commemorated much more than the deceased. In 1805 Lord Nelson's (1758–1805) body was transported from the Royal Navy College at Greenwich, where it had lain in state, down the Thames to St. Paul's Cathedral. A huge crowd gathered to witness the funeral procession and filled the cathedral to capacity. The whole ceremony served to emphasize Britain's naval might and its unity with God. When the greatest British soldier of the Napoleonic Wars died, the capital witnessed similar scenes. The Duke of Wellington (1769–1852) was accorded a full state funeral in 1852. He lay in state at the Royal Hospital, Chelsea, where so many people filed past his coffin that two mourners were accidentally crushed to death. Once again the funeral was used to stress Britain's martial prowess and beneficence. Former prime minister William Gladstone (1809–1898) lay in state in Westminster Hall before being buried at Westminster Abbey. Each occasion was carefully used to promote a particular image of Britain. Given the renewed interest in ceremony and ritual in the nineteenth century, it was hardly surprising that Queen Victoria's funeral in 1901 was a perfectly stage-managed propaganda event. It brought together the largest congregation of royalty and potentates ever witnessed. Victoria was also the first monarch to have her body transported to the funeral on a gun carriage pulled by sailors. The cortege was followed by troops of the empire and thus reflected her worldwide significance. It was a stunning advertisement of the reach and importance of Britain.

In the twentieth century, statesmen and monarchs continued to be buried with pomp and ceremony. Significant examples include the lavish funerals of presidents Franklin D. Roosevelt (1882–1945) and John F. Kennedy (1917–1963) in the United States, General Charles de Gaulle (1890–1970) in France, and Winston Churchill (1874–1965) in Britain. Perhaps the most significant burials of the twentieth century were those accorded to the various unknown warriors. At the end of the Great War the British set a precedent by choosing one unknown soldier to repre-

sent all who had died in the service of the empire. Buried on Armistice Day 1920, immediately after George V had unveiled the Cenotaph, this anonymous soldier was interred in a ceremony marked by ritual and deep sadness. The service was far more than a mere burial, for it united the entire empire in a common moment of homage to the king-emperor. Other countries soon followed Britain's example, with the century of the common man marked by funeral ceremonies once reserved for monarchs.

By the end of the twentieth century, funerals were frequently used as media events to draw attention to a political cause. In Northern Ireland, Israel, and the Israeli-occupied territories, funerals became a key venue at which communities demonstrated their grief and displayed their respective political symbols. Terrorist funerals in Northern Ireland frequently included masked gunmen who fired a volley of shots over the grave. The funeral of Diana, Princess of Wales (1961–1997) reflected a number of competing agendas. In the wake of her death, the new prime minister, Tony Blair (1953–), proved rather more successful in capturing the nation's mood than Elizabeth II, Diana's estranged mother-in-law. The royal family hence attempted to use the funeral to reassociate itself with Diana. Diana's brother, Earl Spencer (1964–), used his eulogy to deliver a stinging attack against the royal family and the media, which had "hunted" Diana. In the funeral service the expected elements of national pageantry were mixed with such innovations as the use of a pop song. The British public, meanwhile, mourned on the streets of London and at improvised memorials in town centers. Through such public mourning the funeral became a stage on which hitherto excluded groups in British society—including gay, young, and minority Britons—came forward and demonstrated both their grief and their presence in British life. The funeral reflected the level of social change in Britain in recent years. The funeral of Queen Elizabeth, the Queen Mother (1901–2002), pro-voked a tussle between the Blair government and the British press over the prime minister's alleged attempt to increase his own role in the associated ceremonial.

Mark Connelly

See also Civil War, English; Ireland; Kennedy, John F.; Memorials and Monuments; Perón, Juan Domingo, and Eva Duarte; World War I

References: Ben-Amos, Avner. *Funerals, Politics, and Memory in Modern France, 1789–1996.* Oxford: Oxford University Press, 2000; Fussell, Paul. *The Great War in Modern Memory.* Oxford: Oxford University Press, 1975; Houlbrooke, Ralph, ed. *Death, Ritual and Bereavement.* London: Routledge, 1989; Woodward, Jennifer. *The Theatre of Death: The Ritual Management of Royal Funerals in Renaissance England, 1570–1625.* Woodbridge, UK: Boydell, 1997.

G

Gandhi, Mohandas K. (1869–1948)

This Indian nationalist leader, more commonly known by the title Mahatma (great soul) Gandhi, was born in Kathiawar, India. Gandhi trained as a lawyer in London and practiced law in Bombay. In 1893 he moved to South Africa and spent the next two decades fighting racial discrimination. In 1914 he returned to India and joined the struggle for home rule. Realizing that violent resistance would lead to further violence, he resorted to nonviolent methods of opposition. This approach both frustrated British rule and demonstrated Indian restraint, which deepened the gravity of the Indian cause before a global audience. In 1930 Gandhi led a mass march to the sea, where he proceeded to boil a small pan of seawater and collect the salt residue—in direct violation of the British government's salt monopoly. He repeatedly used the hunger strike as a means of bringing the British to the negotiating table and was frequently jailed for his political activity. Every aspect of his life served as an argument against British domination and in favor of his vision of a return to a purer way of life for India. He wove his own clothes and, whether in India or on a visit to London, sought the company of and championed the poor and the needy. As a lawyer, he also understood the value of the well-turned phrase. When asked about European civilization, he quipped that it sounded like "a good idea." His leadership was instrumental in winning Indian independence in 1947, but his mystical vision of India's destiny was not strong enough to contain the various factions warring within India. Seeing India riven by violence between Hindu and Muslim, Gandhi sought to restore order through a fast for peace. In January 1948 a Hindu fanatic murdered Gandhi on his way to a public prayer service. Gandhi's life illustrated the propaganda value of nonviolence and provided a powerful model for the African American civil rights movement of the 1950s and 1960s.

Nicholas J. Cull

See also Civil Rights Movement; Indian Subcontinent; Ireland; King, Martin Luther, Jr.; Peace and Antiwar Movements (1945–)

References: Gandhi, M. K., *An Autobiography.* London: Penguin, 1982; Watson, Francis. *Gandhi.* Oxford: Oxford University Press, 1967.

Garrison, William Lloyd (1805–1879)

An American abolitionist born in Newburyport, Massachusetts, Garrison displayed an aptitude for journalism and by the age of nineteen had become editor of the town paper. His great cause was opposition to the evils of slavery in the American South. He was not so much an organizer of the abolitionist movement as a communicator, bringing the cause alive as never before. Motivated by religious conviction, in 1831 he founded *The Liberator* to advance these ideas. In 1833 he founded the American Anti-Slavery society. He worked closely with such black American abolitionists as Frederick Douglass (1817–1895). Garrison was a gifted lecturer, well known in both Britain and the United States. He also pioneered the peace movement in the United States, leading one group within the movement that felt it was their moral duty to fight a war against slavery. Following the end of slavery, Garrison devoted his energies to the twin causes of winning votes for women and promoting the just treatment of Native Americans.

Nicholas J. Cull

See also Abolitionism/Antislavery Movement; Civil War, United States; *Narrative of the Life of Frederick Douglass . . . ;* Peace and Antiwar Movements (1500–1945); United States

References: McPherson, James M. *Battle Cry of Freedom: The Civil War Era.* New York: Oxford University Press, 1988; Merrill, Walter McIntosh. *Against Wind and Tide: A Biography of William Lloyd Garrison.* Cambridge, MA: Harvard University Press, 1963.

Garvey, Marcus (1887–1940)

Garvey was the charismatic leader of the Universal Negro Improvement Association (UNIA), the largest mass movement of black people in U.S. history, which was active in the early 1920s, as well as a student and practitioner of propaganda. Born in Jamaica, in 1912 he moved to London, where he worked as a journalist. Garvey realized the role that symbols played in underpinning the political power of the British Empire and resolved to create a similar set of symbols—flags, uniforms, parades—to restore pride and build power for peoples of African descent. In

1916 Garvey traveled to the United States and began building a movement. Finding the black middle class already committed to existing reform movements, Garvey turned to the working class. In 1917 he founded the first chapter of UNIA in Harlem, New York. The following year he established the weekly newspaper *Negro World;* the daily paper *Negro Times* followed in 1922 to disseminate Garvey's ideas to a mass readership.

The core of Garvey's message was racial pride. He taught that black skin was as beautiful as white skin. Although his slogan "Back to Africa" was more a cultural goal than a concrete scheme for migration, Garvey founded the Black Star steamship line to link the peoples of the African diaspora by trade. He designed a tricolor flag: red symbolizing the blood of struggle and revolution; black representing the African race; and green reflecting the vegetation of Africa. Since Garvey believed that "the greatest weapon used against the Negro is disorganization," he founded a host of organizations, including a paramilitary African Legion, a Black Cross Nurses corps for women; choirs; marching bands; and numerous other auxiliary units filled with eager African American recruits. These groups had chapters wherever there was a large population of black Americans; they took part in elaborate rallies and parades. By some estimates, UNIA's total membership in the United States, the Caribbean, and West Africa exceeded ten million. When Garvey called on his followers to demonstrate their strength, the results were often impressive. In August 1920 twenty-five thousand Garveyites marched south from Harlem to fill Madison Square Garden, carrying banners that read: "The Negro Knows No Fear."

Garvey's success alarmed other black leaders, who looked down on his working-class power base. Garvey did not help matters by seeking allies in unusual quarters. In 1922 he began negotiations with one Edward Clarke, second in command of the Ku Klux Klan, on the grounds that both UNIA and the Klan agreed that the black and white races had separate destinies. The rival African American paper *The Messenger* began a "Garvey must go!" campaign. The Black Star shipping line ultimately proved his undoing. Its finances were sloppy and left Garvey open to allegations of corruption. In 1925 he was sent to jail in Georgia for mail fraud. In 1927 his sentence was commuted to exile. He died in obscurity in Britain in 1940.

Garvey's achievement as a propagandist was considerable. He developed both the message of black pride and the media to carry that message to his audience. His teachings were part of the background to the black literary renaissance of the 1920s and reappeared in the anticolonial movements of Africa and the Caribbean in the 1950s and in the American black power movement of the 1960s.

Nicholas J. Cull

See also Caribbean; Civil Rights Movement; Malcolm X; United States

References: Cronon, Edmund D. *Black Moses: The Story of Marcus Garvey and the Universal Negro Improvement Association.* Madison: University of Wisconsin Press, 1955; Stein, Judith. *The World of Marcus Garvey: Race and Class in Modern Society.* Baton Rouge: Louisiana State University Press, 1986.

Germany

German history is renowned for its peculiarities and paradoxes. The "land in the center of Europe," with its constantly shifting boundaries, was also the land of Martin Luther (1483–1546), Ludwig van Beethoven (1770–1827), Johann Wolfgang von Goethe (1749–1832), and Adolf Hitler (1889–1945). Although it is the Third Reich that is synonymous with the abuse of propaganda, consensus politics has largely remained absent from German political culture throughout its nondemocratic route to modernity. Indeed, the term "Germany" had no real political significance at the beginning of the nineteenth century. The numerous states of which it was comprised were loosely bound by their membership in the old Holy Roman Empire while retaining striking regional variations based more on political and cultural history than geography.

Medieval Germany under the Saxon and Salian dynasties was characterized by the feudal organization of society and politics, with the dominance of a military aristocracy. The revival of intellectual life was largely due to the church, with its monasteries and cathedral schools, many of which were revived in the tenth century. The mid-eleventh to the mid-twelfth century was a period of political conflict and religious strife. The great dynasties that were to leave their mark on German history emerged during this period. The aristocracy was essentially a warrior class that developed an elaborate code of honor that informed Middle High German art and literature toward the end of the twelfth century. Lyric poetry (*Minnesang*) gave expression to the ethos of the knightly class. Equally important, narrative poetry, in the form of the first German version of the Tristan and Isolde legend, dates from approximately 1170. Another category was the heroic epic, the most famous being the *Nibelungenlied*.

The period encompassing the end of the twelfth century and the beginning of the thirteenth is associated with the political legend of the great emperor Frederick Barbarossa (c.1123–1190). For many nationalistic Germans of the nineteenth century this was viewed as the golden age of imperial greatness; propaganda techniques took the form of personal display, costume, and pageantry to disseminate the majesty of Frederick I and the development of courtly civilization. In the next three centuries, a series of changes took place that laid the foundation for modern Germany. In the late Middle Ages Germany remained politically decentralized and fragmented, with local princes assuming responsibility for maintaining peace and waging war within their principalities. This patchwork of dynastic and ecclesiastical territories was loosely held together by the wider protection of the Habsburg empire, whose dynastic possessions stretched from the Low Countries to Italy and Burgundy. Consensus politics was not a feature of the Germanic form of kingship, which was a limited monarchy. Propaganda had the dual role of proclaiming the great power of the emperor and obtaining allegiance to the feudal system at the local level.

From the mid-fourteenth to the mid-seventeenth century German society continued to be largely based on feudal agrarian principles. Political relations within the empire were subjected to an explosive new element in the form of the Reformation, which shattered European religious and cultural unity. The years 1525–1526 saw widespread revolts by peasants and common townspeople against the abuses of the existing system and notions of "godly law." The German Reformation did not, however, foster the cause of wider German unity, leading to the enhancement of the powers of local rulers.

Germany thus entered the age of absolutism embodying a unique pattern of political multiplicity. Until its abolition under Napoleonic rule in 1806, the Holy Roman Empire actively encouraged the survival of small principalities at the expense of a centralized state. Broadsheets, illustrated manuscripts, and proclamations were employed to inculcate obedience and servility as subjects rather than as citizens. The emergence of Brandenburg-Prussia was of immense importance. In the nineteenth century Prussia would assume control of "small Germany" *(Kleindeutschland)* from an excluded Austria. Although one should avoid simplistic conclusions, the "enlightened absolutism" that emerged in Germany produced a literate, articulate public that separated the spheres of "power and spirit" ("Macht und Geist") that sustained rather than challenged the existing status quo. Written and visual forms of political persuasion characterized German concepts of propaganda during this period; portraiture, political poems, tracts and treatises, as well as a growing body of political pamphlets—although not on the same scale as in England—were all features of the political culture of the time.

The German Empire, or Second Reich, was created in 1871, founded on an unequal alliance between the national and liberal movements and the conservative Prussian state leadership. It has been stated that Otto von Bismarck (1815–1898), the Prussian chancellor, united Germany as a result of a series of successful military wars. However, closer examination reveals that the conditions for unification had been achieved *before* Bismarck came to power. The result of overt militarism, the creation of the German Empire appeared to have fulfilled Bismarck's prediction of 1862 that Prussia would unite Germany by "blood and iron." In fact, the empire was only established following numerous compromises and was immediately criticized for being incomplete. By and large, however, the majority warmly greeted the achievement of national unity. Following the euphoria of 1871, imperial Germany failed to adapt its institutions to the newly developing economic and social conditions. No firm parliamentary principle was established, such as the government's responsibility to a sovereign parliament; rather, the situation was one of "government of the parties," a system dubbed "chancellor dictatorship." To this end, propaganda and the strict use of censorship, largely controlled by Bismarck and Prussia, continued to whip up nationalist fervor (Pan-Germanism) and stressed the economic advantages of political unity. Propaganda was employed to "sell" Bismarck's social legislation to the whole world as an unrivaled model. In 1874 the *Reichspressegesetz (*Imperial Press Law) rationalized a highly fragmented regional press and provided the basis for a national legal framework. The law also abolished the practice of prepublication censorship *(Vorzensur),* although it retained postpublication censorship *(Nachzensur),* which guaranteed that publications continued to be suppressed. Overcoming draconian state censorship was a problem, but the liberal press continued to attack the status quo and cartoons and caricature (notably in *Simplicissimus*) were especially popular in satirizing political figures (although rarely the Emperor). Propaganda and persuasion continued to be seen as a means of influencing the masses rather than developing a dialogue or consensus. The bureaucratization and militarization of public life and an imperialist foreign policy, which stirred people's emotions at home, bound nationalism and militarism with the monarchist authoritarian state.

With Bismarck's resignation in 1890, Kaiser Wilhelm II (1859–1941) presented himself as the *Volkskaiser* (people's Kaiser); idealized portraits of a statuesque Wilhelm obscured his insecurity and complex personality, masking his stunted body and withered arm from the public. The new policy of imperialism adopted by Wilhelm II represented a final attempt to overcome internal divisions through foreign policy successes. The kaiser's motto remained: "*Weltpolitik* as a task; to become a world power as an aim; and the fleet [military force] as an instrument."

The declaration of war in 1914 was apparently greeted with enthusiasm, and the political parties agreed to a truce *(Burgfrieden)*. The nation appeared united behind the banner of a fully justified war of self-defense. Following the outbreak of war, the German government immediately surrendered to local army commanders extensive political powers over civil administration. General mobilization was accompanied by the proclamation of the Prussian Law of the Siege, which gave sole responsibility for public safety to the deputy commanding generals in each of the twenty-four army corps districts. The military attempted to solve the problem of coordinating propaganda through the *Zivilversorgungsschein*—penetrating civil society with military values.

The impression that emerges from the study of propaganda in the Great War is one of generally uncoordinated improvisation. By the end of the conflict, however, propaganda would for the first time be elevated to the position of a branch of government. It is ironic (in the light of later criticisms from right-wing nationalists) that of all the belligerents Germany had been the only power to pay serious attention to propaganda before 1914. For some years, and with considerable thoroughness, imperial Germany had been attempting to influence popular and official opinion in foreign countries. When war broke out in August 1914, Germany had a distinct advantage over the Allied governments in the field of propaganda. Germany had been developing a semiofficial propaganda network through her embassies, legations, consular offices, and branches of German banks and shipping companies—all of which acted as agents for the dissemination of literature favorable to the fatherland.

The "peculiarities" of German history led—although not inevitably—to Nazism. During the Weimar Republic the state continued to mingle in and control broadcasting. Ownership of the press was concentrated in the hands of the right-wing Hugenberg press empire, which greatly facilitated the rise of the National Socialists. When Hitler came to power, Joseph Goebbels (1897–1945) was appointed to head the Reichsministerium für Volksaufklärung und Propaganda (Ministry for Popular Enlightenment and Propaganda). It is not surprising that propaganda in Nazi Germany should have been considered important enough to warrant an entire government ministry; in *Mein Kampf* Hitler had stressed the importance of propaganda as a vehicle of political salesmanship in a mass market and laid down the broad lines along which Nazi propaganda was to operate. Indeed, the Nazi rise to power is often viewed as a classic example of political achievement by means of propaganda. The two most important ideas that distinguished the Nazis from other political parties and allowed Goebbels's propaganda to mobilize widespread grievances were the notion of the *Volksgemeinschaft* (community of the people), based on the principle of the common good coming before the good of the community, and the myth of the charismatic Führer. Once in power, Goebbels believed that propaganda was to play a central role and that the function of the new Propaganda Ministry was to coordinate the political will of the nation with the aims of the Nazi state. To this end he quickly set about monopolizing the means of communication by a process known as *Gleichschaltung* (coordination), which referred to the obligatory assimilation within the Nazi state of all political, economic, and cultural activities.

Propaganda in Nazi Germany was not, as is often thought, a "catchall" process. The "revolutionary" aim of the Nazi regime to bring about the *Volksgemeinschaft,* the true harmony of all classes, reflects the highly ambitious nature of its propaganda and its continuing success in maintaining its ideology and totalitarian vision. Terror always lurked behind such "consensus" and represented a real fear, but propaganda played a crucial role in securing at least passive support for the regime. After the grandiose edifice of the Third Reich was laid bare in 1945, the Nazi legacy resulted in a deep mistrust of propaganda throughout the world and a new awareness of how easily the mass media could be manipulated to serve the opportunistic purposes of their masters. Propaganda was

The official Nazi Party membership lapel pin: National-Sozialistische-D.A.P (National Socialist German Workers' Party). (Courtesy of David Culbert)

not invented by Joseph Goebbels, although it is largely as a result of Nazi propaganda that the term has come to have such a pejorative connotation.

At the end of World War II the country was geographically truncated and politically divided into the German Democratic Republic (GDR) and the Federal Republic of Germany (FRG). The break with the past was symbolized by the concept of "Stunde Null" (zero hour) and the stress on renewal. The use made by the National Socialists' propaganda machine had a profound influence on the early development of political cultures and media systems in the respective occupied zones. In the GDR a monolithic and oppressive system based on the Soviet model and the pervasive use of state censorship was instituted, while in the FRG allied "reeducation" placed political culture on a democratic and pluralistic basis.

The structure of the media system in the GDR was established on the principle of "democratic socialism." At the pinnacle of this structure was the Politibüro of the Socialist Unity Party (SED), which directly controlled the Press Office of the Council of Ministers, which in turn presided over the State Radio and Television Committees. In 1971 an additional service called "Stimme der DDR" (Voice of the GDR) was established to provide a twenty-four-hour service mixing entertainment and information but aimed at a West German audience and broadcasting propaganda (the GDR counterpart to the FRG's "Deutschlandfunk"). A youth channel ("Jugendradio 64") was also established, and since the mid-1950s "Radio Berlin International" has provided short-wave service for international consumption. The press was similarly controlled; the SED party press consisted of two dailies (*Neues Deutschland* and *Berliner Zeitung*) and fourteen daily SED "district papers." A state news agency, the Allgemeiner Deutscher Nachrichtendienst (AND), provided officially sanctioned news. In practice, however, the party never enjoyed an information monopoly. Most areas of the

GDR received Western television and radio, and in the 1960s the authorities waged an unsuccessful campaign to counter West German broadcasts.

In the FRG the Allied occupation laid the basis for the resurrection of a strong press, freed from the threat of political oppression and abuse. It also had the effect of suppressing all other forms of discourse and concentrating the media in the hands of such giants as Axel Springer (1912–1985), who personified press power in the FDR. He was granted a license to launch a new radio-program magazine, *Hör zu* (Listen), in 1946. He founded the *Hamburger Abendblatt* two years later, and in June 1952 came the mass-appeal *Bild Zeitung*. In the following year he bought *Die Welt* from the British, who had established it as the mouthpiece of their military government in Germany. Springer also established a number of magazines and moved into commercial broadcasting. The right-wing political stance that the Springer media empire adopted beginning in the late 1950s led to an ongoing feud with the country's intelligentsia. In West Germany the Allies were concerned that broadcasting should be decentralized. In 1954 the Arbeitsgemeinschaft der Öffentlich-rechtlichen Rundfunkanstalten der Bundesrepublik Deutschland (ARD; Working Group of the Public Broadcasting Corporations of the Federal Republic of Germany) was formed; consisting of eleven regional public broadcasting organizations, its mandate was to create national radio and television programs while drawing on the resources of regional stations. When the FRG gained full sovereignty in 1955, the federal states were granted full autonomy in broadcasting. The two foreign-language radio organizations operating under federal law are Deutsche Welle (DW; Voice of Germany; literally, German [Air] Wave) and Deutschlandfunk (DL; Radio Germany). Both stations encountered Soviet jamming during the Cold War. Presently the DW's radio broadcasts (which in 1993 took over the DL's foreign-language programs for Europe) consist of ninety-three daily programs in thirty-four

languages. In 1963 the Zweites Deutsches Fernsehen (ZDF; Second [Channel of] German Television) went on the air; located outside Mainz, it is the largest single, centralized organization devoted to television programming and production in Europe. Since 1991 the ZDF has been entrusted with coordinating Europe's cultural television channel, ARTE. Since 1992 Deutsche Welle TV has been broadcasting a magazine-type program fourteen hours each day via satellite, revealing the FRG's commitment to keep a worldwide audience informed about German culture and politics.

The transformation of Germany into two very different states—one democratic and capitalistic, the other Communist—came to an end in October 1990 with the collapse of Communism in Eastern Europe and the unification of the two Germanys. Unification took place very much on Western terms, and this applied to the mass media, where the new system had to conform to the regulatory framework and principles that had evolved in the FRG.

David Welch

See also Art; Atrocity Propaganda; The Big Lie; Engels, Friedrich; Goebbels, Joseph; Hitler, Adolf; *Jud Süss;* Lord Haw Haw; Marx, Karl; *Mein Kampf;* Morale; Peace and Antiwar Movements (1500–1945); Propaganda, Definitions of; Reeducation; RMVP; *Triumph of the Will;* Women's Movement: European; World War I; World War II (Germany); Zimmermann Telegram

References: Eyck, Erich. *Bismarck and the German Empire.* New York: Norton, 1964; Humphreys, Peter. *Media and Media Policy in Germany: The Press and Broadcasting Since 1945.* Oxford: Berg, 1994; Scribner, R. W. *Popular Culture and Popular Movements in Reformation Germany.* London: Hambledon, 1987; Welch, David. *Germany, Propaganda and Total War 1914–1918.* New Brunswick, NJ: Rutgers University Press, 2000; ———. *The Third Reich: Politics and Propaganda.* London: Routledge, 2002.

Goebbels, Joseph (1897–1945)

A politician and Hitler's propaganda minister, Goebbels was arguably one of the most skillful

Joseph Goebbels, German minister of propaganda, attends a demonstration in 1934. (Illustrated London News Picture Library)

and cynical propagandists of the twentieth century.

Although a serious childhood illness left him with a clubfoot, he excelled academically as a student. In 1921 he graduated from the University of Heidelberg with a doctorate. After fruitless attempts to make a living as journalist, writer, or dramatic adviser, he began his political career by joining the Nazi Party (NSDAP). His antibourgeois attitudes made him a sympathizer with the Strasser wing of the party, but in 1926 he took Hitler's side in an internal power struggle and subsequently advanced in the party hierarchy. Hitler appointed him leader of the Berlin NSDAP the same year. Goebbels became one of the party's most prominent and effective speakers, easily exploiting the freedom that a democratic society granted even its fiercest enemies. As editor of the party newspaper Der Angriff (The Attack) he fashioned it into a powerful propaganda weapon. He became a member of parliament in 1928 and served as the Nazi Party's national propaganda leader beginning in 1929. Continuing to organize demonstrations and unrest to disrupt democratic order, he was one of the major figures to turn the NSDAP into a powerful political force. In 1930 he succeeded in persuading the German government to ban

temporarily the film All Quiet on the Western Front (1930).

On 13 March 1933, shortly after the Nazis assumed power in Germany, Goebbels became minister for "Popular Enlightenment and Propaganda." Newspapers, radio, film, and all other cultural activities were brought in line with the dictatorship's principle of coordination (Gleichschaltung). As president of the Chamber of Culture (autumn 1933), it was primarily Goebbels who defined the new "German culture." Despite some competitors in the field like Alfred Rosenberg (1893–1946), Heinrich Himmler (1900–1945), and Hermann Goering (1893–1946), he remained the central figure of propaganda in Nazi Germany. His influence upon Hitler varied, reaching its weakest point during Goebbels's affair with Czechoslovakian actress Lida Baarova (1914–2000), which threatened his ministerial position. The outbreak of war took Goebbels by surprise, but he soon turned the German newsreel into a gripping part of his film program, personally supervising the latest installments. His role became even more important when the nature of the war altered. His rallying cries and the part he took in reorganizing the armaments industry definitely contributed to the prolongation of the war.

As Goebbels often and quite frankly explained, his convictions about propaganda were based on the dual assumption that propaganda and truth had no necessary connection and that the best type of propaganda was that which was not felt by the audience. These assumptions resulted in a mixture of demagogic presentations and seemingly apolitical entertainment. Organizing the anti-Semitic pogroms of 9 November 1938, promoting Hitler as a messiah, and forcing his audience to support "total war" during his infamous speech delivered in February 1943, he proved his ability as a ruthless and effective propagandist. His policy resulted in overtly propagandistic attempts in radio and film combined with a wealth of supposedly nonpolitical works. This combination altered with the political situation, with a preponderance of pure propaganda in the first years of the war. Nevertheless he consistently aimed to keep the people content, which gave his approach to propaganda an undeniable modern touch. An agitator against bolshevism, democracy, and liberalism and a preacher of hate, Goebbels did not merely threaten people or make them obey his message; he also calculated the effects of entertainment sanitized of any forbidden or subversive qualities. His loyalty to Hitler was finally rewarded when the dictator declared him his successor as chancellor (with Admiral Karl Dönitz [1891–1980]) in his last will and testament. A few hours after Hitler committed suicide, Goebbels and his wife poisoned their six children before following the example of their leader.

Rainer Rother

See also *All Quiet on the Western Front;* The Big Lie; Film (Nazi Germany); Film (Newsreels); Germany; Hitler, Adolf; Holocaust Denial; *Jud Süss;* Propaganda, Definitions of; Riefenstahl, Leni; RMVP; White Propaganda; World War II (Germany)
References: Heiber, Helmut. *Goebbels: A Biography.* New York: Hawthorne, 1972; Moeller, Felix. *The Film Minister: Goebbels and the Cinema of the "Third Reich."* Stuttgart: Axel Menges, 2000; Reuth, Ralf Georg. *Goebbels: The Life of Joseph Goebbels.* London: Constable, 1993; Roberts, Jeremy. *Joseph Goebbels: Nazi Propaganda Minister.* New York: Rosen, 2000.

Goya (Francisco de Goya y Lucientes) (1746–1828)

A Spanish painter, Goya was born in Aragon. In 1789 he became court painter to the young Spanish king Charles IV (1784–1819; r. 1788–1808), a position he retained when Spain came under the rule of Napoleon's brother, Joseph Bonaparte (1768–1844; r. 1808–1816). Although sympathetic to some of the Bonaparte regime's liberal reforms, Goya had a keen sense of nationhood and an abhorrence of the violence used by the French to suppress the guerrilla uprisings protesting their rule. His sympathy for the

Spanish cause is clear from his 1814 painting *The Third of May.* Between 1810 and 1814 he executed sixty-five etchings, collected under the title *Los Desastres de la Guerra* (The Disasters of War), showing all manner of atrocities, including limbs hanging from trees and monstrous figures greedily devouring human flesh. Goya's etchings can be considered true antiwar propaganda, opening the way for future artists to represent the horrors of war.

Nicholas J. Cull

See also Art; Atrocity Propaganda; Napoleon; Peace and Antiwar Movements (1500–1945); Spain
References: Edwards, Samuel. *The Double Lives of Francisco de Goya: A Biography.* New York: Grosset & Dunlap, 1973; Holland, Vyvyan Beresford. *Goya: A Pictorial Biography.* Thames & Hudson: London, 1961.

Gray Propaganda

Gray propaganda falls somewhere between white and black propaganda. The source may or may not be identified, and the accuracy of the information is uncertain. During World War I Britain's War Propaganda Bureau, better known as Wellington House (where it was headquartered), conducted a major campaign directed at the then neutral United States through an American branch headed by Sir Gilbert Parker (1862–1932), a Canadian-born writer and British M.P. British propaganda was not explicitly designed to persuade America to enter the war on the side of the Allies; benevolent neutrality was considered infinitely more preferable. Wellington House therefore decided to provide American policymakers with the material they needed to make up their own minds about the issues (unlike the German propagandists, who bombarded American public opinion with their propaganda of exhortation). Wellington House targeted America's elite in the belief that it would, in turn, influence the larger public.

An educated or elite audience likes to believe that it can spot propaganda when confronted by it, and then duly dismiss it as "propaganda." British propaganda therefore required delicate handling. Wellington House had to disseminate material to its target audience that did not appear to be propaganda—or at least not all the time. Rather, it had to take the form of reasoned argument based on the facts—although not necessarily all the facts—and presented in an objective manner. Some of this propaganda material came directly from Wellington House (white), while other portions were disguised (gray). For this purpose, a clandestine publishing operation produced material that was distributed under the imprint of famous commercial publishing houses such as Hodder and Stoughton, John Murray, and Macmillan.

In World War II Britain's Political Warfare Executive (PWE) produced gray propaganda as well as black. An example was the highly praised newspaper for German troops entitled *Nachrichten für die Truppen,* which was delivered by air. The contents of the paper could not possibly be reconciled with official German authorship, but the failure to disclose its true origin permitted the newspaper to express views that might have been embarrassing if attributed to an official British source.

In the late 1940s and early 1950s Western powers attached great importance to psychological warfare, employing propaganda measures to sway international opinion to support the free world and, ultimately, to bring about the disintegration of Communist regimes. In 1948 the British Foreign Office sponsored a peacetime covert propaganda agency, the Information Research Department (IRD), which was intended to counter Soviet and Communist propaganda and defend Western liberal democracy. The IRD was formed in the aftermath of the Communist coup in Prague and increasingly hostile Soviet propaganda. Supported by Foreign Minister Ernest Bevin (1881–1951), the approach adopted was secretive and aggressive, designed to take the initiative away from the enemy. IRD was in many respects a peacetime PWE. Its task was not black propaganda, which was the preserve of the secret intelligence service MI6, but rather gray propaganda, biased information emanating from an indeterminate source. The target was Communist Russia and the task was to attack and expose this ideological enemy and offer "something better." Gray propaganda was adopted because it was more direct and aggressive than white but less likely to offend the Soviets quite as much as black propaganda. The content of anti-Communist gray propaganda was to highlight Western values as a counterpoint to Soviet activities. At one level IRD material consisted of in-depth confidential studies on aspects of Soviet Communism designed for high-level consumption by senior Allied politicians. On a less classified level, radio broadcasts, pamphlets, articles, letters, and speeches were all used and directed at policymakers in Eastern Europe, who could use such material as factual background in their general work without the need for attribution. To distinguish its activities from those of the Americans, the IRD concentrated on areas threatened by Communism outside the USSR. The ability of IRD to disguise its sponsorship of cultural activity until the late 1970s points to the reason for its success, namely, the fact that much of it was not generally recognized as propaganda.

When the Soviet Union invaded Afghanistan, Radio Moscow employed gray propaganda when it attempted to justify its actions. A television documentary entitled "Afghanistan: The Revolution Cannot Be Killed" was broadcast on Christmas Day 1985. The program deliberately gave the impression that the conflict had been started by other powers. Iran and Pakistan were specifically implicated and captured mercenaries claimed that they had been sent to Afghanistan by the CIA. The film ended with pro-Soviet troops being cheered by Afghan crowds. The source of the message was not in question, but the information was largely inaccurate.

In the wake of 11 September 2001 involving terrorist attacks against New York and Washington, D.C., the United States prepared the population of Afghanistan for a planned U.S. air and land war by dropping food containers and radios that could only pick up one signal. The U.S.-run radio station, which did not formally identify itself, simply referred to itself as Afghan FM. Sandwiched between some lively Afghan music an announcement was broadcast "for the attention of the noble people of Afghanistan." The announcer then proceeded to explain that American forces would be passing through the area and that their aim was not to harm the people but rather to arrest Osama bin Laden (1957–) and those who support him.

David Welch

See also Black Propaganda; CIA; IRD; Psychological Warfare; PWE; Terrorism, War on; White Propaganda

References: Qualter, Terence H. *Opinion Control in the Democracies.* New York: St. Martin's Press, 1985; Roetter, Charles. *Psychological Warfare.* London: Batsford, 1974; Taylor, Philip, M. *Munitions of the Mind: A History of Propaganda from the Ancient World to the Present Day.* Manchester, UK: Manchester University Press, 1985.

Greece

The history of propaganda in Greece has much in common with the rest of the Balkan Peninsula, including nationalistic propaganda first for liberation from Ottoman rule and later to redress grievances against neighbors (most famously Turkey but also Bulgaria, Albania, and Macedonia). As elsewhere in the Balkans, nationalistic propaganda has focused on the glories of the pre-Ottoman past; in the case of Greece, this meant the achievements of the classical era.

The Greek struggle for independence from the Ottoman Empire produced much propaganda in the romantic vein, with such foreign champions of the Greek cause as Lord Byron (1788–1824). Greek voices for independence included Alexander Ypsilanti (1792–1828), who headed the secret Philike Hetairia organization and declared independence during a revolt in 1821, and Ionnes

Capo D'Istrias (1776–1831), president of the new Greek state from 1828 to 1831. In 1832 Greece became the first Balkan nation to formally win its independence from the Ottoman Empire. Greece sought to export nationalism to its Balkan neighbors and at one point attempted to sponsor the idea of Balkan unity (under Greek leadership). One of the earliest representatives of this view was the nationalistic eighteenth-century Greek poet Rigas Velestinlis (1757–1798), whose image graces the 20 lepta coin.

The Greek state sought to incorporate other Greek-speaking parts of the region and used propaganda to nurture a sense of nationalism in such areas. The desire for union with Crete led to the Greco-Turkish war of 1897, which Greece lost, though the Great Powers eventually assigned Crete to Greece in 1913. Propaganda concerning the Macedonian question has also been part of Greek politics. Following a long struggle for Macedonian independence (culminating in the Ilinden uprising of 1903), the Macedonian lands were split between Greece, Bulgaria, and Serbia in 1913. Besides vocal Macedonian propaganda for reunification and liberation, this resulted in a well-organized international underground terrorist network, as well as other conspiracies. Greece, like Bulgaria and Serbia, carried out specific assimilationist and propaganda policies to suppress the Macedonian struggle for independence, all of which largely failed.

In 1921 Greece took advantage of the political ferment in Turkey by seeking to extend control of Greek-speaking territories. In 1922 Turkey repelled this Greek intervention (the so-called Smyrna disaster) and Greece lost control over its territories in Asia Minor, resulting in a huge migration of refugees to Greece proper. The loss of these territories gave rise to the irredentist ideology of the *megali* (or great) idea and a sustained history of tension with Turkey, including mutual claims of atrocities connected to 1922.

From 1924 to 1935 Greece was a republic, but in 1936, with the support of the monarchy, General Iannis Metaxas (1871–1941) established a pro-Italian, semifascist regime (with centralized censorship). The regime fell following Metaxas's death in 1941. Germany occupied Greece, together with Bulgarian and Italian participation. After the war, evidence of atrocities committed during the war was used as a powerful indictment against those who had aligned themselves with the Nazis. The resistance in Greece was split into Communist (EAM-ELAS) and monarchist (EDES) factions, which became antagonists in a bitter civil war. At the end of World War II, Greece was the only Balkan country left in the Western sphere of influence; the government, aided first by Britain and then by the United States, fought its civil war with the Communists. The last Communist enclaves fell in 1949. That year twenty thousand children were sent abroad (some under coercion) to escape the war, mostly to Communist countries. The incident was widely used for propaganda purposes.

The postwar period saw a revival of tension with Turkey, particularly during the anti-Greek riots in Istanbul in 1956. The Greek government also encouraged the dream of *enosis* (reunification) with the Greeks of the diaspora, especially the Cypriots. Supporters of *enosis* on Cyprus included Archbishop Makarios (1913–1977) and General George Grivas (1898–1974). In 1955 Grivas's EOKA organization (Ethniki Organosis Kyprion Aghoniston [National Organisation of Cypriot Fighters]) launched a guerrilla war against British rule on the island. The British made tactical use of propaganda in their counterinsurgency campaign. *Enosis* was strongly opposed by the not insignificant Turkish minority of the island and was subsequently forbidden in 1960 under the terms of Cypriot independence. In 1974, following a Greek-backed coup against Makarios (who had been president since 1960), Turkey invaded and occupied part of the island. The United Nations intervened to separate the hostile parties, but the situation still remains unresolved, result-ing in mutual accusations and propaganda between Greece and Turkey.

Memories of the Greek civil war ensured a strain of anti-Communism in postwar Greek government propaganda. This reached its peak during the rule of the Greek military junta (1967–1974), which also saw widespread political violence. Although the Communist Party had been illegal in Greece since the civil war, it still had many sympathizers. Dissidents included the composer Mikis Theodorakis (1925–), who led the Lambrakis Youth Organization, which was named after Grigoris Lambrakis, one of the murdered leaders of the democratic left. Lambrakis's murder in 1963 also provided the basis for the acclaimed film *Z* (1969) by Greek expatriate director Constantin Costa-Gavras (1933–). Theodorakis was forced into exile by the junta. Another outspoken critic of the colonel's regime was actress Melina Mercouri (1923–1994).

In 1974 Greek democracy returned. Early issues included the referendum on the issue of the monarchy, which rejected such a restoration. Greek propaganda has also included an anti-American strain, which was evident in the 1960s when George Papandreou (1888–1968), who served as prime minister from 1964 to 1965, attacked "paternalistic capitalism." Anti-Americanism returned (with lesser intensity) in the Pan-Hellenic Socialist Movement (PASOK) government of Papandreou's son, Andreas Papandreou (1919–1996), who was elected to office in 1981. That same year Greece joined the European Union. International campaigns have included demands from Mercouri (as culture minister) for the return of antiquities of historical and symbolic importance, including the Elgin Marbles, which are presently housed at the British Museum.

The 1990s saw a diversification of the media in Greece. Until 1990 the state had enjoyed a monopoly in the broadcasting industry and intervened frequently to further its political ends. Restrictions on the media in Greece include regulations outlawing attacks against the church and a law forbidding "unwarranted publicity for terrorists." Terrorist-group operations in Greece include the small left-wing November 17th movement, whose "propaganda by action" included the assassination of a British military attaché in 2000. In the 1990s the Macedonia question returned. Despite fierce Greek propaganda against its statehood, in 1991 Macedonia managed to establish its independence within the borders of the "Former Yugoslav Republic of Macedonia," which, at the insistence of Greece, remains the country's official name on the grounds that calling itself Macedonia implied a claim to the Greek province of the same name. Internal Greek politics has led to a heated debate over the return of Greeks from the territories of the former Soviet Union, as well as a wave of immigrants from Albania, who relocated as a result of the "right of return" policy for Albanian citizens of Greek descent. The Greek Orthodox Church has proved a major source of nationalistic propaganda. Tensions with Turkey remain, including a 1999 dispute over an uninhabited tiny island. As a result of major earthquakes in both countries that same year, feelings improved somewhat following mutual offers of aid. The government's plan to improve Greece's international image by hosting the 2004 Olympic Games was tempered by problems encountered during the early stages of preparation.

Dina Iordanova

See also Balkans; Cold War; Counterinsurgency; Olympics; Poetry

References: Brewer, David. *The Flame of Freedom: The Greek War of Independence, 1821–1833.* London: John Murray, 2001; Brewer, David, and Misha Glenny, *The Balkans, 1804–1999: Nationalism, War and the Great Powers.* New York: Viking, 2000; Mazower, Mark. *The Balkans.* London: Weidenfeld and Nicholson, 2000; Woodhouse, C. M. *Modern Greece: A Short History.* London: Faber, 1984; Zaharopoulos, Thimios, and Manny E. Paraschos. *Mass Media in Greece: Power, Politics and Privatization.* Westport, CT: Praeger, 1993.

The Green Berets (1968)

This Warner Brothers film was the first major Hollywood production to deal with the issue of the Vietnam War. It was the pet project of its star, John Wayne (1907–1979), who also acted as codirector with Ray Kellogg (1906–1976). Wayne sought to rally public sympathy for an increasingly unpopular war. The U.S. military cooperated in its production. The film tells the story of an elite Special Forces unit and its mission to assist the South Vietnamese. It tried to make the Vietnam War appear to be as moral, exciting, and successful as World War II, with which John Wayne was so closely identified as an actor. Subplots include the conversion of a skeptical journalist to the cause of the war, camaraderie among the soldiers, and a special friendship between a Vietnamese orphan and a kindly G.I. Most critics found the film overly long and too blatant in its propaganda. Screenings became a focus for protests against the war, and although box office receipts were the tenth largest for a film that year, it would take a decade before mainstream Hollywood ventured back to the issue of Vietnam.

Nicholas J. Cull

See also Film (Feature); United States; Vietnam War

References: Anderegg, Michael. *Inventing Vietnam: The War in Film and Television.* Philadelphia: Temple University Press, 1991; Wills, Garry. *John Wayne: The Politics of Celebrity.* New York: Simon and Schuster, 1997.

Grierson, John (1898–1972)

A Scottish-born pioneer in the field of documentary filmmaking, Grierson was active in both Britain and Canada, serving as the latter's wartime minister of information. While studying in Chicago in the early 1920s, Grierson developed an interest in propaganda and public opinion. In an article written in 1926, he developed the notion of what he called "documentary" film, which he defined as "the creative treatment of actuality." Beginning in 1928, he applied these ideas in Britain as a member of the Empire Marketing Board, promoting awareness of empire-related products. His first film, *Drifters* (1929), was a documentary about herring fishing. Beginning in 1933, he headed the General Post Office (GPO) film unit, commissioning documentaries that he hoped would educate the British public about the working classes. His most famous GPO film, *Night Mail* (1936), which followed a mail train from London to Scotland, was directed by Harry Watt (1906–1987) and Basil Wright (1907–1987).

In 1938 Grierson quarreled with the British government over the sorts of films it wished to show at the New York World's Fair of 1939. He accepted a mission to Canada to consult on the foundation of a National Film Board to promote national cohesion through film. With the coming of World War II Grierson agreed to remain as director of the board. A string of powerful documentaries followed. His activities also included feeding captured German newsreel to filmmakers in the then neutral United States to ensure that U.S. audiences understood the German way of war. In 1943 Grierson's responsibilities expanded to include all Canadian propaganda activity. Grierson had the ear of William Lyon Mackenzie King (1874–1950), the prime minister of Canada, and his War Information Board. At the end of the war he resigned his post in order to develop documentary film production and distribution in New York, but this scheme foundered. Grierson then fell under suspicion during Canada's early Cold War witch-hunts. From 1946 to 1948 he served as director of mass communications for UNESCO, and from 1948 to 1950 he worked as controller of films for Britain's peacetime government information bureau, the Central Office of Information. Although the nature of his legacy has been questioned, his views of documentary film and propaganda have remained a starting point for scholars as well as filmmakers.

Nicholas J. Cull

See also Britain; British Empire; Canada; Film (Documentary); United Nations

References: Hardy, Forsyth. *John Grierson: A Documentary Biography.* London: Faber, 1979; Evans, Gary. *John Grierson and the National Film Board: The Politics of Wartime Propaganda.* Toronto: University of Toronto Press, 1984.

Guernica (1937)

This painting (1937) by Pablo Picasso (1881–1973) is one of the best-known examples of art as propaganda. The picture protests the bombing of the Basque town of Guernica on the night of 26 April 1937 by German flyers in the service of the Nationalist (fascist) side in the Spanish Civil War. The Republican (socialist) government commissioned Picasso to paint the work for exhibition in the Spanish pavilion at that summer's Paris International Exposition; hence the painting is also tied to the use of exhibitions for propaganda. He completed the painting in six weeks. Drawing on images and a cubist technique already well established in his work, Picasso created a monumental canvas. The painting incorporated a frenzied horse, a stamping bull, and four women distorted as though by the violence of the bombing. One woman clutches a dead baby, while another runs from a burning house. Overhead a light bulb swings madly and on the ground lie the screaming head and lifeless limbs of a soldier. In 1945 Picasso explained his belief that art could be "an instrument of war for attack and defense against the enemy." In *The Charnel House* (1944–1945) Picasso used art to protest against senseless destruction in World War II; in *Massacre in Korea* (1951) and *War and Peace* (1952) he did the same for the Korean War; and in the series entitled *The Rape of the Sabines* (1962–1963) he responded to the Cuban Missile Crisis.

Nicholas J. Cull

See also Art; Civil War, Spanish; Exhibitions and World's Fairs; Peace and Antiwar Movements (1500–1945); Spain

References: Barr, Alfred H., Jr. *Picasso: Fifty Years of His Art.* New York: Museum of Modern Art, 1946; Huffington, Arianna S. *Picasso: Creator and Destroyer.* London: Weidenfeld and Nicolson,

1988; Wiener, Malcolm H. "Picasso and the Cuban Missile Crisis." *Apollo* (October 2001): 3–9.

Pamphlets dropped on Iraqi lines during the Persian Gulf War in 1991. The leaflets fell both before and after U.S. bombing using the 15,000-pound BLU-82/B "Daisy Cutter" bomb. The first leaflet (left) reads in Arabic, "Flee and save your life, or remain and meet your death!" The second reads, "You have suffered heavy losses because we have used the most powerful and destructive conventional bomb of this war. It is more powerful than 20 Scud Missiles in respect of explosion capability. We warn you! We shall bomb your position again. Kuwait will be liberated from Saddam's aggression. Hurry and join your brothers from the south. We shall treat you with all our love and respect. Abandon this position. You will never be safe!" (Reuters NewMedia Inc. / CORBIS)

Gulf War (1991)

This war against Iraq for the liberation of Kuwait was waged between 16 January and 28 February 1991 by an alliance led by the United States. The war saw both the battlefield use of psychological warfare and attempts at news management on both sides. On 2 August 1990 the Iraqi regime of Saddam Hussein (1937–) invaded neighboring Kuwait and took control of its oil fields. The administration of U.S. president George Bush (1924–) knew that effective action against Iraq required a coalition of Western and Middle Eastern countries and deployed public diplomacy to ensure that the region understood the motives and limits of his country's actions. As the coalition moved its military into Saudi Arabia in the first phase of its response—Operation Desert Shield—the Bush administration summed up the stakes in the campaign as "a battle for the New World Order." The U.S. government and commercial media both tended to personalize the campaign as a war against the Hitler-like Saddam. In order to maximize the legitimacy of the campaign, Bush secured a UN resolution calling for military action against Iraq before launching Operation Desert Storm.

Both the Iraqis and the United States had Vietnam in mind as they formulated their propaganda strategies for the Gulf War. Saddam, claiming that the United States lacked the will to fight and sustain significant casualties, acted on this assumption. The Bush administration similarly hoped the war would produce minimal American casualties, aiming for the strictly limited objective of liberating Kuwait. Unlike the relatively free reporting in Vietnam, the United States sought to manage reporting from the Gulf War by instituting a system of press pools with its armed forces. A limited number of journalists were brought on board and encouraged to become part of the "team." At the regional headquarters, a larger number of journalists enjoyed regular briefings from Gen. Norman Schwarzkopf (1934–), the commander of U.S. forces, who proudly displayed images of U.S. "smart weapons" in action. The official U.S. view of the war emphasized technology and precision, striving to obliterate the image of bloodshed and death from the U.S. bombardment of Iraq. Contrary to the impression that this created in the Western media, the "smart weapons" campaign accounted for only 8 percent of the bombing effort.

The government of Kuwait used propaganda to support the liberation of its country, using the front organization Citizens for a Free Kuwait to engage the American public relations firm Hill and Knowlton Public Affairs Worldwide at a cost of some $10.8

million. Hill and Knowlton's tactics included a staple of propaganda: the "atrocity story." On 10 October 1990 a distraught Kuwaiti teenager identified only as Nayirah told a hearing of the U.S. Congressional Caucus on Human Rights that invading Iraqi soldiers had stolen incubators from a maternity hospital in Kuwait and had left babies to die on the floor. The report subsequently became a fixture in Western human rights stories and was included in President Bush's denunciations of Saddam. Nayirah had not witnessed the events but was simply the daughter of the Kuwaiti ambassador to the United States. Once the war had begun, innovations in American propaganda included the extensive use of images of the environmental damage allegedly caused by Saddam's tactics—such as his use of crude oil as an anti-invasion measure—in Kuwait; in an environmentally sensitive era, television pictures of oil-soaked cormorants and chemical fires in Kuwait had a marked impact on European (particularly German) opinion. Analysis after the campaign revealed that the pictures of seabirds, while genuine, predated the particular crime they were used to illustrate.

Iraqi propaganda began with Saddam Hussein's efforts to intimidate his enemies—who were massing in Operation Desert Shield—by pledging "the mother of all battles." Radio Baghdad broadcasts by a female announcer—nicknamed "Baghdad Betty"—aimed to demoralize U.S. troops. She alleged that their wives were home "having sex" with movie stars but lost credibility when she included the animated character Bart Simpson on her list of offenders. Most analysts felt she actually helped boost American morale in the autumn of 1990. Saddam Hussein often appeared on Iraqi television alongside Western captives taken from planes in transit in Kuwait at the time of his invasion. The captives included Stuart Lockwood, a five-year-old British child whom he proceeded to pet. The broadcast did not endear him to Western viewers. During Operation Desert Storm

Iraq attempted to demoralize the coalition by parading prisoners of war. The wider Iraqi media policy rested on Western news broadcasts from Baghdad during the latter's attack. The presence of journalists like Peter Arnett (1934–) of CNN or John Simpson (1944–) of the BBC ensured that it was possible for viewers around the world to watch the effects of the Western bombardments. The Iraqi Ministry of Information steered journalists to sites of civilian damage, such as a factory identified—in what was clearly a recently painted sign in English and Arabic—as a powdered-milk plant whose product was ostensibly intended for babies, and waived all censorship to facilitate reporting of the extensive civilian casualties at a public air raid shelter in the Amiriya district of Baghdad. Coalition analysts later claimed that both targets had duel military and civilian functions and suggested that instigating damage to civilian targets was part of Saddam's propaganda strategy. Other Iraqi tactics included the creation of a black propaganda radio station—Holy Mecca Radio—designed to ferment opposition within Saudi Arabia.

On the battlefield the United States deployed the techniques of psychological warfare. As on the eve of D-Day in June 1944, the United States undertook a considerable campaign of deception to convince the Iraqis that the land assault on Kuwait would begin with a seaborne invasion; in actuality troops crossed the frontier from Saudi Arabia. The United States attempted to sow dissent by creating black propaganda stations like The Voice of Free Iraq and Radio Free Iraq, which purported to be the voice of opposition groups within Iraq. A white propaganda station, the Voice of the Gulf, broadcast war news to the Iraqi front lines. Between 30 December 1990 and 28 February 1991 the United States dropped around twenty-nine million leaflets over Iraqi lines. These included safe-conduct passes to encourage mass surrender, as well as intimidating leaflets warning of imminent aerial bombardment. Loudspeaker teams broadcast instructions on how to surrender, and sixty thousand Iraqi troops did so, greatly accelerating the progress of the Western campaign. The experience boosted U.S. confidence in the power of psychological warfare.

The restrictions of the UN resolution and the fragility of the coalition meant that the Bush administration had to limit its campaign in Iraq. The war ended with the liberation of Kuwait. The United States also appreciated the value of the "clean war" image to bolster domestic and international support. Analysts have noted that the United States ended the war at precisely the moment that the world saw the effect of its bombs on the Iraqi army's evacuation route, the Basra Road, which was subsequently dubbed the "Highway of Death." Saddam remained in office and proceeded to consolidate his dictatorship by attacking the Shiite Muslim opposition in the south and the Kurdish opposition in the north. The coalition had held for the duration of the conflict, but many in the Islamic world were not convinced of the wider benevolence of American involvement in the region. The spectacle of American troops operating from Saudi Arabia, a land holy to Muslims, enraged a number of religious extremists, including Osama bin Laden (1957–), whose actions would precipitate the next major Western intervention in the region ten years later. The media aspects of the war represented a high point of the post–Cold War Western domination of the global media. In subsequent campaigns the United States had to contend with alternative voices on both the Internet and non-Western satellite news channels.

Nicholas J. Cull

See also Arab World; Censorship; CNN; Hussein, Saddam; Israel; Morale; Opinion Polls; Psychological Warfare; Public Diplomacy; Satellite Communications; Terrorism, War on; United Nations

References: Kellner, Douglas. *The Persian Gulf TV War.* Boulder, CO: Westview, 1992; Manheim, Jarol B. *Strategic Public Diplomacy and American Foreign Policy: The Evolution of Influence.* New York: Oxford University Press, 1994; McArthur, John R. *Second Front: Censorship and*

Propaganda in the Gulf War. Berkeley, CA: University of California Press, 1993; Taylor, Philip M. *War and the Media: Propaganda and Persuasion in the Gulf War.* Manchester: Manchester University Press, 1992.

Gulf War (2003)

The war to remove Saddam Hussein (1937–) as the leader of Iraq began on 19 March 2003 with an invasion by the United States and Great Britain. The decision to invade was opposed by much of the Arab world, as well as by France, Germany, Russia, and China, all of whom promised to veto such a move if a vote were taken by the United Nations Security Council. U.S. President George W. Bush (1947–) and Britain's Prime Minister Tony Blair (1953–) chose to bypass the Security Council vote, putting the future of the United Nations at risk, for a war whose aims remained unpersuasive to most Europeans and most intellectuals in the United States. Officially, the war was related to the campaign against international terrorism (the connection to the 11 September 2001 incidents), including weapons of mass destruction, but also became a plan to "liberate Iraq" by "Coalition Forces," the latter a propaganda device to describe the United States and Britain in flattering terms. The taking of Basra by British forces and the taking of Baghdad by U.S. forces on 9 April marked the end of the overt conquest of Iraq, although long-term ramifications remained unclear.

The buildup to war in late 2002 and early 2003 saw intense domestic and international propaganda activity on the part of the U.S. and UK governments as they sought to justify their hard-line diplomacy and the impending conflict. Key moments included U.S. Secretary of State Colin Powell's address to the UN Security Council. During this period the British government issued a succession of dossiers on Iraqi weapons programs and human right abuses. The revelation that one of these dossiers was heavily plagiarized from a thesis written some years previously by a graduate student in California dented the Blair administration's reputation for skillful "spin."

Media reporting of the war and the war's psychological dimension are of particular concern to the student of propaganda. In both areas, the Gulf War of 2003 can claim a number of firsts. Clearly this was a war of swift military action, but also of competing information systems, a war in which television reporting of the war was a weapon for both Iraq and the United States and Britain, particularly with an eye toward influencing European as well as Arab public opinion. The United States controlled channel 3 of Iraqi state television, broadcasting directly to the Iraqi people. Direct e-mail and SMS (sent to mobile phones) text messages contacts with large numbers of Iraqi citizens provided a communication from the United States over the heads of the Iraqi government, part of the campaign for the "hearts and minds" of the Iraqi people.

The war produced a number of media innovations, particularly the decision to send reporters and television journalists as actual members of the invasion forces, on the one hand allowing a direct immediacy never before possible and on the other hand introducing a new intensity of information overload. Britain's Foreign Secretary Jack Straw argued that twenty-four-hour news changed the reality of warfare, now actually compressing time scales. All three of Britain's rolling news channels—Sky, BBC News 24, and the ITV News Channel—experienced early increases in numbers of viewers, with Sky winning the ratings war. For viewers of cable news in the United States, it was possible to watch the war twenty-four hours a day on Rupert Murdoch's Fox News (the largest cable news audience in the United States, with 3.4 million viewers at the war's outbreak), CNN, and MSNBC. Some 600 reporters, "embedded" in advancing units, with satellite phones and live visual feeds, could actually report a fire fight while it occurred. This represents a sharp departure from previous wars, in which re-

porters were generally, because of censorship concerns, far from actual scenes of battles or able to report only after filing reports to be approved by an official military censor. In 2003, war correspondents were not allowed to reveal exact information as to location, so the viewer was rarely able to place fighting within a particular geographical context. Journalists who violated this rule were expelled from the theater of war. Critics feared the new information policy would make cheerleaders of those who reported the war as part of the invasion forces. Media journalists made use of the videophone, allowing reporters to send an imprecise visual report by satellite directly from the field of battle, albeit with low resolution. The videophone also allowed direct conversation with news anchors halfway around the world.

By 2003, television news had adopted a form of print communication as well—the news crawl, in which news bulletins streamed across the bottom of the screen, a relief if what was being shown lacked interest, a distraction if not. Roughly a full third of the screen was thus filled with competing textual forms of information at all times, including information about the stock market. In Britain, critics termed this obsession with styles of graphic information "war porn," dismissing such round-the-clock broadcasting as relentless images lacking context or explanation. In sum, technology was better able to increase the speed and directness of communication than to provide greater accuracy, detailed information, or balance.

The three major U.S. television networks, ABC, CBS, and NBC, had reporters covering the war, often from inside neighboring Kuwait, but also in the form of numerous stringers, many of them British nationals. The war also offered opportunities for veteran journalists, some of whom posed in front of American tanks wearing simple t-shirts. Both CNN and the three major networks stationed news anchors, regularly in New York, on location in Kuwait. A number of journalists, including several who were killed by American "friendly fire," covered the invasion from inside Baghdad.

The print media did a good job of covering the war, even if at some distance from fast-moving events. Technology served the cause of print graphics. Aerial topography, brilliant graphic design, and the use of color allowed the *New York Times* to run daily full-page maps showing precisely what was happening, even inside metropolitan Baghdad, thanks to detailed photographic enlargements superimposed on an aerial map of the city.

Reporting an Arab or Iraqi perspective proved more difficult. In the first Gulf War, CNN's Peter Arnett (1934–) was able to report the war from Baghdad, a first for television news: a reporter describing the impact of missile strikes from the heart of enemy territory. Now such reporting comes from competing channels of information. Since 1996, Al Jazeera, the Arab television network in Qatar, has provided the Arab world with news programming of considerable independence. The United States included Al Jazeera correspondents among the "embedded" journalists travelling with invasion forces. American shells killed two Al Jazeera correspondents in central Baghdad. Peter Arnett, back reporting the war from Baghdad, was fired when he gave an interview on Iraqi state television in which he insisted that most Americans opposed the war, a claim that suggested he was giving aid and comfort to Saddam Hussein's forces. Arnett's firing suggests something about what may or may not be done by foreign reporters inside enemy territory.

Western reporters (generally non-U.S. citizens) in Baghdad during the invasion, hoping to discover the sentiment of the Iraqi people, had to conduct their interviews in the presence of official government "minders," with predictible results: those Iraqis interviewed were obliged to find only good things to say about Saddam Hussein. BBC correspondents in Baghdad, such as Rageh Omaar (1967–), had more success than U.S. reporters in getting a more representative sample of Iraqi public opinion. For Arabs, Al Jazeera is the most significant television source, one available to Arabs in the United States who have the necessary satellite reception. Saddam Hussein was able during the invasion to broadcast directly to Western audiences in feeds from Iraqi state television that were taken by numerous Western television networks, often with a news crawl in Arabic, allowing the Arab speaker to know for sure the original intent of an Iraqi soundbite.

Iraq's propaganda war swiftly became a comedy of errors. The central figure, Minister of Information Mohammed Saeed al-Sahhaf (1940–), attracted much amusement in the West for his unflinching optimism in the face of American advances. He earned the nicknames "Baghdad Bob" in the United States and "Comical Ali" in the UK. Websites in those countries swiftly began to offer mugs, t-shirts, and even talking dolls featuring his slogans: "God will roast their stomachs in hell at the hands of the Iraqis" or "We will kill them all . . . most of them." Al-Sahhaf became a symbol of the absurdity of the Iraqi regime, which had sustained itself through propaganda, attempting to save itself through propaganda alone, and a reminder that propaganda needs to be underpinned at some point by a physical ability to deliver what is promised.

The conflict between Western media coverage of the invasion and Arab coverage has largely turned on the issue of gore—that is, what will or will not be shown of the war's violence. A reporter for Al Jazeera was quoted as saying that "we don't see any of those killed by the American forces." Howell Raines of the *New York Times* indicated a different attitude: "the avoidance of the gratuitous use of images simply for shock value." Self-censorship may play a role, but to date American media have revealed little in terms of violent images. Still photographs, whether in newspapers or newsmagazines, have been mostly in color, technically excellent, but curiously lacking in interest. As Susan Sontag notes: "War is about dead people, not gorgeous-looking soldiers."

U.S. and British forces have intensified the use of psychological operations, known as "psy-ops." The United States engaged in a comprehensive airwaves campaign to soften its enemy and soothe its population at home. Spearheading the electronic propaganda campaign were converted C-130 cargo planes transmitting a mixture of Arabic and Western music, along with announcements to the troops and citizens of Iraq, urging them to lay down their weapons. These planes were the coalition's weapons of mass persuasion. The radio transmissions were backed up with an intense leaflet-dropping campaign. Over 17 million leaflets were dispersed in the first week of the war, offering detailed information about how to signal surrender to advancing coaliation troops. Warnings printed on the leaflets included "Attacking coalition aircraft invites your destruction. Do not risk your life and the lives of your comrades. Leave now and go home. Watch your children learn, grow and prosper." Or "Military fiber optic cables have been targeted for destruction. Repairing them places your life at risk."

The war to eliminate Saddam Hussein was officially connected to a war against international terrorism, particularly to the events of 11 September, a connection that remains to be demonstrated persuasively. U.S. (and British) justifications required the uncovering of evidence of biological and chemical weapons of mass destruction, something that had not been found by teams of UN arms inspectors after months of effort. In the absence of such evidence, many questioned the necessity of the invasion, although the success of that invasion muted some vocal opposi-

tion. If such evidence is found, it will make it harder to justify the value of the United Nations in keeping world peace.

There are many additional unanswered questions at this time about the unilateral invasion: whether the long-term impact will be to hasten the collapse of the United Nations; whether there will be long-term damage to the Security Council or NATO; whether the invasion will intensify hatred of the United States in the Arab world; and whether the invasion will lead to trade boycotts of U.S. products. It is clear that propaganda will play an important part in a post-Saddam Iraqi government and that Iraqi citizens will question the goodwill of U.S. and British occupation forces, wondering, for example, how much credence to give to a widely distributed British leaflet (in English) to those around Basra: "This time we won't abandon you. Be patient. Together we will win." If the actual invasion was quickly successful, the work of nation-building is certain to prove a far more difficult task.

David Culbert and David Welch

See also Gulf War (1991); Hussein, Saddam; Memorials and Monuments; Terrorism, War on

References: Bobbitt, Philip. *The Shield of Achilles: War, Peace, and the Course of History.* New York: Knopf, 2002; Hamza, Khidhir, with Jeff Stein. *Saddam's Bombmaker: The Inside Story of the Iraqi Nuclear and Biological Weapons Agenda.* New York: Scribner, 2002; Kuttab, Daoud. "The Arab TV Wars," *New York Times Magazine,* 6 April 2003, 44–47; McCarthy, Michael. "Iraq Information Minister Strikes Pop-Culture Chord." *USA Today,* 4 May 2003. McLuhan, Marshall. *Understanding Media: The Extensions of Man.* New York: Vintage Books, 1964; Sontag, Susan. *Regarding the Pain of Others.* New York: Farrar, Straus, 2003.

Health

The promotion of public health has become a staple subject of propaganda for governmental and nongovernmental organizations around the world. Government-sponsored health campaigns first appeared during World War I, although at this early stage they were rarely coordinated. Most of the belligerent states worried about the spread of venereal disease and launched campaigns to warn of the danger of unprotected sex. In World War II health campaigns figured more prominently in official propaganda. The wartime emergency meant that citizens had to be physically fit in order to fight, work in industry, cope with air raids, and endure hardship caused by food and other shortages.

In Britain during World War II adequate food supplies were recognized as a key factor in the maintenance of morale. The British government mobilized a number of ministries to explain official policy and to stress the importance of good health for the successful conclusion of the war effort. The Ministry of Food was one of the largest spenders on publicity, issuing a constant flow of leaflets, press advertisements, and short films explaining the rationing system and providing information on wartime recipes and ways of making limited supplies last

longer. The Ministry of Agriculture was responsible for increasing land under cultivation in order to grow more vegetables to feed the population. One of the most famous slogans of the war was "Dig for Victory." In 1943 Ernest Brown (1881–1962), the minister of health, was responsible for the booklet *How to Keep Well in Wartime,* which offered commonsense advice on a range of health issues. One particular health problem singled out was the need to combat venereal disease. A striking poster that accompanied the campaign depicted the "easy" girlfriend, as a skull in a fancy hat, as a source of VD.

A major concern for the authorities was the spread of germs, resulting in large-scale absenteeism from work. One of the most famous wartime slogans on posters was: "Coughs and Sneezes Spread Diseases." The booklet urged people to cough or sneeze into a handkerchief and denounced any failure to do so as a "rude and disgusting habit." Popular film stars and celebrities were recruited to add weight to these health campaigns. In 1942, for example, the comedian Arthur Askey (1900–1982) appeared in a short film documentary entitled *The Nose Has It!*

The maintenance of good health was a major concern of the fascist regimes as well. Health education figured prominently in Nazi propaganda, although this was largely in support of its sinister racial and eugenics campaigns. In July 1933 the "Law for the Prevention of Hereditarily Diseased Offspring" permitted the compulsory sterilization of people suffering from a number of allegedly hereditary illnesses. Less well known is the world's most aggressive antitobacco health campaign, launched by the Nazi government in the 1930s. Nazi policies included bans on smoking in public places, increased tobacco taxes, advertising bans, and research into links between tobacco and lung cancer. A massive antismoking propaganda campaign was launched (and maintained) with posters showing smokers being swallowed by cigarettes, bearing the caption: "You don't smoke it—it smokes you!" Hitler was also drafted to support the program. The caption beneath a picture of a determined-looking Hitler reads: "Our Führer Adolf Hitler drinks no alcohol and does not smoke . . . His performance at work is incredible."

In the 1980s a new global threat posed by the AIDS epidemic persuaded many governments around the world to launch campaigns (mainly television and advertising posters) warning of the dangers of unprotected sexual intercourse. A British campaign warned: "AIDS: Don't Die of Ignorance." Some of these campaigns broke new ground in terms of their explicit reference to sexual practices and the stark honesty about the scale of the epidemic. Some critics argued that they proved counterproductive because the message was so bleak that it scared people, who "turned off" or chose not to listen. Major sources of international information on AIDS included the UN's World Health Organization (WHO) and broadcasters such as the Voice of America.

Occasionally health propaganda has provoked a backlash. As Alan Winkler has noted, during the American occupation of the Italian island of Lampedusa toward the end of World War II, the citizens took exception to new rules and exhortations in the U.S. army propaganda newspaper against defecating in

public. A group of male inhabitants protested by gathering on the main piazza, and "with one accord they struck a blow for freedom."

David Welch

See also Drugs; Hitler, Adolf; MoI; *Reefer Madness*; United Nations; World War I

References: *Persuading the People: Government Publicity in the Second World War.* London: HMSO, 1995; Jowett, Garth, and Victoria O'Donnell. *Propaganda and Persuasion.* London: Sage, 1992; MacLaine, Ian. *Ministry of Morale: Home Front Morale and the Ministry of Information in World War II.* London: Unwin, 1979; Proctor, R. H. *Racial Hygiene: Medicine Under the Nazis.* Cambridge, MA: Harvard University Press, 1988; Winkler, Alan. *The Politics of Propaganda.* New Haven, CT: Yale University Press, 1978.

Hearst, William Randolph (1863–1951)

William Randolph Hearst was a successful American newspaper publisher who built up a readership through the technique of yellow journalism, which emphasized the sensational, lurid, entertaining, and scandalous elements in news coverage. In 1887 Hearst's father handed over control of his inconsequential *San Francisco Examiner* to his son, who modeled it after Joseph Pulitzer's (1847–1911) *New York World.* Hearst doubled its circulation in less than a year by stressing themes that were sure to please the masses: love, sex, crime, and violence. His most effective tool for publicity and propaganda was the "crusade," often in the form of exposés attacking police graft or government corruption.

In 1895 Hearst bought the *New York Morning Journal* and sought to dominate the New York newspaper scene. He placed public acceptance ahead of profit—or at least publicly claimed that this was the case. His championing of social reform seemed to improve his circulation figures. Involvement in international events culminated in his most important crusade: "Cuba Libre!" Hearst attacked Spain's treatment of Cubans. His approach to the Cuban question reflected the self-righteous mentality of many Americans of the 1890s. When staff artist Frederic Remington requested permission to return from Cuba, complaining that no war seemed likely, Hearst allegedly replied: "Please remain. You furnish the pictures and I'll furnish the war." More recently Joseph Campbell, a historian of journalism, has suggested that this story is just too good to be true. Hearst and his rival Pulitzer insisted that America had to go to war with Spain over the issue of Cuban independence. President William McKinley (1843–1901) obliged.

Hearst used his publishing empire to run (unsuccessfully) for both mayor and governor of New York. He unsuccessfully opposed American involvement in World War I. His publishing empire went into a steep decline by the end of the 1930s. Hearst is the subject of Orson Welles's (1915–1985) film masterpiece *Citizen Kane* (1941), in which all of Hearst's psychological problems are subsumed within his quest for "Rosebud," that elusive element missing from his childhood.

Brian Collins

See also Spanish-American War; United States (Progressive Era)

References: Campbell, W. Joseph. *Yellow Journalism: Puncturing the Myths, Defining the Legacies.* Westport, CT: Praeger, 2001; Procter, Ben. *William Randolph Hearst: The Early Years, 1863–1910.* New York: Oxford, 1998; Robinson, Judith. *The Hearsts: An American Dynasty.* Newark: University of Delaware Press, 1991; Swanberg, W. A. *Citizen Hearst.* New York: Scribner's, 1961.

Herzl, Theodor (1860–1904)

Journalist, playwright, essayist, and the founder of modern Zionism, Herzl was born into an assimilated Austrian Jewish family, although his commitment to Jewish causes did not feature prominently in his early life. After earning his doctorate from the University of Vienna, Herzl became a journalist for the Viennese *Neue Freie Presse,* which enabled him to travel extensively. Although initially a proponent of assimilation, in the 1890s Herzl became frustrated by the increasing level of anti-Semitism. Although he later claimed that it was his coverage of the Dreyfus Affair that made him a Zionist, his epiphany was actually a gradual process. In the aftermath of Dreyfus's public degradation and the vulgar anti-Semitism associated with it, Herzl concluded that only through the creation of a Jewish homeland could the problem of anti-Semitism be resolved. In 1896 he published his most famous work, *Der Judenstaat* (The Jewish State), which envisioned a multiethnic, polylingual nation similar to the Austro-Hungarian Empire. Herzl dedicated the rest of his life to the furtherance of the Zionist agenda.

Although known primarily for his diplomatic efforts and organizational ability on behalf of the Zionist movement—in particular the creation of the World Zionist Organization—Herzl was also extremely cognizant of the importance of publicity. Herzl's Zionist ideology sought to unify European Jewry behind a distinct secular national vision intent on regaining the ancestral homeland of the Jews. Herzl's major goal was to create a "New Jewish Man" through various Zionist cultural and educational program, and to disseminate these ideas in the print and visual media. For example, Herzl's statement following the First Zionist Congress (held in Basel, Switzerland, in 1897) that he had "created the Jewish State" must be seen in the context of generating excitement for the new movement. Herzl himself was presented as the archetype of the "New Jew" that Zionism sought to create through art and literature. Herzl and the Zionists were pioneers in the use of visual images. Indeed, Herzl believed that it was crucial for people to "think in images" since they provided the primary motivation for action. As a journalist Herzl recognized the powerful symbolic impact of music and other cultural activities on an educated middle class. The earliest publicity materials of Herzlian Zionism consisted of a series of postcards and delegates' cards produced in connection with the First Zionist Congress. Although crude by later standards, they helped introduce to a wider audience the pantheon of Zionist heroes—such as Herzl and Max Nordau (1849–1923)—who formed the mainstay of Zionist imagery until the end of World War I. After his death in 1904, Herzl's imagery took on epic proportions in both print and visual formats. Various portraits of him continued to circulate during subsequent Zionist congresses, and his life was presented as the quintessential journey from assimilation to Zionism.

Frederic Krome

See also Anti-Semitism; Israel; "J'Accuse"; Zionism

References: Berkowitz, Michael. *The Jewish Self-Image in the West.* New York: New York University Press, 2000; Kornberg, Jacques. *Theodor Herzl: From Assimilation to Zionism.* Bloomington: Indiana University Press, 1993. Robertson, Ritchie, and Edward Timms. *Theodor Herzl and the Origins of Zionism.* Edinburgh: Edinburgh University Press, 1997.

Hitler, Adolf (1889–1945)

Dictator of Nazi Germany and arguably the twentieth century's most notorious exponent of propaganda, Hitler was born in Austria. After training as an artist, he served and was wounded in the German army during World War I. By his own account (*Mein Kampf*) his war service taught him the power of propaganda. He saw how British propaganda destroyed German morale and paved the way for Germany's surrender. In 1919, while supposedly spying on extremist political activity for the army, he actually joined a tiny group, which he swiftly renamed the National Socialist German Workers' Party (NSDAP). In 1923 Hitler's Nazi party took part in an unsuccessful putsch in Munich. Following a period in jail, he began the slow task of building the Nazi Party into a serious political force. Hitler was a gifted orator whose rhetorical style was far more complex than the newsreel footage of his impassioned speeches suggests. His opening remarks often seemed clumsy and faltering, and he would build upon the sympathy of his listeners. He knew how to seek out and express the hidden feelings of his audience, hammering away at the idea of the uniqueness of the German people and stressing the way in which their destiny had been betrayed by their leaders and was now threatened by the two great evils of Communism and a Jewish world conspiracy.

By the early 1930s Hitler had become a force to be reckoned with. He campaigned relentlessly, using all the methods of mass communication to extend his reach and the airplane to maximize his personal appearances. In January 1933 mainstream German conservatives voted him into the government as chancellor in the hope that he could thereby be controlled. Instead, he lost no time in consolidating his power. Propaganda was at the heart of Hitler's state, whose embodiment was in the person of Hitler himself. The Nazi Party was organized according to the "leadership principle" (*Führerprinzip*), with every man obeying his appointed commander, and Hitler was the leader of all Germany. His image was everywhere, strong and staring into a distance at a glorious future that only he could see. A favorite Nazi slogan proclaimed the union of Germany, the state, and Hitler: "One people, one empire, one leader." He paid particular attention to education and censorship, creating an environment dominated by the Nazi view of the world. Hitler's Third Reich became famous for its great propaganda spectacles, such as the Nuremberg rallies, the monumental architecture of Albert Speer (1905–1981), and propaganda films directed by Leni Riefenstahl (1902–), including the spectacular *Triumph of the Will* (1935). Despite the latter, the Ministry for Popular Enlightenment and Propaganda (RMVP) spent much more time commissioning escapist fantasy art and films.

With the outbreak of World War II, German propaganda moved overseas. Hitler used propaganda like an artillery barrage to soften up his enemy before the decisive blow. Here Hitler's personal role sometimes proved a liability. He weakened the credibility of Germany's case by issuing needlessly grandiose

German Chancellor Adolf Hitler receives the ovation of the Reichstag in Berlin in March 1938 after announcing the "peaceful" acquisition of Austria. (National Archives)

statements that became hostages to fortune, as was the case in July 1940, when he announced that the war had been won, or in July 1941, when he proclaimed the defeat of the USSR. As early victories gave way to a stalemate on the steppes of the USSR, and the noose of Allied air power tightened around Germany's neck, Hitler and Joseph Goebbels (1897–1945), his propaganda minister, attempted to use propaganda to rally the German public for a total war. At this point Nazi Germany paid the price for its "leadership principle." Hitler—as though believing his own propaganda—assumed personal command of numerous military operations and refused to acknowledge that victory had deserted him. No amount of propaganda could prevent the destruction of Hitler's Germany in 1945.

Nicholas J. Cull

See also Anti-Semitism; Austrian Empire; The Big Lie; Civil Defense; Fascism, Italian; Germany; Goebbels, Joseph; Health; Holocaust Denial;

Lord Haw-Haw; *Mein Kampf;* Poland; Portraiture; Portugal; Propaganda, Definitions of; Psychological Warfare; RMVP; Rumor; World War II (Germany)

References: Domarus, Max. *Hitler: Speeches and Proclamations 1932–1945.* 4 vols. Wauconda, IL: Bolchazy-Carducci, 1990– ; Kershaw, Ian. *The Hitler Myth: Image and Reality in the Third Reich.* Oxford: Oxford University Press, 1987; Welch, David. *The Third Reich: Politics and Propaganda.* 2d ed. New York: Routledge, 2002.

Holland

See Netherlands, Belgium, and Luxembourg

Holocaust Denial

This term is applied to any individuals, groups, or institutions that seek to dispute or minimize the events relating to the destruction of European Jewry during World War II. The primary goal of the deniers is to rehabilitate Hitler and Nazi ideology by belittling what they believe to be the prime event that discredited Nazism, namely, the Holocaust. Holocaust deniers cast themselves as "revisionists," thereby attempting to lay claim to historical legitimacy by arguing that they are merely trying to examine the "other" side of the issue in order to uncover the true facts. The basic tenets of the deniers' arguments involve one or more of the following themes: (1) Hitler never intended to destroy the Jews and was unaware of what was happening—no document bearing Hitler's signature can be found ordering the destruction of the Jews. (2) Hitler's plan was to force the emigration of the Jews. Accordingly, Jews were rounded up and herded into camps. Because of the Allied blockade and bombings, the available food supply was drastically reduced, and many Jews died of hunger and disease, although the total number was less than six hundred thousand. Allied action also led to the deaths of hundreds of thousands of innocent Germans—thus the Allies and the Nazis are moral equals. (3) The Jews, in conjunction with Soviet Russia, engineered the escape of the Jews eastward and then blamed the German people for genocide. (4) Auschwitz was not a death camp and no one was gassed there. (5) The Holocaust was an anti-German propaganda myth spread by the victorious Allies and orchestrated by the Jews to justify harsh reparations. The unifying subtext behind all these theories is a Jewish conspiracy. Although many deniers refuse to acknowledge it, anti-Semitism motivates most adherents of Holocaust denial.

Holocaust deniers use a variety of tactics to justify their claims. One employs the old Roman legal maneuver whereby if one part of a testimony is found to be false, the entire testimony is invalidated. Deniers consequently look for small inconsistencies in either survivor testimony or historical works, claiming that these mistakes invalidate the entire narrative. One such effort, which occurred in the 1970s, revolved around the old story that the Nazis used the body fat of their victims to make soap. When legitimate

historians found that canard to be untrue, deniers leaped into the fray, arguing that it brought into question the entire story of the Holocaust.

Another common tactic of the deniers is to engage in historical inquiries that on the surface appear legitimate but upon closer examination prove to be based on pseudoscience. One prominent example was the investigation of the Auschwitz gas chambers by Fred Leuchter (1944–), who bore the nickname Dr. Death because he earned his living making execution devices for prisons. Leuchter, who claimed to be an engineer, went to Auschwitz in 1988 and took samples off the walls of the gas chambers and crematoria in order to test for the presence of cyanide. His conclusion that these chambers could not have been used to gas people was applauded and publicized by the deniers. Detailed study of the "Leuchter Report" revealed that it was based on erroneous assumptions (cyanide does not penetrate deeply into concrete). It also emerged that Leuchter had falsified his credentials and overstated his expertise. Despite this, his report is still cited by deniers.

Perhaps the most serious inroads of the deniers into legitimate historical circles resulted from the writings of David Irving (1938–). A self-trained British historian, Irving had written a number of popular history books about World War II and wartime personalities. Although specialists in the field often criticized his work as pro-Nazi and careless in its treatment of primary sources, Irving was often accepted as a reputable scholar who had uncovered new sources on the Nazi era. Claiming to have been won over to the revisionist camp by the "Leuchter Report," Irving became the primary spokesman for the notion that Hitler had not known about the plight of the Jews and that no one was gassed at Auschwitz. His biography of Joseph Goebbels attracted special attention by claiming that it was Goebbels and not Hitler who was behind all the anti-Semitic activities. After his publisher cancelled the book's publication in 1997, Irving depicted himself as a free-speech martyr, the victim of a Jewish conspiracy. Irving later sued American historian Deborah Lipstadt (1947–) for libel in a British court after she had branded him a Holocaust denier. Irving, who represented himself during the trial (January–April 2000), lost his suit and was assessed a heavy monetary fine.

Holocaust denial is the special provenance of the Institute for Historical Review (IHR), a California-based organization, which held its first annual convention in 1979. In addition to its meetings, IHR publishes a journal and maintains a website. Between 1990 and 2001 Holocaust denial reached a broader audience through the Internet. One such organization is the Committee for the Open Debate on the Holocaust (CODOH), run by Bradley R. Smith (1939–). Smith routinely sends full-page ads to college newspapers challenging the validity of the Holocaust under the guise of open debate. The most significant inroads of Holocaust denial have been in the Islamic world, where it has become an integral part of the ongoing Israeli-Palestinian/Israeli-Arab conflict. Islamic Holocaust denial is based on the notion that it was Western guilt over the Holocaust that led to the creation of the State of Israel. Since the Holocaust is a creation of Zionist propaganda, and since Israel uses the Holocaust to "drum up sympathy" in the Western world, according to this argument, the exposure of the "myth" of the Holocaust is necessary in order to eliminate Western support for the Jewish state. Holocaust denial has thus become part of the conventional wisdom of Islamic polemics, which seeks to delegitimize Israel.

Frederic Krome

See also Anti-Semitism; Arab World; Internet; Israel

References: Evans, Richard J. *Lying about Hitler: History, Holocaust, and the David Irving Trial.* New York: Basic Books, 2001; Lipstadt, Deborah E. *Denying the Holocaust: The Growing Assault on Truth and Memory.* New York: Free Press, 1993; Shermer, Michael, and Alex Grobman. *Denying* *History: Who Says the Holocaust Never Happened and Why Do They Say It?* Berkeley: University of California Press, 2000.

Horst Wessel Lied (1929)

The Horst Wessel Lied ("Die Fahne hoch!"—Raise the Flag!) became the second national anthem in Nazi Germany between 1933 and 1945. It was easy to sing and was meant to be sung by persons marching in uniform. The song's success in 1930 owes much to Joseph Goebbels' (1897–1945) propaganda and publicity tactics in Berlin. The song's author, Horst Wessel (1907–1930), was the son of a prominent Lutheran pastor in Berlin who served as military chaplain before his death in 1915. Wessel joined the SA (Nazi storm troopers) and published the text of his song in a Nazi newspaper in the autumn of 1929. Early in 1930 Wessel was shot by Communists in his Berlin apartment; he had moved in with a prostitute whom he planned to make an honest woman. When Wessel died in a hospital room on 23 February 1930, Goebbels arranged for a lavish funeral.

Wessel's song became so ubiquitous after 1933 that it threatened to replace "Deutschland, Deutschland über Alles" in the affections of many an ardent Nazi, in part because the song's range was easier for the amateur singer. Wessel did not write the tune, though he was officially credited as its composer. The tune shares many similarities with earlier German folksongs, but the exact source was a familiar sailor's song dating from the early 1900s. Nevertheless, the official Berlin publisher To-Ma credited Wessel with tune and text. This was the first Nazi marching song released as a record (1930) and was available in an amazing number of arrangements, including mandolin quartet, guitar solo, and harmonica, to say nothing of vocal arrangements for women's choruses and school choirs. The first verse runs: "Die Fahne hoch, die Reihen dicht geschlossen, / S.A. marschiert mit mutig festem Schritt. / Kam'raden, die Rot front und Reaktion erschossen, / marschier'n im Geist in unsem Reihen mit." (Raise the flag! Close ranks! / The SA marches calmly with purposeful tread. / Comrades killed by the Red Front and reactionaries / march with us in spirit.)

David Culbert

See also Goebbels, Joseph; Music

References: Baird, Jay W. *To Die for Germany: Heroes in the Nazi Pantheon.* Bloomington: Indiana University Press, 1990; Murdoch, Brian. *Fighting Songs and Warring Words: Popular Lyrics of Two World Wars.* London: Routledge, 1990; Welch, David. *Propaganda and the German Cinema, 1933–1945.* London: I. B. Tauris, 2001.

Hungary
See Austrian Empire

Hussein, Saddam (1937–)

Saddam Hussein was born in 1937 in Tikrit, near Baghdad. In the 1950s he became involved in the Ba'ath Party, which combined socialism and Iraqi and Arab nationalism in a potent blend. Like European fascists of the early 1920s, its leaders preached that violence could be a creative force. Saddam took part in two unsuccessful coups (1959 and 1964) before playing a key role in the revolution of 1968. During the 1970s he came to dominate the revolutionary government in Iraq, emerging as president in 1979.

Propaganda was at the heart of Saddam's Ba'ath Party regime. He controlled the media and nurtured the sort of personality cult familiar from other twentieth-century dictatorships. Saddam's portrait was ubiquitous in Iraq and was often rendered as a vast mural. The chief architect of his image in print was the poet and journalist Abdul-Amir Malla. Part of Saddam's brand of nationalism included appealing to the past glories of Iraq. Murals frequently depicted him as one of the great rulers of Iraq's past. To this end he sponsored vast archeological excavations at such ancient sites as Nineveh and Babylon, which included massive reconstructions. Modern propaganda projects intended to boost his image included some eighty-three palaces and an enormous victory arch in Baghdad—an immense sculpture consisting of crossed swords erected to mark the end of the eight-year war with Iran, which included an extended radio propaganda duel. Saddam also deployed one of the most ancient propaganda devices, claiming genealogical descent from Ali, the fourth caliph of Baghdad.

Iraqi 25-dinar note bearing the likeness of Saddam Hussein. The notes were overprinted for use as occupation currency when Iraq controlled Kuwait after the invasion, August 1991. (Courtesy of David Culbert)

Hoping to use Kuwaiti oil revenues to speed his postwar reconstruction, in 1990 he invaded Kuwait. He remained in power long after the victorious Western forces in the Gulf War of January and February 1991 forced him to leave that country. During this armed conflict Saddam pursued a number of propaganda strategies. He addressed himself to the people of the Arab world as a truer representative of the people's aspirations than their ruling elites and sought the approval of the region by launching missile attacks against Israel. In his approach to the West Saddam sought to exploit the so-called Vietnam Syndrome, gambling that the U.S.-led coalition could not sustain massive casualties. His tactic of revealing Iraqi casualties resulting from bombardment to the Western media and steering correspondents like Peter Arnett (1934–) of CNN to such scenes proved effective.

Contrary to Western expectations, Saddam survived the Gulf War and the Shi'ite and Kurdish rebellions that followed. His control of the media sustained the regime, and in 2002 he orchestrated a public display of his popularity by organizing a plebiscite and winning around 99 percent of the vote. He continued to present himself to the world as the man who had defied the West and whose people suffered "unjust" sanctions and periodic U.S. and British air attacks.

In late 2002 Saddam engaged in an international propaganda duel with the United States and Britain, insisting that he had no weapons of mass destruction and hence could not be in violation of UN resolutions. The United States refused to compromise and in March 2003 led a war to oust Saddam from power. Saddam was seldom seen during this war. The burden of representing the regime in public fell to the minister of information, Mohammed Saeed al-Sahhaf (1940–), who became famous for his absurdly overoptimistic press briefings. Within three weeks Saddam's regime lay in ruins. The demolition of statues of Saddam provided potent images for his defeat: propaganda from the destruction of propaganda. Saddam's exact fate, like that of Osama bin Laden following the U.S. war in Afghanistan, soon became a matter for propaganda claims and counterclaims. As with bin Laden, defiant taped messages purporting to be from the missing leader were released to the press. Given the simultaneous news that Saddam's family had absconded with billions of dollars from the Iraqi treasury—enough to build a pile of banknotes three times as high as New York City's Empire State Building—Saddam out of power seemed unlikely to have much of a future as a folk hero in Iraq or elsewhere.

Nicholas J. Cull

See also Arab World; Gulf War; Israel; Memorials and Monuments; Terrorism, War on
References: Karsh, Efraim, and Inari Rautsi. *Saddam Hussein: A Political Biography.* London: Brasseys, 1991; Taylor, Philip M. *War and the Media: Propaganda and Persuasion in the Gulf War.* Manchester: Manchester University Press, 1992.

I

Iceland
See Scandinavia

Ignatius of Loyola, Saint (1491–1556)

The founder of the Jesuit Order and pioneer of systematic propaganda, Iñigo Lopez de Recalde was born in Loyola, northern Spain, to a wealthy family. He began his religious activity in 1522, after a war wound cut short a promising military career. Ignatius of Loyola's core idea was to apply military discipline and structure to religious enterprise. In 1534 he and his associate Francis Xavier (1506–1552) founded the Society of Jesus in Paris. In 1539 he traveled to Rome, and beginning in 1540 he operated with the authority of Pope Paul III (r. 1534–1549). The original objective of the order was to convert the Islamic world to Christianity, but the Jesuits were soon redeployed in the struggle against the Reformation and again to win new converts in the lands then being opened up to European trade. Ignatius of Loyola himself sent missionaries to Brazil, India, and Japan. He realized the importance of education to the propagation of Catholic doctrine. Members of his order used the term "propaganda" to describe their work. In 1622 the Vatican made him a saint.

Nicholas J. Cull

See also Latin America; Reformation and Counter-Reformation; Religion; Switzerland

References: Meissner, W. W. *Ignatius of Loyola.* New Haven, CT: Yale University Press, 1992; Caraman, Philip. *Ignatius Loyola: A Biography of the Founder of the Jesuits.* San Francisco: Harper and Row, 1990.

Indian Subcontinent

The history of propaganda in the Indian subcontinent is unique thanks to the linguistic, socioeconomic, and cultural diversity of the region. Propaganda became a central feature of the state during British colonial rule. Though news writers (known as *waquiah nawis*) were already present during the Mughal period (1526–1857), the birth of modern newspapers made propaganda central to government and public discourse in India. Britain's East India Company made extensive use of news reporters, who used newsletters to disseminate "speedy and up-to-date information about the market, business transactions, shipping, [and] decisions of the administration" to the Indian capitalist class, which had emerged under British patronage. In 1780 James Augustus Hicky, a "disgruntled" employee of the company, launched the first newspaper, the *Bengal Gazette or Calcutta General Advertiser,* with the aim of "effecting more easy circulation of such information as are either useful or entertaining and tending to promote the trading concerns of industrious individuals."

In the colonial era British state propaganda was covert and indirect and took the form of suppression and censorship. The period between 1780 and 1818 witnessed stringent government regulation and control. Lord Wellesley (1760–1842), who served as the governor general between 1798 and 1805, appointed an official censor to inspect all newspaper copy well in advance of publication. Failure to submit papers for censorship was a punishable offense and on several occasions led to editors being deported without benefit of trial. Many others were censured and forced to apologize.

With the abolition of censorship in 1818 by the then governor general, Lord Hastings (1754–1826), the reins of control over public opinion loosened. This trend continued until the end of the 1860s. Of Hastings's successors neither Lord Amherst (1773–1857) nor William Bentinck (1774–1839) insisted on the enforcement of existing regulations. The period 1818 to 1868 was most conducive for the nationalistic media to take root and flourish. In fact, newspapers became potent instruments in the hands of an emerging bourgeois middle class, who advocated socioreligious movements under the influence of liberal Western ideas and were largely beholden to the patronage of the colonial administration. They also reflected the increasing clash of interests between foreign rulers and the rising nationalistic middle class. For the latter, press and education were significant factors that could effectively counter the incursion of the state into the ideological realm. By the end of the 1870s the propaganda function of the press was widely recognized and a clear distinction was visible between a pro-Raj press and a nationalistic, anticolonial press.

A number of laws were passed between the late eighteenth and twentieth centuries with the objective of limiting public exposure to "antistate" views and opinions. Three of them deserve mention. The Vernacular Press Act of 1878 discriminated against Indian-language newspapers. Many papers had to publish entirely in English following the act. The Newspapers (Incitement to Offences) Act of 1908 was passed "in view of the close connection between the perpetration of outrages by means of explosives and the publication of criminal incitements in certain newspapers." In such cases the administration was empowered to confiscate the printing press used in the production of the newspaper and to stop its lawful issue. The Indian Press Act of 1910 had a wider scope. Apart from incitements to murder and acts of violence, the act dealt with other "specified classes of published matter, including any words or signs tending to seduce soldiers or sailors from their allegiance to duty, to bring into hatred or contempt the British Government, any native prince or any section of His Majesty's subjects in India or to intimidate public servants or private individuals."

With the change in the colonial government's attitude to the question of India's freedom, some of these acts were subsequently either amended or repealed. Such events as the end of World War I, the Jalianwalla Bagh massacre in 1919, and the homecoming of Mahatma Gandhi (1869–1948) in 1921 gave a fillip to the freedom movement, which in turn generated hunger for news among the public. Both the English- and regional-language press fostered such eagerness through consistent coverage.

The years 1930 to 1945 witnessed a significant transformation in the organizational patterns and ideological moorings of the media. By then it had become increasingly difficult even for successful newspapers to remain in production without sustained financial support and the patronage of big business. Although many of the nationalistic Indian newspapers had brilliant editors, their printing and composing machines were totally outdated and worn out. This made it impossible for them to compete in get-up and "class" with the privileged few, who not only received large subsidies in the form of government advertisements but also could afford to hire trained and experienced staff and buy expensive modern equipment. Having realized the significance of financial patronage, newspapers like the *Free Press Journal, Sentinel, Hindustan Times,* and *National Call* were "flirting with" or trying to woo big businesses—to help the mill owners in the name of *swadeshi,* boost Indian insurance in the name of nationalism, and support Indian shipping because it was a national enterprise. *National Call* campaigned on behalf of General Motors and Dunlop in return for finances to run the paper.

The pro-independence Congress Party proved well able to mobilize mass support through propaganda. Gandhi proved a master of propaganda through symbolic action. This reached a climax in 1930 with the launch of the civil disobedience movement. The center of Congress Party activity shifted form urban to rural areas. There was heightened propaganda to mobilize the rural masses through a committed cadre and by using a variety of instruments, including newspapers and volunteer organizations. This shift eventually led to the radicalization of congress and an ideological transformation in the direction of socialism. However, despite limited success in organizing different segments of the society—peasants, workers, students, and women—and winning the support of cultural organizations, the spokesmen for socialist ideas could not hold a hegemonic position in the nationalistic propaganda.

Censorship was used effectively by the British administration during World War II (1939–1945) both to counter the Japanese short-wave propaganda and the "Quit India" campaign of congress. Food and financial incentives were used to gain the support of the poor, the laboring class, and the educated middle class for the military in eastern India. Newspapers were ensured of liberal supplies of newsprint and suitable news material to sustain wartime nationalism and a negative propaganda against congress, which declared its opposition to the war. Also, a Film Advisory Board was introduced in 1940 with a view to creating the necessary infrastructure of documentary production to aid the war efforts. In 1943 two other agencies—the Information Films of India and the Indian News Parade—were launched to broaden film production and distribution. The exhibitors were asked to include two thousand feet of government-approved propaganda film.

It may be noted that the religious rift in the freedom movement became apparent in the first decade of the twentieth century when the All-India Muslim League was formed with a view to protect and advance the political rights and interests of the Muslims of India. The formation of the league signified the "emergence of Muslim nationalism in an organised form." Throughout the four decades that followed, under the political and intellectual guidance of leaders like Muhammad Ali Jinnah (1876–1948) and Allama Iqbal (1875–1952) the league actively campaigned to gain more support from Indian Muslims. A consolidated northwest Muslim Indian state (consisting of Punjab, North-West Frontier Provinces, Sind, and Baluchistan) within or outside the British Empire had become its cardinal demand by 1930. In 1940 Jinnah declared that Muslims were a nation according to any definition of a nation and had a right to their homeland, their territory, and their state. This had the potential to become a slogan to rally the Muslim masses. Under these circumstances, in contrast to the decision of the congress to oppose the British involvement in World War II, the league supported it on the condition that the latter accepted its demands.

The immediate postindependence years constituted one of the most tumultuous periods in the history of the subcontinent. The British left behind two nations—Pakistan, which chose to be an Islamic country, and India, which sought to remain secular—thus redrawing the political map of South Asia. Like the country, the provinces of Punjab and Bengal were divided, leading to bloody riots within these divisions. There was a complete separation of religious communities in the northwestern province of Punjab.

Both India and Pakistan inherited ruined economies. Their charismatic leaders—including Gandhi, Jinnah, and Allama Iqbal—lost their lives not long after the end of colonial rule. The newly independent India, under the premiership of Jawaharlal Nehru (1889–1964) and Pakistan, under the prime ministership of Liaquat Ali Khan (1895–1951), defined their foreign policy in terms of carving out distinct spaces for themselves in global politics as uncommitted nations. Liaquat Ali Khan, like Nehru, was a staunch supporter of nonalignment. Ironically, from the 1950s through the 1970s the foreign policies of both countries were molded and modified by the politics of the Cold War between the United States and the USSR, each superpower possessing military and political aspirations in the Asian region. Pakistan's need for economic aid and international safeguards for its sovereignty and security eventually drew it closer to the United States, whose agenda was to contain Communist China in the continent. Pakistan was considered by the United States as a potential "advocate of Western policies that can exert a moderating influence on extreme nationalism and anti-Western attitudes." Under the presidency of General Muhammad Ayub Khan (1907–1974), since the early 1960s Pakistan had also taken steps to develop a closer understanding with China. At the other end, the USSR nurtured ties with India to counterbalance China in the region and to check the advance of Western capitalism. The Indo-Soviet relationship culminated in the Treaty on Peace, Friendship and Cooperation of 1971. This treaty is considered by many as a major political and strategic factor that restrained both China and the United States from intervening militarily in the Indo-Pakistan war of 1971. Since the Cold War has become a thing of the past, and given the strengthening of nonproliferation norms and antiterrorism propaganda, political relations within and outside the subcontinent are undergoing realignment.

The elite who came to power in free India projected themselves as strong champions of freedom of expression. In his address to the All-India Newspapers Editors' Conference held in 1950, Nehru stated that it is better to have a completely free press, with all the dangers resulting from the misuse of that freedom, than a suppressed or regulated press. The Indian press has remained the one with the least political control, with the exception of the Emergency period (1975–1977) imposed by Indira Gandhi (1917–1984), Nehru's daughter and the then prime minister, during which the press was subjected to censorship and owners were threatened with seizure and the transfer of their property. As a result, it was forced to play a docile role. While this episode exposed the weakness of the Indian fourth estate, it also provided the champions of freedom of expression with a hard lesson in democracy. The Anti-Defamation Bill, introduced by the Rajiv Gandhi (1944–1991) government in 1988 to curb the investigative role of the press, failed to become law in the face of widespread protests.

The press in Pakistan cannot claim to be free to the same degree, though it is considered one of the most outspoken in the region. It has suffered heavily at the hands of authorities—both elected governments and martial regimes—who have resorted to repressive legal and constitutional measures to make them toe the official line. The Press and Publication Ordinance (PPO) promulgated in 1963, which was repealed and replaced by the Registration of Printing Press Ordinance (RPPO) in the mid-1980s, is by far the strongest instrument used by the government to close down newspapers and silence the press. Governments could also indirectly curb the press since it controlled the allocation of newsprint and the release of public advertisements. In the absence of adequate democratic and constitutional safeguards to protect their interests, journalists have been compelled either to work under a self-imposed censorship or to engage in political propaganda that suits the government. Efforts are now being made to enhance the scope of media freedom in Pakistan. Newsprint quotas were abolished in 2000 and a customs duty on newsprint was reduced. In 2001 the government presented a model freedom of information act for wider public debate.

Interestingly, in the case of television in India, the involvement of the private sector has become significant since the mid-1990s. Until then the government had maintained total control over this media institution. The party in power has always used television to influence and alter the terms of political debate. For instance, it has been argued that the soap-opera serialization of the *Ramayana* on national television from January 1987 to September 1990 helped the Hindu right propagate and assert its political agenda, which centered on the issue of the reconstruction of the Ram temple in Ayodhya. On the other hand, radio, which was introduced to the subcontinent in 1921 as an experiment and was made into a state monopoly in 1930, remained an important arm of state propaganda machinery until the mid-1990s. Legislation was passed to make both radio and television autonomous. In the case of Pakistan, the electronic media is virtually owned by the government. This has given rise to the criticism that this segment of media "presents an unrealistically positive and sanitized version of reality." The mutual banning of media broadcasts by Pakistan and India has figured centrally in the conflict between the two countries. For instance, in June 1999 India banned the relaying of Pakistan Television (PTV) programs, saying that they contain malicious matter. In September 2001 Pakistan banned the airing of Indian cable and satellite programs because of their purported anti-Pakistan propaganda.

More recently even the Indian press has been accused of playing a propaganda role in specific contexts. The most conspicuous instance is the partisan role played by a section of the English and regional language press—especially the Hindi press—in the early 1990s when the Hindutva ideology was being propagated vehemently by such right-wing parties as the Bharatiya Janata Party. Capitalizing on the sentiments of the upper castes during the antireservation agitation of the late 1980s, this party rekindled the federating tendency of the essentially caste-centered electoral politics in the country around a common platform called "Hindutva." The phenomenal growth of the Hindi-language press in the post-1979 period is directly linked to this tendency.

Tara S. Nair

See also British Empire; Gandhi, Mohandas K.

References: Brass, Paul R. *Language, Religion and Politics in North India.* Delhi: Vikas, 1975; Chakravarty, Nikhil. "The Press: Changing Face of the Watchdog." *India,* 15 August 1997; Mahmood, Safdar. *Pakistan: Political Roots and Development.* New Delhi: Sterling, 1990; Media Watch. *State of the Media and Press Freedom Report, Pakistan, 2000–2001.* Islamabad, Pakistan: Green Press, 2000–2001; Moitra, Mohit. *A History of Indian Journalism.* Calcutta: National Book Agency, 1969; Nair, Tara S. "Growth and Structure of the Indian Press." Ph.D. dissertation. Centre for Development Studies, Trivandrum and Jawaharlal Nehru University, New Delhi, 1998; Ram, N. "An Independent Press and Anti-Hunger Strategies: The Indian Experience." In *The Political Economy of Hunger.* Vol. 2, *Famine Prevention.* Ed. Amartya Sen and Jean Dreze. Oxford: Clarendon Press, 1990; Sahni, J. N. *Truth About the Indian Press.* Bombay: Allied Publishers, 1974.

Indonesia

Indonesia is the fourth largest country in Asia, with the fourth largest population in the world (estimated at almost 213 million in 2000). It comprises some fourteen thousand islands, many tiny and uninhabited; two thirds of its population resides on a handful of these islands, including Java and Bali. The vast majority of Indonesia's inhabitants are Muslim. Propaganda has figured centrally in each religion's efforts to capture the hearts and minds of the three hundred ethnic groups in today's Indonesia. It has been a staple in the nationalistic-colonialist struggles of the twentieth century. To Westerners Indonesia evokes powerful associations with a primitive "otherness," sometimes viewed simply as exotic but also viewed as offering a more truthful alternative to Western civilization, as popularized by American anthropologist Margaret Mead (1901–1978) in her writings of the 1930s. Today's Indonesia is a blend of enormous urban congestion and extreme rural isolation, the latter imposed by the need for water transportation.

Indonesia came under Dutch control in 1602, when the Dutch East India Company seized power, operating a highly lucrative trade with the Netherlands until 1798. The latter's government itself controlled the Netherlands East Indies, as Indonesia was then known, from 1816 until 1941. Japan assumed power from 1942 to 1945. On 17 August 1945 Ahmed Sukarno (1907–1970) declared the independence of Indonesia; on 17 December 1949 the Dutch granted Indonesia full independence. In 1966, following months of political turmoil and the assassination of many of the most powerful Indonesian generals, Lt. Gen. Mohamed Suharto (1921–) replaced Sukarno and was reelected every five years until 1998. After additional turmoil, Megawati Sukarnoputri, Sukarno's daughter (1947–) became president in 2001.

The story of Indonesian nationalism pitted against Dutch colonialism is a familiar tale, but there are important differences that will be of particular interest to the student of propaganda since they are occasioned by media campaigns of persuasion. For example, when the Japanese established a protectorate in 1942, they brought Sukarno back from exile, making him the leader of his country, though to the Dutch he simply became a wartime collaborator with the enemy. These issues are dealt with in a film by Joris Ivens (1898–1989), who in 1946 resigned as Dutch film commissioner for Indonesia, subsequently releasing *Indonesia Calling,* a documentary made in Sydney, Australia, with the support of the major Australian dockworkers' unions. Ivens's outspoken appeal for Indonesian independence was a prototype for later Third World solidarity films. The film caused the Dutch to strip Ivens of his citizenship, leading an unidentified contemporary enthusiast to note that "this film explains why his waits for sponsorship have often been long."

Much of Indonesian history since 1975 has involved a variant form of nationalism, the effort by Indonesia to impose itself militarily on East Timor, half of a large island east of Bali that had been a Portuguese colony until gaining independence in 1975. East Timor's inhabitants, reflecting centuries of Portuguese rule, were primarily Roman Catholic. Its independence movement, using the acronym FRETILIN, waged a guerrilla war against Indonesia from the western part of Timor. UN observers estimate that some sixty thousand people were killed as a result of ethnic cleansing, in which Muslim West Timor attacked Catholic East Timor. On 30 August 2001 East Timor's independence was confirmed in UN-supervised free elections. World media attention focused on the bombing of mostly Australian tourists at a Bali nightclub in 2002, the act of Muslim terrorists.

The student of propaganda should not neglect the contribution of ethnographic writing, photography, and film to Western perceptions of an idyllic "precivilized" world. For example, Margaret Mead became a household name in the United States in the 1930s thanks to her publications based on fieldwork as a young anthropologist, first in Samoa and then in Bali. She took thousands of photographs, a selection of which appeared in book form in 1942. She also filmed tribal customs, often emphasizing the culture's sexual freedom, a subject that found wide interest in American mass-circulation magazines of the 1930s. *A Balinese Family* (ca. 1942) illustrates Mead's approach. In the words of an anonymous reviewer, this film is "a study of a Balinese family showing the way in which father and mother treat the three youngest children . . . There are scenes showing the father giving the baby his breast." Subsequent ethnographic films of Indonesia include Robert Gardner's *Dead Birds* (1964), a powerful study of symbolic warfare among the Dani of western (Indonesian) New Guinea.

Given the remoteness of so many of the smaller islands and the enormous ethnic diversity of the country, it is impossible to publish a single national newspaper. In Jakarta, the capital, *Kompas* is the leading newspaper, with a circulation of over 500,000. In 1995 there were 28.1 million radios, not nearly enough to permit one to say that radio reaches all 213 million inhabitants. Television was introduced in 1962. By 1995 the country had 11.5 million sets. There are three major television networks: TV Indonesia (TVRI), Rojawali Citra TV, and a small educational network in Jakarta. Officially there is no censorship of the press, but this does not extend to foreign journalists or foreign films and television programs, which might be more inclined to comment on domestic affairs. Since 1975 Indonesian electronic media have used a great deal of American programming, as well as American commercials—the latter, of course, edited for local consumption and with Indonesian voice-overs. As one Indonesian official noted, Indonesia is a country that wants a national mass media but needs the technological assistance of outsiders. It is a dilemma that makes virtually every television program or foreign feature film a source of interest to the student of propaganda.

David Culbert

See also Australia; Philippines; Southeast Asia; Sukarno; United Nations; World War II (Japan)
References: Anderson, Michael. "Transnational Advertising and Politics: The Case of Indonesia." *Asian Society* 20 (December 1980): 1253–1270; Foerstel, Leonota, and Angela Oilliam. *Confronting the Margaret Mead Legacy: Scholarship, Empire, and the South Pacific.* Philadelphia: Temple University Press, 1992; Mead, Margaret, and Gregory Bateson. *Balinese Character: A Photographic Analysis.* New York: New York Academy of Sciences, 1942; Schwarz, Adam. *A Nation of Waiting: Indonesia in the 1990s.* Boulder, CO: Westview, 1994.

Intelligence

The relationship between intelligence and propaganda involves a fine—and sometimes controversial—distinction. Intelligence agencies can provide invaluable guidance to propagandists and have frequently engaged in psychological-warfare activities. Propaganda agencies have also set up their own intelligence apparatus to monitor the content of their output. The most spectacular example of cooperation between intelligence and propaganda is probably the Zimmermann telegram of 1917, when a German telegram intercepted by British intelligence became an explosive piece of propaganda after being leaked to the U.S. press.

The case of Britain during World War I provides a clear example of the structural problems that can arise in the area of intelligence. The Ministry of Information (MoI) and the Foreign Office (FO) argued over who was responsible for intelligence activities. When the Department of Information (DOI) was set up in January 1917, intelligence became a branch of the newly formed DOI, but under the 1918 reconstruction it was transferred to the FO and the Political Intelligence Department (PID). The ensuing struggle between the MoI and the FO over the PID reflected their differing perception of the role of propaganda and intelligence. Lord Beaverbrook (1879–1964), who headed the MoI, believed that matters of political intelligence (for example, the enemy's morale) were only of value to the propagandist and tried unsuccessfully to secure the intelligence for his new ministry. The FO, on the other hand, argued successfully that intelligence work was not solely concerned with propaganda. Rather, its function was to compile periodic summaries, based on a wide sampling of diplomatic sources, for policymakers on the political situation in foreign countries. In World War II this realization led to the setting up of the Political Warfare Executive (PWE) and the Special Operations Executive (SOE). The British government and the MoI decided that there was a need to establish a system of intelligence to monitor what the public was thinking about the war. In January 1940 the ministry set up its Home Intelligence Division, with responsibility for compiling weekly intelligence reports for use by ministers and top officials. When victory seemed certain at the end of 1944, the reports were discontinued. In Nazi Germany, by contrast, intelligence operations were largely directed by the Abwehr and remained separate from propaganda.

During World War II U.S. intelligence was carried out by a special warfare bureau, the Office of Strategic Services (OSS), which grew out of the Office of the Controller of Information, founded in 1940. Propaganda was among the duties carried out by the OSS. The Central Intelligence Agency (CIA), founded in 1947, also engaged in covert activities and was largely responsible for subsidizing anti-Communist propaganda.

It is difficult to draw a clear distinction between "intelligence" and "propaganda." In the 1950s, after the British and French humiliation during the Suez Crisis, the Soviet Union stepped up its propaganda offensive. The British responded by using cultural propaganda to ensure that British interests were being fostered abroad and, through its intelligence organizations, to counter Soviet propaganda on its own covert terms. The CIA secretly sponsored short-wave radio stations such as Radio Free Europe (RFE) and Radio Liberty (RL) and funded the British magazine *Encounter*. It also supported the Congress for Cultural Freedom, a group of European intellectuals disseminating anti-Communist literature. For its part the Soviet secret police (KGB) planted fabricated stories in the international media as part of its "disinformation" campaign.

David Welch

See also Beaverbrook, Max; CIA; Cultural Propaganda; Disinformation; IRD; KGB; MoI; Okhrana; PWE; RFE/RL; World War II (United States); Zimmermann Telegram; Zinoviev Letter

References: Beesley, Patrick. *Room 40: British Naval Intelligence, 1914–1918.* Oxford: Oxford University Press, 1984; Sanders, Michael, and Philip M. Taylor. *British Propaganda during the First World War.* London: Macmillan, 1982; Saunders, Francis Stoner. *Who Paid the Piper? The CIA and the Cultural Cold War.* London: Granta, 1999; Taylor, Philip M. *British Propaganda in the Twentieth Century: Selling Democracy.* Edinburgh: University of Edinburgh Press, 1999.

International (Communist and Socialist)

This term describes a succession of international alliances of left-wing parties established since the nineteenth century. The internationals have not only successfully coordinated socialist movements and propaganda but have also become a stage for major ideological struggles, including the split between anarchism and socialism in the nineteenth century and communism and socialism in the twentieth. The first international gave its name to the song "The Internationale."

Karl Marx (1818–1883) founded the First International (or International Workingmen's Association) in London in 1864, but the organization became mired in a dispute with the anarchist Mikhail Bakunin (1814–1876). The First International expelled Bakunin and his faction in 1872, gradually declining thereafter until it was finally dissolved in 1876. The Second (or Socialist) International was founded in Paris in 1889, with Friedrich Engels (1820–1895) among its leaders. It established an International Socialist Bureau in Brussels under Émile Vandervelde (1866–1938) and successfully nurtured the growth of trades unions across Europe, as well as Social Democratic parties, especially in Germany (led by August Bebel, 1840–1913), and Russia (led by Georgi Plekhanov, 1857–1918). The movement lost momentum at the outbreak of World War I in 1914, with the international working-class movement collapsing in the face of rampant nationalism. Following the Russian Revolution of 1917, the Bolsheviks, led by Vladimir Lenin (1870–1924), claimed the leadership of the world socialist movement and established the Third International (the Communist International, or Comintern) in 1919. This became a major channel of Communist propaganda in the interwar years. The moderate European Social Democratic parties responded by reviving the Socialist International, which merged with a second alternative grouping (the Vienna International of 1921) in 1923. In 1938 the followers of Leon Trotsky (1879–1940) established the militant Fourth International, which later broke into splinter groups.

The Comintern ceased operation in 1943 as Stalin, seeking cooperation with the Allied powers, pulled back from a global socialist mission and switched Soviet propaganda to more nationalistic themes. During the early Cold War the Comintern's functions passed to a new Soviet propaganda agency, the Communist Information Bureau, or Cominform (1947–1956). The Socialist International continued (and still continues) to operate, having been reconstituted in 1951 at the Frankfurt Congress. It embraces Labour, Socialist, and Social Democratic parties from around the world. Its secretariat is located in London, and publications include the magazine *Socialist Affairs*, as well as press releases and statements on such issues as human rights and economic exploitation. Willy Brandt (1913–1992), the former chancellor of West Germany, served as president from 1976 to 1992. Pierre Mauroy (1928–) former prime minister of France, served from 1992 to 1999, whereupon the post passed to António Guterres (1949–), the Socialist

prime minister of Portugal. The Socialist International adopted the red rose grasped by a fist as its logo. It holds twice-yearly council meetings and congresses every three years. The twentieth congress took place in New York City in 1996, and the twenty-first congress convened in Paris in 1999, where it issued a declaration on globalization. Recent campaigns have included pressure for the cancellation of Third World debt.

Nicholas J. Cull

See also Comintern; Engels, Friedrich; "The Internationale"; Lenin, Vladimir Ilyich; Marx, Karl; Russia; Stalin, Joseph; Trotsky, Leon

References: Braunthal, Julius. *History of the International.* 3 vols. London: Nelson, 1966, 1967, 1980; Joll, James. *The Second International, 1889–1914.* London: Routledge, 1974; Katz, Henryk. *Emancipation of Labour: A History of the First International.* London: Greenwood, 1992.

"The Internationale" (1871–1888)

The rousing anthem of the international Socialist movement and one of the best-known propaganda songs since "La Marseillaise." The words appeared as a poem written in June 1871 by the French Communard Eugène Pottier (1816–1887) following the bloody defeat of the Paris Commune. The tune was composed in 1888 by a Lille wood-carver named Pierre Degeyter (1848–1932). The song opens with the following couplet: "Debout les damnés de la terre. Debout les forçats de la faim," which in the American version reads: "Arise you starvelings from your slumbers, Arise you wretched of the earth."

The title derives from the First International, the alliance of Socialist parties formed by Karl Marx (1818–1883) and Friedrich Engels (1820–1895) at a congress, held in London in 1864, which Pottier had attended. After penning the song's text, Pottier went into exile to escape government reprisals, eventually returning to France, where he died penniless in 1887. Degeyter composed the tune for the choir of the Lille section of the French Worker's Party. Degeyter's brother Adophe (1858–1917) contested its authorship, which gave rise to an eighteen-year lawsuit that was decided in Pierre's favor. The song rapidly became popular in France, which hosted the Second International (1889) soon after its composition. In 1910 the International Socialist Congress in Copenhagen adopted it as its official Socialist anthem. In January 1913 Lenin (1870–1924) wrote an admiring article in *Pravda* to mark the twenty-fifth anniversary of Pottier's death, calling him "one of the greatest propagandists in song." From 1917 to 1943 it served as the national anthem of the Soviet Union. It was dropped by Stalin as part of his attempt to redefine the USSR in more nationalistic terms.

The phrase "les damnés de la terre" was used by the anticolonial activist Frantz Fanon (1925–1961) as the title of his 1961 call for anticolonial revolution in Africa. In 1989 Chinese students sang the song in Tien'anmen Square. The "Internationale" has also been recorded by activist singers such as Pete Seeger (1919–) in the United States and Billy Bragg (1957–) in Britain. Negative uses of the song include a scene in the Nazi propaganda film *Hitlerjunge Quex* (1933), in which a Communist father bellows the song in his young son's face and forces him to sing along while bullying him.

Nicholas J. Cull

See also Engels, Friedrich; International; "La Marseillaise"; Lenin, Vladimir Ilyich; Marx, Karl; Russia

References: Borkenau, Franz. *World Communism: A History of the Communist International.* Ann Arbor: University of Michigan Press, 1962; Brochon, Pierre. *Eugène Pottier.* St.-Cyr-sur-Loire, France: Christian Pirot, 1997; Lenin, V. I. *Collected Works.* Vol. 36. Moscow: Progress, 1950; Miller, Peter [director]. *The Internationale.* New York: First Run Icarus Films, 2000.

Internet

Also known as the World Wide Web, the interconnection of computers has created one of the most potent media of mass communication spanning the end of the twentieth and the beginning of the twenty-first centuries. The Internet began in 1969 with the linking of key U.S. defense computers to enable them to cope with a nuclear strike. This system developed into the ARPAnet (Advanced Research Projects Agency Network). In the 1980s it was superseded by the NSFnet (created by the National Science Foundation in the United States), and the privately operated World Wide Web followed in the 1990s. The Internet performed two major communications roles: virtually instant transmission of letters in the form of e-mail and access to websites displaying easily updatable information in the form of hypertext. Access from personal computers took off thanks to a major breakthrough in software in 1993.

At its most benign the Internet accelerated the dissemination of news and dramatically increased the availability of information worldwide, yet in the process it also changed the sort of information available. Because it is arranged horizontally without the same sort of government or big business "gatekeepers" who control newspapers and broadcasting, the Internet made it possible for small organizations to reach mass audiences. It also proved very hard to censor. Nevertheless, the Chinese government managed to restrict Internet access within its borders. The Internet soon became a favorite propaganda medium for the extreme right and a major forum for such ideas as Holocaust denial and the antigovernment militia movements in the United States. The Internet has proved a medium ideally suited to the circulation of rumor—and a major outlet for the circulation of stories relating to the unpresidential activities of former U.S. president Bill Clinton (1946–). During the Kosovo conflict in 1999, both sides used the Internet to state their respective cases. Yugoslavian gambits included a puppet show featuring a caricature of Tony Blair (1953–), the British prime minister. Computer hackers have also been able to slip their own propaganda messages into frequently visited websites. Some international radio stations, including the Voice of America, used the Internet to supplement (and, in some cases, replace) broadcasts in individual foreign languages. The Internet figured as an issue in the U.S. presidential election of 2000 because of the special contribution of Democratic candidate Al Gore (1948–) to the development of the information superhighway. The Republicans taunted Gore for exaggerating his role by "claiming to have invented the Internet."

Nicholas J. Cull

See also ADL; Black Propaganda; China; Clinton, William Jefferson; Disinformation; Holocaust Denial; Kosovo Crisis and War; Laden, Osama bin; Rumor; Scandinavia; Southeast Asia; United States

References: Moschovitis, Christos, Hilary Poole, and Tami Schuyler. *History of the Internet*. Santa Barbara, CA: ABC-CLIO, 1999; Taylor, Philip M. *Global Communications, International Affairs and the Media Since 1945*. London: Routledge, 1997.

Iran

The Islamic Republic of Iran, known until 1935 as Persia, has a long history of propaganda but is now best known for the Iranian Revolution of 1979, in which relatively simple media—primarily consisting of smuggled cassette tapes—helped precipitate a major revolution, culminating in a religious dictatorship.

Persia entered the early modern period under the leadership of Shah Ismail (1484–1524), who in 1502 founded the Safavid dynasty. Ismail made Shiite Islam his state religion, hence setting Iran apart from the rest of the Islamic world—especially the Sunni Ottoman Empire. The Safavid dynasty reached its zenith under Abbas the Great (1557–1629; r. 1587–1628), whose propaganda methods included the magnificent architecture he created for his capital city of Esfahan. The dynasty fell following an Afghan invasion in 1722. Persia recovered under the brutal rule of Nadir Shah (1688–1747; r.

1736–1747), who briefly attempted to reunite the Sunni and Shiite factions. Nadir Shah named his monarchy "the peacock throne" after a trophy brought back from an invasion of India. Between 1794 and 1925 Persia was ruled by the Qajar dynasty, whose leaders faced the mounting tide of western European and Russian influence. With the British telegraph to India crossing Persia, the latter became better connected to the outside world than other countries in the region, facilitating both political modernization and the birth of newspapers in the late 1890s. The period 1905–1911 saw a constitutional revolution during which the press played a significant role in popularizing Western political concepts of democracy and human rights. Iran unveiled the office of prime minister in 1907. Foreign interest in Persia deepened in the twentieth century thanks to the discovery of oil. Russia and Britain established themselves as the dominant powers, and in 1907 they divided Iran into spheres of influence.

In 1921 an army officer named Reza Khan (1877–1944) seized power and established a military dictatorship. In 1925 he successful ousted the last Qajar shah and proclaimed himself the first shah of the Pahlavi dynasty. The dynastic name was a propagandistic reference to the language of the Sassanid dynasty (224–640) and the lost "golden age" before Arab domination of Persia. The dynasty also sought to evoke the glories of ancient Persia by developing an architectural style for public buildings modeled upon those of Persepolis, with columns and rampant lions. Like Atatürk (1881–1938) in Turkey, Reza Shah insisted on modern dress and renamed his country Iran. He also kept tight control on the press. The chief target of the regime's propaganda was the left-wing Tudeh Party. In 1939 the regime established what amounted to a propaganda ministry as the Office for the Education and the Guidance of Public Opinion. Programs, whether magazines or lectures on health, were liberally interjected with propaganda supporting the shah. Despite these measures, the Reza Shah seemed

Campaign poster featuring the late Ayatollah Khomeini and Ali Khamenei. (BAHAR / IMAX / CORBIS SYGMA)

too pro-German for Allied tastes, and when British and Russian forces occupied Iran he abdicated in favor of his son, Muhammad Reza Shah Pahlavi (1918–1980).

The career of the second Muhammad Reza Shah was intimately bound up with the U.S. presence in the region. At the end of World War II Iran became the scene of Western-Soviet tension. Britain and the United States nurtured the shah accordingly. In 1952 he fled Iran because of the leftist rule of the Nationalist prime minister, Muhammad Mossadeq (1881–1967), who wished to institute constitutional rule and to nationalize the oil industry. Mossadeq was a skilled politician and a particularly effective broadcaster, but in 1953 the United States, which had now succeeded Britain as the dominant foreign power in the country, stepped in, with the CIA backing a coup to restore the shah to power.

This coup effectively cut short the development of a Western-style public sphere in Iran, leaving the Islamic clerics as the chief alternative to the shah. Both the coup and subsequent nation-building projects in Iran owed much to U.S. propaganda. In the 1960s the shah offered up a program dubbed the "White Revolution." Reforms included the enfranchisement of women. Americans also facilitated the arrival of television in Iran, which appeared in 1967 as a tool of state propaganda. The regime staged events for the cameras, including an elaborate coronation in 1967; spectacular celebrations in 1971 marking the twenty-five hundredth anniversary of the founding of the empire of Cyrus the Great (r. 550–529 B.C.E) ; and the unveiling of a new calendar in 1976, dating from the coronation of Cyrus. As Annabelle Sreberny has noted, it is possible that these events and ubiquitous royal speeches actually overexposed the shah and contributed to his decline. By the 1970s the shah employed a brutal secret police force (SAVAK) to repress dissent. In 1978 the discontent erupted in demonstrations across the country that united radical political and religious positions and in which women figured prominently.

Much criticism came from the clerics, including a dissident refugee from the regime, Ayatollah Ruhollah Khomeini (1900–1989), who had been living in exile in Iraq since 1964 (and latterly in Paris). His views were circulated widely throughout religious networks by means of cassette tapes. Underground newspapers and eye-catching posters also carried his message. In the autumn of 1978 the strength of this propaganda was enhanced when revolutionaries caused frequent power outages, which crippled the state broadcasting apparatus. In January 1979, as demonstrators surged through the streets, the shah fled the country and the Ayatollah Khomeini returned from exile to lead the new religious government of Iran. The regime gave short shrift to its erstwhile reformist allies and reintroduced the veil for Iranian women. Propaganda strategies included strict censorship, the use of posters, portraits of the Ayatollah, and rallies interspersed with slogans couched in religious terminology. The United States, a rallying point for the regime's emotional zeal, was dubbed "the Great Satan." The regime staged massive open-air theatrical spectacles based on Shiite religious themes, sometimes altering original texts to give them a contemporary twist. The new regime restructured broadcasting under the Voice and Vision of the Islamic Republic (VVIR). In November 1979 Iranian students seized the U.S. embassy in Tehran. They held 52 Americans hostage for 444 days, demanding that the United States surrender the shah so he could be tried. The incident had great symbolic value both in the United States and in Iran. Following a failed American attempt to rescue the hostages in April 1980, the affair swiftly turned into a massive propaganda debacle for the administration of U.S. president Jimmy Carter (1924–), paving the way for the election of Ronald Reagan (1911–) later that year.

In September 1980 Saddam Hussein (1937–) of Iraq invaded Iran, seeking to redress a long-standing border dispute. Iran retaliated by proclaiming a holy war, rallying its men and women to engage in a struggle that included the use of "human wave" tactics on the battlefield. Iranian propaganda stressed the duty (and virtue) of self-sacrifice. The war—which included a prolonged radio propaganda duel—ended in a stalemate in 1988. Meanwhile, Iran became a major sponsor of propaganda through direct action, that is, terrorism. Iran's international propaganda is generally expressed in terms of religious piety; hence the regime's much publicized attack against British author Salman Rushdie's (1947–) novel *The Satanic Verses* (1989) as blasphemy and the death sentence, declared in absentia, on its author. Iranian politics was clearly split between two forms of power. The clerical power concentrated in the *rahbar* (leader) of the revolution: the Ayatollah Khomeini, the president during the 1980s, and Sayid Ali Khamenei (1939–), the *rahbar* following the Ayatollah's death in 1989. This clerical power has been in conflict with popularly elected representatives. Reformers such as Mohammed Khatami (1943–), the minister of culture from 1982 to 1992, made some attempts to ease censorship but was forced from office by charges of permissiveness.

In 1989 Hashemi Rafsanjani (1934–), who had openly opposed the shah, became president of Iran. He served two terms (1989–1998). His government increased Iranian propaganda overseas. VVIR began satellite television broadcasts to Europe in response to a number of opposition television channels based overseas, including a U.S. government channel organized under the auspices of Radio Free Europe. The elections of 1997 returned Khatami to the presidency. His government faced internal criticism from conservatives, such as Khamenei, and radical reformers. Beginning in 1999, Khatami tightened censorship regulations, resulting in prodemocracy demonstrations. Increased access to the World Wide Web ensured a freer flow of news into the country than had been the case earlier. The U.S. propaganda strategy with regard to Iran has

been to underplay any reform and to maintain pressure on the country as a pariah and "sponsor of terrorism." Iran figured prominently in U.S. rhetoric during the War on Terrorism (2001) and its aftermath, appearing as one of the pariah nations in the Bush administration's "Axis of Evil."

Nicholas J. Cull

See also Arab World; Cold War; Hussein, Saddam; Novel; Ottoman Empire/Turkey; Posters; Religion; RFE/RL; Terrorism; Terrorism, War on

References: Avery, Peter, Gavin Hambly, and Charles Melville, eds. *The Cambridge History of Iran*. Vol.7, *From Nadir Shah to the Islamic Republic.* Cambridge: Cambridge University Press, 1991; Hiro, Dilip. *Iran under the Ayatollahs.* London: Routledge, 1985; Rosen, Barry, ed. *Iran Since the Revolution.* New York: Columbia University Press, 1985; Sreberny-Mohammadi, Annabelle, and Ali Mohammadi. *Small Media, Big Revolution: Communication, Culture and the Iranian Revolution.* Minneapolis: University of Minnesota Press, 1994.

IRD (Information Research Department)

The British Foreign Office's Information Research Department (IRD) was formed in 1948 by the Labour government, marking Britain's entry into the Cold War. Although Ernest Bevin (1881–1951), the foreign secretary, had initially been reluctant to launch a propaganda offensive to counter the growth of Soviet ideological and military influence, the increasingly hostile propaganda attacks launched by the Soviets against Britain finally convinced him to take up the weapon urged upon him since 1946 by his officials at the Foreign Office. The paper presented to the cabinet by the Foreign Office gave the mistaken impression that the IRD would be conducting a positive campaign for social democracy as much as a negative campaign against Communism.

The IRD grew rapidly as the Cold War intensified; at its peak in the mid-1950s it employed a staff of three hundred researching, compiling, and distributing material throughout the world. The approach adopted was to be secret, direct, and aggressive. While the IRD occasionally strayed into "black" propaganda activities—particularly secret radio stations—its role was largely to disseminate "gray" propaganda, by which was meant the dissemination of biased information from an indeterminate source. Indeed, the IRD had close, if informal, links with MI5 and MI6 (domestic and overseas British intelligence), with personnel moving between the organizations and, in certain cases, working for both. The IRD also established a working relationship with the CIA despite concern that the Labour Party would object should this collaboration become known.

Although the IRD never attempted to construct anything like the orchestrated propaganda directed by the CIA against the Soviet Union, it was quite prepared to respond to Soviet targets and to escalate the propaganda offensive by forcing the enemy to defend itself and its policies. The IRD has been likened to a peacetime Political Warfare Executive (PWE); indeed, its first head was Sir Ralph Murray (1908–1983), who, together with a number of his staff, had worked in the PWE during the war.

The majority of propaganda produced by the IRD was solidly based upon fact, and one of its working slogans was "anything but the truth is too hot to handle." Factual evidence would be utilized in order to back the argument that the briefing or publication was attempting to make. One of the formats in which the IRD presented its "factual" material was a series of pamphlets. The themes of these "information reports" were—at least in the first few years—all anti-Communist, examining such topics as "forced labor in the USSR," "the Communist peace offensive," and "Russian imperialism and Asian nationalism." The international distribution network built up by the IRD included the BBC, Reuters, bogus radio stations and news agencies, and a host of "clients," many of whom were well-known journalists, as well as information officers in diplomatic posts overseas.

One of the most contentious activities of the IRD was its involvement in seeking to influence opinion within the British Labour movement—particularly by means of the Labour Party International Department. In 1955 the latter began receiving the IRD's new bimonthly publication *Quotations*. By far the largest IRD publishing operation consisted of a series of books, collected under the title of "Background Books," which began appearing in 1951. Over the next thirty years over a hundred titles were published. The main target audience, as far as the IRD was concerned, was the educated middle class, particularly in the Third World. Information officers would distribute the books free of charge. These books were also available in Britain. In 1977 the IRD shut down on the orders of David Owen (1938–), the Labour foreign secretary. For thirty years the IRD had conducted a covert propaganda war aimed at influencing opinion both internationally and domestically.

David Welch

See also BBC; Black Propaganda; CIA; Cold War; Gray Propaganda; Intelligence; PWE

References: Crozier, Brian. *Free Agent: The Unseen War, 1941–1991.* London: HarperCollins, 1994; Lasmar, Paul, and James Oliver. *Britain's Secret Propaganda War, 1948–1977.* Stroud, UK: Sutton, 1998; Lucas, W. Scott, and C. J. Morris. "A Very British Crusade: The Information Research Department and the Beginning of the Cold War." In *British Intelligence Strategy and the Cold War.* Ed. Richard Aldrich. London, Routledge: 1992; Rothwell, Victor. *Britain and the Cold War, 1941–1947.* London: Jonathan Cape, 1982.

Ireland

Since 1500 Ireland has been shaped by propaganda from within and without. The Irish people have been stereotyped in the international media. Irish politics produced eloquent writing and rabble-rousing oratory in the conflict between Catholic and Protestant communities and the struggle to achieve independence from Great Britain. In the twentieth century the government of the Republic of Ireland made extensive use of propaganda—especially censorship—to shape the development of the country.

As with so much Irish history, the story of propaganda in Ireland is inextricably linked to England. Ireland entered the sixteenth century with English power concentrated around Dublin. With the arrival of the Reformation, Catholic Ireland seemed like an ideological threat to the Protestant English crown. Hence between 1534 and 1603 the armies of the Tudor dynasty conquered Ireland inch by inch. Tudor anti-Irish images, such as John Derrick's series of woodcuts entitled *Image of Ireland* (1581) laid the foundation for English stereotyping of the Irish that would endure up to the present. With Ireland under English rule, Protestant settlers moved from Scotland and established themselves in the northeastern province of Ulster, where English military power was strongest. These settlers used oral and print culture to develop a vigorous sense of themselves as an embattled minority with a destiny to remain on Irish soil. A Catholic uprising in 1641 generated numerous accounts of atrocities against the settlers, the most famous being Sir John Temple's best-selling *History of the Irish Rebellion* (1646), with its numerous gory woodcuts. But the Catholic community had its own atrocity stories, especially the brutal campaign of 1649, during which the army of the English Parliament led by Oliver Cromwell (1599–1658) crushed Irish support for the cause of the pro-Catholic English King Charles I (1600–1649). Memories of such atrocities established the battle lines for the war of 1689–1691 between forces loyal to the former English king, the Catholic James II (1633–1701), and his Protestant successor, William III, also known as William of Orange (1650–1702). The events of this war, including the climactic Battle of the Boyne of 1690, would in turn be mythologized by propaganda generated in later years.

The seventeenth century saw the development of a rich vein of Irish political rhetoric, which followed in the footsteps of the first great Irish political tract, *The Case of Ireland* (1698), by William Molyneux (1656–1698). The greatest voice of the era was that belonging to the clergyman and satirist Jonathan Swift (1667–1745). Swift's works included his *Proposal for the Universal Use of Irish Manufacture* (1720), which called for the boycott of English products, and *A Modest Proposal* (1729), in which he satirized the British exploitation of Ireland by suggesting that the Irish eat their own children. British tactics used to assert control in Ireland included regulation of the educational system. The Catholic population improvised "hedge schools" to teach the basics of a Catholic education in secret. The French Revolution and the Napoleonic Wars brought a flurry of nationalistic feeling and pamphleteering to Ireland. The United Irishman's Rebellion of 1798 was fueled by the popular newspaper *The Northern Star.* After the failure of the rebellion, Ireland was formally incorporated into the United Kingdom.

The early nineteenth century saw a flowering of Irish political rhetoric reflected in the careers of men like Daniel O'Connell (1775–1847), whose skill in rousing those attending mass meetings was legendary. O'Connell used press advertisements and a network of reading rooms around Ireland to spread his ideas. The great famine of 1845–1849 accelerated the existing movement of Irish people to seek new lives overseas, but they met a surge of anti-Irish, racist propaganda in Britain and the United States. Drawing on three centuries of stereotypes, the Victorian press on both sides of the Atlantic transformed the Irish working-class immigrant into the pariah of the age. Irish people were presented as lazy oafs, drunkards, superstitious, with excessively large families. In Ireland, however, a major nationalistic revival was in progress. The Fenian movement's ideas were spread through newspapers such as *The Irish People* and *The Irishman.* Interest in the Gaelic language culminated in the founding in 1893 of the Gaelic League by such academic activists as Douglas

Hyde (1860–1949), author of the tract *The Necessity for De-anglicising the Irish People* (1892). Associated Gaelic League propaganda included the newspaper *Claidheamh Soluis* (Sword of Light) and Irish-language poetry. The era also saw a revival in Gaelic sports.

In the early years of the twentieth century Irish nationalism reached a new level of intensity and organization, culminating in the creation of a new party, Sinn Féin (Ourselves Alone), in 1905. However, this was matched by equally determined voices in Northern Ireland for continued union. In 1795 Protestants in the north of Ireland had established the Orange Order, a political lodge society similar to the Freemasons, dedicated to preserving the memory of King William of Orange. The Orange Order had dissolved in the 1830s but had reemerged as a focus for Protestant Unionism in the 1880s. In 1910 Ulster Protestants formed their own Ulster Unionist Parliamentary Party, led by skilled orator Edward Carson (1854–1935). Events came to a head during World War I. Irish nationalists had always understood the power of the emotive event. To achieve this end they sought to rally Ireland to their cause by mounting an uprising in Dublin during Easter 1916. The event was threatening to become a military fiasco but was effectively transformed into an act of martyrdom when the British executed the ringleaders. A guerrilla war against British rule followed in 1919, leading to the compromise peace of 1922, according to which the six counties of Northern Ireland remained part of the United Kingdom, while the south reconstituted itself as an autonomous Irish Free State.

The government of the Irish Free State proved as keen to regulate the country's media as London had been. It sought to nurture a sense of national identity, which was generally identified during this period with the morality set down by the Catholic Church. The twin threats to Irish identity were the two cultural giants that lay to the east and the west: England and America. The government's chief tool of propaganda was the promotion of "traditional" Irish culture (including the Gaelic language) and regulation of the print media through censorship. In 1926 the Irish Free State government founded a "Committee on Evil Literature." Religious pressure groups demanded more. An Irish Censorship Board followed in 1929, possessing sweeping powers to ban books and periodicals that it felt promoted crime or favored such social evils as contraception or abortion. The same priorities affected the development of radio broadcasting in Ireland, which began in 1926. Similarly, Irish film censors tried to hold back the tide of Hollywood "immorality." Between 1923 and the end of the 1970s they banned over one thousand films and edited out scenes involving sex or criminal acts from ten thousand more. In Protestant-controlled Northern Ireland the provincial government also sought to monitor the images reaching its citizenry; targets included Soviet propaganda and films sympathetic to the nationalist cause in the south.

The history of postindependence Ireland was dominated by Eamon de Valera (1882–1975). A formidable rhetorician and major figure in the war of independence, he dissented from the compromise peace and in 1926 founded the Fianna Fáil (Soldiers of Ireland) Party. He became president of the Executive Council in 1932 and prime minister under the new constitution of 1937. De Valera kept Ireland neutral in World War II and was hence the focus of both Allied and Axis propaganda. The government's resolve was not shaken. De Valera's wartime emergency powers included censorship. The film *Casablanca* (1942) was considered too politically charged to be released before June 1945.

The 1960s brought troubling issues to the government of Northern Ireland. The economy of the province was heavily dependent on the shipbuilding industry, which was in decline. The political status quo—which amounted to a Protestant hegemony—was underpinned by that community's domination of the media and a cycle of public events that emphasized the Protestant view of history. The annual marches by branches of the Orange Order were an eloquent form of propaganda in which one community's version of the past was remembered and that community's power demonstrated in the potent ritual of marching through minority neighborhoods to the beat of an enormous drum. In 1967 Protestant power was suddenly called into question by a Catholic civil rights movement, which drew inspiration from the contemporaneous achievements of African Americans. The movement used marches and rallies to focus world attention on basic grievances. Its success provoked a violent backlash from parts of the Unionist community. The crisis escalated beyond the control of the provincial government. In August 1969 the first British troops arrived in Ulster, ostensibly to protect the Catholic minority. As the British army attempted to contain Catholic anger, they too were drawn into a cycle of violence.

By the early 1970s the situation in Northern Ireland had produced a perverse stalemate. Paramilitary groups based in each community—the Provisional Irish Republican Army and Irish National Liberation Army representing the Catholic/Nationalist; the Ulster Defence Association and Ulster Volunteer Force representing the Protestant/Unionist—were locked in a piecemeal war of retaliatory bloodshed. Nationalist violence was also directed at the British security forces in Northern Ireland, which eventually spread to military and civilian targets on the British mainland. Each side had its newspapers and leaflets, and each sought to garner sympathy through such events as elaborate funerals. Communities also developed a distinctive style of visual propaganda in the form of murals on the gable ends of houses, which often featured flags, images drawn from Irish history, or romanticized portraits of paramilitary activists. Republicans became particularly adept at promoting their cause in the United States, where Irish-American sympathizers rallied to the cause with financial support.

The most dramatic propaganda event of "the troubles" was a protest by Republican prisoners at the Maze prison in 1976–1981. The issue was the withdrawal of the special "political status" granted to paramilitary prisoners. The Labour government sought to undermine the media position of the IRA by treating its prisoners as criminals rather than prisoners of war. Resistance began with the so-called dirty protests, where prisoners refused to wear clothes and soiled their cell walls with human waste. The newspaper and television pictures flashed around the world did little to enhance the reputation of the British government. In 1981, two years into the government of Margaret Thatcher (1925–), the prisoners took the protest to another level by beginning a hunger strike. Such protests had a long tradition in Irish Republican political action, dating back to the aftermath of the Easter Rising. Although its alleged precedents could be found in Irish folk tradition, the hunger strike owed more to the experience of the Suffragettes and, later, the tactics of Gandhi (1869–1948) in India. Ten prisoners died in the protest, including Bobby Sands (1954–1981), who had by that time been elected an M.P. The hunger strike consolidated support for Sinn Féin in the Catholic community and marked the apex of international sympathy for the Republican cause.

The violence in Northern Ireland created profound issues for the media in both Great Britain and the Irish Republic. In 1971 the Irish government attempted to clamp down on coverage of illegal terrorist activities. In 1972 Radio Telefís Éireann (Irish Radio and Television; RTE) had its authority withdrawn because the station had carried an interview with an IRA spokesman. In Britain censorship on Northern Irish issues was commonplace. This reached a climax in 1988 when Margaret Thatcher, seeking to deny terrorists what she had called "the oxygen of publicity," adopted the practice of the Irish Republic and banned the broadcasting of the voices of terrorists. British broadcasters responded by employing actors to dub their remarks. Thatcher's successor, John Major (1943–), lifted the ban in 1994. The British government was also an active player in the Irish propaganda war, circulating its own version of events internationally and within the domestic media of Britain.

In the 1990s the entrenched positions of factions in Northern Ireland began to soften. The years 1994–1995 brought hope in the form of an IRA cease-fire. Britain's Northern Ireland Office began a new propaganda campaign bearing the slogan "Rat on a Rat," which utilized television appeals for information on terrorism. On Good Friday 1998 the parties to the conflict agreed to seek a new and mutually acceptable form of government for the province centered on a Northern Irish assembly. The Northern Ireland Executive convened in late 1999, and it seemed that Irish politics had entered a new era. Symbolic points remained moot, with intense debate over such issues as which flags would fly and what the name of the police force ought to be. However, the executive stalled over the issue of "arms decommissioning," and rule from London returned. By 2001 the Irish struggle had fragmented once again, with the mainstream faction of the IRA agreeing to decommission its arms, thereby clearing the way for cooperation within the terms of the Northern Ireland Executive, and splinter groups calling themselves the "Continuity IRA" and the "Real IRA" continuing their struggle.

Nicholas J. Cull

See also BBC; BIS; Britain; Censorship; Counterinsurgency; Funerals; Poetry; Prisoners of War; Temperance; Terrorism; Thatcher, Margaret

References: Cull, Nicholas J., ed. "Irish Media History" [special issue]. *The Historical Journal of Film, Radio and Television* 20 (August 2000); Curtis, Liz. *Ireland: The Propaganda War: The British Media and the Battle for Hearts and Minds.* Belfast: Sásta, 1998; Foster, R. F. *Paddy and Mr. Punch.* London: Penguin, 1995; Hutchinson, John. *The Dynamics of Cultural Nationalism: The Gaelic Revival and the Creation of the Irish Nation-State.* London: Allan and Unwin, 1987; Lee,

J. J. *Ireland, 1912–1998: Politics and Society.* Cambridge: Cambridge University Press, 1990; Mac Cuarta, Brian, ed. *Ulster 1641: Aspects of the Rising.* Belfast: Queens University, 1993; Miller, David. *Don't Mention the War: Northern Ireland, Propaganda and the Media.* London: Pluto, 1994.

Israel

As a state that avows allegiance to the principles of Western democracy, Israel is repelled by the very idea of "propaganda." The term is applied only to others—primarily its Arab enemies—or to defined periods in democratic regimes, such as election campaigns or in wartime, during which propaganda activities are condoned and conducted openly.

For these reasons, and perhaps as part of an overall strategy, when propaganda is deemed necessary Israeli officials prefer to substitute the more refined Hebrew term *hasbara,* which has several interrelated meanings, including "information," "explanation," "publicity," and, of course, "propaganda." Among Western democracies, such nomenclature is apparently unique to Israel. The Hebrew word for propaganda proper, *taamula,* is said to derive from at least two etymological sources. One possible root means "work," perhaps applied in the slang sense of "doing a number on someone." Another points to the Arabic term *amil* (agent), whose meaning is similar to that of the Latin root of "propaganda," alluding to the dissemination of values, ideas, views, or opinions. The Hebrew euphemism for propaganda, in turn, signifies a kind of reaction, an act of defense, a more positive kind of propaganda to be distinguished from the negative, hostile variety. In time the distinction between the two became firmly rooted in the Hebrew language: While "others," the proverbial "bad guys" (primarily political rivals), engage in *taamula,* in Israel the "good guys" practice *hasbara.* (In the present essay the term "propaganda" is translated as either *taamula* or *hasbara* unless the context specifically mandates otherwise.) An aphorism popular among officials declares that the difference between the two terms is that propaganda works.

Over the years, the State of Israel has invested considerable effort in the development of various types of propaganda. Generally speaking, Israeli propaganda may be classified according to at least two features: front and target audience (see accompanying table).

Sociological propaganda aimed at reinforcing collective identity was part of the national struggle even during the days of the British Mandate. As in similar situations involving the establishment of a new state, nation-building, and perhaps even national rebirth, the political leadership of the pre-state Jewish community in Palestine—as well as the successive governments of Israel—had to rally the public around common national goals. The mass influx of immigrants intensified the need for a dynamic melting pot in which the various ethnic groups and their cultural heritage were gathered together or perhaps simply tossed.

Sociological propaganda practices that helped forge a national identity were of considerable concern to scholars studying Israeli society. Ceremonies and texts were devised through which the Zionist ethos could be disseminated and the bond between the land and its new residents could become institutionalized in the secular culture of the State of Israel. The political leadership during the Mandate recruited the cultural elite to help further this cause: writers, artists, composers, and other intellectuals applied their skills and talents to nurture an affinity with Jewish sources and the land of Israel, as well as to revitalize the Hebrew language. The principles of the Zionist ethos were disseminated not only through a well-developed educational system but also in routine leisure-time cultural activities. At that time (and, to a lesser extent, even today) community singing was a popular pastime, with themes reflecting longing and love for the new homeland. The rhythms of the hora and *debka* mingled with those of original local folk dances. Group hikes, some of which included games proposed by the Jewish National Fund, enriched the fund of knowledge of the new land and strengthened the physical attachment to the soil.

With the establishment of the State of Israel, the new demographic realities created two national camps consisting of a Jewish majority and an Arab minority. The latter collectivity was not ignored in the country's propaganda campaigns. Various means were employed, especially through the broadcast media, to encourage local Arabs to legitimize their permanent status as a minority and to accept Jewish majority rule and the new order as legitimate.

Activity considered acceptable in all new states was accorded special priority because

Types of Propaganda in Israel

| Front | Target Audience | |
	Jews	Non-Jews
Domestic	Sociological propaganda to cultivate national identity. Routine and emergency propaganda. Election propaganda.	Propaganda to promote consensus and reconciliation with the State among its minorities.
Foreign	Sociological propaganda to reinforce national identity among Diaspora Jews. Agitprop to encourage immigration to Israel.	Initiative and reactive propaganda toward enemy states and others. Wartime propaganda aimed at Arab states. Peace propaganda toward Western states.

of the new state's extended armed conflict with its neighbors, entailing a struggle for legitimization of its very right to exist among the family of nations, especially those of its own region. To a great extent, domestic and foreign propaganda were considered part of the State of Israel's battle for survival.

Fluctuations in the severity of the conflict between Israel and the Arab states and the Palestinians have left their mark on propaganda efforts on Israel's domestic and foreign fronts alike. The frequent wars demanded several types of propaganda activities, conducted on different fronts and aimed at various audiences, including war-mongering against the Arab states and wartime propaganda aimed at its own soldiers and civilian populations. In the Six-Day War (1967) Israel aimed its Arab-language broadcasts at Egyptian soldiers, seeking to weaken their morale and motivation and encouraging them to abandon the battlefield and surrender to Israeli troops.

The Jewish Diaspora has always been considered a peripheral reserve of human and economic capital for the State of Israel. Consequently, special propaganda efforts were directed at Jewish communities worldwide, particularly those of affluent Western countries, if only to reinforce national identity among Jews and their affinity to Israel, both symbolic and instrumental, including the readiness to extend economic and occasionally also political assistance to the new and resource-poor state. Agitprop was directed at Jews in distressed countries—Islamic states and those of the Communist bloc—encouraging their immigration to Israel, a key component of Zionist ideology known by the value-laden Hebrew term *aliyah* (ascension).

To carry out its widespread propaganda work, the State of Israel equipped itself with a variety of tools and systems, including nongovernmental organizations (NGOs) not directly identified with the state or its objectives. Even before the formal establishment of Israel, the Jewish Agency and the Jewish National Fund were involved in a variety of Zionist publicity efforts, in particular instilling values and symbols vital to the Jewish collective identity and raising economic resources for the pre-state Jewish community; both continued these efforts even more vigorously after 1948. NGO activity became essential thereafter as well, especially in places and at times that restricted or precluded official state access. NGOs were thus found to be effective cultural propaganda disseminators. For example, they succeeded in penetrating the Iron Curtain and rehabilitating the national identity of Soviet Jews, encouraging many of them to emigrate to Israel—first on a highly limited scale and then, as of the late 1980s, with no restrictions whatsoever. NGOs were also recruited to mount international propaganda campaigns, such as securing the release of Israeli prisoners by their captors in Arab countries. Two Israeli websites are operated by NGOs to influence world public opinion, with one focusing on Israeli POWs and MIAs whose fate has been unknown for periods ranging from several to as many as twenty months.

For their overseas propaganda efforts, NGOs and ancillary bodies are likely to rely on materials produced by various government agencies. The Israel Foreign Ministry's Public Affairs Division distributes up-to-date information about Israel through its representatives worldwide, while the Ministry of Tourism maintains an overseas branch of the Tourism Marketing Authority, whose emissaries and brokers "sell" Israel as a tourist attraction to individual visitors and groups and host travel agents and journalists from all over the world. At the same time, the Ministry of Education's Information Center is ostensibly responsible for disseminating information to the Israeli public; in practice it continues to develop public ceremonies and to promote the internalization of national symbols by the public.

The Jewish Agency operates a series of educational programs aimed at reinforcing ties between Diaspora Jewry and the State of Israel, including the Jewish Identity Project, in which Hebrew teachers help Jews all over the world rediscover their national identity. Furthermore, Israel is assisted in no small measure by the activities of Jewish lobbies throughout the world, such as the American Israel Public Affairs Committee (AIPAC), which helps Israel explain its positions to the U.S. administration. Other bodies develop support for the Israeli government's policies and seek to build a national consensus. A well-oiled government public relations machine has expanded over the years.

In Israel, as in other countries, the government initiates periodic information campaigns—in both peacetime and wartime—rallying the public around specific policies, such as water-conservation campaigns in arid regions and during dry spells. The most successful nationwide campaign of this kind was conducted during the 1960s, reflecting the young society's concern for nature preservation and endangered wildflower species. By contrast, at the height of the economic crisis during the extended Intifada of 2001, private groups attempted to raise morale by illuminating the Azrieli Towers, the tallest buildings in the Middle East, with a giant image, visible throughout Tel Aviv and beyond, depicting a hand holding the national flag aloft and bearing the legend "It's in our hands." Other public affairs campaigns involve preventing traffic fatalities, personal safety (gas mask kits), cancer prevention, the war on narcotics, plastic bottle recycling, and the like.

An additional distinction can be made with respect to the two types of propaganda mentioned earlier, namely, initiative versus reactive propaganda. An external propaganda campaign aimed at a non-Jewish audience may be either initiative—for example, if it precedes the adoption of a new policy—or reactive, such as campaigns following a decline in or total loss of positive world public opinion. Irrespective of circumstance, reactive propaganda appears to follow a likely four-stage cycle. During the first stage—irritation—some issue and/or stimulus arouses the need for action and is attributed to the lack of sufficient propaganda. Political inferiority, for example, whether actual or perceived by world public opinion, spurs the government to initiate propaganda activity accordingly. Alternatively, a real or perceived worsening of conditions, such as an increase in domestic violence—or in its media coverage—generates pressure for a solution. At this stage some may even designate a factor putatively responsible for the situation—a scapegoat, as it were—dismissing enemy propaganda gains as exaggerated in their perceived efficacy. Such rhetorical claims lay the groundwork for the next stage—redeployment—in which financial and human resources are invested to reinforce existing propaganda devices or, alternatively, to create new ones and prepare for emergencies, such as the hiring of advertising agencies in Israel or overseas. During the third stage—standby—national leaders await the positive results of the propaganda campaign, which in itself alleviates immediate pressure for a solution. At times the propaganda campaign serves as a kind of safety valve for the release of tension, rejecting criticism and/or evidence of the government's resolve to deal with a given situation. During the final stage—resignation—national leaders are exposed to real-world exigencies and tend to resign themselves to prevailing conditions, including the limitations of propaganda.

In each case the same principle is applied: success is credited to the propaganda campaign, whereas failure is attributed to some other factor, be it the enemy or some uncontrollable force. If a situation does not improve—such as Israel's status in the international arena—well-worn and familiar rhetorical claims are immediately adduced, such as "the few against the many," "the whole world is against us," or "a hostile media," whether Israeli, Palestinian, or foreign. In contrast, a change for the better, such as a decline in road accidents or in worldwide criticism of Israeli policies, will immediately be credited to intensified propaganda efforts.

One well-known reflection of this cyclical process was discerned in the mid-1970s. In response to a sense of increasing diplomatic distress over international criticism of Israel's control of territories conquered in the Six-Day War, the government decided to concentrate propaganda efforts in a special official body, the Information Ministry, entrusted to Brig. (res.) Aharon Yariv (1920–1994), a former intelligence chief in the Israeli Defense Force (IDF) responsible for political contacts with Egypt. The ministry disappeared once that government's term of office ended. Similarly, in 2001 Zippi Livni (1958–), one of the ministers without portfolio in Ariel Sharon's (1928–) extensive cabinet, was placed in charge of *hasbara,* this time without setting up a special ministry. This decision aroused internal tension, especially in the Foreign Ministry, which is traditionally responsible for Israeli propaganda throughout the world.

Above all, this cyclical process reflects Israeli political conceptions regarding the importance of propaganda and propagandists, a view that does not lack a factual basis. In at least two dramatic cases, propaganda and propagandists proved essential, underscoring their absence in other critical situations. During the Six-Day War, in Israel's pretelevision era, Israel Radio offered military commentary by Brig. (res.) Chaim Herzog (1918–1997), who acted as a kind of "spokesman to the nation." In the early 1990s, then IDF spokesman Nahman Shai held this position during the Gulf War, when Israeli residents barricaded themselves in sealed rooms, equipped with gas masks to protect them against attack by Iraqi dictator Saddam Hussein.

In contrast, in the remaining wars and crises, the Israeli public was left to its own devices, with no national voice to guide it. The presence—and absence—of a spokesman for the nation clearly indicates that the public hungers for propaganda in the sense of the production of ongoing events. The significance of propaganda has become institutionalized in Israeli domestic politics. This change is strikingly and dramatically reflected in election propaganda and is identified with the sweeping Americanization of Israeli politics.

Dan Caspi

See also Arab World; Cold War in the Middle East; Elections (Israel); Herzl, Theodor; Olympics; Public Diplomacy; Religion; Terrorism; Zionism

References: Arieli, D. "Nature as a Builder of Culture: The Case of the Society for the Protection of Nature in Israel" (in Hebrew). *Megamot* 38 (1966): 189–206; Bar-Gal, Y. *An Agent of Zionist Propaganda: The Jewish National Fund, 1924–1947* (in Hebrew). Haifa: Haifa University Press, 1999; Horowitz, D., and M. Lissak. *The Origins of the Israeli Polity.* Chicago: University of Chicago Press, 1978; Mishory, A. *Lo and Behold: Zionists Icons and Visual Symbols in Israeli Culture* (in Hebrew). Tel Aviv: Am Oved, 2000; Shavit, S. "Filling in the Missing Cultural Layer: Between Official and Unofficial Popular Culture in Israeli National Culture" (in Hebrew). In *Popular Culture: A Research Anthology.* Ed. B. Z. Kedar. Jerusalem: Zalman Shazar Center, 1966.

Italy

Propaganda, a term that first appeared on the Italian peninsula during the Reformation, has played a central role at key moments in modern Italian history, including the development of fascism and the establishment of democracy. Earlier in Italy's history it was instrumental in the Risorgimento, which led to the creation of an Italian state. Stimulated by the French Revolution, the appearance of the Risorgimento in 1815 coincided with the desire for self-governance and independence from Austria, the pope, and the Kingdom of The Two Sicilies. The old ruling elites implemented political censorship to avoid the dissemination of the new nationalist ideals. The Austrians tried to block pro-Italian appeals in the press and the arts. A powerful contribution to independent thought was provided by the music of Giuseppe Verdi (1813–1901).

Masked by other themes, Verdi's operas inflamed the hearts of their listeners, transforming each performance into a celebration of patriotism.

Three prominent nationalistic leaders and propagandists emerged during this period. Giuseppe Mazzini (1805–1872), a member of the famous secret society Carbonari and a long-term exile in France, founded the periodical *Giovane Italia* (Young Italy), which championed the cause of Italy's need for self-governance and change. The journal appeared on 18 March 1832 and ran until July 1834, publishing a total of six issues, each from one to two hundred pages in length. A front-page quote by the Italian poet Ugo Foscolo (1778–1827) summarized its message: "Raise your voice in the name of all and tell the world that we may have misfortune but we are neither blind nor cowardly." Count Cavour (1810–1861), leader of Piedmont, founded the newspaper *Il Risorgimento* in 1847. A masterful journalist and diplomat, Cavour sought Italian unification by separating northern Italy from Austria and gradually incorporating the south into an Italian state through a campaign of plebiscites. In 1860 Giuseppe Garibaldi (1807–1882), a charismatic figure, led an army of one thousand in the conquest of Sicily and Naples. Garibaldi's army selected red shirts as part of their uniform purely by chance; initially meant for Argentinean butchers, the shirts were available at low cost. Garibaldi took advantage of the color, transforming the red shirts into a potent republican symbol of independence, freedom, and courage.

After Italy's unification in 1870, the parliamentary democracy, led by the monarchy, was faced with the difficult task of imposing a sense of uniformity on the diverse population and the disparate territories. In 1892 industrial workers founded the Partito Socialista (Socialist Party), and 1896 saw the appearance of Democrazia Cristiana (Christian Democratic Party).

At the beginning of the twentieth century, journalists looked to the wealthy industrial classes to finance new publications. Newspapers around World War I were loosely controlled by prominent figures in various industrial sectors, as well as by the government. Both industry and the state understood the importance of the press but did not exert their influence in a clearly organized, systematic way. The first reputable national newspapers, both originating in northern Italy, were Alfredo Frassati's (1868–1961) *La Stampa* (The Press) and Luigi Albertini's (1871–1941) *Il Corriere della Sera* (The Evening Courier). Both men were wealthy entrepreneurs. Despite their divergent political views, they were united in their desire to publish objective journalism based on British and German models. However, both newspapers primarily represented the political views of their founders since objectivity was understood as expressing one's own views rather than fairly representing all opinions. Other newspapers served as forums for debate on Italian politics, such as Sidney Sonnino's (1847–1922) conservative *Il Giornale d'Italia* (The Journal of Italy), Giuseppe Prezzolini's (1882–1982) *La Voce* (The Voice), and Enrico Corradini's (1865–1931) *Il Regno* (The Kingdom) and *L'Idea Nazionale* (The National Idea).

In 1902 Guglielmo Marconi (1874–1937) granted to the Italian government the free use of his radio patent for twenty years. Promulgated in 1910, a special law guaranteed the state the right to award to an Italian-owned private enterprise the concession for broadcasting equipment "to be built for scientific, educational, and also public or private service." Significantly, the administrative functions for the actual management of the new electronic medium were to be decided by the government itself and by a permanent consulting committee appointed by the government. Control soon also extended to film. The Ministry of the Interior's decree of 1914 established censorship regulations that banned all films considered "injurious to the national fame and self-respect, or against the public order . . . that would lessen the name and fame of public institutions and authorities, or of the offices and agents of the law."

In 1912 Italy became the first country to use leaflets dropped from airplanes as a form of propaganda. Specifically, these appeals to surrender were dropped near enemy lines in North Africa during the Italo-Turkish War. When Italy joined World War I (1915), the same technique was used against Austria. Italian airmen dropped as many as two hundred thousand leaflets over Vienna. World War I and the unsettled postwar period temporarily halted wider media development in Italy, although radio had demonstrated its military potential in combat. During the war Italy received much British, French, and German propaganda. Of the newspapers, *La Stampa* took a neutral position regarding Italian involvement in the war, while the *Corriere* favored intervention, exalting war efforts and ignoring criticism. The Italian press was eventually placed under the control of the Press and Propaganda Bureau for the duration of the war.

At the end of the war, Italy experienced a period of financial and political instability. The era saw the creation of three new political parties, each with an accompanying surge of propaganda: the Partito Popolare (a continuation of Democrazia Cristiana); the Communist Party, which was founded in 1921 by Antonio Gramsci (1901–1937); and the right-wing Fasci di Combattimento (combat action groups) founded in 1919 by Benito Mussolini (1883–1945), which was nationalistic, (initially) anti-Communist, antichurch, and primarily voicing the frustrated aspirations of World War I veterans. In 1922, with Mussolini in control of the parliament, the Fasci di Combattimento became the Partito Nazionale (National Party). Italy's Fascist era had begun.

Mussolini sought to use propaganda to create a "culture of Fascism" in Italy centering on himself as "Il Duce," or the leader. The press became the main agent of this system, followed by radio, film, and Mussolini's famous staged balcony speeches. Using pre-arranged audience responses and rhetoric appealing to the glory of the Roman Empire, Mussolini was initially successful in winning over the crowds. However, Fascist propaganda became increasingly less credible, culminating in the defeats of World War II, the Allied liberation of Rome in 1943, and Mussolini's flight to the north. By the time of Mussolini's death in 1945, the last remains of Fascist propaganda and ideology had been shattered.

Mussolini left Italy a war-ravaged nation with a defunct ideology. In 1943 the Allies took over the key organs of Italian mass communication, such as Radio Bari, for their own propaganda purposes. Paradoxically, in so doing the British and the Americans introduced Italian journalists to a new type of broadcasting freedom. Many journalists had been imprisoned for their political beliefs and felt a kinship with the Allies based on the common hatred of Fascism and a desire to rebuild the nation's communications infrastructure.

Allied propaganda concentrated on anti-Fascist programs intended for German-occupied territories and aimed at winning the approval of the Italian public. A good example was "Italia Combatte," the most famous military program of the time. Broadcast by Radio Bari, the program started with the "Bollettino della Guerra Partigiana," which emphasized a policy of unconditional surrender. The more interesting part of the program, in line with BBC strategy, discredited the enemy through fake intercepted correspondence, offered valuable information about the German army, and revealed espionage activity.

The leading force in postwar Italian politics was the Democrazia Cristiana. With the help of the British, the Americans, and the church, this party became the leading political force in the country, leaving the left isolated and weak. The church played a fundamental role in helping the party grow. On 8 July 1949 Pius XII passed a decree proclaiming opposition to "materialistic and atheistic Marxism" and threatening to excommunicate all who "professed Marxist ideas or were active in Communist parties." But the church alone was not enough to ensure the party's success. Part of the latter's appeal was that, following an initial reassessment of political life during the postwar period, the Italian middle class, the aristocrats, and the industrialists all felt that their interests converged in this Catholic party. Meanwhile, as the Cold War intensified, Britain and the United States recognized the Democrazia Cristiana as the only party that could protect the country against Communism.

The United States played an active role in postwar Italian politics, bankrolling the Democrazia Cristiana and conducting much propaganda for the free-enterprise system under the auspices of the Marshall Plan. The election of April 1948 became one of the first set-piece confrontations of the Cold War, with the United States doing all it could through overt and covert propaganda to defeat the left. The Christian Democrats won by an overwhelming majority. The victory also sealed the party's hegemony within the national broadcasting corporation (RAI) as well. At a 1952 convention RAI was granted exclusive radio and television broadcasting rights for another twenty-five years. Despite the efforts of the left and discussions on the importance of fair political representation and objectivity of information, radio was already under the tight control of the dominant government party. For the next twenty-five years, such control would become apparent in RAI's news broadcasts and programming.

By the end of World War II, the Italian cinema had tried to distance itself from the Fascist era. Its filmmakers attempted to create a new genre, dubbed "neorealism," which aimed to reach the masses with films that contrasted with both Fascist propaganda films and the light, Hollywood-based models of earlier years. Films like Roberto Rossellini's (1906–1977) *Rome Open City* (1946), as well as Vittorio de Sica's (1902–1974) *The Bicycle Thief* (1947) presented the grim reality of postwar Italy. Audiences, however, turned their backs on neorealist films, preferring more escapist, mass-produced Hollywood fare.

Italian newspapers remained the propaganda tools of the multiparty system. Both news reports and editorial views covered a wide spectrum of Italian political views. Newspapers became (and remain) platforms of opinion and debate, affirming their own political ideologies and criticizing opposing points of view. Between 1954, which saw the birth of television, and 1975, the year in which RAI reform was passed, Italy witnessed a chaotic blend of dominant control by the Democrazia Cristiana, political struggles on the part of the opposition, and experimental coalitions between the center and the left. The reform of 1975 was intended to reduce government influence within RAI while providing Italian media with more freedom to reflect the pluralistic interests of the Italian electorate. Unfortunately, it did not fulfill the expectations of its promulgators.

In 1976 new legislation permitted independent television stations to broadcast locally, marking the beginning of commercial television. The next twenty years were characterized by the steady decline of RAI's influence as a result of the erosion of its monopoly. In these years Silvio Berlusconi (1936–) created a media empire (MEDIASET) that transformed Italy's broadcasting scene from a monopoly to a "duopoly." On the one hand, RAI struggled to find a new identity; on the other, private stations expanded rapidly, facilitated by ineffective antitrust legislation.

The "clean hands" investigation of 1992 brought newer political forces to the fore. Berlusconi became heavily involved in politics and filled top RAI positions with trusted members of his new party, Forza Italia (Go, Italy!). As the reelected prime minister of Italy, Berlusconi has had a dominant influence on the media, causing bitter political wars between right- and left-wing parties. The latter have not yet succeeded in forcing the prime minister to resolve the conflict of interest between his political career and his media monopoly. Berlusconian policy makes use of the mass media in a totalitarian way. The prime minister also owns some print media, including the newspapers *Il Giornale* and *Libero,* and Mondadori, Italy's largest publishing company. Independent newspapers such as *La Repubblica* and *Il Corriere della Sera,* as well as the international press, have condemned the prime minister's media monopoly and his many conflicts of interest.

Livia Bornigia

See also Art; CIA; Fascism, Italian; Health; Marshall Plan; Mussolini, Benito; Psychological Warfare; Reformation and Counter-Reformation; Religion; Sport; Women's Movement: European; World War I

References: Arnold, W. V. *The Illusion of Victory: Propaganda and the Second World War.* New York: Peter Lang, 1998; Caretti, P. *Diritto Pubblico dell'Informazione.* Bologna: Il Mulino, 1994; Elwood, D. "Italy: The Regime, the Nation and the Film Industry: An Introduction." In *Film & Radio Propaganda in World War II.* Ed. K. R. M. Short. Knoxville: University of Tennessee Press, 1983, 220–229; MacDonald, C. "Radio Bari: Italian Wireless Propaganda in the Middle East and British Countermeasures, 1934–38." *Middle Eastern Studies* (1991): 195–207; Monteleone, F. *Storia della Radio e della Televisione in Italia.* Venice: Saggi Marsilio, 1992; Reeves, Nicholas. *The Power of Film Propaganda.* London: Cassell, 1999; Sassoon, D. *Contemporary Italy.* New York: Longman, 1986.

J

"J'Accuse" ("I Accuse") (1898)

This open letter addressed to French President Félix Faure (1841–1899) attacking official anti-Semitism was written in January 1898 by the French novelist and radical Émile Zola (1840–1902). The letter, published in *L'Aurore,* accused the French army of anti-Semitism in its treatment of Alfred Dreyfus (c. 1859–1935), a Jewish officer convicted of spying for Germany. The letter did not so much win readers over to the Dreyfus cause as much as it forced the issue out into the public domain. The succeeding political storm surrounding the Dreyfus affair divided the French political and intellectual establishment. Zola found himself on trial and fled to England to escape imprisonment. The French courts twice retried Dreyfus and twice reconvicted him, but the presence of anti-Semitism was evident in each instance. The president of France intervened, granting Dreyfus a pardon. The guilty party, in the person of Maj. Hubert Joseph Henry (1846–1898), the chief of French military intelligence, confessed to forging Dreyfus's signature and subsequently committed suicide.

Nicholas J. Cull

See also Anti-Semitism; France; Herzl, Theodor
References: Bredin, Jean-Denis. *The Affair: The Case of Alfred Dreyfus.* London: Sidgwick and

Jackson, 1987; Halasz, Nicholas. *Captain Dreyfus: The Story of Mass Hysteria.* New York: Simon and Schuster, 1955.

Japan

In the centuries leading up to the 1590s, Japan had been reduced to a state of constant warfare among competing regional warlords. Through a series of stunning battles and by sheer force of will, the warrior Oda Nobunaga (1534–1582) initiated a process of unification. His henchman, the samurai leader Toyotomi Hideyoshi (1536–1598), expanded this initiative and amalgamated the formerly hostile regional fiefdoms. Hideyoshi dictated that large castles be built to demonstrate both the splendor and strength (*tenka*) of his realm. He began employing Confucian terminology to justify his reign. Hideyoshi attempted to suppress powerful Buddhist groups that opposed his rule. Japan, he claimed, was the land of the gods and he was its ruler. Neither Hideyoshi nor the other shoguns (literally, barbarian-subduing general) who followed him ever attempted to usurp the imperial title from the emperor of Japan, instead ruling in his name. This act of fiat resulted in a major social upheaval 250 years later. In the 1850s, during the onset of the Meiji Restoration, Japan witnessed fierce ideological struggles. On one side stood the imperial supporters who argued that the emperor should once again head Japanese society to guard against the encroaching West. On the other side stood the rapidly declining shogun and his band of conservative administrators, who wished to maintain the status quo.

The shogun's authority rested on imperial concession and the concept of *kogi* where public welfare takes precedence over individual rights. The Tokugawa authorities, the ruling house that assumed power from Hideyoshi in the early 1600s, put this quasi-Confucian concept into practice through extensive public laws, posted outside towns and villages, that restricted movement from region to region and controlled the bearing of arms; through ornate imperial processions; and through sumptuary laws. A subsequent ban on Christianity and the use of Buddhist temples to register local inhabitants helped consolidate villages. These measures essentially closed the country off to the outside world for the next 250 years.

By the mid-nineteenth century, Japan was no longer able to keep its doors closed to the outside world. The legitimacy of Tokugawa rule began to wane in the face of increasing economic, military, and cultural threats from the West. Regardless of government efforts, through a multitude of state-sponsored media, to denigrate foreign ideas and peoples as unworthy, the reality of Japan's helplessness proved too shocking to ignore any longer.

For the newly appointed official bureaucrats of Meiji Japan the problem was one of how to convince a population taught to loathe the nonnative to accept foreign ideas. This shift was nothing if not phenomenal. Initially the fledgling government initiated a series of laws, called the *kaiishiki jorei* that attempted to get the populace to dress and comport itself differently. Japan wanted to look good in Western eyes and—just as important—to make the distinction between itself and the "not yet modernized" China even

more apparent. A proliferation of newspapers and illustrated magazines helped both the literate and illiterate populations to understand what was happening. Of course, government censorship continued, with the difference that it became more difficult for the authorities to inspect the wealth of information now available.

Even before the government concentrated on reining in the nascent press, it focused its efforts on the theater and popular entertainment. The government hired various entertainers and teachers, as well as religious clergy, to lecture to the population and urge the masses to support the new government and its ideology. The Meiji state eagerly identified itself with the native Shinto religion. The authorities hoped to draw the entire population into the fold of Shintoism, with state holidays and ceremonies reflecting Shinto rituals and practices. Entertainers had to be licensed. In addition, they were admonished not to perform profane acts or beg openly in the streets.

As the Meiji era progressed, the concept of a single emperor under which the country could be united gained in importance in the eyes of the oligarchy that actually governed the nation. From the late 1860s through the 1880s, the new government, under the leadership of men such as Ito Hirobumi (1841–1909), paraded the Meiji emperor around the entire country and orchestrated lavish ceremonies designed to accustom the population to recognize their new leader. By the turn of the century, schools were required to mark the beginning of each day with the recitation of an oath to the emperor, whose image hung in the schoolroom. These measures proved exceedingly successful. Within thirty years of opening up to the outside world, Japan was victorious in a battle against China in what historians have described as Japan's "first modern war." During the 1894–1895 Sino-Japanese War, the Japanese populace eagerly read comic books mocking the Chinese, but real modern propaganda would not be utilized until the Japanese gov-

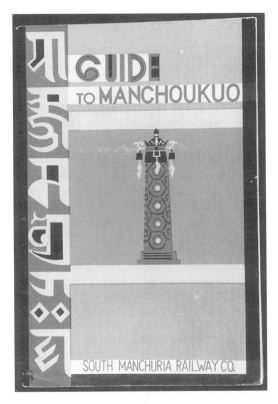

An English-language Guide to Manchoukuo, *published by the South Manchuria Railway Company, 1934. The book attempted to justify Japanese aggression in Manchuria, now under Japanese control with Emperor Pu Yi as titular leader. (Courtesy of David Culbert)*

ernment mobilized the entire country for war with Russia in the Russo-Japanese War of 1904–1905.

The Japanese government now realized it had to influence both domestic and foreign opinion in order to remain in control. Japanese press authorities issued strict orders governing foreign coverage and began sending newspaper reporters over to China. These reporters linked up with military platoons and sent stories back to the censors. Film companies were permitted to send over authorized crews, and their resulting efforts brought about mass support for the war.

Throughout World War I Japanese media analysts and government bureaus continued to research British and German propaganda methods. With the outbreak of hostilities with China in the mid-1930s, the Japanese government commandeered several agencies concerned with propaganda. Along with the institutions that would eventually give rise to the Cabinet Board of Information, the Japanese military ran its own separate media divisions. The South Manchurian Railway Company, a quasi-governmental conglomerate with offices all over the world, also had sophisticated propaganda operations afoot in mainland China and Soviet border areas. Following Japan's invasion of China and subsequent war against the West, Japanese propaganda activities continued to escalate but remained far from unified.

After the disastrous experience of World War II, the Japanese found themselves occupied by the U.S. military. The Allies, led by the Americans, set themselves the task of dismantling all the supposed operations that had led Japan into war, including propaganda (relying largely on the paradigm used to explain U.S. entry into World War I). U.S. reforms included a new constitution, a free press that still had to conform to occupation policies, an end to censorship, and major changes within the Japanese educational system. Teachers were required to sever all connections with the old regime and new textbooks were published. Ironically, due to the extremely small number of Westerners fluent in Japanese, combined with the expansive nature of the occupation, most key posts were filled by the same Japanese propagandists who only months earlier had supported Japan's war in Asia. This shift was paralleled by the transformation of the workforce of Domei, one of the largest media monopolies, into Dentsu, the largest advertising agency in the world. At the same time, the new push to align Japan with American policy led both the Allied authorities and the Japanese bureaucracy to develop systematic surveys of public opinion in Japan. In pursuit of this ideal, the headquarters of the occupation forces created a Civil Information and Education Section. In order to persuade and assuage the newly defeated Japanese, it was first necessary to assess and influence Japanese public opinion. Prior to surrender, emperor worship and a belief in Japan's imperial mission in Asia had been a core focus of an increasingly nationalistic educational system developed under state-controlled media. A belief that democratization involved the molding of minds mandated the study and measurement of public opinion.

On the cultural front, the United States sought to remold Japan, in part by gaining the cooperation of the six major domestic film studios (much as the OWI had worked with Hollywood during the war). As in the print media generally, the United States discouraged active discussion of the Japanese past, including the atrocities committed on the Chinese mainland and throughout Asia. More important, unlike Germany, in Japan blame for the war was placed squarely on the shoulders of the Japanese military establishment; until recently few citizens have proactively researched civilian responsibility. U.S. authorities also routinely repressed images of damage caused by the dropping of the atomic bomb. In part to promote a new sense of openness, scenes reflecting the new Japan, such as images of couples kissing in public, were now permitted by the film authorities. As the Cold War hit East Asia, the United States slowed its ideological reconstruction of Japan and turned its attention to the rapid development of the Japanese economy. Extensive media operations appear to have been implemented in Japan, where U.S. officials secretly financed feature films, TV programs, thousands of hours of radio programming, hundreds of books, and numerous intellectuals to bring Japan under the aegis of American policy.

The Japanese government and private interests engaged in international publicity and propaganda to promote the new image of postwar Japan. The central event in this campaign was the Tokyo Olympics of 1964. Public diplomacy has included an emphasis on technology and both traditional and contemporary achievement in the arts. Domestic-propaganda issues have included both a lively antinuclear movement and the persistence of nationalism. The best-known nationalist-oriented propagandist outside Japan was the novelist Yukio Mishima (1925–1970). Controversies have included accusations by Chinese and Korean observers that the government had amended school textbooks to underplay atrocities committed during World War II.

Barak Kushner

See also China; Churchill, Winston; Korea; Olympics; Pacific/Oceania; Philippines; Public Diplomacy; Reeducation; Southeast Asia; Sukarno; Tokyo Rose; World War II (Japan)

References: Berry, Mary. *Hideyoshi.* Cambridge, MA: Harvard University Press, 1982; Garon, Sheldon. *Molding Japanese Minds.* Princeton, NJ: Princeton University Press, 1997; Gluck, Carol. *Japan's Modern Myths: Ideology in the Late Meiji Period.* Princeton, NJ: Princeton University Press, 1985; Hirano, Kyoko. *Mr. Smith Goes to Tokyo: Japanese Cinema under the American Occupation.* Washington, DC: Smithsonian, 1992; Huffman, James L. *Creating a Public: People and Press in Meiji Japan.* Honolulu: University of Hawaii Press, 1997; Ikegami, Eiko. *The Taming of the Samurai.* Cambridge, MA: Harvard University Press, 1995; Ooms, Herman. *Tokugawa Ideology.* Princeton, NJ: Princeton University Press, 1985. Smith, Dennis B. *Japan Since 1945.* London: Macmillan, 1995.

John Bull

A symbolic figure representing England and/or Great Britain and often used in political cartoons, this character is usually depicted as a plump, middle-aged, clean-shaven man often dressed in a Union Jack waistcoat. John Bull first appeared in print in 1712 in a pamphlet by Scottish-born satirist and court physician John Arbuthnot (1667–1735). It is unclear whether Arbuthnot, an associate of Jonathan Swift (1667–1745), invented John Bull or drew upon an existing character. The first pamphlet, entitled *Law is a Bottomless Pit or a history of John Bull,* used the story of a wildly expensive court case to attack the Whig government and its foreign policy. The satire also included a French character called

Lewis Baboon. Four subsequent pamphlets followed, establishing John Bull firmly in the British imagination. The character became a favorite of satirists, a familiar figure in plays and pageants, and a staple of cartoons by artists like James Gillray (1757–1815) and contributors to such illustrated magazines as *Punch.* In 1906 Horatio Bottomley (1860–1933), a scandal-mongering journalist, politician, and notorious fraud, established a weekly newspaper called *John Bull,* which was aimed at working-class readers. The paper claimed a readership of one and a half million. In 1914 this paper and Bottomley became a fount of jingoistic propaganda in support of World War I. The image of John Bull figured on recruiting posters for the Great War, though it was not as ubiquitous as that of his American equivalent Uncle Sam.

Nicholas J. Cull

See also Britain (Eighteenth Century); Uncle Sam
References: Bower, Alan W., and Robert A. Erickson, eds. *The History of John Bull by John Arbuthnot.* Oxford: Clarendon Press, 1976; Huggett, Frank E. *Victorian England as seen by "Punch."* London: Sidgwick and Jackson, 1978; Hyman, Alan. *The Rise and Fall of Horatio Bottomley: The Biography of a Swindler.* London: Cassell, 1972.

Jud Süss (1940)

This was one of the most notorious and successful pieces of anti-Semitic film propaganda produced in Nazi Germany. Directed by Veit Harlan (1899–1964), who also wrote the script, *Jud Süss* represented a reworking of a celebrated historical novel of the same name by Lion Feuchtwanger (1889–1958), which was sympathetic to its subject, as was a film on the same subject produced by the Gaumont British studios in 1934.

The historical figure of Jud Süss was not the stuff of transparent virtue. In fact, he was notorious, so the Nazi production, overseen by Joseph Goebbels, the minister of propaganda, showed villainous behavior to best effect.

Süss, an official in eighteenth-century Württemberg, committed serial adultery, raised taxes to unheard-of levels, and was in fact hanged as a Jew within an enormous iron cage. *Jud Süss* was successful thanks to the talents of Germany's finest actors and as a result of splendid production values. Millions paid to see a film with a virulent anti-Semitic message. Although the film encouraged a dislike of all Jews, there is no evidence to suggest that this particular film made every German a willing executioner.

David Culbert

See also Anti-Semitism; Film (Nazi Germany); Goebbels, Joseph; Hitler, Adolf; World War II (Germany)
References: Etlin, Richard A., ed. *Art, Culture, and Media under the Third Reich.* Chicago: University of Chicago Press, 2002; Taylor, Richard. *Film Propaganda: Soviet Russia and Nazi Germany.* London: I. B. Tauris, 1998; Welch, David. *Propaganda and the German Cinema, 1933–1945.* Oxford: Clarendon Press, 1983 (rev. ed., London: I. B. Tauris, 2001).

K

Kennedy, John F. (1917–1963)

Thirty-fifth U.S. president and arguably the finest American orator of the twentieth century, John Fitzgerald Kennedy was born into a well-to-do family. His father, Joseph P. Kennedy (1888–1969), groomed him for a political career. He served with distinction in the navy during World War II and entered Congress as a Democrat in 1947. In 1952 he won the junior Senate seat for Massachusetts and by 1960 was able to run for the presidency. As a senator he had a keen eye for publicity, and his doings were frequently reported in the press. His reputation grew with the success of his book *Profiles in Courage* (1956). During the election campaign Kennedy paid particular attention to his appearance. His clean-cut image contrasted startlingly with that of his Republican contender, Richard Nixon (1913–1994), during their famous television debate. Kennedy also made the image of the United States into a campaign issue, claiming that a secret United States Information Agency (USIA) poll had revealed that America had fallen in world esteem. Following a lively campaign, Kennedy won the presidency by a narrow margin.

Attempting to develop a distinctive rhetorical style, in his inaugural address Kennedy set out his agenda by borrowing a phrase that had been used to good effect by many, including the headmaster of his school: "Ask not what your country can do for you—ask what you can do for your country." He loved this sort of sentence construction and used it throughout his presidency. Kennedy got along well with the Washington press corps, drawing them into the spirit of what he called the "New Frontier." With his press secretary, Pierre Salinger (1925–), he became a master of the press conference. Kennedy was the last American president to benefit from a bipartisan media that considered itself as having a stake in the success of the administration. The press turned a blind eye to such things as his ill health and his sexual adventures.

Kennedy gave new leadership to the institutions of American propaganda overseas. He persuaded veteran broadcaster Edward R. Murrow (1908–1965) to serve as USIA director; the Kennedy era was later remembered as a golden age for that agency. He also understood the need for the United States to be active in world affairs. To this end, Kennedy adopted a number of policies with a strong propaganda component designed to meet the challenge of the Soviet Union head on. These included: the creation of the Peace Corps, whose volunteers served in develop-

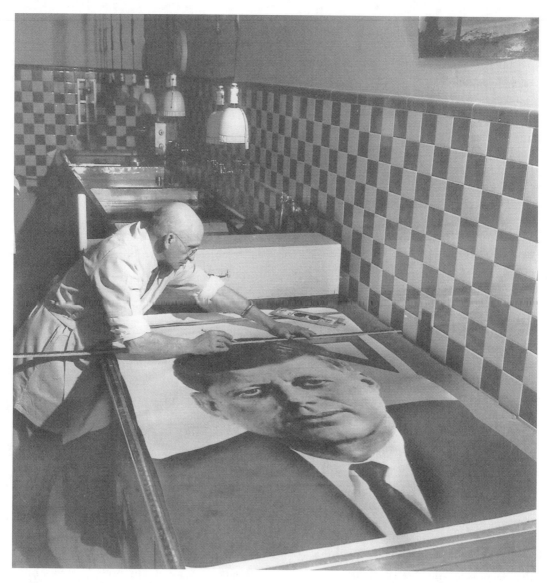

The United States Information Agency prepares giant pictures of Kennedy for export at the time of his inauguration in 1961. (National Archives)

ment projects overseas; the expansion of the American space program, with the declared objective of placing a man on the moon within the decade; and high-profile military actions. The last proved the weakest. Kennedy's support for the invasion of Cuba at the Bay of Pigs in 1961 was a public relations disaster, and his policy of providing aid to the government of South Vietnam created problems for his successor. Nevertheless Kennedy remained a skilled player in the image game. No president was ever so loved or admired in Europe. Following the standoff of the Cuban missile crisis, he convinced the Soviet Union to participate in talks leading up to a nuclear test ban treaty. Kennedy's death in November 1963 at the hands of an assassin gave the United States a martyr, but it also robbed the country of a perceptive leader who understood both the potential and the limits of propaganda.

Nicholas J. Cull

See also Castro, Fidel; Cold War;
   Counterinsurgency; Elections; Funerals; Latin
   America; Murrow, Edward R.; Nixon,
   Richard; *Silent Spring;* United States; USIA;
   Vietnam; Vietnam War
References: Reeves, Thomas C. *A Question of
   Character: The Life of John F. Kennedy.* New York:
   Free Press, 1991; Salinger, Pierre. *With
   Kennedy.* New York: Doubleday, 1966; Sperber,
   A. M. *Murrow: His Life and Times.* New York:
   Freundlich, 1986.

KGB (Committee of State Security, Soviet Union)

The KGB was officially charged with defending the Soviet Communist regime against domestic and foreign enemies. The KGB's principal internal function was surveillance of the Soviet population. The suppression of anti-Soviet behavior was largely achieved through intimidation but could be enforced by means of incarceration in special prisons, forced labor camps, and even corrective psychiatric hospitals. A key internal group targeted for surveillance and control were intellectuals, particularly writers, while the flow of information emanating from the West was considered the primary external threat. Thus, much KGB activity was focused on either repressing or countering "enemy" propaganda.

The KGB, established in 1954, was the last in a long line of institutions of repression employed by Russian regimes since the reign of Ivan the Terrible (1530–1584). In terms of form and function, the committee was certainly a worthy successor to the prerevolutionary Okhrana secret police. Officially it was the successor to a series of state security agencies, including the Cheka, OGPU, NKVD, and the MGB/MVD.

The KGB was constituted as an organ of the Soviet Council of Ministers. The Committee of State Security also organized and administered subordinate committees of state security within individual republics as well as at district and city levels. The ultimate master of agencies operated by the Soviet Union's Communist allies was the KGB. The latter's propaganda techniques overseas included the use of "disinformation"—well-placed rumors or faked stories calculated to undermine the enemy.

Graham Roberts

See also CIA; Cold War; Disinformation;
   Okhrana; Revolution, Russian; Russia; Stalin,
   Joseph
References: Nove, Alec, ed. *The Stalin
   Phenomenon.* New York: St. Martins, 1993;
   Shentalinksky, Vitaly. *The KGB's Literary Archive.*
   London: Harvill, 1997.

King, Martin Luther, Jr. (1929–1968)

An African American civil rights leader, King successfully won the support of the liberal white community for basic reform and attracted worldwide media attention concerning race relations in the United States. Born in Atlanta and the son of a preacher, King attended Boston University and thereafter worked as a Baptist minister in Montgomery, Alabama, gaining recognition in 1955 as a result of his leadership of that city's 382-day bus boycott, which eventually resulted in a law ending desegregated buses. By 1957 he had been elected president of the Southern Christian Leadership Conference (SCLC) and used nonviolent direct action to coordinate high-profile sit-ins, freedom rides, boycotts, and protest marches throughout the South. His most successful campaigns occurred in Birmingham, Alabama, in 1963, when he made certain that the media bore witness to violent police attacks against young black protesters, and the August 1963 March on Washington (250,000 strong), where he delivered his famous "I Have a Dream" speech. In 1963 alone he delivered approximately 350 speeches and traveled 275,000 miles. He won *Time* magazine's Man of the Year Award, followed by the Nobel Peace Prize in 1964. His popularity among white Americans fell after 1965 as he turned his attention to poverty in northern cities and spoke

Martin Luther King Jr. delivers his "I Have a Dream" speech from the Lincoln Memorial during the March on Washington, August 1963. (Flip Schulke / CORBIS)

out against the war in Vietnam. King was harassed by the FBI and criticized by the growing militant "black power" movement. On 4 April 1968 King was assassinated. His death led to outbreaks of violence in several major cities.

King's propaganda skill lay in the art of eloquent and persuasive public speaking, derived from the vibrant oral tradition of the black church in which he had grown up. He used simple words and imagery and stressed basic moral truths. King was not so much original or intellectual but rather personal and inspirational; he spoke often of his own suffering and willingness to die for his cause, which elicited intense emotions from his audiences. Although King's approach owed much to the nonviolence practiced by Mahatma Gandhi (1869–1948) in India, he always appealed to traditional American symbols, including the Declaration of Independence and the memory of Abraham Lincoln (1809–1865), and stressed his belief in the American dream and the "Americanness" of his campaign. His

strategic alliances with northern whites bolstered his success in terms of influencing public opinion throughout America. Liberal white audiences approved of his moderate approach to reform, while blacks were encouraged by his talk of equality and the gradual improvements taking place. King was an ideal promoter of the civil rights movement, presenting the public image of an educated and well-spoken Christian. He frequently appeared on live debates and talk shows, but he was most eloquent when preaching. King also clearly understood the power of visual images and relied on the medium of television to dramatically convey acts of white violence.

By the 1980s his image had become part of the collective American memory, which stood at odds with the radical approach of his later years. His family successfully campaigned to make his birthday (15 January) a federal holiday, and it was first celebrated as such in 1986.

Samantha Jones

See also Civil Rights Movement; Gandhi, Mohandas K.; Malcolm X; NAACP; United States

References: Cook, Robin. *Sweet Land of Liberty? The Black Struggle for Civil Rights in Twentieth-Century America.* London: Longman, 1998; Oates, Stephen B. *Let the Trumpet Sound: The Life of Martin Luther King, Jr.* London: Search, 1982; Taylor, Branch. *Parting the Waters: America in the King Years, 1954–63.* New York: Simon and Schuster, 1988; ———. *Pillar of Fire: America in the King Years, 1963–65.* New York: Simon & Schuster, 1998; Washington, James Melvin, ed. *A Testament of Hope: The Essential Writings of Martin Luther King, Jr.* New York: Harper and Row, 1986.

Korea

Korea has experienced the propaganda of outsiders, not least that of its powerful neighbors China and Japan, but its rulers have deployed propaganda of their own since the Yi dynasty (1392–1910). Modern times produced the cult of personality around North Korea's leader Kim Il Sung (1912–1994).

The Yi dynasty came to power with the help of China, legitimizing its rule with reference to Chinese culture—especially Confucianism. The architecture of its new capital of Seoul underpinned its dynastic power. In 1443 scholars, under the supervision of King Se-jong (1418–1450), developed *Han'gul* (Korean writing), a phonetic alphabet that permitted Korean to be printed efficiently utilizing a movable typeface, thereby increasing the impact of the dynasty's ideology. The kingdom based its civil service on the Confucian examination model and practiced rigorous censorship. The system sustained the Yi dynasty for five centuries, an achievement unmatched elsewhere in Eastern or Western history. On occasion scholars launched ideological initiatives to reform the state along more perfect Confucian lines, as in the notable campaign by Cho Kwang-jo in the early 1500s.

Having resisted Japanese invasion in the 1590s, in 1636 Korea fell to the armies of the Manchu during their campaign to conquer Ming China. Although Korea now entered a long period of isolation from the non-Chinese world, foreign ideas still managed to filter into the country. Koreans learned of Christianity from diplomatic visits to China; before the first missionaries had even reached Korea, the state passed preemptive laws to halt the spread of this "dangerous" belief system, with its "intolerable irreverence for ancestors" and its rejection of Confucian ritual. Christian missionary activity met with persecution. Meanwhile, a reformist movement among the scholar class known as "practical learning" reflected the first stirrings of the Western concept of nationhood. By the nineteenth century Korean culture had rejected rigid Chinese models. Literary and artistic works of this period would become the staples of the cultural nationalists of the twentieth century.

In the 1860s a powerful religious movement called *Tonghak* (Eastern Learning) rocked Korea. Founded by a scholar named Ch'oe Che-u (1824–1864), it borrowed from multiple Eastern religions and set out to purge secret Christian sects and challenge the power of the West. The Yi dynasty clamped down and embarked on a conservative, anti-Christian campaign of its own under the leadership of the regent, or *Taewongun,* Yi Ha-ung (1821–1889). In 1871 Korean guns fended off a U.S. attempt to "open" Korea as it had earlier done in Japan, but in 1876 the Japanese themselves accomplished the same feat. A pawn in Sino-Japanese politics, economic conditions in Korea deteriorated and the Tonghak cult grew. Members demonstrated with drums and bells outside the royal palace as part of a campaign to win its founder a posthumous pardon. When Tonghak supporters rebelled again in 1894, Japan intervened, precipitating the Sino-Japanese War of 1894–1895, which Japan won. The aftermath resulted in a flowering of nationalistic feeling—including propaganda—in Korea. Its chief advocate was So Chae-p'il, who returned from exile in the United States to found both the Korean-language newspaper the *Independent* and a network of "Independence Clubs." In 1898 the court suppressed this reform movement.

In 1905 Japanese troops entered Korea and crossed it to fight Russia. They stayed and dominated the country. The Yi emperor appealed to international opinion—to no avail—and in 1910 Korea became a Japanese imperial possession. Korean resistance to Japan included the so-called *Samil* demonstration of 1 March 1919, which consisted of a day of national protest during which leaders across the country simultaneously read a Proclamation of Independence. Utilizing the language of Western nationalism, it was intended to win the support of Western leaders who had gathered at the Versailles conference. Japan violently crushed the movement. Japanese domination of Korea included a policy of cultural assimilation—especially in the educational system—whereby the use of both the Korean language and Korean names were banned during the 1930s. The Korean nationalist movement formed a government-in-exile in Shanghai under Syngman Rhee (1875–1965).

During World War II Allied propaganda pledges included a promise to restore an independent Korea. This aim was frustrated by the entry of the USSR into the war against Japan. The Soviets established control over the northern, industrialized portion of the country, north of the thirty-eighth parallel. By 1948 the division had produced two separate regimes: the Communist Democratic People's Republic of Korea in the North, under Kim Il Sung, and the Republic of Korea in the South, under Rhee. In June 1950 the Moscow-trained Kim Il Sung launched a massive invasion of the south. The three-year Korean War followed, ending in a cease-fire along the same border. The latter became part of a geographical table tennis match involving propaganda exchanges that has lasted until the end of the century and beyond.

Although based on the ideas of Marx and Lenin, North Korean ideology and propaganda parted company with the rest of the Communist bloc and became an idiosyncratic projection of the "Great Leader" and "sun of the nation" Kim Il Sung. Kim demanded the usual trappings of a personality cult (massive statues, ubiquitous portraits), establishing his own version of Marxist-Leninism known as *Juce,* which emphasized the significance of the leader. Kim's personal propaganda included his name; born Kim Sung Chu, he had taken the name of a guerrilla leader who resisted the Japanese early during the occupation. The exact nature of his wartime activity is open to dispute; he claimed to have led resistance forces against the Japanese. In due course he also emphasized his role in resisting the "American Imperialists" during the Korean War; monuments dedicated to the "great leader" were linked to the lavish memorials to the dead at the end of the Korean War. Following Kim's death in 1994, the leadership passed to his son, Kim Jong Il (1942–), who had served as regent during his father's decline.

Despite economic hardship (which was more acute following the end of Communism in the USSR and reform of the old Chinese Communist ally), North Korea has consistently invested heavily in propaganda at home and overseas. The key to North Korean propaganda remains Radio Pyongyang, which broadcasts to most of the world. North Korea figures frequently as a pariah in U.S. propaganda and was one of the seven nations singled out for special vilification in early 2001 as a sponsor of terrorism.

The South Korean state also began with an authoritarian figure, namely, Rhee. Student protests against the rigging of the 1960 presidential election were effective not so much because of the content of their words as the savagery of Rhee's response, following which he fled the country. Between 1961 and 1979 the military ruled South Korea in the person of Gen. Park Chung-hee (1917–1979). Following Park's death at the hands of his own intelligence chief, power passed to Gen. Chun Doo-hwan (1931–). Chun's regime dealt brutally with prodemocracy demonstrators, massacring hundreds of individuals in Kwangju in 1980. Despite some liberalization and reform, the regime continued to be marked by considerable corruption. Both Chun and his successor, Roh Tae-woo (1932–), were later jailed for corruption. South Korea's international propaganda gambits have included the hosting of the 1988 Seoul Summer Olympics, as well as various cultural ventures sponsored by the privately funded International Cultural Society of Korea and King Se-jong Foundation. The South Korean government also maintains the Korea Overseas Information Service to handle its press relations and has used the services of commercial public relations firms to influence American public opinion.

The South Korean media has developed along Western lines, with a plurality of newspapers and television stations in addition to the state-controlled Korean Broadcasting Service. Regulations imposed on the media include restrictions on the transmission of Japanese popular culture (a sensitive issue related to Korea's colonial experience). Free expression in the media was—and remains—circumscribed by the fact that many papers were either owned by or dependent upon advertising revenues from the big industrial combines. Journalists who broke ranks and criticized the government or praised North Korea were subject to intimidation or worse. The most significant voice of opposition to authoritarian rule in South Korea was that of Kim Dae-jung (1924–). A veteran writer and prodemocracy campaigner, Kim ran for the presidency in 1971, 1987, and 1992. In the interim he endured periods in jail, assassination attempts, and exile. In 1997 he finally won the presidential election. Korean regimes and protestors in both North and South Korea have used patriotic appeals for reunification as a staple of their propaganda. Kim similarly launched the "Sunshine Policy" of cross-border reconciliation. In recognition of his successful easing of tensions and his lifelong fight to promote

democracy in his region, he was awarded the Nobel Peace Prize in 2000.

Nicholas J. Cull

See also Art; Atrocity Propaganda; China; Japan; Korean War; Olympics; Public Diplomacy; Terrorism; Terrorism, War on

References: Cumings, Bruce. *The Two Koreas.* New York: Foreign Policy Association, 1984; Fairbank, John K., Edwin O. Reischauer, and Albert M. Craig. *East Asia: Tradition and Transformation.* Boston: Houghton Mifflin, 1989; Kang Hyeon-dew. *Media Culture in Korea.* Seoul: Seoul National University Press, 1993; Kim Chie-woon and Lee Jae-won, eds. *Elite Media Amidst Mass Culture: A Critical Look at Mass Communication in Korea.* Seoul: Nanam, 1994; Manheim, Jarol B., *Strategic Public Diplomacy and American Foreign Policy: The Evolution of Influence.* New York: Oxford University Press, 1994; Oliver, Robert T. *A History of the Korean People in Modern Times: 1800 to the Present.* Newark: University of Delaware Press, 1993.

Korean War (1950–1953)

This was the first major military conflict of the Cold War period, one that greatly intensified the propaganda struggle between East and West. The war erupted suddenly in June 1950 when the North Korean army, supplied and supported by the USSR, invaded South Korea. Within a week, the United States had formed a coalition under the auspices of the United Nations and had sent military forces to push back the North Korean invaders. During the next six months the conflict escalated, with UN forces routing the North Koreans at Inchon, which in turn provoked the intervention of Communist China. By the summer of 1951 the war had reached a stalemate, with the belligerents agreeing to armistice negotiations at Panmunjom, which dragged on for two years. During this period, the great powers (the United States, USSR, and China) hoped to restrict the actual fighting to the Korean peninsula. At the same time, with relations between East and West having deteriorated markedly, both Washington and Moscow redoubled their efforts to wage the wider Cold War, mobilizing inter-

A U.S. soldier loads propaganda leaflets into a hollow bomb case during the Korean War. This picture was used by the U.S. government to counter Communist claims that such cases found empty on the battlefield were evidence of American use of germ warfare. (National Archives)

nal resources, cementing their respective alliance blocs, and appealing for support among emerging Third World nationalist groups. Consequently, between 1950 and 1953 propaganda played an important role not just in the actual Korean conflict but also in the broader ideological struggle between East and West.

In the year before the Korean War, both superpowers had already established significant propaganda capabilities. The Communist Party had always exerted tight control over the flow of information inside the Soviet Union. In 1947 Stalin (1879–1953) set up the Cominform, which coordinated activities in the international Communist movement and vehemently attacked U.S. policies in Europe. In 1950 the USSR also encouraged peace groups within the West, like the Stockholm Peace Appeal, which gathered millions of signatures on petitions protesting against nuclear warfare. The United States was quick to respond. Aware that the American public had long been suspicious of anything that smacked of domestic propaganda, the Truman administration often relied on a network of private groups to sell its policies at home. With the revival of the Voice of America (VOA) in 1948, U.S. propagandists were also in a position to appeal to "captive nations" under Communist control.

The Korean War gave a tremendous boost to propaganda efforts on both sides. The U.S. Congress tripled funds for America's propaganda program (the "Campaign of Truth") enabling the Truman administration to intensify its efforts at home, and provided the VOA with the facilities to broadcast to more than a hundred countries in forty-six different languages. Given their firm faith in the efficacy of propaganda, the Communist powers made an even more concerted effort. By the end of 1950, Soviet short-wave programming was able to reach more countries in more languages than anything the Americans could muster.

These channels were principally used to disseminate simplistic and ideological messages. The Korean War greatly sharpened the tendency on both sides to paint the world in black and white terms. For American propagandists, Red China was now clearly depicted as part of the monolithic Communist conspiracy. Not only were Chinese Communists portrayed as puppets of Moscow; they were also attacked as brutal and savage, responsible for a range of atrocities against POWs, from brutal executions to the "brainwashing" of captured G.I.s. The Communist states responded in kind. At the start of the war, Mao Zedong (1893–1976) launched a "Hate America" campaign aimed at "unmasking American imperialism." In 1952 the Soviet Union constructed an elaborate and false propaganda story, charging Americans with using biological warfare in North Korea and northeast China.

Such arguments were largely intended for domestic consumption. Even in the authoritarian Communist bloc, leaders deemed it essential to drum up domestic support. This was especially true in China, where the Communist regime had only just come to power after a long and bloody civil war. For Mao the "Hate America" campaign offered an ideal way of mobilizing domestic support and establishing legitimacy for Communist Party rule. Rallying the public was also vital in the United States, particularly since the war had become increasingly unpopular during 1951. As opposition mounted at home, President Harry Truman (1884–1972) found it necessary to explain to Americans why Korea was vital to U.S. security. Truman also had to combat Republican charges—most vociferously and recklessly voiced by Joseph McCarthy (1909–1957)— that his administration was soft on Communism and to challenge the claim of his military commander, Douglas MacArthur (1880–1964), that the United States should expand the fighting in Asia to obtain a complete and total victory.

Nationalistic groups in Asia were another target for propagandists. Coming just months after Mao's success in the Chinese civil war, the conflict in Korea had shifted the focus of the Cold War from Europe to Asia. Attempting to gain the upper hand in this new theater, both the United States and the USSR hoped to rally support in countries like India, Indonesia, and Indochina. One of the most important forums for doing so was the United Nations. At the start of the Korean War, the Soviet boycott of the United Nations enabled the United States to intervene in Korea under the auspices of this international body, backed by the votes of fifty-nine countries around the world. Naturally, this cloak of international legitimacy remained at the heart of America's propaganda message throughout the war. The USSR tried hard to regain the initiative, returning to the United Nations to suppress debate and constantly claiming that the UN action in Korea was illegal, but Moscow's initial absence from the body cost it dearly in the battle to win over neutral opinion.

As the war dragged on into 1952 and 1953, the armistice talks in Panmunjom became yet another arena in which the two sides exchanged propaganda tirades, from charges of bad faith to accusations of war crimes. Only after a change in leadership in Washington and Moscow was an armistice finally concluded in July 1953, demonstrating that, despite the intensified propaganda battle, East and West could still reach a limited agreement, and paving the way for the slight thaw in superpower relations during the mid-1950s. However, the Cold War remained very much alive, with the propaganda capabilities that the two sides had expanded and refined during the Korean conflict continuing to play an integral part in this protracted ideological struggle between East and West.

Steven Casey

See also Atrocity Propaganda; Brainwashing; China; Cold War; *Guernica;* Korea; Mao Zedong; McCarthy, Joseph R.; Prisoners of War; United Nations; VOA

References: Clews, John C. *Communist Propaganda Techniques.* London: Methuen, 1964; Hixson, Walter L. *Parting the Curtain: Propaganda, Culture and the Cold War,* 1945–1961. Basingstoke, UK: Macmillan, 1997; Lucas, Scott. *Freedom's War: The U.S. Crusade against the Soviet Union, 1945–1956.* Manchester: Manchester University Press, 1999; Stueck, William. *The Korean War: An International History.* Princeton, NJ: Princeton University Press, 1995.

Kosovo Crisis and War (1999)

The Kosovo crisis was an extreme case of the use of propaganda by all sides in a late-twentieth-century Western war of intervention. The crisis consisted of four main phases. The first phase, beginning in January, involved a successful attempt by the Kosovo Liberation Army (KLA) to provoke a confrontation between the United States, representing North Atlantic Treaty Organization (NATO) powers, and the Serbian government. The second phase, which began in mid-March, saw the launching of a Serbian military campaign of "ethnic cleansing" to drive out the ethnic Albanian population of Kosovo. The third phase, which began on March 24, was marked by a NATO bombing campaign against Serbia. The Serbs conducted no military action against NATO other than antiaircraft defense. Their main response to the NATO bombing was a propaganda campaign intended to maintain support at home, win it internationally, and to dissuade NATO from launching a ground war. NATO countries viewed the maintenance of public support for their actions at home as a critical area of vulnerability. This was also the first war in which the Internet featured as a significant part of the information and propaganda campaign. The final phase, on June 9, involved the acceptance by Serbia of the presence of the NATO-led peacekeeping force KFOR (Kosovo Force), which entered Kosovo unopposed, thereby permitting the Albanians to return. The formal end to the air war came on June 20 after all Serb forces left Kosovo.

Despite the termination of the Bosnian crisis and war in 1995, diplomatic confrontations continued between Serbia, under Slobodan Milosevic (1941–), and the United

States, which were exacerbated by the continuing separatist tendencies among the other states and regions of the former Federal Republic of Yugoslavia. (Serbia and Montenegro both continued to refer to themselves as Yugoslavia in 1999, but Montenegro distanced itself from Serbia during the crisis.) By 1999 the United States had concluded that Milosevic himself must relinquish power in order for a peaceful settlement to be reached.

Kosovo, a region rather than a state under the 1974 Yugoslav constitution, with a majority of ethnic Albanians, had been agitating for independence since 1992. This included a propaganda campaign directed chiefly at the United States. A first crisis occurred in September 1998 when Serbian troops began an "ethnic cleansing" campaign within Kosovo, only to back down under NATO pressure. An American-led "Kosovo Verification Mission" coincided with the Serbian massacre of Albanians on 15 January 1999 at the village of Racak, an event that was fully exploited for its propaganda value by the KLA. This led to negotiations, supervised by the NATO powers near Paris, leading up to a peace settlement whereby a NATO-led protection force would occupy Kosovo. The Serbian rejection in March 1999 of the "Rambouillet Accords" led to war.

Claiming the right of intervention, the NATO countries denied that they were at war with Serbia, arguing that the bombing campaign was justified by UN Security Council (UNSC) resolutions passed in 1998 calling for a halt to ethnic cleansing in Kosovo. NATO also relied on precision ("smart") bombing, largely avoiding city centers and hitting targets of low political sensitivity in order to minimize Serbian civilian casualties. This was in keeping with media-sensitive targeting policies going back to the 1991 Gulf War. Information strategies directed at the home populations of NATO countries were based on the "sand castle" model of popular support and consent, the belief that these could erode rapidly if not continually bolstered. Methods included daily special government press conferences and updates of Internet websites. After a decade of experiencing the pace of a television war, most countries took these structures and methods for granted. NATO, as an institution, had no comparable structures, and as the war progressed serious deficiencies were revealed in its approach.

By 1999 the Serbs—and particularly Milosevic—had been so completely demonized by the Western media and its governments that critics of NATO found it virtually impossible to argue the Serbian cause. Instead, criticisms were voiced by small but vocal minorities claiming that the bombing was illegal or immoral—and largely ineffectual—in preventing the ethnic cleansing campaign. Some critics also condemned Western information campaigns as propaganda intended to mislead their own people.

The response of the Serbian government to the bombing campaign was directed both at their own people and at NATO. Home propaganda included frequent references to the bombing of Belgrade in April 1941 by the Germans, accusations of NATO war crimes, and the portrayal of Serbia as the weak and innocent victim of superpower aggression. Propaganda directed at NATO emphasized the difficulties of mounting a ground war and the cost in NATO casualties. Serbia also coordinated its propaganda war with its military operations in Kosovo extremely well. Overseas reporters were encouraged to remain in Belgrade, but access to Kosovo itself was severely restricted by both sides until the very end of the crisis. NATO media specialists were critical of this lack of information—above all of visual images—from Kosovo, which they felt allowed Serbia to dictate the pace and nature of the propaganda war.

The Kosovo crisis and war witnessed the first systematic use of the Internet for communication and propaganda on both sides, including nongovernmental players. The extent of institutional and informal mass media available meant that the media and propaganda permeated this war to an extent and in a manner that had not been previously seen. It was also argued that a combination of informal media and institutional controls meant that the days of the independent television or newspaper "war correspondent" were over.

Milosevic fell from power a year after the war and went on trial for war crimes at The Hague, which he used as a platform for displaying his defiance. The reasons behind Milosevic's acceptance of KFOR in 1999 remain obscure, and the relative importance of the propaganda campaign on both sides is still being debated. Concern about possible fighting led the KFOR to use a media "pool" for the first twenty-four hours following its entry into Kosovo—the first use of such a pool since the 1991 Gulf War. Modeled on IFOR, which grew out of the Bosnian crisis and war, KFOR also possessed similar information capabilities and plans.

Stephen Badsey

See also Balkans; Blair, Tony; Bosnian Crisis and War; Censorship; Internet

References: Badsey, Stephen, and Paul Latawski, eds. *Britain, NATO and the Lessons of the Balkan Conflict.* London: Frank Cass, 2002; Carruthers, Susan L. *The Media at War.* London: Macmillan, 2000; Chomsky, Noam. *The New Military Humanism: Lessons from Kosovo.* London: Pluto, 1999; Hammond, Philip, and Edward S. Herman, eds. *Degraded Capability.* London: Pluto, 2000; Knightley, Philip. *The First Casualty: The War Correspondent as Hero and Myth-Maker from the Crimea to Kosovo.* Rev. ed. London: Prion, 2000.

L

Labor/Antilabor

Labor propaganda techniques have included posters, banners, and a succession of memorable songs, but on the whole they must be considered a failure. Workers and their organizations have never really received evenhanded treatment from the media organs of society in which labor has lived and operated. Whether in the capitalistic industrialized countries or in the socialist states, even when lip service is paid to them, workers and their labor organizations are given short shrift. For example, the actual reasons behind strikes are often lost in superficial media coverage, whether in the popular press at the end of the last century, television and film media in the twentieth century, or, more recently, electronic media.

Consider how newsreels in the United States dealt with labor unrest during the 1930s. Although hundreds of thousands of workers struck the textile industry nationally in 1934 (one of the largest walkouts ever in U.S. labor history), on American movie screens audiences only saw worker violence that had been engendered by management intransigence. When, during another strike in 1937, newsreel cameras caught the Chicago police turning against the workers (killing ten), this footage was temporarily suppressed.

Conversely, in the USSR in 1936 that country's propaganda machine used Communists everywhere to play up the new constitution, which supposedly guaranteed Soviet workers rights denied them in capitalist countries. The reality was quite different. Internal passports were issued that could tie workers to their jobs like serfs. The year 1936 also marked the beginning of the Stalinist terror, which eliminated or placed in the Gulag most of the ostensible leaders of Soviet trade unions as well as many workers.

Attempts by workers worldwide to place before the public often quite limited and reasonable demands have foundered for lack of a proper forum—since they were usually controlled by those who wish to squelch labor or use it for their own political ends. Weimar Germany saw a wide variety of efforts on the part of a dedicated left to propagandize on behalf of workers. Like agitprop theater, these efforts had a certain cultural impact, but they ultimately gave little voice to labor. Interestingly enough, Hitler (1889–1945) and his cohort won over the salaried classes and wage earners after crushing organized labor through propaganda that stressed unity at the expense of individuality, the Labor Front instead of unions.

Antilabor forces (such as the Nazis) generally succeeded because they had the resources necessary to sell and implement their ideas and to eradicate any program that organized labor might wish to promote. This was done in Britain during the General Strike of 1926 as well as under the Thatcher government. During the late nineteenth and early twentieth centuries in the United States, antilabor forces were willing not only to apply extralegal force but also to propagandize successfully about their use of it as they wrapped themselves in the cloak of "Truth, Justice, and the American way of life."

During the heyday of the 1930s, the Congress of Industrial Organizations (CIO) attempted to unionize America's industrial workers. Management stalled that very forceful drive using what was dubbed the "Mohawk Valley Formula," which involved disseminating propaganda about the need for "law and order" and the threat of "outside agitators" through a friendly or bribed media, thereby obfuscating such real issues as hours, wages, and working conditions. Variations of that successful technique, which was based on earlier initiatives, are still in use in the United States.

Other countries may possess a less violent labor history than the United States, where strikes often led to pitched battles that organized labor, however successful in the field, generally lost in the media. Opponents of labor in these countries successfully utilized the forces of propaganda. In the 1930s in France, the Popular Front lost out to the cry "Better Hitler than Blum"—an appeal to anti-Semitism at the expense of the Socialist prime minister Léon Blum (1872–1950). In the decades following World War II, an anti-Communist smear campaign succeeded in discrediting militant unionism in France and Italy. Whatever kernels of truth may have been present, the labor movement was tarred with a Red brush and the charge ceaselessly broadcast that the Communists worked not in the interests of the worker but rather that of the Soviet Union.

Workers do have friends and supporters who speak out for labor, but, as has become clear in the United States, labor organizations tend to work through the political process. The picket line and the strike cannot, despite labor's efforts, garner sufficient support. As was the case with New Labour in Britain, despite a great deal of hoopla, workers did not benefit as a result of political action. Unions in the non-Communist world are well positioned to plead their case—possessing sufficient funds, savvy staffs, and sound political connections—but antilabor propaganda continues unabated.

In the 1980s President Ronald Reagan (1911–) crushed the Air Traffic Controllers' Union but managed, through clever manipulation of the media, to retain the support of many workers, the so-called Blue Dog Democrats, who opposed the policies of their party's leaders. The German unions are powerful and have trumpeted their success at achieving "Mitbestimmung,"(participation in decision-making), but, notwithstanding their boasts, the propaganda is much better than the results. Worker representation on company boards does not seem to have made much of a difference.

Organized labor seems to have fallen into a state of stasis despite a handful of energetic vocal leaders. They do not hesitate to find a forum to speak out, but it is generally not one that is a major component of the mass media. Throughout much of the second half of the twentieth century, organized labor tried to fund its own radio stations to sponsor programs, make films, and win over public opinion, but what can justifiably be called "Big Labor" in various parts of the world has not been able to overcome hostile propaganda. Antilabor forces continue to be successful in utilizing the media to promote their ideas.

Daniel Leab

See also BBC; International; "The Internationale"; Marx, Karl; Reagan, Ronald; Thatcher, Margaret

References: Dubofsky, Melvyn, and Foster Rhea Dulles. *Labor in America*. 6th ed. Wheeling, IL:

Harlan Davidson, 1999; Slomp, Hans. *Labor Relations in Europe: A History of Issues and Developments.* New York: Greenwood, 1990.

Laden, Osama bin (1957–)

An Islamic militant and exponent of terror as a means of political communication, Osama bin Laden was born into a wealthy Saudi family that had made its fortune in the construction business. At the time of the Soviet war with Afghanistan, he underwent a religious awakening to militant Islamic fundamentalism, specifically Saudi Arabia's Wahhabi sect. After a period devoted to raising funds for the struggle against the USSR, he traveled to Afghanistan and used his family's wealth and equipment in support of the resistance. In particular, he became associated with two 1987 battles against the Russians at Jaji and Ali Khel. After the war he became a regular speaker in mosques throughout Saudi Arabia. Recordings of his powerful speeches were widely circulated. He argued that the victory over the Russians showed that a jihad (holy war) could not be stopped and that Islam was the wave of the future. The Saudi regime initially supported bin Laden but subsequently distanced itself following the Iraqi invasion of Kuwait in 1990. Bin Laden called for the liberation of Kuwait by means of a religious jihad, but the Saudi government preferred to join the United States and accomplish the task through a more conventional campaign. Now a persona non grata, bin Laden relocated to the Sudan in East Africa. The presence of U.S. troops on the holy soil of Saudi Arabia was an outrage to bin Laden and led him to consider the United States the epicenter of evil.

U.S. Navy SEALs hold an Osama Bin Laden propaganda poster found in an Al Qaeda classroom, 14 January 2002. (Reuters NewMedia Inc. / CORBIS)

Sudan was the base for a number of Islamic militant organizations with which bin Laden became associated, including the International Muslim Brotherhood and Al Qaeda (The Base), which began as a financial network; its activities originally included aid to Muslim fighters in Bosnia. Propaganda emanating from the Sudan included an Iranian-sponsored radio station. In 1992 the United States committed troops to nearby Somalia. Bin Laden was active in mobilizing an Islamic opposition in support of Somali "warlord" Muhammad Farah Aydid (1936–1996). In a 1997 CNN interview bin Laden claimed that his followers had been behind the killing of eighteen American soldiers in Somalia in 1993. These deaths proved a humiliation for the United States and further increased bin Laden's reputation.

Bin Laden made use of the fax and the Internet to extend his reach. He moved frequently but spent part of 1994 as a resident in London. Although his campaign included religious-based arguments against the United States, Israel, and the pro-Western governments of Egypt and Saudi Arabia, he increasingly looked to dramatic acts of terrorism to publicize his message and humiliate his enemies. Early incidents associated with bin Laden include a 1995 car bombing in Riyadh. Bin Laden then issued a declaration of war against the United States. The first major blow in this war fell in August 1998 when bombs exploded at the U.S. embassies in Kenya and Tanzania, killing 224 mostly local people. This simultaneity, which multiplied the psychological impact of the attacks, became a trademark of bin Laden's activities. Foiled plans included plots to hijack and destroy two planes in Hong Kong and eleven planes in U.S. airports. He also sought out prestige targets, with plans to attack the World Cup Soccer match in France in 1998. Successful operations ascribed to bin Laden included a suicide attack on the U.S.S. *Cole* in the Gulf of Aden. In 1996 bin Laden returned to Afghanistan,

where the ultrareligious Taliban regime offered a safe haven to Al Qaeda to construct and operate terrorist training camps. Bin Laden's political activities within Afghanistan included one of the most potent acts in the region: intermarriage with the family of Taliban leader Mullah Mohammad Omar (1962–). In the wider Middle Eastern region, bin Laden became a folk hero to the poor and disenfranchised: his picture appeared in bazaars in Pakistan and was placed in the hands of demonstrators in the Gaza strip. No Arab leader had commanded such popular appeal since Gamal Abdel Nasser (1918–1970) in the 1950s.

On 11 September 2001 Islamic terrorists crashed hijacked planes into prestige targets in the United States: the World Trade Center in New York City and the Pentagon in Washington, D.C. Bin Laden denied direct responsibility but endorsed the action. As a U.S.-led coalition mounted a War on Terrorism against his Afghan strongholds, bin Laden issued statements to the outside world in the form of video messages, broadcast on the Qatar-based satellite TV channel Al Jazeera. As the war progressed, bin Laden lost this link with the outside world. Despite the military success of Allied air power and the anti-Taliban Northern Alliance on the ground, it was clear that the threat of Islamic terrorism was bigger than one man, and that, dead or alive, bin Laden would remain a rallying point for dissent and anti-Western feeling.

Nicholas J. Cull

See also Arab World; Gray Propaganda; Gulf War; Satellite Communications; Terrorism; Terrorism, War on

References: Bearden, Milton. "Afghanistan, Graveyard of Empires." *Foreign Affairs* 80 (Nov.–Dec. 2001): 17–30; Bergen, Peter L. *Holy War, Inc: Inside the Secret World of Osama bin Laden.* New York: Free Press, 2001; Bodansky, Yossef. *Bin Laden: The Man who Declared War on America.* Rockilin, CA: Forum, 1999; Reeve, Simon. *The New Jackals: Ramzi Yousef, Osama Bin Laden and the Future of Terrorism.* Boston: Northeastern University Press, 1999.

Latin America

From its colonial period, through liberation struggles and revolutions, to the Cold War, Latin America has been both a battleground for propaganda and has itself spawned some masters of the art. European contact with the Americas following the voyage of Columbus sparked one of the great surges of propaganda as writers, in addition to the church and state, sought to digest and disseminate news of the "discovery" and exploit it to suit their own ends. Enthusiasts for the colonial project, such as the Englishman Walter Raleigh (1552–1618), sought to spur conquest of the region with tales of the fabulous wealth of El Dorado. Raleigh's inability to deliver the promise of his propaganda led to his execution. The conquest of the Americas led to the production of maps, with vast swathes of territory claimed for a particular European power. The terminology adopted carried powerful meanings: "New World" implied a careful distinction between Europe and the Americas, establishing the latter as a blank page on which the newcomers could write as they pleased. Other motivating ideas included the belief that the natives were not just different but the inverse of Europeans— "children of the devil," as Europeans were "children of God."

Priests accompanied the Spanish and Portuguese conquistadors. The Americas first witnessed religious propaganda for initial conversion and then the inquisition as the church sought to ensure that the initial conversions were genuine. The conquest and the inquisition became a major subject of anti-Spanish and anti-Catholic atrocity propaganda during the Reformation, particularly in the Netherlands. Catholics questioning the validity of the stories of excess dubbed this "the black legend."

As Latin Americans sought to move beyond their colonial relationships, they looked to propaganda techniques of the French Revolution. The aftermath of that revolution provided an opportunity in Napoleon's conquest of their master, Spain. Simon Bolivar (1783–1830) had lived in Paris at the time of the Revolution and rallied first Venezuela and then other colonies of the region against Spain. His skill as a self-publicist and his understanding of slogans and stage-managed events—like his victorious entry into Caracas in 1813—established him as a major force. By the end of his life he had liberated not only Venezuela and Columbia but also Ecuador and Peru.

The nineteenth century saw the emergence of a characteristic figure in Latin American politics in the person of the *caudillo,* or regional boss. These figures combined financial and military power with bonds of family loyalty to guarantee their political control; many also added a newspaper to their business interests, viewing a "kept press" as part of their hold on power. In places this linkage between individual politicians and the media endured throughout the twentieth century. In Argentina the nineteenth century saw a flowering of literary propaganda. Esteban Echeverría (1805–1851) used poetry and prose to nurture a love of country and to attack the brutal dictatorship of Jean Manuel de Rosas (1793–1877). Echeverría's political novels included *El Matadero* (The Slaughterhouse, 1837). Another critic of de Rosas was Domingo Faustino Sarmiento (1811–1888), whose works included *Facundo, o Civilización i barbarie* (Life in the Argentine Republic in the Days of the Tyrants, 1845). Some years after the fall of de Rosas, Sarmiento served as president of Argentina. In 1888 in Brazil the writer Joaquim Nabuco (1849–1910) led a campaign for the abolition of slavery. He subsequently campaigned for Pan-American cooperation and presided at the Pan-American Conference of 1906.

In the twentieth century, U.S.-based companies exported radio technology to Latin America. U.S. private radio programming aimed at Latin America developed in the 1930s. Latin America looked to Europe for its political models and developed the equivalent of propaganda-driven dictatorships. The region produced a succession of fascist-style leaders, each with their own radio style, feeling for their people, taste in uniforms, and censorship requirements. Examples include Getulio Vargas (1883–1954) of Brazil and the formidable husband-and-wife team of Juan and Eva Perón in Argentina.

During World War II Latin America became a major theater of the propaganda struggle between the Allies and the Nazis. The Nazis used propaganda to promote sympathy for their cause; their agents appealed to national opinion, unveiling extravagant plans to redraw the continent's boundaries—usually at the expense of whichever neighbor seemed most in disfavor at the time. The British scored a major success by stealing such a map, altering it to exaggerate Nazi designs, and passing it on to Franklin Delano Roosevelt (1882–1945), who in October 1941 cited it as evidence of the need for a strong defense against Nazi Germany. To promote hemisphere defense, in 1940 the United States created the Office of the Coordinator of Inter-American Affairs (CIAA), led by Nelson D. Rockefeller (1908–1979). The CIAA broadcast shortwave propaganda, trained local radio workers in U.S. methods, and placed readymade programs with Latin American stations. It also promoted "suitable" Hollywood films and persuaded U.S. distributors to withhold films from theaters that screened Axis newsreels. U.S. propaganda activity continued in the Cold War. As the Soviet Union flooded the region with print propaganda through Montevideo, Uruguay, the United States struggled to keep up with cultural programs of its own.

In 1959 the Cuban revolution established a major and enduring figure in the regional propaganda war in the person of Fidel Castro (1927–). Castro mixed charisma with rigid censorship and the suppression of dissent. Cuba now sent propagandists and revolutionaries into the region, including the Argentine-born Ernesto "Ché" Guevara (1928–1967), whose photograph became an icon for a generation of student radicals throughout the Western world. The United States mobilized such organs as USIA for a lively holding action. Particular U.S. initiatives included President John F. Kennedy's (1917–1963) Alliance for Progress and publicity surrounding the Peace Corps. Other novelties in U.S. propaganda in South America included the creation of, by USIA, a TV soap opera called *Nuestra Barrio* (Our Neighborhood). Originally intended for Mexican audiences, this series eventually won sizable audiences across the entire region.

American aid seemed only to strengthen the old order. During the 1960s many of Latin America's fledgling democracies slipped back into military rule, with its attendant press censorship. The election of left-wing Salvador Allende (1908–1973) in Chile in 1970 prompted a notorious campaign of CIA support for the right-wing opposition, which included the payment of some $1.6 million to the newspaper *El Mercurio* to attack Allende. This opposition culminated in Allende's murder during a violent military coup in 1973. Despite its dictatorships, the region produced a lively anti-American intellectual discourse on the theme of "dependency" and American economic imperialism. Propagandists against the dictatorships included Catholic priests in what became known as "Liberation Theology."

In 1976 UNESCO called a meeting of twenty Latin American nations to discuss the issues of politics and control of communications in the region. The conference called for wider participation and access to the airwaves. At the time this goal seemed far off, but by the early 1980s the so-called southern cone of the continent moved toward democracy. Liberalization of the press and an easing of censorship constituted one of the first signs of this change. Censorship ended in Brazil in 1978. The press's exposure of state-sanctioned torture in Chile and Brazil accelerated the fall of the dictatorships.

The 1980s saw a renewal of the Cold War in Central America and the Caribbean. The key theaters of this Cold War struggle were a propaganda war between the United States and Cuba and struggles by proxy in El Salvador and Nicaragua. In El Salvador the Reagan administration supported an anti-Communist government in its war against the guerrillas of the Frente Farabundo Martí para la Liberación Nacional (Farabundo Martí National Liberation Front; FMLN). Issues in the propaganda war included the precise level of Cuban and Soviet support and the extent of atrocities attributable to the government's "death squads," which included the assassination of Archbishop Oscar Romero (1917–1980) in 1980 and the rape and murder of three U.S.-born nuns and a church worker. In Nicaragua the declining days of the Somoza family dictatorship (founded in 1937) witnessed some of the crudest methods of media control, including acts of terror against the press, most notably the murder of Pedro Joaquín Chamorro (1924–1978), the editor of the opposition paper *La Prensa*. In 1979 the Somoza regime fell to a coalition led by the left-wing Sandinista guerrilla movement, their name derived from guerrilla fighter Augusto Sandino (1895–1934), who had opposed the Americans in the early years of the century. As the Sandinistas accepted Cuban and Soviet aid and began to build a socialist state (with accompanying propaganda campaigns), the United States sponsored the opposition. U.S. tactics including training the so-called Contra rebel army in the sort of guerrilla warfare and propaganda tactics that had been a trademark of the Communists since the 1960s. A guerrilla war followed. During the 1980s the newspaper *La Prensa* continued its role as an oppositional voice, and in 1990 its owner, Pedro Chamorro's widow, Violeta Barrios de Chamorro (1929–), won the presidential election and moved the country toward peace.

The most notorious propaganda campaign in the region during the 1980s was that of the Maoist guerrilla movement Sendero Luminoso (Shining Path) in Peru. Founded in 1970 by a philosophy lecturer called Abimael Guzmán Reynoso (Chairman Gonzolo; [1934–]), the Shining Path preached a potent mixture of Marxist and Maoist teaching combined with Andean folk law and elements of Catholicism. Guzmán used posters and pamphlets decorated with a symbolic black-and-red color scheme symbolizing the struggle between the revolution and the state, but his most emotive weapon was terrorist violence. In 1992 Peruvian president Alberto Fujimori (1938–) instituted martial law and successfully jailed Guzmán. The movement dwindled, with the image of the jailed Guzmán serving as propaganda for Fujimori. He himself was no stranger to the world of propaganda, having won a masterful election in 1990 by donning blue jeans and campaigning as a "common man." Columbia's Medellín drug cartel later claimed to have funded his campaign to the tune of a million dollars. Once in office, Fujimori clamped down on expressions of opposition. In 2000, beset by corruption scandals, Fujimori fled into exile. Powerful anti-Fujimori propaganda included the broadcast, in September 2000, of a videotape of Vladimiro Montesinos (1947–), his intelligence chief, bribing a Peruvian congressman to vote Fujimori's way.

In the final years of the twentieth century the region became the focus of a number of key ideological global battles, including issues relating to the environment—in particular the destruction of the rain forests—poverty, and the fate of indigenous peoples. In Brazil a diary written on scraps of paper by one Carolina María de Jesus (1914–1977) and published under the title *Child of the Dark* provided insight into the lives of people forced to reside in that country's slums, while the memoir *I Rigoberta Menchú* (1983) by the Guatemalan activist Rigoberta Menchú (1959–) attracted world attention to the cause of the Mayan Indians living in that country. In 1992 (symbolically marking the five hundredth anniversary of the voyage of Columbus) Menchú won the Nobel Peace Prize. In 1999 the book attracted criticism for having altered key facts in Menchú's life. The region remained the site of large-scale religious propaganda, this time on behalf of Christian evangelical denominations. In Central America the tradition of the *caudillo* seemed alive and well in the form of media-savvy drug barons, who regularly appeal to anti-Communism, patriotism, and regional pride. The drug cartels have proved masters of propaganda by bestowing lavish gifts—a sports stadium here or a new school there. The wider South American media has come under the control of a small number of media conglomerates. The most powerful of these is the Brazilian Globo conglomerate, established by Roberto Marinho (1904–1998). The media played a major role in the rise of Fernando Collor (1949–), the first elected president of Brazil since 1960. In 1989 Collor ran a highly sophisticated TV campaign for the presidency, attacking certain exploitative civil servants he dubbed "Maharajas." With the Globo conglomerate on his side, he rapidly became an unstoppable force. However, the combination of media criticism of his corruption and the ire of the newly aggrieved Globo conglomerate brought about his resignation in 1992 under threat of impeachment. Globo's assault on Collor included attacks in the country's most popular medium, the soap opera.

Nicholas J. Cull

See also Castro, Fidel; CIA; Falklands/Malvinas War; Mexico; Perón, Juan Domingo, and Eva Duarte; Spain

References: Alisky, Marvin. *Latin American Media: Guidance and Censorship.* Ames: Iowa State University Press, 1981; Cull, N. J. "Faked Boundaries: Latin America, 'Nazi Maps' and Britain's Secret War Against U.S. Neutrality." *LABSA [Latin American British Studies Association] Journal* 1 (July 1997): 9–20; Fox, Elizabeth. *Latin American Broadcasting: From Tango to Telenovela.* Luton, UK: University of Luton Press, 1997; Fox, Elizabeth, ed. *Media and Politics in Latin America: The Struggle for Democracy.* London: Sage, 1988; Lee, Rensselaer W. *The White Labyrinth: Cocaine and Political Power.* New Brunswick, NJ: Transaction, 1989.

Leaflet

The leaflet is a common device in the arsenal of the propagandist, dating from shortly after the invention of the printing press. There is, however, some confusion as to terminology. A leaflet (a nineteenth-century term) is a printed—usually folded—handbill or flyer intended for free distribution. A flyer (a nineteenth-century American word) is a pamphlet or circular intended for mass distribution. According to William Safire (1929–), "flyer" and "handbill" are used interchangeably to mean a cheap circular devoted to an issue or calling attention to an upcoming event or visit; he further states that the term "circular" is no longer in current use in politics. The propagandist is nevertheless likely to see these pieces of paper intended to persuade enemy soldiers to surrender (or an enemy public to give up a hopeless quest) variously described as leaflet, flyer, or handbill. The flyer or leaflet is the inexpensive staple of every politician. The neophyte may literally hand out such materials personally to constituents.

The leaflet also plays a significant role in wartime by demoralizing the enemy. Napoleon Bonaparte (1769–1821) once famously declared that "in war, the moral is to the physical as three is to one." As a result, armies have long sought to sow doubt and divide loyalties by dropping leaflets into enemy hands. For example, in 1806 the British Navy used kites to carry notes to France. In World War I some nine million leaflets urging surrender were transported by aerial balloon to German troops. It is unclear how effective such strategies were since at the time little thought was given to assessing their impact by, say, interviewing enemy troops or examining the enemy press to see if such leaflets were discussed.

World War II saw the massive use of leaflets by virtually all of the major combat-

Nazi propaganda leaflet, Italy, 1944, aimed at the American soldier: "Rich Man's War—Poor Man's Fight." The businessman is depicted as stereotypically Jewish, with large paunch and cigar. (Courtesy of David Culbert)

ants. German flyers dropped behind advancing Allied lines emphasized preexisting prejudices or class divisions. One flyer, printed in red and black, is entitled: "Rich Man's War—Poor Man's Fight." A sorrowful-looking wounded G.I., his arm in a splint, is contrasted (in the background) with a stereotypical anti-Semitic caricature showing an obese businessman, cigar in hand, who looks contentedly at a safe decorated with a victory wreath. The message on the reverse is not very subtle: "While you are fighting and dying in the scorching heat of Italy thousands of miles away from your family, the war profiteers and war slackers back home are safe and sound." Americans dropped some seven million leaflets each week over various parts of Europe between 1944 and 1945, thanks in part to the invention of a leaflet bomb, a cylinder composed of laminated paper that held some eighty thousand leaflets. When the bomb was a thousand feet above the ground, it opened automatically. If not an exact system of delivery, it was a notable improvement over what went before, namely, simply tossing leaflets from a great height and relying on the vagaries of wind and weather as to where they landed. A particularly successful American leaflet was a "Safe Conduct Pass," which was printed in German and English and encouraged German soldiers to surrender: "The German soldier who carries this safe conduct is using it as a sign of his genuine wish to give himself up. He is to be disarmed, to be well looked after, to receive food and medical attention as required, and to be removed from the danger zone as soon as possible." Another effective American leaflet dropped over German cities in 1944 asked: "Wo ist die Luftwaffe?" ("Where is the Luftwaffe? . . . Now, in broad daylight, masses of American bombers fly over Berlin. Ask Goering! Ask Hitler!") In their revisionist article Philip Taylor and N. C. F. Weekes have argued that leaflets designed to encourage the surrender of German soldiers in 1944–1945 (as, for example, "What Capitulation Means") were an important and effective part

of psychological warfare, but that not enough energy went into targeting the German soldier—the significant military target—as opposed to the German populace generally.

Leaflets played a definite role in the Vietnam War, though the actual results are still the subject of debate. They were dropped by American planes over Vietcong strongholds and distributed by American troops to the Vietnamese. Leaflets played a role in the Gulf War of 1991–1992, as well as the war in Afghanistan in 2001. The Fourth Psychological Operations (Psyops) Group at Fort Bragg, North Carolina, which is part of the U.S. Army Civil Affairs and Psychological Operations Command, prepared a leaflet campaign for use in Afghanistan. These days such leaflets are tested on focus groups composed of native speakers, including captured enemy prisoners. In short, to be effective the leaflet must speak directly, in idiomatic language, to its intended audience—the same quest that concerns the intelligent advertising executive.

David Culbert

See also Psychological Warfare; Revolution, American, and War of Independence; World War I; World War II (Britain); World War II (United States)

References: Lerner, Daniel. *Sykewar: Psychological Warfare against Germany.* Cambridge, MA: MIT Press, 1974; Rhodes, Anthony. *Propaganda, The Art of Persuasion: World War II.* New York: Chelsea House, 1976; Taylor, Philip M., and N. C. F. Weekes. "Breaking the German Will to Resist, 1944–1945: Allied Efforts to End World War II by Non-Military Means." *Historical Journal of Film Radio and Television* 18 (March 1998): 5–48.

Lenin, Vladimir Ilyich (Ulyanov) (1870–1924)

Lenin (pseudonym of Vladimir Ilyich Ulyanov) was a Russian revolutionary and political theoretician, leader of the Bolsheviks, and consequently the architect of the USSR (Union of Soviet Socialist Republics) and the creator of the Soviet Union.

Lenin was born in Simbirsk, on the middle Volga, on 22 April 1870, the son of a success-

An official portrait of Lenin from the postrevolutionary period. (Courtesy of Bernard O'Callaghan)

ful government official. In 1887 his elder brother was executed for plotting the assassination of Tsar Alexander III (1845–1894). Lenin was immediately expelled from Kazan University and sent into exile within Russia. While in exile he read the works of Karl Marx (1818–1883). He went on to work as a lawyer for the poor in Samara, on the Volga, before moving to St. Petersburg in 1893. In 1895 he helped create the St. Petersburg Union for the Struggle for the Emancipation of the Working Class. The police soon arrested the leaders of this organization. After another period in exile, Lenin went abroad, where he joined Georgi Plekhanov (1857–1918) and other Russian Marxists. Lenin was a key figure in creating the party newspaper entitled *Iskra* (The Spark). Lenin's grasp of propaganda was primarily based on Plekhanov's views. His original contribution was one of praxis. His goal-orientated pragmatism guided the Bolsheviks to seize and maintain power. His masterpiece of organiza-

tional theory, *What Is to Be Done?* (1902), laid out his plan for a revolution centered on a highly disciplined party of professional revolutionaries who would serve as the "vanguard of the proletariat." Lenin's insistence on professional revolutionaries caused a split among the Russian Marxists. Lenin's faction emerged with a small majority at their 1903 congress—thus they were dubbed Bolsheviks (the majority), while his opponents were permanently damned as Mensheviks (the minority) whether they won succeeding votes or not.

Lenin viewed World War I not as a disaster but as an opportunity to ferment the revolution that would destroy the old empires. When the war broke out in Russia, Lenin gained safe passage through Germany in a sealed train. He arrived at the Finland Station in Petrograd and immediately repudiated the policy of cooperation with the provisional government. Under the slogan "All Power to the Soviets" the Bolshevik Party took control of the workers' organizations and thus assumed political power. After setbacks experienced during the summer, Lenin went into hiding and wrote his (rather idealistic) blueprint for Socialist government entitled *State and Revolution* (1917). He convinced his comrades to risk an armed uprising, which was successfully executed on November 7. After the Bolsheviks engineered a coup that left them in control of all the institutions of government, Lenin was elected chairman of the Council of People's Commissars. He continued to exhibit a pragmatic approach to the process of administration, including the acceptance of Germany's terms under the Brest-Litovsk peace treaty, as well as the ruthless suppression of political resistance (utilizing the newly formed security police, the Cheka). Victorious in the civil war of 1918–1921 yet uncertain of continued support, Lenin was able to promulgate the New Economic Policy, which permitted a partial return to a market economy but asserted even tighter political control over Soviet society—and his own party in particular.

Lenin suffered his first stroke in May 1922, following which he was never again able to resume an active role in government or his party. He suffered a second stroke in March 1923. Lenin died in Gorkii on 21 January 1924. Following his death, Lenin became a central icon of Soviet Communism. The city of Petrograd was renamed Leningrad in his honor. His image became ubiquitous, with his well-preserved body, lying in its tomb on Moscow's Red Square, serving as a destination for pilgrims. The tomb became the focal point for propaganda events, such as the annual May Day parade.

Graham Roberts

See also Marx, Karl; Revolution, Russian; Russia; Stalin, Joseph; Switzerland; Trotsky, Leon

References: Fischer, Louis. *The Life of Lenin.* London: Phoenix, 2001; Service, Robert. *Lenin: A Biography.* London: Pan, 2003; Volkogonov, Dmitri. *Lenin, Life and Legacy.* London: HarperCollins, 1994.

Lincoln, Abraham (1809–1865)

A politician and the sixteenth president of the United States, Lincoln used his considerable gifts as a speaker first in the cause of antislavery and then to lead the United States in its war against the Confederacy. Born in 1809 in Kentucky, Lincoln grew up on the then Illinois frontier. He studied and practiced law and moved up in state politics in the 1830s and 1840s. Campaigning for the Whig Party, he was not above the use of such dirty tricks as circulating anonymous letters accusing the opposition candidate of fraud. In the 1850s he became a founding member of the antislavery Republican Party. In 1858 he came to national attention when he ran for the Illinois Senate seat against incumbent Stephen A. Douglas. Lincoln challenged Douglas's view that the issue of slavery could be settled by "popular sovereignty" at the state level, arguing that "a house divided against itself cannot stand." (speech in Springfield, Illinois, 16 June 1858). Although Douglas won the Senate race, Lincoln's performance won him the Republican nomination for president in 1860. His campaign successfully articulated the candidate's image as a "rail-splitting" frontiersman, using the log cabin as a logo. His reputation as an uncompromising antislaver was such that even before he took office the slave-holding states of the South had seceded from the Union.

In the Civil War the Union benefited from Lincoln's skill as an orator. He relied on simple, homespun metaphors and Biblical language. Lincoln combined this skill with a keen understanding of the value of ideals to mobilize mass participation in the Civil War effort. When the Union's fortunes hit a low point in the autumn of 1862, he effectively transformed what had originally been a war to rebuild the Union into a crusade to free the slaves and (as stated in the Gettysburg Address of November 1863) to bring about a national renewal, "a new birth of freedom." Lincoln's ability to express the war aims of the Union paid dividends both at home and overseas.

As the war drew to an end, Lincoln turned his attention to the future of the Union, setting out a vision of reconciliation "with malice toward none and with liberty and justice for all," as was memorably stated in his second inaugural address of March 1865. One month later, an assassin ended Lincoln's life before he could put these words into practice. His death transformed Lincoln into a national icon, a symbol of wise leadership and racial tolerance. The year 1922 marked the completion of the Lincoln Memorial in Washington, D.C., a monumental seated sculpture of Lincoln by Daniel Chester French (1850–1931). The memorial—and Lincoln's legacy as a whole—has been variously appropriated, most famously in 1963, when it provided the venue for the climax of the great civil rights march on Washington and the "I Have a Dream" speech by Martin Luther King Jr. (1929–1968).

Nicholas J. Cull

See also Abolitionism/Antislavery Movement; Civil War, United States; King, Martin Luther,

Jr.; Memorials and Monuments; Nast, Thomas; United States

References: Donald, David Herbert. *Lincoln.* New York: Simon and Schuster, 1995. McPherson, James M. *Battle Cry of Freedom: The Civil War Era.* New York: Oxford University Press, 1988; Wills, Garry. *Lincoln at Gettysburg: The Words That Remade America.* New York: Simon and Schuster, 1992.

Livingston, William (1723–1790)

An American political writer and colonial politician, Livingston is frequently cited as a propagandist of the American Revolution, primarily because his use of a pseudonym functioned not only to shield him from prosecution but also to deceive his readers as to the social background of the author. Livingston's talent lay in his ability to appeal to a wide swath of society and to motivate American colonists to address their common injury, to the point of engendering a sense of hatred against their British oppressors. Philip G. Davidson has argued that his propaganda shows "a real knowledge of crowd psychology."

William Livingston was born in Albany, New York, into a prominent political family. After graduating from Yale, he practiced law in New York, actively engaging in politics. Inspired by such English pamphleteers as Addison, Steele, Trenchard, and Gordon, in the 1750s and 1760s Livingston published the *Independent Reflector,* launching frequent attacks against his family's political rivals, the De Lanceys, using the pseudonyms "American Whig," "Sentinel," and "Watch Tower." His controversial attack on the Anglican establishment and defense of religious tolerance drew Livingston into radical politics.

In 1772 Livingston moved to Elizabethtown, New Jersey. Increasingly involved in the colonial resistance to British policy, in 1774 he was elected to represent New Jersey at the Continental Congress and took command of the East Jersey militia. In 1776 Livingston was elected the first governor of New Jersey, a post he was to hold until 1790. He continued to take an active hands-on role in the War of Independence, becoming the target of a number of loyalist assassination plots. His greatest contribution was his awareness that the Revolution was a campaign of the mind. Davidson has remarked that while Livingston was "above rather than of the people, he knew them shrewdly, and was one of the few who . . . realized the urgency of reanimating their enthusiasm."

Livingston established the *New Jersey Gazette* to promote support for the war. He wrote a prolific number of essays and broadsides under twenty different pseudonyms ("Adolphus," "Hortentius," and "Cato") designed not only to appeal to republican rhetoric but also—by being identified as "a Pennsylvania Dutch farmer" or "a New Jersey gentleman"—to capture distinct constituencies. For example, during the visit of the Peace Commission he used different signatures to sign several letters urging support for the war—including an appeal to patriotic women to use their influence on their menfolk, signed "Belinda."

Livingston's political vision reflected a traditional "country" republicanism that championed agrarian virtue, yet his support for commerce and western settlement also demonstrated an unusual sympathy for the common man. Despite his patrician background, Livingston adopted radical causes, such as antislavery and land redistribution, and embraced the confiscation of loyalist property as an opportunity for social reform. In 1787 he served as a delegate to the federal Constitutional Convention, lending his written support to the federalist faction.

Karen M. Ford

See also Britain (Eighteenth Century); Revolution, American, and War of Independence; United States
References: Davidson, Philip G. "Whig Propagandists of the American Revolution." *American Historical Review* 39, 3 (1934): 442–453; Klein, Milton M. *The American Whig: William Livingston of New York.* New York: Garland, 1993.

London Can Take It (1940)

This was one of the most potent pieces of documentary film propaganda produced in Britain during World War II. Directed by Humphrey Jennings (1906–1950) and Harry Watt (1906–1987) for the Ministry of Information (MoI), it showed daily life in London during the German Blitz. The film was specifically aimed at the neutral United States; to this end, it was scripted and narrated by Quentin Reynolds (1902–1965), an American journalist who was covering the war for *Collier's Weekly.* Although Reynolds identified himself as a "neutral reporter," he went on to extol the virtues of Londoners in a most unneutral way. The MoI arranged for the film to be distributed in the United States by Warner Brothers. It was screened without an indication that it represented anything other than the views of Reynolds. Such films, as well as sympathetic coverage of the Blitz by journalists like Reynolds or broadcasters like Edward R. Murrow (1908–1965), paved the way for American aid to Britain in 1941 and arguably made the entry of the United States into the war all but inevitable.

Nicholas J. Cull

The cover for the sheet music for "Every Man a King" (1933), with words and music by Huey P. Long and Castro Carazo. It became the theme song for Louisiana Governor Huey Long, whose Share Our Wealth Clubs were found in every state in the spring of 1935. (Courtesy of David Culbert)

> **See also** Britain; Film (Documentary); MoI; Murrow, Edward R.; World War II (Britain); World War II (United States)
> **References:** Aldgate, Anthony, and Jeffrey Richards. *Britain Can Take It: The British Cinema in the Second World War.* Edinburgh: Edinburgh University Press, 1994; Cull, Nicholas J. *Selling War: British Propaganda and American "Neutrality" in World War Two.* New York: Oxford University Press, 1995.

Long, Huey (1893–1935)

A Depression-era politician in the American South, Huey Pierce Long was President Franklin D. Roosevelt's (1882–1945) most powerful opponent. Long served as governor of Louisiana (1928–1932) and U.S. Senator (1930–1935). He died following an assassination attempt inside the Art Deco–style state capitol he had ordered built in Baton Rouge as architectural propaganda to underline his commitment to change. Aside from attending the University of Oklahoma Law School for one term and spending one year at Tulane Law School in New Orleans, Long possessed no formal higher education, becoming a lawyer after passing a special oral examination. He was elected railroad commissioner in 1918, representing his first political office. Long built up his career by portraying himself as a friend of the downtrodden. His national prominence coincided with the Great Depression; hard times made millions of Americans eager to hear about Long's Share Our Wealth Clubs (which had chapters nationwide), a program meant to redistribute wealth so that one out of every four families in America would have a guaranteed yearly income of $5,000 at a time when one could purchase an automobile for $750. Critics noted that Long's economic plan did not add up; his vision of hope mattered more to listeners than whether he had his facts and figures straight.

Long was a master propagandist, second only to Roosevelt as the most gifted American radio personality of his generation. His catchy theme song "Every Man a King" claimed that everyone could "be a millionaire." Long's autobiography of the same title (1933) was distributed widely and proved to be an effective piece of self-promotion. He started his own newspaper, *American Progress,* and insisted that every state employee subscribe to it. Long was deemed newsworthy enough to receive numerous invitations to speak on NBC-Red, the most prestigious national radio network in America. He threatened to run for president as a third-party candidate in 1936; his ability to organize political clubs all across the country made his candidacy a serious threat. His sense of humor made him a natural for newsreels, always on the lookout for a colorful personality.

Long died on 10 September 1935, two days after allegedly being shot by Baton Rouge physician Carl Weiss (1906–1935); it is now believed that he died from bullets fired at Weiss by Long's bodyguards. His career is described in one of America's greatest political novels, *All the King's Men* (1946) by Robert Penn Warren (1905–1989), who taught English at Louisiana State University during Long's heyday. Long was accused of being a fascist and of having dictatorial ambitions. His desire for power seemed boundless, but he never lacked for political opponents. His plan to censor the Louisiana newspapers that opposed him backfired, through the unanimous U.S. Supreme Court decision in the matter of *Grosjean v. American Press Co.,* in February 1936, occurring after Long's death.

David Culbert

See also Roosevelt, Franklin D.; United States (1930s)

References: Brinkley, Alan. *Voices of Protest: Huey Long, Father Coughlin, and the Great Depression.* New York: Knopf, 1982; Long, Huey. *Every Man a King.* New Orleans, LA: National Book Co., 1933; Warren, Robert Penn. *All the King's Men.* New York: Harcourt, Brace, 1946; Williams, T. Harry. *Huey Long.* New York: Knopf, 1970.

Lord Haw-Haw

This was the nickname of Nazi radio propagandist William Joyce (1906–1946), who broadcast to Britain during World War II. Joyce was born in Brooklyn to Irish parents. He grew up in Ireland and Britain, where he became involved in extreme right-wing politics. He split from the British Fascist leader Oswald Mosley (1896–1980) on the grounds that Mosley was insufficiently anti-Semitic. On the eve of World War II he fled to Germany and volunteered his services as an anti-British broadcaster on Radio Hamburg. The name Lord Haw-Haw was coined in October 1939 by Jonah Barrington of the *Daily Express* as a nickname for the German broadcaster (probably Wolf Mittler), who possessed an upper-class British accent. Joyce inherited the name. With an estimated six million listeners, his broadcasts became part of the folk culture of life in Britain during the early years of the war and were even the butt of the popular song "Lord Haw-Haw the Humbug of Hamburg." The British press, attempting to deal with the broadcasts through humor, only succeeded in publicizing them.

Lord Haw-Haw's broadcasts followed the classic propaganda tactic of divide and conquer. He stressed class differences within Britain, alleged that the rich didn't care about working-class casualties in the Blitz, and mocked Churchill (1874–1965) as a warmonger. He spread rumors of severe bomb damage. Occasionally he scooped the BBC with major war news, throwing doubt on the British media. Later in the war he stressed differences between Britain and the United States, and on 16 April 1943 he dropped a monkey wrench in the area of Allied relations with the Soviet Union by revealing evidence of the mass murder of Polish officers by the USSR in the Katyn forest. In a diary entry for March 1941 Joseph Goebbels (1897–1945) recorded his admiration for Joyce as "the best horse in my stable."

The Nazi regime operated other propaganda-driven radio stations that targeted niche audiences during this period, including the Christian Peace Movement, Radio Caledonia (aimed at Scotland), and Worker's Challenge. Other "traitor" broadcasters included John Amery (1912–1945; son of British cabinet minister Leo Amery [1873–1955]) and renegade soldier Norman Baillie-Stewart (1915–1966). At the end of the war, the British government resolved to make an example of Joyce, even though he was not legally a British subject, by ordering both his and Amery's executions for treason.

Nicholas J. Cull

See also Germany; Goebbels, Joseph; Radio
   (International); RMVP; Tokyo Rose; World
   War II (Britain); World War II (Germany)
References: Cole, John Alfred. *Lord Haw-Haw
   and William Joyce: The Full Story.* London: Faber
   and Faber, 1964; Doherty, M. R. *Nazi Wireless
   Propaganda: Lord Haw-Haw and British Public
   Opinion in the Second World War.* Edinburgh:
   University of Edinburgh Press, 2000.

Luther, Martin (1483–1546)

A German religious leader and founder of the Reformation, Luther was the son of a miner. He was ordained a priest in 1507. Beginning in 1508 he lectured at the University of Wittenberg. After a visit to Rome in 1510–1511, he began to preach against corruption in the church—especially attempts to raise money through the sale of "indulgences," which gave the purchaser dispensation from a certain number of future sins. In 1517 he formulated a list of ninety-five theses objecting to this practice and nailed it to the cathedral door in Wittenberg, with others soon rallying to adopt his position. He developed his case against the Vatican in such works as *On the Babylonist Captivity of the Church of God* (1520). With the German states in an uproar over Luther's ideas, Protestant doctrine was codified in the Augsburg Confession of 1530. Luther was a gifted preacher and writer whose output included learned theological works and popular hymns. He was skilled in face-to-face debate and con-

Portrait of Martin Luther, sixteenth-century German theologian and instigator of the Protestant Reformation. (Library of Congress)

fronted his critics directly. He knew the value of a symbolic act, such as nailing his theses to the door or publicly burning a papal writ issued against him. Luther's activity unleashed an ideological storm that, despite the Vatican's attempts to rein it in, gave the world the term "propaganda."

Nicholas J. Cull

See also Germany; Ignatius of Loyola, Saint;
   Reformation and Counter-Reformation;
   Religion
References: Edwards, Mark U. *Printing,
   Propaganda, and Martin Luther.* Berkeley:
   University of California Press, 1994; Mee,
   Charles L. *White Robe, Black Robe: Pope Leo X,
   Martin Luther and the Birth of the Reformation.*
   New York: Putnam, 1972.

Luxembourg

See Netherlands, Belgium, and Luxembourg

M

Malaysia

See Southeast Asia

Malcolm X (1925–1965)

A controversial figure in the struggle for black liberation in America who became larger in death than he had been in life, Malcolm X was born Malcolm Little in Michigan, the son of a preacher who was active in the Garvey movement. Having lost both his parents at a young age, he moved first to Boston and then to New York. Here he led a life of crime, eventually being sent to prison for burglary in 1946. There he fell under the influence of Elijah Muhammad (1897–1975) and his black nationalist religious movement, Nation of Islam (NOI). Behind prison walls he quickly emerged as a powerful orator. Upon his release, he took the name Malcolm X (the NOI believed that names could be used as propaganda, so members rejected their "slave names"). Malcolm rose quickly through the ranks. He helped establish the movement's first nationally distributed newspaper, *Muhammad Speaks,* and became well known as an orator. His rhetoric was confrontational. He refused to work within the framework of American nationalism like his southern contemporary Martin Luther King Jr. (1929–1968). Whereas King spoke of the "American dream," Malcolm X pointed to the "American nightmare" of inner-city poverty. Television appearances brought Malcolm X to national attention. The American media tended to view Malcolm X as a convenient counterpoint to the moderation exemplified by King.

Malcolm X quarreled with Elijah Muhammad over the former's widely reported remark that the "chickens had come home to roost," which was made at the time of John F. Kennedy's assassination. In 1964, following a pilgrimage to Mecca, Malcolm X formed the Muslim Mosque, Inc., an Islamic movement devoted to working within the political sphere. Malcolm X's thinking departed from his earlier radical and anti-integrationist opinions and moved toward a broader humanism. In 1965 he died at the hands of assassins loyal to Elijah Muhammad.

Since his assassination, Malcolm X has attracted many followers and gained a symbolic status in the eyes of young black people on both sides of the Atlantic. In life he spoke their language and encouraged them to take pride in their heritage and culture. Inspired by Third World examples, he pointed to black nationalism—"taking control of the politics of your community"—as the way for black Americans to advance. In death he became a martyr and an undisputed icon for angry young men. Many activists have associated themselves with his name and cited him as an inspiration, including Huey Newton (1942–1989) and Bobby Seale (1937–), who formed the Black Panthers in 1966. His autobiography, dictated to journalist Alex Haley (1921–1992), became a cult text, and his speeches were published widely. In the 1980s, as mainstream politics seemed to leave black America behind, he reemerged as an icon of street culture. His message, determination, and passion have endured through black folklore, and his popularity with the young has been maintained through rap music, black-pride literature, and the 1992 film *Malcolm X*, directed by Spike Lee (1957–). Over the years people eager to profit from his cult status have distorted many of his original ideas. His precise ideology is still being contested because his life was cut short just as his thinking was reaching maturity.

Samantha Jones

See also Civil Rights; Garvey, Marcus; King, Martin Luther, Jr.; United States

References: Dyson, Michael Eric. *Making Malcolm: The Myth and Meaning of Malcolm X.* New York: Oxford University Press, 1995; Fairclough, Adam. *The Civil Rights Movement in America, 1941–1988.* London: Macmillan, 1995; Malcolm X, *The Autobiography of Malcolm X,* with the assistance of Alex Haley. London: Penguin, 1968.

Mao Zedong (1893–1976)

A Chinese Communist leader and the focus of personality cult, Mao was born in 1893 into a "middle peasant" family in Hunan province in the south of China. In 1921, while a university librarian in Shanghai, Mao became a founding member of the Chinese Communist Party. The party initially cooperated with the wider Chinese Nationalist movement, led by Chiang Kai-shek (1887–1975), but in 1927 the Nationalists turned on the Communists in a bloody purge. The Communists regrouped first in Jiangxi province in southeast China,

where Mao and others developed a brand of Communism more suited to rural life than Marx's and Lenin's more industrial model. In 1934, as the Nationalists closed in again, the Communists began a two-year, six-thousand-mile "Long March" to the town of Yan'an in mountainous Shaanxi province. During this period Mao emerged as the preeminent leader of Chinese Communism, with the Long March becoming an integral part of the mythology surrounding him. His image in the West was greatly enhanced thanks to his lengthy conversations with American journalist Edgar Snow (1905–1972), which became the foundation for the book *Red Star over China* (1937).

Mao understood the importance of propaganda and put much effort into disseminating Communist ideology. Moreover, he realized that in what he called a "people's war" there could be no disparity between what the party claimed and how its army behaved. Mao understood that daring guerrilla raids against the Nationalists or the Japanese during World War II had as much propaganda as military value. The guerrilla approach saw the Communist movement through its wilderness years and provided a solid foundation for the more conventional Communist victory over the Nationalists in the postwar period. However, recent research suggests that the Communists were not as militarily successful as their propaganda maintained, and one of their great retrospective victories was to minimize the Nationalist government's war effort against the Japanese.

In 1949 Mao established the People's Republic of China, which maintained direct control over the mass media and the educational system in China. The party used a wide range of propaganda techniques—including mass meetings, posters, and theater—to communicate an easily understandable message that became closely identified with its leader; a personality cult around Mao, "the Great Helmsman," soon followed. Partly as a result of Mao's proclivity for believing his own propaganda, by 1960 the

Chinese poster from 1968 encouraging the people to "respectfully wish Chairman Mao eternal life." (Stefan Landsberger)

country was in the grips of a horrendous famine. After being sidelined by his colleagues, Mao relaunched himself in the mid-1960s by reaching out first to the army and then to China's youth with an anthology of his writings, *Quotations from Chairman Mao*. In 1966 he unleashed the Cultural Revolution, which was marked by successive waves of violence and propaganda until 1969. By the time of his death in 1976, his significance as a propagandist was being felt far beyond China. Other movements in Asia, Africa, and Latin America (with and without formal Chinese aid) have sought to adapt his model of guerrilla warfare.

Nicholas J. Cull

See also China; Korean War; Latin America;
Quotations from Chairman Mao; Terrorism
References: Fairbank, John K., and Edwin O.
Reischauer. *China: Tradition and Transformation.*
Boston: Houghton Mifflin, 1989; Schram,

Stuart. *The Thought of Mao Tse-tung.*
Cambridge: Cambridge University Press,
1989; Snow, Edgar. *Red Star over China.* London:
Gollancz, 1937.

"La Marseillaise" (1792)

A marching song of the French Revolution and later the national anthem of France, this is arguably the most potent use made of a song for propaganda purposes. Both its words and music were composed on 25–26 April 1792 by Claude Joseph Rouget de Lisle (1760–1836), an officer of engineers in the French Army of the Rhine. The new revolutionary government in Paris had just declared war on Austria, and as the army mustered in Strasbourg for an advance into the German states, the mayor of that city noted that they lacked any appropriate marching songs. He commissioned Rouget de Lisle, whose musical skill he admired, to write something appropriate. The result was originally entitled "The War Song of the Army of the Rhine" but was renamed after being used in action by a battalion from Marseilles as it stormed the Tuileries Gardens in August 1792. Its simple tune and rousing words ("Come, children of the fatherland / The day of glory is here!") made it an infectious propaganda vehicle for the spirit of the Revolution. Rouget de Lisle subsequently questioned the Revolution and narrowly escaped execution. Under Napoleon he attempted (unsuccessfully) to use his authorship of the song to secure a position of influence in the French musical establishment. His enemies questioned whether he had actually written the tune. *La Marseillaise* is also the popular title (more properly called *The Departure of the Volunteers*) of a dramatic relief sculpture by François Rude (1784–1855) that adorns the Arc de Triomphe (1806–1836) in Paris, as well as a 1938 film on the Revolution by Jean Renoir (1894–1979). "La Marseillaise" has been featured in music promoting Russian nationalism—the "1812 Overture" by Tchaikovsky (1840–1893)—and peace—the Beatles' "All You Need is Love." One emotive use in twentieth-century propaganda is the 1942 feature film *Casablanca,* where it is used to symbolize the defiant spirit of the Allied nations.

Nicholas J. Cull

See also *Casablanca;* France; "The Internationale";
    Music; Revolution, French
References: Arnold, Eric A., Jr. "Rouget de Lisle
    and the *Marseillaise.*" *Proceedings of the Western
    Society for French History* 5 (1978): 61–70;
    Hobsbawm, Eric. *Echoes of the "Marseillaise."*
    London: Verso, 1990.

Marshall Plan (1947–1951)

Also known as the European Recovery Program (ERP), the Marshall Plan was an economic aid program launched by the United States following World War II. When the European countries signed on for the Marshall Plan, each accepted a clause that allowed for the dissemination within their borders of "information and news" on the workings of the plan itself. From these premises there sprang arguably the greatest international propaganda operation ever seen in peacetime.

With the unveiling of the Marshall Plan, the United States had invented a new method for projecting its power into Europe. What started out as a suggestion from Secretary of State George Marshall (1880–1959) to jump-start Europe's ailing postwar reconstruction process quickly evolved into a wide-ranging effort to modernize Europe's industries, markets, unions, and economic control mechanisms. The means used were economic loans and grants, technical assistance, "missions" established in each country, and as much advice and exhortation as the plan's technocrats thought they could get away with.

Such crucial Marshall Plan concepts as "counterpart," the dollar gap, productivity, and European integration were not only quite new to European ears but difficult to communicate in the best of circumstances. As the Marshall Plan's administrator, former car salesman Paul Hoffmann, explained later, there were but two objectives: "One to promote economic recovery and the other to promote understanding of the Marshall Plan itself. We had to move quickly and vigorously in order to get results." The key countries were France, the bi-zone (British and U.S.-occupied Germany) and Italy. This was followed by a second group that included Greece, Turkey, Austria, Trieste, and the French zone of Germany. A third group consisted of England and Sweden, with a fourth group encompassing the rest.

It was in Italy that the largest Marshall Plan campaign emerged, the one considered "tops" in the Paris field headquarters. It followed hard on the heels of a massive U.S. effort to ensure the defeat of the Communists in its 1948 elections (including covert CIA aid to the anti-Communists). The Marshall Plan campaign in Italy, which began in June 1948, continued this effort, aiming to reach the people it was benefiting in order to channel attitudes, mentalities, and expectations in the direction of mass production for mass-consumption prosperity. Italians were told that the United States was a land of full shelves and shops crammed to the rafters, thanks to increased productivity and good wages, and that its prosperity might be emulated elsewhere by those willing to work toward this goal.

The operating principles arrived at in Italy were spelled out more clearly than elsewhere, and although similar to the methods used in the other Marshall Plan countries, they were probably applied more intensively after the experience of the 1948 elections, hardly changing until the outbreak of the Korean War. A January 1950 report from the Rome mission insisted: "Carry the message of the Marshall Plan to the people. Carry it to them directly—it won't permeate down. And give it to them so that they can understand it." The basic thrust was for a truly massive program using "every method possible . . . to reach Giuseppe in the factory and Giovanni in the fields," or, as the Paris office put it, "slugging it out way down among the masses." This came to mean carloads of documentary films, hundreds of radio programs, thousands of mobile film screenings, millions of copies of pamphlets, and tens of millions of spectators who attended exhibitions and films.

When applied on the ground, the methods proved extremely flexible. No idea seemed too large or too daring for the information program in its heyday. Millions of balloons were launched from Marshall Plan events in countries bordering the Iron Curtain. Waterborne shows toured the canals of Holland, Belgium, and northern Germany, as well as the islands of the Aegean. A Marshall Plan train stopped at major European railway stations, while trucks brought mobile exhibits to fairs the length and breadth of the Continent.

In addition to the traditional media, in Italy there were also Marshall Plan–sponsored

concerts, essay contests, art competitions, radio variety shows, trains, and ceremonials. Troubadours sang the tale of Marshall Plan–sponsored miracles in Sicilian villages. Even mobile puppet shows were provided "to bring the Marshall Plan message ostensibly to children but actually through the children . . . to semi-literate or illiterate adults." In terms of print propaganda, there were calendars, cartoon strips, postage stamps, and atlases.

Film was the preferred medium for getting the message across—especially to difficult "target groups" such as Communist workers in factories. The aim was not to preach democracy or even to teach the latest American industrial techniques but rather to find a nonpropagandistic point of contact with such an audience. "Even though these films do not openly praise the American way of life," explained the embassy in Rome, "they reflect a part of it in the way the workers dress, the shining conditions in the factories, the technical excellence of the machinery, etc."

According to a July 1950 report to Congress, in the whole of Western Europe fifty Marshall Plan–sponsored documentaries and newsreels were being seen every week by upwards of forty million people (thirty million of whom watched newsreels and ten million, documentaries). "Our inquiries in various countries," said the report, "have shown to us the great potential of the cinema in transmitting information in ways that spectators can understand, believe and remember."

Summing up the results of its efforts after two years of activity, the Information Division in Rome calculated that at least thirty million citizens could now be considered "well informed" concerning the Marshall Plan. Of the entire population, 52 percent considered it good for the country, while 11 percent perceived it negatively. Women and young people were considered the key target groups from a long-term perspective. The plan's objectives had evolved on the strategic level, now being defined as "the mobilization of the Italians around the idea that only on the basis of a free economy can a strong, democratic and free Italy be constructed, together with a peaceful and prosperous Europe." In fact, the division considered the enthusiasm of the Italians for European unity (together with the growth of a nonconfessional trade union movement where none had existed before) among its greatest successes.

In private, however, there were many doubts about the effectiveness of the message and the overall results. As early as February 1949 a high-level official in the Paris headquarters noted: "The European worker listens listlessly while we tell him we are saving Europe, unconvinced that it is his Europe we are saving."

An opinion poll carried out by the Economic Cooperation Administration (ECA) in mid-1950 had interviewed almost two thousand people, including citizens from France, Norway, Denmark, Holland, Austria, and Italy. On average, approximately 80 percent of those interviewed knew about the Marshall Plan, and 75 percent approved of it. Between 25 and 40 percent of those interviewed understood its functioning. But, as the official sponsors of the poll commented, it was among the minorities "not on the team" that the most important target groups—workers and peasants—for whom the persuasion strategy was intended were still to be found. They still seriously doubted the motives behind American action, just as Communist propaganda had prompted them to do.

The greatest challenge to American action in Europe from summer 1950 onward was the battle against the effects of the Korean War. It is impossible to overestimate the impact throughout Europe of this decisive moment marking the escalation of the Cold War. The Korean War brought in its wake a qualitative change, an unprecedented intensification in the ideological and psychological commitment to the anti-Communist crusade. For its part the left-wing opposition insisted—with some success—that the entire episode confirmed its prediction that the purpose of

NATO was to drag Europe into America's wars. Henceforth problems of military security would override economic reconstruction in terms of U.S. priorities in Europe. The militarization effort, coinciding with the prospect of general rearmament, cost the promoters of productivity and prosperity dearly.

Throughout the ECA it was assumed that the strains of rearmament could lead to "internal security crises" in France and Italy, or at best skeptical neutralism already evident in a number of other countries. However, ECA men on the ground had already decided that there was no contradiction between defense and the Marshall Plan's objectives, it being just a matter of bending the existing policy goals to the new requirements.

The Americans were under no illusions as to the difficulties they faced. In a top-level analysis carried out for the Paris headquarters and lasting two and a half years, it was admitted that knowledge of the Marshall Plan and its popularity were stagnant by that time (November 1950). While the percentage of the population opposing the plan in countries such as France and Italy was smaller than the Communist vote, doubts still persisted in "much too great a segment of the European population" surrounding the question of whether America's aims were genuinely to improve living standards or simply to shore up the existing system.

Senior-level Americans in Europe felt they had been "led down the garden path" in countries such as France, Germany, and Italy, where their investments showed few signs of paying visible social or political dividends. Only from this point forward was there an awareness that the effectiveness of the messages ultimately depended on their being adapted to local circumstances. In the early months it was considered more important to have available press articles and formulas for radio shows, exhibitions, and films that could be used in any country in Europe—and even be shown on American television.

In a country like Italy, the need for more meaningful contact with native residents led to local scriptwriters and directors being recruited to fabricate the film propaganda material based on schemes furnished by the sponsor, which they would then translate into the symbolic, visual, and spoken language of the Italian audience. In this way the Organizzazione Epoca was born, set up not to proclaim but to conceal the American origins of its operations. No one, however, was taken in.

In its discussion of the Marshall Plan, today's European historiography emphasizes the capacity of the European governments of the era to elude, neutralize, or ignore American exhortations. Outside France few comprehensive or coherent strategies were ever drawn up for the use of American aid, this despite incessant ECA pressure in this area. Hardly any of the reforming, modernizing methods proposed by the Americans for the national states and economies were ever adopted. Yet in a more diffuse, cultural sense the Marshall Plan in all its manifestations did place the American challenge of psychological and technical modernization on national agendas. Current speculations regarding the overall impact of the Marshall Plan on the participating countries see it not only in macroeconomic terms but also as a sort of psychological plasma. The limits of its innovative goals have become clear, as has the crudeness of its insistence on the American way as the solution to every problem. Intended to serve as a weapon in the Cold War, the Marshall Plan failed to stop the growth of Communist parties and trade unions in France and Italy, while in Greece more forceful methods were needed to stop the revolutionary left. Even so, the combination of the Marshall Plan and NATO left no room for doubt as to America's commitment to the security and prosperity of Western Europe, and at a time of widespread despair it greatly revived the Old World's faith in its own potential for renewal.

The Marshall Plan ended prematurely in December 1951, giving way to the Mutual Security Program. But the underlying effec-tiveness of its energizing impulses soon became clear. In Italy government, industry, and the public all bet on the future in these years. At the dawn of the era of the economic "miracle," it quickly became apparent that the same psychological processes had been operating in Italy, as in other Western countries, since the end of the war. In the striking phrase coined in 1949 by Harlan Cleveland, an economist and senior Marshall Plan official, the transformation became known as "the revolution of rising expectations." According to Enzo Forcella, a veteran left-wing intellectual, "The American myths kept their promises and won through." In his post–Cold War discussion of the impact of American culture on the radicalized Italy of the 1950s, Forcella was referring to the images offered by Marshall Plan documentaries of the American way of life, specifically those showing workers arriving at factories behind the wheel of their own cars—an unthinkable notion in the Italy of 1949.

David Ellwood

See also Cold War
References: Carew, Anthony. *Labour under the Marshall Plan.* Manchester: Manchester University Press, 1987; Cheles, L., ed. *The Art of Persuasion: Political Communication in Italy from 1945 to the 1990s.* Manchester: Manchester University Press, 1999; Ellwood, D. W. *Rebuilding Europe: America and West European Reconstruction.* London: Longmans, 1992; Kipping Matthias, and Ove Bjarnar, eds. *The Americanisation of European Business.* London: Routledge, 1998.

Marx, Karl (1818–1883)

Founder of Communism, historian, and philosopher, Marx was born in 1818 in the German Rhineland. His family was originally Jewish, but his father had converted to Christianity to avoid anti-Semitism. Marx studied philosophy in Bonn and Berlin and in 1842 began work as a radical journalist in Cologne. Having angered the state government, in 1843 Marx fled to Paris and began to develop the notion of a worker's revolution as a means

Karl Marx. The full beard was a virtual trademark.
(Illustrated London News Group)

of social change. While in Paris he met his lifelong friend and collaborator, Friedrich Engels (1820–1895). The two men fled to Brussels and wrote *The Communist Manifesto* (1848), a masterpiece of political propaganda. The core of Marx's teaching was the idea that all history was a driven by the engine of conflict between social classes and that this conflict would inevitably produce a revolution following which power would pass to the working classes. In 1848 he returned to Cologne to edit the *Neue Rheinische Zeitung,* but after the collapse of the paper the following year he sought refuge in London. His study *Das Kapital* appeared in three volumes in 1867, 1884, and 1894. From 1864 to 1872 he was a leading figure in the First International. He spent the remaining years of his life writing and relying on Engels for financial support, eventually dying in relative obscurity. Despite the brilliance and accessibility of the *Manifesto,* Marx's achievement is not so

much that of a communicator as a theorist and philosopher. The full impact of his ideas became apparent through the intercession of more gifted rhetoricians such as Lenin (1870–1924) and Mao Zedong (1893–1976).

Nicholas J. Cull

See also *The Communist Manifesto;* Engels, Friedrich; International; "The Internationale"; Lenin, Vladimir Ilyich; Mao Zedong

References: Katz, Henryk. *Emancipation of Labour: A History of the First International.* London: Greenwood, 1992; McLellan, David. *Karl Marx: His Life and Thought.* London: Macmillan, 1973; Raddatz, Fritz J. *Karl Marx: A Political Biography.* London: Weidenfeld and Nicolson, 1979.

McCarthy, Joseph R. (1909–1957)

A virulent American anti-Communist propagandist, Joseph McCarthy was born into a poor Catholic family. He rose from lawyer to judge in 1939, earning a reputation for arranging quick divorces. In 1942 he joined the Marine Corps and served in the Pacific. Although his war record was undistinguished, it became the foundation of his postwar political career. He campaigned successfully as "tail-gunner Joe" for a Senate seat in 1946, promising to represent the interests of the veteran in Washington, D.C. His early Senate career was also undistinguished, and he feared he might not be reelected. After seeking advice from friends, he hit on anti-Communism as the cause that would advance his career. McCarthy launched his campaign against Communism on 9 February 1950 in a speech to the Republican women's club in Wheeling, West Virginia. He claimed that he had a list of 57 Communists working at the State Department; by the end of the month he had raised this number to 205. The American political lexicon had a new term: "McCarthyism," a term allegedly coined by the political cartoonist Herblock.

An immediate investigation of McCarthy's claims found no evidence of Communists in the State Department, but this news was dwarfed by the arrest of Julius (1917–1953) and Ethel (1916–1953) Rosenberg on spy charges and the outbreak of the Korean War. McCarthy's accusations offered a convenient explanation for the apparent reversal of political fortunes. McCarthy's alarmism won him reelection and a position of considerable power as chairman of the Senate's Permanent Subcommittee on Investigations beginning in January 1953. From this platform he conducted a round of investigations into alleged subversion in high places, at one point disparaging America's official propagandists, the Voice of America and the United States Information Service, which he alleged were run by dangerous liberals. McCarthy's charges became ever more extreme and his targets more diverse in an attempt to maintain political momentum. In 1954 he attacked the U.S. Army, conducting thirty-six days of nationally televised hearings, which eventually proved his undoing. Under the sustained purview of the camera he came across as a crass bully. McCarthy was outmaneuvered by skilled defense attorney Joseph Welch (1890–1960), who won over the American public with his simple rebuke: "Have you no sense of decency, sir?" Edward R. Murrow's (1908–1965) contemporaneous CBS documentary in the "See It Now" series also did much to expose McCarthy as a demagogue, with the latter's hectoring response in a "right to reply" piece the following week only making matters worse. In December 1954 the Senate passed a vote of censure. His power broken, McCarthy died of acute alcoholism in 1957.

McCarthy, like Titus Oates (1649–1705), the notorious English perjurer of the 1670s, proved that a demagogue can go far if his claims are extreme enough and repeated often enough. Yet it should also be remembered that he was a creature of his times. He based his approach on the heritage of midwestern mistrust of Washington and all things foreign that had shaped the populist movement of the 1880s and interwar isolationism. President Harry Truman (1884–

1972) had himself used similar scare tactics in his early attempts to rally the United States to the cause of the Cold War. Other militant anti-Communists proved more dexterous and adaptable. McCarthy fell in 1954, but Richard Nixon (1913–1994), who also built his career on postwar Communist witch-hunting, went on to become president. McCarthyism remains one of the most potent terms of abuse in the Anglo-American political lexicon.

Nicholas J. Cull

See also Canada; Cold War; Murrow, Edward R.; Oates, Titus; Television; United States; VOA

References: Fried, Richard M. *Men Against McCarthy.* New York: Columbia University Press, 1976; Reeves, Thomas C. *The Life and Times of Joe McCarthy: A Biography.* New York: Stein and Day, 1982; Rovere, Richard. *Senator Joe McCarthy.* New York: Harcourt, 1959.

Mein Kampf (1925)

This foundational work of Nazi propaganda was written by Adolf Hitler (1889–1945) and first published in 1925. The significance of *Mein Kampf* (My Struggle) is often overlooked by historians. The book may be turgid and irrational, but mere stylistic analysis overlooks the propaganda aspects of the work.

The failure of the Munich putsch (1923) and a period of imprisonment elevated Adolf Hitler from an obscure, provincial, right-wing politician into a national figure. The nine months he spent in Landsberg Prison provided Hitler with the opportunity to write *Mein Kampf.* Unable to address his audience in person, Hitler dictated his ideas. The text of *Mein Kampf* is thus a piece of political demagoguery in prose, an outpouring of Hitler's half-baked ideas and prejudices. It was clearly written as a work of propaganda.

The extent to which *Mein Kampf* constituted a blueprint that the Nazi Party systematically implemented when it came to power in 1933 remains a source of intense debate. Hitler devoted two chapters to the study and practice of propaganda. His thoughts on war propaganda largely reflected the prevailing nationalist claims that Allied propaganda was responsible for the collapse of the German Empire in 1918. Convinced of the essential role of propaganda in any movement intent on gaining power, Hitler saw propaganda as a vehicle of political salesmanship in a mass market, arguing that the consumers of propaganda were the masses and not the intellectuals. According to Hitler, the masses were malleable and corrupt, "overwhelmingly feminine by nature and attitude." As such, their sentiment was not complicated "but very simple and consistent." In other words, they were led not by their brains but by their emotions.

In *Mein Kampf* Hitler laid down the broad outlines along which Nazi propaganda was to operate. The function of propaganda was to "see that an idea wins supporters . . . it tries to force a doctrine on the whole people." To achieve this, propaganda was to bring to the attention of the masses certain facts, processes, and necessities "whose significance is thus for the first time placed within their field of vision." Accordingly, for the masses propaganda had to remain simple, concentrating on as few points as possible, which then had to be repeated many times, focusing on such emotional elements as love and hatred. Through the continuity and sustained uniformity of its application, Hitler concluded that propaganda would lead to results "that are almost beyond our understanding." Unlike the Bolsheviks, Hitler and the Nazis did not make a distinction between agitation and propaganda. In Soviet Russia agitation was concerned with influencing the masses through ideas and slogans, while propaganda served to spread the Communist ideology of Marxist-Leninism. Hitler, on the other hand, did not view propaganda as merely an instrument for reaching the party elite but rather as a means to persuade and indoctrinate all Germans. During World War II Allied propagandists quoted from and published portions of *Mein Kampf* to illustrate the scale of Hitler's ambitions.

David Welch

See also Anti-Semitism; The Big Lie; Germany; Goebbels, Joseph; Morale; Propaganda, Definitions of; Psychological Warfare; World War I; World War II (Germany)
References: Bramsted, Ernst. *Goebbels and National Socialist Propaganda, 1925–1945.* East Lansing: Michigan State University Press, 1965; Welch, David. *Hitler: Profile of a Dictator.* London: Routledge, 2001; Welch, David. *The Third Reich: Politics and Propaganda.* London: Routledge, 2002.

Memorials and Monuments

Mankind has been erecting memorials and monuments since ancient times. Memorials have been used to commemorate a wide range of human endeavor and emotions: to mark great victories and discoveries and to celebrate the lives of great men and women, but also to commemorate moments of great stress, sorrow, or loss. Memorials are an extremely important propaganda medium, capable of imparting a wide range of messages. However, it is equally remarkable how little they have changed in design and function over the centuries.

Egyptian and Assyrian civilizations both built memorials, and their traits can be seen in the use of memorials by other classical civilizations. The Romans were great monument builders, using them to illustrate battles and mark great victories. Columns became a favorite device for relating the stories of war campaigns. Some are still extant today, one of the most important being Trajan's Column in Rome. The Romans also built arches and gates to mark important events. Triumphal arches, like columns, were used to provide narratives and to commemorate the accomplishments of emperors and generals. All of these devices were passed down throughout European civilization. However, the medieval world did not show quite the same reverence for memorial architecture. The commemoration of martial prowess was most often embodied in the architecture of the tomb itself. Great kings and princes were often entombed beneath effigies of themselves in full armor.

The Renaissance, with its revival of interest in the classical world, inspired a return to greater diversity in the use and design of memorials. Following the Great Fire of London in 1666, Sir Christopher Wren (1632–1723) used the classical column to provide a memorial to mark the event. The base of the monument contains inscriptions relating the story of the fire; one, added in 1681, was deliberately aimed at maintaining the Protestant ascendancy of England by implying that the fire was started by Catholics. Another panel contains a bas-relief of Charles II (1630–1685), in Roman dress, directing the relief of the sick and the destitute, linking him with Christian charity and the wisdom and power of the ancient world.

By the eighteenth century, with the arrival of the Enlightenment, memorial architecture not only mirrored the diversity and ubiquity it had achieved in the classical world but was equally dedicated to the dissemination of messages and images. Columns and arches proliferated, as seen in such memorials as the column to Horatio Nelson (1758–1805) in London and the Arc de Triomphe in Paris. Both memorials were meant to impress the people with the significance of their nation and its national traits. The French revolutionary wars and the growing importance of the nation-state and its citizens affected the appearance of such memorials. Precursors of twentieth-century memorials can be seen in the Guards' Crimean Memorial at the foot of Regent Street in London. The memorial is surmounted by an angel of victory holding aloft a laurel wreath and is fronted by bronze statuary depicting ordinary guardsmen rather than a great commander.

The two great wars of the twentieth century turned war memorials into potent symbols of the political landscape. Smaller memorials built at the community level tended to stress the element of grief and loss, whereas larger schemes expressed pride in victory and the glory of war. The British Empire and Commonwealth instituted an Imperial War Graves Commission in 1917. The commission employed the finest architects in the empire to create cemeteries and memorials that reflected the glory, dignity, and power of the British Empire. After World War II the commission completed a new set of memorials and cemeteries. Now renamed the Commonwealth War Graves Commission, it continues to care and maintain such sites across the globe.

Memorials such as that to the United States Marine Corps in Arlington, Virginia, fulfill a similar purpose. Based on the famous photograph showing marines hoisting the Stars and Stripes over Iwo Jima, the memorial is intended as a powerful reminder of the might and resolution of the United States. In complete contrast is the Vietnam War memorial, completed in 1982. The memorial, designed by Maya Lin (1959–), tried to heal the deep wounds created by the war in American society by remaining simple, dignified, and rather austere. Consisting of a reflective black surface, the wall contains the names of the 58,000 U.S. war dead and missing. Representing a call to quiet reflection and contrition, it is far removed from the Marine Corps memorial.

Totalitarian powers also used memorials as reminders and imparters of a certain ideology. For example, the Soviet Union erected statues to their revolutionary heroes with almost spendthrift enthusiasm, and memorials abounded in Saddam Hussein's Iraq. The destruction of a giant statue of Saddam, seen worldwide on live television, became a defining image of the U.S. victory in the Gulf War of 2003. Similar images defined the collapse of Communist power in Eastern Europe in the early 1990s.

Mark Connelly

See also Art; British Empire; Funerals; Hussein, Saddam; Lincoln, Abraham; Portugal; Revolution, American, and War of Independence; Russia; Spain; World War I; World War II (Russia)

References: Borg, Alan. *War Memorials, from Antiquity to the Present.* London: Leo Cooper, 1991; Curl, James. *A Celebration of Death.* London: Batsford, 1993; Mosse, George L.

Fallen Soldiers: Reshaping the Memory of the World Wars. Oxford: Oxford University Press, 1990.

Mexico

From buttressing the empire of the Aztecs to present-day struggles for social justice, propaganda issues have been at the core of Mexican history. Aztec architecture and ritual served to perpetuate this group's control over the peoples of the region, establishing the Aztec "chief speaker" as a descendant of the gods, with a responsibility to practice the ceremonies necessary to keep the cosmos in motion. At the heart of Aztec rituals was the practice of human sacrifice. As the Aztecs extended their reach across Mexico, the scale of their sacrifices grew. Although the practice underscored the Aztecs' power over their subject peoples, it predisposed the latter to join forces with an outside "liberator" in the person of the Spanish explorer Hernán Cortés (1485–1547). The Europeans also used the Aztec understanding of war to their advantage. Aztec war included a ritual and symbolic content, with combat taking place between powerful individuals, and with limited aims, such as the capture of prisoners for later sacrifice. The Aztecs were not prepared for a European-style war of annihilation.

Upon arriving in Mexico in 1519, Cortés attempted to utilize Old World symbols, such as a banner of the Virgin Mary. In his attempts to convince potential allies to join his campaign against the Aztecs, he scored a breakthrough when he came upon a multilingual woman nicknamed "La Malinche" (ca. 1500–ca. 1551), who acted as his translator during the conquest. In the twentieth century this woman, known to the Spanish as Dona Marina, has been a major figure in Mexican literary propaganda, branded as a traitor in nationalistic texts but reconfigured as a complex mother of mixed-race Mexico in feminist writing.

Between 1519 and 1526 Cortés wrote a series of five self-serving letters ("cartas de relación") describing the conquest, which served as propaganda for his own cause. The Spanish court responded by banning the circulation of his first and last letter, but the others became famous across Europe and did much to establish the idea of Mexico as a mirror image of Europe and ripe for colonization. While Cortés was busy subduing the country militarily, Catholic priests attempted the ideological conquest of Mexico under the leadership of Bishop Juan de Zumárraga (1468–1548). Doubts over the completeness of Mexico's "conversion" led to subsequent waves of inquisition. The alleged behavior of both the Spanish and their priests in Mexico became a favorite subject for early Protestant propaganda then emerging from the Low Countries.

The mixture of Spanish and indigenous cultures produced new symbols. The most enduring was "Our Lady of Guadalupe." In December 1531 an Aztec peasant, Juan Diego, saw a vision of the Virgin Mary speaking in his language on a hill sacred to the Aztec goddess Tonastsi. A miraculous painting of this Aztec madonna appeared on his cloak, which became an object of veneration across the region. The Virgin of Guadalupe figured as an icon in the conversion of Mexico to Christianity, but one could argue that it was far more significant in later Mexican propaganda campaigns, from the struggle for freedom from Spain through the revolutionary movements of the twentieth century. In 2001 the Virgin of Guadalupe remains a potent symbol of Mexican and Chicano/Chicana (Mexican American) identity and can be found everywhere, from church publications and public murals to car hubcaps and even tattoos.

Mexico was the first country in the Americas to have a printing press and hence also the first to produce news sheets resembling newspapers. The press played an important role in church mission activity. The first printer in the country was Juan Paoli, or Pablos, an agent of the Casa Cromberger in Seville, Spain, who established his press around 1536. The Spanish ruled the New

World with recourse to censorship in the name of "public morality." By the eighteenth century this censorship had become overtly political and was directed at oppositional *pasquines,* or pamphlets. The first Mexican newspaper appeared on 1 January 1722. The *Gazeta de México y Noticias de Nueva España* (Mexico Gazette and News of New Spain) was published monthly, edited by Dr. Juan Ignacio de Castorena Ursua y Goyeneche (1668–1733), priest in the cathedral of Mexico City and later bishop of Yucatan.

Full-scale rebellion in Mexico followed hard on the heels of the French Revolution and Napoleon I's conquest of Spain. A mixed-race priest named Miguel Hidalgo y Costilla (1753–1811) organized an uprising against Spanish rule. His propaganda campaign, which mixed religion and class consciousness, can be summed up in his "Grito de Dolores" (Cry of Dolores) of September 1810, which demanded racial equality and land for the peasants. Although Hidalgo managed to assemble an army of eighty thousand people, the rebellion foundered in 1811. However, the flame of independence in Mexico now burned brightly. Newspapers of the revolutionary era included *El Despertador Americano* (American Alarm Clock). Mexico was granted independence from Spain in 1821.

Mexico's rulers in the nineteenth century included Antonio López de Santa Anna (1794–1876), who used a personality cult to rule dictatorially for three terms (1832–1855). He became an enduring bogeyman in U.S. propaganda as a result of his massacre of Texans at the Alamo in 1836. Liberal figures included Benito Juárez (1806–1872), who first opposed Santa Anna and then the French army of Napoleon III (1808–1873), with his "marionette emperor" Maximilian (1832–1867), during the war of French intervention (1863–1867). Juárez, Mexico's first president of Indian descent, served from 1858 until his death during a rebellion, becoming an enduring icon akin to Abraham Lincoln in the United States. In France memorable treatments of Maximilian (in propaganda aimed at Napoleon III rather than Mexico) included a rendering by Édouard Manet (1832–1883) of the emperor's death before a firing squad.

In 1876 Porfirio Díaz (1830–1915), Juárez's former general, seized power in Mexico. He consolidated his power by appeasing the church and U.S. business interests and allowing only token debate or opposition. He nurtured his state with all the usual propaganda techniques of the era, including ostentatious uniforms, flattering portraits, and lavish public ceremonies. Díaz began the Mexican practice of sending propagandists to the United States to promote his regime and encourage investment in Mexico.

Cinema came early to Mexico. In July 1896, the Lumière brothers sent French cameramen, a camera, and the projector used in the first public film performance in the world (given in Paris just six months previously). Mexico's first film performance was held privately for Díaz on 5 August 1896; the following days saw performances for journalists and for the public. The first movies, or *vistas,* were images of Mexico and scenes of Don Porfirio, the Pane Baths, the Military School, and the Canal de la Viga. The first Mexican fiction films appeared in 1907. Meanwhile antigovernment publications multiplied; they included Francisco Madero's (1873–1913) *La Sucesión Presidencial en 1910* (The 1910 Presidential Succession), published in 1908. In 1910 Madero campaigned against Díaz for the presidency, only to be defeated as a result of election fraud. Jailed and subsequently released, he fled to the United States but later returned to lead a successful revolution against Díaz in 1911. Soon after becoming president, in early 1913 he died at the hands of the forces of a new contender for power, Gen. Victoriano Huerta (1854–1916).

Huerta knew the propaganda value of the symbolic deed. On seizing power he attempted to build nationalist credentials by provoking the United States. In April 1914 his contrived insults to American prestige (he was described at the time as dishonoring the U.S. flag) led U.S. president Woodrow Wilson to seize the port of Vera Cruz. A further U.S. intervention followed in 1916.

The continuing revolutionary struggle of the poorest Mexicans—first against Díaz, then Huerta, and finally against the liberal "Constitutionalists"—resulted in a barrage of slogans, cartoons, and songs about the rebel leaders of the period, such as the charismatic peasant generals Emiliano Zapata (ca. 1879–1919) and "Pancho" Villa (ca. 1877–1923). Villa had a keen sense of the media and went so far as to sign a film deal with Hollywood's Mutual Film Company. He obliged its director, Raoul Walsh (1887–1980), by staging action when and where the light was best. He allegedly also executed a few federal troops for the cameras, but the studio cut these scenes for reasons of taste. In the final version of the film, which was called *The Life of General Villa* (1914), Walsh himself played Villa as a youth.

During World War I the combatants vied for Mexican opinion. German propaganda, trading on resentment against U.S. interventions, was particularly intense. Wireless broadcasting played an important role. President Venustiano Carranza (1859–1920) allowed German agents to rig up large transmitters and receivers atop Mexico City's Chapultepec Heights, which were used to send and receive war and propaganda messages, including (from 1917) press bulletins about the war for Central American newspapers. In 1917 Mexico figured in British propaganda to draw the United States into World War I. British intelligence intercepted and leaked the Zimmermann telegram, a communication from the German foreign minister that offered Mexico U.S. territory in exchange for entering the war.

The war years also saw the launch of two of the most significant Mexican newspapers: *El Universal* (1916) and *Excélsior* (1917). Meanwhile, in Mexico the new president, Constitutionalist leader Venustiano Carranza, unveiled a new constitution. He then wisely embarked on a campaign of public diplomacy in the United States, sending speakers north to establish his regime's liberal credentials and to discourage further U.S. intervention. From 1917 the United States conducted propaganda in Mexico through the Committee on Public Information (CPI). Its chief agent was Robert H. Murray, a foreign correspondent of the *New York World*. The CPI placed particular emphasis on the teaching of English.

By 1920 the revolution had ended. The postrevolutionary government sought to use propaganda to build a sense of Mexican identity and nationalism. The government experimented with broadcasting in 1924. The Ministry of Public Education (under José Vasconcelos) commissioned a massive nationwide program of mural painting. Its three most famous exponents ("Los Tres Grandes") were José Clemente Orozco (1882–1949), David Alfaro Siqueiros (1896–1974), and Diego Rivera (1886–1959), who later painted politically tinged murals in the United States. The muralists used a rich historical vocabulary of national struggle, including images of the conquest and Mexico's Aztec past, to build a sense of Mexican identity. Working on a smaller scale but toward similar ends, during the 1930s a group of artists called Taller de Gráfica Popular (Workshop of Popular Graphics) revived earlier opposition print techniques as a means of educating the masses and spreading the cause of antifascism. Specific issues of political propaganda within Mexico included the bitter clash in the late 1920s between the revolutionary state and the church. State anticlericalism (which included propaganda, the closure of religious schools, and a ban on church services) sparked the so-called Cristero Rebellion of 1926–1929 in western Mexico. Peace between church and state was not established until 1940, when newly elected president Manuel Ávila Camacho (1897–1955) memorably declared: "I'm a believer."

Commercial radio broadcasting in Mexico dates from September 1930, when XEW went on the air from Mexico City. It grew into the most influential commercial station in Latin America, and during the 1950s its young owner, Emilio Azcárraga Milmo (1930–1997), became the region's first great television mogul. In January 1938 President Lázaro Cardenas (1895–1970) launched the Departamento Autónomo de Prensa y Publicidad (DAPP), very similar to European ministries of information. The DAPP controlled all federal ministry briefings. It attempted (and failed) to increase government ownership and direction of the media and later adopted a more pragmatic course. From 1940 the new president, Manuel Avila Camacho established secret agreements, which his successors maintained, for full support with the owners of the mass media.

On 18 March 1938, President Cardenas signed a wildly popular decree nationalizing the foreign-owned oil industry in Mexico. Protests by the affected companies and the British, U.S., and Dutch governments only intensified the wave of national feeling. These attitudes were very fresh at the outbreak of World War II and had to be counteracted by Britain and the United States during the first years of the war.

As in World War I, Mexico leaned toward Germany during World War II. From 1936 on, the German Legation in Mexico City undertook an intense propaganda campaign to spread Nazism. In 1939 the British Ministry of Information fought back by establishing the Inter Allied Committee of Propaganda, by which French and English companies worked to manipulate the treatment of the war in the Mexican media through selectively increasing or cutting their advertising. The Allied Information Office under Robert H. K. Marett (an Englishman resident in Mexico City) used much the same tactics as the Nazi chief propagandist, Arthur Dietrich. In June 1940 Mexico's government pledged itself to the Allied cause, and by 1941 the British had effective control of all the key media channels in Mexico. U.S. propagandists operated extensively in wartime Mexico

under the auspices of the office of the Coordinator of Inter-American Affairs (CIAA), founded in 1940. CIAA initiatives included covert subsidies to develop the Mexican film industry.

Mexico's postwar propaganda was marked by repeated attempts to market the nation in the United States as well as prestige projects such as the Inter-American Highway. For much of the postwar period Mexico's ruling Partido Revolucionario Institucional (Institutional Revolutionary Party; PRI) enjoyed a cozy relationship at home with the state broadcaster Mexico Televisa. The highlight of postwar Mexican propaganda was supposed to have been the prestigious staging of the 1968 Olympic Games, though the event was hijacked by agendas other than that of President Gustavo Díaz Ordaz (1911–1979) when students took advantage of the presence of cameras to stage massive protests against the regime. Since the 1970s Mexico Televisa has attempted to export programming elsewhere in Latin America and to the Hispanic population of the United States, where its ownership of the popular Univision network sparked U.S. cries of "cultural imperialism." In 1992 Mexico conducted a large-scale public relations and lobbying campaign in the United States to lobby for the passage of the North American Free Trade Agreement (NAFTA).

In the latter half of the twentieth century Mexico's indigenous population achieved a number of breakthroughs in the field of political communication. The Worker-Peasant-Student Coalition of the Isthmus of Tehuantepec (COEI), founded in 1973 to represent the Zapotec Indians, made local gains against the PRI by campaigning in the Zapotec language and promoting its indigenous culture. In 1981 the COEI won the municipal election in the city of Juchitán and established a "People's Government," which the PRI removed by force in 1983. The COEI remains a major force in the region. On 1 January 1994—the very day on which Mexico became a member of NAFTA—an uprising of Mayan Indians in the province of Chiapas captured the attention of the Mexican and world media. The rebels called themselves the Ejército Zapatista de Liberación Nacional (EZLN), or Zapatista National Liberation Army, thereby claiming the mantle of the revolutionary hero Emiliano Zapata. Having seized a string of major towns in Chiapas, they proved adept at presenting themselves to the broadcast media. Their masked, eloquent, non-Indian leader "Subcomandante Marcos" began by reading a "Declaration of the Lacadón Jungle" to the TV cameras, claiming that the rebellion's national goal was the establishment of a democratic socialist government. Over a hundred thousand supporters rallied in Mexico City. In the months that followed, the Zapatistas provided an articulate challenge to the slick publicity machine of the PRI, thereby hastening the fall of President Carlos Salinas de Gortari (1948–). Marcos and the Zapatistas had proved that the propaganda mechanisms of the international media could work for the weak as well as the strong.

Nicholas J. Cull

See also Art; Latin America; Olympics; Religion; Spain; Zimmermann Telegram
References: Britton, John A. *Revolution and Ideology: The Image of the Mexican Revolution in the United States.* Lexington: University Press of Kentucky, 1995; Carrasco, Davíd. *City of Sacrifice: Violence from the Aztec Capital to the Modern Americas.* Boston: Beacon, 1999; Carrasco, Davíd, ed. *The Oxford Encyclopedia of Mesoamerican Cultures.* New York: Oxford University Press, 2001; Fox, Elizabeth. *Latin American Broadcasting: From Tango to Telenovela.* Luton, UK: University of Luton Press, 1997; Krauze, Enrique. *Mexico: Biography of Power.* London: HarperCollins, 1997; MacLachlin, Colin, and William Beezley. *El Gran Pueblo: A History of Greater Mexico.* Englewood Cliffs, NJ: Prentice-Hall, 1994; Ortiz Garza, José Luis. *La guerra de las ondas.* México City: Planeta, 1992; ————. *México en guerra.* México City: Planeta, 1989.

Milton, John (1608–1674)

An English poet who turned to propaganda during the civil war, Milton's early works of propaganda (1641–1642) attacked the power of bishops and the marriage laws in England. His best-known rhetorical work was *Areopagitica: A Speech for the Liberty of the Unlicensed Printing* (1644), an eloquent defense of the freedom of the press for all except Catholics, who, he felt, were too great a threat to the freedom of others. Milton worked as a licensor, effectively administering state censorship policies. In 1649 Milton wrote a passionate defense of the execution of King Charles I (1600–1649) called *The Tenure of Kings and Magistrates.* This led to his appointment as Latin Secretary to the Council of State (or "Secretary of Foreign Tongues"), with associated responsibility for explaining the new regime's policies overseas. His Latin arguments were widely read in Europe. This role anticipated that of public diplomacy of the twentieth century. Milton held this post until 1660, coinciding with the restoration of Charles II (1630–1685) to the throne. After spending a brief period in jail, he was released thanks to the intervention of fellow poet Andrew Marvell (1621–1678). Now blind, Milton resumed his poetic career, completing *Paradise Lost* in 1665 and *Paradise Regained* in 1671. Milton's *Areopagitica* remains one of the great masterpieces of persuasive writing and is still quoted whenever the freedom of the press is threatened.

Nicholas J. Cull

See also Britain; Civil War, English; Poetry
References: Fallon, Robert Thomas. *Milton in Government.* University Park: Pennsylvania State University Press, 1993; Raymond, Dora Neill. *Oliver's Secretary: John Milton in an Era of Revolt.* New York: Minton, Balch, 1932.

Mission to Moscow (1943)

During World War II, following the German invasion of the Soviet Union in 1941, each of the major Hollywood studios agreed to promote better friendship between America and its "awkward" ally, the Soviet Union, by releasing a feature film with a Russian theme. Warner Brothers produced *Mission to Moscow*

(1943), one of the most notorious pieces of feature film propaganda ever released in the United States. Like *Casablanca* (1942), it was directed by Michael Curtiz (1886–1962). Unlike the latter, it was a docudrama, purporting to provide an accurate account of Soviet politics in the 1930s, as seen through the eyes of American ambassador Joseph E. Davies (1876–1958). Although it appeared that Franklin D. Roosevelt (1882–1945) controlled the content of the film, in fact it was Davies who did. The result was a ridiculous puff piece glorifying a kindly Stalin and justifying the Moscow purge trials as a necessary evil to rid Russia of the supporters of Leon Trotsky (1879–1940), who is revealed in the film to be in the employ of Nazi Germany. The release of the film did not proceed as intended by those who controlled production. It created an uproar when its silly falsifications were exposed, and despite enormous production costs, it enjoyed a poor run and never returned its production costs—in short, it was a flop. One can say that the making of this film is a tale of zeal gone awry, of misplaced enthusiasm, of government officials at cross-purposes, a story of the buck never stopping anywhere.

After 1945, this film's falsehoods helped persuade many that Hollywood was controlled by Communist enthusiasts. It helped prepare the way for Sen. Joseph McCarthy (1909–1957), for in promoting untruth as truth, as a conspiratorial "revealed" history, it helped promote the method later used by McCarthy, while giving a specious substance to the burden of his allegations of betrayal of American institutions from within.

David Culbert

See also Cold War; Film (Feature); McCarthy, Joseph; World War II (United States)
References: Culbert, David. *Mission to Moscow.* Madison: University of Wisconsin Press, 1980; Davies, Joseph E. *Mission to Moscow.* New York: Simon and Schuster, 1941; Doherty, Thomas. *Projections of War: Hollywood, American Culture, and World War II.* New York: Columbia University Press, 1993; Koppes, Clayton R., and Gregory D. Black. *Hollywood Goes to War: How Politics, Profits, and Propaganda Shaped World War II Movies.* New York: Free Press, 1987.

MoI (Ministry of Information)

This was the name of the British propaganda ministry during both World Wars I and II. Writing in the BBC's handbook for 1941, Harold Nicolson (1886–1968), the ministry's parliamentary secretary, observed that the MoI was "the most unpopular department in the whole British Commonwealth of nations," as a result of the public's "healthy dislike for all forms of government propaganda." During World War II the MoI was restricted to domestic propaganda and censorship, as well as propaganda in neutral and Allied countries. Since British propaganda policy had been designed for a news-rich environment, it faired especially badly during the news-depleted "phony war" period (September 1939 to April 1940). Critics condemned the MoI for overstaffing and patronizing slogans. Its reputation improved steadily when Lord Hugh Macmillan (1873–1952), the ineffective original minister, was replaced first by Lord John Reith (1899–1971) in January 1940, next by Alfred Duff-Cooper (1890–1954) in May 1940, and finally by Brendan Bracken (1901–1958) in July 1941. The MoI's attempts to survey British public opinion through mass observation sparked criticism and the label "Cooper's Snoopers." Individual success stories included the production of documentary films by the Crown Film Unit, assisting in American coverage of the Blitz, and communicating war-related news to the United States before American entry into the war. In 1945 the Central Office of Information (COI) took over the domestic publicity functions of the MoI, while overseas functions passed to the relevant foreign or colonial office department.

Nicholas J. Cull

See also BBC; BIS; Bracken, Brendan; Britain; Censorship; Churchill, Winston; Health; *London Can Take It;* Morale; Murrow, Edward

R.; Orwell, George; Reith, Lord John; World
War II (Britain)

References: Aldgate, Anthony, and Jeffrey
Richards. *Britain Can Take It: The British Cinema
and the Second World War.* Edinburgh: Edinburgh
University Press, 1994; Cole, Robert. *Britain
and the War of Words in Neutral Europe,
1939–1945.* London: Macmillan, 1990;
MacLaine, Ian. *Ministry of Morale: Home Front
Morale and the Ministry of Information in World War
II.* London: Unwin, 1979.

Morale

The spirit of a nation's armed forces or its
population has long been recognized as a central concern for any leader and a key target
for an enemy. Morale became a central issue
for propagandists in the twentieth century.
Although it is difficult to arrive at a working
definition of morale during wartime, there
appears to be a consensus that behavior and
action are involved. Morale is often viewed as
meaningless, or at least ineffective, unless it
promotes action.

One of the most significant lessons to be
learned from World War I was that public
opinion could no longer be ignored by governments. Unlike previous wars, the Great
War was the first "total war" in which nations
and not just professional armies were locked
in mortal combat. The war served to increase
the level of popular interest and participation
in affairs of state. The gap between the soldier at the front and civilians at home narrowed substantially since the full resources of
the state were mobilized. In "total war,"
which requires civilians to participate in the
war effort, morale came to be recognized as
a significant military factor.

Writing in *Mein Kampf,* Adolf Hitler
(1889–1945) claimed that Allied propaganda
had undermined civilian morale and was responsible for the collapse of the German Empire in 1918. There is, in fact, compelling evidence to suggest that Allied propaganda had
greater success in driving a wedge between
the German armed forces and the political
and military leadership. This theme of creat-

ing divisiveness between the kaiser and the
German people became one of the main elements in American propaganda once the
United States entered the war in 1917; the
same scenario occurred in British propaganda
once Lord Northcliffe (1865–1922) was appointed director of propaganda in enemy
countries in 1918. Leaflets, flyers, small pamphlets, and booklets were dropped behind
German lines by aircraft and unmanned balloons. This material combined words and images in the form of cartoons, photographs, or
maps showing German soldiers the quickest
route home. The Allied propaganda offensive
was directed against the evils of the German
government, caricaturing the kaiser or attacking Prussian militarism and German imperialism. One of the most famous leaflets
contained a drawing that depicted the kaiser
and his six sons in full military regalia—all
unscathed by war—marching blindly past
hundreds of skeletal arms reaching out to
them in anguish. The caption read: "One
family which has not lost a single member."

Sustaining civilian morale was considered
to be even more important in World War II.
Modern technology affected the nature of
warfare, with mass bombings killing thousands of civilians and injuring many more.
Moreover, the needs of modern war required
the mass mobilization of people and the
economy to provide fighting forces and the
equipment necessary to sustain their efforts.
In Britain the Ministry of Information (MoI)
set up a Home Intelligence Division. In October 1941 Stephen Taylor (1910–1988), its
head, submitted a report indicating that good
morale depended on such material factors as
adequate food, warmth, rest, a secure base,
and the safety of dependants. Morale was also
affected by mental factors, including belief in
victory, equality of sacrifice, the justice of the
war, and efficient leadership.

The need to address morale applied equally
to such totalitarian regimes as Nazi Germany
and Soviet Russia. During World War II belligerent states used propaganda to undermine
the morale of the enemy. The Japanese, for ex-

ample, invested a great deal of its resources in creating short-wave propaganda aimed at the United States. Little of this propaganda adversely affected morale because the Japanese failed to devise messages that were meaningful to their intended target; it also failed to realize that the attack on Pearl Harbor was sufficient justification for U.S. participation in the conflict. To compound their mistakes, the Japanese claimed that Americans had become decadent and "soft" and were unable to withstand the pressures of war in the face of the superiority of the Japanese fighting forces and its immense spiritual strength. Such propaganda is more likely to stiffen rather than weaken morale. Similar Iraqi broadcasts from "Baghdad Betty" during the Gulf crisis and war (1990–1991) seem to have improved morale among U.S. troops in Saudi Arabia as a result of their unintended comic value.

David Welch

See also Austrian Empire; Gulf War; Hitler, Adolf; *Mein Kampf;* Psychological Warfare; World War I; World War II (Japan)

References: MacLaine, Ian. *Ministry of Morale: Home Front Morale and the Ministry of Information in World War II.* London: Unwin, 1979; Roetter, Charles. *Psychological Warfare.* London: Batsford, 1974; Welch, David. *Germany, Propaganda and Total War, 1914–18.* New Brunswick, NJ: Rutgers University Press, 2000.

Murdoch, Rupert (1931–)

This Australian-born communications entrepreneur's global News Corporation empire includes: Twentieth Century-Fox films; the London *Times* and the Chicago *Sun-Times;* the Sky satellite TV news and cable network; and HarperCollins publishers. Murdoch has also invested heavily in direct digital broadcasting. Although the latter part of the twentieth century produced a number of powerful media magnates—such as Axel Springer (1912–1985) in Germany, Roberto Marinho (1904–1998) in Brazil, and Ted Turner (1938–) in the United States—no one has exercised the same degree of control over such a diverse media empire.

Murdoch was born in Melbourne into a distinguished newspaper family. His father, Keith Murdoch (1885–1952), had made his name as a crusading war correspondent during World War I. Following his father's death, Murdoch inherited his paper, the *Adelaide News.* After establishing a chain of papers in Australia, in 1969 Murdoch moved into international publishing by buying the London *News of the World* and *The Sun.* In the 1970s he purchased the *New York Post.* He gained a reputation as the king of the tabloids, increasing circulation by catering to the lowest common denominator—scandal. In 1981 he purchased the London *Times.* In 1985 Murdoch became a U.S. citizen, clearing the way for his purchase of domestic U.S. media conglomerates Metromedia and Twentieth Century-Fox, over which he assumed full control in 1992.

In propaganda terms, his papers have supported such conservative politicians as Ronald Reagan and Margaret Thatcher. In 2000 Murdoch seized a substantial share of the U.S. TV news market with his flagrantly partisan Fox News broadcasts. Regular targets include the European Union. For all its domestic conservatism, Murdoch's empire has been notoriously soft on the People's Republic of China, where his News Corporation has commercial interests. For example, in 1998 Murdoch ordered HarperCollins to reject the book *East and West* by Chris Patten (1944–), the last governor of Hong Kong, purportedly because it included anti-Chinese statements.

Nicholas J. Cull

See also Blair, Tony; CNN; Falklands/Malvinas War; Reagan, Ronald; Satellite Communications; Terrorism, War on; Thatcher, Margaret

References: Bagdikian, Ben H. *The Media Monopoly.* 6th ed. Boston: Beacon, 2000; Chenoweth, Neil. *Virtual Murdoch.* New York: Secker and Warburg, 2001; Shawcross, William. *Murdoch.* New York: Simon and Schuster, 1992.

Murrow, Edward R. (1908–1965)

An American radio and television broadcaster, subsequently appointed director of the United States Information Agency (USIA), Murrow was born in North Carolina and raised in the Pacific Northwest. His undergraduate studies in speech and rhetoric equipped him for a career in the emerging radio industry. In 1935 Murrow joined the Columbia Broadcasting System (CBS) and in 1937 began coverage of the growing international crisis from London. Although frustrated by Britain's appeasement of Nazi Germany, Murrow advised the British on how best to facilitate American coverage of the coming war. The officials at the Ministry of Information (MoI) soon grew to trust Murrow, giving him and his colleagues privileged access to the British war effort and restricting conventional propaganda appeals to the U.S. public. Murrow's live broadcasts of the Nazi Blitz of London in September 1940 brought the war into American homes and played a key part in turning the tide against isolationism. Later governments would use press reporters to achieve similar ends, including Harrison Salisbury (1908–1993) in Hanoi during the Vietnam War and Peter Arnett (1934–) in Baghdad during the Gulf War of 1991.

In postwar America Murrow pioneered current affairs broadcasting in the new medium of television. His "See It Now" program (first broadcast in 1951) championed numerous causes, achieving lasting fame for effectively exposing the bullying propaganda techniques of Sen. Joseph McCarthy (1909–1957).

In 1961 Murrow agreed to join President John F. Kennedy's (1917–1963) administration as director of USIA. Although he continued to publicly emphasize the importance of open media and balanced reporting (showing America "warts and all"), he expected his principle organ, the Voice of America, to toe the line in terms of fairly rigid Cold War propaganda. Murrow oversaw new initiatives in overt American propaganda, including increased expansion in the Third World. Although illness prevented him from playing a significant role in the Cuban Missile Crisis, his agency performed well. By the time of the Kennedy assassination, Murrow was already seriously debilitated by the lung cancer that would bring about his early retirement in January 1964 and death in 1965. Nevertheless his agency played an important role in easing the trauma of the transition from Kennedy to President Lyndon B. Johnson (1908–1973) overseas, and developed Kennedy's image as a champion of the highest political ideals.

Nicholas J. Cull

See also Kennedy, John F.; McCarthy, Joseph; MoI; Radio (International); United States; USIA; World War II (Britain)

References: Cull, Nicholas J. *Selling War: British Propaganda and American Neutrality in World War Two.* Oxford: Oxford University Press, 1995; Sperber, A. M. *Murrow: His Life and Times.* New York: Freundlich, 1986.

Music

Although a basic tool of the propagandist, music inevitably is more meaningful to those with professional training or who are attracted to it than those for whom music remains at best something to while away the time in an elevator or while waiting for a telephone call to be completed. The ancient Greeks used a primitive trumpet at the Olympic Games. According to the Old Testament (and the spiritual tune based on this story), Joshua won the battle of Jericho by sounding a trumpet "and the walls came tumblin' down." In the preindustrial era, martial music—drums, fifes, bagpipes, trumpets—played an enormous role in boosting morale in battle, encouraging troops to ever greater heroic achievements. Music plays a similar role in modern sporting events.

Music can serve a variety of purposes, all of which can benefit the student of propaganda. It can be patriotic, romantic, or escapist. It can function in the popular media, as in film scores, or as a form of high culture. In organized religion, the required "leap of faith" is abetted by music, which forms part of the act of worship. Martin Luther's hymn "A Mighty Fortress Is Our God," for which he provided both melody and text, is universally considered the national anthem of the Protestant Reformation. The success of Methodism is directly related to the melodies and texts of John Wesley (1703–1791) and his younger brother Charles (1707–1788). In the United States, the spiritual served as a central device for comprehending the religious piety and militant protest of slaves in the antebellum South.

Popular song includes folk songs as well as popular music. Although popular music traditionally relates romantic tales of boy-meets-girl or boy-loses-girl, it can also serve as a mechanism of social protest. During the 1960s in the United States, Bob Dylan's (1941–) "Blowin' in the Wind" was one of many protest songs attacking the Vietnam War. Attempting to define the parameters of the protest movement of the 1960s, one scholar has argued that it encompasses every single person who listened to such songs—a rough interpretative device at best. Certainly folk song has been coopted by those singing songs of protest in general, such as various labor organizers. The best known of all worker songs is "The Internationale," which was written in Paris after the Commune of 1871 and served as the official national anthem of the former Soviet Union from 1917 to 1943.

Music lends itself to patriotic appeals since the latter depends upon an emotional response, and music is well suited to the expression of emotions. The first truly great national anthem is still "La Marseillaise," composed by Claude Joseph Rouget de Lisle in 1792. As a direct response, Franz Joseph Haydn (1732–1809) composed the Austrian national anthem in 1797, whose tune was so good that the Germans adopted it for their national anthem, "Deutschland, Deutschland über Alles." The national anthem of the United States, "The Star-Spangled Banner," was only made official in 1931; it combines a stirring text by Francis Scott Key (1780–1843) with the popular English drinking song "Anacreon in Heaven" by John Stafford Smith (1750–1836). Although millions of individuals can sing the simple melody of England's "God Save the Queen" with ease, America's national anthem has a melody that has notes so high that few can sing it properly, including the amateur soloists who open many a sporting event.

High culture often includes a predilection for classical music. In this sense all such music is a form of cultural propaganda, a way of defining one's status. But classical composers have on occasion also dealt with matters of war and peace in memorable ways. Sergei Prokofiev (1891–1953) wrote the score for director Sergei Eisenstein's (1898–1948) film *Alexander Nevsky* (1938), which contains a memorable depiction of the defeat of the German Teutonic knights at the Battle of Lake Peipus (1242). The programmatic music conveys a clear message to even the nonmusical listener, making it clear that a moral distinction separates the barbaric German invaders from the peace-loving Russians. In 1942 Aaron Copland (1900–1990) wrote a short piece for brass and percussion entitled "Fanfare for the Common Man," which is correctly considered a form of civil religion. The title indicates that the composer wished his music to speak directly to the average person, whom he considered a modern hero.

Nazi Germany dealt with music in a specifically racist fashion by banning jazz and the music of Jewish composers. For example, not a note of Mendelssohn could be played in Germany between 1933 and 1945. The Holocaust has produced a substantial musical response, both by composers who died in concentration camps and by those writing music that comments on the meaning of the Holocaust.

One of the least imaginative forms of musical propaganda is the Hollywood feature film, where unimaginative directors have insisted on pedestrian musical scores. Romantic melody still reigns when boy meets girl. The concerns of Theodor Adorno (1903–1969) and Hanns Eisler (1898–1962), whose

Composing for the Films (1947) is still the best book written on the subject, suggest that in film music the endless recycling of musical clichés is all that is required—which is to say that another gibe continues to have currency: "In Hollywood, everyone knows his business, and music."

David Culbert

See also Horst Wessel Lied; "The Internationale"; "La Marseillaise"; Peace and Antiwar Movements (1945–)

References: Adorno, Theodor, and Eisler, Hanns. *Composing for the Films.* London: Athlone, 1994; Reed, W. L., and M. J. Bristow, eds. *National Anthems of the World.* 8th ed. New York: Cassell, 1993; Sonneck, Oscar. *Report on "The Star-Spangled Banner," "Hail Columbia," "America," and "Yankee Doodle."* (1909). Reprint. New York: Dover, 1972.

Mussolini, Benito (1883–1945)

The Italian Fascist leader, Mussolini was born near Forli in northeastern Italy. His father, a blacksmith, was an active Socialist and Mussolini's early forays in the field of propaganda were also left-wing. In 1913 he became editor of the Socialist newspaper *Avanti!* (Forward!). World War I saw his dramatic conversion to nationalism, with Mussolini supporting Italy's entry into the war on the Allied side. In 1914 he founded his own daily paper, *Popolo d'Italia* (People of Italy), to advance this cause. Beginning in 1915, he drew a substantial subsidy from the French government's propaganda budget. After a period of war service, Mussolini resumed his editorship of the newspaper in 1917. The latter became a key platform from which he organized his Fasci di Combattimento (Fascist Party) in 1919.

Mussolini's rise to power rested on nationalistic propaganda, a personality cult, and a willingness to engage in street violence. Mussolini utilized many tools of paramilitary propaganda, including uniforms (the Black Shirt), flags, and parades to create a sense of belonging among his followers. He borrowed much from the earlier nationalistic perfor-

Benito Mussolini, in a characteristic braggadocio pose. (Illustrated London News Group)

mances of playwright Gabriele D'Annunzio (1863–1938), including frenzied balcony speeches and the straight-arm "Roman" salute. Mussolini's first major success came in 1921 when he and thirty-four other Fascists were elected to the Chamber of Deputies. In 1922 he used the tactic of a massive "March on Rome" to force the king to name him prime minister. Mussolini swiftly consolidated his control of the media. His international propaganda efforts included a famous series of articles (1927–1934) for the Hearst newspaper chain in the United States.

Mussolini placed himself at the center of his regime's propaganda, with slogans proclaiming that "Mussolini is always right." He stage-managed rallies and speeches; ensured a flattering appearance in the papers and newsreels by adopting athletic or energetic poses; and supported everything from larger families to increased levels of agricultural production. Mussolini's drive to project his regime as the successor to the Roman Empire brought forth grandiose public works and even overseas military adventures, such as the conquest of Abyssinia in 1935–1936, which resulted in the expulsion of Italy from the League of Nations. As an international pariah, Mussolini grew closer to his onetime imitator Adolf Hitler (1889–1945), with whom he concluded the Axis pact of 1936 and the "Pact of Steel" in 1939. He joined Hitler's war against the European democracies in 1940, but in July 1943, with the Allies landing on the Italian mainland, found himself out of office through the simple expedient of having been sacked by the king. After being rescued by German paratroops, Mussolini ruled a puppet Italian National Socialist Republic (Salo) in northern Italy. In April 1945 he was captured, tried, and executed by partisans. In death this inveterate propagandist himself became an icon; his body was exhibited up-side down, the traditional fate of traitors during the Renaissance in the Florentine republic.

Nicholas J. Cull

See also Civil War, Spanish; Fascism, Italian; Hitler, Adolf; Italy; Perón, Juan Domingo, and Eva Duarte; Sport

References: MacSmith, Denis. *Mussolini.* London: Paladin, 1985; Whittam, John. *Fascist Italy.* Manchester: Manchester University Press, 1995.

N

NAACP (National Association for the Advancement of Colored People)

The most significant and enduring African American civil rights organization, the National Association for the Advancement of Colored People (NAACP) began its work during the Progressive Era as a response to a rise in antiblack violence, specifically two lynchings in Springfield, Illinois, in 1908. White and black activists, led by a white woman, Mary White Ovington (1865–1951) convened at a conference in New York City in 1909 and formed the NAACP. When the organization started operations in 1910, its key propagandist was the African American sociologist W. E. B. Du Bois (1868–1963), who edited its house organ, *Crisis*. At first Du Bois was the only black board member. *Crisis* swiftly built up a circulation of a hundred thousand. Early campaigns included picketing of the film *The Birth of a Nation* (1915) and a silent march through New York to protest the brutal race riot in East St. Louis in 1917. In 1920 the organization appointed its first African American secretary, the writer James Weldon Johnson (1871–1938).

In the 1940s, under the leadership of Walter White (1893–1955), the organization launched a legal initiative through the NAACP Legal Defense and Education Fund. It won high-profile victories against U.S. army segregation and, most important, precipitated the 1954 Supreme Court decision in the case of *Brown v. Board of Education of Topeka, Kansas*. The NAACP's national network became the framework upon which the civil rights movement was built. In the 1950s segregationists attacked the organization for being a communist front. The NAACP responded by purging left-wing members. In the 1960s black radicals attacked the NAACP (as they had in the 1920s) for being too middle class and limited in its goals. The NAACP weathered both storms and remained active under the leadership first of Roy Wilkins (1901–1981) and then of Benjamin Hooks (1925–). After a spate of financial scandals in the early 1990s, the leadership passed to former congressman Kweisi Mfume (1948–).

Nicholas J. Cull

See also *The Birth of a Nation;* Civil Rights Movement; United States (Progressive Era)
References: Finch, Minnie. *The NAACP: Its Fight for Justice.* Metuchen, NJ: Scarecrow, 1981; Wilson, Sondra Kathryn, ed. *In Search of Democracy: The NAACP Writings of James Weldon Johnson, Walter White, and Roy Wilkins (1920–1977).* New York: Oxford University Press, 1999; Zangrando, Robert L. *The NAACP*

Crusade Against Lynching, 1909–1950.
Philadelphia: Temple University Press, 1980.

Napoleon (1769–1821)

Napoleon had the advantage of inheriting the lessons of the French Revolution, which used pamphlets, art, architecture, music, plays, and festivals to convert the public to its ideology. Napoleon Bonaparte—he was not called by his first name until he became emperor in 1804—needed propaganda as much as his revolutionary predecessors since he first gained power through a coup (1799) rather than by virtue of inheritance or by being elected and therefore had to establish his legitimacy. Moreover, he needed propaganda to muster support for his ongoing warfare against other European powers, which lasted all but fourteen months of the period in which he led France.

Napoleon never used the term "propaganda," but he was keenly aware of the importance of shaping public opinion. "The truth," he once asserted, "is not so important as what people think to be true." He understood the importance of public opinion while still an army officer. He had been promoted to general because of his leadership in commanding the artillery at Toulon, which had been handed over to the British. Napoleon's recapture of this important naval base on the Mediterranean coast in 1793 was celebrated in all the media of the day, catapulting him into public prominence.

Later, as the commander of the French army in Italy in 1796, he publicized his exploits effectively in speeches, dispatches, and commissioned works of art. As he rose to power, he considered an appropriate symbol. Although the bee represented his family name, it did not have enough prestige for public use. He considered three powerful animals: the elephant, the lion, and the eagle. He commissioned an elephant fountain for the place de la Bastille, had a huge model built near the site, but never carried the idea through to completion. He also realized that the lion was too closely associated with the British. Finally he chose the eagle. Not only did it soar high in the heavens and pounce on its prey with powerful talons, but it also reminded the public of imperial Rome and its dominance of western Europe and the Mediterranean.

As Napoleon rose from first consul to consul for life to emperor, he utilized a variety of governmental agencies to control and direct public opinion. The Ministry of Police kept careful watch over public opinion in the streets. The Postal Administration supervised the dissemination of information. The Department of the Interior controlled theaters and the arts. The Ministry of Public Worship made sure that churches and synagogues toed the official line. The Ministry of Finance and the Ministry of the Public Purse subsidized those media that influenced public opinion. In addition to these ministries, there were personal functionaries who assisted in specialized areas of propaganda. Thus, the bureaucratic state, modernized by the Revolution, was mobilized to create a favorable image of the leader, his civic administration, and his military exploits.

Since the press was still the major means of disseminating information, it received special attention. The Napoleonic regime first reduced the number of Parisian newspapers from seventy-three to eighteen and then to only four. In the regional departments, newspapers were reduced to only one per department. The newspapers that remained were subject to censorship and were forbidden to treat certain sensitive topics. The government occasionally even appointed editors favorable to the emperor and his regime. Other forms of print were likewise controlled. Books were censored, distribution was carefully supervised, and certain authors were subsidized. At the same time, minor forms of print such as pamphlets, handbooks, posters, and proclamations were tightly regulated. When all these controls failed to work satisfactorily, the government used financial constraints.

The other media were not neglected. Revolutionary festivals were suppressed and new ones substituted, such as Napoleon's birthday, the anniversary of the battle of Jena (October 1806), the coup of 18 Brumaire (November 1799), the coronation of Napoleon as emperor (December 1804), or the victory at Austerlitz (December 1805). Other special festivals were staged to celebrate such events as the marriage of Napoleon to Marie-Louise (March 1810) or the birth of an heir, the king of Rome (1811). These periodic or special festivals combined parades, band music, poetry readings, speeches, and fireworks. Such festivals were, however, much more militaristic and involved much less popular participation than their revolutionary prototypes. Frequently government agents mingled with the crowd in order to spread rumors favorable to the regime.

The Napoleonic government also paid close attention to education in the widest sense of the term. The regime trained teachers, selected textbooks, and suppressed rival publications. Catholic and Protestant churches and Jewish synagogues were employed as branches of education; they were ordered to read bulletins, pray for the emperor, and use catechisms that taught the legitimacy of the emperor and his successors. Theaters were also considered a branch of public education. The number of theaters was controlled, productions were censored, and certain topics were proscribed. There could be nothing dealing with the Bourbons, the private life of Napoleon, usurpation of the throne, punishment of a tyrant, or a victory over France. At the same time positive themes were encouraged, such as those about 18 Brumaire, military victories, peace settlements, or the birth of the king of Rome.

Napoleon and his agents also mobilized the fine arts. A program was unveiled to dot the landscape with imperial buildings, columns, and triumphal arches. Printers and engravers were commissioned to glorify the military feats of the emperor and the achievements of the civil administration. A series of medals was issued to commemorate similar achievements. Caricatures were also employed to ridicule the enemy and counter its claims.

In the long run this propaganda was not completely successful. The public came to realize that the media only published what the government wanted it to know. Foreign news was sometimes able to filter into France. Finally, there was no way for a ruler and a regime that always portrayed itself as invincible to overcome military defeat. Even so, a myth grew up around Napoleon that became a powerful political force in the nineteenth century, eventually leading to the Second Empire under Napoleon III (1808–1873), who ruled from 1852 to 1870. Moreover, appropriately named monuments and place names continued to stir up memories of Napoleon and his "grande armée."

James A. Leith

See also David, Jacques-Louis; France; Goya; Portraiture; Revolution, French; Spain

References: Boime, Albert. *Art in an Age of Bonapartism, 1800–1815.* Chicago: University of Chicago Press, 1990; Collins, Irene. *Napoleon, First Consul and Emperor of the French.* London: Historical Association, 1986; Holtman, Robert B. *Napoleonic Propaganda.* Baton Rouge: Louisiana State University Press, 1950; Leith, James, and Andrea Joyce. *Face à Face: French and English Caricatures of the French Revolution and Its Aftermath.* Toronto: Art Gallery of Ontario/Musée des Beaux-Arts d'Ontario, 1989; Wilson-Smith, Antony. *Napoleon and His Artists.* London: Constable, 1996.

Narrative of the Life of Frederick Douglass, an American Slave, written by himself (1845)

This autobiography of runaway slave Frederick Douglass (1817–1895) was first published in 1845 by the Boston Anti-Slavery Society. Its impact as abolitionist propaganda was surpassed only by Harriet Beecher Stowe's novel *Uncle Tom's Cabin* (1852). As a firsthand account, Douglass's work had immediacy and moral conviction. The narrative included multiple beatings and Douglass's

Frederick Douglass. (Perry-Castaneda Library)

eventual escape from slavery. His eloquence as a writer gave the lie to the Southern claim that an African American was intellectually inferior, suited only to perform manual labor. Subsequent volumes of his autobiography dealt with his work in the abolitionist movement. He also served as a diplomat for the U.S. government.

Nicholas J. Cull

See also Abolitionism/Antislavery Movement; Civil War, United States; *Uncle Tom's Cabin*
References: Douglass, Frederick. *Narrative of the Life of Frederick Douglass.* London: Penguin, 1982; McFeely, William S. *Frederick Douglass.* New York: Norton, 1991.

Nast, Thomas (1840–1902)

Nast, a German-born illustrator and cartoonist who transformed American visual communication, invented the elephant as an emblem

for the Republican Party, popularized the donkey as an emblem for the Democratic Party, and established modern representations of both Uncle Sam (lean visage, sporting a goatee) and Santa Claus (rotund, with full beard). Nast arrived in the United States in 1846. He began work on *Frank Leslie's Illustrated Newspaper* and in 1859 moved to *Harper's Weekly,* where he worked for nearly thirty years. He covered the war in Italy in 1860 (for the *New York Illustrated News* and other papers) and then returned to the United States to illustrate the Civil War. Nast contributed numerous propaganda images during the Civil War, including conditions in prison camps and alleged Confederate guerrilla atrocities, typical of which was his "John Morgan's Highwaymen Sack a Peaceful Village in the West" (*Harper's,* 30 August 1862). Santa Claus first appeared with a wartime spin, dressed in the stars and stripes and cheering up Union soldiers by handing out gifts—specifically a rather ghoulish statue depicting Confederate President Davis with his neck in a noose (*Harper's* cover of 3 January 1863).

Nast's pictures had a great visual impact, frequently covering large double-page spreads. His illustrations were utilized as presidential election posters for Abraham Lincoln (1809–1865) and, later, Ulysses S. Grant (1822–1885). The most famous targets of Nast's postwar work were Lincoln's successor, Andrew Johnson (1808–1875), whom he lampooned as a caesar or "King Andy," and the notoriously corrupt New York city politician William "Boss" Tweed (1823–1878), who was also depicted as a Roman emperor. In the 1860s and early 1870s Nast pursued Tweed relentlessly, rendering his Tammany Hall political machine as a tiger. His images became so well known that when Boss Tweed fled to Spain, he was recognized from a Nast cartoon and arrested. Nast stopped working for *Harper's* in 1886. His images frequently reflected anti-Irish stereotyping, and in the later 1880s he drew regularly for the anti-Catholic propaganda paper *America.* In 1892 he attempted to launch his own paper, *Thomas*

Thomas Nast, in a formal portrait late in life. (Library of Congress)

"Neo-militias" is a term used to describe the armed military groups that have been forming in recent years. These "new'" militia groups often refer to themselves as "unorganized militia." They do not approve of modern American society or its government and seek to return to the past and the spirit of the Founding Fathers. The stereotypical neo-militia member is a strict nationalist, Caucasian Protestant (leaning toward cultural and religious lack of tolerance), conspiracy theorist, gun-rights activist, and avowed enemy of oppressive "big government."

Neo-militia groups believe that less government is better and that civil liberties are best protected by individuals themselves. Crucial to such thinking is a strong desire to own firearms as a necessary precondition for the protection of individual liberties. Common to many of the conspiracy theories held by such groups is the fear that they may be attacked by agencies of their own government. Religious militia groups often cite a turning away from God or even a coming apocalypse. Most groups claim that society is disintegrating and view themselves as the last bulwark against such decline. Consistent with their conspiracy theories, neo-militia groups are highly critical of what they view as the liberal-biased media. Neo-militia groups cited media coverage of the 1995 bombing of the Alfred Murrah Federal Building in Oklahoma City and the subsequent conviction of Timothy McVeigh (1968–2001) as further evidence of bias and misrepresentation of their aims. As a result new militias tend to eschew the "controlled media" and instead disseminate their propaganda via the Internet and publish their own right-wing literature. The steady flow of propaganda from neo-militia groups is carefully monitored by opponents such as the Anti-Defamation League.

Nast's Weekly, but it failed after only thirteen issues. Nast died in 1902 while serving as a diplomat in Ecuador.

Nicholas J. Cull

See also Cartoons; Civil War, United States; Lincoln, Abraham; Uncle Sam

References: Hess, Stephen, and Sandy Northrop. *Drawn and Quartered: The History of American Political Cartoons.* Montgomery, AL: Elliott and Clark, 1996; Keller, Morton. *The Art and Politics of Thomas Nast.* New York: Oxford University Press, 1975.

National Anthems

See Music

Neo-Militia Groups

Militia groups have existed in the United States since the founding of the colonies.

David Welch

See also ADL; Internet; Revolution, American, and War of Independence; United States

References: Dees, Morris. *The Gathering Storm: America's Militia Threat.* New York: Harper Collins, 1996; Diamond, Sara. *Roads to*

Dominion: Right-wing Movements and Political Power in the Unites States. New York: Guilford Press, 1995; Hoffman, David. "The Web of Hate: Extremists Exploit the Internet." Anti-Defamation League Research Report, 1996.

Netherlands, Belgium, and Luxembourg

The Low Countries were an ideological hotbed during the early modern period, witnessing both the Protestant Reformation and the Dutch Revolt of 1566–1581. The golden age of the seventeenth century saw the flowering of national propaganda. The nineteenth century saw the emergence of Belgium as an independent kingdom after centuries of foreign rule. In the twentieth century the Low Countries endured the propaganda of two German occupations. The Netherlands and Luxembourg have both played a significant part in broadcasting history. Enduring issues in the region include the clash between Catholic and Protestant (the Netherlands still has sectarian newspapers, trade unions, political parties, and broadcasting organizations) and between the French and Flemish/Dutch languages.

The Low Countries entered the early modern period with a highly developed intellectual and print culture, being one of the heartlands of the Protestant Reformation. Netherlandish engraving was world famous and would become a powerful weapon of political propaganda in the sixteenth century when the northern provinces opposed the rule of the Habsburg dynasty, which had acquired the region in a series of marriage alliances. The problem began in 1555 when Emperor Charles V abdicated his rule to his son, Phillip II of Spain (1527–1598). Phillip's attempts to reassert Catholicism in a region of religious diversity and toleration provoked a revolt in the northern provinces, led by William the Silent, Prince of Orange (1533–1584). William had the advantage of the family color, which figured in the tricolor flag of the country he effectively founded; his

orange color became as potent a symbol of his cause as the green flag of Irish nationalism or the red flag of the revolutionary left.

A key propagandist of the anti-Spanish cause was Philips van Marnix (1540–1598), William's secretary and chief publicist. Marnix's works included a widely read anti-Catholic pamphlet called *De Biënkorf der Roomsche Kercke* (The Beehive of the Roman Church, 1569), but rebel propaganda tended to avoid religious issues (William himself was slow to convert to Calvinism), focusing instead on the idea that Netherlandish freedom had been violated by Spain. Marnix's works in this vein included the *Vraye Narration et apologie* (True Narrative and Apology) of 1567. Writing in a similar vein, Jacob van Vesembeeke (1524–1575) produced a series of tracts in 1568–69 on the "natural ingrained freedom" of the Netherlands. This articulation of an abstract concept of freedom was a legacy of the Dutch Revolt and proved influential in the wider development of Western political thought.

The rebel cause swiftly accumulated a repertoire of rousing songs, the best known being "Wilhelmus van Nassauwe" (William of Nassau), which became the national anthem of the Netherlands in the late nineteenth century. As the revolt unfolded, the printing presses of the Netherlands produced visual atrocity propaganda dealing with the "Black Legend" of Spanish brutality in Spain, the Netherlands, and the New World. The particular villain, in the eyes of the Dutch, was the Duke of Alba (1507–1582), who governed the Netherlands from 1567 to 1573. Among his excesses was the notorious "Court of Blood" established in Brussels, which executed eighteen thousand people. Later atrocities included the "Spanish Fury," an attack against Antwerp in 1576. Like prints and engravings, coins also played an important role in the propaganda of the Dutch Revolt, utilizing a rich iconography in which the Netherlands was represented as a lion and the Spanish king as a tyrant in armor. These coins first popularized the image of a cap to denote liberty and used the image of a circular fence to represent historical restrictions on the power of kings in the region.

The upsurge of national feeling growing out of opposition to Spanish rule led to the political union of the northern provinces under the Pacification of Ghent (1576) and Union of Utrecht (1579), by which they effectively declared independence from Spain as the United Provinces. In 1580 William himself sent a defiant *Apologie* to Philip II explaining his actions in terms of principles of liberty and denouncing Spanish atrocities at home and abroad. The document, actually written by William's chaplain, was published in French, Dutch, English, German, and Latin and was aimed at a wide European audience. It thus foreshadowed the international propaganda of the modern age. Spain did not acknowledge the independence of the United Provinces until the Treaty of Westphalia (1648), which ended the Thirty Years' War. The remaining Spanish lands (modern Belgium) passed to Austrian rule in 1714.

The United Provinces remained a hotbed of propagandist writing and art, shaping the public image of the state and its rulers. Engravers often returned to the iconic events of the Dutch Revolt, and the notion of liberty, which proved very real for the Protestant and Jewish refugees who had found safety in the Netherlands at this time. The image of the circular fence evolved into a fertile garden symbolic of the Netherlands' prosperity; other symbols of wealth that appeared on coins included a plump cow. Writers like jurist Hugo Grotius (1583–1645) and artists Rembrandt van Rijn (1606–1669) and Otto van Veen (1556–1634) embroidered on the national mythology by retelling the story of ancient resistance to Rome by the Batavi tribe. The Netherlands also produced a lively genre of propaganda that influenced the ethical behavior of its citizens. The virtuous household became a particularly important theme in the work of poets like Jacob Cats (1577–1660) and Jan Luiken (1649–1712). A series of wars with England inspired British

anti-Dutch propaganda, the best known example of which was a poem by Andrew Marvell entitled *The Character of Holland* (1651). Marvell insulted the people of the Netherlands by comparing them to the silt on which they lived, which he called "indigested vomit of the sea." The court of William III (1650–1702) drew upon the services of the prolific engraver Romeyn de Hooghe (1645–1708) and the epic poet Lucas Rotgans (1654–1710); William's formidable propaganda arsenal proved its worth during the Glorious Revolution, following which William III became king of England in 1689.

The ideas of the French Enlightenment, popularized in the Netherlands by writers such as Joan Derck van der Capellen (1741–1784) and newspapers like *Politieke Kruijer* (Political Courier; 1783–1787), sowed the seeds of opposition to the rule of the House of Orange. Many welcomed the occupation of the Netherlands by a French revolutionary army in 1795. France established the Batavian Republic (again harking back to the classical history of the region), which lasted until 1806. Napoleon created the kingdom of Holland as a throne for his brother, Louis. In 1814 the Congress of Vienna restored the ancient Grand Duchy of Luxembourg in the south and combined the United Provinces of the Netherlands with the former Austrian territories (Belgium) under a restored House of Orange.

In 1830 Belgium declared its independence from the Netherlands. Britain intervened to prevent Dutch reconquest. Belgium industrialized rapidly and produced a lively socialist movement. The Second International (1889) established an International Socialist Bureau in Brussels under Émile Vandervelde (1866–1938), which nurtured the left-wing and trade union movement across Europe. Vandervelde served as Belgium's foreign minister in the 1920s. Belgian politics included a conflict between church and liberal factions over education and the struggle of the Flemish population to assert its language within the Walloon-dominated (and French-speaking) government; the year 1898 saw a major victory, as Flemish translations of laws were finally declared as valid as those in French. State propaganda gambits included the staging of and participation in fairs, a tradition that lived on into the twentieth century, most memorably in the Brussels World's Fair of 1958. In part for reasons of prestige, the Belgian crown obtained colonies in the Congo basin in West Africa; propaganda exposing colonial excesses included the novel *Heart of Darkness* (1898) by Polish-born novelist Joseph Conrad (1857–1924).

Despite their status of neutrality, in 1914 the German army invaded the Low Countries and occupied them for the duration of World War I, much of which was fought on Belgian soil. German occupation propaganda in Belgium followed a strategy called *Flamenpolitik,* which targeted the Flemish speakers and promoted their division from the French. The suffering of "gallant little Belgium" became a major issue in British war propaganda at home and abroad, especially in the United States. The United States also emphasized the theme after joining the war in 1917. Belgium was somewhat disappointed that the wealth of wartime Allied sympathy did not translate into peacetime support and attempted to sustain its wartime image well into the 1920s. Following the war, Belgium abandoned neutrality and formed a political alliance with France and an economic union with Luxembourg. Active anti-German propagandists during the war included Louis Raemakers (1869–1956), the cartoonist of the Amsterdam newspaper *Telegraaf,* whose work became famous in British and, later, American newspapers.

In 1927 the Netherlands became the first European country to begin regular short-wave radio broadcasts when the Philips Corporation inaugurated radio service to the Dutch East Indies (now Indonesia). Multilanguage services followed the next year. The station had the call sign PCJ, which an enterprising announcer (Edward Startz) claimed stood for Peace, Cheer, and Joy. Radio Lux-embourg, a station founded by an international consortium with the blessing of the grand duke, came on the air in 1934 with an immensely powerful medium-frequency signal. The station caused a headache for the BBC since it challenged the corporation's monopoly over the British news. Despite this, Radio Luxembourg enjoyed a close relationship with British intelligence. With Britain hiding behind the official neutrality of Radio Luxembourg, the station became a mechanism for black propaganda. During and following the Munich crisis of September 1938, the British used Radio Luxembourg to broadcast German translations of key statements and appeals. Hence the words of the British prime minister Neville Chamberlain (1869–1940) and U.S. President Franklin D. Roosevelt (1882–1945) reached the German people directly through an "innocent" station just ten miles across the frontier, which, unlike the BBC, was audible on most German radio sets.

The Great Depression produced small but extreme right-wing movements in the Low Countries. In the Netherlands A. A. Mussert (1894–1946) founded the National Socialist Beweging (Movement; NSB); in francophone Belgium Léon Degrelle (1906–1994) formed the catholic Rexist movement; Flanders (Flemish Belgium) produced the *De Vlag* (the flag) movement. Degrelle, a charismatic speaker and writer, achieved a modest degree of electoral success in 1936. His propaganda outlet included the daily newspaper *Le Pays Réel* (The Real Country). In April 1940, following a sustained propaganda campaign of intimidation, Nazi Germany invaded the Low Countries. The indigenous far right proved eager collaborators, and Degrelle formed the SS Brigade Wallonie, which he led on the eastern front. The nationalistic message of the Rexists and the NSB was compromised by their cooperation with Nazi rule. Elements of the region's media continued to operate under the Nazis, including Belgium's famous cartoonist Hergé, the pseudonym of Georges Rémi (1907–1983), who introduced anti-America (and arguably anti-Semitic) material into his Tin-Tin story "The Shooting Star."

Belgian resistance included the symbolic emblazoning of the letter "V" for victory on walls, one of the best known examples of graffiti as propaganda. In London the BBC adapted the "V" as part of it propaganda campaign aimed at occupied Europe, and the "V" hand gesture became the trademark of Winston Churchill (1874–1965). The Dutch government-in-exile in London broadcast home over the BBC as Radio Oranje (Radio Orange). The Nazis suspended prewar Dutch broadcasting (which had been organized along sectarian lines by associations such as the Katholieke Radio Omroep (KRO; Catholic Radio Broadcasting), creating a single counterpropaganda station aimed at the Dutch public, which was first called Rijksradio Om-roep (State Radio Broadcasting) and later Nederlandsche Omroep (Netherlands Broadcasting). When this failed to capture much of an audience, the Nazis confiscated all radios. Most citizens either handed over their old radios or improvised homemade sets, thereby maintaining a substantial audience for Radio Oranje from London. As the liberation of Europe began in 1944, Radio Luxembourg became a major weapon in Allied radio propaganda to Germany, while Dutch broadcasters established a radio station in the liberated portion of their country called Radio Herrijzend Nederland (Radio Resurrected Netherlands) that broadcast into German-occupied territory. In 1947 this station formally became the multilingual Radio Netherlands International, which played an important role during the Cold War. The sectarian broadcasting associations resumed their prewar role in the postwar Netherlands, extending operations into the new field of television.

Following a second experience of wartime occupation in a generation, the Low Countries became key advocates of European security through cooperation and eventually union. The three countries joined NATO in 1949 (with Belgium hosting the headquarters) and formed the Benelux union in 1958. The Netherlands played a prominent role in the Cold War antinuclear movement, generating major opposition to the deployment of American cruise missiles in the 1980s. In Belgium language played a key role as both a vehicle of and issue in propaganda. Belgium developed two separate broadcasting systems—one in Flemish and one in French—each with its own international divisions. A 1962 law sought to broker a compromise by recognizing the Brussels region as bilingual, Flemish as the official language of Flanders, and French as the official language of Wallonia (including separate rights for German speakers); but the issue remained unresolved and in 1968 it brought down the government. In 1993 the three regions gained even more autonomy under a new constitution.

Nicholas J. Cull

See also Art; Exhibitions and World's Fairs; International; Latin America; Marshall Plan; Radio (International); Raemakers, Louis; Reformation and Counter-Reformation

References: Conway, Martin. *Collaboration in Belgium: Léon Degrelle and the Rexist Movement, 1940–1944.* New Haven, CT: Yale University Press, 1993; Israel, Jonathan. *The Dutch Republic: Its Rise, Greatness and Fall, 1477–1806.* Oxford: Oxford University Press, 1995; Kossmann, E. H. *The Low Countries, 1780–1940.* Oxford: Oxford University Press, 1978; Schama, Simon. *The Embarrassment of Riches: An Interpretation of Dutch Culture in the Golden Age.* London: Collins, 1987; Schama, Simon. *Patriots and Liberators: Revolution in the Netherlands, 1780–1813.* London: Collins, 1977; Taylor, Philip M. *British Propaganda in the Twentieth Century: Selling Democracy.* Edinburgh: Edinburgh University Press, 1999; Wansink, H., ed. *The Apologie of William of Orange Against the Proclamation of the King of Spaine.* Leiden: Brill, 1969.

New Zealand

The New Zealand press began in 1840, the year Britain assumed sovereignty over the country. From the start newspaper proprietors were interested in serving their communities by printing classified advertisements and news. But news was a scarce commodity in settlements that, until the end of the 1860s, often remained isolated for months at a time. The raison d'être for the newspapers was persuasion, propaganda favoring a particular political view. Newspaper proprietors were deeply involved in the political life of the colony, and their newspapers were there to ensure that the development of the nascent country took an acceptable form. From Wellington *The New Zealand Gazette and Wellington Spectator* argued the case for the New Zealand Company, a private, colonizing enterprise always at odds with the Crown Colony Government. In the north, first from Russell and then from Auckland, *The New Zealand Advertiser* and various successor journals were short-lived since they dared to present settlers' views before being closed down by the Crown Colony Government— in the early years the owner of the only printing press in the region.

Beginning in the mid-1840s, two newspapers were advocates for the Crown Colony Government. The rest were firmly allied with the settlers and led the charge for self-government, a provincial form of which was granted by the British Parliament in 1852. From that point on newspapers became allies of individual politicians. In all provinces leading politicians owned or otherwise controlled the local newspapers. It was accepted as proper that the task of a newspaper was partisan political propaganda in support of its politician-owner. If one did not agree with a paper's politics, the alternative was to start one's own and not question the propriety of partisan journalism. The 1860s saw the appearance of a new type of commercially oriented and economically profitable journalism, which coincided with the spread of the telegraph and steamer-based shipping, as well as a general surge in the population. It emphasized news and a doctrine of objectivity while resting securely and independently on the financial base of advertising revenues.

Advertising managers, and later advertising agencies and display advertising, became influential in determining the success or failure of a newspaper. A style of journalism developed that purported to speak for the entire community while at the same time continuing to represent a decidedly partisan political understanding of the proper course for the country. Moreover, the new commercial journalism was gradually seen as itself a form of propaganda, both politically partisan and supportive of a particular economic understanding of the country's future.

Journalism among the Maori, the indigenous population, was mainly concerned with convincing the Maori of the advantages of European settlement. A variety of publications, the best known being *Te Karere Maori* (Maori Messenger), were sponsored by the government. Most were written in Maori, an oral language that took a written form soon after the arrival of missionaries early in the nineteenth century. Literacy—though not Christianity—was immediately embraced by the Maori; in the mid-nineteenth century the Maori had higher literacy rates than the European population. Arguably the first genuine Maori newspaper was *Te Hikioi o Nui Tirini e Rere atu na* (The War Bird of New Zealand Soaring Above), which began publication in 1861 in support of Maori nationalism. Its advocacy was countered by a government newspaper, *Te Pihoihoi Mokemoke i Runga i te Tuanui* (The Lonely Sparrow on the Housetop). The latter had a short existence; its printing press was seized and its offices were sacked by Waikato Maori. This act of defiance helped to start the Waikato war, during which *Te Hikioi* also ceased publication, its lead type melted down and reconfigured as musketshot.

The country's various daily newspapers gradually coordinated their efforts and formed press associations. In the 1870s political input remained strong, with the first national association under the control of the prime minister, Julius Vogel. However, this marked a turning point for such direct control of the press. Member newspapers regularly complained that press telegrams "are supervised with paternal care in high places." Gradually commercial imperatives and a wider political ideology neutralized the newspapers' ability to offer unwavering support for individual politicians. Beginning in 1880 the country's newspapers formed a cooperative press association that provided a cheap and reliable news source while protecting individual newspapers from competition. Only one current daily, Wellington's *Dominion,* has been established since that date. New Zealand newspapers represented a cohesive conservative force united in their opposition to new political developments, especially those having to do with socialism and the politics of the developing Labour movement. For example, a press association directive in 1919 required newspapers not to report anarchist utterances nor to help spread the creeds of Bolshevism and the International Workers of the World movement. Newspapers presented views supportive of government policy and suppressed alternative views. This practice was most noticeable during World War I, when the press collaborated with government and the military to publish propaganda for the assumed good of the country and its war effort. Such efforts were not peculiar to New Zealand, resulting in general postwar disillusionment with the newsprint medium.

The introduction of film gave New Zealanders a new source of entertainment, providing a glimpse of activities in the rest of the world—but it also brought a strict system of censorship to ensure that the New Zealander's eye was not opened too widely. Censorship was cultural, moral, and political and was regularly fueled by moral crises over the supposed injurious influences of the new medium. The decisions of the censor—a "clean, average man" according to the minister—could not be appealed until the 1930s.

The start of radio broadcasting in the 1920s was accompanied by a concern that broadcasting be used for cultural elevation. Classical music and English programming were favored, with alternative fare suppressed. In particular, popular music, along with programs from the United States—especially the new genre of radio serials—gained public favor but official opprobrium. Indeed, only in the 1960s did popular programming from the United States gain official acceptance. Radio's introduction was also accompanied by a regulation that the new medium "shall not be used for the dissemination of propaganda of a controversial nature." The regulation was interpreted strictly and resulted in the absence of news and serious discussion from the airwaves. Even sermons were jammed during religious broadcasts when such controversial topics as the prohibition of alcohol or the reading of the Bible in schools were mentioned. The most famous cases occurred during the 1930s, when figures such as Major (Clifford Hugh) Douglas (1879–1952), the advocate for Social Credit, and the Indian philosopher Krishnamurti (1895–1986) were denied the right to broadcast. Only George Bernard Shaw (1856–1950), a man of enormous stature in the English-speaking world, was considered beyond the state's ability to censure. In a famous radio talk in 1934, which caused much embarrassment for his broadcasting hosts, Shaw admirably argued that New Zealand was a communist nation second only to Russia. The most important instance of government censorship for New Zealanders took place during the 1935 election campaign, when broadcasts from 1ZB, a private Auckland station, were jammed on the eve of the election, while support was voiced for the Labour Party, which won the election—its first victory.

Propaganda took a new turn when the government nationalized all radio stations in order to create a new government department intended to counter opposition from the country's newspapers. Direct broadcasts of parliamentary proceedings were introduced—a first. Less positively, the new government began its own news service. News broadcasts were prepared in the prime minister's office and were required to be broadcast without any alterations. There was no secrecy about the practice, with Michael Joseph Savage (1872–1940), Labour's inaugural prime minister, openly acknowledging this method of bringing his government's message to the people. "Propaganda of a controversial nature" was banned from radio, with the meaning of the term defined politically, thereby effectively denying broadcasting rights to government opponents. Even after the defeat of the Labour government in 1949, the incoming National government, a conservative alternative, continued the practice, along with daily control of all programming. Examples of the practice are legion. Among the most significant were the broadcasts in support of military conscription during the 1949 conscription referendum. Both press and radio were fulsome in their support of the proposal. Peter Fraser (1884–1950), the Labour prime minister, initially refused to permit conscription opponents to broadcast. Eventually he granted them some airtime while ensuring that it remained ineffective by nominating those groups that could broadcast and vetting their material. The National government illustrated its willingness to use similar tactics during the 1951 waterfront dispute, one of New Zealand's longest-lasting and most bitter industrial battles. It introduced emergency regulations stipulating that both radio stations and newspapers were available only to government supporters. These laws made it a criminal offense to offer opposing views.

The system was overturned in the 1960s, a decade that saw not only the advent of television broadcasting but also the political acceptance that broadcasting should be controlled by an independent corporation rather than by a government department. The emergence of public broadcasting also introduced the view that news broadcasts were a proper activity for broadcasters. Independent news broadcasts matured during this decade. They were also of considerable influence on the country's newspapers. Responding to the increased competition, they permitted a broader range of journalism. A new freedom of expression swept the country, which was further extended in broadcasting with the advent of private radio. This began forcefully with the Auckland station *Radio Hauraki,* which began life as a pirate, broadcasting from offshore international waters. Its popularity resulted in a grudging political acceptance and, beginning in 1970, a shore-based future. Any further extension of private broadcasting was restrained by successive governments and was only extended to television in 1989. That move was part of a radical reordering of government activities in the belief that much of what had previously been considered proper state activity was best conducted privately.

Since that change, ownership of New Zealand newspapers, radio, and television has increasingly shifted to the same international corporations that are dominant in many other countries. The various media have expanded beyond anything previously imagined, thanks to the introduction of computers, communications satellites, and fiber-optic technology. In broadcasting, local programming is essentially funded by the state Broadcasting Commission. While the political slanting of news and programming has not disappeared, a new emphasis has emerged in which international interests—from sports, fashion, and entertainment to news, fast food, and a consumer lifestyle—and greater advocacy of globalization have become dominant voices. Propaganda has expanded, moving from political advocacy and the suppression of alternatives to a wholesale endorsement of a new way of life.

Patrick Day

See also Australia; British Empire; Censorship; Environmentalism; Pacific/Oceania; World War I

References: Day, Patrick. *The Making of the New Zealand Press.* Wellington, NZ: Victoria University Press, 1990; ———. *The Radio Years: A History of Broadcasting in New Zealand.* Vol. 1. Auckland, NZ: Auckland University

Press: 1994; ———. *Voice and Vision: A History of Broadcasting in New Zealand.* Vol. 2. Auckland, NZ: Auckland University Press, 2000; Meiklejohn, G. M. *Early Conflicts of Press and Government.* Auckland, NZ: Wilson and Horton, 1954; Scholefield, G. H. *Newspapers in New Zealand,* Wellington, NZ: A. H. and A. W. Reed, 1958; Watson, Chris, and Roy Shuker. *In the Public Good? Censorship in New Zealand.* Palmerston North, NZ: Dunmore, 1998; Williams, John F. *Anzacs, the Media and the Great War.* Sydney: University of New South Wales Press, 1999.

Nixon, Richard (1913–1994)

Coming from a poor family, in 1946 Richard Nixon entered politics as a Republican congressman representing Southern California. In 1948 he came to national attention for his role in exposing Alger Hiss (1904–1996) as a former Communist in hearings conducted by the House Committee on Un-American Activities. Nixon was elected to the U.S. Senate in 1950. In 1952 he served as Dwight D. Eisenhower's (1890–1969) vice-presidential running mate. In 1960 Nixon lost his bid for the U.S. presidency to John F. Kennedy. Undaunted, Nixon ran again and was elected president, serving from 1969 to 1974. Facing conviction on three impeachable offenses relating to a failed attempt on 17 June 1972 to bug the Democratic National Committee headquarters (at the Watergate apartment building—hence the appellation "Watergate affair"), Nixon resigned the presidency on 9 August 1974.

Nixon's career as propagandist is closely tied to the medium of television. He first appeared on national television on 23 September 1952 to defend his integrity in what has become known as the "Checkers" speech (during which he adroitly introduced a red herring near the end of the broadcast by promising that his daughters would not return a black-and-white cocker spaniel named Checkers sent to Nixon as a gift). In 1960, now a front runner, Nixon agreed to a series of four one-hour televised debates with John F. Kennedy, his less-well-known

Richard Nixon, official presidential photograph. (Library of Congress)

Democratic opponent. Nixon was widely thought to have lost the first round because of his evident discomfort before the cameras—something that was easy to see but not to hear, as radio listeners attested. Television covered Nixon's tearful farewell speech to his White House staff on the morning of 9 August 1974, an emotional moment in which Nixon came as close as he ever would to apologizing for the Watergate cover-up, which he admitted having orchestrated. A now-obsolete technology provided the evidence that forced Nixon's resignation: voice-activated tapes recorded every conversation held in the Oval Office; it is unclear what kept Nixon from destroying these tapes of his. Although Nixon is remembered for his strong stand against Communism, in time he may also be thought of as a prime example of the long-term survivor in American politics, as well as a pioneer in the use of television as a medium of political persuasion.

David Culbert

See also Cartoons; Elections (United States); Kennedy, John F.

References: Ambrose, Stephen E. *Nixon.* 3 vols. New York: Simon and Schuster/Touchstone, 1991; Bernstein, Carl, and Robert Woodward. *All the President's Men.* New York: Simon and Schuster/Touchstone, 1974; Kutler, Stanley I. *Abuse of Power: The New Nixon Tapes.* New York: Simon and Schuster/Touchstone, 1997; Nixon, Richard. *Six Crises.* New York: Simon and Schuster/Touchstone, 1990.

Northcliffe, Lord (1865–1922)

A pioneer of the popular press in Britain and propagandist during World War I, over the course of his long career he built up a publishing empire that included regional newspapers—he reshaped the British press by introducing such American techniques as banner headlines—as well as a host of popular educational and self-improvement books.

Born Alfred Harmsworth in Ireland, and raised in London, he plunged into journalism immediately after leaving school. In 1896 he launched the *Daily Mail* and in 1908 he bought the London *Times.* In 1917 he led the British War Mission to the United States, using publicity to consolidate the transatlantic alliance. In 1918 he directed Britain's propaganda offensive against the Central Powers: the Department of Enemy Propaganda, located in London's Crewe House, which many observers, including Adolf Hitler (1889–1945), claimed played a major role in destroying German and Austrian morale. Displaying alarming symptoms of nervous collapse, he died shortly after war's end. Lord Northcliffe's service at Crewe House ensured that for the generation following World War I his name would become synonymous with propaganda, as that of Joseph Goebbels (1897–1845) was for the generation following World War II.

Nicholas J. Cull

See also Austrian Empire; Britain; Morale; Psychological Warfare; World War I
References: Pound, Reginald, and Geoffrey Harmsworth. *Northcliffe.* London: Cassell, 1959; Sanders, Michael, and Philip M. Taylor. *British Propaganda During the First World War.* London: Macmillan, 1982.

Norway

See Scandinavia

Novel

Fictional narratives, a key mode of human expression, have played their part in the story of propaganda. Early examples of novels used as propaganda include religiously inspired works such as John Bunyan's (1628–1688) *Pilgrim's Progress* (1678) and political satires such as Jonathan Swift's (1667–1745) *Gulliver's Travels* (1726). In the nineteenth century the novel became a vehicle for emerging nationalist aspirations (especially in Latin America and Eastern Europe). It was also used to propound reformist messages, such as Harriet Beecher Stowe's (1811–1896) *Uncle Tom's Cabin* (1852), which dramatized the evils of slavery. The works of Émile Zola (1840–1902) in France and Charles Dickens (1812–1870) in Britain revealed the need for social reform. The British labor movement drew inspiration from *The Ragged Trousered Philanthropists* (1914) by Robert Tressell, the pen name of the Irish-born working-class novelist Robert Noonan (1870–1911).

In the twentieth century those opposing war have been particularly well served by novels, the classic example being Erich Maria Remarque's (1898–1970) *All Quiet on the Western Front* (1928). In the United States Ernest Hemingway (1899–1961) wrote in support of the cause of the Spanish Republic in the Spanish Civil War. John Steinbeck (1902–1968) highlighted the misery of the dust bowl migrants in *The Grapes of Wrath* (1939). More controversially, Eugene Burdick and William Lederer's *The Ugly American* (1958) argued in favor of American counterinsurgency operations in Vietnam and helped build a consensus for U.S. intervention in that country. Novels were also an important means of expressing dissent within the Soviet Union. The regime sought to suppress the works of dissident novelists like Boris Pasternak (1890–1960), author of *Doctor Zhivago* (1958), and Alexander Solzhenitsyn (1918–), author of *The Gulag Archipelago* (1973). Their works were published in the West, were circulated clandestinely in the USSR, and frequently figured in radio broadcasts beamed back to Russia over stations such as RFE/RL. More recently, the Islamic regime in Iran denounced *The Satanic Verses* (1989) by Salman Rushdie (1947–), calling it blasphemy and placing a death sentence (in absentia) on its author.

While the novel has had a distinguished history as an oppositional medium, literary criticism has demonstrated the extent to which novels have also underpinned the dominant cultural order in terms of racial, class, and gender stereotyping. In his book *Culture and Imperialism* (1994) Edward Said (1935–) argued that much European literature—including Jane Austen's *Mansfield Park* (1814), Joseph Conrad's *Heart of Darkness* (1898), and Albert Camus's *L'Étranger* (The Stranger; 1942)—implicitly bolstered imperialism.

Nicholas J. Cull

See also *All Quiet on the Western Front;* Austrian Empire; Britain (Eighteenth Century); British Empire; Caribbean; Censorship; Defoe, Daniel; Japan; Latin America; Mexico; Orwell, George; Ottoman Empire/Turkey; Peace and Antiwar Movements (1500–1945); Peace and Antiwar Movements (1945–); Russia; *Uncle Tom's Cabin;* United States (1930s); United States (Progressive Era)

References: Foulkes, A. P. *Literature and Propaganda.* London: Methuen, 1983; Said, Edward. *Culture and Imperialism.* New York: Knopf, 1994; Thompson, Oliver. *Easily Led: A History of Propaganda.* Stroud, UK: Sutton, 1999.

O

Oates, Titus (1649–1705)

English anti-Catholic propagandist, cleric, and convicted perjurer, Oates was born in Rutland. His early career gave ample indication of his fondness for lying. He was expelled from school, discharged from service as a naval chaplain, and narrowly escaped a term in jail for libel. In the mid-1670s he fell in with Israel Tonge (1621–1680) and the two men became fixated on the danger of Catholicism to the crown of England. Following a false conversion and a period spent in Jesuit colleges in France and Spain to gather evidence, in 1678 Oates established himself as England's foremost authority on the Catholic conspiracy, spreading his ideas through a stream of leaflets and at public meetings. Specifically, Oates alleged that the Jesuit order planned to murder King Charles II (1630–1685) and substitute his brother, James, to rule England in his place. His allegations caused a sensation at court—especially after the magistrate to whom Oates had presented his allegations was found murdered. With London in an uproar, the king granted Oates a fat pension. The search for conspirators now began in earnest. Some thirty-five people were executed during the course of the investigation. By 1680 the popular fever for the "Vile Popish Plot" had passed and Oates had lost credibility. In 1685 Oates was convicted of perjury and sentenced to life imprisonment, with an annual public pillorying and flogging. He was freed in the wake of the English Revolution, married a rich widow, and lived out his life on a state pension. The career of Titus Oates, like that of Sen. Joseph McCarthy (1909–1957) in the twentieth century, demonstrates what a demagogue can achieve when building on existing suspicion.

Nicholas J. Cull

See also Britain; Fakes; McCarthy, Joseph R.; Reformation and Counter-Reformation; Religion

References: Kenyon, John. *The Popish Plot.* London: Heinemann, 1972; Lane, Jane. *Titus Oates: The First Biography.* London: Andrew Dakers, 1949.

Okhrana

The Russian tsarist security police was initially formed by Tsar Ivan IV—Ivan the Terrible (1530–1584)—to serve as his personal bodyguard. The Okhrana (like its postrevolutionary extensions) was not so much a propaganda organ as an antipropaganda institution. Nonetheless this supposedly secret organization was very keen to project an image of all-pervasive, ruthless power. Its functions included infiltrating revolutionary or seditious groups and generally harassing any group that could be seen as a threat to tsarist hegemony. When not contributing to the general fear ingrained in the Russian ruling class, much of the Okhrana's time and effort was expended in seizing and preventing the distribution of dangerous materials. Although the organization was known by various names under Nicholas I's reign (1825–1855), it was referred to as the "third section"—Okhrana remained the generic term. The golden age of the Okhrana began in 1881 with the "Reaction" to the attempt on the life of Alexander III (r. 1881–1894). Okhrana activity increased again in 1912–1914 concomitant with an increase in labor unrest following the assassination of Petr Stolypin (1862–1911), the minister of the interior. Okhrana agents were undoubtedly working behind the scenes; the massacre of workers in Siberia's gold fields was caused by agents provocateurs. The Okhrana filed reports of peasant unrest in 1916 and of the actions of revolutionary groups in February 1917. Although the organization was officially disbanded by the provisional government, its traditions were revived in 1918 by the Cheka and, later, the KGB.

Graham Roberts

See also KGB; *Protocols of the Elders of Zion;* Revolution, Russian; Russia

References: Smith, Edward Ellis. *The Okhrana.* Stanford, CA: Hoover Institution, 1967; Zuckerman, Frederic. *The Tsarist Secret Police in Russian Society, 1880–1917.* Basingstoke, UK: Macmillan, 1996.

Olympics (1896–)

The first modern Olympic Games were held in Athens in 1896. The games were largely the brainchild of a Frenchman, Baron Pierre de Coubertin (1863–1937), who certainly had a political agenda in mind. He saw the revival of the ancient Olympics as a way of promoting peace among nations through a friendly sports competition. His ideas reflected the coming together of many nineteenth-century ideals. European liberalism believed in free and unbridled discourse among nations, which, it was hoped, would promote peace, happiness, and progress worldwide. The development of "Muscular Christianity" encouraged the idea of "manly" godliness. "Christian Gentlemen" sought to improve and test themselves in the pursuit of physical excellence. The games were consequently full of symbolic import, reflecting the dominant ideals of the Western world at that moment in history.

Given the British obsession with sports, it is perhaps unsurprising that de Coubertin's inspiration came as much from Britain as it did from ancient Greece. He was much impressed with the Much Wenlock Olympian Games, initiated by Dr. William Penny Brooks (1809–1895) in 1850, which he witnessed in 1889. The first few games remain rather hazy affairs. Though competitors were nominally connected with national teams, there was a greater feeling of individual effort and competition. By the 1908 games, which were held in London, the concept of the national team was beginning to take shape. The Olympics thus became an important stage for propaganda—and hence were more highly politicized—as nations sought to stress the virtues of their own society. The International Olympic Committee (IOC) and the various national committees have always denied this combination, but the conjunction of the two is difficult to ignore.

In 1920 the games took place in Antwerp, marking the rehabilitation of Belgium after the devastation of the Great War. The IOC banned Germany, Austria, Hungary, and Bulgaria from competing. Germany returned in 1928 for the games in Amsterdam. After World War II international political statements and the Olympics became even more intimately linked. The 1964 games were awarded to Tokyo, marking Japan's return to the fold as a rehabilitated nation, and introduced the world to the Japanese economic miracle. This was also the year in which South Africa was banned in response to its apartheid laws. The next games, held in Mexico in 1968, were used as an overt propaganda platform. Mexican students rioted to protest the money lavished on the games while the poor starved. Several black American athletes also used the opportunity to give the black power salute during the medal ceremony in order to highlight the problems of racism in U.S. society. Four years later in 1972 Palestinian terrorists used the Munich games to highlight their cause by kidnapping members of the Israeli team; nine Israeli athletes died as a result of the kidnap attempt and bungled rescue.

The most overtly political and propagandist games in modern times were those held in Berlin in 1936. The Nazi government invested vast sums in the games, believing it would provide an excellent test of Nazi racial theories. Stage-managed to the hilt, the games introduced a significant innovation. Dr. Carl Diem (1882–1962) had the idea of bringing the Olympic torch from Mount Olympus itself. In July 1936 fifteen Greek maidens—clad in short tunics imitating the robes of the priestesses of ancient Olympia—gathered at dawn on the plain by the mountain. The rays of the morning sun, reflected off a concave mirror, lit the torch. A relay of runners then brought the torch to Berlin. The imagery was unmistakable: Nazi Germany was hereby claiming for itself the legacy of ancient Greece as the home of civilization and defender of Western ideals. The games were given added propaganda value by filmmaker Leni Riefenstahl (1902–) in her brilliant film *Olympia* (1938). Today the games are best remembered for the performance of African American athlete Jesse Owens (1913–1980), who won four gold medals and almost single-handedly deflated Nazi racial arrogance.

Beginning in 1945, the Olympics became a stage for the Cold War, though the USSR first joined the games as late as 1952 in Helsinki. At times the games appeared as if their sole intention was to pit the United States against the Eastern bloc; it was clear that the press was most interested in this aspect. In 1956 the Melbourne games were dominated by the Soviet invasion of Hungary, which led to the first boycott in modern Olympic history, when the Dutch, Spanish, and Swiss teams refused to take part. Matters reached their nadir in 1980, when the United States led a boycott of the Moscow games in response to the Soviet invasion of Afghanistan. Sixty-three nations stayed away, including West Germany, Japan, China, and Canada. At the opening ceremonies many nations made a propaganda statement by using the Olympic flag instead of their national flag and by performing the Olympic hymn instead of their national anthem during the medals ceremonies. The tit-for-tat response came in 1984 when much of the Eastern bloc boycotted the Los Angeles games. These games were notable for their overt show-biz razzmatazz and promotion of the "American Way of Life." Full-blooded capitalism and nationalism were everywhere as many of the European nations, in particular, complained that the American press and television did not appear to notice that any other nation was taking part. The whole thing was a triumph of Reaganism. Controversy had still not died down by 1988, when the next games were held in South Korea, a state much of the Eastern bloc did not recognize, though most of its member countries did attend. The Seoul games sought to reproduce the success of Tokyo in 1964, but the result actually had more in common with the Mexico games, for prodemocracy activists staged protests to use the extra media attention to their advantage.

The millennial games were held in Sydney in September 2000. The choice marked the importance of the Pacific Rim to the world economy and also gave Australia an opportunity to project a new multicultural image. The IOC awarded the 2004 games to Athens, and in 2001 it voted to hold the 2008 games in Beijing. The decision promised to deliver a propaganda coup for the Chinese government, but it also prompted a storm of criticism concerning China's abysmal human rights record.

Mark Connelly

See also Cold War; Exhibitions and World's Fairs; Germany; Greece; Japan; Korea; Mexico; Satellite Communications; Spain; Sport

References: Buchanan, Ian, and Bill Mallon. *Historical Dictionary of the Olympic Movement.* Lanham, MD: Scarecrow, 1995; Espy, Richard. *The Politics of the Olympic Games.* 2d ed. Berkeley: University of California Press, 1981; Hargreaves, Jenny, ed. *Sport, Culture and Ideology.* London: Routledge, 1982; Kanin, David B. *A Political History of the Olympic Games.* Boulder, CO: Westview, 1981; MacAloon, John J. *This Great Symbol: Pierre de Coubertin and the Origins of the Modern Olympic Games.* Chicago: University of Chicago Press, 1981; Manheim, Jarol B. *Strategic Public Diplomacy and American Foreign Policy: The Evolution of Influence.* New York: Oxford University Press, 1994; Senn, Alfred Erich. *Power, Politics and the Olympic Games.* Champaign, IL: Human Kinetics, 1999.

Opinion Polls

Formal surveys of public opinion first appeared in the 1930s and have since become a central feature of democratic government. They can set an agenda for propaganda, showing how and when the public needs to be persuaded, but they can also be part of propaganda itself since slanted or loaded questions or polls cited out of context can be used to sway the public. Many nations ban polling in the period immediately preceding an election.

Napoleon once famously remarked: "Power is based on opinion. What is a government not supported by opinion? Nothing." Theoretically democracy is the political expression of mass opinion according to which a government should respond to the popular will. In reality the relationship is far more complex. In a democratic state the views of ordinary members of society are taken into account. The government and its institutions must be shown as representative of the majority of individuals through a sampling of individual opinion. This democratic process centers on the idea of "public opinion," which since the mid-twentieth century has been conducted through polling. The concept of public opinion, however, is problematic, for there is no such thing as a single opinion or public. Public opinion may be distinguished from "norms" or "customs." Its effectiveness in bringing about change depends on the political and societal context in which it operates. Nevertheless polling has become increasingly sophisticated, particularly in specialized areas like voting behavior, and is now generally accepted as representing public attitudes across a wide range of issues. There have been occasions when opinion polls have turned out to be completely misleading, most notably the 1948 and 1960 U.S. presidential elections and the British general election of 1970.

Opinion polling is both a commercial activity and a political intervention staged within the media. Political polling in the broadest sense is undertaken largely by specialized firms commissioned by newspapers, television, political parties, and other interest groups. The polls that influence public perceptions and debate are those that appear in the mass media. By the 1930s there was a growing recognition that participation in the war, coupled with greater access to education and the extension of the franchise, legitimized mass participation in the democratic process. The question was to determine how public opinion could be measured and acted upon. In 1935 George Gallup (1901–1984), a professor of journalism and director of research for the advertising agency Young and Rubicam, founded the American Institute of Public Opinion Research. The following year British anthropologist Tom Harrison and journalist Charles Madge founded Mass Observation. Although much of its material was unscientific when compared to Gallup's organization, Mass Observation's findings added a new dimension to social investigation and public attitudes, one that was coopted by the British government during World War II as a means of gauging civilian morale. As historian Thomas E. Mahl has shown, while the United States was still neutral, British intelligence successfully penetrated the Gallup organization and subtly manipulated polls in order to undermine the popular isolationist position and stimulate a "bandwagon" of support for Britain.

Despite the remarkable growth in both the use and accuracy of public opinion surveys since the mid-1930s, some problems remain. Public opinion polls have a natural appeal in a democratic society. While many political figures claim to speak for the people, or maintain that "pubic opinion will not support a particular course of action," opinion polls let the people speak for themselves. At best, polling can amplify the public's voice so that it may be heard over the clamor of special interests. As George Gallup claimed: "Public opinion research is a necessary and valuable aid to a truly representative government." However, since the mid-1970s the number of polls conducted and reported has increased exponentially. Rather than providing clarity, this wealth of polling data can actually distort the public's voice. Moreover, an underlying assumption is that public attitudes as expressed through opinion polls reflects a rational process, whereby the public makes decisions after all the facts are known. Yet most important public decisions result from crises that demand immediate action to effect some crudely defined yet necessary goal—with the full knowledge that all the facts are not known. On many issues large segments of the public want only a result and have no definite view about how to achieve it; for example, the public wants peace, but individuals may not feel that they have greater insight into how to achieve peace than their elected officials. Thus, the relationship between the public's view, at a specified moment, about what the government does is far from a mirror image. Another problem with opinion polls is that the public's response to an issue may change daily and be wildly inconsistent. George Bush (1924–) allegedly decided to end the Gulf War (1991) after seeing a poll

showing that the American public wanted it to stop. A week later another poll indicated that a substantial number of voters now believed that the war should have been continued until Saddam Hussein (1937–) had been captured or deposed.

Opinion pollsters have long recognized that subtle changes in the wording of a question can produce dramatically different responses. For example, the percentage of Americans supporting aid for the contras in Nicaragua between 1983 and 1986 varied from 13 percent to 42 percent, depending on how the question was worded. If the question explicitly mentioned President Reagan (1911–) or the contras, more Americans supported the aid, whereas if the question mentioned the amount of the aid or presented both sides of the issue, fewer Americans supported aid to the rebels. Faulty or incomplete readings of survey results or problems with the surveys now generate as much research and analysis as the original opinion polls. In the 1990s—especially in Britain—governments increasingly used focus groups rather than the more unwieldy polls in such delicate matters as policy development.

David Welch

See also Elections; Elections (Britain); Elections (Israel); Morale

References: Gallup, George H. *The Gallup Poll: Public Opinion, 1935–1971.* New York: Random House, 1972; Hennessy, Bernard. *Public Opinion.* Monterey, CA: Brooks/Cole, 1985; Lippmann, Walter. *The Phantom Public.* Macmillan: London, 1953; Mahl, Thomas E. *Desperate Deception: British Covert Operations in the United States, 1939–44.* Washington, DC: Brasseys, 1998; Mills, C. Wright. *The Power Elite.* Oxford: Oxford University Press, 1956.

Orwell, George (1903–1950)

British novelist and sometime propagandist, Orwell (the pen name of Eric A. Blair) was born in India. He attended Eton College in England and then joined the Burma police force before launching a career as a left-wing writer and journalist. His writing was unashamedly political. "All art" he once wrote "is to some extent political." In his 1946 essay "Why I Write" he explained: "What I have most wanted to do . . . is to make political writing into an art." Orwell used his writing to raise public consciousness about such issues as poverty—in *Down and Out in Paris and London* (1933) and *The Road to Wigan Pier* (1937)—and the Spanish Civil War—in *Homage to Catalonia* (1938). During World War II he worked for the BBC Eastern Service, writing and producing propaganda broadcasts to Asia. His firsthand experience of censorship and intimate knowledge of such things as the 850-word language called Basic English which was occasionally used in BBC broadcasts—provided the foundation for his account of a future propaganda state in the novel *Nineteen Eighty-Four* (1949).

Orwell's experiences in the Spanish Civil War, during which the faction on whose side he fought (the POUM) was brutally suppressed on the orders of the Soviet Union, its supposed ally, instilled in him an enduring bitterness toward Stalin. In 1945 he published *Animal Farm,* an allegorical fable of the Russian Revolution. The novel was widely circulated during the Cold War, with the CIA subsidizing translations and even an animated film adaptation. Orwell was a willing participant in the propaganda campaign of the early Cold War, secretly briefing British intelligence on fellow writers whom he considered untrustworthy.

Nicholas J. Cull

See also Bracken, Brendan; Britain; CIA; Civil War, Spanish; Cold War; Novel

References: Crick, Bernard. *George Orwell: A Life.* London: Penguin, 1980; West, W. J. *Orwell: The War Commentaries.* New York: Pantheon, 1985.

Ottoman Empire/Turkey

The Ottoman Empire (named for the ruling Osmanli family) mobilized propaganda to facilitate its conquest and legitimize its dominion over a vast swath of Asia Minor, the Middle East, and the Balkans. It also inspired much propaganda from others, not least in Europe, where the Turkish threat remained a perennial theme. In the nineteenth century the sultan faced challenges from without and within, responding with a vigorous reassertion of state ideology. The Turkish national state that emerged from the ashes of the Great War produced one of the most impressive personality cults of the twentieth century, namely, that of Atatürk.

Following its capture of Constantinople in 1453, the Ottoman Empire used propaganda to hide the dynasty's nomadic origins, developing the ideological core of the empire as a potent fusion of Byzantine and Turkish traditions. Pageantry and architecture underpinned the image of ruler Mehmet II (1430–1481), who pointedly constructed his Topkapi Palace on the site of the Byzantine acropolis. The Ottomans prospered in the sixteenth century under rulers like Selim I (1467–1520) and his son, Suleyman I (1494–1566; known as Suleyman the Magnificent and Suleyman the Lawgiver). Selim I's propaganda strategies included his assumption of the title of caliph following his conquest of Egypt in 1517. In doing so the Ottoman emperor claimed both political and religious authority, assuming the role carried out in previous centuries by the immediate associates of the prophet Muhammad. Suleyman the Magnificent cultivated this connection, presenting the title of caliph as a counterweight to that of his Christian competitor, Charles V (1500–1558), the Holy Roman Emperor. The Ottoman Empire maintained an effective propaganda machine and a broad administrative network, which included a remarkable level of tolerance for non-Islamic religion and diverse cultural practices.

By the beginning of the nineteenth century the Ottoman Empire faced multiple challenges. In the Balkans the flame of the French Revolution had spread to Greece as well as other national groups, precipitating the Greek War of Independence (1821–1827). The Russians remained eager to roll back Ottoman power (as seen in the Russo-Turkish War of 1828–1829) and put themselves forward as champions of the Slav cause. In Arabia the teachings of Muhammad ibn Abd al-Wahab (1703–1791) roused followers to holy war against non-Arab rule. The Wahhabis remained a major challenge for much of the nineteenth century, reemerging in the early twentieth century to threaten the Ottoman hold on Arabia as the ideology behind Ibn Saud (1880–1953). The Egyptians defied the empire under the leadership of Muhammad Ali (1769–1849).

The empire responded by initiating reforms. Mahmud II (1785–1839), who became sultan in 1808, made broad use of internal propaganda. He adopted the non-Islamic practice of displaying his portrait in the manner of a European monarch and "guiding" the preaching of Friday sermons in mosques. The content of Mahmud II's propaganda included justification of the bloody annihilation in 1826 of the Janissary Corps, which had once been the heart of the Ottoman army; with its political power compounded by Shiite religious beliefs in the ranks, it was now viewed as a threat to the Sunni state. Following Mahmud II's death in 1839, his son, Sultan Abdülmecid (1823–1861), launched the first in a series of reforms known as the *Tanzimat* (reorganization). This period saw a flowering of "Young Ottoman" oppositional culture. Two individuals came to the fore: Ibrahim Sinasi (1826–1871) and Namik Kemal (1840–1918). Educated in France, Sinasi founded modern Turkish journalism and was a pioneer in a number of fields, including science, in addition to introducing the concepts of modernization and democracy. He wrote not merely for the elite but to win over public opinion. His works of satire include *The Marriage of a Poet* (1860), the first Turkish play. He edited the newspaper *Tercüman-I Ahval* (Interpreter of Events) until being sacked for a provocative editorial on the principle of "no taxation without representation." He fled the country in 1865. Namik Kemal succeeded him as editor of the

paper. His writings included biographies of the great Ottoman and Arab rulers of the past, the play *Silistre* (Fatherland; 1873) and the poem *Ode to Freedom*. Working while exiled in Paris, Kemal and other Young Ottomans, including the poet Ziya Pasa (1825–1880), organized the journal *Hüriyet* (Freedom) to advance their ideas for the future of the Ottoman Empire.

Responding to pressure from reformers, in 1876 Sultan Abdülhamid II (1842–1918) introduced a new constitution, revoking it the following year and rallying the empire to seek war with Russia (1877–1878). He utilized propaganda extensively to legitimize his rule. For example, he reasserted the idea of the Ottomans as caliphs and appealed to dynastic history by placing renewed emphasis on genealogies (of dubious authenticity) and building elaborate tombs on the alleged sites of Ottoman ancestral graves. State-sponsored religious teachers (*da'iyan*) worked to promote Sunni Islam across the empire, while secondary schools promoted the Turkish language. The Hamidian state paid particular attention to its image overseas. Its policies ranged from making lavish contributions to various world's fairs to bribing Western journalists in Istanbul. Ottoman embassies protested against unflattering or overly exotic representations of their culture, targets that ranged from a comedy sketch in Amsterdam set in a harem and featuring eunuchs to a group of dervishes performing for money in the streets of New York. The sultan presented photographic collections to the Library of Congress and the British Library that reflected the "preferred" view of the modern empire. Contradicting these state-approved images was an ample supply of critical depictions of Ottoman behavior, including William Gladstone's (1809–1898) popular pamphlet *Bulgarian Horrors and the Question of the East* (1876), which sparked mass demonstrations in London, as well as the equally emotional reports of the Armenian massacres of 1894–1896. Despite the state's efforts, by the end of the century the image of Turkey in the West had seldom been more dismal.

While Abdülhamid's "ideological regeneration" apparently rallied the masses in the empire, the emerging middle class did not accept his political repressions passively. Resistance lived on in the Young Turk movement, which developed a powerful hold on the Ottoman military establishment. Literature remained a key method of political persuasion. In addition to established reformist writers like Namik Kemal, Mehmet Akif Ersay (1873–1936) called for an Islamic revival, Tevfik Fikret (1867–1915) for modernization along Western lines, and Ziya Gökalp (1876–1924) for Turkish nationalism. Others soon followed their lead. Fatma Aliye Hanim (1864–1936) argued for reform in the treatment of women in novels such as *Muhazarat* (Disputations; 1892).

The Young Turk–inspired revolution of 1908 led to the deposition of Abdülhamid II by parliament in 1909, but in 1913 (following the disastrous Balkans wars) the military assumed dictatorial power. A committee of officers known as the Committee of Union and Progress (CUP), which included Enver Pasha (1881–1924), ruled Turkey from 1913 to 1918. It brought Turkey into World War I on the side of Germany, the Ottoman state's long-standing ally. During World War I the CUP government attempted to maintain the empire by emphasizing Islam, only to be challenged in Arabia by the Wahhabis, who were now armed by the British in a full-scale Arab revolt. Closer to home, the government appealed to Turkish ethnicity, which apparently prevented large-scale desertions from the army but set the Young Turks at odds with minority populations, including the Christian Armenians of the northeast. In April 1915 an isolated Armenian revolt in the town of Van triggered a second spate of mass killings of Armenians across the Ottoman empire. The genocide became a staple of British propaganda against Turkey's German ally, including a substantial report published by historian Arnold Toynbee (1889–1975) in 1916. In the United States Armenians and sympathetic Americans formed the American Committee for Armenian and Syrian Relief, which propounded an enduring image of Turks as eager participants in atrocities real and imagined.

As the Ottoman Empire became fragmented, the army provided a measure of cohesion under the leadership of Mustafa Kemal (1881–1938). At the end of World War I he organized a nationalistic movement that drew upon Turkish outrage at the Greek military presence in Asian Turkey. In Ankara Kemal created a nationalistic alternative to the Constantinople-based sultan. In 1921–1922 he led a brilliant campaign to drive out the Greeks, which remains a source of propaganda claims and counterclaims. In 1923 the parliament of the new Turkish republic elected Kemal as president. A formidable speaker, his performances included a legendary six-day speech delivered in 1927 at the opening of the third national assembly.

Kemal spearheaded multiple reforms, the most important of which was his insistence on a secular state. He abolished the caliphate in 1924 and religious orders in 1925. Islam ceased to be the state religion in 1928. His cultural policies included the rooting out of imagery reflecting the Greek presence and such symbols of Ottoman religiosity as the fez, the characteristic headgear. He introduced Latin script and adopted a Swiss legal system. A "language reform" policy removed works with Arabic or Persian roots. Kemal even dropped his own Arabic honorific *Gazi* (warrior). In 1935 Turkey switched over to the Western twenty-four-hour timekeeping system, the Gregorian calendar, and adopted the concept of the "weekend," with Sunday as a day of rest. Such changes were aimed at creating a cultural break with the past. Moreover, Kemal sought to nurture pride in the national language, literature, and history of Turkey. In 1934 he adopted the name Atatürk, meaning father of the Turks. His *Cumhuriyetci Halk Partisi* (Republican People's Party) was the only political party in the country between 1923 and 1946. At the end of the century Atatürk remained the central symbol of Turkish identity and, according to the constitution of 1982, "immortal leader and unequaled hero." His portrait is everywhere in Turkish shops and homes, and criticism of his life or legacy remains largely taboo.

During World War II both Axis and Allied propaganda vied for the attention of neutral Turkey. At war's end the country became the focus of Cold War tension. In 1947 President Truman made his famous "Containment" speech to rally U.S. support and aid for the Turkish government in its struggle against the domestic Communist threat. In 1950 Atatürk's successor, President Ismet Inönü (1884–1973), organized the first free general elections, which he and his party lost. The new administration, with Celâl Bayar (1884–1986) as president, advanced what would become an enduring element in Turkey's international image, namely, commitment to the Cold War alliance with the United States. After a potent piece of propaganda by deed—fighting in the Korean War—Turkey became a full member of NATO in 1952 and a founding member of the Central Treaty Organization (CENTO) in 1954. At home Bayar extended religious freedom, permitting mosques to broadcast religious programs.

Freedom in the Turkish press has varied. In the late 1950s the press faced serious repression, with journalists jailed by Prime Minister Adnan Menderes (1899–1961). In 1960 a military coup removed his government. A new constitution followed in 1961. Political turmoil in 1980 led to the declaration of martial law by Gen. Kenan Evren (1917–), who remained head of state until 1989.

In the 1990s Turkey remained a key regional base for U.S. armed forces, playing an important role in supporting U.S. operations during the Gulf War (1991). Against this positive image, Turkey faces powerful negative criticism, including human rights abuses, repression of Kurds, and the penal system. Such issues loomed large during Turkey's application to join the European Union. At home a serious challenge to the principle of a secular state came from religious politicians,

specifically Necmettin Erbakan (1926–), leader of the Refah Partisi (Welfare Party) and prime mover in its predecessors, the National Order Party (banned 1971) and the National Salvation Party (banned in 1980). The Welfare Party gained the most seats in the parliamentary election of 1995, and during a coalition period Erbakan, as prime minister, worked to advance Islamic education and culture at home and to align Turkey with Islamic regimes (including Iran). His propaganda strategies included denouncing capitalism as a Zionist conspiracy. The military reacted by pressing Erbakan to resign. In 1998 the Welfare Party became illegal, though its members regrouped to form the Fazilet Partisi (Virtue Party).

Nicholas J. Cull

See also Arab World; Atrocity Propaganda; Austrian Empire; Crimean War; Reformation and Counter-Reformation; Religion; World War I
References: Ahmad, Feroz. *The Young Turks.* Oxford: Oxford University Press, 1969; Deringel, Selim. *The Well-Protected Domains: Ideology and the Legitimation of Power in the Ottoman Empire, 1876–1909.* London: I. B. Tauris, 1998; Hale, William. *Turkish Foreign Policy, 1774–2000.* London: Frank Cass, 2000; Kinross, Lord. *Atatürk: The Rebirth of a Nation.* London: Weidenfeld and Nicolson, 1964; Lewis, Bernard. *The Emergence of Modern Turkey.* 3d ed. New York: Oxford University Press, 2002; Mardin, Serif. *The Genesis of Young Ottoman Thought.* Princeton, NJ: Princeton University Press, 1962.

OWI (Office of War Information)

America's overt propaganda office during World War II, the Office of War Information (OWI) was created by executive order in June 1942 and operated until August 1945. It consolidated an array of agencies created during the buildup leading up to U.S. entry into the war. These included: embassy press bureaus; the Foreign Information Service, which had been part of the Office of the Coordinator of Information (later the Office of Strategic Services); and the new radio station the Voice of America. OWI's director, journalist Elmer Davis (1890–1958), had come to public attention as one of the CBS radio network's chief commentators on war news. In this capacity he had argued for a unification of the U.S. news and information apparatus. Davis worked on the same sort of "propaganda with fact" approach used by the British Ministry of Information (MoI). His motto was: "This is a people's war, and the people are entitled to know as much as possible about it."

The OWI included the Domestic Branch, directed by journalist Gardner Cowles Jr. (1903–1985). This branch operated the News Bureau, which released information and news about the war effort to the domestic audience—and withheld information in conjunction with the Office of Censorship. A separate Overseas Branch, directed by Robert Sherwood (1896–1955), a playwright and Franklin D. Roosevelt's speechwriter, distributed American news and information overseas, operated the Voice of America, and coordinated propaganda policy with Allied nations. Sherwood received over 80 percent of the OWI's budget. Much of the OWI's domestic propaganda effort involved managing the commercial channels of American mass communication through its War Advertising Council and its Motion Picture Branch, located in Hollywood and directed by Lowell Mellett (1884–1960). The Motion Picture Branch urged U.S. film producers to ask themselves: "Will this picture help to win the war?" Other notable employees of the OWI included the theatrical producer John Houseman (1902–1989) and the anthropologist Ruth Benedict (1887–1948).

The OWI soon became the focus of controversy. Its constituents fought each other rather than the Germans. The military proved intransigent with respect to releasing information, and Republican politicians attacked the organization as too partisan. Cowles resigned in 1943 following allegations that he was "managing" the news. He was succeeded by E. Palmer Hoyt (1897–1979). In the aftermath of the war, the OWI became a major target of McCarthyite anti-Communist attacks on the grounds that it had been soft on Stalin. Elmer Davis, in turn, became a major figure in the media counterattack against McCarthy.

Nicholas J. Cull

See also Roosevelt, Franklin D.; VOA; World War II (United States)

References: Roeder, George H. *The Censored War: American Visual Experience During World War Two.* New Haven, CT: Yale University Press, 1993; Shulman, Holly Cowan. *The Voice of America: Propaganda and Democracy, 1941–1945.* Madison: University of Wisconsin Press, 1990; Steele, Richard W. *Propaganda in an Open Society: The Roosevelt Administration and the Media, 1933–1941.* Westport, CT: Greenwood, 1985; Winkler, Allan M. *The Politics of Propaganda: The Office of War Information, 1942–1945.* New Haven, CT: Yale University Press, 1978.

P

Pacific/Oceania

The inhabitants of the Pacific islands (ethnologically divided into Melanesia, Micronesia, and Polynesia and known in the West historically as the South Sea Islands), who possessed their own rich traditions of social and political communication, were exposed to Western methods in the nineteenth and twentieth centuries through Christian missionary activity and colonial educational projects. In the second half of the twentieth century Oceania generated propaganda for independence and both contributed to and figured in environmental propaganda campaigns.

The traditional societies of the Pacific drew on a rich and infinitely varied mix of creative arts, including wood carving, mask making, tattooing, and dances. These arts described and perpetuated a complex world of religious and kinship obligations, affirming leadership structures and confirming roles. Contact with the West can be traced back to the sixteenth century. The Portuguese reached Sumatra (which had been known to the Arabs for centuries) in 1509; the Spanish reached Guam in 1521 and the Solomon Islands in 1568. The seventeenth and eighteenth centuries saw a succession of pathbreaking European expeditions, beginning with those led by the Dutch explorers

Willem Cornelis Schouten (ca. 1567–1625) and Abel Tasman (ca. 1603–1659) and reaching a climax with the voyages of the Englishman Capt. James Cook (1728–1779). The propaganda elements in these "first contact experiences" ranged from a display of portraits of European monarchs and products to pointed demonstrations of European firearms. Such experiences continued into the 1930s, with some captured on film.

During the nineteenth century the Pacific Islands became the focus of European interest. The islands experienced a gradual increase in economic activity and frenzied competition between Catholic and Protestant missionaries (and even among various Protestant denominations). The key institution in the region was the London Missionary Society (LMS), which was founded in 1795 and sent missionaries to Tahiti and Tongatapu in 1797. These missionaries included William Ellis (1794–1872), who established a printing press and devised a written form of the Hawaiian language, and John Williams (1796–1839), who not only "discovered" the island of Rarotonga in 1823 but also translated the Bible into the island's native language. Reverend Williams became a celebrated figure in Victorian Britain. He raised substantial sums to finance a missionary expedition and his book *Narrative of Missionary Enterprises* (1837) became well known. His fate—being eaten by the inhabitants of Errogmango in the New Hebrides in 1839—led to his being called the "Apostle of Polynesia." A staple of Victorian religious propaganda, his tale, which attracted new recruits, created an enduring image of Oceanic culture.

The sexual frankness of the art appalled missionaries, resulting in the wholesale destruction of cultural artifacts, especially in Polynesia. What offended the missionaries attracted others, most famously the artist Paul Gauguin (1848–1903), whose eroticized images of Tahitian women perpetuated race and gender stereotypes. Conversely, Fijians (and, no doubt, other islanders) were appalled by the short intervals between the pregnancies of missionaries' wives, imagining the husbands themselves to be grossly lustful.

In many places the missionary presence precipitated political control, as was the case in the Cook Islands, which was proclaimed a British protectorate in 1888. Mission schools imposed Western-oriented education and values. This sometimes included bans on teaching in indigenous languages. (The government of New Zealand only approved Maori schools in the 1960s.) Mission schools elevated the "mother country," which in some places reflected changing diplomatic relations. At the turn of the nineteenth century Germany traded part of the island of Bougainville for parts of British Samoa. French missionaries predominated in the Marquesas and Society Islands, which were annexed by France in 1842, with Tahiti following in 1844. In 1903 the French government established French Polynesia as an administrative entity.

The twentieth century saw continued missionary activity and colonial education projects. In Papua Australia took control from Britain in 1905. World War I brought Australia and New Zealand into a more active role, with mandates by the League of Nations to administer formerly German islands, including Western Samoa (New Zealand) and New Guinea (Australia). The Japanese held a similar mandate with respect to the Marshall and Caroline Islands. Japan's bid to conquer the Pacific during World War II involved little in the way of propaganda to island groups. Ideological control in New Guinea included the imprisonment of indigenous church workers. The United States held several possessions in the region, including Hawaii (which was finally annexed in 1898), Guam (1898), and Eastern Samoa near the port of Pago Pago (1899). It extended its cultural presence in the region dramatically during the war with Japan. The wartime presence of Allied war material in Melanesia sparked a surge in the indigenous millenarian movements, which contained elements of cultural resistance and even nationalism. After the war the United States assumed responsibility for the Marshall and Caroline Islands. In 1961 the United States launched a major development program on American Samoa, including the pioneering use of television for educational instruction. After a promising start, the scheme foundered, in part owing to power supply problems.

During the Cold War the Pacific region figured prominently in propaganda as a result of the testing of nuclear weapons there by Britain, France, and the United States. Local and international groups protested against these tests, the best known of these being the voyages of the *Golden Rule, Phoenix,* and *Everyman I, II,* and *III.* The issue of nuclear testing was still alive in the 1980s. The French secret service struck back in July 1985 when it sank the Greenpeace vessel *Rainbow Warrior* in Auckland Harbour, New Zealand. The incident became a massive propaganda backfire resulting in the resignation of the French minister of defense. In August 1985 the islands of the South Pacific signed the Rarotonga Pact, asserting their nuclear-free status. In 1996 France announced the end of its nuclear testing program.

Influential broadcasters in the region have included the Australian Broadcasting Corporation (ABC), Radio France Overseas (RFO), and the Central Pacific Network of the U.S. Armed Forces Network (AFN). As territories in the region gained their independence, they established state-run broadcasting companies, though programming remained dominated by the West. Radio endured as an important medium of state and religious propaganda. Indigenous movements with active propaganda campaigns include the autonomy movements in French Polynesia. In the late 1950s Pouvanaa A. Oopa (1895–1977), a veteran of the French Resistance, led the Democratic Assembly of the Tahitian People (RDPT) against French rule. His campaign met with censorship, arrest, and exile in France (1960–1968). At the end of the twentieth century the Polynesian Liberation Front remained active. Fiji gained its independence from Britain in 1970 under the leadership of Ratu Sir Kamisese Mara (1920–), who, as Fiji's first prime minister, attempted to create a form of regional leadership. Papua New Guinea gained independence in 1975 under Sir Michael Somare (1936–).

Since independence, secessionist movements in the region have challenged the integrity of colonially established states. In 1980 the island of Espiritu Santo attempted to break away from the newly independent Vanuatu (formerly the New Hebrides). Australia and Papua New Guinea helped to quell the revolt. In 1988 Papua New Guinea experienced a secessionist uprising on the island of Bougainville, during which a propaganda radio station (Radio Free Bougainville) managed to keep broadcasting into the mid-1990s by running generators powered by coconut oil. Other political problems in the region include a dispute between the South Asian and ethnically Polynesian inhabitants of Fiji and an independence movement among the ethnically Melanesian inhabitants of Indonesian-ruled Irian Jaya.

Groups from across the region have profited from international freedom movements. Maori demonstrations in New Zealand in 1975 drew inspiration from the U.S. civil rights and black power movements. Oceania has also taken part in international indigenous/aboriginal rights campaigns. In 1994 the United Nations sponsored a global conference on small islands in Barbados, which adopted a convention designed to assist in both economic development and cultural and environmental conservation on island nations worldwide. Many of the Pacific nations made their first foray into international propaganda in the final years of the twentieth century over the issue of global warming at venues such as the United Nations Earth Summit in Rio de Janeiro, Brazil, in 1992, or the Climate Summit in Kyoto, Japan, in 1998. Nations such as the Marshall Islands stressed the problem of rising sea levels, which pose an obvious threat to a country where the highest elevation is less than seven feet above sea level.

Nicholas J. Cull

See also Australia; British Empire; Environmentalism; New Zealand; Peace and Antiwar Movements (1945–); Religion
References: Campbell, I. C. *A History of the Pacific Islands.* Christchurch, NZ: University of Canterbury Press, 1989; Denoon, Donald, et al., eds. *The Cambridge History of the Pacific Islanders.* Cambridge: Cambridge University Press, 1997; Northcott, Cecil. *John Williams Sails On.* London: Hodder and Stoughton, 1939; Robie, David. *Blood on Their Banner: Nationalist Struggles in the South Pacific.* London: Zed, 1989; Scarr, Deryck. *The History of the Pacific Islands.* London: Macmillan, 1990.

Paine, Thomas (1737–1809)

A political writer and professional propagandist for the revolutionary cause on both sides of the Atlantic, Thomas Paine was born in Thetford, England. After immigrating to America in 1774, he began his writing career in Philadelphia editing *The Pennsylvania Magazine*. His political career was launched meteorically in January 1776 with the publication of *Common Sense*, a pamphlet calling for American independence under the future Continental Congress. The pamphlet is often

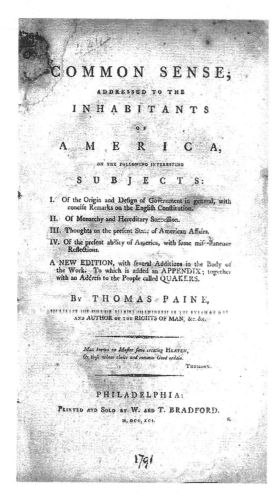

The cover of the 1791 Bradford edition of Thomas Paine's Common Sense. (Library of Congress)

credited with shifting popular opinion from loyal protest to independence, although Paine's point was that the British did this themselves by opening fire on the militia at Lexington in April 1775, an act he compared to that of a brutal mother devouring her young.

Paine served as aide to Generals George Washington (1732–1799) and Nathanael Greene (1742–1786) during the Revolutionary War, but his greatest contribution to the war effort was maintaining morale. In December 1776 he wrote the first of the "Crisis" papers, meant to rally support for a war that the colonists appeared to be losing, which began: "These are the times that try men's souls. The summer soldier and the sunshine patriot will, in this crisis, shrink from the service of their country; but he that stands it now, deserves the love and thanks of man and woman. Tyranny, like hell, is not easily conquered; yet we have this consolation with us, that the harder the conflict, the more glorious the triumph." Washington ordered the paper to be read to the starving, freezing volunteer troops on Christmas Eve, before launching his successful attack on Trenton. The astonishing triumph of the ragtag colonial army over the mighty British Empire emerged from this pivotal moment.

Between 1777 and 1778 Paine served as secretary to Congress's new Committee of Foreign Affairs; he was forced to resign after denouncing the war profiteer Silas Deane (1737–1789), which proved an embarrassment to the French government. Although Paine was part of the radical "constitutionalist" faction supporting the democratic Pennsylvania Constitution of 1776, he was also a vocal supporter of stronger union, drawing him into early federalist circles. The Articles of Confederation assigned no tax-levying powers to the United States, thus crippling the war effort. Attempts by the Continental Congress to raise funds by printing paper notes not backed by gold resulted in a devastating inflation. Paine traveled to Rhode Island, where he published six letters in the *Providence Gazette* in an attempt to convince the tiny state to agree to a 5 percent duty to pay for the war. At the behest of Robert Morris (1734–1806), the government's superintendent of finance, beginning in 1782 Paine was awarded an annual salary of $800, drawn from secret service funds, to write in support of Congress and taxation. Although sometimes accused of "prostituting his pen," Paine vigorously defended his integrity. He wrote primarily to spread his ideas, frequently donating the proceeds of his writings to the revolutionary cause.

In 1787 Paine traveled to Europe to find backers for a bridge design. English reformers greeted him as a hero. The outbreak of revolution in France spurred Paine to return to politics. Edmund Burke's (1729–1797) *Reflections on the Revolution in France* (1790) generated a furious debate in Britain. Paine responded by penning *The Rights of Man* (1791), which proved a best-seller: 50,000 copies were sold in the first three months alone, with perhaps 200,000 in the first year, to a population of only 10 million. Public readings of it were widespread in the new popular political societies, causing perhaps 40,000 working-class people to engage in political debate for the first time. Numerous towns and cities planted "Liberty Trees," and rioters in the streets of Edinburgh were heard to cry out "Tom Paine and no King!" *The Rights of Man Part Second* (1792) called for the creation of a constitutional convention in Britain to reform Parliament from the outside. Prime Minister William Pitt (1759–1806) responded with unprecedented acts of repression. The government prosecuted Paine for seditious libel against the constitution. Now mobs burned him in effigy, popular poems and songs denounced him, and medals depicted him hanging from a gibbet. A royal proclamation banned his book, and five Scotsmen were sent to the penal colony in Australia for disseminating his ideas. Moncure Conway, Paine's modern biographer, has claimed that Pitt went to war with France in 1793 not over the fate of Louis XVI but in order to halt the spread of the ideas contained in *The Rights of Man.*

Revolutionary France embraced Paine, electing him to their National Assembly as deputy for Calais in 1792. Associated with the Girondin faction, Paine attracted the hostility of the Jacobin dictatorship. He was imprisoned for eleven months, during which time he published *The Age of Reason* (1794), which challenged the idea of the Bible as "revealed text." He returned to the United States in 1802 but was shunned for his religious ideas. Since his death, Paine's ideas and image have been appropriated by numerous causes. In 1819 the English radical William Cobbett (1763–1835) dug up Paine's bones

for symbolic use in his political campaign, only to be lost sometime thereafter. Up until the 1850s Paine's birthday was celebrated by radical societies in Britain and by labor unions in the United States. His rhetoric has been employed by politicians as diverse as the British M.P. Tony Benn (1925–) and U.S. president Ronald Reagan (1911–).

Karen M. Ford

See also Revolution, American, and War of Independence; United States
References: Aldridge, Alfred Owen. *Thomas Paine's American Ideology.* London: Associated University Presses, 1984; Claeys, Gregory. *Thomas Paine: Social and Political Thought.* London: Unwin Hyman, 1989; Conway, Moncure D., ed. *The Writings of Thomas Paine.* 4 vols. 1908. Reprint, New York: Burt Franklin, 1969; Foner, Eric. *Tom Paine and Revolutionary America.* Oxford: Oxford University Press, 1976; Ford, Karen M., ed. *Property, Welfare and Freedom in the Thought of Thomas Paine.* New York: Edwin Mellen, 2001; Keane, John. *Tom Paine: A Political Life.* London: Bloomsbury, 1995; Philp, Mark. *Paine.* Oxford: Oxford University Press, 1989.

Pakistan
See Indian Subcontinent

Peace and Antiwar Movements (1500–1945)

Although most closely identified with war, propaganda has also been a staple of those either seeking peace or voicing opposition to a particular war, from the writings of the Dutch scholar Erasmus (1466–1536) against the brutality of the religious wars of his time to street demonstrations against the bombing of Afghanistan in 2001. Arguments for peace have been based on the horrors of war, religious feelings, and humanist philosophy derived from ancient Greek thought. Early depictions in art include the works of Jacques Callot (ca. 1592–1635) (in response to the Thirty Years' War). The best-known sectarian preaching against war was that of the Religious Society of Friends or Quakers, founded by George Fox (1624–1691). Other sects preaching peace included the Mennonites and Brethren. In 1693 Quaker colonist William Penn (1644–1718) wrote "An Essay towards the Present and Future Peace of Europe, by the establishment of an European Diet, Parliament or Estates." The same idea of a league of states to underwrite peace surfaced in the work of Charles Irénée Castel, Abbé de Saint-Pierre (1658–1743), who in 1713 published his *Projet de la Paix Perpétuelle* (Scheme for Perpetual Peace).

The Napoleonic Wars sparked artistic condemnation of the excesses of war in the works of Goya (1746–1828) and among non-sectarian peace organizations on both sides of the Atlantic. These groups founded newspapers such as the *Herald of Peace* (1819) in Britain and *Friend of Peace* (1821) in the United States. The idea of a "Congress of Nations" was popular with numerous state-level American peace organizations of the early nineteenth century, which came together in 1828 to form a national, nonsectarian American Peace Society (APS) under the leadership of William Ladd (1778–1841). Unfortunately the APS soon split over the issue of whether it was moral to fight a defensive war. William Lloyd Garrison (1805–1879) believed that it was not and organized the breakaway New England Non-Resistance Society. This organization also split over the morality of the American Civil War, which Garrison, being an abolitionist, endorsed. In 1862 Garrison's chief opponent on the issue, Alfred Henry Love (1830–1913), published *An Appeal in Vindication of Peace Principles and Against Resistance by Force.* Love argued: "Let us seek to convert rather than coerce." In 1866 Love presided over the founding of the Universal Peace Union, which attracted many prominent female members. Although it matched the APS in its endorsement of an international organization, it extended its antiwar arguments to include war-inspired toys and violent sports.

The mid-nineteenth century saw the establishment of a series of international peace congresses, beginning in London in 1843 with the First Universal Peace Congress. The second (Brussels, 1848) combined arguments for an international organization with calls for disarmament. Prominent European pacifists in the era included the Frenchman Ferdinand Edouard Buisson (1841–1932), Russian novelist Leo Tolstoy (1828–1910), and Austrian author Bertha von Suttner (1843–1914), best known for her internationally popular 1889 novel *Die Waffen nieder* (Lay Down Your Arms). Younger activists included Alfred Hermann Fried (1864–1921), founder of the Deutsche Friedensgesellschaft (German League for Peace). The major powers seemed responsive, attending the First International Peace Conference in 1899 and establishing an international tribunal at The Hague in Holland. These years also saw the founding of the Nobel Peace Prize. The emerging peace movement, however, could not prevent the coming of World War I. The latter provoked a lively antiwar movement variously led by liberal humanists, sectarian pacifists, and socialists. Leaders in Britain included Bertrand Russell (1872–1970), who at war's end was jailed for his views. The leading antiwar activist in the United States was the Socialist presidential candidate Eugene V. Debs (1855–1926), who was likewise imprisoned from 1918 to 1921. Those draftees in Britain and the United States who refused to bear arms were arrested as conscientious objectors (a term coined during the war). Groups supporting them included the Fellowship of Reconciliation and the American Union against Militarism, whose propaganda included the exhibition of a dinosaur as a warning against human extinction. Hollywood produced a number of feature films with a pacifist message, the most famous being *Civilization* (1916), directed by Thomas H. Ince (1882–1924). Jane Addams (1850–1935) helped found the Women's International League for Peace in 1915, which four years later became the Women's International League for Peace and Freedom (WILPF). Antiwar activity led to the founding (also with Addams's help) of the American Civil Liberties Union (ACLU) in 1920. Internationally the experience of the Great War energized the peace movement as never before.

The interwar peace movement had no shortage of remarkable polemical material, including novels such as *All Quiet on the Western Front* (1928) by Erich Maria Remarque (1898–1970), in Germany (which was turned into a classic film in 1930), and *A Farewell to Arms* (1929) by Ernest Hemingway (1899–1961). British fiction included plays like *Journey's End* (1929) by R. C. Sherriff (1896–1975) and polemical essays by writers like Sir Norman Angell (1872–1967) and even A. A. Milne (1882–1956). The focus for much of this effort was the League of Nations Union, which was organized to support the international body established in 1919. As the hope of world peace crumbled with the rise of Hitler and Mussolini new polemical works appeared, among the most famous being Pablo Picasso's painting *Guernica* (1937).

In the United States pressure from peace activists like Dorothy Detzer (1893–1981), who was a Washington lobbyist for WILPF, resulted in a congressional hearing on the arms industry. During these "Merchants of Death" hearings (1934 and 1935), Sen. Gerald P. Nye (1892–1971) exposed the willingness of arms manufacturers to exploit war to suit their own ends. These ideas became orthodoxy in pacifist films of the era, such as William A. Wellman's *The President Vanishes* (1934), in which arms manufacturers kidnap the president and try to start a war. Similar views surfaced in 1938 in the first adventure of the comic book hero Superman. U.S. pacifism added additional weight to the preexisting isolationist trend in American politics, resulting in a complex web of neutrality acts passed between 1935 and 1939 to keep the United States out of future wars. Pacifist arguments remained central to U.S. isolationist politics and could be found in student movements, same-sex organizations (such as WILPF, or the National Women's Committee to Keep the United States Out of War, led by Katherine Curtis), labor-based movements, and farmers. The Na-

tional Council for the Prevention of War coordinated these disparate groups.

Eloquent antiwar novels included a graphic account of the suffering of a mutilated solider in *Johnny Got His Gun* (1939) by Dalton Trumbo (1905–1976), which was turned into a film in 1971. Propaganda against U.S. intervention in World War II included arguments that fell short of the high ideals of pacifism. The emotive radio broadcasts of Father Charles Coughlin (1891–1971) and later speeches by the aviator Charles Lindbergh (1902–1974) were not opposed to war per se but just a war against Hitler "on behalf" of Britain and "the Jews." It is a mark of the success of the pacifists in the interwar years that World War II concluded with universal agreement on the need for an international organization. Doctrines first promulgated in pacifist and liberal international writing in the nineteenth century became aims in Allied wartime propaganda, leading to the establishment of the United Nations in 1945.

Nicholas J. Cull

See also *All Quiet on the Western Front;* Garrison, William Lloyd; Goya; *Guernica;* Peace and Antiwar Movements (1945–); Switzerland; Women's Movement: European; World War I

References: Brock, Peter. *Pacifism in the United States from the Colonial Era to the First World War.* Princeton, NJ: Princeton University Press, 1968;———. *Twentieth-Century Pacifism.* Syracuse, NY: Syracuse University Press, 1999; DeBenedetti, Charles. *The Peace Reform in American History.* Bloomington: Indiana University Press, 1980; Martin, David. *Pacifism: A Historical and Sociological Study.* London: Routledge, 1965.

Peace and Antiwar Movements (1945–)

Although 1945 brought hope in the form of the United Nations, it also saw the new threat of atomic weapons. The A-bomb gave added intensity to the pleas of peace activists, who for the first time could claim that the survival of the human race would be at stake

A protester holds a banner stating "Don't Attack Iraq" before an antiwar demonstration in London, 15 February 2003. (Reuters NewMedia Inc. / CORBIS)

in a future war. The first formal statement of this position appeared in the 18 August 1945 issue of the *Saturday Review of Literature* in an editorial entitled "Modern Man Is Obsolete" by Norman Cousins (1915–1990). In 1957 he became a founding member of SANE (National Committee for a Sane Nuclear Policy), which launched a campaign against atmospheric nuclear testing. In Britain antinuclear activists formed the Campaign for Nuclear Disarmament (CND), whose activities included a mass march at Easter 1958 from London to the British government's nuclear arms laboratory at Aldermaston. Protests proved particularly large and effective in Scandinavia, where in 1959 the Swedish Action Group demanded its government abandon nuclear research—at least officially.

The antinuclear protests of the Cold War used nonviolent direct action of the sort that had been pioneered by the Indian pacifist and nationalist Mahatma Gandhi. Protests in-

cluded mass vigils entering nuclear-testing sites on land (such as those in Nevada) and sea (such as attempts by the ships *Golden Rule* and *Phoenix* to sail into areas in the Pacific in 1958). Novels highlighting nuclear dangers have included *On the Beach* (1957) by Nevil Shute (1899–1960) and *Fail-Safe* (1962) by Eugene Burdick and Harvey Wheeler (both of which were later turned into films). The most enduring antinuclear work was the film *Dr. Strangelove* (1964), directed by Stanley Kubrick (1928–1999). The protests began to pay dividends in 1963 when the United States and the USSR concluded the nuclear test ban treaty. However, the Cold War continued by proxy in Vietnam, which became the focus of world peace activism for the rest of the decade.

The Vietnam War united activists in the United States across lines of color, class, religion, and age. Organizations opposing the war included: Students for a Democratic Society (SDS), founded in 1962; the Women's International League for Peace and Freedom; the War Resisters League; and the Student Nonviolent Coordinating Committee (SNCC). Prominent figures endorsing the cause included the pediatrician Benjamin Spock (1903–1998) and civil rights leader Martin Luther King Jr. (1929–1968). Methods ranged from mass protests, concerts, and draft card burnings (two Catholic priests symbolically doused draft cards in blood) to teach-ins at universities. The movement communicated its message through songs— including the protest songs of Bob Dylan (1941–) and Joan Baez (1941–)—poetry, and the graphic arts, becoming a marker of generational identity. The most dramatic protests occurred when three peace protestors burned themselves to death (emulating Vietnamese monk Quang Duc).

Antiwar membership and activism surged when President Richard Nixon (1913–1994) invaded Cambodia in 1970 but declined once he stopped drafting students. The movement remained strong among Vietnam Veterans against the War (VVAW), which was founded in 1967. VVAW members returned their Vietnam War medals in 1971 and arranged the "Winter Soldier" hearings in Detroit, which revealed the true scope of U.S. atrocities in Vietnam. Debate continues as to the precise impact of the movement on the war. According to some estimates, aggregate membership of U.S. peace organizations reached four million during this period. In Europe the 1960s also saw mass protests against the Vietnam War, frequently with a radical anticapitalist and anti-American flavor, including a celebrated riot outside the U.S. embassy in London in 1968.

Although active throughout the 1970s, the peace movements returned to prominence toward the end of the decade when U.S. president Jimmy Carter (1924–) announced the deployment of the neutron bomb. The scale of protests forced him to scrap the idea but did not prevent his successor, Ronald Reagan (1911–), from deploying cruise

missiles in Europe. The United States spawned the Nuclear Freeze movement, whose advocates included journalist Jonathan Schell (author of the 1982 book *The Fate of the Earth*) and scientist Carl Sagan (1934–1996), who propounded the theory of "nuclear winter," claiming that nuclear war would result in catastrophic climatic changes. In Britain the CND returned to the fore under the joint leadership of Labour politician Joan Ruddock (1943–), historian E. P. Thompson (1924–1993), and Catholic priest Bruce Kent (1929–). Its techniques included a widely circulated pamphlet called *Protest and Survive* that parodied the British government's civil defense literature; mass rallies; and screenings of the film *The War Game,* originally commissioned for the BBC in 1965 but never aired, which used a documentary style to dramatize the effect of a nuclear bomb on London. Other significant polemical works included the strip cartoon book *When the Wind Blows* (1982) by Raymond Briggs, which followed an elderly couple through the aftermath of a nuclear explosion to their deaths from radiation sickness. Methods used across Europe included commemorations of the anniversary of Hiroshima, and mass "die-ins" simulating the casualties of a nuclear strike. Cities, including Manchester and Leicester in Britain and Tromsö in Norway, declared themselves to be nuclear-free. Women established "peace camps" outside the Greenham Common air base in Oxfordshire and the Viborg nuclear bunker in Denmark.

The second wave of the antinuclear and peace movement overlapped with the developing environmental movement. The best-known environmental organization, Greenpeace, began life in 1971 by protesting nuclear testing in Alaska. With the end of the Cold War, the environmental movement maintained the impetus of activism and continued to use many of the tactics pioneered by the peace movement, including mass incursions into "off limits" sites and filming violators on location, as from Greenpeace's vessel *Rainbow Warrior.* Although neither the Gulf

War nor the war in Bosnia sparked large-scale peace movements, the memory of 1960s activism served as a break on U.S. foreign policy and that of other governments through the 1990s. Succeeding U.S. presidents assumed that the American people would object to a large or prolonged military commitment and sought to fight wars in ways that did not jeopardize U.S. lives, such as the use of airpower or "smart weapons."

Nicholas J. Cull

See also Capa, Robert; Environmentalism; Music; Peace and Antiwar Movements (1500–1945); Scandinavia; United Nations; Vietnam War; *The War Game*

References: Carter, April. *Peace Movements: International Protest and World Politics Since 1945.* London: Longman, 1992; Chatfield, Charles. *The American Peace Movement: Ideals and Activism.* New York: Twayne, 1992; Garfinkle, Adam. *Telltale Hearts: The Origins and Impact of the Vietnam Antiwar Movement.* New York: St. Martins, 1994; Wittner, Lawrence S. *Rebels against War: The American Peace Movement, 1933–1983.* Philadelphia: Temple University Press, 1984;———. *The Struggle against the Bomb: A History of the World Nuclear Disarmament Movement.* 3 vols. Palo Alto, CA: Stanford University Press, 1993–2002.

Perón, Juan Domingo (1895–1974) and Eva Duarte (1919–1952)

The president and First Lady of Argentina in the period following 1946, this formidable husband-and-wife team possessed a potent understanding of the power of the media. Juan Perón had studied the techniques of Benito Mussolini while a military attaché in Fascist Italy. His mistress Eva Duarte worked as an actress and radio broadcaster. In 1943 Perón was one of a number of army officers who seized power in a military coup. He took a backseat as minister of labor, but his compelling oratory earned him the admiration of Argentinean workers. In 1945 a group of army and navy officers attempted to end his rise to power by jailing him, but the pressure of an already adoring public mobilized by Eva Duarte brought his speedy release. In 1945

Juan and Eva married and together they campaigned for the presidency of Argentina, which he won in 1946. She consolidated his position by buying three of the country's major newspapers and winning over the poor, whom she emotively named "los descamisados" (the shirtless). The Perón regime was characterized by a personality cult focused on both Eva (Evita) and Juan, which was buttressed by posters, press and radio propaganda, and stage-managed events. Eva carved out a prominent role for herself in the field of both women's rights and welfare. She replaced the old welfare system with a personal charity named after herself. Perón lost ground following her death in 1952. In 1955 Perón fled the country. However, his popular support remained, permitting his triumphant return from exile to assume the presidency in 1973. He died in 1974. The cult of Eva Perón lasted long after her death, transforming her physical remains into a potent political symbol. Her body was variously stolen, hidden, reburied in exile, and reburied in state before being moved to its final resting place in her hometown of Recoleta in 1976.

Nicholas J. Cull

See also Funerals; Latin America; Mussolini, Benito

References: Barager, Joseph R. *Why Perón Came to Power: The Background to Peronism in Argentina.* New York: Knopf, 1968; Potash, Robert A. *The Army and Politics in Argentina, 1945–1962: Perón to Frondizi.* London: Athlone, 1980.

Philippines

From early missionary activity to contemporary political turmoil, propaganda has loomed large in the history of the Philippine islands. In the fourteenth century Arab traders introduced Islam to the southern islands. The first European contact occurred in 1521 during the voyage of Ferdinand Magellan (ca. 1480–1521). In 1542 an expedition from New Spain (Mexico) named the islands in honor of Philip II (1527–1598), the heir to the Spanish throne, but this was a symbolic gesture rather than one based on political reality. Spain did not launch its conquest of the islands until the 1560s. Catholic missions—specifically the Jesuit order—soon followed. Although by the late sixteenth century the Philippines had become a hub of trade between the West and the East, popular unrest was never far below the surface, with the Moro (Muslim) population remaining a particularly thorny problem.

By the nineteenth century the church had become the most powerful force in the lives of ordinary Filipinos. This, combined with the abuses of Spanish colonial rule, proved fertile ground for a Philippine independence movement. The preeminent propagandist of this movement was José Rizal (1861–1896). A physician, poet, and writer whose academic career took him to Europe, in 1886 (while in Berlin) Rizal published a novel called *Noli me tangere* (The Lost Eden). This stinging attack on the church and Spanish rule resulted in Rizal's exile. In 1891 (while in Hong Kong) he wrote a sequel entitled *El Filibusterismo* (The Subversive). He then returned to the Philippines but was promptly banished to the southern island of Mindanao. When a rebellion broke out in 1896, the Spanish tried and executed Rizal as its instigator. His death proved as powerful a piece of propaganda as his poems or novels, with the government soon facing a full-scale revolution under the leadership of Emilio Aguinaldo (1870–1964).

In 1898 the Philippine revolutionaries received a substantial windfall in the form of the Spanish-American War. After sinking the Spanish fleet at the battle of Manila, the United States armed Aguinaldo and gave its blessing to his cause. At this point the imperial lobby in the United States unleashed a considerable amount of propaganda about the religious needs and economic potential of the Philippines. When President William McKinley (1843–1901) bowed to pressure and purchased the islands from Spain, the United States found itself in a bitter guerrilla war against Emilio Aguinaldo, which lasted from 1899 until his capture in 1901.

The U.S. government ruled the Philippines with an eye to appeasing nationalistic sentiment. Thanks to the agitation of leader Manuel Quezon (1878–1944), the Americans first promised Filipinos their independence as early as 1916. As a stage in this process, in 1935 the Philippines became a commonwealth under American protection and elected Quezon as their first president. In December 1941 the Japanese attacked the Philippines. By the spring of 1942 the U.S. and Filipino army were fighting a hopeless rearguard action in defense of the Bataan peninsula and island of Corregidor, which became a staple of U.S. wartime propaganda. The Japanese established a puppet regime in the Philippines and attempted to win over the population by employing teams of local propagandists. Their recruits included the father of postwar Philippine politician Ferdinand Marcos. The Japanese used the aging Aguinaldo to broadcast propaganda for "the Greater East Asian Co-Prosperity Sphere." Both nationalists and Communists organized resistance groups. The latter took the name Hukbalahap (People's Anti-Japanese Army), or Huks for short.

In 1946 the Philippines became a fully independent republic, but the Huks mounted an antigovernment insurrection on the island of Luzon. The United States assisted President Ramón Magsaysay (1907–1957) in suppressing the Huks. Advisers in the campaign included Colonel Ed Lansdale (1908–1987), who taught propaganda techniques and helped build the image of Magsaysay. Success against the Huks bolstered American confidence in unconventional warfare, marking a step on the path to U.S. involvement in Vietnam. The Philippines served as a key regional outpost for U.S. Cold War propaganda. In 1950 the State Department established a Regional Service Center (RSC) in Manila to print propaganda for use across the region; it was here that the United States printed the leaflets it dropped in such quantities over Vietnam. The Philippines eventually became part of the U.S. image war in South Vietnam by sending a medical team (and eventually some military engineers) to the war in what was known as the "Many Flags." The scale and nature of this involvement became a major diplomatic issue, with the Philippine government extracting a high price in U.S. aid money for a small show of support.

Anti-Communism offered an ideal channel for a Philippine politician to win American support. The man who cornered the market was Ferdinand Marcos (1917–1989), who was elected president in 1965. Marcos's propaganda techniques included shameless exaggeration of his career as a wartime resistance fighter, saber rattling over his country's territorial claims against Malaysia, and the rapid construction of a personality cult. He retained CIA advisers from the Magsaysay era. Internal problems included a new uprising by the Communist Huks and a rebellion of the Moro (Muslim) population on Mindanao, which called itself the Moro National Liberation Front (MNLF). In the summer of 1972 Marcos staged a series of propaganda events, including the seizure of a Communist arms shipment containing "terrorist" bombs, in order to justify declaring martial law and claiming dictatorial powers. He took control of the media and launched the New Society Movement. His wife, Imelda Marcos (1929–), emerged as a powerful figure, sharing state-scripted media adulation, wooing Western leaders, and heading prestigious cultural projects.

In 1981 Marcos ran for election and won amid allegations of fraud. Marcos's camp sought to strengthen its hand by getting rid of the opposition. However, the murder of Benigno Aquino (1932–1983) as he returned from exile in the United States, like the Spanish execution of Rizal ninety years earlier, merely provided a focus for protest. Aquino's widow, Corazon "Cory" Aquino (1933–), now assumed the leadership of the opposition. The presidential election of 1986 ended indecisively, with Marcos claiming victory and Aquino alleging fraud. Aquino rallied a tide of popular support and forced Marcos to flee the country. Aquino's techniques included the use of a protest color, designated yellow. This display of what was called "People Power" was widely cited in the West as an example of the dawn of a new era in both the East and the West, linking reform in the Soviet Union and the Solidarity movement in Poland. As in Poland, the Catholic Church played a major role in the revolution under the leadership of Jaime Cardinal Sin (1928–).

Although Cory Aquino failed to deliver on many of the promises of her campaign, reforms included the creation of a new constitution in 1987 guaranteeing freedom of the press. Faced by economic crises, civil unrest, and multiple attempts to unseat her, she did not stand for reelection in 1992. Fidel Ramos (1928–), a senior figure in the Marcos military whose defection had proved a turning point in the revolution, succeeded her. In 1996 the Muslim population won a measure of self-determination in the autonomous region on Mindanao, but the Moro Islamic Liberation Front (MILF) faction continued fighting. The thirty-year-old insurgency of the New People's Army (NPA) also continued.

In 1998 Joseph Marcelo "Erap" Estrada (1937–) won the presidency, campaigning vigorously on the slogan "Elect Erap as President of the Masses." As he had done during his term as vice president (1992–1998), Estrada traded on nationalism, anti-American rhetoric, and his 1960s celebrity as a film star. He swiftly gained a reputation for corruption. During 2000 public opposition to Estrada mounted critics included the church, led by Cardinal Sin. In January 2001 demonstrators mounted a mass protest at the Edsa religious shrine, using messages sent on mobile phones to coordinate activities. Estrada resigned in favor of his vice president, Mrs. Gloria Arroyo (1947–). Arroyo faced multiple challenges, including deciding what to do with her predecessor, continuing civil unrest, and the activities of the Muslim separatists—particularly Abu Sayyaf (Sword of God), which kidnapped Westerners to draw attention to its demands.

Nicholas J. Cull

See also Counterinsurgency; Japan; Southeast Asia, Spanish-American War; Terrorism, War on; Vietnam War; World War II (United States)

References: Bonner, Raymond. *Waltzing with a Dictator: The Marcoses and the Making of American Policy.* London: Macmillan, 1987; Karnow, Stanley. *In Our Image: America's Empire in the Philippines.* New York: Random House, 1989; Seagrave, Sterling. *The Marcos Dynasty.* New York: Harper and Row, 1988.

Photography

Photography is the process of producing images on a sensitized surface through the action of radiant energy (light). A photograph freezes a moment in time. The first photograph, the daguerreotype, was made by Louis Daguerre (1789–1851) in 1839. His process involved a copper plate coated with silver iodide and exposed to light for a short time. This created a latent image enhanced in the darkroom through the use of mercury vapor. Brief exposure to light, followed by a process of development to bring out the latent image, is still the heart of the photographic process.

Early photography centered on portraits, landscapes, and architecture. An outstanding portrait, seeming to reveal something of the psychological makeup of the subject, is Robert Howlett's (1831–1858) portrait entitled *Isambard Kingdom Brunel Standing before the Launching Chains of the* Great Eastern (1857), portraying the engineer as hero posing before the largest ship afloat. Abraham Lincoln (1809–1865) was frequently photographed during the Civil War; the cost of leadership is seen in the suffering apparent in his face. Roger Fenton (1819–1868) photographed various aspects of the Crimean War, just as Mathew Brady (ca. 1823–1896) and Alexander Gardner (1821–1882) did for the American Civil War. Because of technical constraints, such as lengthy exposure, these images rarely capture the face of battle. For example, though the American Civil War was the bloodiest ever fought by Americans, with most wounds requiring amputation in the field, there is only a single extant image of an operation—and even this is lacking in detail because of inadequate interior light. The few images of battlefield dead remind us of entire subject areas rarely photographed.

The student of propaganda is most concerned with documentary photography, which can be used to prove or back up assertions made either with accompanying text or through the use of explanatory captions. Although documentary photography apparently bears a close resemblance to official documents, such as photographs used to identify someone on a driver's license, documentary photographers always insist that the true documentary image is a blend of fact plus emotion (generally pity) and that a documentary photograph does not merely reflect the attempt to record the appearance of something but rather a call for action on the part of the viewer. For example, in *How the Other Half Lives* (1890) Jacob Riis (1849–1914) used photography to awaken the conscience of comfortable, middle-class, suburban viewers to the slum conditions of the "other half," the poor of the inner city. Photography proved an important tool for Progressive Era reformers, such as Riis and Lewis Hine (1874–1940). The latter photographed instances of child labor abuse, including preadolescent girls working in textile mills in the South whose stature is dwarfed by the machines they are employed to operate. Late in his career Hine turned to photography to celebrate the patriotic embrace of laborers helping to construct the Empire State Building. His *Men at Work* (1932) consciously attempts to find in the construction of what was then the world's tallest building a spirit of optimistic hope in the future.

President Franklin D. Roosevelt's (1882–1945) New Deal used a small group of photographers, employed by the Farm Security Administration (FSA), to photograph rural America, focusing on such problems as malnutrition,

A 1936 example of New Deal propaganda by Farm Security Administration photographer Walker Evans. Evans arranged the interior of this Alabama tenant farmer's kitchen to show middle-class viewers that the poor were driven by the dicates of tidy housekeeping. (Courtesy of David Culbert)

soil erosion, and endemic poverty. The best known of these photographers was Walker Evans (1903–1975), who was less interested in people than in creating beautiful compositions depicting worn or abandoned structures. Dorothea Lange (1895–1965) captured the spirit of survival in hard times in "Migrant Mother," the best-known image of the FSA years.

World War II was a time of unprecedented importance for photographers, both on the home front and the battle front, and for all of the major combatants. Nor should one forget the amateur photographer, for the war was of interest to countless millions of persons who owned both simple and quite elaborate equipment. For example, photographs taken by German soldiers in the Soviet Union became an important source of documentation for the Holocaust. Yevgeny Khaldei (1917–1997) photographed the raising of the Russian flag atop the burning ruins of Berlin's Reichstag on 2 May 1945; he was allowed to retouch his official image a few days later when someone noted that one Russian soldier had wristwatches on both arms, a sure indication of looting. Joe Rosenthal (1912–) an Associated Press photographer, captured the second flag raising atop Iwo Jima on 23 February 1945, the iconic American image of World War II, subsequently inspiring the larger-than-life sculpture known as the Marine Monument in Arlington, Virginia. Photographers brought the reality of the Holocaust to disbelievers in gruesome shots of piles of dead bodies that greeted soldiers at the opening of such concentration camps as Bergen-Belsen in the spring of 1945.

Photography for propaganda purposes often entails manipulation. For example, every shot emphasizes something by purposely omitting something else. A smiling, well-fed, well-clothed child can be used to reflect a general sense of well-being, whereas the opposite can be implied through the use of a tearful, emaciated, shabbily dressed child. A close-up of a small number of persons can be used to suggest an enormous crowd. Photomontage involves the conscious construction of an image from bits and pieces of other photographs to create a new image that may bear little resemblance to the original photographs. Careful cropping or retouching can make an artistic or aesthetic statement out of what would otherwise not be as visually satisfying. The digital image and the digitalization of images has led some to wonder if 2000 marks the end of the photograph's power to persuade based on the latter's presumed relationship to visual truth. What may be more significant in the short run, however, is the ability of the amateur or professional photographer to see whether the desired image has been captured in appropriate fashion without undertaking a trip to the darkroom. Digitization also makes possible the transmission of photographic images literally around the world at low cost, assuming that the computer possesses sufficient resolution capability. The painted image may not be suitable for digitization, but photography certainly is. It seems clear that this is the most significant technological advance in photography in the past century.

David Culbert

See also Capa, Robert; Civil War, United States; Crimean War; Riis, Jacob; United States (1930s); United States (Progressive Era); Vietnam War

References: Curtis, James. *Mind's Eye, Mind's Truth: FSA Photography Reconsidered.* Philadelphia: Temple University Press, 1989; Faber, John. *Great News Photos and the Stories behind Them.* 2d ed. New York: Dover, 1978; Goldberg, Vicki. *The Power of Photography: How Photographs Change Our Lives.* New York: Abbeville, 1991; Hambourg, Maria Morris, et al. *The Waking Dream: Photography's First Century.* New York: Abrams, 1993.

The Plow That Broke the Plains (1936)

This documentary film, one of the most innovative pieces of propaganda for President Franklin Roosevelt's (1882–1945) New Deal, was directed by Pare Lorentz (1905–1992) for the Resettlement Administration.

The film tells the story of the mechanized cultivation of the prairies to feed the world during World War I and the disastrous effect of "high winds and sun" on the land during the 1930s. Lorentz's images of the Dust Bowl, many featuring the children of the region, are made even more poignant by a powerful musical score by Virgil Thomson (1896–1989). Although it was well made, as a documentary the film's impact was limited, thanks in part to low production values. Millions more were affected by the photographs of Dorothea Lange (1895–1965) or the powerful novel *The Grapes of Wrath* (1939) by John Steinbeck (1902–1968).

Nicholas J. Cull

See also Film (Documentary); Roosevelt, Franklin D.; United States; United States (1930s)

References: Lorentz, Pare. *FDR's Moviemaker: Memoirs and Scripts.* Reno: University of Nevada Press, 1992; Snyder, Robert L. *Pare Lorentz and the Documentary Film.* Reno: University of Nevada Press, 1968.

Poetry

Although poetry shares many characteristics with other cultural artifacts identified as propaganda, it is not itself regularly identified as such by mainstream literary discourse. Yet poetry is often used by publishers, politicians (among other agents), and poets themselves as a vehicle for the dissemination of "information" and "emotion" meant to alter opinion on matters great and small, and hence has been and continues to be an instrument of statecraft, politics, and social struggle.

Indeed, Plato (ca. 428–ca. 348 B.C.E.) feared poets for their radical misuse of the potent resources of rhetoric, in that they played with false statements in order to induce emotion in their audiences and could threaten state security by manipulating the masses with their seductive lies. In his ideal state, as portrayed in *The Republic,* he considered them persona non grata.

The main strategies and elements that poetry shares with propaganda are briefly noted below, covering the period between roughly 1500 to the present. First is the expression of national aspiration, supremacy, or uniqueness. Poets have consistently written poems that celebrate, justify, and call into being particular nation-states and empires, often based on ethnic or linguistic groupings. Narrative-based poetry—first in Homer (ca. 700 B.C.E.) and later in Virgil (70–19 B.C.E.)—consists of epic poems reflecting the struggle of opposing armies and nations, followed by the founding of just states pleasing to the gods. This jingoism is most evident during times of war, when the poetic genre of "war poetry" is practiced. Rudyard Kipling (1865–1936) was the Victorian poet most emphatically associated with such patriotism, and his mostly vernacular verse remained, until late in World War I (when he lost a son in battle), an almost uninterrupted love letter to Britannia's empire and military victories—and the lowly soldiers who make such victories possible. His poem "Dane-Geld" is a clear call to fight against German expansionism at all costs.

Not all war poetry takes sides, but it is usually inherently infected with subjective and ideological positioning in favor of the poet's "own" forces. The case of the American modernist poet Ezra Pound (1885–1972) provides a startling example of the inversion of this principle, for he took active aim against the United States during World War II and was later arrested as a traitor for his seditious broadcasts from Italy. On the other hand, Dylan Thomas (1914–1953), who often used his wonderful performing voice on radio, obliquely slanted some poems toward the anti-Nazi cause, such as "A Refusal to Mourn the Death, by Fire, of a Child in London," which describes the aerial bombardment of London during the Blitz. Other poets, such as Lord Byron (1788–1824), were leading figures in the struggle for independence (in Byron's case on behalf of Greece). Slovenia's national poet, France Preseren (1800–1849), imported his native language into his poetry and espoused his people's desire for liberty and self-governance while subjugated by imperial Austria, especially in the collection entitled *Poems* (1847), which helped to inspire the 1848 uprisings. So did the legendary and provocative poems of Hungarian rebel Sandor Petofi (1823–1849), who published his call-to-arms in the poem "National Song" (which he read on the steps of the National Museum) on 15 March 1848, setting off a revolt that is still celebrated to this day. W. B. Yeats (1865–1939) maintained a similar relationship, through his poems, to the Easter Rising in Ireland.

Church or government sponsorship is a third important factor. Throughout recorded history poets have sought and received protection and support from powerful men and women, organizations, and rulers. In exchange for money, official positions of cultural and diplomatic significance at court, or abroad, and titles (including that of England's poet laureate), poets have been willing to dedicate poems and verse plays to their benefactors, praise the latter's aims and achievements, and promote the patron's belief systems through their written works. John Milton (1608–1674) issued inflammatory pamphlets and took sides during Britain's political conflicts, leading to charges of treason that were only dropped thanks to the influence of his friends at court. His *Paradise Lost* (among other works) is considered by some critics to be a veiled allegory on Cromwell and the regicidal government of his day, for which he had worked as a propagandist.

Yevgeny Yevtushenko (1933–), the Soviet-born poet, wrote poems early in his career that celebrated Stalin's worldview, which made him a national hero and led to his poems being recited before stadium-size crowds. In 1956, in his long poem *Stantsiia Zima* (Winter Station), he turned against Stalin, following revelations of Stalin's atrocities made during the Twentieth Party Congress. In this way he worked the system and continued to provide material of value to the state machinery.

A fourth characteristic involves a defense of linguistic and societal norms or, conversely, attacking said norms. Poets by definition work through language and are identified with particular linguistic communities in the course of their career. Many poets practice a de facto chauvinism against other cultural communities and languages, which can amount to a sort of propaganda. Philip Larkin (1922–1985), a key figure in English poetry of the mid-twentieth century, expressed his disdain for things foreign and/or non-British in poems, letters, and criticism. The Scottish poet Christopher Murray Grieve (1892–1978), better known as Hugh MacDiarmid, combined a strong interest in establishing a unique Scots-based (literary) language for his nation with—in such later, rambling poems as *Third Hymn to Lenin* (1955)—exceptionally didactic Marxist pronouncements.

A point worth noting is that the poet's rhetorical arsenal is inherently militaristic. Poets have long cherished a close relationship with militaristic themes and tropes. During the Elizabethan period, many leading court poets were soldiers; some were even accused of being spies, as was the case with Christopher Marlowe (1564–1593).

It is no accident that modernist poets living in Europe in the early twentieth century were described as being in the "avant-garde" together with other artists. The issuing of "poetic manifestos"—for example, by the Fascist Futurists in Italy under Mussolini—clearly echoes the tactics of such master propagandists as Lenin. Finally, the aim of poetry is subtly to convey strong impressions, emotions, images, and ideas. Unlike prose, which tends to be a vehicle for lucid exposition, poetry is characterized by enigmatic, opaque, and even gnomic statements, phrases, allusions, and references that are, in some ways, subliminal. Just as with any "good" propaganda, a good poem operates below the radar of a reader's conscious mind, enabling disturbing, inspiring, or irrational forces to penetrate the latter's defenses. By using such mnemonic devices as rhyme, rhythm, and meter, the poem engages the reader by means of seductive properties designed to convert the reader to often-aphoristic "truths" that defy logic and are nearly impossible to refute. This enables strong poets to influence the opinion of their age through the sheer force of their poetic ability, assuming near-oracular status. For example, T. S. Eliot (1888–1965) single-handedly created a consensus on what was and was not canonical— and hence worthy of cultural attention— while masking his anti-Semitism and conservative social values in a cloak of poetic objectivity. It is this "Big Brother" iconic function assumed by major poets that most resembles the propagandistic constructions of consensus normally associated with political movements and dictators.

Todd Swift

See also British Empire; Crimean War; Fascism, Italian; Germany; Ireland; Latin America; Milton, John; Peace and Antiwar Movements (1945–); Shakespeare, William; Vietnam

References: Bergonzi, Bernard. *Wartime and Aftermath: English Literature and Its Background, 1939–1960.* Oxford: Oxford University Press, 1993; Eliot, T. S. *Points of View.* London: Faber and Faber, 1941; Hanák, Péter. *The Corvina History of Hungary.* Budapest: Corvina Books, 1991; Larkin, Philip, ed. *The Oxford Book of Twentieth Century English Verse.* Oxford: Oxford University Press, 1973; Preseren, France. *Poems.* Ljubljana: DZS, 1997; Quiller-Couch, Arthur, ed. *The Oxford Book of English Verse.* Oxford: Oxford University Press, 1931; Redman, Tim. *Ezra Pound and Italian Fascism.* Cambridge: Cambridge University Press, 1991; Scarfe, Francis. *Auden and After: The Liberation of Poetry, 1930–1941.* London: George Routledge & Sons, 1945; Schmidt, Michael. *Lives of the Poets.* London: Weidenfeld and Nicolson, 1998; Sutherland, John. *Literary Lives.* New York: Oxford University Press, 2001; Todd, Albert C., and Max Hayward, eds. *20th Century Russian Poetry,* sel. Yevgeny Yevtushenko. New York: Anchor, 1994.

Poland

Poland has both produced propaganda—especially in the cause of nationalism during years of foreign rule—and been the target of propaganda, not least during World War II and the Communist era. As with many European countries, the early modern period in Poland saw propaganda on behalf of the royal house (and opposition nobles), in connection with the Reformation and Counter-Reformation, and at the beginnings of a popular print culture. Poland witnessed the publication of Eastern Europe's oldest vernacular newspaper, *Merkuriusz Poliski Ordynaryjny* (Polish Common Mercury), which was founded in Krakow in 1661. In the eighteenth century Poland suffered a series of partitions (1772, 1793, 1795) during which the country was divided between neighboring Austria, Prussia, and Russia (which took the largest share of territory). Nationalistic movements, with attendant patriotic propaganda, culminated in a rebellion led by Tadeusz Kosciuszkó (1746–1817), a veteran of the American Revolution. Kosciuszkó was a master of the emotional appeal, as exemplified in his 1794 plea to the nation to rise up, which he delivered in the market square in Krakow symbolically attired in the Polish national costume. He remained a key figure in Polish national propaganda. Art embodying a political agenda is exemplified in the poem "Myszeidos" (Mouse Poem), an allegory on political disorder by Ignacy Krasicki (1735–1801).

The Napoleonic Wars did little to improve the lot of Poland, sparking a revival of nationalistic feeling. In 1830–1831 the Russians crushed the so-called November Uprising in "their" Polish territory. This led to a large-scale migration to Paris, which became the locus of Polish émigré activity and propaganda for the remainder of the century. Leading émigrés included the pianist and composer Frédéric Chopin (1810–1849). Chopin's music regularly included pieces in such specifically Polish idioms as the mazurka and the polonaise, which served as nationalistic propaganda in musical form. Equivalent figures in the field of poetry included Adam Mickiewicz (1798–1855), Juliusz Słowacki (1809–1849), and Zygmunt

Krasinski (1812–1859). Art by painters like Piotr Michalowski (1800–1855), which frequently celebrated Kosciuszkó and his battles, circulated widely in print form.

Russian- and Austrian-occupied Poland rose up in 1848, with the former again revolting in 1866 during the January Revolution. In the wake of these rebellions, the Russians in the east and Prussians in the west both began campaigns of Russification and Germanization, respectively, which included censorship, propaganda, and educational controls, as well as the renaming of places. Opponents of this policy included Count Mieczisław Ledóchowski (1822–1902), archbishop of Poznan, who in 1874 refused to obey the Prussian order not to teach in the Polish language. The Prussians were involved in a wider conflict with the church during the period known as the Kulturkampf (cultural struggle). Artists who promoted Polish nationalism included the painter and dramatist Stanisław Wyspiański (1869–1907) and the novelist Stefan Żeromski (1864–1925). Political activists involved in the Polish independence movement later in the century included the young Józef Piłsudski (1867–1935), who in 1894 launched the underground left-wing journal Robotnik (Worker).

During World War I Piłsudski led the Polish army against Russia, but he also quarreled with the Central Powers. In 1918 he declared an independent Polish republic, which was confirmed by the Treaty of Versailles in 1919. The 1920s saw a heated debate over the nature of the Polish state. Lithuanian-born Piłsudski favored a multiethnic Poland with a place for Germans, Jews, and Ukrainians. Included among the ethnic nationalist propagandists who disagreed with this approach was Roman Dmowski (1869–1939), who had assembled an anti-German army during the Great War, was editor of Przegląd Wszech-polski (All-Polish Review) and served as minister of foreign affairs in 1923. Dmowski's arguments were frequently racist and anti-Semitic. Seeking to maintain his broader vision, Piłsudski seized power in a coup in 1926. Between 1926 and his death in 1935 he dominated Polish politics (both as premier and minister of war). His successor, Edward Rydz-Śmigły (1886–1941), joined with the nationalists, resulting in a rise in anti-Semitism. The interwar period thus witnessed a mixture of nationalistic propaganda and the exuberant expression of Polish culture in an increasingly right-wing political context. Overseas propaganda enterprises included a sizable Polish pavilion at the New York World's Fair of 1939.

In September 1939 Adolf Hitler (1889–1945) invaded Poland, triggering World War II. The early months of the war saw what amounted to a new partition of Poland, with Hitler sharing the spoils with Stalin (1879–1953), his new ally. In occupied Poland the resistance operated an underground press with strong propaganda content. The Polish government-in-exile, led by Władysław Sikorski (1881–1943), worked hard to communicate news of Nazi atrocities in Poland to the outside word, publishing reports and photographs smuggled out by the underground Polish Home Army. The Polish Ministry of Information-in-exile was among the first institutions to provide news of the genocide of European Jews, which was downplayed as a war atrocity story by many. Beginning in 1941, the Poles were technically fighting on the same side as their old enemy, Russia, a relationship that was made more complicated in 1943 with the discovery of a mass grave of Polish officers murdered by Russians in the Katyn Forest near Smolensk—the news of which proved a coup for Nazi propaganda. The issue became the subject of charge and countercharge in wartime and postwar propaganda, and it was not until 1990 that the Russians admitted responsibility and apologized.

Despite Allied propaganda at the beginning of the war stressing the need to defend Poland, World War II ended with the de facto acceptance by the Allies that Poland lay within Stalin's sphere of influence. The extent to which President Franklin Roosevelt

(1882–1945) had "betrayed" Poland at the Yalta Conference of 1945 became an issue in domestic U.S. party propaganda in the post-war years. The Lublin Poles, a pro-Soviet faction that had spent the war in the USSR, dominated the new Polish government, and Poland swiftly became an integral part of the emerging Soviet bloc. Significant events during this period included: rigged elections in 1947, which returned a Communist government to power; membership in the Communist economic organization COMECON in 1949; the unveiling of a Soviet-style constitution in 1952; and membership in the Warsaw Pact military alliance in 1955. Communist Poland experienced rigid party control of education and the media, which included the licensing of journalists. State sponsorship of the arts produced the Polish equivalent of Soviet-style Socialist Realism. "Ideologically sound" writers included the poet Konstanty Ildefons Gałczyński (1906–1953). Following the death of Stalin, Poland experienced a period of media liberalization during the early administration of Władysław Gomułka (1905–1982), who had come to power in 1956, but by the 1960s the party propaganda machine was back in full swing.

External anti-Communist propaganda aimed at Poland included U.S. government-sponsored broadcasts of the Voice of America (VOA) and Radio Free Europe (RFE). Indigenous anti-Communist propaganda circulated in the form of underground newspapers, the largest being *Tygodnik Mazowsze* (Mazovian Weekly). The economic crisis of the 1970s widened the gap between Polish government propaganda and reality. The church remained a center of oppositional thought and received a massive moral boost with the election in 1978 of Polish pope John Paul II (1920–) and his emotional visit to Poland in 1979. Liberal voices in film included Andrzej Wajda (1926–), whose 1978 film *Cztowiek z Marmuru (*Man of Marble) questioned the legacy of the leaders from the 1950s. Political dissidents included Adam Michnik (1946–), who was jailed six times for his views.

In 1980 workers at the Gdansk shipyards went on strike under the leadership of Lech Wałęsa (1943–), who had organized the Solidarity trade union, whose slogan was: "There is no freedom without Solidarity." The union's demands included an end to censorship and biased media coverage. A substantial proportion of Polish media workers joined the union. Solidarity's publications included the newspaper *Jednosc* and the national magazine *Tygodnik Solidarność* (Solidarity Weekly). Wajda documented the upheaval in his 1981 film *Czlowiek z zelaza* (Man of Iron). The Communist government clamped down, imposing martial law from 1981 to 1984. Poland became a major issue in international propaganda in the revived Cold War. Examples included the United States Information Agency's (USIA) star-studded television special *Let Poland Be Poland* (1982), which was broadcast worldwide by satellite. Wałęsa presented himself as the embodiment of the gritty, Catholic, patriotic Polish worker. He captured the imagination of the Western media, making repression of the movement much harder. Other important figures included the articulate academic Bronisłav Geremek (1932–). Solidarity's leaders seemed all the more inspiring when compared to the stiff Gen. Wojciech Jaruzelski (1923–), whose appearance was rendered significantly more sinister thanks to his dark glasses, which he was forced to wear for medical reasons. In November 1988 Wałęsa confronted Mieczslaw Rakowski the prime minister of Poland, in a live television debate. In 1989 Solidarity negotiated political reforms, including free elections. The government allowed the opposition to publish a daily newspaper to cover the election. Entitled *Gazeta Wyborcza* (Election Gazette), this paper drew many of its staff from the underground *Tygodnik Mazowsze*. Walesa recruited Adam Michnik (1946–) as editor. Solidarity won a majority in the resulting elections. The Communist era in Poland had ended. *Gazeta Wyborcza* remains one of Poland's leading newspapers, although it split with Wałęsa in 1990.

Post-Communist Poland saw a proliferation of political parties and a lively culture of interparty propaganda. Although Wałęsa won the presidency in 1990, the country went though eight prime ministers in rapid succession. In 1995 Wałęsa lost the presidential election to Aleksander Kwaśniewski (1954–), a former Communist propagandist who had made his mark as a student activist in the 1970s and editor of the reformist party journals *ITD* (Et Cetera) and *Sztandar Młodych,* who now led the Democratic Left Alliance (SDL). Jerzy Urban (1933–), another veteran of Communist propaganda and General Jaruzelski's press officer, reinvented himself for the post-Communist era by launching the muckraking satirical weekly *Nie* (No). The magazine soon commanded a circulation over seven hundred thousand and claimed a readership in excess of 2 million. Its declared targets were "nationalism, clericalism, and bigotry, rightist parties and factions, Solidarity and Lech Wałęsa." The success of *Nie* reflected the scale of dissatisfaction with the media following the collapse of Communism. Many Poles felt that "black (church) censorship and propaganda were replacing the red." Criticism of the church, abortion law, women's rights, and anti-Semitism seemed stifled in the mainstream media. In 1999 Poland joined NATO, a substantial coup for Kwaśniewski that helped him win reelection in 2000.

Nicholas J. Cull

See also Atrocity Propaganda; Austrian Empire; Elections; Philippines; Religion; Russia; Stalin, Joseph; World War II (Germany)

References: Ash, Timothy Garton. *The Polish Revolution: Solidarity, 1980–82.* London: Granta, 1991; Davies, Norman. *God's Playground: A History of Poland.* 2 vols. Oxford: Clarendon, 1981; Goban-Klas, Tomasz. *The Orchestration of the Media: The Politics of Mass Communications in Communist Poland and the Aftermath.* Boulder, CO: Westview, 1994.

Portraiture

Historically the role of portraiture was acknowledged in the Renaissance as serving one of two purposes in art. German master Albrecht Dürer (1471–1528) expressed this as preserving the "likeness of men after their death." Portraits naturally raise a number of considerations when being viewed. They are the result of the interplay between artist and sitter. Their aesthetics are conditioned by the traditions of the genre and the requirements of the patron or buyer. Their intention is often highly fluid. Questions as to why the work was commissioned and for what end purpose are always prevalent in all genres, but in portraiture this assumes a more prominent place. It is a truism that the patron or purchaser determines the final image and what can be inferred from an examination of the work. This intent is often revealed in the setting, which helps to define the sitter's place in society. The spectator learns of the latter's interests and values through the resulting appropriation of objects and symbols reflecting social mores.

This is not to say that portraiture may only be read in terms of iconography. The development of individual portrait types indicates that different styles of portraiture serve differing purposes. Full-length portraits have mostly been reserved for royalty and nobility. In such cases direct communication with the viewer is aided by presenting different views of the subject's features. Profile views, which are often used in elite circles as well, are derived from classical forms and were perceived in the Renaissance and thereafter as representing a dignified character in a hieratic manner. In all these cases the use of the individual portrait demonstrates the social standing of the sitter as an autonomous individual. Group portraits consequently define the social status of those portrayed. Often they depict various hierarchies within a given group through the use of complex compositional techniques to indicate this. Portraits of couples or families are often concerned with creating the impression of the nuclear family, in line with the conventions of the age. This complexity is revealed through rhetorical gestures and facial expressions, coupled with the iconography of emblems and attributes. In short, the very nature of portraiture is propagandist: the projection of an image—which may or may not be true—to a passive audience.

Early portraiture reflected the grandeur of the Renaissance. The rise of humanism gave the practice of portraiture a conceptual dignity as a result of theoretical and cultural factors. Earlier portraiture was mainly religious in nature, with the subject often shown performing an act of veneration toward a saint or holy person. The frontal depiction of the face was reserved solely for Christ; prior to Dürer's self-portrait (1500), which appropriated the traditional image of Christ to further the claims of the artist as creator, few portraits adopted this approach (a notable exception was the depiction of Napoleon). The portrait developed along didactic lines. The prominence of physiognomy in intellectual theory meant that often portraits were thought to provide an insight into the personalities of the model. As a result, portraits were often painted as realistically as possible, although in time idealization and monumentality prevailed in the portraits of the ruling classes.

Portraits served as a potent type of propaganda in the depiction of rulers. Early-eighteenth-century diplomatic protocol saw the vicarious use of portraiture as representing the subject as actually present. The portrait could thus serve a "representative" function, a frank demonstration of power, hegemony, and prestige. Portraits of ruling princes often reflected a desire for power, as, for example, in equestrian portraits, where military prestige was viewed as the foremost duty of a prince. Hence Titian's (ca. 1488–1576) *Emperor Charles V after the Battle of Muhlberg* shows the subject in a historical context, having defeated his rival Protestant princes. Such imagery is not always realistic. For example, in 1653 Antonis Mor (ca. 1519–ca. 1575) portrayed Philip II of Spain in armor prior to the "War of San Quentin" purely for propaganda purposes. Phillip II was, in fact, never

at San Quentin, although the image suggests that he is riding forth to win a crucial battle.

In France many painters depicted Napoleon as emperor and military leader, especially Jacques-Louis David (1748–1825), Baron Antoine-Jean Gros (1771–1835), and most notably Jean-Auguste-Dominique Ingres (1780–1867), whose *Napoleon on His Imperial Throne* (1806) transformed the subject into an otherworldly figure, complete with imperial paraphernalia and presented in the frontal posture recalling late medieval representations of God. In this ambitious work the hero worship surrounding Napoleon had made tenable his removal from the constraints of the physical world into a timeless realm.

During this period portraiture in the form of caricatures and cartoons was becoming popular, particularly of prime ministers and other leaders. In Britain the rise of print shops established a wide market for such works. It is a moot point as to the extent the caricatures of James Gillray (1757–1815) played in the downfall of Charles Fox (1749–1806). Britain's imperial policy also represents a prime example of the use of portraiture as propaganda, particularly through the erection of statues of Queen Victoria (1819–1901) in India, which, as symbols of allegiant nationalism, were intended to inspire a sense of patriotic feeling in the local natives. Often these took on the form of allegory; in Calcutta the queen is depicted as a Roman goddess and elsewhere she is generally shown as matriarchal, suggesting fair treatment for those under the British yoke.

Portraiture within avant-garde art holds little in the way of propaganda value. The avant-garde's stress on art's autonomy removed portraiture from the realm of politics in most cases, assuming a more critical stance toward the subject. This was compounded by the rise of abstraction. This autonomy of art was compromised under political dictatorships. Hitler (1889–1945) and Stalin (1879–1953) both saw the importance of controlling state culture. In both cases the ideology and culture of the political parties merged with the personality of the leader, with aesthetics largely a reflection of the leader's taste. Official art in general veered toward the conservative and the grandiose, with the figure of the leader being depicted as alternately paternal, caring, and vengeful. The iconography may have differed slightly from one dictatorship to another, but the message generally remained the same: the hopes and fears of a nation were focused on one man, who was most often depicted as a warrior-leader. This naturally expressed itself through portrait cycles or iconic history paintings. Examples of these genres are evident in all totalitarian regimes; for example, Hubert Lanzinger's (1880–1950) *The Protector of German Art* and Heinrich Knirr's (1862–1944) modern depiction of Hitler executed in the style of an eighteenth-century English portrait.

Stalin was more intimately and personally depicted in painting than in print. Often, in an act of political legitimation, he is dwarfed by a statue of Lenin, as Grigori Shegal's (1889–1956) *Leader, Teacher and Friend* (1936/7). This was a popular motif in both Social Realist art depicting Stalin and in political posters. Gustavs Klucis's (1895–1944) *Raise the Banner of Marx, Engels, Lenin and Stalin* (1937) and *Long Live the Stalinist Order of Heroes and Stakhanovites!* (1936) are two prime examples of Soviet propaganda fostering Stalin's personality cult. Such imagery was frequent and commonplace, particularly after the suppression of the Russian avant-garde and the return to iconic subject matter.

The association of figurative art with totalitarian states has led to the gradual rejection of portraiture as a dominant art form in postwar art. Portraiture is still paramount in art, although not in the mainstream avant-garde, where abstraction has led to the dissolution of the art object. The rise of photography has also struck a blow to this once popular art form.

Daniel Cooper

See also Art; Austrian Empire; Britain; Cartoons; David, Jacques-Louis; Elizabeth I; France; Napoleon; Russia; Spain; Stalin, Joseph

References: Archer, Mildred. *India and British Portraiture, 1770–1825.* Karachi, India: Oxford University Press, 1979; Campbell, Lorne. *Renaissance Portraits: European Portrait-Painting in the 14th, 15th and 16th Centuries.* New Haven, CT: Yale University Press, 1990; Halliday, Anthony. *Facing the Public: Portraiture in the Aftermath of the French Revolution.* Manchester: Manchester University Press, 2000; Pointon, Marcia Rachel. *Hanging the Head: Portraiture and Social Formation in Eighteenth-Century England.* New Haven, CT: Yale University Press, 1993; Wilton, Andrew. *The Swagger Portrait: Grand Manner Portraiture in Britain from Van Dyck to Augustus John, 1630–1930.* London: Tate Gallery, 1992; Woodall, Joanna. *Portraiture.* Manchester: Manchester University Press, 1997.

Portugal

A country such as Portugal—which has experienced Islamic, Catholic, Masonic, fascist, and even quasi-Marxist forms of government—has naturally been subjected to many forms of indoctrination and persuasion over the past eight hundred years. The longest-running confidence game in history must surely be the claim that in medieval Portugal the Christians were the legitimate rulers of the land and the Muslims the alien usurpers. The Christians of the north, with their pre-Christian overlay of Celtic culture and their Burgundian aristocracy, had no better claim to ethnic purity than the Muslims of the south, with their strong Roman traditions of architecture and their lyrical Arabic poetry. History, however, belongs to the victors, and when Christian crusaders from England sacked Muslim Lisbon (en route to further exploits involving plundering in the Mediterranean), the Portuguese of the north worsted the Portuguese of the south and eventually captured not only the great plains beyond Lisbon but also appropriated the Algarve—the crown of the Muslim "Kingdom of the West." So persuasive was the propaganda relating to these religious civil wars that when a Portuguese academic was recently asked to deliver a paper on Portuguese "independence" to an international seminar, he spoke neither of the liberation from Spanish rule in 1640 nor of the ending of British rule in 1820 but rather the Christian "victories" of the Middle Ages.

One of the beneficiaries of the Christian conquest of Muslim Portugal was Prince Henry (1394–1460), a commander of the Order of Christ with a papal license to plunder the lands of the "infidels." The Lancastrian prince, a grandson of John of Gaunt—onetime claimant to the thrones both of Castile and of England—was the younger son of the king of Portugal and a past master of political propaganda. It is said that "he who pays the piper calls the tune," and Henry's piper, one Azurara, whose chronicles the next fifteen generations of historians treated as evidence rather than as propaganda, was second to none in the art of praising. At the age of sixteen Henry embarked on a catastrophic venture into Muslim North Africa—hitching a ferry ride on a large but ill-fated international expedition commissioned by the pope—and although the little Moroccan port of Ceuta was seized, Henry had to sacrifice his elder brother, murdered for want of an adequate ransom. Like Churchill (1874–1965) at Dunkirk, Henry's propagandists turned bitter defeat into songs of victory over the Islamic "forces of darkness," and four centuries later Victorian Englishmen dubbed Henry "the Navigator," although he is not known ever to have set foot on a boat again. Instead he commissioned the fishermen of the Algarve to raid the coast of Morocco for Moorish slaves to work the conquered latifundia of the Portuguese main. He even managed to claim credit for his brother's shrewd efforts to bring Italian bankers and sea captains to Lisbon, where they alleviated the city's periodic bread famines by initiating the first overseas colonization and planting of wheatfields on the Atlantic islands. By the twentieth century Prince Henry had become the idol of imperialism and was the ubiquitous symbol of power during Portugal's half-century of fascist-style autocracy.

A century after Henry's death Portugal still believed it had the right to conquer the lands beyond the Pillars of Hercules in the name of Christ—and imperial profit—but the expedition of 1578 into Morocco, led by King Sebastian (1554–1578), proved a fiasco. When the long-lamented warriors failed to return from Africa, Philip II of Castile, the widowed former king-consort of England, took over Portugal, claiming that he had "inherited it, bought it, *and* conquered it." He thereafter used the Portuguese fleet, the Armada, to attempt the capture of England. By 1640 Portugal had become as closely integrated into Spain as Catalonia or Andalusia, but the Castilianized aristocracy in Lisbon greatly feared that heavy taxation and large military levies might lead to a peasant revolt, as had already happened in 1637. They were also concerned that the court at Madrid would be so preoccupied in suppressing revolts in richer provinces that it would not have the military resources to suppress a revolt against the landowners of Portugal. Thus it was that on 1 December 1640 the aristocracy seized local power in Lisbon, persuaded the duke of Braganza (1604–1656) to adopt the style of "king," and announced, with all the propaganda devices at their disposal, that they were restoring *l'ancien régime* of King Sebastian and claiming independence for Portugal. It took twenty-eight years of civil and international war—part of the Thirty Years' War that settled the future of early modern Europe—for Spain, France (which had a powerful court faction at Lisbon), and the papacy (which had refused to consecrate any bishops for the Portuguese church during hostilities) to accept Portuguese independence under English patronage. This patronage, however, cost Portugal dearly, and in exchange for agreeing to take the Portuguese princess Catherine of Braganza (1638–1705) as his bride, Charles II of England (1630–1685) demanded the remnants of the Portuguese empire in North Africa—Tangier—and the safe haven of the Portuguese in India—Bombay—as a dowry. Portugal's "oldest ally" demanded its pound of flesh and its pint of blood. In 1703 the neocolonial dependency between Portugal and England was consolidated by John Methuen (ca. 1650–1706), but the terms of his famous treaty were not as unequal as Portuguese patriots and propagandists would have their readers believe, with England agreeing to buy quantities of occasionally inferior Portuguese wine in return for a guaranteed Portuguese market for English woolens.

The propaganda and counterpropaganda relating to the Methuen Treaty rumbled on for three centuries, but in 1755 an earthquake destroyed Lisbon and its government was taken over by a quasi-enlightened despot, the future Marquis of Pombal (1699–1782), who devoted considerable skill to the rewriting of history. His postings as chargé d'affaires in both Vienna and London had given him powerful insights into both the Old World aristocracy and the New World merchant bourgeoisie. Following the earthquake, Pombal wrongly claimed all the credit for "feeding the living and burying the dead," banishing the true leaders of the philanthropic recovery program to remote monastic houses. He then set about spreading a campaign of disinformation about Portugal's aristocrats, who had allegedly been disloyal to the crown, and eventually killed some of them with an excessive public display of cruelty—a symbolic use of power politics that was fearfully recalled by ordinary Portuguese when a new police state was established in the 1930s. Pombal gave power and status to the king, his feeble patron, even obliterating the names of the benefactors from the towering Lisbon aqueduct and anachronistically attributing the grand structure to his tame master. Although claiming to be a great patriot, Pombal in fact sold commercial rights to largely English foreigners when he established the quality port wine trade to replace the dwindling colonial revenues of Brazil. Two centuries later the Portuguese Republic claimed Pombal as one of its sources of inspiration, and the Masonic lodges helped fund the erection of one of Lisbon's most potent statues honoring brute power.

After Wellington's (1769–1852) Peninsular Wars, the English army, under the command of Field Marshal William Carr Beresford (1768–1854), ruled Portugal for a decade and began a century-long process of English modernization. Although some of this modernization proved effective, a great deal was window dressing in the style adopted by provincial officials in Catherine the Great's (1729–1796) Russia. The phrase "para o inglês ver"—putting on appearances for the benefit of the English—became one of the country's most frequent sayings as aspiration failed to match reality. But change did occur: the monasteries were dissolved and the land was given to a merchant bourgeoisie, which turned itself into a British-style House of Lords while the generals played musical chairs with seats in the cabinet and the house of Saxe-Coburg took over the monarchy. The English were constantly breathing down the necks of the Portuguese. Lord Palmerston (1784–1865) was heard to mutter: "I occasionally find it necessary to administer a sound chastisement to the semibarbarous nations of the world such as China or Portugal." This arrogant style of politics finally exploded in 1890 when Portugal's claim to a natural sphere of influence in Central Africa—from Angola across the Zambezi River and the Zimbabwe highlands to Mozambique—was absentmindedly dismissed by Lord Salisbury (1830–1903) in London, an insult that still rankled in Portugal a century later but was scarcely noticed at the time in England.

The twentieth century began violently for Portugal when the king was assassinated in 1908 and Portugal was once more disputing with England over the continuing trade in colonial slaves captured in Angola and Mozambique. No amount of sugarcoating could disguise the fact that Britain was buying Portuguese cocoa from slave-run plantations, and soon thereafter the trade was banned and the Saxe-Coburg dynasty was overthrown by a working-class conspiracy fomented in secret *carbonari* cells. A subsequent revolution was orchestrated by middle-class Freemasons. The propaganda spread by the republic from 1910 to 1926 blamed the country's ills on aristocrats, clergymen, and the foreigners who dragged Portugal into the Great War of 1914, thereby bankrupting the exchequer. The outlawed Catholic Church fought back by blaming the postwar depression on Masonic incompetence, encouraging Catholic army officers to oust their Masonic counterparts, which occurred in the military coup d'état of May 1926. To hold on to its power the army turned to Antonio Salazar (1889–1970), a part-time journalist and lecturer in bookkeeping who proved to be one of the century's most adept (if mendacious) manipulators of information and propaganda. Salazar was a modest landowner and a one-time fledgling priest with a taste for wine and women that outstripped his income but not his ability to market himself as an ascetic recluse and a financial genius. By adopting a crude form of early monetarism and denying both the theory and the morality of Keynesian economics, he was able to cut back on social expenditures so savagely that his ministry of finance could afford to pay the upper echelons of the army enough to live in idle comfort. He presented himself as a messiah, though he rapidly eschewed the posters of himself as a sword-bearing crusader and instead adopted the social restraints perfected by Mussolini (1883–1945) in Italy, though without imitating the latter's bombastic speeches or the grand popular marches. Although Salazar never left his country, through shrewd diplomacy he maintained working relations with both Franklin Roosevelt (1882–1945) and Adolf Hitler (1889–1945) until their deaths, enabling him to survive—along with his much-despised neighbor, Gen. Francisco Franco (1892–1975) of Spain—while other fascist dictatorships fell. He billed himself as a stalwart anti-Communist fit to be admitted to the North Atlantic Treaty Organization (NATO) and even attempted to claim

that his regime's minuscule and carefully vetted electoral elite represented "democracy." Salazar's greatest coup was to present himself as the champion of white "civilization" just when the United Nations seemed about to be flooded with black Third World applicants, and in 1955 Portugal was admitted to the organization as though it had been an approved democracy.

However, the admission of Portugal as a white counterweight at the United Nations soon backfired in a most spectacular and ironic fashion, and Salazar once again had to summon all his skills in political persuasion. In 1961 the Portuguese colonies rebelled against two generations of cruel economic exploitation that utilized forced labor and centuries of virulent racial abuse. The propaganda machine denied that forced labor was practiced, claiming that Africans were naturally idle and would never become "civilized" unless forced to adopt methodical work practices. During a particularly severe bout of compulsory cotton cropping in 1945, Salazar is alleged to have remarked: "Famine is a figment of the Bantu [African] imagination." He was even more incensed by the accusations of racism leveled against Portugal, and the city of Lisbon was plastered with posters proclaiming that black and white were equal in his great empire. One of the most peculiar features of the hysteria was the claim that the mixed-race mestizo element of the colonial population was a symptom of equality rather than an indication that however well the modesty of white girls might be protected by church and state, African women were fair game for all; even novices in convents lost their virginity to lustful colonial officials, while other black girls were taken at will by their employers or by conscripted soldiers for whom sex was almost the only solace in a lonely posting. Even so, the propaganda machine continued to blare out the message that Portugal did not abuse and exploit nonwhites in the way South Africa had commonly done.

Strident rhetoric was less effective than silent diplomacy in protecting the Portuguese empire for another half generation, and Salazar was able to force U.S. president John F. Kennedy (1917–1963) to reverse an American policy of proclaiming "Africa for the Africans" by threatening to close the mid-Atlantic airfields on the Portuguese islands. The Washington climb-down enabled Salazar quietly to divert weapons issued to Portugal for the defense of the North Atlantic against the USSR to bomb rebel colonies in Africa back into submission. No amount of diplomacy and papal lobbying, however, enabled Portugal to recover its Indian colonies, and the thousands of monotone posters proclaiming "Goa is ours" began peeling along the colonnades of Lisbon shopping arcades. Meanwhile, in Africa white vigilantes butchered any educated blacks they could lay their hands on, exploding once and for all the myth of colonial racial harmony. In the end, colonial propaganda failed not only in the colonial and international spheres but also in the domestic one as a hundred thousand Portuguese turned their backs on the rose-colored empire of the propaganda images and, hidden under freight trains, set off to work illicitly in the "miracle" factories of postwar France. The captains of Portuguese industry soon abandoned the myth of imperial propaganda too, tired of government development plans often based on fictitious statistical projections prepared for propaganda purposes and then recycled as hard data. The industrialists joined forces with young army officers—many of whom had not made adequate speculative profits out of colonial black markets and currency speculation—and between them they overthrew the dictatorship of Salazar's dauphin, Marcelo Caetano (1906–1980). Young soldiers marched into Lisbon as ecstatic crowds thronged to put carnations in their rifle barrels, while businessmen prepared to enter the European Union.

Before Portugal made the full transition from imperial pariah to industrial democracy, it underwent a phase of political experimentation in which propaganda scribbled on walls was at its most colorful and exuberant.

Old Moscow-style Communists participated in new governments, while more energetic left-wing political groups painted every available wall in Lisbon with graffiti advocating everything from free love to land nationalization. The radicalism of the daily street demonstrations and the gaudiness of nightly spray-can artistry persuaded some Portuguese to emigrate, but the majority waited for the tide to turn. Twenty-five years later many people were not even sure whether the "revolution of the carnations" had been a revolution at all, though the verbal barrage had been nothing if not exhilarating.

David Birmingham

See also Africa; International; Reformation and Counter-Reformation; Spain
References: Birmingham, David. *A Concise History of Portugal.* Cambridge: Cambridge University Press, 1993;———. *Portugal and Africa.* Basingstoke, UK: Palgrave, 1999; Boxer, C. R. *Race Relations in the Portuguese Colonial Empire.* Oxford: Oxford University Press, 1963; Macaulay, Rose. *They Went to Portugal.* London: Jonathan Cape, 1946; Maxwell, Kenneth. *The Making of Portuguese Democracy.* Cambridge: Cambridge University Press, 1995; Nogeira, Franco. *Salazar.* 6 vols. Coimbra, Portugal: Atlantida, 1977–1985; Pélissier, René. *Explorar. Voyages en Angola et autres lieux incertains.* Orgeval, France: Pélissier, 1979; Saramago, José. *The Year of the Death of Ricardo Reis.* London: HarperCollins, 1992; White, Landeg. *The Lusiads of Camoes.* Oxford: Oxford University Press, 1997.

Postage Stamps

Postage stamps are receipts for prepaid delivery of envelopes or packages, but they can convey messages displayed on them along with the amount paid. Thus, they can serve as little posters, which make up for their small size by the scale and scope of their distribution. Canada, for instance, has produced stamps displaying images of the monarch, political leaders, church leaders, the maple leaf, distinguished authors, outstanding artists, flags of the ten provinces, national flora and fauna, discoveries by Canadians, national aviation history, distinctive artifacts, national parks, aboriginal peoples, important cities, expositions, ships, and sports heroes. In this way Canada seeks to project a favorable image of its country.

The United States has produced similar stamps, plus some conveying American ideology. During World War II its stamps and cancellations featured slogans such as "Defense Comes First," "Let's Go U.S.A.," "Keep 'Em Flying," "Speed Up for Victory," and "Nations United for Victory" (with the American bald eagle often appearing with its powerful wings forming a "V"). These stamps also bore images of various allies holding swords to symbolize their united military power. In the half century since the war, the United States has disseminated its ideology by producing stamps about religious freedom, freedom of the press, world peace through law and trade, NATO united for freedom, John Kennedy's Alliance for Progress, food for peace, and freedom from hunger. Often stamps have appeared with quotations by Washington, Franklin, and Lincoln. Space exploration has also been a popular theme.

Revolutionary and totalitarian regimes use stamps, along with other instruments of mass persuasion, in a deliberate way to mold the opinions of their citizenry toward the regime. During the twelve years of Germany's Third Reich, the commonest image on postage stamps was that of Hitler, usually flanked by Nazi symbols such as the swastika, torches, giant swords, huge eagles, and powerful steeds (a symbol of Aryan power in the sense of pure breeding) pulling a chariot driven by the goddess Victory. To make him appear more human, Hitler was often shown alongside mothers and children. During World War II many stamps featured an array of transport vehicles, such as armored tanks, submarines, airplanes, and gun ships. Sometimes Hitler was depicted facing Mussolini with a slogan that read: "Zwei Volkes, Ein Krieg" (Two peoples, One War). Cancellations also featured a huge sword emerging from a giant swastika penetrating into the east with the slogan: "Gegen Bolshevismus" (Against Bolshevism).

During its eighty-five years of existence, the Soviet Union likewise promoted favorable images of its ideology and accomplishments, although, unlike Hitler, Stalin seldom appeared. On the other hand, Marx, Engels, and Lenin appeared often. Typical Soviet symbols included the red star, hammer and sickle, and flags of the federated Soviet states, along with mine workers, peasants, and soldiers. The success of each Five-Year Plan was underscored with images of factories, blast furnaces, hydroelectric power stations, tractors, and new public buildings. As in Nazi Germany, during World War II Soviet postage stamps depicted military hardware, naval ships, the defense of Stalingrad, and Red Army scouts and snipers. Stamps also reminded the public of Soviet exploits in space, famous Soviet writers, and victories in international sports, especially hockey.

Postage stamps issued by Communist China are especially interesting. Beginning in 1927, Chinese Communists began using postage stamps for propaganda in their base territories. Their crude stamps exhibited the red star, the hammer and sickle, and the globe with red spreading across its surface to signify the worldwide scope of the movement. (Red has been associated with violent events since the French Revolution, but crimson or *hones* red has had a special appeal to the Chinese, symbolizing joyous events.) After losing their foothold in southeastern China and the Long March to the north, the Communists issued similar stamps in liberated regions. Once the Chinese Communists won national power in 1949, they began to produce better-quality stamps designed to impress the masses. Popular themes included: the *Communist Manifesto*, Russia's October Revolution, China's May Fourth Movement (1919), the founding of the Chinese Communist Party, the Long March, the inauguration of the People's Republic of China, and the "liberation" of Tibet (showing cattle grazing peacefully alongside the Communist Chinese flag). With the start of the Cultural Revolution in 1966, the look of Chinese stamps changed in terms of size and theme. Chairman Mao's sayings (either in type or in his own handwriting) appeared alongside his likeness. Other stamps featured heroes who had died, terraced hillsides symbolizing the conquest of nature, scenes from Mao's wife's new revolutionary operas, and the integration of women into the workforce.

James A. Leith

See also Black Propaganda; China; Posters; Russia; Spain

References: Altman, Dennis. *Paper Ambassadors: The Politics of Stamps.* North Ride, Australia: Angus and Robertson, 1991; Leith, James A. "Postage Stamps and Ideology in Communist China." *Queen's Quarterly* 78, 2 (1971): 176–186; Stoetzer, Carlos. *Postage Stamps as Propaganda.* Washington, DC: Public Affairs Press, 1953;Strauss, Harlan J. *Subliminal Propaganda: The Postage Stamp.* Eugene: University of Oregon Press, 1972.

Posters

Posters are handwritten or printed notices, announcements, and advertisements displayed in a public space. Posters have been around ever since people began to write announcements on parchment or paper and mounted them on buildings, especially in conspicuous places such as public edifices and streetcorners. After the invention of printing by means of movable type, such announcements could be disseminated with ease and in much greater numbers. Until the nineteenth century most posters consisted of large headings with smaller type underneath. Such printed posters were issued primarily by political and religious groups. At the start of the French Revolution posters still consisted mainly of printed words with the royal coat of arms at the top, whereas after the overthrow of the monarchy in 1792, such announcements appeared with Liberty Bonnets or a female figure representing Liberty as the sole graphic work.

Most posters continued to consist primarily of printed messages until the spread of lithography (literally "writing on stone") in the nineteenth century. Lithography had been invented in the 1790s by the German named Aloys Senefelder (1771–1834), who used Bavarian limestone. The lithographic process is based on the mutual antipathy of oil and water. The drawing is made in reverse directly on a smooth, flat stone using crayon or ink containing a greasy substance. The fatty substance interacts with the stone to form an insoluble layer that accepts printer's ink but rejects water. In other words, those portions of the stone that have been drawn on have an affinity for ink while the rest of the wet stone rejects it.

Lithography proved a relatively fast way of producing illustrated posters. Later improvements permitted drawings to be transferred from paper onto stone by means of pressure, avoiding the necessity for the artist to reverse his image. Color lithography was made possible by using as many stones as the colors needed in the design. With the invention of photolithography, a negative was exposed over a gelatin-covered paper. Wherever the light did not strike the gelatin the latter remained soluble, while the rest remained insoluble. The soluble sections were then washed away, with the drawing inked and transferred to stone.

These techniques developed concurrently with the rise of a consumer society. In the late nineteenth and early twentieth centuries striking posters advertised consumer products such as tonics, alcoholic beverages, cigarettes, clothing, bicycles, and sewing machines, as well as concerts, plays, cabarets, and sporting events. As railways linked European countries, eye-catching posters advertised trips to beach and mountain resorts. Companies representing transatlantic and Mediterranean ocean liners produced appealing posters advertising trips to exotic destinations. With the advent of automobiles in the early twentieth century, rival manufacturers advertised their vehicles on a large scale.

With the outbreak of World War I in 1914, illustrated posters became indispensable as the belligerent powers waged "total war" against their enemies. Such warfare involved the mobilization of huge armies, the production of vast quantities of military supplies, and the raising of huge amounts of money. Recruitment posters generally depicted a military leader or a soldier who pointed a finger at the onlooker, asking: "Have you volunteered?" Recruitment campaigns also used posters in which wives and sweethearts appealed to their men to enlist immediately. Many posters urged citizens to finance the war effort, while others called on those behind the lines to produce more food and weapons. Still others warned citizens not to discuss what they knew about military operations lest the enemy glean valuable information. To whip up popular support, all the warring states produced images of alleged atrocities by the enemy, especially against women and children.

Like total war, revolutions demand poster propaganda. Revolutionary leaders need to discredit the old regime, create support for their new ideology, stimulate recruitment for the revolutionary army, and convey the advantages of the new order. The Paris Commune of 1871 set a precedent when both Communards and Anti-Communards produced a flood of lithographed words and images. The Russian Revolution in 1917 resulted in thousands of posters denouncing tsars, priests, and wealthy farmers (kulaks) while glorifying workers and peasants. In the 1920s many posters were designed in a constructivist style, with a stress on the evils of the old regime and the promises of the new one. A typical poster portrayed (in the upper left) the old regime in black with poorly dressed peasants carrying oil lamps and living in dilapidated log houses, while (in the lower right) in red one saw well-dressed peasants using electric lights and living in modern homes. Red, of course, was the international symbol of radical revolution since the French Revolution. El Lissitzky (1890–1941) created a famous abstract poster showing a large red triangle piercing a white circle—white being the color of counterrevolution—with the slogan "Beat the Whites with the Red Wedge." Posters were affixed to walls, storefronts, on canal boats, and on propaganda trains. The widespread use of posters continued after 1928 under Stalin, but they were less modernistic and cluttered with wordy exhortations.

Twentieth-century revolutions on the right in Italy, Spain, and Germany all used posters to rally people to their cause. Nazi posters featured swastikas, eagles, huge swords, images of leaders—especially Hitler—and repellant depictions of Jews. During World War II many posters featured soldiers in armed conflict, planes, ships, and submarines. Italian Fascist posters were similar except for prominent fasces—an ancient Roman image consisting of a bundle of rods tied closely together, with an axe in the center—a symbol of state power and corporate union. During the Spanish Civil War both the right and the left made widespread use of posters to rally support. When Francisco Franco's (1892–1975) right-wing Falangist Party won the war in 1939, it employed posters to consolidate power.

Despite the advent of radio and moving pictures, World War II, like World War I, made heavy use of posters. Since then there have been occasional upsurges in the utilization of posters: during the Chinese civil war and the Communist victory in 1949, especially throughout the Cultural Revolution, from 1966 onward; following Castro's conquest of Cuba in 1959; during the student-worker insurrection in France in 1966; and during the Iranian revolution in 1979. In the West they continue to be used to promote consumer products, but they are also employed widely in political campaigns and demonstrations. It seems reasonable to predict that despite the current popularity of the electronic media, they will continue to be mobilized in the twenty-first century.

James A. Leith

See also Art; China; Elections (Britain); Flagg, James Montgomery; Health; Iran; Russia; Uncle Sam; World War I; World War II (Russia)

References: Barnicourt, John. *Posters: A Concise History.* London: Thames and Hudson, 1988; Bonnel, Victoria A. *Iconography of Power: Soviet Official Posters under Lenin and Stalin.* Berkeley: University of California Press, 1997; Evans, Harriet. *Picturing Power in the People's Republic of China: Posters of the Cultural Revolution.* Lanham, MD: Rowman and Littlefield, 1999; Gallo, Max. *The Poster in History.* New York: American Heritage, 1972; Leith, James A., ed. *Images of the Commune / Images de la Commune.* Montreal and London: McGill–Queen's University Press, 1967. Rickards, Maurice. *Posters of Protest and Revolution.* New York: Walter, 1970.

Pravda (Truth)

The official organ of the Central Committee of the Communist Party of the Soviet Union, the paper began as the title of the Bolshevik faction of the Russian Social Democrats in 1912. The naming of the official voice of Soviet Communism as "truth" gives a clear indication of the unquestioned value of official pronouncements within the Soviet Union. In a similar fashion the official newspaper of the Supreme Soviet was named *Izvestiya* (The News). Editors of *Pravda* included the then rising star Joseph Stalin (1879–1953) and Nikolai Bukharin (1888–1938).

Graham Roberts

See also Lenin, Vladimir Ilyich; Revolution, Russian; Russia; Stalin, Joseph

References: Roxburgh, A. *Pravda: Inside the Soviet News Machine.* London: Gollancz, 1987.

Prisoners of War

Prisoners of war (POWs) have been both actively and passively enmeshed in propaganda. In the aftermath of war, prisoners have often been transmuted into mythic figures and popular cultural icons, but POWs have also become the direct target of propagandistic initiatives aimed *at* them. The closed conditions of POW camps facilitate far-reaching attempts to reshape prisoners' attitudes and manipulate their behavior toward specific ends: to render prisoners docile, extract intelligence, or compel them to participate in propaganda activities aimed at their country of origin. North Korea's and China's alleged brainwashing of British and American prisoners during the Korean War (1950–1953) caused an intense moral panic in the United States in the mid-1950s. Ironically, both British and American authorities themselves engaged in attempts to reeducate POWs, including German POWs during World War II (as part of the wider denazification effort), and in Korea, where hundreds of thousands of Communist prisoners were persuaded to renounce North Korea for South Korea at the conclusion of hostilities.

It is hardly surprising that the presence of captured personnel in enemy hands should arouse anxiety not only over the prisoners' *treatment* but also their *behavior* while in captivity. Various agreed-upon conventions—at least on paper—govern the treatment of POWs by their captors and the behavior their own armed forces expect of them should they fall into enemy hands (for example, making clear that "collaboration" may be an offense punishable by court-martial). Strictly speaking, the Geneva Conventions prohibit captors from requiring more information from their prisoners than their name, rank, and serial number. The conventions also outlaw other abuses, including attempts either to influence prisoners' attitudes while in captivity or to manipulate POWs for propaganda purposes.

These safeguards notwithstanding, POWs remain in a uniquely exposed and vulnerable position, with internationally agreed-upon codes of conduct commonly breached. Wars in which combatants develop mirror-image conceptions of their opponents' inhumanity are unlikely to generate propitious circumstances for humane treatment of surrendered or captured enemy personnel. Moreover, even states that *do* recognize the Geneva Conventions balk at extending its protective clauses to prisoners captured in conflicts that fall short of declared war (as seen early in 2002 with regard to the Al Qaeda/Taliban fighters transported by the United States to

Viet Cong prisoners captured during Operation Starlite await transfer by helicopter to a prisoner-of-war camp in August 1965. The Marine search-and-destroy operation south of Chu Lai resulted in 599 Viet Cong casualties. (National Archives)

Guantanamo Bay in Cuba). The treatment of "terrorist suspects" thus poses particularly vexing questions concerning the legal status of those incarcerated in what is nominally peacetime. Prisoners may demand the political status that a state is keen to deny them by treating their actions as criminal, and such contests readily become the site of intense propaganda. In the case of the IRA hunger strikes (1980–1981), the election of participant Bobby Sands (1954–1981) to Parliament, followed by his death, helped galvanize support for the nationalist cause both within Northern Ireland and overseas as the IRA placed itself within a long tradition of Irish martyrdom at English hands.

Subject to abuse, exploitation, and brutalization, POWs provide much material for popular iconography and national myth-making. In the twentieth century POW heroism—and the camaraderie of camp life—inspired a plethora of feature films, television series, comics, and novels. World War II loomed large, inspiring multiple representations of Allied escapes from notorious Nazi strongholds, such as Colditz (the subject of a British film and television dramas). Likewise, Japan's treatment of Allied POWs during World War II has been well documented in fiction and film, perhaps most memorably in David Lean's movie *The Bridge on the River Kwai* (1957). But while tales of resistance and endurance or, alternatively, of escape form staples of POW mythology, POWs have also inspired much controversy, with less heroic behavior in captivity sometimes taken as illustrative of failings of "national character." After the Korean War, for example, a number of prominent American social critics charged that POWs had never before failed to escape, succumbed to disease and death, or collaborated with the enemy in such numbers. Diverse sources of the national characterological malaise were identified, ranging from suffocating mothers to material affluence, that had sapped the psychic and physical vigor of a young generation of postwar Americans.

During and following the Vietnam War, U.S. prisoners again became a source of controversy. In the wake of Vietnam, however, the issue of POWs and those missing in action (MIA) has generally been framed around government misconduct rather than prisoners' improprieties. Unlike their counterparts in Korea, U.S. prisoners in Vietnam have repeatedly been depicted as victims of sadistic Communist mistreatment who were betrayed and abandoned by their government. In line with Hollywood's cinematic interventions, at best the POW/MIA lobby has charged the U.S. government with making insufficient requests to Hanoi to secure the release of American soldiers in captivity; at worst with conniving with Hanoi in their disappearance. Unleashing much emotion, the POW/MIA issue bedeviled Washington's attempts to restore diplomatic relations with Vietnam in the 1980s and early 1990s.

As controversy in Western Europe in 2002 over conditions at the U.S. military prison at Guantanamo Bay again demonstrated, prisoners can readily become the focus of political disputes and popular sentiment. As both subjects and objects of propaganda, POWs inspire passions far beyond the scene of their captivity and long after it has ended.

Susan Carruthers

See also Australia; Brainwashing; Ireland; Korean War; Reeducation; Terrorism; Terrorism, War on; Vietnam War

References: Biderman, Albert. *March to Calumny: The Story of American POWs in the Korean War.* New York: Macmillan, 1963; Franklin, H. Bruce. *MIA or Mythmaking in America.* New York:

Lawrence Hill, 1992; Gruner, Elliot. *Prisoners of Culture: Representing the Vietnam POW.* New Brunswick, NJ: Rutgers University Press, 1993; Kinkead, Eugene. *In Every War But One.* New York: Norton, 1959; O'Malley, Padraig. *Biting at the Grave: The Irish Hunger Strikes and the Politics of Despair.* Belfast, UK: Blackstaff, 1990; White, William Lindsey. *The Captives of Korea: An Unofficial White Paper on the Treatment of War Prisoners.* New York: Scribner's, 1957.

Propaganda, Definitions of

What are the characteristic features of propaganda? In his book on Communist propaganda techniques, John Clews describes propaganda as "the vogue word" of the twentieth century. While the word itself originated with the seventeenth-century Roman Catholic Commission of Cardinals set up by the pope for the propagation of the Catholic faith, in the course of the twentieth century it has come to have pejorative associations. Modern synonyms for propaganda include "lies," "deceit," and "brainwashing." The *Penguin Political Dictionary* (1957) has defined propaganda as "statements of policy or facts, usually of a political nature, the real purpose of which is different from their apparent purpose . . . a statement by a government or political party which is believed to be insincere or untrue, and designed to impress the public at large rather than to reach the truth or to bring about a genuine understanding between opposing governments or parties." More recently the *Pocket Oxford Dictionary* (1984) provided a colloquial definition of propaganda as "biased information."

Such definitions are not helpful, perpetuating the misleading belief that propaganda has to do with "good or bad," "right or wrong." As Harold Lasswell (1902–1978) has maintained, propaganda as a mere tool is no more moral or immoral than a pump handle. One of the problems confronting the student of propaganda is the veritable plethora of definitions. Some are distinguished by their brevity: Jacques Driencourt's all-encompassing assertion that "Toute est propagande" (everything is propaganda) is not very helpful. Equally unhelpful are those definitions that attempt to encapsulate in a single sentence larded with qualifiers all the distinctive and distinguishing features of propaganda. Most writers on the subject agree that propaganda is concerned with influencing opinion. Frederick Lumley (1880–1954) and William Albig, among others, regard secrecy or a concealed source as an essential defining element in propaganda; as soon as the source is revealed, as in advertising, the activity ceases to be propaganda. Others stress the controversial element in propaganda. Harold Lasswell has argued that while the spread of controversial attitudes is propaganda, the spread of accepted attitudes and skills is a form of education. Similarly, Leonard Doob (1909–2000) has suggested that propaganda is "the attempt to affect the personalities and to control the behavior of individuals toward ends considered unscientific or of doubtful value in a society at a particular time." Some writers stress the emotional as opposed to the intellectual appeal of propaganda. Lasswell has argued that propaganda is concerned with attitudes of love and hate, whereas education is concerned with the transmission of skills and is therefore not propaganda. Lasswell has referred to propaganda as the "manipulation of collective attitudes by the use of significant symbols (words, pictures, tunes)." Writing in *Mein Kampf*, Adolf Hitler (1889–1945) claimed that the masses were influenced not by their brains but by their emotions: "In consequence, all effective propaganda must be limited to a very few points and must harp on these in slogans until the last member of the public understands what you want him to understand by your slogan." Other writers have emphasized the importance of the mechanisms of transmission in their definitions of propaganda. Terence Qualter, for example, has defined propaganda as the deliberate attempt to control or alter opinions through the use of the instruments of communication. French sociologist Jacques Ellul (1912–1994) has insisted that only suc-

cessful propaganda is true propaganda. However, all these definitions fail precisely because each of them excludes activities that should clearly be defined as propagandistic.

Where better to begin than with the propagandist himself? How important to the definition of propaganda is the purpose of the propagandist or his sense of purpose? Doob regards the question of purpose as irrelevant, arguing instead that the decisive factor is the use of suggestion: "If individuals are controlled through the use of suggestion . . . then the process may be called propaganda, regardless of whether or not the propagandist intends to exercise the control." It is difficult to see how Doob can maintain that propaganda can suggest something that it was not intended to suggest. There is a degree of deliberation in the notion of suggestion that this writer does not allow for.

A similar objection can be raised to A. J. Mackenzie's definition, where the use of "attempt" also implies a degree of deliberation. An attempt to disseminate propaganda must be both conscious and deliberate. The "purpose" of the propaganda is therefore the key. Without purpose propaganda can have no aim and direction, and therefore no distinctive function differentiating it from other social and political activities. Propaganda is an attempt at targeted communication with an objective that has been established a priori. Propaganda is best seen as the deliberate attempt to influence public opinion through the transmission of ideas and values for a specific purpose, not through violence or bribery. As Lindley Fraser has stated: "To affect a donkey's behavior by whipping is not propaganda, nor is plying it with carrots. But if the owner shouts at it in a threatening manner, or tries to coax it with winning words, then the word begins to become appropriate."

Modern political propaganda is consciously designed to serve the interests, either directly or indirectly, of the propagandists and their political masters. The aim of propaganda is to persuade its subject that there is only one valid point of view and to eliminate all other options. What follows is a brief chronological survey of the variety and scope of definitions of propaganda over the course of the twentieth century.

Pre-1918
"A propagandist presents many ideas to one or a few persons; an agitator presents only one or a few ideas, but he presents them to a mass of people." Georgi Plekhanov. "What Is to Be Done?" (1902). Quoted in V. I. Lenin, *Collected Works*. Vol. 5. London: Lawrence and Wishart, 1961, p. 409.

1920s
"Our system of education turns young people out of the schools able to read, but for the most part unable to weigh evidence or to form an independent opinion" (p. 34). "Propaganda, conducted by the means which advertisers have found successful, is now one of the recognized methods of government in all advanced countries, and is especially the method by which democratic opinion is created . . . There are two quite different evils about propaganda as now practiced. On the one hand, its appeal is generally to irrational causes of belief rather than to serious argument; on the other hand, it gives an unfair advantage to those who can obtain most publicity, whether through wealth or through power" (p. 35). Bertrand Russell. "Free Thought and Official Propaganda" (1922 Conway Memorial Lecture). In *Let the People Think: A Selection of Essays*. London: Watts, 1941.

"The task of propaganda is to attract followers; the task of organization is to win members. A follower of the movement is one who finds himself in agreement with its aims; a member is one who fights for it" (p. 163). "The receptivity of the great masses is very limited, their intelligence is small, but their power of forgetting is enormous. In consequence, all effective propaganda must be limited to a few points and must harp on these in

slogans until the last member of the public understands what you want him to understand by your slogan" (p. 165). Adolf Hitler. *Mein Kampf* (1925), trans. Ralph Manheim. Boston: Houghton Mifflin, 1943.

"Propaganda is the management of collective attitudes by the manipulation of significant symbols . . . One propaganda group may flourish in secret and another may invite publicity . . . Democracy has proclaimed the dictatorship of palaver, and the technique of dictating to the dictator is named propaganda" (Harold D. Lasswell. "The Theory of Political Propaganda." *American Political Science Review* 21 [1927]: 627). "Propaganda may be defined as a *technique* of social control, or as a species of social *movement*. As technique, it is the manipulation of collective attitudes by the use of significant symbols (words, pictures, tunes) rather than violence, bribery or boycott. Propaganda differs from the technique of pedagogy in that propaganda is concerned with attitudes of love and hate, while pedagogy is devoted to the transmission of skill . . . The spread of controversial attitudes is propaganda, the spread of accepted attitudes and skills is education" (idem. "The Person: Subject and Object of Propaganda." *Annals of the American Academy of Political and Social Science* 179 [1927]: 189).

"Propaganda is the executive arm of the invisible government" (p. 20). "Propaganda will never die out. Intelligent men must realize that propaganda is the modern instrument by which they can fight for productive ends and help to bring order out of chaos" (p. 159). Edward L. Bernays. *Propaganda*. New York: Liveright, 1928.

1930s
"Propaganda is not education, it strives for the closed mind rather than the open mind. It is not concerned about the development of mature individuals. Its aim is immediate action. The propagandist merely wishes you to think as he does. The educator is more modest, he is so delighted if you think at all that he is willing to let you do so in your own

way." Everett Dean Martin. *The Conflict of the Individual and the Mass.* New York: Henry Holt, 1932, p. 29.

"Propaganda is promotion which is veiled in one way or another as to (1) its origin or sources, (2) the interests involved, (3) the methods employed, (4) the content spread, and (5) the results accruing to the victims— any one, any two, any three, any four, or all five." Frederick E. Lumley. *The Propaganda Menace.* New York: Century, 1933, p. 44.

"May the bright flame of our enthusiasm never be extinguished. It alone gives light and warmth to the creative art of a modern political propaganda . . . It may be a good thing to possess power that rests on arms. But it is better and more lasting to win the heart of a people and to keep it." Joseph Goebbels speaking at the 1934 Nuremberg rally. Quoted in David Welch, *The Third Reich: Politics and Propaganda.* London: Routledge, 2002, p. 25.

"If individuals are controlled through the use of suggestion . . . then the process may be called propaganda, regardless of whether or not the propagandist intends to exercise the control. On the other hand if individuals are affected in such a way that the same result would be obtained with or without the aid of suggestion, then this process may be called education, regardless of the intention of the educator." Leonard W. Doob. *Propaganda: Its Psychology and Technique.* New York: Henry Holt, 1935, p. 80.

"Propaganda refers to the conscious attempt to manage the minds of other and usually more numerous publics." Harwood L. Childs. Quoted in *The American Political Scene.* Ed. Edward B. Logan. New York: Harper, 1936, p. 226.

"Propaganda gives force and direction to the successive movements of popular feeling and desire; but it does not do much to create those movements. The propagandist is a man who analyses an already existing stream. In a land where there is no water, he digs in vain." Aldous Huxley. "Notes on Propaganda." *Harper's* 174 (December 1936): 39. "There

are two kinds of propaganda—rational propaganda in favor of action that is consonant with the enlightened self-interest of those who make it and those to whom it is addressed, and nonrational propaganda that is not consonant with anybody's enlightened self-interest, but is dictated by, and appeals to passion." Idem. "Propaganda in a Democratic Society." In *Brave New World Revisited.* London: Chatto & Windus, 1959.

"Propaganda is an attempt, either unconsciously or as part of a systematic campaign by an individual or group holding certain beliefs or desiring certain ends, to influence others to adopt identical attitudes." A. J. Mackenzie. *Propaganda Boom.* London: John Gifford, 1938, p. 35.

"We shall here limit propaganda to intentional special pleading" (p. 285). "There is deliberate distortion by selection . . . The objective of the propagandist is to achieve public acceptance of conclusions, not to stimulate the logical analysis of the merits of the case" (p. 286). "Propaganda is a special term referring to the intentional dissemination of conclusions from concealed sources by interested individuals and groups" (p. 287). "Propaganda is essential to the development of tribes or simple folk pieces" (p. 296). [On page 305 Albig maintains that advertising is *not* propaganda because its sources are revealed.] "Propaganda is pervasive in our time. There has always been some propaganda, but in the modern age it is organised, intentional and relatively more effective. However, modern propaganda emphasises distortion and derationalises the public opinion process. It usually does not help the individual to come to a rational understanding of public issues but rather attempts to induce him to follow nonrational emotional drives" (p. 309). "[Bertrand Russell] maintains that successful propaganda essentially makes people hold more emotionally to their opinions and beliefs, rather than develop new opinions" (p. 317). William Albig. *Public Opinion.* New York: McGraw-Hill, 1939.

1940s

"It is a part of the regular method of propaganda to use the symbol, which stirs the sentiment, always in an atmosphere of stress, strain or crisis. Thus the generalisations which fit the sentiments will be met by that enthusiastic sweeping away of criticism which fits the emotion." Sir Frederic C. Bartlett. *Political Propaganda.* Cambridge: Cambridge University Press, 1940, p. 65.

"Propaganda in itself has no fundamental method. It has only purpose—the conquest of the masses." Joseph Goebbels (then Nazi German minister for propaganda). Quoted in *Political Propaganda,* by Frederic C. Bartlett. Cambridge: Cambridge University Press, p. 66.

"The power of propaganda, as of all other weapons, must depend very largely upon the time when it is used. In the early stages of war its weight is not so great as in the last stages, when it can prove decisive. There is no dispute about the fact that propaganda against victory in arms is powerful, but when victory in arms is on your side, propaganda can press the results of victory miles further. Then propaganda can shorten the period required for the achievement of victory by months, possibly by years, and it is therefore in these early days that we should gradually perfect the machinery of propaganda, in order that when the time comes we may be ready to strike. We cannot tell yet how soon that time may come. It has been said in this Debate that it was propaganda which decided the last war. That again, if I may say so, is the result of the mistaken view that has grown up in many people's minds owing to German propaganda in the last few years. It was not propaganda that won the last war; it was the efforts of our soldiers and sailors. It was the great attack on the Western front that finally smashed German resistance, and we can still see in our mind's eye the German soldiers retreating in their hundreds and throwing up their hands. At the same time, taking full advantage of these victories, our propaganda, busy in Germany, produced the revolts and mutinies, which spread. I ought to remind those people who believe that it was on the home front among the wicked communists and the Jews, as the Nazi story has it, that the revolution in Germany started. The revolution did not start in any city. It was the German Navy that was first to mutiny. We shall make full use of the weapon of propaganda and we must be busy in perfecting it during these months." Alfred Duff Cooper (then British minister of information) in a speech to the House of Commons on 3 July 1941. *Hansard,* 3 July 1941, col. 1622.

1950s

"Propaganda in the broadest sense is the technique of influencing human action by the manipulation of representations. These representations may take spoken, written, pictorial or musical form." Harold D. Lasswell. "Propaganda." In *International Encyclopedia of the Social Sciences.* Vols. 11–12. New York: Macmillan, 1950, pp. 521–522.

"Propaganda in the sense of diffusion of conclusion while discouraging the subjects from examining the reasons for the positions which they are asked to accept, has existed throughout the history of human society. Leaders and institutional representatives are always desirous of furthering their objectives without argument. They wish to win converts and to reproduce (*Propagare*) the conclusions, the essential statements and values of their ideology." William Albig. *Modern Public Opinion.* New York: McGraw-Hill, 1956, p. 293.

"Propaganda may be defined as the activity, or the art, of inducing others to behave in a way in which they would not behave in its absence" (p. 1). "The central element in propagandist inducements, as opposed to compulsion on one side and payment, or bribery, on the other, is that they depend on 'communication' rather than concrete penalties or rewards. To affect a donkey's behavior by whipping is not propaganda, nor is plying it with carrots. But if its owner shouts at it in a threatening manner, or tries to coax it with winning words or noises then the word begins to become appropriate" (p. 3). "Perhaps a better metaphor is to call it a burning glass which collects and focuses the diffused warmth of popular emotions, concentrating them upon a specific issue on which the warmth becomes heat and may reach the firing-point of revivals, risings, revolts, revolutions" (pp. 196–197). Lindley Fraser. *Propaganda.* Oxford: Oxford University Press, 1957.

1960s

"Propaganda is thus defined as the deliberate attempt by some individual or group to form, control, or alter the attitudes of other groups by the use of the instruments of communication, with the intention that in any given situation the reaction of those so influenced will be that desired by the propagandist. The propagandist is the individual or group who makes any such attempt." Terrence H. Qualter. *Propaganda and Psychological Warfare.* New York: Random House, 1965, p. 27.

"Propaganda is made, first of all, because of a will to action, for the purpose of effectively arming policy and giving irresistible power to its decisions . . . Ineffective propaganda is no propaganda" (p. x). (Quoting Lasswell): "Propaganda is the expression of opinions or actions carried out deliberately by individuals or groups for predetermined ends and through psychological manipulations" (p. xii). "The propagandist uses a keyboard and composes a symphony" (p. 10). "The aim of modern propaganda is no longer to modify ideas but to provoke action. It is no longer to change adherence to a doctrine, but to make the individual cling irrationally to a process of action. It is no longer to lead to a choice but to loosen the reflexes. It is no longer to transform an opinion, but to arouse an active and mythical belief" (p. 25). "Propaganda is a set of methods employed by an organized group that wants to bring about the active or passive participation in its actions of a mass of individuals, psychologically unified

through psychological manipulations and incorporated into an organization" (p. 61). Jacques Ellul. *Propaganda: The Formation of Men's Attitudes.* New York: Knopf, 1965.

"Propaganda is the relatively deliberate manipulation, by means of symbols (words, gestures, flags, images, monuments, music, etc.), of other people's thoughts or actions with respect to beliefs, values, and behaviors which these people ("reactors") regard as controversial." Bruce L. Smith. "Propaganda." In *International Encyclopedia of the Social Sciences.* Vols. 11–12. New York: Macmillan, 1968, p. 579.

1980s

"[Propaganda is] the systematic propagation of information or ideas by an interested party, especially in a tendentious way in order to encourage or instil a particular attitude or response." Terrence H. Qualter. *Opinion Control in the Democracies.* London: Macmillan, 1985, 124.

1990s and After

"The systematic propagation of a doctrine or cause or of information reflecting the views and interests of those people advocating such a doctrine or cause." *American Heritage Dictionary of the English Language,* 3d ed., s.v. "propaganda."

"Modern political propaganda can be defined as the deliberate attempt to influence the opinions of an audience through the transmission of ideas and values for the specific purpose, consciously designed to serve the interest of the propagandists and their political masters, either directly or indirectly." David Welch. "Powers of Persuasion." *History Today* 49 (August 1999): 24–26.

"Propaganda is a deliberate attempt to persuade people to think and then behave in a manner desired by the source; public relations, a branch of propaganda, is a related process intended to enhance the relationship between the organization and the public. Both in turn are related to advertising." Bill Backer, in *The Care and Feeding of Ideas* (New

York: Crown, 1993), suggests that advertising and propaganda are half brothers. An advertisement connects something with human desires; propaganda shapes the infinite into concrete images." David Culbert. "Government, Propaganda and Public Relations." In *The Oxford Companion to American Military History*. Ed. John Whiteclay Chambers II. New York: Oxford, 1999, 571–572.

"The usually organised spreading of ideas, information, or rumors designed to promote or damage an institution, movement, etc." *The New Penguin English Dictionary*. London: Penguin, 2000.

David Welch

See also The Big Lie; Black Propaganda; Brainwashing; Goebbels, Joseph; Gray Propaganda; Hitler, Adolf; Lenin, Vladimir Ilyich; Psychological Warfare; Public Diplomacy; Reformation and Counter-Reformation; White Propaganda

Protocols of the Elders of Zion (1903)

This is both the most notorious use of a fake for propaganda purposes and a central document in the history of anti-Semitism. First published in August–September 1903 in Saint Petersburg, Russia, in the anti-Semitic newspaper *Znamya* (The Banner), these writings next appeared in book form in 1905 as the appendix to the apocalyptic work of a religious mystic named Serge Nilus. The *Protocols* purported to be a collection of lectures by and for Jewish leaders outlining methods for world domination. Highlights included the revelation that underground railways had been built to allow the Elders to dynamite the great capitals of the world. In all probability, this document was requested by Pyotr Ivanovich Rachovsky, head of the overseas branch of the Okhrana, the tsarist secret police, who planned to use anti-Semitism as a rallying point for a nationalist political party. The document combined myths that had been part of the Christian world since the Middle Ages and soon was used to justify

pogroms against the Jews of Russia. In the aftermath of the Russian Revolution, the *Protocols* found a wider readership across Europe and the rest of the world. In May 1920 the London *Times* presented a serious discussion of its contents. In Germany the *Protocols* found an eager champion in Alfred Rosenberg (1893–1946), the Nazi "intellectual" whose book on the subject, *"The Protocols of the Elders of Zion" and Jewish World Politics*, appeared in 1923 and became an instant bestseller. The *Protocols* became a mainstay of Nazi propaganda underpinning the Holocaust. In the United States the *Protocols* inspired a series of anti-Semitic articles in the *Dearborn Independent*, a newspaper belonging to industrialist Henry Ford (1863–1947), which were collected and published in book form as *The International Jew*. After World War II the *Protocols* were wholly discredited. Nevertheless, their slanderous arguments surfaced again in the rhetoric of Arab nationalism and remain a perennial theme in American neofascist circles.

Nicholas J. Cull

See also Anti-Semitism; Arab World; Fakes; Germany; Holocaust Denial; Neo-Militia Groups; Okhrana; Russia

References: Bernstein, Herman. *The Truth about the "Protocols of Zion": A Complete Exposure* (1935). Reprint, New York: Ktav, 1972; Cohn, Norman. *Warrant for Genocide: The Myth of the Jewish World-Conspiracy and the "Protocols of the Elders of Zion."* London: Eyre and Spottiswoode, 1967.

Psychological Warfare

This is the planned use of propaganda to influence enemy audiences in times of war. In 1950 one official document defined psychological warfare as consisting of "activities, other than physical combat, which communicate ideas and information intended to affect the minds, emotions, and actions of the enemy, for the purpose of disrupting his morale and his will to fight." The British government, which conceptually pioneered modern psychological warfare in World War

German soldiers surrender in Brittany, France, in 1944, carrying the "safe conduct" passes dropped in an Allied psychological warfare campaign. (National Archives)

I, divided its Ministry of Information (MoI) into departments of home, allied, neutral, and enemy propaganda. Psychological warfare can be distinguished from other forms of external propaganda in that it is directed at an "enemy" rather than peoples of neutral or friendly nations. Sometimes known as combat propaganda, psychological warfare has gradually come to have wider applications at the strategic and political levels, no longer being confined to formal war situations, which is why psychological operations (psyops) is now the preferred term. Like propaganda in general, psychological warfare can assume black, white, and gray forms. Psychological warfare has become a characteristic of conflict in the twentieth century, figuring not only in both world wars but also in the ideological "peacetime" warfare that culminated

in the Cold War. It has also played a role in endemic smaller wars, including Korea, Vietnam, and the Gulf War, as well as counterinsurgency conflicts in Kenya and Malaya.

Sun Tzu (active ca. 500–350 B.C.E.), an ancient Chinese thinker on the art of war, wrote that "to subdue the enemy without fighting is the acme of skill." Preliterate ages used frightening sounds, scary images, and rumors spread by word of mouth to weaken the enemy's morale. During the American Revolution, American forces encouraged British troops to desert by wrapping such messages around stones and throwing them behind the British lines. Printed leaflets aimed at Hessian mercenaries proved particularly effective and may have accounted for the high level of desertion among these soldiers—by some estimates five or six thousand of the thirty-thousand-strong force. The modern period can be said to have begun with the dropping of millions of leaflets by balloon and aircraft over enemy lines during World War I. This "paper war" was designed to undermine the will of the enemy to continue the fight, to sow doubts about his government's aims and honesty, sap his morale, and ultimately to induce desertion, defection, and even insurrection. Pioneered by the British, who referred to it generically as political warfare, the U.S. Army used the term "psychologic warfare" after joining the war in 1917. Britain's campaign was at first conducted by the War Office and its branch MI 7, reaching its climax in 1918 when Lord Northcliffe (1865–1922) was appointed to head the department of propaganda in enemy countries, with headquarters at Crewe House. The British and their allies principally used leaflets, pamphlets, and trench newspapers written in all the enemy languages to play up ethnic and political differences. After the Bolshevik takeover, the Russians concentrated on exploiting social discontent. The principal psychological warfare campaigns during World War I included: Britain, France, and Italy against Austria-Hungary, Germany, and Bulgaria; Germany and Austria-Hungary against Italy; and Soviet Russia against both of the Central Powers.

At the conclusion of the war both victors and losers made extensive claims for the effectiveness of psychological warfare. In 1919 the *Times* of London concluded that "good propaganda probably saved a year of war, and this meant the saving of thousands of millions in money and probably at least a million lives." General Erich von Ludendorff (1865–1937), the German chief of staff, claimed that "we were hypnotized by the enemy's propaganda as a rabbit is by a snake." General Hindenburg (1847–1934), German commander in chief, wrote that "besides bombs which kill the body, his [i.e., the enemy's] airmen throw down leaflets which are intended to kill the soul . . . Unsuspectingly many thousands consume the poison." Both men claimed that psychological warfare was a principal factor contributing to the final collapse of Germany in November 1918, a conclusion with which Adolf Hitler (1889–1945) agreed in *Mein Kampf* (1925). Of course, they each had good reasons for blaming the defeat of Germany on causes other than either the military conduct of the war or the fighting abilities of German soldiers.

In 1920 some military historians were predicting that in the future physical combat would be "replaced by a purely psychological warfare, wherein weapons are not used or battlefields sought." A new factor after 1918 was the emergence of Soviet Russia, followed by Fascist Italy and then Germany. The commencement of ideological warfare, which lasted until 1989, made psychological warfare a permanent feature of international relations; it was often conducted by newly emerging secret intelligence services. The British called it "that aspect of intelligence in which information is used aggressively to manipulate opinion or to create special conditions by purely intellectual means." The Germans preferred the term *"Geistige Kriegsführung"*(intellectual warfare).

During World War II, the British government continued to use the term "political warfare"—based on its Political Warfare Executive (PWE)—until the Americans joined in after 1941, when the term "psychological warfare" replaced it. Allied Psychological Warfare branches were established in the various theaters of action. The largest of these was set up in North Africa in November 1942. As part of the preparations for the invasion of Europe, a Psychological Warfare Division was established at Supreme Headquarters Allied Expeditionary Forces (PWD/SHAEF). Although this suggested greater inter-Allied cooperation than was, in fact, the case, the British and Americans were united in their overall approach to psychological warfare, which was based on a distinction between "white" propaganda, which manifestly emanates from the government, and "black" propaganda, which appears to emanate from somewhere else. In white propaganda—best exemplified in the BBC's broadcasts to occupied Europe as well as Germany and her allies—the approach was "propaganda with truth." Hugh Carleton Greene (1910–1987) of the BBC defined it as "to tell the truth within the limits of the information at our disposal and to tell it consistently and frankly . . . It is a strategic weapon and must not deviate from the truth for tactical reasons." The emphasis on truth and credibility was shared by Richard Crossman (1907–1974), the assistant chief of PWD/SHAEF, who gained the reputation of a "propaganda genius" thanks to his almost clairvoyant ability to transport himself into the mind of the enemy. He later served as a Labour M.P. and cabinet minister.

A group of fictitious radio stations—which gave the impression in their broadcasts of conversations between underground cells of disaffected German soldiers but were, in fact, put out by a secret transmitter in Britain whose code name was Aspidistra—constituted the principal black propaganda technique employed by the Allies, reinforced by secret agents disseminating false rumors. Since it was purportedly coming from within occupied Europe, black propaganda did not have to worry about lies or false promises. For example, following the Casablanca Conference of 1943, Allied policy was one of unconditional surrender, which implied that negotiation would not be possible even if the German people rose up against their Nazi rulers. Black propagandists, on the other hand, could suggest that if "we" get rid of "Hitler's gang," then "our" situation might well improve.

Most post-1945 studies of psychological warfare assumed that it was both a necessary and legitimate response to the growing political, military, and ideological threat posed by international communism. Following North Korea's invasion of South Korea, in 1950 U.S. president Harry Truman (1884–1972) established the Psychological Strategy Board

in the White House to coordinate the wider effort, both overt and covert. A bolstering of the white propaganda machinery occurred first within the State Department in the form of the International Information Administration (IIA). In 1953 U.S. president Dwight Eisenhower (1890–1969), who had seen the potency of psychological warfare on the battlefields of Europe, established the autonomous United States Information Agency (USIA), with the Voice of America (VOA) as its white broadcasting arm. The CIA funded Radio Free Europe and Radio Liberty as gray broadcasting organs. The degree to which the activities of these groups were effectively coordinated is doubtful, with each branch going its separate way until the Bay of Pigs disaster of 1961 exposed the myth of a coordinated psychological effort.

Psychological warfare (psywar) was used episodically in Vietnam, but with the defeat of the United States it went into disrepute in western military thought. The Soviets retained their faith in it, terming it "active measures" and scoring some notable Cold War successes, in particular the campaign surrounding the neutron bomb and later campaigns accusing the United States of manufacturing the AIDS virus in a biological warfare lab. President Ronald Reagan revived U.S. psychological warfare in the 1980s in the form of the Department of Defense's "psyops Master Plan" of 1985 and its application since then in the form of psychological operations. Psyops played a role in U.S. intervention in Panama, the Gulf War, Bosnia, Kosovo, and the War on Terrorism of 2001.

Philip M. Taylor

See also Austrian Empire; Black Propaganda; Britain; Cold War; Counterinsurgency; Crossman, Richard; Disinformation; Germany; Gulf War; Italy; KGB; Korean War; Kosovo Crisis and War; Northcliffe, Lord; PWE; Radio (International); United States; Vietnam War; World War I; World War II (Britain); World War II (Germany); World War II (Japan); World War II (Russia); World War II (United States)

References: Cruickshank, Charles. *The Fourth Arm.* Oxford: Oxford University Press, 1981;

Daugherty, William E., and Morris Janowitz, eds. *A Psychological Warfare Casebook.* Baltimore, MD: Johns Hopkins University Press, 1958; Lerner, Daniel. *Psychological Warfare against Nazi Germany.* New York: G. W. Stewart, 1949; Roetter, Charles. *Psychological Warfare.* London: Batsford, 1974.

Public Diplomacy

This term has been used in the United States since 1965 to describe transnational cultural propaganda and press management activities. In 1997 a State Department planning team defined the term as follows: "Public Diplomacy seeks to promote the national interest of the United States through understanding, informing and influencing foreign audiences." It is therefore distinguished from private diplomacy, which aims to cultivate only professional diplomats. The term itself is in some ways propaganda, but the United States wished to avoid the negative connotations of "propaganda" to describe the activities of agencies like the United States Information Agency (USIA) and the Voice of America (VOA). A well-known example of U.S. public diplomacy is the Fulbright Program, established at the end of World War II by Senator William Fulbright (1905–1995) of Arkansas to promote international educational exchanges.

The term is thought by some to have been coined by the American diplomat Edmund Gullion (1913–1998). Although Gullion denied this, he promoted its use as director of the most significant professional school connected with this type of work, namely, the Edward R. Murrow Center for Public Diplomacy at the Fletcher School of Law and Diplomacy, Tufts University, which was established in 1965.

Public diplomacy is not a one-way street. Jarol B. Manheim has charted the extensive public diplomacy activities of other nations seeking to influence the U.S. government. In so doing he has developed the concept of strategic public diplomacy, according to which the objectives of international communication are best served by a targeted application of the fruits of political and social science research—usually by highly paid public relations firms. The best known firm representing foreign nations within the United States is Hill and Knowlton Public Affairs Worldwide, whose clients included the Kuwaiti government during the Gulf War. Manheim called their image management "the *real* smart weapon of the Gulf Conflict." In terms of targeted lobbying and public relations, top spenders within the United States include Japan and Israel. Individual success stories include the promotion of Pakistan as a "partner in democracy" in the late 1980s and Mexico's lobbying for the passage of the North American Free Trade Association (NAFTA) resolution. Such campaigns have prompted Manheim's preliminary conclusion that "when it comes to strategic public diplomacy the United States gives far less than it gets."

Since 1999 and the dissolution of the USIA, responsibility for public diplomacy has passed to the undersecretary of state public diplomacy and public affairs at the State Department. In the George W. Bush administration the post was first held by Charlotte Beers (1935–), a former advertising executive. When asked about the incongruity of this past experience, Colin Powell (1937–), the then secretary of state, replied: "She got me to buy Uncle Ben's rice." Charlotte Beers resigned in early 2003 after criticism of a high-profile campaign of television advertisements in the Middle East featuring Arab Americans. The cultural approach to international relations associated with public diplomacy is supported by the Public Diplomacy Foundation, which includes many USIA alumni. During the 2001 War on Terrorism public diplomacy in support of the war was overseen by a Coalition Information Center established under the auspices of the White House, which later coordinated a wider public diplomacy campaign against anti-Americanism worldwide.

Nicholas J. Cull

See also Cultural Propaganda; Gulf War; Israel; Japan; Korea; Mexico; Milton, John; Propaganda, Definitions of; Terrorism, War on; USIA; VOA

References: Becker, Elizabeth, and James Dao. "Bush Will Keep Wartime Office Promoting U.S." *New York Times,* 20 February 2002; Hansen, Allen C. *USIA: Public Diplomacy in the Computer Age.* 2d ed. New York: Praeger, 1989; Klein, Naomi. "Brand USA." *Los Angeles Times,* 10 March 2002; Manheim, Jarol B. *Strategic Public Diplomacy and American Foreign Policy: The Evolution of Influence.* New York: Oxford University Press, 1994; Tuch, Hans N. *Communicating with the World: U.S. Public Diplomacy Overseas.* New York: St. Martins, 1990.

PWE (Political Warfare Executive)

Britain's World War II propaganda and subversion agency, the Political Warfare Executive (PWE) was established in 1941, with former journalist Robert Bruce Lockhart (1887–1970) in charge as of 1942. The PWE was the third attempt to organize British psychological warfare against the enemy (its predecessors were a secret Foreign Office unit called Electra House, established in the immediate prewar period, which in 1940 became "SO1," the propaganda branch of the Special Operations Executive (SOE). PWE activities ranged from supplying staff and propaganda material to the clandestine press operating in occupied Europe and shaping BBC broadcasts beamed into enemy and occupied Europe to battlefield loudspeaker operations to encourage desertion. The PWE's best-known operation was its bid to undermine Nazi Germany through the use of black radio propaganda, specifically a PWE radio station called Gustav Siegfried Eins that claimed to be run by an anti-Nazi general but in reality was manned by former *Daily Express* journalist Sefton Delmer (1904–1979). More troubling to Delmer was the PWE's practice of sending food parcels via Switzerland to the family of dead German soldiers with a note saying that their loved one, realizing that the Nazi cause was lost, had deserted and wanted his family to have the food. Later Delmer would explain that although the hope was false, the ham was genuine.

Nicholas J. Cull

See also Britain; Black Propaganda; Crossman, Richard; Psychological Warfare; Radio (International); Rumor; World War II (Britain)

References: Cruickshank, Charles. *The Fourth Arm: Psychological Warfare, 1938–1945.* Oxford: Oxford University Press, 1981; Delmer, Sefton. *Black Boomerang.* London: Secker and Warburg, 1962; Garnett, David. *The Secret History of PWE: The Political Warfare Executive, 1939–1945.* London: St. Ermin's Press, 2002; Howe, Ellic. *The Black Game.* London: Michael Joseph, 1980.

Q

Quotations from Chairman Mao (translated 1966)

This work consists of a selection of short political aphorisms by Mao Zedong (1893–1976), who was the chairman of the Chinese Communist Party and paramount Chinese leader from 1949 to 1976. The collection, which was also known as the "Little Red Book," exhorted readers to practice self-sacrifice and exhibit devotion to the revolutionary spirit. It was not compiled by Mao himself but rather by Lin Biao (1908–1971), his defense minister, who in the early 1960s assembled the quotations from Mao's voluminous published writings and distributed them in book form among the soldiers of the People's Liberation Army, the armed forces of the People's Republic of China. By 1963 millions of soldiers were encouraged to memorize the quotations and use them in political discussions, thereby increasing the reverence in which Mao was held as China's foremost ideologist. The book was read more widely during the Cultural Revolution (1966–1976), when student revolutionaries, known as Red Guards, used it as ammunition during their attempts—which were endorsed by Mao—to overthrow the existing social and political structures. First published in the West in translation in 1966, the book also became popular among student radicals, who felt that its iconoclasm echoed their attempts to overthrow existing structures in capitalist society.

Rana Mitter

See also China; Mao Zedong

References: *Quotations from Chairman Mao Tse-tung.* Beijing: Foreign Languages Press, 1966; Schram, Stuart. *The Thought of Mao Tse-tung.* Cambridge: Cambridge University Press, 1989.

R

Radio (Domestic)

The standard format for modern radio broadcasts—a blend of short, digestible musical selections, snippets of news, or half-hour talk shows interrupted by advertisements—is not how broadcasting evolved in the 1920s. Once considered a powerful tool of mass persuasion and social influence, radio today is largely devoted to providing entertainment and superficial information.

In the early twentieth century, wireless communication was primarily of interest to the navies of the world. World War I saw the birth of radio as a medium for propaganda. In 1918 listeners around the world heard U.S. president Woodrow Wilson (1856–1924) discuss his plan for peace in his Fourteen Points radio address. Wilson used America's government station (call sign NFF) to appeal directly to the German people, calling on them to overthrow the kaiser. Radio news broadcasts in the United States began in November 1920 with coverage of election returns. Network broadcasting began in 1926. By the end of 1928, the newly formed National Broadcasting Company (NBC) estimated that there were 9.6 million radio sets—with more than 40 million listeners—in use in the United States. NBC had two networks, NBC-Red and NBC-Blue. The weaker Blue network became the American Broadcasting Company (ABC) in 1942. The Columbia Broadcasting System (CBS) began operations in 1927. In Britain radio broadcasting began in 1922 with the formation of the British Broadcasting Company (later Corporation) (BBC), which played a key role in bolstering the government case during the General Strike of 1926.

Radio was the primary medium of mass communication in the 1930s, with radio sales booming during the Great Depression. Radio simultaneously emerged as a tool of mass persuasion and propaganda. Adolf Hitler's (1889–1945) rise to power was aided by his radio broadcasts, in which he promised to restore German power. Hitler preferred to speak before a live audience because he did not like the sound of his voice on radio. In 1933 Franklin D. Roosevelt (1882–1945) gave the first of his "fireside chats," which involved a more informal style of speaking than was common in the 1930s. Radio also boosted the careers of such Roosevelt critics as Huey Long (1893–1935) and Father Charles Coughlin (1891–1971), both of whom offered visions of a secure economic future that appealed to millions of unemployed workers.

Radio's influence peaked during World War II. The average American turned first to radio for war news. Such popular commentators as Edward R. Murrow (1908–1965), H. V. Kaltenborn (1878–1965), Elmer Davis (1890–1958), and Fulton Lewis Jr. (1903–1966) gave listeners both the headlines plus their personal opinions—which were sometimes rather simplistic. With the end of the war and the rise of television, 1945 marked the demise of radio's central role in American life. In the 1950s radio network broadcasting seemed an endangered species.

But radio found a new position in American society, both through the FM frequencies (earlier network broadcasting had all been AM) and the growth of community-supported Public Broadcasting System (PBS) stations. Talk radio stations permitted those with strong conservative or religious views to reach millions of listeners. For example, Rush Limbaugh (1951–) has a mostly male, mostly middle-aged listenership that relishes his denunciations of feminists (which he refers to as "femi-nazis") or the evasions of the politically correct. Once counted out as a mass medium, radio has found an important niche—at least in the United States—as an outlet for political commentary.

Brian Collins

See also BBC; Murrow, Edward R.; Radio
(International); Reith, Lord John
References: Barnouw, Erik. *A History of Broadcasting in the United States.* Vol. 1, *A Tower in Babel;* Vol. 2, *The Golden Web.* New York: Oxford, 1966–1968; Culbert, David H. *News for Everyman: Radio and Foreign Affairs in Thirties America.* Westport, CT: Greenwood, 1976.

A government-organized protest against Voice of America (VOA) broadcasts in Hungary in 1949. VOA is mocked as a quacking duck. Such events were a sign of the effectiveness of U.S. broadcasts and the fear they engendered in the Communist governments of Eastern Europe. (National Archives).

Radio (International)

International radio propaganda began during the closing months of World War I as the United States and Soviet Russia both broadcast Morse code messages about peace terms. For the Soviet Union radio offered both a means of communicating with the masses worldwide and a way of associating the Bolshevik cause with the technology of the future. The USSR used radio to broadcast to Romania in 1926 and made a series of propaganda broadcasts to celebrate the tenth anniversary of the Russian Revolution in 1927. Radio Moscow, which was founded in 1929, was not the first regular international radio station; that distinction belongs to Radio Netherlands, which began a service to the Dutch Empire in 1927. Regular Soviet broadcasts caused a hurried response from the West. The late 1920s and early 1930s saw a host of broadcasters on the shortwave band (which could bounce off the earth's ionosphere and hence travel across vast distances). New stations included Radio Vatican (1931) and the BBC Empire Service (1932).

Beginning in the mid-1920s the U.S. government began broadcasting to Latin America to promote the cause of Pan-American unity, but it was slow in developing this activity. Boston-based station WIXAL, the first major U.S. commercial station aimed at overseas listeners, began broadcasting in 1933. Commercial broadcasts opposed all proposals for large-scale U.S. government sponsorship of radio propaganda, such as the 1937 plan devised by Rep. Emmanuel Celler (1888–1981) to broadcast anti-Nazi messages to Latin America. The pressure surrounding World War II led to the founding of the Voice of America (VOA). The BBC acted as a midwife, providing advice and allowing the VOA to use its transmission facilities.

The Cold War led to the creation of new propaganda stations, including the CIA-funded Radio Free Europe and Radio Liberty (RFE/RL). The United States also maintained a station called Radio in the American Sector (RIAS) in West Berlin, which eventually became part of the United States Information Agency (USIA). RIAS played an important role in encouraging the East German rising of June 1953. The Cold War introduced the phenomenon of jamming, whereby a high-powered signal containing just noise was broadcast on the same frequency as the foreign station. Stations affected often moved their frequency slightly so as to dodge the jammers in a radio game of cat and mouse. English-language broadcasts to the USSR were not jammed and allegedly served as a welcome source of news for senior Communist Party officials.

Germany's international radio station Deutsche Welle (Voice of Germany; literally German [Air] Wave) was originally founded in 1929. It began life broadcasting in German to German-speaking populations around the world. In 1953 the station was relaunched by ARD, the West German broadcasting federation, and soon diversified into foreign-language broadcasting. Since 1960 it has been operated by the federal government.

International broadcasting has seen numerous black propaganda stations, that is, radio stations purporting to represent one group but actually subsidized by another. The most famous of these was the British station Soldaten Sender Eins (Soldier's Radio One), which was beamed at Germany during World War II and pretended to be an anti-Nazi station operated by dissidents in the German army. Along similar lines, East Germany operated a number of clandestine Cold War radio stations, including: Deutsche Soldaten Sender (German Soldier's Radio), aimed at West Germany; the Voice of Greeks Abroad; "Our Radio," intended for Turkish guest workers in West Germany; and Radio Vlatava, which attempted to undermine the Czech uprising of 1968. Radio Swan (named after its base on Great Swan Island, off the coast of Honduras) broadcast to Cuba from 1960 to around 1967. Claiming to be sponsored by the Gibraltar Steamship Line, it was actually funded by the CIA and hence produced a fount of propaganda against the regime of Fidel Castro (1927–).

International radio played an important part in the collapse of Communism. Radio gave ordinary citizens of the Soviet bloc the chance to hear uncensored news about their own country. In 1986 Eastern Europe learned about the Chernobyl nuclear accident from Western radio stations, while the Soviet media attempted to suppress the story. Incidents like this severely undermined the credibility of the Communist regimes. As the latter began to crumble, Western radio broadcasts kept the Eastern bloc informed of developments. Subsequently radios were displaced somewhat by satellite television broadcasts and the World Wide Web.

In 2001 international radio returned to the fore during the War on Terrorism, if only because the Taliban regime had suppressed the medium of television. In 2002 the United

States introduced a new radio station called Radio Sawa (Arabic for "Together"). Aimed at young Arab listeners, its lively format included plenty of music mixed in with American propaganda. That same year a group of Zimbabwean expatriates living in London organized SW Radio Africa. With the handle "the voice of independent Zimbabwe," the station broadcast news over the shortwave frequency to a country dominated by the extremist dictator Robert Mugabe (1924–). The station took great pains to carry both the Mugabe government's line as well as the opinions of ordinary people, which it gathered by means of frequent phone-in programs, with callers often using mobile phones.

Nicholas J. Cull

See also BBC; Black Propaganda; Canada; Castro, Fidel; CIA; Cold War; Falklands/Malvinas War; Germany; Lord Haw Haw; Netherlands, Belgium, and Luxembourg; Psychological Warfare; Reith, Lord John; RFE/RL; Russia; Suez Crisis; Terrorism, War on; Tokyo Rose; United States; VOA; White Propaganda; World War II (Britain); World War II (Germany); World War II (Japan); World War II (Russia); World War II (United States)

References: Brown, Donald R. *International Radio Broadcasting: The Limits of the Limitless Medium.* New York: Praeger, 1982; Nelson, Michael. *War of the Black Heavens: The Battles of Western Broadcasting in the Cold War.* London: Brassey's, 1997.

Raemakers, Louis (1869–1956)

A Dutch cartoonist whose anti-German images became a staple of British propaganda in the United States during World War I, Louis Raemakers was already well established as a cartoonist at the outbreak of war. His work frequently appeared in the Amsterdam newspaper *Telegraaf.* His wartime images caricatured Germans as bloated, half-human militaristic monsters and dramatized their alleged atrocities on the western front. The value of these images to British propagandists lay not only in their inherent persuasive power but also in the fact that their creator

was from a neutral country. In 1916 John Buchan (1875–1940), director of Wellington House, Britain's propaganda office with responsibility for the United States, began to promote Raemakers's work there. By the end of the year a significant number of American newspapers had begun to carry the cartoons. Interest in Raemakers's work increased considerably with the U.S. entry into the war. By November 1917 over two thousand newspapers carried his images. After the war Raemakers was attacked as an anti-German hatemonger. In 1940 he moved to the United States, a refugee as a result of the Nazi invasion of Holland.

Nicholas J. Cull

See also Atrocity Propaganda; Britain; Cartoons; Netherlands, Belgium, and Luxembourg; World War I

References: Murray, Allison. J. *Raemakers' Cartoon History of the War.* London: Bodley Head, 1919; Sanders, Michael, and Philip M. Taylor. *British Propaganda during the First World War* London: Macmillan, 1982.

Reagan, Ronald (1911–)

Hollywood actor and president of the United States from 1981 to 1988, Reagan was arguably the most able propagandist ever to occupy the White House. Born in Illinois in 1911, Reagan formed his political views during the Republican domination of American politics following World War I. He worked as a sports announcer at a local radio station, where he invented the play-by-play commentary to match the wire description of baseball games in other cities. In 1937, while in Hollywood on a baseball assignment, he took a screen test at Warner Brothers and subsequently became a leading man for that studio. Although a number of Reagan's films fall into the category of propaganda—for example, the pro-British *International Squadron* (1941) and wartime shorts and informational films made for the U.S. military—far more significant than his film roles was his work as president of the Screen Actors Guild beginning in 1947. In this capacity Reagan became a

Ronald Reagan, official presidential photograph. (Library of Congress)

prominent anti-Communist voice, supporting the investigations of the House Committee on Un-American Activities (HUAC). He also acted as corporate spokesman for the General Electric company.

Reagan's marriage to actress Nancy Davis (1923–) in 1952 linked him to one of the most powerful political families in California's Republican Party. He first appeared nationally in 1964, rallying the party faithful to endorse Senator Barry Goldwater's (1909–1998) bid for president. In 1966 Reagan won the governorship of California (he served until 1975) and achieved a national reputation as a hard-line conservative by clamping down on student activism and the anti–Vietnam War movement. He became a perennial contender for the Republic presidential nomination, which he finally won in 1980. Reagan's blend of down-home charm and Cold War saber-rattling fitted the mood of the times, especially since former president Jimmy Carter (1924–) had appeared weak as a result of the Iranian hostage crisis and the

Soviet invasion of Afghanistan in 1979. One TV ad featured a sinister Soviet bear crashing through the woods, while another asked pointedly: "Do you think the Soviets would have invaded Afghanistan if Ronald Reagan had been President?" Reagan excelled in the televised debates with Carter, demolishing the president with the perfectly timed dismissive line: "There you go again."

Once in office, Reagan invested heavily in U.S. propaganda overseas, appointing his trusted friend Charles Z. Wick (1917–) to the directorship of the United States Information Agency (USIA) and endorsing such propaganda initiatives as Radio Martí broadcasts to Fidel Castro's (1926–) Cuba. Reagan's multimillion-dollar Strategic Defense Initiative (SDI)—nicknamed "Star Wars" by the Democrats—had a strong propaganda component, functioning better as a psychological lever to force the Soviets back into arms talks than as a piece of technology. Reagan also used the U.S. military as an extension of the national image, committing it to short but highly visible missions, such as the liberation of the island of Grenada in 1983. The Reagan administration also aided anti-Communist regimes and guerrilla movements in Central America. This commitment required a considerable White House propaganda effort to minimize the links between America's allies in the region and "death squads." One important conceptual breakthrough in U.S. propaganda was due to Jeane Kirkpatrick (1926–), a professor of international relations and ambassador to the UN, who argued that there was a difference between Communist *totalitarians* and the *authoritarian* regimes sponsored by the administration, since the latter were capable of reform at a later date.

At home Reagan earned the nickname "the Great Communicator." Despite widening social inequalities during this era, he achieved broad popularity. He successfully dramatized the doctrines of the "neoconservative" writers of the era, arguing that far from being the solution to America's problems, "Government *is* the problem." He "played the president" with the confidence of a great actor and won the 1984 presidential election by a substantial margin, insisting that America was once again "standing tall." Reagan had substantial input into scripting his television speeches, developing a powerful rhetorical style that owed much to both Franklin D. Roosevelt (1882–1945) (whom he greatly admired) and the Cold War rhetoric of Harry Truman (1884–1972). Although he appeared to be speaking spontaneously, he was not at his best in improvisational situations, on occasion requiring to be rescued by the first lady. Perhaps his best performance was his broadcast to the nation following the explosion of the space shuttle *Challenger* in 1986.

The later years of Reagan's presidency witnessed a series of summits and a path-breaking disarmament treaty with Mikhail Gorbachev (1931–), the new Soviet leader. Despite various challenges, such as the scandal surrounding the Iran-Contra affair (which made headlines in 1986), Reagan left office in January 1989 with his reputation intact. In 1994 he announced publicly that he was suffering from Alzheimer's, hoping that the revelation would increase public awareness of this debilitating disease.

Nicholas J. Cull

See also Caribbean; Civil Defense; Cold War; Counterinsurgency; Drugs; Labor/Antilabor; Latin America; Opinion Polls; Paine, Thomas; Psychological Warfare; Thatcher, Margaret; United States; USIA; VOA; Wick, Charles Z.

References: Cannon, Lou. *President Reagan: The Role of a Lifetime.* New York: Simon and Schuster, 1991; Dallek, Robert. *Ronald Reagan: The Politics of Symbolism.* Cambridge, MA: Harvard University Press, 1999; Morris, Edmund. *Dutch.* New York: HarperCollins, 1999; Noonan, Peggy. *What I Saw at the Revolution: A Political Life in the Reagan Era.* New York: Random House, 1990.

Reeducation

This term was given to the information policy of the United States and Britain toward Germany and Japan, the defeated enemies of World War II, the major themes of which were the promotion of democracy and teaching the message that "war doesn't pay." Reeducation began before the end of the war in prisoner-of-war camps. German prisoners were screened and divided into three groups: black (diehard Nazis), gray (politically neutral), and white (actively anti-Nazi). Although most reeducation of POWs took the form of optional group discussions, all prisoners were required to see a film depicting German atrocities at Bergen-Belsen and Buchenwald. As the Allies advanced into Germany, the Political Warfare Division (PWD) of the Supreme Headquarters Allied Expeditionary Force (SHAEF) set up an Information Control Division (ICD) under General Robert McClure (1897–1957) to oversee the media in occupied Germany. The Allied military authorities issued newspapers and a newsreel called *Welt im Film* (World in Film), which devoted an entire issue to evidence of the Holocaust. The newsreel series ran from 1945 to 1952. The United States also created and distributed a documentary called *Todesmühlen* (Death Mills), directed by Hanus Burger, on the concentration camps. Such activities limited any immediate attempts to deny the Holocaust.

The administration of the U.S. zone was quick to license new publications, staffed mainly by refugees from Nazi Germany, along American lines, including the newspaper *Neue Zeitung* and the magazine *Der Monat* (The Month). Other U.S.-sponsored activities included the founding of Radio in the American Sector (RIAS) in West Berlin. The United States opened a chain of libraries and information rooms known as *Amerika Häuser* (American Houses). The British licensed the newspaper *Die Welt* as the voice of their occupation. The key figure in the British occupation was Robert Birley (1903–1982), the former head teacher of the prestigious school, Charterhouse, while the prime mover in the American zone was Hungarian-born writer Hans Habe (1911–1977), who became the first editor of *Neue Zeitung*.

In Japan reeducation was managed by the Civil Information and Education (CIE) Section of Allied General Headquarters in Tokyo. A CIE press code forbade criticism of the Allies. Film censors banned the patriotic historical epics of prewar Japan and encouraged films based on new themes and featuring new social mores, such as public kissing. The occupation worked to discredit the reputation of the wartime military regime and to put an end to the cult of the emperor. In Japan, as in Germany, the occupation forces paid particular attention to school textbooks, dropping old ones and commissioning new textbooks from writers sympathetic to the democratic project. A committee of trusted Japanese administrators screened teachers and removed some three thousand thought to be too closely connected to the old regime. One of the most beneficial legacies of reeducation was the promotion of mass higher education in Japan.

In both West Germany and Japan reeducation became increasingly politicized beginning in 1948 as democratic nations prepared for the Cold War. Although democratic practices flourished in both countries, the role of reeducation should not be overestimated. Both countries had indigenous liberal traditions, which moved to the fore during these years.

Nicholas J. Cull

See also Germany; Japan; Marshall Plan; Prisoners of War

References: Pronay, Nicholas, and Keith Wilson, eds. *The Political Reeducation of Germany and Her Allies after World War II*. London: Croom Helm, 1985; Tent, James F. *Mission on the Rhine: Reeducation and Denazification in American-Occupied Germany*. Chicago: University of Chicago Press, 1982; Willett, Ralph. *The Americanization of Germany, 1945–1949*. London: Routledge, 1989.

Reefer Madness (1936)

This American public health information film was designed to warn of the evils of smoking marijuana. Originally released under the title *Tell Your Children* and known by a variety of alternative titles—including *The Burning Question* and *Love Madness*—*Reefer Madness* was directed by French-born Louis Gasnier (1875–1963). The film shows how a group of young Americans are lured into drug use, with murder, madness, and suicide the consequences. Another film in a similar vein was *Marihuana: The Devil's Weed* (1935)—also known as *Marihuana, the Weed with Roots in Hell*—whose tag line was: "Weird orgies! Wild Parties! Unleashed Passions." It showed how drugs led youngsters to participate in fatal nude swimming sessions. Later examples of antidrug film propaganda include *She Shoulda Said No* (1947). By the 1960s such films had reached cult status among a new generation of young Americans, who were able to compare their personal drug-related experiences with the hysterical fears of their parents' generation. *Reefer Madness* is still available on video and DVD in the United States, where it retains a substantial following as an example of camp filmmaking.

Nicholas J. Cull

See also Drugs; Film (Feature); Health; United States

References: Starks, Michael. *Cocaine Fiends and Reefer Madness: An Illustrated History of Drugs in the Movies*. New York: Cornwall, 1982; Stevenson, Jack. *Addicted: The Myth and Menace of Drugs in Film*. London: Creation, 2000.

Reformation and Counter-Reformation

The Reformation was a religious movement of the sixteenth century that began as a bid to reform the then universal Roman Catholic Church but eventually led to the creation of Protestant Christianity. The struggle between Protestant and Counter-Reformation forces—the attempt of the Catholic Church to regain its power—produced a stream of propaganda that lasted well into the seventeenth century. The word "propaganda" is derived from the title of a Vatican institution founded to reassert Catholicism, namely, the

Reefer Madness, *a 1936 film denouncing the addictive power of marijuana, was re-released in 1972 by the National Organization for Reform of Marijuana Laws with this ironic poster. (Bettmann / CORBIS)*

Sacra Congregatio de Propaganda Fide (Sacred Congregation for Propagation of the Faith) of 1622.

Although the Reformation began as a movement calling for internal reform, when the Roman hierarchy condemned reformers like Martin Luther (1483–1586) in Germany and Hulderich Zwingli (1484–1531) and John Calvin (1509–1564) in Switzerland as heretics, the resulting split led to the establishment of separate, so-called Protestant churches. The turning point occurred in 1521 at the German Diet of Worms, where Martin Luther declared that he would not yield to pressure by the pope or the emperor.

The Protestants were greatly aided by their skillful oral and printed propaganda. Both language and images were strong— even vulgar—with the pope portrayed as the Whore of Babylon and Catholic priests shown kissing the rear ends of animals. Catholic anti-Protestant propaganda demonized the person of Martin Luther, a former monk who had married a former nun, praised sexuality, and enjoyed eating and drinking. The negative image of Martin Luther was fleshed out in a book by the Catholic polemicist Johannes Cochlaeus (1497–1552) entitled *Commentary on the Acts and Writings of Martin Luther* (1549). Cochlaeus tried to explain Luther's conflict with the Roman Catholic Church by pointing to defects in the reformer's character. According to Cochlaeus, Luther was a self-centered man driven by pride and lust and lacking in religious seriousness. A parallel to this highly personal form of propaganda, which was used by the Roman Catholic Church as late as the twentieth century, was the demonization of Luther by the English king Henry VIII (r. 1509–1547). Henry broke with Rome and abolished the monasteries, instead founding a national Catholic English church with the king as its master, thereby distancing himself from Lutheranism. In Luther's view, education was a necessity since everyone was supposed to study the Bible. The Reformation was promoted through the establishment

of new educational institutions, which added to the prestige of the new religious movements. Some tried to stay within the Roman Catholic Church, hoping to reform it from the inside, while others broke away from it. In the first camp were men like the humanist scholars Erasmus of Rotterdam (c. 1466–1536) and Guillaume Budé (1467–1540), neither of whom broke officially with Roman Catholicism. Nevertheless Erasmus helped the cause of Protestantism by criticizing the established church and the educational system; he also published an edition of the Bible in Greek. Provided with royal support, Budé founded the Collège de France in Paris as an alternative to the reactionary Catholic university at the Sorbonne.

The Roman Catholic Church remained in a defensive position spiritually until the appearance of Ignatius Loyola (1491–1556), a Basque-Castilian nobleman and warrior who made himself general of a new religious order, the so-called Jesuits, a spiritual army that served the pope. Loyola supplemented his military background, which was influenced by the Spanish tradition relating to the Moorish wars, with humanistic studies in Paris. It was there, in 1534, that Loyola and six followers founded a clandestine society whose first priority was the conversion of Muslims in the Holy Land. It quickly changed course to fight against a more immediate threat to Catholicism, namely, the Protestants. In this fight the means justified the ends. Thus, Loyola devised a secret manual for Jesuits in England, who tried to build up a conspiracy against King Henry VIII. In 1540 the Jesuit order obtained papal recognition and quickly became the heart and soul of the movement known as the Counter-Reformation.

By the 1540s Protestantism dominated Scandinavia and northern Germany, apparently being close to taking over the rest of Germany and Poland, Bohemia-Moravia, and Hungary-Transylvania. It was dominant in Switzerland, had a strong position in France, and was only under control in Spain and Portugal, where the Inquisition had thus far managed to suppress it. The Jesuits used the first part of the Council of Trent (1545–1547), the leadership of which they in effect took over, to strengthen papal authority over the church and to formulate alternative Catholic positions to the Protestant ones. These were spread by means of education and propaganda. The Jesuits worked both secretly and openly to provide the Roman Catholic Church with well-educated people who could act as agents for it in societies apparently already "lost" to Protestantism. They used laymen as well as clerics, princes as well as scholars. They were supported by most of the Habsburg emperors as well as forces in society—particularly in Poland—that worried about the social revolutionary potential of Protestantism.

Protestant education and propaganda proved particularly attractive to the middle classes and those ethnic groups eager to emancipate themselves by substituting their mother tongue for Latin as the language of church and school. The Jesuits, however, deployed a pincer movement, aiming at the elite and at the uneducated masses in the countryside. Protestantism remained mostly an urban phenomenon. The Jesuits used refined learning to convince noble disciples to support the Roman Catholic Church, whereas it reverted to such populist means as processions and other mass events centered around saints and relics to influence the broader population. The Jesuit order spread quickly. In 1544 there were only nine Jesuit colleges and no provinces. By the time of Loyola's death in 1556, the order had a hundred colleges and twelve provinces, with members scattered all over the world, from Japan to Latin America. They typically served as doctors and professors at universities, as confessors of princes, and as secret agents proselytizing for the Catholic faith.

In the 1550s and 1560s Jesuit propaganda, combined with state repression in the Netherlands, led to a radicalization of Protestantism there. The more anti-Catholic Calvinist church essentially eradicated Lutheranism. This led to a religious war between Philip II (r. 1556–1598), the Spanish Catholic king and sovereign of the Netherlands, and William of Orange (William the Silent) (1533–1584), leader of the northern provinces, which were fighting for religious and political freedom. Calvinist propaganda was more politically outspoken than the Lutheran version, John Calvin himself being a professed republican.

Around 1600 most of the cities of the Habsburg Empire, like Vienna and Prague, were Protestant. But the Jesuits, supported by the Habsburg emperors, were very active and gradually managed to gain ground for the Counter-Reformation. The Vatican in Rome had begun to structure its holding action in Europe by creating an organization consisting of three cardinals known as the Cardinals' Commission for Propagation of the Faith (*de propaganda fide*), established during the reign of Pope Gregory XIII (r. 1572–1585). In 1622 Pope Gregory XV (r. 1621–1623) created a new framework for this mission in the form of the Sacred Congregation for the propagation of the faith, composed of thirteen cardinals, which he explicitly charged with the task of extending the faith in the "new" lands of Asia and America and turning back the tide of Protestantism. The organization prospered, especially when Maffeo Barberini (1868–1644), one of the thirteen cardinals, succeeded to the papacy as Urban VIII (ruled 1623–1644). The organization effectively gave the world the word "propaganda."

During the Thirty Years' War, which began in 1618 in Prague, the Protestants made the Calvinist count Frederick (1596–1632), Elector of the Palatinate, king of Bohemia in 1619. Following the decisive battle at the White Mountain, outside Prague, in 1620, Frederick was forced to flee the country. The Counter-Reformation now prevailed. Bohemia was totally purged of Protestantism by means of executions, confiscation of property, and the zealous missionary work of the Jesuits. The same fate later befell the Protestants in Austria. In Hungary-Transylvania the Protestants were saved by the Ottoman occupation. Print propaganda on both sides emphasized the enemy's atrocities and the religious virtue of the home side.

One of the problems of the Protestants was the split between Lutherans and Calvinists, whereas the Catholics were now united under Pope Urban VIII and his spiritual guards, the Jesuits. The Protestants were denounced as heretics and unpatriotic for failing to support the emperor in his fight against Christian and Muslim infidels. The Jesuit Wilhelm Lamormaini (1570–1638), adviser to Habsburg emperor Ferdinand II (1578–1637), described the attitude of his emperor as follows: "The false and corrupt policies, which are widespread in these times, he, in his wisdom, condemned from the start. He held that those who followed such policies could not be dealt with, since they practice falsehood and misuse God and religion." In the 1630s, after the defeat and withdrawal from Germany of the Danish Lutheran king Christian IV (r. 1596–1648) and the death of Gustav II Adolf (r. 1611–1632) of Sweden, his more successful neighbor and fellow Lutheran, the odds of Protestantism dominating Germany were slight.

Just when the emperor seemed about to restore both the Holy Roman Empire and the Roman Catholic Church in Germany, France intervened in the person of Catholic Cardinal Richelieu (1585–1642). After having marginalized the position of Protestants in France, Richelieu used every means to stabilize and strengthen them in Germany. He was helped by the stubborn refusal of the Habsburg emperor to compromise with the Protestants. In 1648 the Habsburgs were forced to compromise under the terms of the Treaty of Westphalia. The boundaries between Protestantism and Catholicism were fixed according to a political agreement whereby Catholic France and Protestant Sweden were allied and emerged as winners. The high tide of religious propaganda in continental Europe was over, but within the British Isles (especially Ireland) it remained a major factor in political life until the end of the century and beyond.

In the eighteenth century the Counter-Reformation was ultimately defeated by the Enlightenment. Political pressure on the Vatican from the leaders of Portugal and Spain led to the abolishment of the Jesuit order. The Jesuits and Counter-Reformation propaganda were revived in the nineteenth century in the form of Roman Catholic propaganda against political liberalism, and later against Communism. Late-twentieth-century attempts to reconcile Lutherans and Catholics attempted to annul mutual accusations made back in the sixteenth century. This effort was only partly successful. Despite ecumenical cooperation, the impact of the theological propaganda and counterpropaganda of the past has not yet been eliminated. One reason is that propaganda helped form the identity of both branches of Christianity.

Karsten Fledelius

See also Atrocity Propaganda; Austrian Empire; Britain; France; Germany; Ignatius of Loyola, Saint; Ireland; Latin America; Luther, Martin; Netherlands, Belgium, and Luxembourg; Portugal; Religion; Scandinavia; Spain; Switzerland

References: Bireley, Robert. *The Refashioning of Catholicism, 1450–1700: A Reassessment of the Counter Reformation.* Basingstoke, UK: Macmillan, 1999; Edwards, Mark U. *Printing, Propaganda, and Martin Luther.* Berkeley: University of California Press, 1994; Garstein, Oskar. *Rome and the Counter-Reformation in Scandinavia.* 2 vols. Oslo: Universitetsforlaget, 1963–1980; Scribner, Robert W. *For the Sake of Simple Folk: Popular Propaganda for the German Reformation.* Cambridge: Cambridge University Press, 1981.

Reith, Lord John (1889–1971)

John Reith was born in Scotland, trained as an engineer, and served and was wounded in World War I. In 1922 Reith became general manager of what was then called the British Broadcasting Company. In 1926 Reith became the first director-general of the British Broadcasting Corporation (BBC). In deciding on programming, he was guided by the belief that broadcasting must be educational as well as entertaining. He allowed the BBC to be an instrument of propaganda for the British government during the General Strike of 1926. During the 1930s he oversaw the inauguration of the BBC Empire Service, which transmitted British news and "values" to citizens overseas. In 1938 he assumed the chairmanship of Imperial Airways. Appointed in 1940 as the second minister of information by Prime Minister Neville Chamberlain (1869–1940), he helped to reinvigorate Britain's wartime propaganda effort. In May 1940 Winston Churchill (1874–1965) transferred Reith to the Ministry of Transport. He was also made a peer. Churchill dropped Reith from the cabinet in 1942. He felt painfully underused by the government and spent the rest of his life waiting for a call to high office that simply never came. The "Reithian" tradition lived on at the BBC long after his departure. His name remains synonymous with the idea of public-service broadcasting that is both morally and intellectually uplifting rather than just entertaining.

Nicholas J. Cull

See also BBC; The Big Lie; Britain; Censorship; MoI; Radio (International); World War II (Britain)

References: Boyle, Andrew. *Only the Wind Will Listen: Reith of the BBC.* London: Hutchinson, 1972; McIntyre, Ian. *The Expense of Glory: A Life of John Reith.* London: HarperCollins, 1993.

Religion

Religion can be defined as a belief in something greater and more powerful than mankind. Religious movements have used propaganda techniques to spread their message. Religion is often used in propaganda because, once established, it rules out all other arguments, such as human rights, vested interests, political privileges, or property rights. It is the ultimate instrument of political power.

Royal authority has traditionally been supported by religiously based propaganda. The notion of the holiness of kingship goes back to prehistoric times. With respect to Christianity, it is linked to the notion of the anointed kings of Israel, specifically David (ca. 1000 B.C.E.) and his son, Solomon (ca. 1015–977 B.C.E.). The divine act of anointing, later elaborated in a coronation ceremony, made the king untouchable and his murder an act of sacrilege. In Britain Oliver Cromwell (1599–1658) deliberately tried to break that link by having Charles I (1600–1649) executed in 1649 and the regalia of the crown annihilated. But both kingship and regalia were recreated in 1660 with the restoration of the British monarchy under Charles II (1630–1685).

The particular holiness of emperorship was established by the first century and given a Christian basis in the fourth. It has been used by all later Christian rulers, most notably the Habsburgs of Austria (1452–1806), emperors of the so-called Holy Roman Empire. The Romanovs of Russia (1613–1917) drew heavily on religious propaganda for their emperorship, which did not prevent four of the eight Russian tsars from being assassinated. The use of religion as propaganda by the monarchy made antireligious propaganda very important for revolutionaries since the 1790s. Notable examples include Thomas Paine's (1737–1809) *Age of Reason* (1794–1796) and critiques of religion advanced by Karl Marx (1818–1883).

The Vatican in Rome is the most obvious example of an institution entirely based on religious propaganda. The very word "propaganda" is derived from the sixteenth-century organization for religious propaganda, *Sacra congregatio de propaganda fide* (Sacred Congregation for the Propagation of the Faith). Papal propaganda became particularly evident after Italy annexed the papal state in 1870. Popes have been fighting against democracy, political liberalism, left-wing parties, female reproductive rights, and liberation theology—often supporting right-wing dictators like Francisco Franco (1892–1975) in Spain and Augusto Pinochet (1915–) in Chile. Pope

John Paul II (1920–) used modern mass media to fight Communism, materialism, and to promote conservative family and societal values.

Despite the constitutional separation of church and state in the United States, political speeches are frequently imbued with religious rhetoric. Outstanding examples include the civil rights speeches of the 1950s and 1960s, which were influenced by Southern Baptist preachers like Martin Luther King Jr. (1929–1968), or the speeches of radical black Muslim leader Malcolm X (1925–1965). In the 1980s Republican politicians like Ronald Reagan (1911–) and George Bush (1924–) used much religious rhetoric, while TV evangelists like Jerry Falwell (1953–) lobbied on behalf of marital fidelity and against abortion, themes taken up by conservative political leaders.

Modern religious propaganda since the 1980s has witnessed a decline in traditionally antireligious Marxist ideology. The same period has also witnessed a rise in nationalistic rhetoric, which is frequently combined with religion. In 1992 the radical Serb leadership in Bosnia used the defense of Orthodox Christianity as the basis for breaking away from the multireligious state of Bosnia and creating a separate state. The value of religion as propaganda seems to have been enhanced during the 1990s, replacing political ideology as the most important source of propaganda. This is also true in states whose constitution requires the separation of church and state.

In the Islamic world the interpretation of the Koran by right-wing Moslem clerics brought religion into international politics. In 1979 the Ayatollah Ruhollah Khomeini (1900–1989) successfully engineered the overthrow of the shah of Iran by making use of such simple means of mass communication as audiocassettes of his sermons and political speeches, which were smuggled into the country. Religiously based propaganda has been used by both sides in the Israeli-Palestine conflict, with both sides claiming a divine right to the land.

The late twentieth century saw the emergence of Islamic religious terrorism—especially in the Arab world. An early example involved the assassination in October 1981 of Egyptian president Anwar Sadat (1918–1981) by radical Muslims, with the terrorists subsequently exploiting media coverage of their trials to bolster their cause. Unlike the clerical revolution in Iran, the new brand of militant Islam looked to laymen, with propaganda disseminated by organizations like al-Jamaa al-Islamiya in Egypt or the Al Qaeda network targeted at the masses. Some opposition to radical Islamism actually comes from Muslim theologians who reject the militant layman's one-sided and politically biased interpretation of the Koran. The propaganda of radical Arab Islamism is as much directed against local Arab rulers as against the "unbelievers" of the West. Not only secular regimes like those of Egypt and Algeria have suffered; so, too, have fundamentalist Muslim rulers like King Fahd (1922–) of Saudi Arabia, who himself had financed Koran schools in Asia and Europe. Radical Islamist clerics have achieved success among immigrant Arab circles in Western cities like New York, London, Brussels, and Hamburg. Suicide terrorism is the most notorious product of this religious propaganda. Polite, well-educated young men from good families became instruments of terror, fueled by the promise of a life of pleasure in paradise attended by seventy or seventy-two naked virgins. Documents published following the attacks against the United States on 11 September 2001 revealed the religio-political character of the propaganda used to prepare the attackers, silence their doubts, and nurture a feeling of being the instrument of God. By choosing prominent targets and timing their attacks to ensure maximum global media coverage, the religiously motivated suicide pilots of 11 September united traditional martyrdom with modern communications technology.

Karsten Fledelius

See also Arab World; Balkans; Ignatius of Loyola, Saint; Iran; Ireland; Italy; Laden, Osama bin;

Luther, Martin; Marx, Karl; Netherlands,
Belgium, and Luxembourg; Ottoman Empire;
Pacific/Oceania; Paine, Thomas; Philippines;
Poland; Reagan, Ronald; Reformation and
Counter-Reformation; Revolution, French;
Switzerland; Temperance; Terrorism;
Terrorism, War on; United States

References: Bruce, Steve. *The Rise and Fall of the New Christian Right: Conservative Protestant Politics in America, 1978–1988.* Oxford: Clarendon Press, 1988; Noll, Mark, ed. *Religion and American Politics: From the Colonial Period to the 1980s.* New York: Oxford University Press, 1990; Sahliyeh, Emile, ed. *Religious Resurgence and Politics in the Contemporary World.* Albany: State University of New York Press, 1990; Sivan, Emmanuel, and Menachem Friedman, eds. *Religious Radicalism and Politics in the Middle East.* Albany: State University of New York Press, 1990.

Revolution, American, and War of Independence (1764–1783)

American independence was accomplished in a war of ideas in which propaganda was the most important weapon. John Adams (1735–1826) claimed that a revolution in the minds of the colonists took place before a drop of blood was shed, as a result of the political campaigns between 1764 and 1775. The patriots opposed the authority of the British Parliament to impose duty on goods and services in the colonies. The colonial elite engaged in a systematic effort to gain public support, described by Philip G. Davidson as propaganda, demanding that the right to raise taxes in the colonies would be determined solely by American colonial assemblies. Their intention was not to prepare the people for independence, which was not considered until 1776. John Dickinson's (1732–1808) "Letters from a Pennsylvania Farmer" (1767–1768) rallied popular support against the Townshend Acts (1767), invoking an oppositional "country" ideology familiar to British politics, championing the merits of the British constitution and the rights of Englishmen, while at the same time asserting the corruption of the present court and house.

The propaganda campaign created an atmosphere of hostility and fear, the escalation of which drew the patriots reluctantly into an anticolonial war. So convinced were the colonists that the British government intended to extinguish traditional English liberty that even minor expressions of legal authority were resisted. In 1770, when troops fired on a riotous crowd, killing five men, the "Boston Massacre" was used as evidence of oppression. In 1775, when British troops engaged with colonial militia in Lexington and Concord, Massachusetts, the incident was widely regarded as a great injustice despite the context of resistance against lawful authority. Thomas Paine's (1737–1809) pamphlet *Common Sense* (1776) proposed American independence as the only feasible goal.

During the War of Independence (1776–1783), the focus turned to maintaining morale. For example, Paine's sixteen pamphlets collectively known as *The Crisis* (1776–1783) reinforced the rightness of the colonists' cause and doubted the supremacy of British forces. After the British surrender at Yorktown in 1781, the debate on the future of the colonies continued in newspapers and pamphlets, particularly in relation to the terms of the Peace of Paris (1783), the jurisdiction over western frontier lands, and the Federal Constitutional Convention (1787–1788). *The Federalist,* comprising a series of articles by Alexander Hamilton (1755–1804), John Jay (1745–1829), and James Madison (1751–1836), sought popular support for ratification but met with a vigorous anti-Federalist campaign.

Print was by far the most important medium in spreading political sentiments. Such political debates took place in articles, letters, official documents, poems, sermons, and speeches printed in newspapers, almanacs, and broadsides. By 1775 there were thirty-eight newspapers, transformed by rebellion from "newspapers without news" into forums for political debate and centers of resistance. The most useful tool for extended

American revolutionary Paul Revere's famous engraving of the Boston Massacre, entitled The Bloody Massacre Perpetrated in King Street. *(National Archives)*

political argument was the pamphlet. Ranging from short squibs to technical treatises, between 1750 and 1776 over four thousand pamphlets were published bearing on the colonial crisis. Pamphlets were cheap to produce and provided a quick response to events, often resulting in protracted debates. While the latter often ended in vituperative personal attacks, pamphlet literature generally consisted of reasoned argument motivated by a sense of injustice rather than hate. Despite their use of satire—a common device in British pamphleteering—these authors were amateurs, mostly lawyers, clergy, merchants, and planters; with the exception of Paine and William Livingston (1723–

1790), they never attained the level of professional English penmen.

Official documents such as the Declaration of Rights and Grievances (1774) also appealed to public opinion. Although unlikely to effect a change in British policy, such documents were intended to justify concerted action to the public. The Declaration of Independence, which informed the world that the colonists no longer considered themselves subjects of the British crown, has been seen as "performative" propaganda, for "only as men fought for it did they give meaning to it."

Speeches, sermons, and plays reached an uneducated audience whose support for the revolution was vital. Preachers borrowed from the religious enthusiasm and engagement of the "Great Awakening" (1734–1760). "Mob orators" like Ebenezer Mackintosh (1737–1816) of Boston made intense emotional appeals to the crowd. Oral persuasion, though independently effective, was reinforced and disseminated in print. Songs and parodies set to popular tunes, such as John Dickinson's (1732–1808) "The Liberty Song" (1768) were performed and printed in broadsides. Printed engravings, such as Paul Revere's (1734–1818) widely circulated illustration of the Boston Massacre, provided visual news. Paper money bearing patriotic emblems and slogans was printed and issued by state legislatures and the Continental Congress to fund the war effort. Flags also employed symbols, such as the liberty tree, the rattlesnake (the latter bore the slogan "Don't tread on me"), and the thirteen stars and stripes, which was adopted by Congress in 1777.

Street festivities, while often spontaneous, can also be seen as a medium for the dissemination of propaganda, recreating written and oral rhetoric in terms of ritual. During the Stamp Act crisis of 1765, angry colonists performed a "funeral of liberty" procession in the street. The Declaration of Independence was greeted and endorsed by a ritual burial and destruction of royal statuary and arms.

Parades to liberty trees, public toasts to ancient liberties, continental fasts and thanksgiving days—which included civic feasts, gun salutes, and orations—marked significant events and anniversaries. Campaigners also used "patriotic numbers" as symbols. Initially the number 45 linked their cause to British political rebel John Wilkes (1727–1797), publisher of antigovernment *The North Briton No. 45*. In 1766 the colonists added the number 92, reflecting the majority opinion in the Massachusetts Assembly opposing British rule. Thus, a crowd in Charleston, South Carolina, lit their liberty tree with 45 lights, followed by a celebration involving 45 bowls of punch, 45 bottles of wine, and 92 glasses. After the signing of the Declaration of Independence, the numbers 76 and 13 became the preferred symbols of liberty.

Loyalist propaganda was restricted to the print medium, disparaging popular appeals. The Tory counterattack reached a fever pitch in 1774–1775, using personal exposé and public accusation. Some loyalist pamphlets were well respected, such as *Plain Truth* (1776), which went into several editions. Tory opposition was tolerated less during the war. Tories were publicly tarred and feathered and marched out of town. Nevertheless, in 1778 loyalists appealed for peace by manipulating anti-French and anti-Catholic sentiments.

The interpretation of the American Revolution as propaganda is associated with Progressive historians Charles Beard (1874–1948) and Arthur M. Schlesinger (1888–1965), who have argued that the revolution was motivated by class interests rather than political ideas. Carl Becker (1873–1945) claimed that the colonists modified their political theory to "suit their changing needs." Since the colonists did not suffer from poverty or significant oppression, he argued, the revolutionaries employed the rhetoric of "slavery," "corruption" and "massacre" as "mere propaganda." By contrast, the ideological interpretation of the Revolution, which is associated with Bernard Bailyn and Gordon

S. Wood, sees political ideas as the determinant of the patriots' interpretation of events. Bailyn has argued that the colonists understood the terms "slavery" and "corruption" within the paradigm of the commonwealth tradition and genuinely felt their oppression.

Nevertheless, a descriptive conception of propaganda recognizes that the revolutionary literature did amount to a partially orchestrated campaign to effect mass persuasion. Several writers deliberately manipulated readers emotionally in addition to utilizing rational argument. Philip G. Davidson has demonstrated that pamphleteers intended to "hoodwink" the people. For example, Dickinson pretended to react to reader's questions despite the fact that entire series of letters had been completed before publication. In response to the Peace Commission, William Livingston sent several letters to the *New Jersey Gazette* under assumed names, including "Belinda." H. S. Stout has argued that manipulative propaganda could not flourish in the absence of mass society. The educated elite numbered only three thousand college graduates in 1776. However, Paine's *Common Sense* is estimated to have reached one sixth of the population. The need to persuade the common man, evidenced by the distinctly oral orientation of patriot propaganda, "psychologically enfranchised" the masses in a society characterized by an unusual degree of social equality. The unintended effect of the "decidedly disingenuous" democratic rhetoric employed by the elite was an inevitable turn toward political equality.

The American Revolution assumed a central position in the national mythology of the United States and hence became a key reference point in U.S. home-front war propaganda. Icons of such campaigns included Tompkins Harrison Matteson's (1813–1884) painting *Spirit of '76* (1845) and sculptor Daniel Chester French's (1850–1931) *Minute Man* (1875), which figured in U.S. war bond promotions in both world wars. In the early years of the Cold War, documents from the Revolutionary period toured the United States on the Freedom Train as part of a patriotic propaganda initiative.

Karen M. Ford

See also Britain (Eighteenth Century); Freedom Train; Livingston, William; Paine, Thomas; Psychological Warfare; United States

References: Bailyn, Bernard. *The Ideological Origins of the American Revolution.* Cambridge, MA: Belknap Press of the Harvard University Press, 1967; Beard, Charles. *An Economic Interpretation of the Constitution of the United States.* New York: Macmillan, 1913; Becker, Carl. *The Declaration of Independence: A Study in the History of Political Ideas.* New York: Harcourt and Brace, 1922; Davidson, Philip G. "Whig Propagandists of the American Revolution." *American Historical Review* 39, no. 3 (1934): 442–453; ———. *Propaganda and the American Revolution, 1763–1783.* Chapel Hill: University of North Carolina Press, 1941; Maier, Pauline. "John Wilkes and American Disillusionment with Britain." *William and Mary Quarterly* (3d ser.) 20, 3 (1963): 373–395; Schlesinger, Arthur M. *Prelude to Independence: The Newspaper War on Britain, 1764–1776.* New York: Knopf, 1958; Stout, H. S. "Religion, Communications and the Ideological Origins of the American Revolution." *William and Mary Quarterly* (3d ser.) 34, 4 (1977): 519–514; Waldstreicher, David. "Rites of Rebellion, Rites of Assent: Celebrations, Print Culture and the Origins of American Nationalism." *Journal of American History* 82, 1 (1995): 37–61; Wood, G. S. *The Creation of the American Republic, 1776–1787.* Chapel Hill: University of North Carolina Press, 1969.

Revolution, French (1789–1799)

This period of political upheaval in France ended the monarchy but was itself subsumed by the rise of Napoleon Bonaparte (1769–1821). The French revolutionaries of 1789 and after spoke of creating a new human being to suit the new regime. To this end they mobilized all the available media—printed texts, visual images, theatrical productions, popular songs, stately hymns, games, playing cards, and architecture—to impress, accommodate, and serve the masses. At first much of this propaganda was created spontaneously, with prorevolutionary and royalist advocates engaged in a battle to control people's minds. As the Revolution progressed, however, there was growing pressure from the national government, municipal authorities, and political clubs to support the revolutionary cause. This pressure intensified after the advent of the Terror in 1793, during which the revolutionary government took on many of the features of a totalitarian state.

The printed word was the principal medium for spreading or opposing the revolutionary gospel. It requires a thick volume just to list the myriad newspapers that appeared once royal authorization was no longer required. Early in the Revolution prorevolutionary and opposition newspapers were allowed to compete, but as the Revolution intensified royalist newspapers were suppressed and their editors arrested. During the Terror the revolutionary government supervised and subsidized the press. Printed propaganda, however, extended far beyond newspapers to include caricatures, declarations of rights, almanacs, catechisms, lists of adages, revolutionary commandments, Republican calendars, songbooks, children's primers, revolutionary board games, and playing cards.

Art was likewise mobilized to serve the revolutionary cause. Although many artists continued to paint landscapes, portraits, and still lifes based on apolitical classical or religious themes, others attempted to immortalize contemporary events—the Tennis Court Oath, the storming of the Bastille, the overthrow of the monarchy—and such political martyrs as Louis-Michel Lepelletier (1760–1793), Marie-Joseph Chalier (1747–1793), and Jean-Paul Marat (1743–1793). At the peak of the Revolution, the Committee of Public Safety sponsored an ambitious contest that utilized state patronage as a means of increasing the number of works of art depicting revolutionary events, political heroes, and allegorical compositions in praise of new revolutionary ideals.

Plays were also used to disseminate revolutionary messages. Even before the Revolution, some authors had advocated turning the theater into a school for civic education. As the royal monopoly of the theater disappeared, scores of new theaters were opened and hundreds of new plays were produced. Again pressure was exerted on playwrights by the central government, municipal authorities, and patriotic clubs to produce plays with revolutionary themes. During the Terror the central government issued lists of approved plays. At the same time, attempts were made to change the physical layout of theaters. Auditoriums were redesigned without boxes and separate sections so that audiences could mingle.

Those who were not avid readers, did not care for art, or did not attend the theater could be reached through music. Thousands of revolutionary songs and hymns were written during the decade-long Revolution, peaking during the Terror (1793–1794). Songs were reproduced on single sheets, in newspapers, in civic manuals, and collected in little songbooks. They were sung on street corners, in homes, and in political clubs by soldiers and the general populace during state festivals. (The revolutionary government selected the music for such festivals and their massed choirs.) At the peak of the Revolution the government itself sponsored a National Institute of Music that produced two musical publications, one containing popular songs and the other more elevated compositions suitable for formal state occasions. Architecture also served the revolutionary cause. From the very beginning of the Revolution, ambitious architects sought state commissions to design towering columns, triumphal arches, revolutionary temples, and other public buildings. Such structures were meant to impress the public through their monumental size, official inscriptions, symbols, and allegorical figures. Still other edifices were designed to accommodate citizens in revolutionary meetings and festivities. Civic leaders strove to demonstrate their concern for the masses by planning such public facilities as fountains, lavatories, public

baths, swimming pools, libraries, museums, and schools. The effort to impress, accommodate, and serve the masses reached a peak in the spring of 1794, when the Committee of Public Safety called upon sculptors and architects to create revolutionary monuments of various kinds, Temples of Equality, *Temples decadaires* for worship on the tenth day (the Republican substitute for Sunday), Republican schools, and various urban amenities. The plans also called for a revolutionary public park in the heart of Paris. If successful, these projects would have created a new ideological landscape to replace the former Christian one.

It was at the revolutionary festival, however, where all the media came together to serve the Revolution. In the great festivals celebrating the anniversary of the storming of the Bastille, the overthrow of the monarchy, the inauguration of the Republican constitution, revolutionary victories, the "Cult of the Supreme Being," or the commemoration of Republican martyrs, there were always speeches, printed programs, parades of officials marches by the common people, bands and choirs, ephemeral statues, triumphal arches, floats bearing allegorical figures—all funneling into a large area where the participants gathered around the Altar of the Fatherland.

French revolutionary propaganda was not an immediate success. The Revolution went through a constitutional monarchy, a moderate republic, a radical republic, and a conservative one, culminating in a coup by Napoleon Bonaparte. It wasn't until a decade after the establishment of the Third Republic in 1870 that most of its major goals were achieved. The French Revolution had been too unstable for Republican propaganda to bear immediate fruit. It did, however, provide a prototype for future regimes on the left and right anxious to mold their citizens in the image of a new order.

James A. Leith

See also Architecture; Art; David, Jacques-Louis; France; "La Marseillaise"; Napoleon; Paine, Thomas

References: Carlson, Marvin. *The Theater of the French Revolution.* Ithaca, NY: Cornell University Press, 1966; Kennedy, Emmet. *A Cultural History of the French Revolution.* New Haven, CT: Yale University Press, 1989; Leith, James A. "Music as an Ideological Weapon in the French Revolution." *Canadian Historical Association Annual Report, 1966.* Ottawa,1967, 126–140; ———. *Media and Revolution: Moulding a New Citizenry in France during the Terror.* Toronto: Canadian Broadcasting Corporation, 1968; ———. *The Idea of Art as Propaganda: A Study in the History of Ideas.* Toronto: Toronto University Press, 1965; Ozouf, Mona. *Festivals and the French Revolution.* Cambridge, MA: Harvard University Press, 1988.

Revolution, Russian (1917–1921)

The Russian Revolution, also known as the Great Revolution or the October Revolution, was the second revolution to occur in 1917; it followed February's successful attempt to overthrow the autocracy, which resulted in the abdication of the tsar. The Provisional Government—a coalition hastily cobbled together by a state Duma (parliament)—was not used to the exercise of power and was intended only as a temporary measure until an election could be held. The Provisional Government could not withdraw from World War I against Germany and found it impossible to organize the day-to-day affairs of a vast nation at war—not least because it needed the support of the Petrograd soviet, the organization of workers and soldiers who had taken control of that city following the February Revolution.

The Bolsheviks, the most radical revolutionary party, seized on this inactivity. Once their leader Vladimir Lenin (1870–1924) arrived in April and coopted Leon Trotsky (1879–1940) to the cause, they scorned the Provisional Government and claimed their right to act. They gained the support of the soviets through the slogan "Peace, Bread, and Land!" The Provisional Government, led by Alexander Kerensky (1881–1970), became more and more unpopular. On the night of

25 October 1917 the Bolsheviks seized control of the Winter Palace in Petrograd almost without firing a shot, proving that no one was willing to fight for the Provisional Government.

Lenin, the master of "agitation," announced to the Revolutionary Military Committee of the Petrograd Soviet of Workers' and Soldiers' Deputies: "The cause for which the people have fought, namely, the immediate offer of a democratic peace, the abolition of landed proprietorship, workers' control over production, and the establishment of Soviet power—this cause has been secured . . . Long live the revolution of workers, soldiers and peasants!" ("To the Citizens of Russia!" *Worker and Soldier* 8, 1–2 [25 October 1917]).

The offer was attractive, the facts were simple, and the tone was one of absolute confidence. There was to be nothing "provisional" about the Bolshevik's approach. Lenin's rhetoric to the general populace was even more direct: "Comrades—workers, soldiers, peasants and all working people! The workers' and peasants' revolution has definitely triumphed in Petrograd . . . The victory of the workers' and peasants' revolution is assured because the majority of the people have already sided with it . . . We shall go forward firmly and unswervingly to the victory of socialism—a victory that will be sealed by the advanced workers of the most civilized countries, bring the people lasting peace and liberate them from all oppression and exploitation" ("To the Populace." *Pravda* 4 [19 November 1917]; this speech was written before the uprising).

As soon as he gained power, Lenin made clear what he intended to do. The "Decree on Land" nationalized the latter on behalf of the people who farmed it. This was followed by the "Decree on Peace" announcing that the war with Germany was over. Despite giving the people "Peace, Bread, and Land!" the Bolsheviks came in second after the Social Revolutionaries in the elections. Lenin's response was simple. When the new Russian parliament, the Constituent Assembly, met on 5 January 1918, it was dispersed and Lenin's cabinet continued to rule. Much like their tsarist predecessors, the Bolsheviks were energetic in cutting off the publicity options of their opponents. Other political parties were banned, newspapers were censored, and a secret police force was set up. The Cheka, led by Felix Dzherzhinsky (1877–1926), enforced revolutionary discipline to the point of executing thousands of people.

Britain, France, and the United States landed troops in Russia in 1918. Ukrainians, Cossacks, and other minorities seized their chance to gain independence. Russian counterrevolutionary forces—the Whites—obtained foreign backing and organized armed resistance against the new regime, but the Bolsheviks proved to be better equipped, more highly organized, and better disciplined. In any event, since few Russians wanted to return to tsarist rule, they were at least potentially receptive to Bolshevik agitation.

Lenin agreed wholeheartedly with Georgi Plekhanov (1857–1918) both in terms of the necessity to spread ideas and to distinguish between *agitatsiia* (agitation) and *propaganda*. In *What Is to Be Done?* (1902) Lenin took the moderate Menshevik Yulii Martov (1873–1923) to task for obscuring Plekhanov's distinction: "The propagandist . . . must present 'many ideas.' So many, indeed, that they will only be understood as an integral whole only by a (comparatively) few persons. The agitator, however, . . . will direct his efforts to presenting a *single idea* to the 'masses.'"

Leaving aside the niceties of Marxist propagandistic strategy, the new government of Russia had to achieve cultural hegemony. The Bolsheviks were faced with the difficulties of having triumphed in a coup d'état without having gained control of the country except for a few major cities—and with no guarantee of continued support by the industrial workers or soldiers. The citadel had been stormed but the trenches—in which counterrevolution could breed—were still intact. As Lenin put it in *On Cooperation* (1922): "In our country the political and social revolution preceded the cultural revolution."

In view of the urgent need to spread the Bolshevik ideology, justify the seizure of power, and raise education levels—not to mention increase economic efficiency—the Narkompros (People's Commissariat) quickly set up an agitprop machine to spread "enlightenment." It is hardly surprising that right after seizing power the Bolsheviks also took control of the film industry. The importance given to film can be gauged by the fact that the first head of the Narkompros film subsection was Lenin's wife, Nadezhda Krupskaia (1869–1939).

The Bolsheviks had the twin advantages of controlling what was left of the transportation infrastructure (via the trade unions) and energetic cadres well versed in revolutionary agitation. The first "agit-train"—naturally named the *V. I. Lenin*—was dispatched to provide ideological guidance to the troops fighting to regain the Kazan area from the rampaging Czech Legion. The train contained a printing plant and a theater group. Eduard Tisse (1897–1961), who was later to work with filmmaker Sergei Eisenstein (1898–1948) on *Battleship Potemkin* (1926), was placed on board to lead a film crew. Soon this material was being shown in Moscow. It was then circulated to the growing network of "agit-stations" and onto the trains and boats whose mission was to enlighten, educate, and motivate those areas still held by the Reds.

If agitation and/or propaganda failed to work, the Bolsheviks could always rely on Lenin's taste for the pragmatic New Economic Program (NEP) or the draconian, as exemplified in his brutal response to the growing opposition among the Red Army rank and file at Kronstadt in March 1921. By the spring of 1921 the White armies had all been defeated, internal dissent had been quelled, and the Bolsheviks controlled much of the former Russian Empire. The Revolution had been effectively (and victoriously) concluded.

Graham Roberts

See also *Battleship Potemkin;* Comintern; Eisenstein, Sergei; Lenin, Vladimir Ilyich; Marx, Karl; *Pravda;* Russia; Stalin, Joseph; Trotsky, Leon; Women's Movement: European; World War I

References: Figes, Orlando. *The People's Tragedy.* London: Jonathan Cape, 1997; Hosking, Geoffrey. *A History of the Soviet Union.* London: Fontana, 1992; Kenez, Peter. *The Birth of the Propaganda State.* Cambridge: Cambridge University Press, 1985; Pipes, Richard. *Russia under the Soviet Regime.* London: HarperCollins, 1994.

RFE/RL (Radio Free Europe/ Radio Liberty)

These were the two American shortwave radio stations during the Cold War. Radio Free Europe (RFE) was incorporated in 1949. Purportedly funded by public subscription through the National Committee for a Free Europe, in reality it received secret funding from the Central Intelligence Agency (CIA). It was beamed at the "captive nations" of Eastern Europe. Its sister station, Radio Liberty (RL), was originally known as Radio Liberation from Bolshevism. It began to broadcast to the USSR in 1951 as a project of the National Committee for Freedom of the Peoples of the USSR, Inc. Both stations sought to be regarded as surrogates for domestic radio stations. Instead of carrying the sort of international news that could be heard on the Voice of America (VOA), they carried local news and features. Both were heavily jammed. In 1956 RFE was criticized for having encouraged the Hungarian uprising, which the U.S. government was unable to support. Another CIA-funded station called Radio Free Asia broadcast to China intermittently between 1951 and 1955.

In 1967 the *New York Times* revealed the secret funding and political pressure mounted for both radio stations to be shut down. In 1973 they were placed under the supervision of the new Board of International Broadcasting. The greatest triumph for both stations occurred during the second Cold War of the

1980s. The role of RFE and RL in encouraging the political change was well argued on Capitol Hill by Sen. Joseph Biden (1942–) in whose state (Delaware) the stations were incorporated. The Clinton administration preserved the stations within a revised International Broadcasting Board, which also incorporated the VOA. RFE/RL soon diversified, adding broadcasts aimed at Iraq and Radio Free Asia to their stable. In 2001 they received unwelcome evidence of their effectiveness in the form of news of a terrorist plot—involving Iraqi intelligence and one of the September 11 hijackers—to attack RFE headquarters in Prague.

Nicholas J. Cull

See also CIA; Cold War; Poland: Radio (International); Russia; VOA

References: Brown, Donald R. *International Radio Broadcasting: The Limits of the Limitless Medium.* New York: Praeger, 1982; Critchlow, James. *Radio Hole-in-the-Head/Radio Liberty: An Insider's Story of Cold War Broadcasting.* Washington, DC: American University Press, 1995; Mickelson, Sig. *America's Other Voice: The Story of Radio Free Europe and Radio Liberty.* New York: Praeger, 1983; Nelson, Michael. *War of the Black Heavens: The Battles of Western Broadcasting in the Cold War.* London: Brassey's, 1997; Puddington, Arch. *Freedom Radios: How Radio Free Europe and Radio Liberty Broke the Soviet Information Blockade.* Lexington: University of Kentucky Press, 2000.

Riefenstahl, Leni (1902–)

German dancer, actress, and filmmaker, Leni Riefenstahl was responsible for some of the most important and aesthetically striking propaganda films made under the Nazi regime. Between 1933 and 1935 she directed three Nazi party rally films: *Victory of Faith* (1933), *Triumph of the Will* (1935), and *Day of Freedom* (1935). Her greatest international success was *Olympia* (1938). The employment of an ever-growing number of camera teams enabled Riefenstahl to arrange the footage of selected events in shot-reverse-shot patterns. This montage technique, usually associated with fiction writing, gave her films an unusual flowing rhythm that was unattainable for other contemporary documentarians.

Riefenstahl began her career as a solo dancer in 1923. After having suffered an injury, she became an actress in the specialized genre of mountain films directed by Arnold Fanck (1889–1974). She starred in five of Fanck's films, inevitably playing the female lead role in an otherwise almost exclusively male cast. Her first picture, *The Blue Light* (1932), resulted from her close cooperation with writer Bela Balasz (1884–1949) and cameraman Hans Schneeberger (1895–1970). The film tells a romantic story, with Riefenstahl playing a young gypsy outcast. In 1932 Riefenstahl met Hitler. He appointed her artistic director for the party-rally film *Victory of Faith* (1933). Riefenstahl edited the film herself, first using the montage technique that signaled a new propaganda style. As a result, the political meaning of the event was concentrated in a montage exclusively dedicated to illustrate the Führer's power and charisma.

The next party-rally film, *Triumph of the Will,* was far better prepared. With a highly skilled large staff at her disposal, Riefenstahl was able to create the ideal portrait of Nazi party rituals. Screenings in regular movie houses (with Ufa as distributor) plus numerous special showings for party organizations assured it the widest possible audience. Although it was not distributed regularly in foreign countries, it won the prize for best documentary at the 1935 Venice Film Festival and was awarded a gold medal at the 1937 World's Fair in Paris.

Riefenstahl's most ambitious project was *Olympiade,* a film about the 1936 Olympic Games held in Berlin, which premiered on Hitler's birthday and was subsequently shown in most European capitals. In 1939 she began to prepare a large-scale film version of Heinrich von Kleist's (1777–1811) play *Penthesilea.* The outbreak of war brought an end to this project. Riefenstahl at first joined the German troops along with her film crew but quit further work in uniform after witnessing a massacre committed by German soldiers in the Polish village of Konskie. She began work on *Tiefland* (The Lowlands), a film adaptation of the opera by Eugen d'Albert (1864–1932). Held back by various circumstances, the film was only finished in 1954. After the war Riefenstahl was interrogated by the U.S. Army, appeared three times at denazification hearings, and was finally released after being branded as a "sympathizer."

She continued to undertake film projects but never finished any. In the 1960s she traveled to Africa four times. Her book *The Nuba* won her recognition as a photographer, but it also raised questions as to whether her aesthetic position had changed since her party-rally films. In the late 1970s she began to publish a series of underwater photography books. She celebrated her one-hundredth birthday on August 22, 2002, to considerable media attention.

Rainer Rother

See also Film (Documentary); Film (Nazi Germany); Goebbels, Joseph; Hitler, Adolf; Olympics; *Triumph of the Will*
References: Hinton, David B. *The Films of Leni Riefenstahl*. Metuchen, NJ: Scarecrow, 1991; Loiperdinger, Martin. *Rituale der Mobilmachung*. Opladen, Germany: Leske & Budrich, 1987; Rother, Rainer. *Leni Riefenstahl: The Seduction of Genius*. London: Continuum, 2002; Salkeld, Audrey. *A Portrait of Leni Riefenstahl*. London: Jonathan Cape, 1996; Welch, David. *Propaganda and the German Cinema (1933–45)*. Rev. ed. Oxford I. B. Tauris, 2001.

Riis, Jacob (1849–1914)

A pioneer photojournalist and Progressive reformer active in New York City at the turn of the century, Riis was born in Ribe, Denmark. In 1870 he immigrated to the United States, where he made his name as a journalist, working first at the *New York Tribune* and later for the *New York Evening Sun*. He photographed the appalling living conditions in New York slums and published his observations in a book called *How the Other Half Lives* (1890). He was a friend and political associ-

ate of Theodore Roosevelt. His son, Edward Riis, directed U.S. propaganda in Denmark for the Committee on Public Information during World War I.

Nicholas J. Cull

See also Photography; Scandinavia; United States; United States (Progressive Era)
References: Meyer, Edith Patterson. *"Not Charity, but Justice": The Story of Jacob A. Riis*. New York: Vanguard, 1974; Riis, Jacob. *How the Other Half Lives*. 1890. Reprint, London: Penguin, 1997.

RMVP (Reichministerium für Volksaufklärung und Propaganda)

The Nazi propaganda ministry, the Reichministerium für Volksaufklärung und Propaganda (State Ministry for Popular Enlightenment and Propaganda), was established by a presidential decree, signed on 12 March 1933 and promulgated the following day, which defined the task of the new ministry as the dissemination of "enlightenment and propaganda within the population concerning the policy of the Reich Government and the national reconstruction of the German Fatherland."

Joseph Goebbels (1897–1945), who headed the new ministry, is said to have been initially unhappy with the use of the word "propaganda" in the name on the grounds that it was psychologically counterproductive. Given his voluminous writings on the subject and the fact that he felt confident enough to form the Nazi Party Reich Propaganda Directorate in 1930, this claim, based on little substantive evidence, seems totally out of character. In June Adolf Hitler (1889–1945) was to define the scope of the RMVP in even more general terms, making Goebbels responsible for the "spiritual direction of the nation." Not only did this vague directive provide Goebbels with room to outmaneuver his critics within the party, it also gave the seal of approval to what was soon to result in the ministry's wholesale manipulation of the mass media. Nevertheless, Goebbels was constantly involved in quarrels with ministerial colleagues who resented the encroachment of this new ministry on their old domain.

Analyzing the political function of propaganda in the Third Reich is further complicated by the fact that it was simultaneously channeled through three different institutions: the RMVP, the Reichspropagandaamt (Central Propaganda Office) of the party, and the Reichskulturkammer (Reich Chamber of Culture). Moreover, the political structure of the Third Reich was based on the twin pillars of the party and the state. According to Hitler in *Mein Kampf*, it was the task of the state to continue the "historical development of the national administration within the framework of the law," while it was the function of the party to "build its internal organization and establish and develop a stable and self-perpetuating center of the National Socialist doctrine in order to transfer the indoctrinated to the state so that they may become its leaders as well as its disciples." The creation of the RMVP in March 1933 was a significant step in merging the party and the state. Goebbels continued to be head of party propaganda, but he greatly strengthened both his own position within the party and the scope of propaganda by setting up this new ministry—the first of its kind in Germany.

With the creation of the RMVP, propaganda primarily became the responsibility of the state, although its departments were to be supported and reinforced by the party's Central Propaganda Office, which remained less conspicuous to the general public. Indeed, the two institutions were often merged into one unit: not only did their respective organizations and responsibilities correspond closely, but many of the leading positions in the ministry and the Reichspropagandaleitung (Reich Propaganda Directorate) were held by the same officials. Originally Goebbels had planned only five departments for the new ministry to encompass radio, the press, active propaganda, film, theater, and popular education, but by April 1933 it had acquired its basic structure and was divided

into seven departments. (During the war even Goebbels's antibureaucratic stance could not prevent the RMVP from escaping the process of expansion and bureaucratization, with the number of departments actually increasing to fourteen.)

Department 1: Legislation and Legal Problems; Budget, Finance, and Accounting

Department 2: Co-ordination of Popular Enlightenment and Propaganda ("active propaganda"); Regional Agencies of the Ministry; German Academy of Politics; Official Ceremonies and Demonstrations; National Emblems; Racial Questions; Treaty of Versailles; Opposing Ideologies; Youth Organizations; Public Health and Sports; Eastern and Border Questions; National Travel Committee

Department 3: Radio; National Broadcasting Company (Reichsfunkgesellschaft)

Department 4: National and Foreign Press; Journalism; Press Archives; News Service; National Association of German Press

Department 5: Film; Film Picture Industry; Film Censorship; Newsreels

Department 6: Theatre

Department 7: Music; Fine Arts; People's Culture

The RMVP began with only 350 administrative and executive officials. Goebbels retained a notoriously low opinion of civil servants and once confided to his diary: "Just as you cannot expect a cow to lay eggs, so you cannot expect a bureaucrat to look after the interests of the state properly." As a new organization, the RMVP was at first staffed by fanatical young Nazis, generally with better educational qualifications than the average Nazi activist. Goebbels had declared that his staff should never exceed 1,000. He also agreed to offset the costs of running the RMVP by collecting radio-licensing fees.

Fortunately for the new minister, the purchase of radios increased dramatically in the Third Reich, and it has been estimated that over 80 percent of the ministry's expenditures were recovered from this source. Goebbels saw the RMVP as the main policy- and decision-making body, providing direction and delegating responsibility to the numerous subordinate agencies that were under its control. The most important of these was the Reich Chamber of Culture. The RMVP set itself the task of reeducating the population for a new society based on National Socialist values. Much of prewar German propaganda was devoted to instilling a military spirit, while the main functions of propaganda during World War II were to mobilize the energy and commitment of the German people for the war effort and to sustain its morale.

David Welch

See also Film (Nazi Germany); Germany; Goebbels, Joseph; Hitler, Adolf; World War II (Germany)

References: Heiber, Helmut. *Goebbels: A Biography*. New York: Hawthorne, 1972; Reuth, Ralf Georg. *Goebbels: The Life of Joseph Goebbels*. New York: Harcourt Brace, 1993; Welch, David. *The Third Reich: Politics and Propaganda*. London: Routledge, 2002.

Rockwell, Norman (1894–1978)

Norman Rockwell is perhaps the best-known American artist of the twentieth century. He was certainly the most beloved illustrator, having created some 322 covers for the *Saturday Evening Post* between 1916 and 1963. The latter had some two million weekly subscribers when Rockwell did his first cover for the magazine. Rockwell has long troubled more elitist viewers, who have traditionally dismissed his art as, according to one critic, "patriotic escapism" or "candied solace and small-town nostalgia." More recently, however, Rockwell's reputation among critics has undergone a sea change, something noted by Rockwell's granddaughter in a November 2001 letter to the *New York Times:* "Paintings

like *Freedom From Want* are ubiquitous in our culture: on calendars, wall-hangings, plates, mugs, statuettes, you name it. They have become iconic. They've become an ethos, an intangible and in large part fantastical aspect of American life; that is, they symbolize the very essence of Americana, the perfect Norman Rockwell world."

As a propagandist, Rockwell is best known for four large paintings illustrating Four Freedoms, an attempt to define American war aims in 1941: *Freedom of Speech, Freedom of Religion, Freedom from Fear, and Freedom from Want* (1943). These *Post* covers were used to sell bonds during World War II, served as official Office of War Information (OWI) poster propaganda, and were widely seen in Britain. Rockwell's *Rosie the Riveter* (1943) is the personification of the emancipated American woman in wartime. Rosie has big muscular arms; her penny loafers are atop a copy of Hitler's *Mein Kampf.* The real Rosie, Mary Keefe, was a petite twenty-one-year-old telephone operator when she posed for Rockwell in 1943.

David Culbert

See also OWI; World War II (United States)

References: Claridge, Laura. *Norman Rockwell: A Life*. New York: Putnam's, 1999; Rockwell, Norman. *Saturday Evening Post*, 13 February 1960.

Romania

See Balkans

Roosevelt, Franklin D. (1882–1945)

Franklin Delano Roosevelt (or FDR) was the only president in American history to have been elected to a fourth full term. (A constitutional amendment now ensures that this cannot happen again.) Roosevelt was born to wealth and position in Hyde Park, New York. He was an average student at Harvard, his major interest being the *Harvard Crimson,* the student newspaper on which he served as editor. For the rest of his life he equated

"Save Freedom of Speech," a war bonds drive poster by Norman Rockwell, 1943. This poster was one of Rockwell's depictions of Franklin Roosevelt's Four Freedoms. (Corbis)

Franklin D. Roosevelt campaigns for president with his daughter, Anna, and wife, Eleanor, in 1932. (Franklin D. Roosevelt Library)

this experience with that of a professional journalist, a testament to his sense of self-esteem. The extroverted, handsome, athletic Roosevelt married his awkward, homely (in her own eyes), humorless distant cousin Eleanor (1884–1962) in 1905. The marriage was not a happy one. After serving as assistant secretary of the Navy during World War I, in 1920 Roosevelt ran for vice president on the Democratic ticket. Roosevelt contracted polio in 1921, and for the remainder of his life he was confined to a wheelchair; since he regained only partial control over his legs, he required heavy metal braces to walk even a few steps. Eleanor encouraged Franklin to return to politics in spite of his physical handicap.

Roosevelt was elected governor of New York State in 1928. In 1932 he was elected president at a time when the Great Depression had deprived millions of Americans of hope for the future. Roosevelt promised them economic aid in the form of the New Deal. He turned to radio as a medium of mass communication. His splendid speaking voice—the finest of any American politician in the twentieth century—gave his words a special impact. Roosevelt spoke directly to the American public in a series of "fireside chats" in which he employed a more informal style of delivery than was common for the day; few in number, they attracted a large listenership. His first inaugural address, delivered on 4 March 1933, is justly regarded as a classic example of presidential oratory, particularly for one memorable sentence: "Let me assert my firm belief that the only thing we have to fear is fear itself." Roosevelt held twice weekly press conferences for much of his presidency. He enjoyed engaging in a game of wits with reporters, many of whom discovered that Roosevelt's charm was often intended to disguise rather than inform.

Roosevelt's physical handicap was largely hidden from most Americans thanks to an arrangement with newsreel and still photographers. No image of FDR was permitted that showed his physical handicap. In practice this meant no shots from the waist down. Those who broke the rule were denied entrance to the White House by the Secret Service. In retrospect, it is difficult to understand this "conspiracy of silence" in the light of constitutional guarantees of freedom of the press. Although Roosevelt was deathly ill when he was reelected to a fourth term of office in the fall of 1944, the severity of his medical condition was kept secret.

Roosevelt is remembered for his skills as a persuasive politician, his ability to attract and win over millions of enthusiastic supporters, and for his national and international leadership during World War II. His legislative accomplishments stem mostly from the spring of 1935 and include the Wealth Tax Act, Social Security, and the Wagner Act, which made possible industrial trade unionism in the United States. After FDR's failed attempt in 1937 to pack the U.S. Supreme Court with extra New Deal appointees, he never again saw the passage of significant domestic reform legislation. Eleanor, a significant political figure in her own right, died in 1962.

David Culbert

See also Long, Huey; OWI; Radio (Domestic); Rockwell, Norman; United States (1930s); World War II (United States)

References: Buhite, Russell D., and David W. Levy, eds. *FDR's Fireside Chats.* New York: Penguin, 1993; Burns, James MacGregor. *Roosevelt: The Lion and the Fox.* New York: Harcourt, 1956; ———. *Roosevelt: The Soldier of Freedom.* New York: Harcourt, 1970; Cohen, Lizabeth. *Making a New Deal: Industrial Workers in Chicago, 1919–1939.* New York: Cambridge University Press, 1990; Winfield, Betty Houchin. *FDR and the News Media.* New York: Columbia University Press, 1994.

Rumor

A propaganda device since time immemorial, well-placed rumors—especially the titillating sort that people *want* to believe—have proved a highly effective way of puncturing an enemy's image or inciting hatred. In *The Arthasastra* (ca. 250 B.C.E.), an ancient Indian text on statecraft, Kautilya recommends sending agents into an enemy's ranks to spread demoralizing stories. The creation of such rumors was turned into an art during World War II by the British Political Warfare Executive (PWE), which referred to rumors as "sibs" (from the Latin *sibilare*, to hiss). The PWE had a Rumour Committee that met every two weeks to devise fresh stories. These rumors were then spread by British agents in the bars of neutral cities like Lisbon, Zurich, Stockholm, and Istanbul in the hope that they would find their way back to Germany. They included various sexual fetishes attached to the Nazi hierarchy and stories of Hitler's plans to flee the country as Allied victories mounted. Domestic rumors included a story of a miracle weapon that had set the sea aflame and torched a German invasion army. The Germans, for their part, spread rumors to promote Anglo-American rivalry and to breed dissent against Franklin D. Roosevelt—including a rumor that he was Winston Churchill's cousin. A macabre rumor used to promote absenteeism from American munitions factories had it that an American woman had gone to her hairdresser, unaware that there were traces of explosive in her hair, and that her head had exploded while under the dryer. During the Cold War the Soviet secret police, the KGB, spread rumors, including the claim, circulated in Africa, that the condoms being distributed by Western aid organizations were actually spreading AIDS. The Central Intelligence Agency's (CIA) use of rumor included a campaign against Jean-Bertrand Aristide (1953–), the exiled president of Haiti.

Nicholas J. Cull

See also The Big Lie; Black Propaganda; Caribbean; Disinformation; Psychological Warfare; PWE

References: Daugherty, William E., and Morris Janowitz, eds. *A Psychological Warfare Casebook.* Baltimore, MD: Johns Hopkins University Press, 1958; Delmer, Sefton. *Black Boomerang.* London: Secker and Warburg, 1962; Taylor, Philip M. *British Propaganda in the Twentieth Century: Selling Democracy.* Edinburgh: Edinburgh University Press, 1999.

Russia

Whether considered as a single nation, an empire, or as the Union of Soviet Socialist Republics (USSR), Russia has remained a major regional and global power for several hundred years; at the height of its power it controlled one sixth of the earth's land surface. During this long history propaganda has been central to its life and politics. This Great Power needs to be understood in terms of its culture as defined by its language (Slavic), religion (Russian Orthodox Church), heritage (Byzantine), and recent Soviet experience.

Russia began as a constantly threatened, heterogeneous, unstable state known as Kiev Rus, located at the edge of Europe. Russia gained its stability as an autocracy. The tsar (emperor)—a title adopted in 1472 by Tsar Ivan III (1440–1505) in a move that was to prove as propagandistic as any in the centuries to come—was not just the head but the embodiment of government. Propaganda was thus the exclusive activity of the realm. Ivan IV, commonly known as Ivan the Terrible (1530–1584), who ruled Russia from 1533 to 1584, consolidated his central authority, orchestrated a state-sponsored glorification of the tsar as Russia personified, and closely identified himself with the Russian Orthodox Church. Ivan's single political achievement was the

Soviet propaganda photograph purporting to show Lenin and Stalin in Gorki in 1922. In reality Lenin sits alone, and Stalin's image was pasted in at a later date to create the impression that he had been Lenin's confidante and hence was his natural successor. (Courtesy of Bernard O'Callaghan)

founding of the Oprichniki—forerunner of the Okhrana (secret police)—which did much more than merely serve as his personal bodyguard. In effect, the Okhrana generally harassed the (very small) ruling class. Its methods prefigured the terror of Stalin (1879–1953), the "Red Tsar" of the twentieth century. After Ivan, a series of weak tsars resulted in a "time of troubles."

In the following centuries a number of rulers took the initiative and relied on self-propaganda rather than their "God-given" authority alone. Peter the Great (1688–1725) drove his people by appealing to their patriotism. ("Remember that you are fighting not for Peter but for the state.") Peter took personal responsibility for making Russia a Western state and built the new capital city Saint Petersburg facing west. Peter's grandiose plans were underpinned by a campaign that encouraged his people to modernize, including the symbolic shaving of beards; noncompliance might result in death.

Catherine the Great, who reigned from 1762 to 1796, was an enlightened despot who utilized the propaganda techniques of such European stars of the Enlightenment as Voltaire (1694–1778) and Diderot (1713–1784). Catherine's Enlightenment was largely for show, as were the model villages built by Grigori Potemkin (1739–1791), her chief minister, which have become proverbial examples in the twentieth century of a state's attempt to impress by means of strategically deployed fanciful projects.

After the innate conservatism of Nicholas I (ruled 1825–1855), whose slogan was "Orthodoxy, Autocracy and Nationalism," Russia under Alexander II ("the Liberator") (r. 1855–1881) was initially marked by a campaign of modernization and reform, the most important being the emancipation of the serfs in 1861 (hence his nickname). Alexander's reforms, while outraging many reactionaries, were regarded as far too moderate by both liberals and radicals. Radical activities increased sharply among the intelligentsia, resulting in a reassertion of repressive policies.

Radical groups responded with terrorist tactics. In 1881, following several unsuccessful attempts, a member of an organization called the People's Will assassinated Alexander with a hand-held bomb. The new tsar, Alexander III (ruled 1881–1894) was already primed for reaction by his tutor (who was later to become chief minister), Constantin Petrovich Pobedonostev (1827–1907). The Okhrana's powers were extended and a new Statute of State Security of 1881 included a tightening of press censorship. Lenin (1870–1924) described this all-consuming restriction as "the de facto constitution of Russia." The University Statute of 1887 closed in on the subversive potential of education. Alexander III also oversaw a campaign of "Russification," with Russian declared the official language. Although this move made it easier to monitor all forms of activity, it also undermined what little cohesion there was between the national groups and the regime.

Alexander III's regime also supported a policy of Pan-Slavism, which promoted international solidarity among the numerous Slavic peoples and nations of Eastern Europe in the nineteenth century. Whatever the ostensibly cultural—even liberating—focus of this movement in the revolutions of 1830 or 1848, state-sponsored Pan-Slavism in the years before World War I came to mean the domestic repression of non-Slavs and the sowing of dissent throughout southeastern Europe. Russia as *the* Slavic state could use the Pan-Slavic movement to mask its expansionist designs.

At home Slavic purism could be brought to bear on the most easily identified outsider group—the Jews. Already legally forced to reside in ghettos, Alexander III sanctioned six hundred new measures against the Jews. His regime gave official support to an anti-Semitic group called the Black Hundreds. This unleashing of violent racial prejudice as recommended activity was supported by a propaganda campaign utilizing myths promulgated in *The Protocols of the Elders of Zion* (1903).

The rule of Alexander III was also characterized by rapid industrialization under Minister of Finance Sergei Witte (1849–1915). The resulting social tensions planted the seeds of the revolutions of the early twentieth century. Opposition to the autocracy centered on the disillusioned (Westernized) intelligentsia and particularly within such new political groups as the (Marxist) Social Democrats and the Social Revolutionaries. Due to the complete disempowerment of the political system, these opponents could do little more than create propaganda, which was usually published in exile.

Georgi Plekhanov (1857–1918) founded the Social Democrats in 1898. At the London conference of 1903, the movement split into two factions, instigated by Vladimir Ilyich Ulianov—better known as Lenin—who in *What Is to Be Done?* (1902) had called for a party as the "Vanguard of the Revolution." This revolutionary elite would be rigorously disciplined through "democratic centralism." Lenin's group somewhat disingenuously—but essential in terms of propaganda—adopted the name Bolsheviks (majority), dubbing their opponents Mensheviks (minority). The Bolsheviks followed Marx's analysis contained in his *German Ideology* (1845–1846): "The ideas of the ruling class are in every epoch the ruling ideas," which became an article of faith.

In 1905 revolutionary activity—including naval mutinies depicted in the celebrated film *Battleship Potemkin* (1926)—reached as far as the capital when Father Georgii Apollonovich Gapon (1870–1906) led a demonstration to the very doors of the Winter Palace. Soviets (workers' councils) were set up in the major cities. Tsar Nicholas II (ruled 1894–1918) responded with the "October Manifesto," which established a Duma (parliament) and guaranteed some civil liberties. A steady retreat from limited liberalism was accompanied by a more strident sanctification of the tsar (culminating in the massive—and highly publicized—celebration of the tercentenary of the Romanov dynasty in 1911). World War I was at least in part the result of the regime's desire to appeal to carefully cultivated patriotic sentiment. The February Revolution of 1917 (March 1917 in the New Style calendar) was largely the result of spontaneous anger. The Bolsheviks came to power based on a combination of Lenin's organizational abilities and such appealingly simplistic slogans as "Peace, Bread, and Land" and "All power to the Soviets."

The Bolsheviks—later known as the Communist Party of the Soviet Union—were driven by one major aim: to stay in power. Many of its leaders and the rank and file believed their survival would make the world a better place; all believed (with Lenin) that politics without power was meaningless. Survival could only be achieved by two interconnected processes: securing and increasing the power of the Soviet state domestically (through industrialization) and internationally (through the Third International, or Comintern) and consolidating the party's hold on the state (resulting in the Red terrors of the early and late 1920s). All of this activity was justified and facilitated by means of a ubiquitous propaganda campaign. The main thrust of all propaganda activity was that the party was the fount of all wisdom. Later this worldview would be modified so that Stalin became the fount of all wisdom; this trick was initially achieved by claiming that he was the true heir of Lenin.

In 1912 Joseph Stalin (1879–1953) joined the Bolshevik Central Committee as the party's general secretary. Thus, his power emanated from his control over the party apparatus. In total control after 1929, he launched a new revolution that abandoned the relative economic liberalism of the 1920s in favor of mass collectivization and industrialization, both justified by his doctrine of "socialism in one country." As many as 10 million people died during the forced collectivization. The rapid industrialization, which began with the launch of the first Five Year Plan in 1928, wasted vast amounts of material and caused massive social dislocation. In line with these seismic changes, a cultural revolution was introduced that utilized all the arts and the media of mass culture—especially film, which was an important tool in a primarily illiterate country. Several of the propaganda devices of the previous revolutionary period, such as the "agit-train" railway campaign, were resuscitated.

Many of the problems faced even by loyal workers within the Soviet arts and media during this period resulted from the famous distinction, devised by Georgy Plekhanov, between *agitatsiia* (agitation) and propaganda—agitation being the approach used to reach the masses and propaganda being the more rarefied ideological indoctrination of the individual. An apparently powerful mass medium, film and the other arts had to be treated as an ideological weapon for *agitatsiia* by the authorities. This led to outside pressure to achieve greater simplicity and directness, which distorted creative development—and quite possibly reduced the effectiveness of art as a propaganda weapon.

Much propaganda activity in the 1930s focused on social, political, and even financial participation. Soviet men and women were constantly urged to buy state bonds (yielding low interest). Regular subscriptions to these loan offers became an index of loyalty. Industrial workers were asked to make "donations" toward the construction of a tank, plane, or ship. The resultant piece of machinery would then be "sponsored." Thus, a postcard dating from the 1930s proclaimed: "Every factory, every shop floor, every brigade—[Join] the ranks of the builders of the dirigible *Klim Voroshilov.*" Individual workers were transformed into national celebrities, or Stakhanovites—named after Aleksei Stakhanov (1906–1977), the "hero coal miner" who mined a hundred tons of coal in a single shift in 1935.

Despite all this well-publicized activity, the Soviet people—not to mention the government's military infrastructure—were woefully unprepared for the German invasion of 1941. In the postwar period control over culture was reinvigorated rather than relaxed. This period became known as the *Zhdanovshchina,* or the time of Zhdanov, named after Andrei Zhdanov (1896–1948), Stalin's minister of culture and the founding father of Socialist Realism. All the arts were held under the steady and suspicious gaze of the Kremlin. An "Artistic Council" met weekly to oversee all film production. A system of serial censorship at the script, production, and postproduction levels was overlaid by an atmosphere of suspicion and uncertainty. Self-censorship made the normal functioning of the creative faculties highly unlikely. Documentary film, newsreel, and later TV programs presented a fantasy world where all was well in the Soviet bloc and where working classes in the rest of the world craved the same utopian lifestyle. Such a fantasy left the Soviet Union vulnerable to news from outside through such foreign media as the Voice of America, Radio Liberty or the BBC World Service radio. The Soviet government periodically jammed these stations, disseminating propaganda of its own through broadcasts by Radio Moscow and an extensive publication program, which focused on the developing world.

The Khrushchev (1894–1971) period (1953–1964) saw the creation of energetic (if vacuous) state schemes that led to reaction during the Brezhnev (1906–1982) period (1964–1982), which was also known as the "period of stagnation." Life for the average Soviet was less dangerous, but there was little left to propagandize. This period saw an exponential rise in the use of the myth of the Great Patriotic War—which is not to downplay the heroic deeds of the Soviet people—immortalized in thousands of war memorials. The most famous one stands by the walls of the Kremlin gardens. The Tomb of the Unknown Soldier bears the following inscription: "Your Name Is Unknown, but Your Feat Is Immortal." It contains a corpse from a common grave 41 kilometers (25 miles) north of Moscow, as well as six urns of sacred earth from across the USSR. The monument was unveiled on 6 May 1967 and remains a pilgrimage site for wedding couples. Around the outskirts of the capital stand the antitank "hedgehogs"—a memorial to Moscow's defenders. Naturally, there is also a most impressive memorial to Leningrad's defenders on Victory Square (erected 9 May 1975).

Assuming power in 1985, Mikhail Gorbachev (1931–), intent on restructuring (*perestroika*) the ossifying Soviet Union, brought a new reality to the public sphere by inaugurating a policy of openness (*glasnost*). The media, including journalists and documentary filmmakers, were welcome to join Gorbachev's historic project as long as they played by his rules. The high-profile documentaries that were shown in movie theaters (with an officially sanctioned and sponsored publicity campaign) had to conform to the Gorbachev view of history (itself an outgrowth of Nikita Khrushchev's view) that the Soviet Union had developed through the heroic efforts of "good" (Communist) leaders—Lenin, the increasingly venerated Nikolay Bukharin (1888–1938), Khrushchev, and Gorbachev himself—while its progress had been hampered by such "bad" leaders as Stalin and Leonid Brezhnev. However, the genie had escaped from the bottle. Gorbachev's gamble regarding the independent media was already spinning out of control before the forces of reaction attempted to oust him in a 1991 coup.

The failure of the coup led to the final humiliation of the Communist Party and the demise of the Soviet Union. The new Russia was to be led by Boris Yeltsin (1931–)—former Moscow party chief and an expert self-publicist, having made his reputation as a vociferous critic of the slow pace of Gorbachev's reforms. President Gorbachev's December resignation sealed the USSR's dissolution. Yeltsin, who became the first popularly elected leader in Russian history, insisted: "It is especially important to encourage unorthodox thinking when the situation is critical."

Yeltsin utilized his support by the media to promulgate a classic scenario of impending crisis interspersed with calls for resilience. Irritated by a conservative parliament, Yeltsin suppressed it in September 1993, following a media onslaught of criticism against non-Russians and "Communists." War with Chechnia, a genuine economic crisis, and a loss of patience with their leader's frequently reported erratic behavior brought increased pressure upon Yeltsin. He dismissed his entire government twice in 1998. His opponents used their own media outlets (including privately owned television stations) to publicize these and other scandals. By the end of 1998 Yeltsin was facing an impeachment vote. Vladimir Putin (1952–), the prime minister, became acting president. He succeeded Yeltsin following official elections held on 26 March 2000. A KGB operative, in 1996 Putin had been recruited as a Kremlin aide from a position in Leningrad's city government. In 1998 Yeltsin appointed Putin head of the Federal Security Service (the successor to the KGB) and in March 1999 he called on him to head Russia's security council.

As a political neophyte Putin has won tremendous popular support. Nonetheless he is an astute manipulator of, if unscrupulous panderer to, public opinion—for example, in his heavy-handed campaign against Chechens, which was turned into a crusade against Islamic citizens and residents of Russia. Putin's supporters in the Unity Party won major victories in the 2001 parliamentary elections. His message of anticorruption and anti-Communism was certain to strike a responsive chord with Russians. He has also publicly worshiped in the Russian Orthodox Church. In 2002 he vociferously protested the treatment of Russian athletes at the Winter Olympics—playing on age-old Russian feelings of injustice. His ability to repackage the church–autocracy–unique Russianness paradigm illustrates that little has changed except the medium employed.

Graham Roberts

See also Art; Austrian Empire; *Battleship Potemkin;* Castro, Fidel; Censorship; Cold War; Cold War in the Middle East; Comintern; Crimean War; Disinformation; Eisenstein, Sergei; Fakes; Film (Documentary); International; "The Internationale"; KGB; Labor/Antilabor; Lenin, Vladimir Ilyich; Marx, Karl; Okhrana; Poland; Portraiture; Postage Stamps; Posters; *Protocols of the Elders of Zion;* Radio (International); RFE/RL; Stalin, Joseph; Trotsky, Leon; Women's Movement: European; World War I; Zinoviev Letter

References: Cooper, Julian, et al. *Soviet History, 1917–1953.* Basingstoke, UK: Macmillan, 1995; Eben, Martin. *The Soviet Propaganda Machine.* New York: McGraw-Hill, 1987; Hosking, Geoffrey. *A History of the Soviet Union.* London: Fontana, 1992; Kenez, Peter. *The Birth of the Propaganda State.* Cambridge: Cambridge University Press, 1985; Pipes, Richard. *Russia under the Old Regime.* Harmondsworth, UK: Penguin, 1990; ———. *Russia under the Soviet Regime.* London: Harper, 1994; Roberts, Graham. *Stride Soviet!* London: I. B. Tauris, 1999; White, Stephen. *Developments in Russian and Post-Soviet Politics.* Basingstoke, UK: Macmillan, 1994.

S

Satellite Communications

Satellites entered the realm of international propaganda as technological symbols rather than useful additions to international communications. The Soviet Union led the way with the launch of *Sputnik* in October 1957 and thereby dealt a massive blow to U.S. prestige. The latter's *Explorer I* followed in February 1958. In December 1958 the United States launched its first satellite designed to transmit an explicit propaganda message. The U.S. army's *Score* satellite carried a tape-recorded message, intermittently transmitted to ground stations for thirteen days, in which President Dwight Eisenhower (1890–1969) delivered a short Christmas goodwill message expressing "America's desire for peace on earth and goodwill toward men everywhere."

Despite *Explorer I* and *Score,* polls taken by the United States Information Agency (USIA) consistently revealed the United States to be behind in the space race until the mid-1960s. The United States recovered somewhat with the launching of its first communications satellite, *Telstar,* in 1962. The satellite *Syncom III* carried television pictures of the 1964 Tokyo Olympics, demonstrating the capabilities of the new medium. In the 1960s both the United States (INTELSAT) and the USSR

(INTERSPUTNIK) formed international consortia to encourage the global expansion of satellite technologies. Despite this effort, for the balance of the decade satellites were few in number; given the cost needed to build them, they remained the province of a few governments, multinational corporations, and wealthy research institutions.

It was not until the 1970s that satellites became a major method for the transmission of international news and telephone traffic. The transition of the U.S. cable industry to satellite distribution in the early 1970s dramatically expanded the use of satellite technologies and consequently lowered the cost. During the Reagan administration the United States sought to develop the propaganda potential of the medium. In 1982 the USIA staged an international satellite hookup as part of its television special "Let Poland Be Poland," launching Worldnet, a television news and U.S. government information service. Worldnet was swiftly outstripped by commercial broadcasters, including the Cable News Network (CNN) and Sky News. News events carried round the world by satellite included the 1989 demonstrations in Tien'anmen Square in China—staged in part, to piggyback on media attention for the simultaneous visit of Soviet premier Mikhail

Gorbachev (1931–)—and the fall of the Berlin Wall later that year.

The power of satellite reports from the battlefield was seen during the Gulf War. The technology gave the Western media the sort of news monopoly not seen since the British cable ship *Teleconia* cut the German undersea cable to the United States at the beginning of World War I. The power of this news monopoly was not lost on observers of the Gulf War. The 1990s saw many nations developing their own launch facilities, launching their satellites from vehicles belonging to other nations, and expanding their television systems to accept more satellite feeds. These new satellites carried news, propaganda, and entertainment; some were used for surveillance. Inspired, in part, by the rapid privatization of the former Soviet satellite industry, the Clinton administration liberalized and privatized the U.S. satellite industry.

The War on Terrorism (2001) unfolded in a far more diverse satellite-broadcasting environment than that of the Gulf War. Stations now included such non-Western broadcasters as the Qatar-based station Al Jazeera, which carried video releases from Osama bin Laden (1957–) and presented news from an Islamic point of view. Like the Internet, satellite technology inherently has the power to transcend national boundaries and hence threatens the censorship abilities of governments. In Singapore, for example, the state has tightly controlled the spread of the technology and satellite dishes cannot be privately owned. A real concern for the future of satellite communications is the extraordinary power it bestows on media moguls such as Rupert Murdoch (1931–). The ability of private news channels to broadcast globally has undermined the position of such state-sponsored radio broadcasters as the Voice of America (VOA) and the BBC World Service. The BBC has responded by launching its own commercial "BBC World" channel.

Nicholas J. Cull

See also BBC; CNN; Gulf War; Murdoch, Rupert; Television (News); Terrorism, War on; USIA; Wick, Charles Z.

References: Dickson, Paul. *Sputnik.* New York: Walker, 2001; Hudson, Heather. *Communication Satellites.* New York: Collier Macmillan, 1990; Taylor, Philip M. *Global Communications and International Affairs and the Media since 1945.* London: Routledge, 1997.

Saudi Arabia
See Arab World

Scandinavia
The nations of Scandinavia—Denmark, Sweden, Norway, Iceland, and Finland—have experienced court and state propaganda under the Swedish and Danish empires, and have been major theaters of propaganda in World War II and the Cold War. In the nineteenth century Norway, Iceland, and Finland all witnessed a flowering of art and literature in the cause of nationalism. The region has played a key role in both the international environmental and peace movements.

The history of early modern Scandinavia was dominated by the competition between the kingdoms of Denmark and Sweden. In 1502 Sweden severed its ties to the Scandinavian (or Kalmar) Union (under which it had been joined to Norway and Denmark in 1397). In 1520 the Danish king attempted to revive the union by force. A mass execution of nobles that occurred during their campaign, known as the Stockholm Bloodbath, became a staple of anti-Danish propaganda in the hands of Gustav Vasa (1496–1560), who led the ultimate break with Denmark. Vasa ruled Sweden as King Gustav I beginning in 1523. Two centuries of intermittent war produced no shortage of further atrocity stories on both sides. Both the Swedish and Danish courts continued to use the three crowns and the enemy's coat of arms as part of their own, indicating, at least, their claim to rule the full union.

Denmark and Sweden both accepted Lutheranism as the state religion with relatively little disturbance. The Danish court flourished, most notably during the reign of Christian IV (r. 1596–1648). The court used the usual Renaissance tools of political propaganda (architecture, portraiture, and so forth). Denmark also claimed to have the first national banner, *Dannebrog* (Denmark's Cloth), consisting of a red field with a white cross. According to Danish legend, in 1219 it miraculously floated down from heaven into the camp of the young king Valdemar II (r. 1202–1241) on the eve of a battle against the heathen Estonians. Its image immediately appeared on coins and was incorporated into existing heraldry. The original banner was carried and lost in battle as late as 1500, but full banners of the same design were already in use. Other Scandinavian nations adopted variations on the *Dannebrog,* the Swedish flag being Gustav Vasa's deliberate counterpoint to the Danish one: blue with a yellow cross. In Denmark the flag remains a key symbol of national identity, used not only for national holidays but also during Christmas and birthday celebrations.

The seventeenth century saw the apogee of Swedish power in Scandinavia and beyond, beginning with the reigns of Gustav Adolf (1594–1632), who acceded to the throne in 1611 and ruled as Gustav II with the assistance of Axel Oxenstierna (1583–1684), a chancellor of legendary ability. Gustav Adolf led Sweden into the Thirty Years' War after the unsuccessful intervention of the Danish king. His success on the battlefield was matched by the calculated manipulation of his own (widely reproduced) image as the paragon of Protestant kingship. To preserve this image of virtue, he imposed rigid discipline on his army, forbidding his soldiers from participating in the looting and rapine typical of the era. However, the Swedish army soon reverted to type following Gustav Adolf's death on the battlefield. Sweden's career as a great power came to an abrupt end in 1718 with the death of its warrior king Charles XII (r. 1697–1718), who perished at the hands of a sniper during the Great North-

ern War (1700–1721) in Norway. Playing up the king's almost supernatural reputation, a widely circulated Swedish/Norwegian story of the time claimed that the sniper used a bullet fashioned from a silver button stolen from Charles's uniform. The death also inspired a generation of assassination conspiracy theories alleging that the shot had been fired from behind Swedish lines. Subsequently Sweden developed a lively parliamentary political culture in the eighteenth century, with freedom of the press guaranteed by law beginning in 1844.

In 1814, following an international propaganda duel, Denmark lost Norway to Sweden (as compensation for Sweden's loss of Finland to Russia during the Napoleonic Wars). In 1864, after the last of a string of wars and much German and Danish nationalistic propaganda, Denmark also lost the border duchies of Schleswig, Holstein, and Lauenburg to Prussia. Danish energy turned inward with the motto: "What is outwardly lost is inwardly won." Typical projects included educational reform. Bishop N. S. F. Gruntvig (1783–1872) established a nationwide system of folk high schools aimed at popular adult education. The schools taught national history, literature, self-improvement skills, and greatly enriched Danish rural life. Although contributing to a sense of nationhood, the schools were not propaganda mills; they served as a humanistic hedge against the more extreme doctrines of the nineteenth and twentieth centuries. Cooperatives established as a result of the movement brought prosperity to the Danish countryside.

For Iceland, Norway, and Finland the nineteenth century witnessed a growing national awareness and sense of selfhood opposed to Danish, Swedish, and Russian rule, respectively. As in contemporaneous movements in Eastern Europe and Ireland, art, literature and language proved key vehicles of propaganda. In Iceland such literary pioneers as poets Bjarni Thorarensen (1786–1841) and Jónas Hallgrímsson (1807–1845) carved out a national idiom. Jón Siguredhsson (1811–

1879), an Icelandic historian and authority on the ancient sagas, founded the nationalist periodical *Ny felagsrit* (New Fellowship Writing; 1841) and campaigned for home rule, which was granted by Denmark in 1874. Iceland gained full independence in 1944. A similar event occurred on the Faroe Islands, a Danish dependency, paving the way for home rule in 1948.

In Norway patriotic writers included Henrik Wergeland (1808–1845) and Bjørnstjerne Bjørnson (1823–1910). The latter also took part in the international peace movement and campaigned on behalf of such oppressed peoples as the Finns and the Slovaks. He won the Nobel Prize in literature in 1903. The linguist and poet Ivar Aasen (1813–1897) developed *landsmål,* a written form of Norwegian that drew on the dialects of the countryside and the language to create a defiantly un-Danish medium. The composer Edvard Grieg (1843–1907) wrote music based on folk themes with a strong national thrust. Norway dissolved its union with Sweden in 1905, thereby gaining independence for the first time in five hundred years. There was an element of national propaganda in the state's support for the polar explorations of Fridtjof Nansen (1861–1930) and Roald Amundsen (1872–1928). In 1933 a huge Norwegian propaganda campaign developed around the country's claim to the eastern coast of Greenland. In 1933 the International Court of Justice upheld Danish sovereignty over the entire island. In the same period the Norwegian press supported the cause of independence for Iceland.

In Finland central figures included the "national poet" Johan Ludvig Runeberg (1804–1877), whose poems (written in Swedish) often dealt with historical subjects. The literary scholar Elias Lönnrot (1802–1884) reconstructed and published the ancient Finnish epic called the *Kalevala* (1835 and 1849), which became a wellspring of Finnish nationalistic art, influencing not only literature but also graphic design, as well as figuring in the music of Jean Sibelius (1865–

1957). Political champions of the Finnish language included the philosopher Johan Vilhelm Snellman (1806–1881). The language gained official recognition in 1863, although at the end of the nineteenth century Russia launched a determined "Russification" campaign. The nationalistic art of the nineteenth century became central to the identity of the Finnish state following its independence from Russia in 1917.

The Scandinavian countries entered the twentieth century with a commitment to neutrality, but, as elsewhere in Europe, the turbulence of the interwar period produced political extremes. In Denmark a coalition of right-wingers formed the Landbrugernes Sammenslutning (Agrarian Revival Movement) and organized a huge march on Copenhagen in 1931 to advance farmer's concerns. A parallel group, the Lappo Movement, developed in Finland. The most notorious, full-blown Fascist party in Scandinavia was the Norwegian Nasjonal Samlung (National Party), modeled after Hitler's Nazi Party, which was founded in 1933 by Vidkun Quisling (1887–1945), the former minister of defense. Quisling proved a willing collaborator following the German invasion of Norway in 1940, serving as the puppet prime minister beginning in 1942. He was executed in 1945. His name, "quisling," has become a synonym for traitor.

The Germans employed propaganda to aid their invasion of Norway and Denmark in April 1940. The advancing Luftwaffe dropped leaflets to explain the necessity of its action, but the confusion of languages in the text (mixing Danish, Norwegian, and German) proved counterproductive. During the Nazi occupation, the Danish king, Christian X (ruled 1912–1947) became the focus of national sentiment. The resistance movement grew out of the unlikely coalition of the Conservative People's Party and Denmark's Communists; propaganda tools included the use of underground newspapers, such as *Frit Danmark* (Free Denmark). Assisted by Britain's Special Operations Executive (SOE), acts of sabotage began in 1942 and had symbolic as well as strategic value. In May 1942 John Christmas Møller (1898–1948), a leading conservative politician, made a dramatic escape by boat to England. There he became chairman of the Free Danish Council and launched a series of patriotic radio broadcasts back home over the BBC, comparable in their impact to those of Churchill to the British people. In addition to acts of sabotage, the resistance coordinated a wave of strikes in August 1943 (which prompted German direct rule to replace the existing puppet government) and a general strike in June 1944. In postwar Scandinavia, Norway, Iceland, and Denmark aligned with NATO, while Sweden and Finland maintained their neutrality. Finland's location on the Soviet border created particular problems. The USSR conducted propaganda in Finland through existing left-wing groups and applied diplomatic pressure on the Finnish government to restrain the country's media. The government obliged and, as Finnish historian Esko Salminen has documented, successfully browbeat the Finnish press into accepting a culture of self-censorship regarding the Soviet Union, which became a key feature of the process known elsewhere in Europe as "Finlandization." In the mid 1970s the philosopher and artist Carl-Gustaf Lilius (1928–1998) drew attention to self-censorship, but the practice continued until the collapse of the Soviet Union.

All of the Scandinavian countries developed strong peace and antinuclear movements, with protests against the Vietnam War and widespread participation in the "Nuclear Free" campaign. In 1985 Iceland declared itself a nuclear-free zone. Scandinavian governments have viewed their role in the media as one of protecting freedom of expression. Freedom of the press is guaranteed by the constitution of Norway and Denmark and by law elsewhere in Scandinavia. In Finland there is also a legal right to reply, though such legal protections did not prevent the self-censorship of the Cold War. In Sweden the government provides a subsidy to all newspapers, regardless of their

politics, and also supports the peace movement with money from the defense budget. The Scandinavian nations all developed state-owned broadcasting systems, which have acted as a hedge against the cultural imperialism of their more powerful neighbors. The legislative brief of the Icelandic National Broadcasting Service explicitly includes a mandate to protect the Icelandic language and culture. Government regulation has tended to be lax, limited to matters of content, such as restrictions on violence in Norway and children's programming in Sweden. The 1990s witnessed the rapid adoption of both digital broadcasting media and the Internet. Major propaganda issues within Scandinavia at the end of the twentieth century included membership in the European Union (Sweden voted to join in the 1990s but Norway voted to stay out) and the future of national currencies. In 2000 Denmark voted to retain the krone by a slim margin of 6 percent. Only Finland adopted the Euro. Issues of race and immigration also figured across the region, with a revival of extreme right-wing politics that utilized the Internet as a propaganda medium. In Sweden the far right revived the image of Charles XII as an icon of Sweden's past.

Nicholas J. Cull

See also Marshall Plan; Peace and Antiwar Movements (1945–); Reformation and Counter-Reformation; Religion; Riis, Jacob; Temperance; Women's Movement: European
References: Derry, T. K. *A History of Scandinavia: Norway, Sweden, Denmark, Finland and Iceland.* London: Allen and Unwin, 1979; Lauring, Palle. *A History of Denmark.* Copenhagen: Høst and Søn, 1981; Roberts, Michael. *The Age of Liberty: Sweden, 1719–1772.* Cambridge: Cambridge University Press, 1986; ———. *Gustavus Adolphus and the Rise of Sweden.* London: Longman, 1992; Salminen, Esko. *The Silenced Media: The Propaganda War between Russia and the West in Northern Europe.* Basingstoke, UK: Macmillan, 1999.

Shakespeare, William (1564–1616)

An English playwright whose work served as dynastic propaganda for the Tudors and who became a staple of British propaganda in the modern world, William Shakespeare was born in Stratford, located in the Midlands. He worked in London under state censorship and regularly performed at court, especially after the accession of King James I (1566–1625) in 1603, whereupon his company took the name The King's Men. Elements of dynastic propaganda are most easily discernable in Shakespeare's history plays. His early play *Richard III* (c. 1593) constitutes a slander on the last king of the Plantagenet line, who was killed in a battle against Henry VIII, the founder of the Tudor line. The historical tragedy *Macbeth* (c. 1606) touches on the origins of the Scottish royal house that produced King James. Other plays make political points on the nature of kingship and the danger of civil war.

By the twentieth century Shakespeare had assumed a centrality in English cultural history. The three hundredth anniversary of Shakespeare's death occurred in April 1916, providing a patriotic windfall for British domestic propaganda during World War I, as well as an opportunity for cultural propaganda in the still neutral United States.

Patriotic speeches extracted from his plays became favorite morale boosters in both world wars, the favorite being John of Gaunt's death speech in *Richard II* (c. 1594)—which is even quoted by Sherlock Holmes at the climax of the Hollywood film *The Secret Weapon* (1942). The most famous wartime use of Shakespeare was *Henry V* (1944), produced, directed, and acted by Laurence Olivier (1907–1989). Elements in his rhetoric clearly influenced Churchill.

Other countries have adapted Shakespeare to serve their own political ends. Verdi (1813–1901) used *Macbeth* as a veiled attack on Austria's misrule of Italy. In Stalin's Russia a bold company famously staged a production of *Hamlet* (c. 1602) in which all the characters were drunk, intended as an attack on the decadent monarchical system. For all his international resonance, Shakespeare still figures prominently in British cultural propaganda overseas, from the activities of the British Council and such trans-Atlantic cultural groups as the English-Speaking Union to tours by the Royal Shakespeare Company (RSC).

Nicholas J. Cull

See also Britain; Churchill, Winston; Cultural Propaganda; Poetry; Theater

References: Cohen, Derek. *The Politics of Shakespeare*. New York: St. Martin's, 1993; Leggatt, Alexander. *Shakespeare's Political Drama: The History Plays and the Roman Plays*. London: Routledge, 1988; Wells, Robin Headlam. *Shakespeare, Politics and the State*. London: Macmillan, 1986.

Silent Spring (1962)

This book by biologist Rachel Carson (1907–1964) drew public attention to the mounting problems of pollution in the United States. Carson warned of a bleak future in which the beauties of nature would be just memories—the silent spring of the title. Her particular target was the "miracle" insecticide DDT, then being used in vast quantities to control agricultural pests. Carson pointed out that such poisons "should not be called insecticides but biocides" since they not only killed insects but also animals, and threatened humans. The book sold two hundred thousand copies within a month, causing worldwide alarm and prompting U.S. president John F. Kennedy (1917–1963) to launch an investigation of the issue. The pesticide industry fought a formidable rearguard action, but in 1970 the newly formed Environmental Protection Agency (EPA) successfully banned the use of DDT within the United States. Carson did not live to see the impact of her work, but her book became for the environmental movement what *Uncle Tom's Cabin* had been to nineteenth-century abolitionism: a foundational text of mass persuasion.

Nicholas J. Cull

See also Environmentalism; United States

References: Hays, Samuel P. *Beauty, Health and Permanence: Environmental Politics in the United*

States, 1955–1985. Cambridge: Cambridge University Press, 1987; Lear, Linda. *Rachel Carson: Witness for Nature.* New York: Holt, 1997.

Songs
See Music

South Africa
See Africa

Southeast Asia

The nations of the Southeast Asian region— Burma, Cambodia, Laos, Malaysia, Singapore, Thailand, and Vietnam—have experienced the propaganda of missionary and imperial activity, national awakening, and revolution and reaction in the second half of the twentieth century. The region has produced both the most extreme propaganda— such as Pol Pot's (1925–1998) regime in Cambodia, which lasted from 1975 to 1979—and models of media control—such as the military regime in Burma (Myanmar), the Communist government in Laos, and the authoritarian capitalist regimes in Singapore and Malaysia. Regional propaganda ploys have included the renaming of countries to indicate a break with the past.

Portuguese missionaries reached the region in the early 1500s, but large-scale colonization was mainly a nineteenth-century phenomenon, with French influence spreading out from Vietnam and British influence emanating from India. Only Siam remained independent. In 1932 a military coup transformed Siam into a constitutional monarchy. Field Marshal Luang Pibul Songgram (1897–1964), one of the coup's leaders, became premier in 1938 and renamed the country Thailand. The entire region was occupied by the Japanese during World War II and was subjected to propaganda couched in a Pan-Asian anti-imperialist rhetoric. Japanese rule was widely contested, as in Burma, where Japan's client anti-British Burmese Indepen-dent Army rebelled as the Anti-Fascist People's Freedom League.

In the postwar period the region saw bitter struggles between Communist insurgents and colonial or postcolonial regimes. Britain responded to the Communist rebellion in Malaya in 1948–1960 by deploying both troops and propaganda. Britain's strategies included denying the crisis status of the war by dubbing it "the Malayan Emergency" and referring to the enemy as "bandits." Field Marshal Sir Gerald Templer (1898–1979), who directed the counterinsurgency effort, coined the phrase "winning hearts and minds" to describe his strategy. Techniques included the use of leaflets urging the enemy to surrender, mobile loudspeakers (including those mounted on aircraft), and film propaganda. The British also printed newspapers in the vernacular and circulated a black propaganda newspaper called *New Path News* that purported to be Communist. Britain's success (especially the "winning hearts and minds" rhetoric) became an influential model for the United States as it contemplated its own counterinsurgency efforts in Thailand and the former French colonies of Laos, Cambodia, and Vietnam.

In the 1950s and 1960s the United States deployed the resources of the Central Intelligence Agency (CIA) and the United States Information Agency (USIA) to combat Communism in the region. In Thailand propaganda methods included the establishment of a television system with communal sets in villages. While anti-Communist activities achieved a level of success in Thailand, regional insurgencies continued, the most damaging being that in South Vietnam, which precipitated the Vietnam War. The United States dropped leaflets (and bombs) over those sections of Laos and Cambodia used by their Vietnamese enemies to infiltrate South Vietnam. The United States also reputedly dropped giant condoms over Laos in order to start rumors concerning the prodigious and intimidating nature of American manhood.

The Vietnam War placed extreme hardship on neighboring countries, especially

Cambodia, which was bombed and invaded by the United States in its campaign against the Vietnamese guerrillas. In 1972 a coup led by Lon Nol (1913–1985) overthrew King Norodom Sihanouk (1922–), the long-term head of state, and the country was renamed the Khmer Republic. Propaganda strategies included intensive anti-Vietnamese campaigns. Sihanouk formed a coalition with the Communists, and in 1975 the Communist Khmer Rouge movement, led by Pol Pot, seized power. Borrowing propaganda methods from the Chinese Cultural Revolution, Pol Pot sought to refashion his country, declaring "year zero" of a new era. Khmer Rouge forces renamed the country Kampuchea and herded the population into the countryside to work on farms. Their propaganda made scapegoats of many groups—including all foreigners, middle-class intellectuals, and people who wore glasses—who were executed in special camps. The Khmer Rouge conscripted the youth of the country and indoctrinated them to turn against their "corrupt" elders. As many as 1.7 million perished in the mass murder and famine that followed. In 1979 Communist Vietnam ended Pol Pot's reign of terror and established a client regime, but the civil war continued. Since 1985 the country has been ruled by Hun Sen (1952–) of the Cambodian Peoples Party. His search for prosperity dictated his renunciation of Communism and a succession of compromises, including renaming the country Cambodia in 1989, restoring Sihanouk as king in 1993, and accepting a coalition with the Funcinpec Party. The exact course of the genocide and the responsibility of various politicians in the events (including ex–Khmer Rouge soldier Hun Sen) remain a staple of propaganda claim and counterclaim in the country.

Since gaining independence, Singapore has been dominated by Lee Kuan Yew (1923–), its autocratic prime minister, in office from 1959 to 1990. State propaganda policies have ranged from poster campaigns publicizing the country's public antismoking policy to an education policy that promoted the English language at the expense of Chinese. Although a multiparty state, Lee's People's Action Party enjoyed a monopoly on power and close links to Singapore Press Holdings, the conglomerate that dominates the newspaper industry. Beyond this, the state has established a rigid system of censorship and controls the spread of the new media. Internet access is regulated and satellite dishes cannot be owned privately.

In Malaysia the government, headed by Mahathir Mohamad (1925–), prime minister since 1981, has also regulated the media, passing a Printing Presses and Publications Act in 1984 and a Broadcasting Act in 1988, which imposed a system of renewable licenses. The state has been particularly keen to regulate Western images for Islamic religious reasons. Symbols of national economic prosperity have included the Petronas Twin Towers, the world's tallest building, which opened in Kuala Lumpur in 1997, on the eve of a massive economic recession.

The region's liveliest media culture developed in Thailand. Despite government and army ownership of television channels, by the 1980s censorship was self-imposed rather than administered by the state. Criticism of the monarchy or army remains rare, but the press functions as an effective watchdog on such issues as corruption and human rights abuses. Issues in domestic state propaganda include public health messages concerning the spread of AIDS.

By the end of the twentieth century the most extreme example of state propaganda in the region was to be found in Burma. The military took control of the postcolonial state in the early 1960s and perpetuated its rule through a combination of force and holding a monopoly on all media outlets, thereby censoring all dissenting views. In 1988 a prodemocracy movement called the National League for Democracy (NLD) gained world attention by staging a mass protest scheduled on the symbolic date of 8 August (8–8–88).

The military government, reconstituted as the State Law and Order Restoration Council (SLORC), responded violently. Propaganda gambits included playing the nationalistic card by renaming the country Myanmar (in 1989) rather than use the Anglicized colonial name Burma. Since 1988 NLD opposition has been led by Aung San Suu Kyi (1945–), the daughter of one of the architects (and martyrs) of Burmese independence, and has relied on nonviolent protest. An able writer and speaker, Aung San Suu Kyi effectively mobilized world opinion against the military regime. In 1990 the military overturned a landslide election that favored the NLD. In the 1990s the key figure in the military regime was Gen. Than Shwe (1933–), a proponent of psychological warfare who made some attempts to ease international criticism of his regime by means of the token release of dissidents. In 1991 Aung San Suu Kyi won the Nobel Peace Prize. The NLD continues to protest against human rights abuses in Burma by supplying information to the Western media (BBC, VOA, and Radio Free Asia) and pressure groups such as Amnesty International. Public pressure successfully forced a number of major multinational corporations—including Texaco, Levi-Strauss, and Pepsi Cola—to withdraw from Burma.

Nicholas J. Cull

See also China; Counterinsurgency; Indonesia; Japan; Philippines; Satellite Communications; Vietnam; Vietnam War

References: Aung San Suu Kyi. *Freedom from Fear and Other Writings.* London: Penguin, 1991; Carruthers, Susan L. *Winning Hearts and Minds: British Governments, the Media and Colonial Counter-Insurgency, 1944–1960.* Leicester, UK: University of Leicester Press, 1995; Khoo Boo Teik, *Paradoxes of Mahathirism: An Intellectual Biography of Mahathir Mohamad.* Kuala Lumpur, Malaysia: Oxford University Press, 1995; McCargo, Duncan. *Politics and the Press in Thailand: Media Machinations.* London: Routledge, 2000; Shawcross, William. *Sideshow: Kissinger, Nixon and the Destruction of Cambodia.* New York: Simon and Schuster, 1979; Thant Myint-U. *The Making of Modern Burma.* Cambridge: Cambridge University Press, 2001; Wong, Kokkeong, *Media and Culture in Singapore: A Theory of Controlled Commodification.* Cresskill, NJ: Hampton, 2000.

Spain

Spain as a political entity was created through the marriage of Ferdinand II of Aragón (1452–1516) to Isabella I of Castile (1451–1504) in 1469. They ruled the joint kingdoms beginning in 1479 and in 1494 were given the appellation "Catholic Kings" by the pope, at that time a significant addition to their propaganda armory. Like their medieval forebears, they continued the tradition of demonstrating their power through devotional images and ceremonies. Examples of the latter included formal entries into cities, the most famous being their entry in 1492 into Granada, the last Muslim kingdom in the Iberian Peninsula to fall in the reconquest by Christians, which spanned four centuries. The monarchs generally boosted their image among nobles and other subjects in traditional ways, emphasizing their role as model Christian kings ruling over a *respublica christiana* by divine delegation and supported by the church as they demonstrated their devotion to it and its works. Religious unity became the hallmark of the Spanish Catholic monarchy as Judaism, Islam, and Christian heresies—which for their successors came to include Protestantism—were rooted out in what was presented as a divinely inspired mission.

The use of portraiture as a propaganda tool was in its infancy under the Catholic kings, as evidenced by the need to import foreign talent. However, this medium of propaganda was fully utilized by their successors from the Habsburg house of Austria: Charles I (1500–1558; r. 1516–1556), who also reigned as Holy Roman Emperor Charles V (1519–1556); and Philip II (1527–1598; r. 1556–1598). Portraiture was for them a means of demonstrating their grandeur; in the case of Charles V, it involved symbolic references to Hercules. Philip II built on the dynastic tradition of elevating family prestige through portraiture and architecture, collecting portraits and displaying them in the Alcázar and Prado in Madrid and, after its completion in 1584, the Royal Monastery of St. Lawrence at El Escorial. The latter was built to demonstrate royal devotion, the remoteness and grandeur of royal power, and dynastic continuity (being the repository of royal remains from Charles I onward). Philip II maintained the providentialist image by continuing the process of evangelization in the New World and combating Protestantism as the ostensible secular arm of the Counter-Reformation. Outside Spain these activities were bitterly caricatured in the "black legend," which portrayed Philip as archetypally cruel and obscurantist. In Protestant northern Europe and its overseas extensions, this legend took hold and provided a powerful negative image of Spain and Catholicism that began to fade only in the late twentieth century.

Beginning in the 1630s, the art of royal portraiture was continued and energized by Diego Velázquez (1599–1660) as court painter to Philip IV (1605–1665; r. 1621–1665), whom he memorably portrayed as an equestrian figure. Philip's sickly and childless successor, Carlos II (1661–1700; r. 1663–1700), was portrayed in a religious manner by court painter Claudio Coello (1642–1693), who showed the king's retinue adoring the miraculous Host of Gorkum. In the eighteenth century court painting continued to be an integral part of royal propaganda under the house of Bourbon, although the increasingly centralized administration, which outlawed Catalan as an official language, and intermittent warfare were the main means of demonstrating royal power at home and overseas. An imposing architectural symbol of the new dynasty's prestige was the royal palace in Madrid, the Palacio de Oriente, which was built between 1737 and 1764. Rusticity and domesticity were in vogue, and Francisco José de Goya y Lucientes (1746–1828), court painter from 1786 to 1824, obliged with a fine portrait of Charles III (1716–1788; r. 1759–1788) in the garb of a huntsman. From a propaganda standpoint, his unflattering portrayal of the family of Charles IV (1748–1819; r. 1788–1808) was probably counterproductive.

Ferdinand VII (1784–1833; r. 1808–1833), who was restored to power in 1814 after the expulsion of the invading French, was also painted by Goya, but it was Goya's painting depicting the execution of alleged Spanish resisters by a French firing squad on 3 May 1808 that was to stir patriotic feelings for decades to come. The revolution of 1820 not only precipitated the loss of Spain's mainland empire but also ushered in a century of liberalism and instability. There were two civil wars (1833–1840 and 1872–1876) as a result of attempts by other members of the Bourbon family, whose followers were known as Carlists, to gain control of the throne. Both were won by the proponents of liberalism, who established political pluralism, though with such a narrow base that the army rather than elections determined governments and regimes until 1874. The pluralistic press was largely regulated by governments, with the number of newspapers and pamphlets burgeoning during revolutionary periods (1854–1856 and 1868–1874). Despite low levels of literacy in the nineteenth century, the printed word—sometimes reinforced by cartoons—came into its own for propaganda purposes, promulgated by political parties and radical groups in the cities. In the rural north the spoken word of the clergy upheld traditional Catholic values, while in Catalonia, Galicia, and (to a lesser extent) the Basque region literary activities reinvigorated regional culture, serving as the basis for future waves of nationalism. Toward the end of the century the propaganda stereotypes of the Freemasons (conspiratorial enemies of Catholicism) and the Jesuits (conspiratorial enemies of progress) emerged, foreshadowing the heated propaganda wars of the twentieth century.

Among the literate, the late nineteenth century saw a surge in patriotic feeling spurred by Spanish attempts to hold on to rebellious Cuba, if necessary by taking on the United States. Jingoistic press campaigns in Spain (matched by similar campaigns in the United States) contributed to the Spanish-American War of 1898, in which a disastrous defeat for Spain led to angry demands for national regeneration. These were spearheaded by the propaganda campaign of reformer Joaquín Costa (1846–1911), which left as its legacy an intellectual movement of criticism of the liberal parliamentary monarchy of Alfonso XIII (1886–1941; r. 1886–1931), which often looked to France as its model. Others sought national regeneration through a return to traditional religious values, as advocated by the polymath and publicist Marcelino Menéndez y Pelayo (1856–1912), as evidenced by missionary and other propaganda campaigns by the clergy.

During World War I the Spanish press remained divided, with conservatives generally campaigning for neutrality and liberals for a more pro-Allied stance. The belligerent powers offered clandestine financial support to newspapers and journalists as needed. In 1923 the unstable parliamentary regime was overthrown by Gen. Miguel Primo de Rivera (1870–1930), who ruled as dictator until 1930. The military had already persuaded the previous regime to avoid criticizing it. Primo de Rivera censored the press and created his own party, Unión Patriótica, and newspaper, La Nación, to firm up support for his rule.

The coming of the Second Republic (1931–1936) saw political warfare carried on mainly in the press. At the national level these included the Alfonsine monarchist ABC, the Carlist traditionalist El Siglo Futuro (The Future Century), the Catholic El Debate (The Debate), the liberal El Sol (The Sun), the Socialist El Socialista, the Anarchist Tierra y Libertad (Earth and Liberty) and the Communist Mundo Obrero (Workers' World). In Catalonia La Veu de Catalunya (The Voice of Catalonia) and L'Opinió (Opinion) represented the right and left wings of regionalism. Most provincial capitals published a daily of each persuasion. The importance of periodicals for ideological indoctrination may be gauged by the creation in 1931 of Acción Española, a review whose purpose was to turn the elite toward traditional monarchy.

The prosperity of the 1920s brought an increase in advertising for personal products that continued into the 1930s. Radio programs were first broadcast in 1924 in Madrid and Barcelona. Though regulated by the state, stations were privately owned and carried commercial advertising. News bulletins arrived in 1930, but during the Republic it was decided not to broadcast parliamentary debates for fear that they might provoke rioting in the streets. Election speeches were first carried in 1933 (the use of airplanes was banned for campaign purposes), but in the polarized election campaign of 1936 only the centrist premier was permitted to broadcast. The potential of radio's use in politics was seen in the 1934 broadcast declaring a revolt in Barcelona, which was answered by the premier in Madrid, and by some rightist conspirators' plans in 1936 to launch a coup by seizing radio installations.

The Spanish Civil War of 1936–1939 was won by the Nationalists, who were led by Generalissimo Francisco Franco y Bahamonde (1892–1975); the victors described the conflict variously as the Spanish Crusade (used in the regime's official multivolume history) or the War of Liberation (from Communism). Throughout the regime its single political organization was known as the National Movement, although until 1958 it was properly called Falange Española Tradicionalista y de las Juntas Ofensivas Nacional-Sindicalistas (FET y de las JONS; Spanish Traditionalist and National-Syndicalist Offensive Groups' Phalanx). Representing an amalgam of all the rightist forces supporting the military uprising of 18 July 1936, until 1958 its ideology was formally that of the Fascist party Falange Española, founded by the dictator's son, José Antonio Primo de Rivera (1903–1936) in 1933, who was shot by Republicans in 1936. The Falange supplied the visual symbol of the regime—yoked arrows of the Catholic kings—seen on war memorials and at the entrances to towns and villages. José Antonio's execution on 20 November was observed as a holiday, as was the date of the uprising on 18 July, which featured a military parade in Madrid with the Caudillo (Chief) taking the salute. The main streets or squares of towns and villages were renamed after José Antonio. Well into the 1960s the main news broadcasts of the day carried by all radio stations ended with a trumpet call and the words "Por los gloriosos caídos por Dios y por España" (For the glorious ones, fallen for God and for Spain), followed by an amalgam of the Falange's anthem "Cara al Sol" (Face to the Sun), the Carlist anthem "Oriamendi" (commemorating that Carlist victory over the British Legion in 1837), and the Royal March of Charles III (the national anthem except during the Republic, when it was the Hymn of Riego, named after the military leader of the coup of 1820). The national red and gold flag replaced the Republican red, gold, and purple one during the civil war. The idea, borrowed from Italy, of redesignating years from 1937 onward as Año Triunfal (Years of Triumph) was soon abandoned. The cult of Franco was propagated by his appearance on coins, where he was proclaimed "Moderator Hispaniae" (Moderator of Spain), and postage stamps in the manner of past monarchs. He claimed he was accountable only to God and history.

Adopting the manner of Philip II, whom extreme ideologues claimed as the founder of the totalitarian state, architecturally the regime commemorated its glory by constructing a gigantic monument, inaugurated in 1959, called Santa Cruz del Valle de los Caídos (Holy Cross of the Valley of the Fallen), a basilica and mausoleum for Franco, José Antonio, and the war dead located near El Escorial. Despite the apparent ideological ascendancy of the Falange's creed in the early 1940s, the regime was in reality a coalition of "families"—monarchist, Catholic, military, and Falangist—and the formal redefinition of

its ideology in 1958 as the installation of a "Catholic, traditional, social and representative monarchy" better reflected the ideals of the coalition. Following approval by a 1947 referendum, Spain had again become a monarchy, but Franco in effect remained as regent until his death, even though Alfonso XIII's grandson, Juan Carlos (1938–), was designated as the future Spanish king in 1969. Francoist constitutionalism was completed in 1967, following the approval by referendum of the Organic Law of the State, but by then the regime's internal propaganda had begun to stress economic progress and peace as the achievements to be praised. The year 1964 saw celebrations (twenty-five years of Spanish peace). In the 1960s Spain experienced the highest rate of economic growth in the world, second only to Japan. These years also saw some relaxation of press censorship in the form of a 1966 law introduced by Manuel Fraga Iribarne (1922–), minister of information and tourism, plus the brief political ascendancy in the economics ministries of members of Opus Dei. Despite the portrayal by others of this Catholic secular institute as a sort of sinister holy mafia, its members followed no single political line, as could be seen in the regime's closure of the liberal newspaper *Madrid,* which had been run by two prominent members of Opus Dei. Prior to this there had been a greater show of unity by its members in producing the cultural review *Arbor* and running Ediciones Rialp, which published a series of neotraditionalist works.

Censorship of the media was the responsibility of the Delegation of Press and Propaganda, while in matters of morals Catholic doctrine was the rigid norm, especially with regard to film, beachwear, and behavior in public. Nevertheless, gradations of political interpretation were permitted, which by the 1960s had turned into incipient pluralism. The Falangists had their national daily *Arriba* (Come On!), the Catholics of the ACNP (National Catholic Association of Propagandists), founded in 1910, had *Ya,* and the monarchists had *ABC*. There were Catholic provincial dailies, but former left-wing and liberal papers were taken over by the Falange. All newspapers were published in Castilian until the 1960s, when regional languages were permitted.

The transition to democracy after Franco's death in 1975 has brought a stable constitutional monarchy into being that has reinstated freedom of the press. Nationally the ideological balance was restored with the founding of the daily *El País* (The Country), a progressive organ sympathetic to the Socialist Party, while *ABC* remains the chief conservative mouthpiece, *Arriba* having gone out of business in 1979 and *Ya* in 1988. There is a flourishing regional press. *Avui* (Today) is a popular Catalan-language daily, while *Deia* (The Call) in Bilbao serves as the mouthpiece of mainstream Basque nationalism.

Surveys have shown that Spaniards get their news mostly from radio and television rather than newspapers. The Franco regime created Radio Nacional de España (RNE; Spanish National Radio) during the civil war and it remains the major network, although it is now run by the state holding company Radio, Televisión de España (RTVE; Spanish Radio and Television) and adheres to the views of the government in power. In Franco's Spain there also existed private stations with low-power nationwide networks. Chief among these was the commercial Cadena SER (Spanish Broadcasting Company Chain), which in 2001 was bought by the group that owns *El País*. The Red de Emisoras del Movimiento (Network of the Movement's Stations), a FET enterprise, was taken over by RTVE in the 1970s and merged into RNE in the 1980s. COPE (Spanish Popular Wavelengths Chain), a church-owned network, came into being in the 1960s and remains popular. Television started up in Spain in 1956, but its true impact dates from the mid-1960s, when it overtook radio as a news source. RTVE's Televisión Española (Spanish Television), which was strictly controlled by successive governments, lost its monopoly in

1988. Media pluralism accompanied political pluralism, with the techniques of advertising being applied to politics, particularly at election time.

Throughout the twentieth century Spanish governments have encouraged cultural and diplomatic links with former colonies, but resources have generally limited the intensity of propaganda campaigns. In Spain 12 October is celebrated as a national holiday, now called El Dia de Hispanidad (Hispanity Day). Primo de Rivera's Ibero-American Exhibition, staged in Seville in 1929, was a major event that promoted Pan-Hispanic ideals. In the 1930s and 1940s ideas were broached of a Hispanic cultural or diplomatic bloc, but their successful propagation was limited by Spanish resources. Although Spanish-American elites (outside Mexico) often shared the Catholic and authoritarian ideals of the Caudillo, there was still suspicion of the former colonial power and competition from Pan-Americanism and Indo-Americanism. The external service of RNE only received adequate transmitters in 1945. Much of its output consisted of anti-Communist propaganda intended for Europe, praising Franco for his prescience in alerting the West to the danger by challenging this menace in the civil war. Otherwise the message was one of Spanish exceptionalism, successfully marketed by Spanish tourist offices to a mass international audience in the 1960s with the slogan "Spain Is Different." This stress on individuality declined with social and economic development and Spain's entry into the European Community (EC) in 1986. Another sign of change from the Francoist past are regular news bulletins in Catalan and Basque on Radio Exterior de España. Major events marketed to boost tourism and national prestige included the Twenty-fifth Olympic Games, held in Barcelona in 1992, which projected a Catalan as much as it did a Spanish image. Perhaps more successful in drawing attention to Spain's contribution to world history on the five hundredth anniversary of Columbus's arrival in the Americas was the world exhibition held in Seville in 1992, with its resonance of the 1929 exhibition and the links to Spanish America.

R. A. H. Robinson

See also Austrian Empire; Civil War, Spanish; Goya; *Guernica;* Latin America; Mexico; Netherlands, Belgium, and Luxembourg; Philippines; Portraiture; Portugal; Posters; Spanish-American War

References: Callahan, William J. *The Catholic Church in Spain, 1875–1998.* Washington, DC: Catholic University Press, 2000; Carr, Raymond. *Spain, 1808–1975.* Oxford: Clarendon Press, 1982; Checa Cremades, Fernando. "Monarchic Liturgies and the "Hidden King": The Function and Meaning of Spanish Royal Portraiture in the Sixteenth and Seventeenth Centuries." In *Iconography, Propaganda, and Legitimation.* Ed. Allan Ellenius. Pp. 89–104. Oxford: Clarendon Press, 1998; Garitaonaindia, Carmelo. *La Radio en España, 1923–1939.* Madrid: Siglo XXI Editores, 1988; Montes Fernández, Francisco José. *Los Orígenes de la Radiodifusión Exterior en España.* Madrid: Editorial Complutense, 1998; Nieto Soria, José Manuel. "Propaganda and Legitimation in Castile: Religion and Church, 1250–1500." in *Iconography, Propaganda, and Legitimation.* Ed. Allan Ellenius. Pp. 105–119. Oxford: Clarendon Press, 1998; Payne, Stanley G. *The Franco Regime, 1936–1975.* Madison: University of Wisconsin Press, 1987; Pike, Frederick B. *Hispanismo, 1898–1936.* Notre Dame, IN: University of Notre Dame Press, 1971.

Spanish-American War (1898)

The war between the United States and the Spanish Empire, fought primarily in Cuba and the Philippines, has become the archetype of a war fomented by domestic commercial media pressure. The war grew from two parallel crises. In Cuba a nationalist rebellion against colonial Spanish rule began in 1895 under the leadership of José Martí (1853–1895). In the United States an economic depression combined with the national malaise arising from the closing of the frontier to suggest the need for a more active foreign policy with naval strength to secure commercial markets. Advocates of naval strength and American Empire included Alfred Thayer Mahan (1840–1914), Senator Albert Beveridge (1862–1927), and the assistant secretary of the navy, Theodore Roosevelt (1858–1919).

In New York City the press had become locked into a circulation war between the *New York World,* owned by Joseph Pulitzer (1847–1911), and the *New York Journal* of William Randolph Hearst (1863–1951). These papers vied for circulation by championing the cause of the Cubans with ever more extreme fervor. The papers attacked a particularly aggressive Spanish general, Valeriano "Butcher" Weyler (1838–1930), whose counterinsurgency methods included the use of "Reconcentration" camps, in which thousands died of disease. Hearst also built up the case an eighteen-year-old woman—Evangelina Cosio y Cisneros—imprisoned for abetting assassination of the island's governor. Spicing the story with sex, Hearst's accounts portrayed her as a child who slew her would-be ravisher. In October 1897 Hearst journalist Karl Decker rescued her from a Havana jail. The Hearst papers also publicized the contents of a letter by the former Spanish ambassador in Washington, D.C., Enrique Dupuy de Lôme (1851–1904), that spoke of the weakness of U.S. President William McKinley (1843–1901). Hearst's circulation soon exceeded a million papers a day.

With U.S. government protests mounting, Spain attempted a compromise and granted the island autonomy. This angered a loyalist faction. In February 1898 the U.S. Navy sent a battleship, the *USS Maine,* on a visit to Havana to deter violence. On the night of 15 February the battleship exploded, killing 266. Although the explosion may have been the result of a boiler fault, the newspapers had no doubt of Spanish perfidy and clamored for war. President McKinley, mindful of the need to keep Republican Party support, duly declared war—an act of propaganda by deed for European audiences. McKinley had grown concerned by German activity in

China and wanted to show that the United States was a force to be reckoned with.

While Theodore Roosevelt raised a volunteer regiment of "Rough Riders" (symbolically beginning his recruitment campaign at the Alamo in San Antonio, Texas), the U.S. Pacific Fleet set sail for the Philippines to engage the Spanish at Manila. This battle on 1 May 1898 proved a stunning success; the United States was in effective control of the islands. The campaign in Cuba was covered by journalists, including Richard Harding Davis (1865–1916) and the artist Frederick Remington (1861–1909), and in their hands became a celebration of American valor. Highlights included the Rough Riders' charge up San Juan Hill (actually Kettle Hill).

Film propaganda figured on the home front. The Vitagraph Company produced a four-minute film that cut from the symbolic replacement of the Spanish flag with the Stars and Stripes to footage of the burial of victims of the *Maine* in Arlington National Cemetery. Both the Biograph and Edison motion picture companies sent cameras to Cuba. Thomas Edison (1847–1931) also made a short fictional film set in the conflict, *Love and War* (1899), which was released with accompanying patriotic songs. The public acclaim for these films helped transform the fledgling film industry from a sideshow attraction into a major business.

The war reporting made a hero of Theodore Roosevelt and prepared the way for his progress first to the governorship of New York, then the vice presidency and a popular presidency, following the assassination of McKinley in 1901. The press and the public mood that it created also influenced the U.S. government to take control of Spanish possessions at the war's end. Although it was required to give independence to Cuba, other portions of the Spanish Empire passed to U.S. control. In the Philippines the Americans found themselves fighting a guerrilla war against their erstwhile allies and adopting much the same counterinsurgency tactics that had sparked the war with Spain in the first place. The irony of this did not escape a growing anti-imperial, isolationist lobby.

Nicholas J. Cull

See also Caribbean; Film (Feature); Philippines; Spain; United States

References: Brown, Charles H. *The Correspondents' War: Journalism in the Spanish-American War.* New York: Scribners, 1967; Fell, John L., ed. *Film before Griffith.* Berkeley: University of California Press, 1983; Linderman, Gerald F., ed. *The Mirror of War: The Spanish-American War and American Society.* Ann Arbor: University of Michigan Press, 1974; Milton, Joyce. *The Yellow Kids: Foreign Correspondents in the Heyday of Yellow Journalism.* New York: Harper & Row, 1989; Musser, Charles. *The Emergence of Cinema: The American Screen to 1907.* New York: Scribner's, 1990; Paterson, Thomas G., ed. *American Imperialism and Anti-Imperialism.* New York: Crowell, 1973.

Sport

Sport has long been a propaganda medium. The rise of the modern industrialized, urbanized state and its stricter delineation between working hours and free time also gave sport a higher profile. A corollary of these developments was the standardizing and codification of the rules of many games and pastimes, thus making sport into an international language with commonly defined laws.

Sport came to be regarded as an important medium of internal cohesion within states, often crossing class and rank divides, and between states. Sports could therefore be harnessed to propaganda messages designed to promote patriotism and competition. The British proved themselves particularly adept at drawing up rules and codes for games. Most of the world's modern sporting practices can be traced back to Britain. Association football (soccer), rugby football, cricket, tennis, golf, track and field events, boxing, even many winter sports were originally given structures and rules by British bodies. As the British Empire grew these sports were exported and played both by expatriates and indigenous peoples. Sport soon became an important solvent of the empire and was promoted as a medium of cooperation and friendly competition. The Empire Games reflected this; they continue to this day as the Commonwealth Games.

In the formal British Empire cricket was the most successful sporting export. A cult of cricket grew up, predicated on ideals the English thought they truly represented—gentlemanliness, good manners, and courage. A strict amateur spirit ruled, dedicated to the idea that taking part was more important than winning. The modern definition of being a "good sportsman" grew from this understanding. Such ideals helped to promote the Anglo-Saxon race as a superior being, detached from petty jealousies and squabbles. But cricket became more inclusive as the nonwhite peoples of the empire took to the game. As *the* imperial game its spirit was often associated with the spirit of the empire itself. For the nations of the empire, however, beating the English at their own game quickly became an obsession. Cricket was then used to support nascent national identity, helping to give greater definition to Australia and New Zealand in the first instance. Since 1945 cricket has played its part in emphasizing the separateness of India, Pakistan, and Sri Lanka, while it has also been a vital source of propaganda and self-pride to the people of the West Indies.

The other great British export, football, took especial hold in the "informal" empire of South America and other regions where British technical expertise was called upon, such as the mining areas of northern Spain and the industrial regions of northern Italy. Britain saw the development of the national associations—England, Wales, Scotland, and Ireland—and from these the first international matches. Followed by enormous numbers of the working and lower middle class, football soon became the world's most important sport. King George V (1865–1936), realizing the significance of this development, insisted on attending and presenting the FA Challenge Cup to the winners. It was a vital propaganda tool in maintaining his image as a monarch in touch with his people.

International matches and competitions soon flourished. Significantly, the British Home Associations, responsible for teams from England, Scotland, Wales, and Northern Ireland, boycotted the World Cup from 1930 until 1950, ostensibly over differences concerning the definitions of amateur players, but this policy contained a strong element of disdain for such frivolous sideshows. Football therefore became a symbol of British aloofness from foreign entanglements and an expression of national culture. However, the Home Nations did take part in international matches, a few of which became notorious for their propaganda value. In 1934 the visiting Italian team was promised massive bonuses by Mussolini if they beat the English at their own game. The Italian team rose to the occasion in one of the most violent matches ever seen in England, dubbed by the press "the Battle of Highbury." Four years later the English team went to Berlin to play in the Olympic Stadium. The game provoked a furor in the British press, as the team gave the Nazi salute at the request of the British ambassador; they also inflicted a 6–3 drubbing on their opponents. Since 1945 England-Germany matches have maintained their importance, more particularly perhaps for England as a nation in decline, feeling ever more overshadowed by its powerful neighbor. Similarly, since the Falklands Conflict of 1982 England-Argentina clashes have been used by Argentina especially as chances to strike a propaganda blow.

Totalitarian regimes have attempted to use sport for overt propaganda purposes. For the Nazis the racial purity of their prize boxer Max Schmeling (1905–2003) was to be the prime asset in his bout with the black American fighter Joe Louis (1914–1981). In 1936 Schmeling won, but Louis prevailed in the 1938 rematch in an astonishing 2:04 minutes. The former Soviet Union and Eastern bloc used sport to highlight the superiority of their culture over the decadence of the Western world. China still dedicates a phenomenal budget to maintaining its prestige in the sporting arena.

But there is little doubt that since 1945 the Western world has been equally keen to use sport to promote national ends. During the Cold War the United States found itself in a constant battle to maintain athletic and sporting prowess over the Communist states. Sport highlights national aims in other ways. The Tour de France, for example, ensures that the French countryside still ravishes the eye, thus maintaining an image of France as a highly civilized land of good living. The varsity boat race, Royal Ascot, and the Henley Regatta in England continue to be used as symbols of the supposedly ancient and unchanging culture of England. Sporting success has also provided a platform for athletes with a political message, the most eloquent being the African American boxer Muhammad Ali (1942–), who became a prominent advocate of civil rights and pointedly refused to serve in the Vietnam War. Probably the most extreme example of sport and politics mixing was the so-called Soccer War of July 1969 between Honduras and El Salvador, in which crowd violence following a series of three soccer games brought an underlying border dispute to a head. A full-scale Salvadoran invasion and Honduran counterattack followed.

Mark Connelly

See also British Empire; Olympics
References: Arnaud, Pierre, and James Riordan, eds. *Sport and International Politics.* London: Spon, 1998; James, C. L. R. *Cricket.* London: Allison & Busby, 1989; Hargreaves, Jenny, ed. *Sport, Culture and Ideology.* London: Routledge, 1982; Hoberman, John M. *Sport and Political Ideology.* Austin: University of Texas Press, 1984; Holt, Robert. *Sport and the British.* Oxford: Clarendon, 1989; Houlihan, Barrie. *Sport and International Politics.* London: Harvester Wheatsheaf, 1994.

Stalin, Joseph (1879–1953)

Revolutionary, political agitator and longest-serving Soviet leader, Iosif Vissarionovich Dzhugashvili, was born 21 December 1879 in Gori, Georgia. He adopted the pseudonym Stalin, meaning "man of steel," in 1907. Dzhugashvili attended the Gori church school and earned a full scholarship to the Tbilisi Theological Seminary. While studying for the priesthood, Stalin read forbidden literature, including the writings of Karl Marx (1818–1883). He left the seminary to become a full-time revolutionary.

Stalin began his career in the Social Democratic Party in 1899 as a propagandist among the Tbilisi rail workers. Between 1902 and 1913 Stalin was arrested eight times; he was exiled seven times and escaped six times. Stalin supported the Bolshevik faction of the party, making himself useful particularly in raising funds by robbing banks. In 1912 Vladimir Lenin (1870–1924) coopted him into the Bolsheviks' Central Committee. He briefly edited the new party newspaper, *Pravda* (Truth), and at Lenin's urging wrote his first major work, *Marxism and the National Question* (1913).

After the Revolution of March 1917, Stalin returned to Petrograd where he resumed the editorship of *Pravda.* Together with Lev Kamenev (1883–1936), Stalin led the party policy of moderation until Lenin arrived in April. After the Revolution Stalin distinguished himself by ruthless military leadership and strengthened his position by organizational work and devotion to administrative tasks. In 1922 he became general secretary of the party: the source of political power. After Lenin's death Stalin joined with Grigori Zinoviev (1883–1936) and Kamenev to lead the country and eliminate Leon Trotsky (1879–1940); their attack included much propaganda. Stalin then reversed course and aligned himself with Nikolai Bukharin (1888–1938) and Aleksey Rykov (1881–1938) to galvanize the party to destroy his old allies in the "left opposition." He then used careful manipulation of the economic data available to the party cadres to destroy the "right opposition." By his fiftieth birthday (1929), he had cemented his position as Lenin's anointed successor and entrenched his power as sole leader of the Soviet Union.

A huge poster of Joseph Stalin adorns a building in Leningrad, 1938. (Hulton-Deutsch Collection / CORBIS)

Stalin used the lack of progress in Soviet agriculture to launch a ruthless collectivization program that was in effect an offensive against the peasantry. This process was linked to thoroughgoing cultural revolution and a wholesale industrialization campaign that raised the Soviet Union to the front rank of the industrial powers able to prosecute a world war. In the mid-1930s Stalin launched a major campaign of political terror. The purges, arrests, and deportations to labor camps were orchestrated via an all-pervasive propaganda campaign to convince the population (and particularly the party cadres) that the whole state was riddled with traitors. Even major figures like Zinoviev, Kamenev, and Bukharin admitted to crimes against the state in show trials and were sentenced to death. Stalin was not a particularly subtle propagandist—and had little to add to the theory of the practice—but his campaigns were audacious, energetic, and total. Unlike his cultured rivals, he had learnt his lessons in the seminary and on the hard stage of revolutionary agitation. The campaigns were undoubtedly helped by the all-pervasive atmosphere of fear instilled by the State security apparatus.

The purges had stripped the Soviet Union of its political and military leadership, and the regime's triumphalist rhetoric had left the state unprepared for the Nazi assault. The "Great Patriotic War" began disastrously. Nonetheless Stalin showed his "steel" by personally directing the defense of the USSR. He rallied the population in part by astute use of nationalist (pan-Slavic) rhetoric. Stalin was also willing to make huge human sacrifices—and make propaganda capital from the sacrifice—including through the sieges of Stalingrad and Leningrad.

After the war his regime extended Communist domination over the countries liberated by the Soviet armies. This campaign—and the single-minded determination to protect the Soviet Union—led to growth in arms production and strident anticapitalist propaganda, which contributed to the mutual suspicions of the Cold War. Stalin died in March 1953 but remained a Soviet icon, although his successor Nikita Khrushchev (1894–1971) engineered a break with this by denouncing Stalin and his cult of personality in a secret speech to the Twentieth Communist Party Congress in 1956.

Graham Roberts

See also Cold War; Comintern; International; KGB; Lenin, Vladimir Ilyich; Portraiture; *Pravda;* Revolution, Russian; Russia; Trotsky, Leon; World War II (Russia)
References: Nove, Alec, ed. *The Stalin Phenomenon.* London: Weidenfeld and Nicolson, 1993; Schapiro, Leonard. *The Communist Party of the Soviet Union.* London: Eyre & Spottiswoode, 1970; Tucker, Robert. *Stalin in Power.* New York: Norton, 1990.

Suez Crisis (1956)

Suez marked a watershed in international affairs, teaching lessons about the importance of public opinion and "winning the propaganda war" that have resonated through the Falklands/Malvinas Conflict and the Gulf War to the present day. The crisis was initiated in July 1956, when Egyptian president Gamal Abdel Nasser (1918–1970) nationalized the Suez Canal Company, thereby taking control of a strategic artery. Suez became the focal point of an international propaganda contest the shape of which was defined not simply by Anglo-Egyptian or French-Egyptian antagonism, but by the broader Cold War struggle, the Arab-Israeli dispute and the regional balance of power in the Middle East, and the forces of nationalism and anti-imperialism across the developing world.

British plotting against Nasser was already well advanced in July 1956. By March, concerned at the negative impact of Cairo Radio's "Voice of the Arabs" broadcasts about Western strategic interests, British and U.S. diplomats had authorized "Omega," a covert plan for a series of political warfare and propaganda measures designed to undermine Nasser's position in Egypt and the Arab world. For the British, the outbreak of the Suez Crisis simply lent new urgency to existing plans to "get Nasser down." The redistribution of propaganda resources away from anti-Communist activities in favor of Middle Eastern operations was hastened and a new organization, the Information Co-ordination Executive, was created to oversee the anti-Nasser campaign. Initially, this campaign sought to present Nasser as an unprincipled treaty-breaker, undermining accepted standards of behavior and posing a threat to the values and commercial interests of the international community. British ministers compared Nasser to Hitler and Mussolini while clandestine French broadcasts denounced the Egyptian president as a Communist. These measures were clearly intended to prepare domestic public opinion for military operations against Egypt.

Among Britain's main objectives was the destruction of Nasser's personal prestige and his pretensions to pan-Arab leadership. Prime Minister Anthony Eden (1897–1977) wanted Nasser exposed as a fool and a failure; British propagandists therefore focused on themes giving the lie to Nasser's claim that Egyptian control of the canal would bring economic benefits to the Egyptian people. British broadcasts floated ideas about alternative trade routes, new oil pipelines, and declining canal revenues, while the intelligence services, through a Cyprus-based radio station posing as an Egyptian opposition group, suggested that a vengeful British government might abuse its position of colonial rule in Uganda to interfere with Egypt's share of the Nile waters, bringing starvation upon the Egyptian people if they failed to rise up against Nasser.

The beginning of military operations against Egypt at the end of October ushered in a new phase in the propaganda war. Unhappy with the performance of the BBC's Arabic Service, British officials in Cyprus commandeered the facilities of the Near East Arab Broadcasting Station for the Foreign Office's "Voice of Britain" broadcasts. Alongside an incompetent army psychological warfare unit and a number of clandestine radio stations, the "Voice of Britain" sought to undermine Egyptian military and civilian morale and create the psychological conditions for Nasser's overthrow. A clandestine French station located near Tours was more extreme, calling for Nasser's assassination on an almost daily basis. Against this background, the official Anglo-French information services attempted to keep up the pretence that the assault on Egypt was a "police action" intended to keep apart warring Israeli and Egyptian forces.

Despite deep U.S. involvement in the formulation of the Omega strategy, American propaganda during the crisis was not dictated by the belief that Suez provided the opportunity to "bring Nasser to heel." The State Department considered that the open use of force against Nasser would alienate Arab and Muslim opinion completely and risk driving the states of the developing world into the arms of the Soviet Union. Once the attack on Egypt occurred, therefore, United States Information Agency (USIA) and Voice of America (VOA) output was calculated to place as much distance as possible between the United States and its European allies. Reflecting Eisenhower's anger at Anglo-French actions, the USIA relentlessly proclaimed America's commitment to the principles of peace, the rule of law, and support for the dignity and independence of the postcolonial world. In propaganda terms, the Anglo-American relationship proved to be of less value than the Cold War struggle for influence in Arab and Asian countries. Furious that Britain had provided a distraction from the Soviet Union's brutal repression of the Hungarian uprising, U.S. propagandists were not slow to take advantage of Eisenhower's stand against "gunboat diplomacy" in order to win new popularity and prestige across the Middle East.

Unquestionably, Nasser emerged as the major victor in the Suez propaganda war. His political and propaganda triumph massively overshadowed the reality of Egypt's military defeat at the hands of the Israelis, and he emerged from the crisis as the undisputed leader of a resurgent Arab nationalist movement. The broadcasts of Cairo Radio (which the British Royal Air Force had signally failed to bomb off the air), and iconic portraits of Nasser himself came to serve as propagandistic symbols of Nasser's new-found status as the hero of the Arab masses across North Africa and the Middle East.

In contrast, Britain's defeat was clear for all to see, and there was little the propagandists could do to disguise it. The flawed policies of the Eden government effectively left British propagandists with an impossible task. Picking up the pieces in the aftermath of a humiliating political defeat, they concentrated on damage limitation, attempting to refute Egyptian claims of atrocities against civilians during the Anglo-French attack on Port Said and, with an eye toward the reestablishment of the Anglo-American alliance, stressing the close links between Nasser and his Communist arms suppliers (a task made somewhat easier by the vocal support for Nasser expressed in Soviet propaganda). Left to explain the disaster, one Foreign Office official summed up the difficulties of Britain's propagandists with the observation that "the Archangel Gabriel transmitting with Infinite Power on The Last Trump could not, prior to an Arab-Israeli settlement, sell British cooperation with France and Israel to the Arab world."

James Vaughan

See also Arab World; BBC; Cold War in the Middle East; Radio (International); USIA; VOA
References: Rawnsley, Garry. *Radio Diplomacy and Propaganda: The BBC and VOA in International Politics.* London: Macmillan, 1996; ———. "Overt and Covert: The Voice of Britain and Black Radio Broadcasting in the Suez Crisis, 1956," *Intelligence and National Security* 11, 3 (July 1996); Shaw, Tony. *Eden, Suez and the Mass Media: Propaganda and Persuasion during the Suez Crisis.* London: I. B. Tauris, 1996.

Sukarno (1901–1970)

Sukarno, Indonesia's president from 1945 to 1968, was both a practitioner and casualty of propaganda. Born in the Dutch East Indian colony of Java, Sukarno was educated at the Bandung Technical Institute, graduating in 1925 as a civil engineer. As a talented orator he soon emerged as a prominent figure in Java's independence movement. He spent the years 1929–1931 in jail and was exiled by the Dutch in 1936. He returned in 1942 and cooperated with the Japanese occupation of the Dutch East Indies. In 1945 he established an independent state of Indonesia under his presidency.

Sukarno ruled by building an elaborate cult of personality. He played his country's Communists against the army and survived in the center with a notoriously lavish lifestyle. In international politics, he sponsored the emergence of the nonaligned movement of so-called Third World countries at the Bandung Conference of 1955. By the early 1960s the Western powers were actively engaged in destabilizing Sukarno's regime, seeing it as an open door for Communism. Both the CIA and Britain's IRD conducted operations to undermine his rule and promote the "forces of order" in the Indonesian army. In 1965 public opinion began to swing dramatically against Sukarno as a result of an attempted Communist coup. Officially he left office in 1968, but real power had passed to the leader of the army faction, General Suharto (1921–), in 1966.

Nicholas J. Cull

See also CIA; Indonesia; IRD
References: Lashmar, Paul, and James Oliver. *Britain's Secret Propaganda War: 1948–1977.* Stroud, UK: Sutton, 1998; Legge, J. D. *Sukarno: A Political Biography.* London: Penguin, 1972.

Sweden

See Scandinavia

Switzerland

The landlocked, multilingual confederation in the mountainous heart of Europe played a central role in the development of European propaganda as a locus of the Reformation and a major center of early printing. As a neutral country Switzerland has provided a refuge to propagandists from other states, from John Knox (c.1514–1572) to Vladimir Lenin (1870–1924). The city of Geneva has been home for the League of Nations (1919–1946), the International Red Cross (from 1864), and other international organizations, including the World Health Organization. The projection of the Swiss national image has been closely tied to its role as an international peacemaker.

Partly because of its mountainous location, medieval Switzerland developed with a tradition of independence and special privilege not seen elsewhere in Europe. In 1291 three cantons (regions) Uri, Unterwalden, and Schwyz, combined to form the Everlasting League of the Three Forest Cantons to defend themselves against Habsburg Austria. Lucerne joined in 1332. These events are memorialized in the legendary campaign of resistance led by the archer William Tell, retold by eighteenth-century historian Johannes von Müller (1755–1809) in his *History of Switzerland* (1786). Tell became a potent symbol of national awakening in Switzerland and beyond during the Enlightenment and the early nineteenth century. He was celebrated as a symbol of freedom in a play of 1804 by the German poet and dramatist Schiller (1759–1805) and as an allegory of Italian nationalism in the opera of 1829 by the Italian composer Rossini (1792–1868).

From 1291 Swiss power grew through successive military campaigns, more cantons joined the league each generation, and in 1499 the Emperor Maximilian (1459–1519) formally recognized the virtual independence of the league. But the growing power of Switzerland was cut short in the sixteenth century, first by defeat at the hands of the French in 1515 but most significantly by the Reformation. Two leading figures of the Reformation worked in Switzerland: the Swiss-born Hulderich Zwingli (1484–1531) in Zurich and Frenchman John Calvin (1509–1564), who was based in Geneva from 1536. The Reformation split the country as the Four Forest Cantons fought to defend their Catholicism. But both sides agreed with the need for neutrality. The Swiss profited from this neutrality in the Thirty Years War

(1618–1648) and received international recognition of their independence under the Treaty of Westphalia, which brought that conflict to an end.

Swiss neutrality was recognized internationally in the Peace of Paris (1815) at the end of the French Revolutionary and Napoleonic Wars, during which the French had imposed on Switzerland the Helvetic Republic (1798–1803). Nineteenth-century Swiss politics was characterized by the clash between the centralizing Radicals and the Catholic cantons, which wished to retain regional power. The struggle involved much sectarian propaganda, and key players on the Catholic side included the Jesuits. In the 1840s the Catholic cantons combined into the Sonderbund (Separate League). This was crushed in the largely bloodless civil war of 1847, and in 1848 Switzerland agreed to a new federal constitution and a ban on the Jesuits operating within the country.

In the twentieth century the Swiss conducted propaganda campaigns during the two world wars to assert their neutrality. During World War II Switzerland became a major theater of the propaganda war as Britain and Germany vied for the sympathy of the Swiss public, but neither side achieved much success. Allied anti-Nazi propaganda seeped across the Swiss border into Germany in the form of mail, news, and rumors.

In the postwar period issues in Swiss politics included the struggle for language rights by the French speakers of the Jura region. In the 1990s the far-right Peoples' Party made gains in Switzerland. The party, led by Christoph Blocher (1940–), traded on anti-immigrant feeling and resentment of the international disapproval of the Swiss role as bankers to Nazi Germany, the scale of which had been revealed during that decade. It won nearly 25 percent of the votes in the election of October 1999, becoming the nation's second most powerful grouping. Switzerland has a record of frequent referenda on key issues, all of which have produced lively political campaigns. In 2002 Switzerland voted to join the United Nations.

Nicholas J. Cull

See also Herzl, Theodor; Lenin, Vladimir Ilyich; PWE, Reformation and Counter-Reformation; Women's Movement: European; Zionism

References: Butler, Michael, Malcolm Pender, and Joy Charnley, eds. *The Making of Modern Switzerland, 1848–1998.* Basingstoke, UK: Macmillan, 2000; Cole, Robert. *Britain and the War of Words in Neutral Europe, 1939–1945.* New York: St Martin's Press, 1990; Head, Randolph C. "William Tell and His Comrades: Association and Fraternity in the Propaganda of Fifteenth- and Sixteenth-Century Switzerland." *Journal of Modern History* 67, 3 (September 1995): 527–557; Johnston, Pamela, and Bob Scribner, *The Reformation in Germany and Switzerland.* Cambridge: Cambridge University Press, 1993.

Syria

See Arab World

T

Television

"Television," the British critic Malcolm Muggeridge (1903–1990) once wrote, "was not invented to make human beings vacuous, but is an Emanation of their vacuity." Television is an electronic system of transmitting changing images, together with sound, along a wire or through space by converting the images and sounds into electrical signals and then reconverting the received signals into images and sound. The word first appeared in *Scientific American* magazine in 1907. The history of television shares many similarities with feature and documentary film—with one basic difference: film was intended as a group experience in a public theater, whereas television was meant to be seen in one's home. Television can be traced back to a German invention in 1884, but television as we know it uses a process dating back to 1930, and even that is remote from television after 1945. In the 1930s Germany, Britain, and the United States all had television programming, but it was available only to the privileged few, and generally as an experimental competitor to radio or film, which were both well established in the 1930s. World War II effectively canceled television programming in all three countries, though some broadcasts continued in the United States, including a propaganda "special" in support of the United Nations.

Television programming is a central source for the cultural propaganda of the producing country. It can be crucial to the electoral process, but it also deserves to be dismissed as a "vast wasteland," as it was in 1962 by Newton Minow (1926–), chairman of the Federal Communications Commission (FCC).

From a practical point of view, television is a post-1945 phenomenon. In Germany television was reluctant to admit to its Nazi past; in Britain the BBC introduced noncommercial television, where, as with radio, each owner paid a yearly license fee. In the United States competing technologies led the FCC to issue an order limiting the total number of television stations for the entire country at just over 100 from 1948 until 1952, a ruling that saw New York City and Los Angeles with seven stations apiece, while many other cities had none. Thus, only after 1953 did television become pervasive in American life, and it did not truly come into its own until 1960. The year 1967 saw the arrival of color broadcasting in the United States, though many viewers enjoyed black-and-white reception well into the 1970s; of course, all earlier programming in black-and-white continues to be rebroadcast as originally produced, though recently some films have been colorized digitally.

In the United States television proved a bonanza for advertisers. The 1950s witnessed the collapse of network radio and the Hollywood system as millions of Americans bought television sets and stayed home to enjoy a new leisure-time activity. Television experienced a brief moment during which productions were aired live, but it soon settled into a pattern that continues to characterize the commercial broadcasts to this day: escapist fare, endless advertisements that interrupt programs at moments when something interesting is about to occur; some news programs; some talk shows; and some local programs. In the 1950s the typical television station was only on the air for a few hours a day; nobody had yet thought of a round-the-clock schedule. In the United States three networks reigned supreme: NBC, CBS, and ABC. (Actually until the 1970s ABC remained a rather feeble third network in terms of station strength, programming, advertising revenues, and numbers of viewers.) In the 1960s commercial television was restricted to the UHF (ultra high frequency) channels; the VHF (very high frequency) channels were difficult to locate given the primitive tuning devices on most sets, so that VHF was left for educators—a sure indication of poor reception.

Cable television, satellite transmission, and video totally changed a viewing world controlled by the three commercial U.S. networks or, in Britain, by the BBC. Britain succumbed to the fare offered by commercial television. The United States broadcast a myriad of offerings from literally hundreds of providers. With the arrival of satellite transmission, the entire world could theoretically be linked through television—but only to those with appropriate receivers. These days television also entails the use of videocassette recorders (VCRs). The entire planet can be divided into three basically incompatible color systems: NTSC (United States); PAL (Britain and most of Europe and Asia) and SECAM (France, the former Soviet Union, and a good bit of Africa). The development of these rival systems was not unrelated to issues of national pride and technology as propaganda.

Cable television, with such world broadcasters as CNN (Cable News Network), Fox News, and MSNBC, has changed the nature of viewing in more than just the United States. Gone forever is the dominance of the three commercial U.S. networks. The advent of the VCR means that viewers are free to record programs on any channel and to view them at a time that seems convenient. In the Arab world Al Jazeera, created by the emir of Qatar in 1996, provides round-the-clock Arabic programming that now reaches some 35 million people in twenty-two countries.

The future of television is driven by technological changes. The Internet and the World Wide Web have affected leisure-time schedules for millions of people. Indeed, the latest technological innovation has advertisers quite worried: digital video recorders record programs and store them on hard disks, making it easy to fast-forward past commercials. This has led one anonymous industry executive to issue a dire warning: "There's no Santa Claus. If you don't watch the commercials, someone's going to have to pay for television and it's going to be you." It seems unlikely that such hortatory appeals will move many viewers.

David Culbert

See also BBC; Blair, Tony; CNN; Elections; Elections (Britain); Elections (Israel); Elections (United States); Film (Newsreels); Ireland; Latin America; Mexico; Nixon, Richard; Television (News); Thatcher, Margaret; USIA

References: Barnouw, Erik. *Tube of Plenty.* New York: Oxford University Press, 1975; Briggs, Asa. *The BBC: The First Fifty Years.* New York: Oxford University Press, 1985; ———. *Sound and Vision.* Vol. 4, *The History of Broadcasting in the United Kingdom.* Oxford: Oxford University Press, 1979; Surgeon General's Scientific Advisory Committee on Television and Social Behavior. *Television and*

Growing Up: The Impact of Televised Violence. Washington, DC: GPO, 1972.

Television (News)

In July 1941 Columbia Broadcasting System (CBS) network began regularly scheduled television newscasts totaling fifteen hours a week, which, however, did not survive Pearl Harbor. In the United States television news—and television as a whole—had to wait until the end of World War II. In 1946 there were roughly 7,000 television sets, 3,000 of which were located in New York City alone. By 1949 there were 10 million sets in operation across the country, in about 100 urban markets.

To radio reporters such as Edward R. Murrow (1908–1965) the term "television news" was a misnomer. Early television news broadcasts had much to be modest about, consisting mainly of "talking heads" plus still pictures and maps. However, being able to see news events appealed to viewers, who forgave television news its poor production values. It became a source of public information in 1954, when CBS broadcast a Murrow "See It Now" episode that attacked Sen. Joseph McCarthy (1909–1957). This broadcast, plus network coverage of the Army-McCarthy Hearings in the spring and summer of 1954, helped bring an end to the phenomenon of McCarthyism. In 1960 four televised hour-long presidential debates gave television news a certain degree of respectability, though Richard Nixon's obvious discomfort before the TV cameras in the first debate

Wisconsin Republican Senator Joseph R. McCarthy, appearing on a television screen during his filmed reply to Columbia Broadcasting System newscaster Edward R. Murrow, tells a coast-to-coast audience on 6 April 1954 that Murrow "as far back as twenty years ago, was engaged in propaganda for Communist causes." McCarthy was answering Murrow's anti-McCarthy program of 9 March. (Bettmann/CORBIS)

helped his less well-known opponent, John F. Kennedy, win popular support. Television news also benefited from the presence of Howard K. Smith (1914–2002), a respected TV news reporter, who acted as moderator.

In 1963 television network news expanded from fifteen to thirty minutes. Coverage of the Vietnam War did not really bring live images of violence into the homes of millions of Americans, since the fighting usually took place at night in remote jungle areas, where the setting up of television camera lights would have been impossible. Still, the most discussed piece of newsfilm to come out of the Vietnam War was captured on 16mm color film by NBC: the execution in February 1968 of a Viet Cong suspect by the chief of the South Vietnamese police at the beginning of the Tet Offensive, which marked a turning point of the Vietnam War. Television coverage of rioting in the streets of Chicago during the 1968 Democratic National Convention helped define public perceptions of political leaders for many years thereafter.

The proliferation of television news increased with the advent of cable. In 1979 the Cable Satellite Public Affairs Network (C-SPAN) went on the air, offering unedited twenty-four-hour news coverage of national events, from political conventions to debates in Congress. In 1980 millionaire Ted Turner (1938–) launched the Cable News Network (CNN), the first round-the-clock news network. The mid-1980s also saw the rise of pseudonews shows such as *Hard Copy* and *A Current Affair,* which consisted of not much news but plenty of glitz and entertainment. In the late 1990s, more twenty-four-hour news channels emerged, including Fox News and MSNBC, with regular news programs as well as news talk-show formats. The hosts of these shows are generally portrayed as aggressive and objective journalists, although self-serving advertisements promote their personalities and/or good looks. CNN was sharply criticized (by older male journalists) in early 2002 for briefly running an advertisement for anchorperson Paula Zahn

(1956–), who was described in the ad as being "provocative, super-smart . . . and just a little sexy."

Television news coverage of the U.S. war on terrorism following the 11 September 2001 attacks on the World Trade Center and the Pentagon brought worldwide attention to Al Jazeera, a twenty-four-hour news channel that serves the Arab world. Formed in 1996 by the emir of Qatar, Al Jazeera has been compared to CNN—favorably by those who like the idea of a pro-Arab television news, unfavorably by those who feel the programming is overtly anti-Israeli and often anti-American. Al Jazeera reaches thirty-five million people in some twenty-two countries.

The power of television to influence opinion throughout the world is well documented. What effect does television news have on the shaping of opinions? Many recognize the agenda-setting function of television news. By addressing certain topics and neglecting others, this medium places emphasis on issues news managers deem significant and important. There is an obvious danger if the average viewer presumes that an unknown and unseen news manager is defining television news, particularly in a time of downsizing in television news bureaus. The rise in popularity of the Internet makes it possible for many people to receive news in an interactive fashion. It seems clear that major media empires and changing electronic technology will determine the future of television news and may affect it in unforeseen ways.

Brian Collins

See also BBC; Civil Rights Movement; Gulf War; McCarthy, Joseph R.; Murdoch, Rupert; Murrow, Edward R.; Nixon, Richard; Satellite Communications; Terrorism, War on; Vietnam War

References: Bliss, Edward, Jr. *Now the News: The Story of Broadcast Journalism.* New York: Columbia University Press, 1991; Cloud, Stanley, and Lynne Olson. *The Murrow Boys: Pioneers on the Front Lines of Broadcast Journalism.* New York: Houghton Mifflin, 1996; Iyengar, Shanto, and Richard Reeves. *Do the Media Govern? Politicians, Voters, and Reporters in America.* London: Sage, 1997; Mickelson, Sig. *The Decade*

That Shaped Television News: CBS in the 1950s. Westport, CT: Praeger, 1998.

Temperance

This essentially religious movement campaigned against the drinking of alcohol in the United States, Britain, and northern Europe in the nineteenth and early twentieth centuries. The "evils of drink" have long been a popular theme in art and written social commentary. The excesses resulting from drunkenness were memorably depicted by the painter Pieter Brueghel (ca. 1520–1569) in the Netherlands and the satirist William Hogarth (1697–1764) in Britain. In the early nineteenth century a religious awakening on both sides of the Atlantic sparked the temperance movement, which saw drink as the root cause of poverty and moral corruption.

Early advocates of temperance included the Irish priest Father Theobald Matthew (1790–1856). The American Temperance Society was founded in 1826, the British and Foreign Temperance Society in 1831, and the United Kingdom Alliance for the Legislative Suppression of the Sale of Intoxicating Liquors in 1853. In 1833 British adherents accidentally acquired their popular sobriquet "teetotalers" when an advocate with a stammer, Richard Turner of Preston, called for "te-te-total" abstinence. Similar movements developed in Sweden, Finland, and Germany. The temperance movement's methods included marches, songs, badges (consisting of white ribbons and a "sacred heart" for Catholics), and the physical act of signing a pledge to abstain from alcohol.

In the United States in particular the movement became closely identified with women. Organizations such as the Woman's Christian Temperance Union (1874) and Anti-Saloon League (1895) viewed temperance not only as part of the moral mission of womanhood but also as a way to prevent domestic violence and alcohol-related family poverty. The activist Carry Moore Nation (1846–1911), whose attention-getting tactics included attacking saloons with a hatchet, was not supported by the mainstream of the movement. The identification between women and temperance meant that brewers actively opposed the enfranchisement of women and funded propaganda to this effect. The movement resulted first in local and eventually nationwide prohibition of alcohol in the United States (1919–1933) as well as in several Scandinavian countries. In Britain the need for a sober workforce during World War I clinched the argument for tighter licensing laws. Following the end of prohibition in the United States, the Anti-Saloon League changed its name first to the National Temperance League and (since 1964) the American Council on Alcohol Problems.

Nicholas J. Cull

See also Drugs; Health

References: Shiman, Lilian Lewis. *Crusade against Drink in Victorian England.* Basingstoke, UK: Macmillan, 1986; Tyrrell, Ian. *Sobering Up: From Temperance to Prohibition in Antebellum America, 1800–1860.* Westport, CT: Greenwood, 1979;———. *Woman's World / Woman's Empire: The Woman's Christian Temperance Union in International Perspective, 1880–1930.* Chapel Hill: University of North Carolina Press, 1991.

Terrorism

The practitioners of terrorism, defined as the political use of violence—especially random violence—use conventional propaganda channels such as leaflets or newspapers to recruit and promote their ideas. For example, Sinn Fein, the political party associated with the Provisional Irish Republican Army, publishes the newspaper *An Phoblacht / Republican News.* Terrorism is fundamentally connected to the mass media. Terrorist actions—kidnappings, bombings, hijackings, the taking of hostages—can be seen as media events staged by those without access to the popular press or television in order to raise awareness of a particular cause in the public's consciousness and/or to spread fear among a targeted population. The propaganda value of an act can

A wall in Falls Road, Belfast, Northern Ireland, is painted with republican slogans and images. It links the objectives of the Palestine Liberation Organization (PLO) with that of the Irish Republican Army (IRA). (Paul Seheult; Eye Ubiquitous/CORBIS)

be modified by the choice of target, claims (or denials) of responsibility, and the release (or execution) of hostages. The connection between terrorism and the media was memorably acknowledged by British Prime Minister Margaret Thatcher (1925–) when she advocated media regulation in order to deny terrorists the "oxygen of publicity." Like the term "propaganda," the word "terrorism" is freighted with negative connotations, having become a staple of contemporary political rhetoric. However, one man's terrorist/bandit/criminal can be another man's urban guerrilla/freedom fighter/soldier. Antiterrorist rhetoric has been used to justify repressive laws in democratic societies, as was the case in West Germany in the 1970s.

Regimes and their armies have long sought to utilize terror as a weapon of war in order to produce an emotional impact on their enemy (or subject population) beyond their military capacity. Atrocities were used for this purpose in sixteenth-century Europe during the Wars of Religion and the Dutch Revolt; in seventeenth-century Europe during the Thirty Years' War; and in the eighteenth century, most famously during the French Revolution, when depictions and descriptions of such events circulated as counterpropaganda. The revolutionary movements of the nineteenth century recognized the power of symbolic violence to draw attention to a cause. The anarchist Mikhail Bakunin (1814–1876) spoke of "le propagande par le fait" (propaganda by means of action) and militant anarchists put this into effect through assassinations and bombings. Notable examples include the assassination of Tsar Alexander II of Russia (1818–1881) and the Haymarket bomb incident in Chicago in 1886. Terrorist acts performed in the cause of Irish nationalism included the Phoenix Park murders of

1882 and other acts committed by the Fenian "Invincibles." By the end of the century, symbolic direct action was well established in the terrorist's political arsenal.

In the twentieth century, attacks on civilians became a regular feature of conventional warfare and revolutionary and anticolonial guerrilla struggles. The Anglo-Irish War (1919–1921) saw the formation of the Irish Republican Army (IRA) and acts of terror on both sides. In China Mao Zedong (1893–1976) theorized the propaganda dimension of guerrilla warfare and advocated what amounted to terrorist activities at the start of a campaign as a tactic by means of which a small movement could build a reputation for heroism among the wider population. His theory became dogma for the anticolonial and "urban guerrilla" movements later in the century, though the latter do not establish the sort of territorial presence seen in Chinese or Vietnamese guerrilla warfare.

The political philosopher Michael Walzer (1935–) has argued that the scale of civilian involvement in World War II redefined the limits of political violence, placing ordinary people rather than just police, soldiers, or leaders in the front lines of the new wave of terrorism that emerged in the postwar years. Part of the reason for this change was due to the colonial dimensions of many postwar terrorist campaigns, in which one ethnic group sought to free itself from rule by another and considered all members of the enemy group to be a legitimate target. Among the advocates of violence as a means of recovering the self following colonial rule was the Caribbean-born writer and psychologist Frantz Fanon (1925–1961). Examples of anticolonial violence against civilian populations in the immediate postwar period include both Jewish and Arab actions in Palestine and Algerian resistance to the French.

Terrorism developed in tandem with the globalization of world news. It moved into a new era in the 1960s and early 1970s. Key examples include: the Palestine Liberation Organization (PLO), founded in 1964, consisting of a number of organizations, the largest being Fatah; Provisional IRA, founded in 1969; and the Basque-separatist organization Euzkadi Ta Azkatasuna (ETA) (Basque Fatherland and Liberty), founded in 1959. Anticapitalist terrorist organizations founded in the 1970s include the Baader-Meinhof gang in Germany, which developed into the Red Army Faction; Brigatte Rossi in Italy, founded in 1969; and Sendero Luminoso (Shining Path) in Peru, founded in 1970.

The Arab-Israeli Six-Day War of 1967 sparked a new wave of Palestinian terrorism, including the Popular Front for the Liberation of Palestine (PFLP), founded in 1969 by George Habash (1925–). In September 1970 the PFLP staged a spectacular series of hijackings, flying three planes to Amman, Jordan, and one to Cairo, Egypt, and then destroying the planes on the ground—all of which the world watched on TV. The kingdom of Jordan retaliated by expelling the Palestinian militants in what became known as "Black September." This action gave its name to the Black September organization (operational 1970–1974), whose exact relationship to the mainstream Fatah was kept deliberately vague as a propaganda strategy. In 1972 the Black September organization kidnapped eleven members of the Israeli team at the Munich Olympics, five of whom died (along with four terrorists) in a botched rescue attempt. In 1974 the United Nations recognized the PLO as the Palestinian government-in-exile, which improved the international standing both of its leader, Yasir Arafat (1929–), and the Palestinian cause.

The later 1970s saw the emergence of the Palestinian Abu Nidal Organization (ANO), which split violently from the PLO in 1974, and Hamas—whose name is the Arabic word for courage—an acronym for Harakat al-Muqawamah al-Islamiyya (Islamic Resistance Movement). Other significant groups that emerged at this time included Hezbollah (Party of God) in Lebanon, which was founded with Iranian support in 1982. Palestinian organizations have launched two concerted uprisings (intifada), the first lasting from December 1987 to September 1993 and the second, Al-Aqsa (named after the mosque in Jerusalem), in September 2000. Both were accompanied by international propaganda offensives. Distinguishing between acts of terrorism associated with the intifada and the violent responses of the State of Israel has been a major preoccupation of Israeli propaganda.

The 1990s saw the emergence of a new wave of militant Islamic organizations linked by such umbrella organizations as the International Muslim Brotherhood or Al Qaeda (The Base). Groups affiliated with these organizations conducted spectacular raids against American and other targets chosen for their symbolic value, culminating in the 11 September 2001 attacks against New York and Washington, D.C.

The condemnation of terrorism has long been a central feature in U.S. propaganda and became central to the War on Terrorism launched in the wake of 11 September. Earlier in 2001 the State Department had released a list of seven pariah states—Cuba, North Korea, Iran, Iraq, Libya, Sudan, and Syria—that sponsor terrorism with arms and/or propaganda facilities. Domestic terrorist groups within the United States have included the left-wing Weathermen (established in 1968) and radical right-wing "antigovernment" terrorists such as those responsible for the attack against the federal building in Oklahoma City in 1995.

Although terrorism is frequently portrayed in state propaganda as both irredeemably immoral and doomed to failure, by the end of the century there was no shortage of leaders associated with terrorist movements who had made the transition to conventional political leadership, including Yasir Arafat, Nelson Mandela (1918–), and Gerry Adams (1948–).

Nicholas J. Cull

See also Arab World; Atrocity Propaganda; Israel; Ireland; Laden, Osama bin; Netherlands, Belgium, and Luxembourg; Olympics; RFE/RL; Terrorism, War on

References: Nacos, Bridgette L. *Terrorism and the Media.* New York: Columbia University Press, 1994; Walzer, Michael. *Just and Unjust Wars.* New York: Basic Books, 2000; Weimann, Gabriel, and Conrad Winn. *The Theater of Terror: Mass Media and International Terrorism.* New York: Longman, 1994; Wright, Joanne. *Terrorist Propaganda: The Red Army Faction and the Provisional IRA, 1968–1986.* New York: St. Martin's, 1990.

Terrorism, War on (2001–)

This U.S.-led campaign, launched in the wake of terrorist attacks against the United States on 11 September 2001, included a military campaign in Afghanistan. Propaganda figured prominently in the War on Terrorism. The terrorist attacks were in and of themselves a form of propaganda by direct action. The terrorists selected their targets with an eye to their symbolic value and cultural resonance. In the aftermath of the attacks, U.S. president George W. Bush (1946–) set about the difficult task of building a coalition favoring retaliation against the Al Qaeda network, its leader, Osama bin Laden (1957–), and the Taliban regime in Afghanistan that condoned their activities.

The key to the U.S. propaganda strategy was to stress that its response was aimed at terrorists rather than Islam in general. This aim was not helped by the early faux pas of President Bush in referring to the campaign as a "crusade"—a term with negative historical echoes in the Islamic world. A second gaffe was committed in dubbing the campaign "Eternal Justice," which implicitly laid claim to two realms that Muslims believe to be the monopoly of God alone. The United States swiftly renamed its operation "Enduring Freedom." As the campaign developed, the West made several more attempts to display cultural sensitivity to the Islamic world. Bush and other world leaders visited mosques and speakers—including British prime minister Tony Blair (1953–)—couched their arguments against terrorism in Islamic terms, stressing the heritage of Islamic tolerance and the Koran's prohibition against killing civilians. The West's presentation of the Taliban stressed their involvement in the drug trade.

The War on Terrorism witnessed the deployment of all the mechanisms of propaganda and psychological warfare. The British announced a news initiative in cultural diplomacy intended to project the moderate views of British Muslims to the rest of the Islamic world. Radio played a key role since economic and religious conditions in Afghanistan ensured minimal TV viewership. The Taliban had used the radio station Radio Shariah as their principal propaganda weapon. In an effort to establish their supremacy, the allies made Radio Shariah an early bombing target. The West also stepped up its broadcasts to the region. The BBC World Service, Deutsche Welle, and the Voice of America all expanded programming. The RFE/RL revived their Reagan-era station Radio Free Afghanistan. The crisis sparked major debate over the content of U.S. radio broadcasts. In the wake of 11 September 2001, the State Department attempted to prevent the Voice of America (VOA) from carrying an interview with Taliban leader Mullah Mohammed Omar (1962–). VOA journalists insisted that their charter demanded evenhandedness and proceeded with the broadcast.

The United States also attempted to win the "hearts and minds" of the inhabitants of Afghanistan by dropping food parcels and leaflets explaining that the war was being fought against the Taliban, not the Afghan people, and criticizing the Taliban in terms of Islamic law. The U.S. psychological warfare aircraft, *Commando Solo,* broadcast similar material from powerful on-board transmitters to Afghan radio listeners. The Pentagon established an Office of Strategic Influence (OSI), under Brig. Gen. Simon P. Worden, to coordinate its psychological warfare against the Taliban the wider campaign against terrorism. The OSI retained the services of an international public relations consultancy, the

Rendon Group, and reserved the right to deal in black propaganda in neutral and allied media, which provoked a brief controversy when it was disclosed in early 2002. The wider effort to explain the war to the rest of the world was entrusted to a White House office called the Coalition Information Center (also known as the War Room), organized by presidential adviser Karen P. Hughes (1956–) in conjunction with Alistair Campbell (1957–), the British prime minister's press secretary. Initiatives included a campaign to highlight Taliban mistreatment of women that drew on the talents of first lady Laura Bush (1946–) and Tony Blair's wife, Cherie Blair (1954–).

Although lacking the technological resources of the West, the Taliban/Al Qaeda network also mounted a considerable propaganda campaign that utilized the popular Qatar-based TV station Al Jazeera. Osama bin Laden based his appeal to the Muslim world on the notion of a religious war between "faith and unbelief," arguing that all Muslims had a duty to defend their fellow believers against the United States. Like Saddam Hussein during the Gulf War, the Taliban made considerable capital by taking Western journalists to the sites of civilian bombing casualties. As the anti-Taliban Northern Alliance advanced, the Taliban finally held their first press conference of the war. In the United States television news stations acted as voluntary propagandists for the war on the home front. The most extreme endorsements came from the Fox network, founded by Rupert Murdoch (1931–) and Roger Ailes (1940–) in 1996. As the *New York Times* reported on 3 December 2001, "Osama bin Laden, according to Fox News Channel anchors, analysts and correspondents, is 'a dirtbag,' 'a monster' overseeing a 'web of hate.' His followers in Al Qaeda are 'terror goons.' Taliban fighters are 'diabolical' and 'henchmen.'"

The liberation of Kabul produced a final propaganda windfall for the United States in the form of a videotaped conversation in which

Osama bin Laden acknowledged responsibility for the attack of 11 September. The United States released the tape as justification for the campaign, although nations believing in Osama bin Laden's innocence contested its authenticity. The close of the campaign brought fresh propaganda challenges for the United States as press coverage of its treatment of Al Qaeda prisoners provoked criticism from Europe. In January 2002 President Bush used his State of the Union address to argue for a wider campaign against nations that sponsor terrorism. He borrowed World War II rhetoric when he referred to "an Axis of Evil" consisting of North Korea, Iraq, and Iran. Bush also wished to retain the OSI and to develop the Coalition Information Center into a coordinating body for all U.S. public diplomacy. In 2003 President Bush justified war against Iraq as part of the war on terrorism.

Nicholas J. Cull

See also Blair, Tony; Cold War; Gray Propaganda; Gulf War (2003); Laden, Osama bin; Murdoch, Rupert; Prisoners of War; Public Diplomacy; RFE/RL; Terrorism; VOA

References: Ahrens, Frank. "Crackling Signals." *Washington Post,* 10 November 2001; Becker, Elizabeth. "In the War on Terrorism, a Battle to Shape Opinion." *New York Times,* 11 November 2001; Dao, James, and Eric Schmitt. "Pentagon Readies Efforts to Sway Sentiment Abroad." *New York Times,* 19 February 2002; Jaffe, Greg. "Spreading the Word: An Elite Army Team Opens a New Front: The Afghan Mind." *Wall Street Journal,* 8 November 2001; Rutenberg, Jim. "Fox Portrays a War of Good and Evil, and Many Applaud." *New York Times,* 3 December 2001.

Thailand
See Southeast Asia

Thatcher, Margaret (1925–)
A former British Conservative prime minister, Margaret Thatcher (née Roberts) was born in Grantham, Lincolnshire. She studied chemistry at Oxford University and later switched to law, which she practiced in the

1950s. In 1959 she entered Parliament as Conservative M.P. for Finchley, in north London. Her regard for the United States was sharpened thanks to a visit in 1967 as part of a U.S. government visitors' program—hence she may be considered a recipient of cultural propaganda. Between 1970 and 1974 she served as secretary of state for education in Edward Heath's (1916–) cabinet, but she soon aligned herself with right-wing opposition to Heath's brand of conservatism and in 1975 was chosen as leader of the Conservative Party.

Thatcher possessed a keen understanding of the importance of one's image in politics. She was the first British politician to hire an image consultant; based on his advice, she lowered her vocal register to avoid sounding too strident. She also engaged the advertising agency Saatchi and Saatchi to manage her propaganda campaign in preparation for the general election of 1979—with stunning results. The best-known image from this campaign was a poster showing a looping line of unemployed people, with the caption: "Labour Isn't Working." Television broadcasts during the campaign used symbolic images; one depicted athletic coaches labeled "Labour Party" stopping a race to strap weights marked "taxes" onto British athletes. The Thatcher era had begun.

Thatcher's approach to politics privileged the leader. She declared that she was "not a consensus politician" and operated her own system of press briefings through Sir Bernard Ingham (1932–), her press secretary, a former journalist. This was a new development in British politics. Personally, Thatcher relished images of the nation and her rhetoric echoed that of Winston Churchill (1874–1965). In 1982 she was in her element, leading Britain's bid to recapture the Falkland Islands from their Argentinean invaders. In 1983 she marshaled these images to win a substantial second general election victory. The Thatcher government was prepared to use censorship in its battle against Irish terrorism. Thatcher argued that terrorists would be defeated if they were denied the "oxygen of publicity." She was also vociferous in her opposition to closer British ties to the European Community. Her great ally was her fellow conservative, U.S. President Ronald Reagan (1911–). Like Reagan, she took a hard line in her approach to the Communist threat. Unlike Reagan, however, she did not pump money into international broadcasting. The BBC World Service was cut back during the 1980s because of Thatcher's desire to reduce public spending and general skepticism about the broadcast media.

By the late 1980s Thatcher had lost her touch. Critics mocked her use of royal syntax in announcing to waiting reporters: "We have become a grandmother." Key members of her own party questioned her judgment, especially with regard to Europe. With an internal party leadership challenge underway, she resigned in 1990. After leaving office, Thatcher continued to promote her conservative ideology.

Nicholas J. Cull

See also BBC; Blair, Tony; Britain; Churchill, Winston; Civil Defense; Elections; Elections (Britain); Falklands/Malvinas War; Ireland; Labor/Antilabor; Murdoch, Rupert; Terrorism; World War II (Britain)

References: Ingham, Bernard. *Kill the Messenger.* London: HarperCollins, 1991; Young, Hugo. *One of Us: A Biography of Margaret Thatcher.* London: Macmillan, 1989.

Theater

Theater entails dramatic literature or its performance. The Greek word for viewing is the root of "theater" and "theory." Live theater requires not only text and actors but also an audience present in the same space. This fact distinguishes theater from film and television, which have much in common with it. The ancient Greeks and Romans loved theater; both civilizations built enormous outdoor amphitheaters, some of which survive intact and are still used on a regular basis. The first performances of preexisting texts occurred in Greece in the fifth century B.C.E. Following the fall of the Roman Empire, theater as an art form seems to have fallen into disuse, but since the Renaissance it has been an important mainstay of many cultures. Shakespeare (1564–1616) in England, Goethe (1749–1832) and Schiller (1759–1805) in Germany, and Racine (1639–1699) and Molière (1622–1673) in France are not only extraordinary playwrights but major interpreters of their respective countries' national cultures. In this sense these classic authors are both sources of cultural propaganda as well as the creators of plays that themselves make propagandistic statements. Theater has been a significant presence in Japan and China as well, though not in so central a fashion as in the West. The Renaissance also saw the development of commedia dell'arte, a popular form of often improvised comedy involving stock characters, some of whom wear masks.

Theater is related to organized religion, but it has historically been viewed as a rival. The early church fathers attacked the theater as a source of pagan thought. The medieval church featured elaborate religious dramas divorced from the popular brand of theater, where both the subject of the play and the actors themselves were considered enemies of morality. Only in more recent times has the theater been openly embraced by many organized religions as a method of bringing religion into the lives of persons not accustomed to regular churchgoing.

Theater is traditionally an urban art. The nineteenth century saw the rise of specialized types of theater for specific productions—often in a single large city. Opera or ballet, light opera, revivals of the classics, new serious works, and such popular types of theater as melodrama, farce, and vaudeville all had a particular group concerned with its production. The system worked well until about 1900, when new types of plays threatened the prevailing system. Soon thereafter film would threaten the very survival of theater itself. Since 1900 regional theaters have provided a venue for experimental productions often associated with artistic and bohemian culture.

Theater is inevitably associated with drama, the Greek word for action. Actors represent human actions by impersonating characters on a stage. Plays and dramas are nearly synonymous, starting with Greek masterpieces such as Aeschylus's (525–456 B.C.E.) *Agamemnon* and *Peace* and Aristophanes' *Lysistrata*. Christopher Marlowe's (1564–1593) *Tamburlaine* (1587) depicts a fourteenth-century Scythian shepherd, Alexander the Great's successor, whose impulse for absolute power leads him to conquer most of the known world. In such dramas the topic of war leads to political commentary on just and unjust rulers or the ability of the weak to triumph over the strong thanks to God's intervention.

Many of the world's greatest plays concern war, cynically defined by the American satirist Ambrose Bierce (1842–ca.1914) in his *A Devil's Dictionary* as a "by-product of the arts of peace." William Shakespeare wrote history plays filled with battles, like *Henry V* (1599), *Richard III* (c. 1593), and *King John* (c. 1594). His play *Othello* (c. 1604) concerns a great soldier undone by jealousy. In *King Lear* (c. 1605) war is rarely from Lear's mind. In more recent times, one thinks of the soldier in Georg Büchner's (1813–1837) *Woyzeck* (published in 1879, though written in 1837). George Bernard Shaw's (1856–1950) *Arms and the Man* (1894), concerns war profiteers; his *Heartbreak House* (1919) ends with a bombardment; and in *Saint Joan* (1923) war and religious faith are united in the figure of Joan of Arc.

One of the most frequently produced of all twentieth-century plays is Bertolt Brecht's (1898–1956) *Mother Courage and Her Children* (1938), which, though set during the Thirty Years' War (1618–1648), actually concerns political courage under the Nazi regime. Some war dramas address history, such as Rolf Hochhuth's (1931–) play *The Deputy* (1963), which concerns the alleged complicity of Pope Pius XII in the killing of the Jews; when first shown, it occasioned protests by Roman Catholics in many European cities. Ts'au Yu's (1911–) *Thunderstorm* (1933), one of China's most often-produced plays, combines ample melodrama with the depiction of an industrialist whose mind-set contributes to the continuing tensions of the Chinese civil war.

David Culbert

See also Britain; China; Peace and Antiwar Movements (1500–1945); Peace and Antiwar Movements (1945–); Shakespeare, William
Reference: Brockett, Oscar G. *History of the Theater.* Boston: Houghton Mifflin, 1982; Gassner, John, and Edward Quinn. *The Reader's Encyclopedia of World Drama.* New York: Viking, 1969; Girard, Rene. *Violence and the Sacred.* Trans. Patrick Gregory. Baltimore, MD: Johns Hopkins University Press, 1977.

Tokyo Rose

The case of Tokyo Rose figures twice in the history of propaganda, first as an element in Japanese World War II radio propaganda against the United States and then as an example of postwar anti-Japanese propaganda within the United States. Tokyo Rose was the name given to Iva Ikuko Toguri d'Aquino (1916–), a Japanese-American woman tried for treason in 1949. Throughout the 1930s Japanese radio broadcast English-language programs aimed at Western audiences. Following the attack on Pearl Harbor in December 1941, the frequency of these broadcasts escalated as the Japanese military deployed radio to weaken the enemy's resolve. The most famous of these broadcasts supposedly headlined a woman who was given the nickname Tokyo Rose by G.I.s. The 1949 treason trial singled out Iva Toguri as the main broadcaster, even though it became increasingly clear that supporting evidence remained scant. The plight of Tokyo Rose reflected the awkward situation of the *nisei,* or Japanese-Americans, who had been stranded in wartime Japan. Some, like Toguri, had worked for various Japanese English-language news organizations in Japan during the war. Ultimately the trial revealed that there was no single Tokyo Rose, nor anyone who referred to themselves as such, but for postwar America the appellation became synonymous with treasonous propaganda for the imperial Japanese.

The U.S. courts convicted Toguri and sent her to federal prison, where she remained until paroled in 1956. As a result of her conviction, the U.S. government stripped her of her American citizenship and initiated deportation proceedings. She successfully appealed to remain in the United States as a stateless person. After long neglecting her case, the Japanese American Citizens' League took action and began to press Toguri to take redress against the government. In 1976, on the day before he was to leave office, U.S. President Gerald Ford (1913–) granted her a full presidential pardon, restoring her rights as an American citizen.

Barak Kushner

See also Australia; Japan; Radio (International); World War II (Japan)

References: Chapman, Ivan. *Tokyo Calling: The Charles Cousens Case.* Sydney: Hale and Iremonger, 1990; Duus, Masayo. *Tokyo Rose: Orphan of the Pacific.* New York: Kodansha International, 1979; Fujita, Frank. *Foo: A Japanese-American Prisoner of the Rising Sun.* Denton: University of North Texas, 1993; Meo, L. D. *Japan's Radio War on Australia.* Melbourne: Melbourne University Press, 1968.

Triumph of the Will (Triumph des Willens) (1935)

This documentary film directed by Leni Riefenstahl (1902–) has become the most famous piece of propaganda associated with the Nazi regime (1889–1945). The film records the Nazi Party rally held at Nuremberg in 1934. Highlights include the majestic descent of Hitler's plane through the clouds and the aircraft's shadow overspreading marching columns of party members on the ground; the adoration of the crowd as Hitler drives by in his car; the vast spectacle of uni-

formed soldiers assembling to hear their Führer speak; and a shot of Hitler and his entourage marching through a human avenue on his way to deliver a speech. Although critics hailed the film as a masterpiece, there is little evidence of its having captured the imagination of Germans at the time. It was not widely circulated overseas during the 1930s, although it won prizes at the Venice Film Festival (1935) and at the Paris World's Fair in 1937. In providing eloquent visual testimony to the regimentation and power of Hitler's regime, the film proved an invaluable resource for Allied propagandists seeking to rally anti-Nazi feeling during World War II; clips of Riefenstahl's film were used to good advantage in the U.S. army's "Why We Fight" series.

Nicholas J. Cull

See also Exhibitions and World's Fairs; Film (Documentary); Germany; Goebbels, Joseph; Hitler, Adolph; Riefenstahl, Leni; Why We Fight

Souvenir program of Leni Riefenstahl's Triumph des Willens (Triumph of the Will), 1935. *The Prussian eagle and the Hakenkreuz. (Courtesy of David Culbert)*

References: Barsum, Richard Meran. *Filmguide to Triumph of the Will.* Bloomington: Indiana University Press, 1975; Hinton, David B. *The Films of Leni Riefenstahl.* Metuchen, NJ: Scarecrow, 1991; Salkeld, Audrey. *A Portrait of Leni Riefenstahl.* London: Jonathan Cape, 1996; Welch, David. *Propaganda and the German Cinema 1933–1945.* London: I. B. Tauris, 2001.

Trotsky, Leon (1879–1940)

The pseudonym of Russian revolutionary Lev Davidovich Bronstein, Trotsky was one of the most brilliant propagandists of the twentieth century. Born into a Jewish family in the Ukraine and educated in Odessa, he became a Marxist in the 1890s. Arrested in 1898 and imprisoned in Siberia in 1900, he escaped to the West in 1902 by utilizing a fake passport in the name of his jailer, Trotsky. In London he cooperated with Vladimir Ilyich Lenin (1870–1924) on the revolutionary journal *Iskra* (Spark). In 1903, when the Social Democratic Party split into Bolshevik and Menshevik factions, Trotsky was a propagandist for the Mensheviks. He returned to Russia and chaired the Soviet in Saint Petersburg during the revolution of 1905. Forced into exile again after the revolution, he worked as a journalist and revolutionary propagandist, arguing against World War I. One of his refuges was New York City, where he edited a journal entitled *Novi Mir* (New World). In the spring of 1917 he returned to Russia, joined the Bolshevik Party, and became a key planner of the Bolshevik-led October Revolution.

Trotsky served in the Bolshevik government as commissar for foreign affairs. Next, as commissar for war, he organized a 5-million-strong Red Army in the civil war against the anti-Bolshevik forces (1918–1921). Following the death of Lenin in 1924, he was involved in a power struggle with Joseph Stalin (1879–1953), which ended with his expulsion from the Politburo in 1926, from the party in 1927, followed by exile to Central Asia in 1928, and finally exile beyond Russia's borders in 1929. In his absence, Trotsky became a key figure in Stalinist propaganda: the traitor behind numerous alleged conspiracies. His so-called confederates suffered in show trials (1936–1938), during which they delivered scripted confessions. Trotsky himself was tried and sentenced to death in absentia in 1937.

Living in exile in Turkey, France, Norway, and finally in Mexico, Trotsky continued to argue against Stalin and produced a stream of newspaper articles and books in support of his vision of a "perpetual revolution," as opposed to Stalin's drive for "socialism in one country." To this end he organized a so-called Fourth International. His books include *History of the Russian Revolution* (1932) and *The Revolution Betrayed* (1937). He was murdered in Mexico City in 1940 on Stalin's orders. Trotsky's commitment to a global revolution and the wit and passion of his writing assured him a global audience for his ideas. Forty years after his death, the three-way struggle between the Trotskyites and Stalinists, on one side, and moderates, on the other, was still being fought out in internecine battles within the left.

Nicholas J. Cull

See also Capa, Robert; International; Lenin, Vladimir Ilyich; Revolution, Russian; Stalin, Joseph

References: Cliff, Tony. *Trotsky.* 4 vols. London: Bookmarks, 1989–1993; ———. *Trotskyism after Trotsky: The Origins of the International Socialists.* London: Bookmarks, 1999; Volkogonov, Dmitri. *Trotsky: The Eternal Revolutionary.* London: HarperCollins, 1997.

Turkey

See Ottoman Empire/Turkey

U

Uncle Sam

A national figure symbolizing the United States, Uncle Sam emerged during the nineteenth century and became a staple of propaganda illustration both for and against the U.S. government in the twentieth century. He is often thought of as the counterpart of the rotund British archetype John Bull.

The earliest national symbols in America (used in Revolutionary-era cartoons) were the goddesslike Columbia (who later became overlaid with the allegorical figure of Liberty) and the self-confident American "everyman" figures like Yankee Doodle and Brother Jonathan. Uncle Sam emerged during the Anglo-American War of 1812. There are two stories concerning his origin. The name Uncle Sam was first attached to a genial meat packer named "Uncle" Samuel Wilson (1766–1854) of Troy, New York. Wilson sold meat to the U.S. army through a merchant, Elbert Anderson, which duly arrived branded with the initials EAUS (Elbert Anderson United States). The soldiers joked that the letters stood for Elbert Anderson and Uncle Sam. At the same time, journalists opposed to the war began to use the term "Uncle Sam" in propaganda as a derisive nickname for American soldiers and customs officials (a reference to the letters *U.S.* on their uniforms). The term swiftly came to signify the entire U.S. government apparatus.

Uncle Sam's costume, consisting of striped trousers and top hat, first emerged in the 1830s but were originally the attributes of a completely different figure named Maj. Jack Downing, a comic Yankee character created by Maine journalist Seba Smith (1792–1868). Jack Downing, the archetypal political office seeker in Jacksonian Washington, D.C., swiftly became a familiar archetype in the cartoons of the era. By the time of the Civil War, Uncle Sam frequently wore the same costume. Celebrated users of the Uncle Sam character include the cartoonist Thomas Nast (1840–1902) of *Harper's Weekly* fame, who gave Uncle Sam his characteristic goatee and lean look, and World War I poster artist James Montgomery Flagg (1877–1960). Uncle Sam has also figured in satirical cartoons and anti-American cartoon propaganda, such as those published in the Soviet magazine *Krokodil* (Crocodile). In 1961 the U.S. Congress formally acknowledged Samuel Wilson as the original Uncle Sam.

Nicholas J. Cull

See also Cartoons; Flagg, James Montgomery; Nast, Thomas; Posters

References: Katchum, Alton, *Uncle Sam: The Man and the Legend.* New York: Hill and Wang, 1959;

World War I recruiting poster by James Montgomery Flagg, based on an earlier British poster, in which Uncle Sam takes the place of Secretary of War Kitchener. (Corbis)

King, Nancy. *A Cartoon History of United States Foreign Policy from 1945 to the Present.* Washington, DC: Foreign Policy Association, 1991.

Uncle Tom's Cabin (1852)

Serialized in 1851 in newspaper installments and published as a book in 1852, this novel represents the most famous example of abolitionist propaganda. Three hundred thousand copies were sold in the United States alone during its first year in print, making it a key text of the abolitionist movement. Harriet Beecher Stowe (1811–1896) used the techniques of sensational women's fiction to highlight the multiple abuses of slavery in the South of the United States. The novel helped set opinion in the North on a collision course with the South that could only be resolved by a civil war. *Uncle Tom's Cabin* was based on authentic documents and testimony about the slave system, which Harriet Beecher Stowe later collected and published, but it was her skill as a novelist that gave the work its impact. Readers on both sides of the Atlantic were captivated by such dramatic moments as the slave girl Eliza scrambling toward freedom across the ice floes of the Ohio River. Abraham Lincoln acknowledged the novel's importance, reputedly greeting Stowe with the words: "So you're the little woman who wrote the book that made this great war." The novel was frequently abbreviated for stage performances known as "Tom Shows," and it was here that the dignified character of the old slave Tom became the shuffling stereotype of the subservient "Uncle Tom." Ironically, a character invented to help free black Americans became as synonymous with their cultural degradation as a work of overt racism like *The Birth of a Nation* (1915).

Nicholas J. Cull

See also Abolitionism/Antislavery Movement; Civil War, United States; Novel

References: Gossett, Thomas. *Uncle Tom's Cabin and American Culture.* Dallas, TX: Southern Methodist University, 1985; Stowe, Harriet Beecher. *Uncle Tom's Cabin.* 1852. Reprint, London: Penguin, 1981.

United Nations

The key international organization, the UN was founded in 1945 following over a century of worldwide campaigning and represented the central promise of Allied propaganda during World War II. Subsequently the UN became a key forum for international debates and attendant propaganda. UN organizations have sponsored health, human rights, and cultural campaigns.

The idea of a parliament of nations first emerged when Quaker colonist William Penn (1644–1718) wrote "An Essay towards the Present and Future Peace of Europe, by the establishment of an European Diet, Parliament or Estates" (1693). The same idea of a league of states to underwrite peace surfaced in the work of Charles Irénée Castel, abbé de Saint-Pierre (1658–1743), who in 1713 wrote his *Projet de la paix perpétuelle* (A Scheme for Perpetual Peace). The idea became a staple of the international peace movement of the nineteenth century and began to take shape at the end of the century, when the first International Peace Conference of 1899 was held at The Hague, the Netherlands. U.S. president Theodore Roosevelt (1858–1919) endorsed the notion of a League of Peace in his Nobel Peace Prize acceptance speech of 1910, and President Woodrow Wilson (1856–1924) made his own vision of a League of Nations the core of U.S. propaganda in World War I (1914–1918).

The Versailles Conference (1919) not only established the League of Nations but also sparked the creation of a network of global international organizations. These organizations ranged from intellectual bodies, such as the United States Council on Foreign Relations and the British Royal Institute of International Affairs (Chatham House) to mass-membership organizations such as the British League of Nations Union, led by Lord

Robert Cecil (1864–1958). The league became a forum for international debate and arbitration. Unfortunately, member states invoked the propaganda tool of resigning in protest and the league (which already lacked U.S. membership) could do little to prevent World War II. The key to future peace resided in establishing a new organization and winning American support for it.

The idea of a new organization for collective security was at the heart of the Atlantic Charter, which the still officially neutral U.S. president Franklin Roosevelt (1882–1945) and the beleaguered British prime minister Winston Churchill (1874–1964) signed in August 1941. The Atlantic Charter became the core of a joint United Nations declaration signed by all the Allied powers on 1 January 1942. The British Inter-Allied Information Committee, formed to feed Allied propaganda to a neutral American audience, now became the United Nations Information Committee (under a U.S. director), which promoted internationalism and awareness of the Allied war effort by supplying material to the U.S. press, promoting United Nations days, and even organizing a television pageant in 1942. Advocates of internationalism within the United States included lawyer and Republican presidential candidate Wendell Willkie (1892–1944) and film mogul Darryl F. Zanuck (1902–1979), who produced *Wilson* (1944), a valentine to U.S. president Wilson and the lost opportunities of 1919. By the end of the war the U.S. public was solidly behind membership in an international organization.

As the powers prepared to meet in San Francisco in 1945 to lay down the foundations of the UN, a group of graphic designers (led by one Oliver Lundquist) from the U.S. Office of Strategic Services (OSS) designed its globe and laurel wreath logo, originally intended only for conference security passes. Early drafts of the globe for the logo cut off the bottom of South America because the design team resented Argentina's support for Fascism. The sky-blue background color was selected to represent peace; the shade was named Stettinius blue in honor of U.S. secretary of state Edward Stettinius (1900–1949). The logo and color was applied more generally and later figured not only on UN flags and vehicles but on the berets and helmets of UN peacekeeping forces.

The UN Charter of 1945 established a benchmark for the fundamental elements of international behavior and gave the UN a mandate to promote human rights around the globe, culminating in the Universal Declaration of Human Rights of 1948. Early UN resolutions included number 59 (I) of 1945, which declared: "Freedom of Information is a fundamental human right," and resolution number 110 (II) of 1947, which condemned propaganda against peace. Successive U.S. secretary-generals have eloquently defended the cause of peace, most notably Dag Hammarskjöld (1905–1961) of Sweden and Kofi Annan (1938–) of Ghana. However, from its inception the UN also became a central venue for international debate and propaganda, and capturing the blue flag became a perennial propaganda tactic of the Cold War and after.

Membership in the UN Security Council has been an issue in its own right, with the United States spending decades defending the position of Taiwan on the council and arguing for the exclusion of the Peoples Republic of China. In 1947 the NAACP attempted to use the moral force of the UN in American domestic politics, presenting an appeal to the United Nations protesting the treatment of black Americans. In 1950 the United States also took full advantage of the UN mandate to wage the Korean War. Leaders such as Nikita Khrushchev (1894–1971) of the USSR and Fidel Castro (1927–) of Cuba used the General Assembly as a platform for their personal agendas. A celebrated U.S. ambassador to the UN was Adlai Stevenson (1900–1965), who countered Communist propaganda during the Cuban Missile Crisis, though not without distorting the truth. As decolonization swelled the ranks of the General Assembly, its resolutions increasingly reflected the needs and views of the developing world. UN resolutions have condemned the apartheid system in South Africa and Israeli actions in the Middle East. The British secured a UN mandate before launching the Falklands/Malvinas War of 1982 and the United States and its allies secured a UN mandate before launching the Gulf War of 1991. Within the United States the UN is a frequent rallying point in right-wing propaganda, from Senate Republicans who successfully blocked payment of UN dues in the 1990s to extreme "Militia" members who warn against a UN conspiracy to conquer and control the United States.

The United Nations has become an active player in the world of international communications through its commissions and agencies. The United Nations Educational, Scientific, and Cultural Organization (UNESCO) in Paris, founded in 1945 (and a UN agency since 1946), has promoted education and intellectual exchange around the world. UNESCO attracted controversy in the 1970s when the Third World membership initiated a drive for a so-called New World International Communications Order. The specifics seemed to play into the hands of the Soviet Union and dictatorships in the developing world at the expense of Western commercial broadcasters. In the mid-1980s the United States and Britain resigned from UNESCO in protest, though Britain rejoined in 1997. Among the other UN agencies, the World Health Organization (WHO), founded in 1948 and based in Geneva, has deployed international propaganda in the cause of public health. The office of the United Nations High Commissioner for Refugees (UNHCR), founded in 1951, and the United Nations International Children's Fund (UNICEF), founded in 1946, have both publicized the plight of people in their care; in the case of UNICEF, their welfare is dependent on maintaining the voluntary funding upon which the agency depends. UN news management during the peacekeeping and negotiation process

in the Bosnian crisis of the 1990s was criticized for partisanship. Some analysts have argued that the UN should develop a capability for conducting tactical psychological operations as part of its peacekeeping mission.

Nicholas J. Cull

See also Bosnian Crisis and War; Grierson, John; Gulf War; Korean War; Peace and Antiwar Movements (1500–1945)

References: Cull, Nicholas J. "Selling Peace: The Origins, Promotion and Face of the Anglo-American New Order during the Second World War." *Diplomacy and Statecraft* 7 (March 1996): 1–28; Finkelstein, Lawrence S., ed. *Politics in the United Nations System.* Durham, NC: Duke University Press, 1988; Stoessinger, John. *The UN and the Superpowers.* New York: Random House, 1977; Taylor, Philip M. *Global Communications, International Affairs and the Media Since 1945.* London: Routledge, 1997.

United States

The United States of America would not have come into being without propaganda, nor would its society exist as currently constituted. Yet the average American continues to take comfort in the notion that propaganda is something one associates with Nazi Germany, neatly distinguishing between propaganda and advertising by defining the latter as dealing with information or persuasion and the former as a form of deception. Collective amnesia is too strong a way to characterize this curious state of affairs, but it takes some doing to live in a society that is the world's greatest consumer of propaganda while at the same time convincing oneself that this is not so.

The history of American governance is largely based on English precedent. The Revolution of 1776 turned on arguments over the limits of royal authority, using not only a common language but a common mode of political propaganda: the broadside. Any successful revolution requires a method to mobilize mass support, and the American Revolution would have been inconceivable without Thomas Paine's (1737–1809) *Common Sense* (1776), a tract that sold perhaps

500,000 copies in a country with three million inhabitants. American governance is also connected to the medium of the newspaper, the first of which, the *Boston News-Letter,* appeared in 1704. Colonial newspapers turned increasingly to issues of governance. In 1735 Andrew Hamilton (1676?–1741) successfully defended the right of journalist John Peter Zenger (1697–1746) to attack the royal authorities, using the defense against seditious libel termed the "right of exposing and opposing arbitrary power." Political propaganda was crucial in selling Americans on the benefits of the conservative Constitution of the United States. Alexander Hamilton (1755–1804), James Madison (1751–1836) and John Jay (1745–1829) wrote *The Federalist Papers* (1787), a series of anonymous articles placed in newspapers to justify an entire series of political compromises, part of the system of checks and balances in place to this day.

Early parliamentary debate in U.S. colonial society was often marked by a coarseness of expression, especially from those no apologist has ever tried to place on a marble pedestal. When Congressman Matthew Lyon (1749–1822) took exception to the remarks of a fellow legislator, he seized a fireplace tool and tried to club his opponent, who had grabbed a tool himself during the fracas in the legislative chamber. The act of persuasion thus contributed the hammer-and-tongs assault to American political discourse. British readers savored an oft-reproduced cartoon depicting the scene, with the English artist making sure to do justice to the appearance of such "refined" gentlemen.

Propaganda and persuasion found constant use in the election campaigns of the Republic's early days. A broadside of 1815 mocked the unhappy timing of Harrison Gray Otis (1765–1848), leader of New England's secessionist Hartford Convention of 1814. Otis set sail for Washington, D.C., bringing news of Andrew Jackson's (1767–1845) victory over the British in the Battle of New Orleans and the end of the War of 1812. The Hartford Convention also marked the end of the Federalist Party and inaugurated the first two-party system in the United States. The broadside showed Otis riding in a chamber pot, while asking his fellow secessionists: "Did you ever know a ship like ours fill from the bottom?" Political oratory traded in deception and false promises—and not simply because much of the electorate was at best semiliterate. In 1820 Rep. Felix Walker (1753–1828) interrupted a House of Representatives debate with a long, dull, irrelevant speech, explaining to his colleagues: "I'm talking for Buncombe" (the North Carolina county he represented). Shortened to "bunk," the word continues to play an important role in American political life, where there is a ready market for pretentious nonsense meant for hometown consumption. Also playing a role in early political propaganda was the "hatchetman," whose function was to clear the way for a military group advancing through the woods; it was subsequently used to refer to partisan attacks clearing the path for a leader who wished to appear "above politics."

Early American political discourse traded heavily in the possibility of self-advancement and the presumptive openness of America to those not well born. From 1840 onward it was a given that every presidential candidate be born in a log cabin even if patently untrue. In a frontier society "stump oratory" was a way of life for candidates. The office seeker stood on a tree stump to address farmers, who had walked for miles to listen to him. Not surprisingly, the term became synonymous with the stump speech, a type of bombastic, inflammatory oratory still current in recent campaigns. Before the Civil War, it was difficult for candidates to reach a large audience. Voices carried only a short distance in the open; newspapers were often published weekly and distributed through a precarious mail system; much of the potential electorate either did not or could not vote. It seemed that a democratic society admired the idea of democratic institutions while lacking the ability to make such institutions function.

The Constitution's Bill of Rights guaranteed a free press and freedom of speech. Yet as early as 1798 Congress passed the Alien and Sedition Acts, making it a crime to criticize John Adams (1735–1826), Federalist president of the United States. Though this notorious legislation was soon permitted to expire, it left behind a legacy threatening to those considering an open attack on any incumbent administration. No propaganda had greater impact than the *Appeal* published in 1829 in Boston by David Walker (ca. 1796–1830), a black man. His lengthy tract urged slaves to use violence to gain their freedom, sending great waves of fear throughout the slaveholding South. Indeed, the entire abolitionist struggle (1820–1860) represents a defining moment in U.S. propaganda. A great moral wrong was debated in special-interest publications, but it was generally not talked about on the floor of Congress; on this subject America's political institutions proved incapable of nonviolent compromise. The one piece of propaganda that did the most to make the abolitionist case was *Uncle Tom's Cabin* (1852), by Harriet Beecher Stowe (1811–1896); it sold 300,000 copies in its first year of publication. It did not cause the Civil War, but it did make the moral case for outright abolition in a way no Southern apologist could match.

It should come as no surprise that in the twentieth century many moral crusades have turned to visual symbolism. The first photograph was made in 1839; that same year photographers had already opened for business in New Orleans. The photographic likeness increasingly became part and parcel of political discourse. Early daguerreotypes could not be reproduced, though likenesses could be transferred to engravings on wood or steel (lithographs) for reproduction in newspapers or broadsides. Abraham Lincoln (1809–1865) was the first American political leader to embrace the photograph as a symbolic means of communication. His singular looks were a ready subject for his self-deprecating humor. Lincoln's presidency coincided with a new technology, making possible the reproduction of photographic images on paper, known as the carte de visite. The human cost of presidential leadership in the Civil War can be seen by contrasting images of Lincoln in 1860 and in the spring of 1865. His homeliness added the word "Lincolnesque" to our vocabulary to describe someone of surpassing ugliness. His features, however, also reflect a sense of integrity and suffering; they are therefore part of his symbolic legacy as America's greatest president.

Propaganda and persuasion are bound up with twentieth-century electronic communication. Increased levels of literacy have resulted in an educated citizenry that requires an underlying reason from those who seek support for specific policies. They are also tied to advertising and its need to create and maintain consumer demand for luxury goods. Effective propaganda is linked to motion pictures. Thomas Edison's (1847–1931) short political films were a hit during the Spanish-American War of 1898. The newsreel *Pathé's Weekly* went into operation in 1911, political broadcasting began on Pittsburgh's radio station KDKA in 1920, and the first American TV station went on the air in 1941. Television was a curiosity for the rich until after 1945; it was not used for political persuasion until the Federal Communications Commission (FCC) lifted its so-called Freeze Order in April 1952.

The electronic media have greatly aided the president's ability to make what Theodore Roosevelt (1858–1919) called a "bully pulpit" to persuade Americans of presidential programs. Franklin D. Roosevelt (1882–1945) adopted an intimate style in his so-called fireside chats, national radio addresses employing a conversational tone to allay public fears about the economic crisis, particularly in 1933–1934. Richard Nixon (1913–1994) saved his political career by appearing on national television in 1952; he explained away charges of campaign irregularities by claiming he would keep his dog "Checkers"—an effective red herring for viewers in that bygone era. Presidential campaigning has involved national radio addresses and (since 1960) televised presidential debates, which have transferred the stump speech to another medium.

War has tempted the government to seek temporary ways of restricting the oppositional potential of the media. The Sedition Act of 1917 and the notorious Espionage Act of 1918 enabled Woodrow Wilson (1856–1924) to send to prison anyone criticizing the war effort; the Supreme Court upheld wartime restrictions on freedom of speech and the press in *Schenck v. United States* (1919), where Justice Oliver Wendell Holmes (1841–1933) famously declared that "no citizen has the right to cry 'fire' falsely in a crowded theater."

Fears of oppositional propaganda mean that the electronic media have not been given full citizenship when it comes to freedom of speech. In the FCC's 1941 Mayflower ruling, broadcasters were told they could not editorialize; this so-called Fairness Doctrine was upheld in *Red Lion Broadcasting v. FCC* (1969), where the courts ruled in favor of denying a broadcast license to someone "not serving the public interest, convenience, and necessity." The print media have never been so rigidly controlled—though not because a journalist believes the federal government cannot do him or her harm.

The Vietnam War was free of official censorship, at least in theory; the result has seemingly given governments the world over a lesson in how not to manage information. The Gulf War in 1991 saw a different approach, in which the U.S. military carefully controlled the flow of information. It seems likely this will continue. Cable television has dramatically altered the way Americans gain information about politicians, products, and services. Today the Internet is already part of this information superhighway, but those who imagine that this marks an end to government news management must keep in mind the potential of electronic eavesdropping, an acute danger for the lobbyist as well

as the average citizen. Propaganda and persuasion are at the heart of a troubling relationship very much a part of today's world: the conflict between a government's eagerness to hide some or all of what it is doing and the citizen's right to full disclosure. It is sometimes alleged that U.S. success often involves a victory in terms of scale. This may very well be the case, as the United States is the largest consumer and disseminator of propaganda and persuasion in history.

David Culbert

See also Abolitionism/Antislavery Movement; ADL; *Birth of a Nation;* Capra, Frank; CIA; Civil Rights Movement; Civil War, United States; Clinton, William Jefferson; CNN; Cold War; CPI; Drugs; Environmentalism; Film (Documentary); Film (Feature); Film (Newsreels); Garvey, Marcus; Gulf War; Holocaust Denial; Internet; Kennedy, John F.; King, Martin Luther, Jr.; Labor/Antilabor; Latin America; Lincoln, Abraham; Malcolm X; Marshall Plan; McCarthy, Joseph R.; Mexico; Murrow, Edward R.; NAACP; Nast, Thomas; Nixon, Richard; OWI; Paine, Thomas; Peace and Antiwar Movements (1900–1945); Peace and Antiwar Movements (1945–); *The Plow that Broke the Plains;* Psychological Warfare; Reagan, Ronald; Religion; Revolution, American, and War of Independence; RFE/RL; Roosevelt, Franklin D.; Spanish-American War; Television; Temperance; Terrorism, War on; Uncle Sam; *Uncle Tom's Cabin;* United States (1930s); United States (Progressive Era); USIA; Vietnam War; VOA; Why We Fight; Women's Movement: First Wave/Suffrage; Women's Movement: Second Wave/Feminism; World War I; World War II (United States)

References: Braestrup, Peter. *Big Story: How the American Press and Television Reported and Interpreted the Crisis of Tet 1968 in Vietnam and Washington.* 2 vols. Boulder, CO: Westview, 1977; Davidson, Philip. *Propaganda and the American Revolution, 1763–1783.* New York: Norton, 1973; Doherty, Thomas. *Projections of War: Hollywood, American Culture, and World War II.* New York: Columbia University Press, 1993; Donovan, Robert J., and Ray Scherer. *Unsilent Revolution: Television News and American Public Life.* New York: Cambridge University Press, 1992; Vaughn, Stephen L. *Holding Fast the Inner Lines: Democracy, Nationalism, and the Committee on Public Information.* Chapel Hill: University of North Carolina Press, 1980; Winfield, Betty

Houchin. *FDR and the News Media*. New York: Columbia University Press, 1994.

United States (1930s)

U.S. propaganda in the 1930s relates directly—but not exclusively—to President Franklin Roosevelt's (1882–1945) New Deal program. Roosevelt himself was a masterful public speaker. His voice had a certain aristocratic quality that he made no attempt to disguise. His sense of timing meant that he understood how to give listeners—radio being the primary mass medium in the United States in the 1930s—enough time to savor a particular phrase. Roosevelt's chief speechwriter was his longtime friend Samuel Rosenman, but many of FDR's memorable phrases were his own, as can be seen by noting Roosevelt's penciled emendations to typescripts prepared by others. For example, in his first reelection speech on 8 October 1940 in Philadelphia, the ironic suggestion that "Republican orators" were shedding "tears—crocodile tears" at the prospect of taking charge of New Deal programs was his own idea—and his audience loved the humor.

Roosevelt felt he was his own best propagandist, although he distrusted the ability of propaganda to cover up official shortcomings. Roosevelt sold his New Deal policies in a relatively few so-called fireside chats, in which the president spoke to the nation in a less formal style than was the custom for presidents. Visitors to the White House saw the fireplace (with fake logs) where Roosevelt made his national radio addresses, carried "as a public service" by the major networks. Roosevelt also sold his programs in a series of newsreel appearances, in which he was almost always shown seated, a convention explained by the unwritten rule that the president was not to be photographed from the waist down in deference to his physical handicap. Finally, for much of his presidency Roosevelt met with the press corps twice a week, a rather extraordinary instance of official openness to the media. In reality, FDR engaged in a game of wits with members of the press corps, often going out of his way to disguise what was going on. Roosevelt enjoyed cordial relations with many reporters—at least through 1940. Later, when his health began to fail, he held press conferences less frequently.

Other New Deal propaganda, very much second in importance to Roosevelt's own efforts, is also worth noting. In the field of documentary film, Pare Lorentz (1905–1992) made *The Plow That Broke the Plains* (1936) and *The River* (1937). The former explained the causes of drought in the Midwest (the dust bowl) as simple greed on the part of farmers. New Deal conservation measures, the narration insisted, would solve the problem. *The River* premiered in New Orleans, Louisiana, which was appropriate for a film about flood control through a series of New Deal dams constructed by the Tennessee Valley Authority (TVA). Again the fault lay with the greed of the shortsighted individual—this time the lumberjack was accused—and the problem was to be remedied through federal conservation measures. Both films featured scores by Virgil Thomson (1896–1989), who used American folk tunes with great skill to underscore the destruction of natural resources by thoughtless businessmen. Much of New Deal propaganda was either explicitly or implicitly antibusiness.

Documentary photography played a significant role as a tool for New Deal propaganda. The Farm Security Administration (FSA) hired a handful of photographers to travel around the United States photographing rural life, especially the poor. Walker Evans (1903–1975) is the best-known photographer who worked for the FSA; his cool, beautifully composed images reveal the neat, orderly interiors of those poor folk who aspire to the middle-class ideal of cleanliness. One should not ignore the work of Russell Lee (1903–1975) or Dorothea Lange (1895–1965); the latter's "Migrant Mother" is an iconic representation of the suffering poor in

Depression America. After Pearl Harbor the remaining FSA photographers turned to images of a bountiful, prosperous land. Federal Arts Projects also projected an image of a revitalized America. Murals (intended for post offices and other public buildings) were commissioned as Works Progress Administration (WPA) relief work. They were painted in an American socialist realist style, where workers tend to be muscular and regional culture is often ennobled. The Federal Theater Project adapted topics favorable to the New Deal in a series of "Living Newspaper" productions. For example, *Power* defended the socialist content of the TVA and openly advocated public control of utilities. Harry Hopkins (1890–1946), head of the WPA, commented on the political content of the play: "People will say it's propaganda. Well, I say what of it?" Other "Living Newspaper" topics focused on the value of labor unions.

Roosevelt even introduced television as a new medium to mark the opening of the New York World's Fair in April 1939. A primitive television camera positioned next to conventional newsreel cameras captured FDR's opening remarks, which were sent by wire to downtown New York City. Roosevelt appeared on television again in 1940 and was seen by a few hundred industry executives at best, but otherwise television as a medium of political communication had to wait until after 1945.

David Culbert

See also Labor/Antilabor; Long, Huey; *The Plow that Broke the Plains;* Roosevelt, Franklin D.; United States

References: Curtis, James. *Mind's Eye, Mind's Truth: FSA Photography Reconsidered.* Philadelphia: Temple University Press, 1989; Molella, Arthur P., and Elsa M. Bruton, eds. *FDR—The Intimate Presidency: Franklin Delano Roosevelt, Communication, and the Mass Media in the 1930s.* Washington, DC: National Museum of American History, 1982; Park, Marlene, and Gerald E. Markowitz. *Democratic Vistas: Post Offices and Public Art in the New Deal.* Philadelphia: Temple University Press, 1984; Steele, Richard W. *Propaganda in an Open Society: The Roosevelt Administration and the Media, 1933–1941.* Westport, CT: Greenwood, 1985; Winfield, Betty Houchin. *FDR and the News Media.* New York: Columbia University Press, 1994.

United States (Progressive Era)

This period of reform in the United States in the late nineteenth and early twentieth centuries coincided with the rise of the mass media and hence witnessed the widespread use of propaganda in support of its aims. Dates vary, but the period 1900–1914 is generally accepted. The election of 1912, in which Theodore Roosevelt (1858–1919) campaigned unsuccessfully for the presidency at the helm of the Progressive Party was probably the zenith of Progressive propaganda. The reformists of the era both drew on and inspired parallel movements in Europe.

The foundation of Progressive thought was contained in the book *Progress and Poverty* (1880) by Henry George (1839–1897), a printer and journalist from California. George reasoned that the cause of poverty lay in limited land ownership and proposed a "single tax" to redistribute wealth. By the early years of the twentieth century his book had sold over two million copies worldwide. Also influential was the novel *Looking Backward, 2000–1887* (1888) by Edward Bellamy (1850–1898), in which a Bostonian named Julian West falls asleep in the 1880s and awakens in 2000 to find that the United States has become a socialist utopia founded on economic equality. The novel became a best-seller and sparked a nationwide chain of Bellamy Clubs dedicated to its economic principles. The novel also prompted socialist reformer and designer William Morris (1834–1896) in Britain to write his own utopian novel entitled *News from Nowhere* (1890).

By the 1890s Progressive ideas had been taken up by a generation of (generally well-born and religiously motivated) Americans who sought to reform U.S. cities. Prominent Progressives included Theodore Roosevelt (1858–1919), who made his name as an innovative police commissioner in New York City and pushed through reforms during his presidency (1901–1909). Also prominent was Jane Addams (1860–1935), who founded Hull House in Chicago in 1899 to promote the welfare of immigrants. Investigative ("muckraking") journalists of the era included Ida Tarbell (1857–1944) and Lincoln Steffens (1866–1936), who both contributed to *McClure's* magazine, and the African-American antilynching campaigner Ida B. Wells-Barnett (1862 –1931). Danish-born photographer Jacob Riis (1849–1914) photographed the appalling conditions in New York's slums and published them in a book entitled *How the Other Half Lives* (1890). Among the novelists whose work contributed to reform one should mention Upton Sinclair (1878–1968), who exposed the filthy conditions in the Chicago meatpacking industry in his novel *The Jungle* (1906).

The Progressive era succeeded in bringing the federal government into a more active role, regulating interstate commerce and other aspects of industry. It also led to the establishment of a number of important pressure groups, including peace organizations, the National Association for the Advancement of Colored People (NAACP), and the Anti-Defamation League of B'nai B'rith (ADL), which sought to combat anti-Semitism. The movement included important campaigns to extend the vote to women, and against alcohol. Although responsible for transforming many aspects of American life and politics, the Progressive era has been viewed by some historians as partially responsible for blunting socialism in the United States and making America safe for big business.

Nicholas J. Cull

See also ADL; Hearst, William Randolph; NAACP; Peace and Antiwar Movements (1500–1945); Riis, Jacob; Temperance; Women's Movement: First Wave/Suffrage

References: Bellamy, Edward. *Looking Backward.* 1888. Reprint, New York: Dover, 1996; Chambers, John Whiteclay, II. *The Tyranny of Change: America in the Progressive Era, 1890–1920.* New York: St. Martin's, 1992; Ekirch, Arthur A., Jr. *Progressivism in America.* New York: New Viewpoints, 1974; Frankel, Noralee, and Nancy S. Dye. *Gender, Class, Race and Reform in the Progressive Era.* Lexington: University of Kentucky Press, 1991; Riis, Jacob. *How the Other Half Lives.* Reprint, London: Penguin, 1997.

USIA (United States Information Agency) (1953–1999)

America's integrated overt propaganda agency was established by President Dwight D. Eisenhower (1890–1969) in August 1953 and operated until its reabsorption into the State Department in 1999. The USIA provided a home for the Voice of America and

The USIA (known overseas as USIS) took pains to reach rural populations in the Third World during the Cold War. Here Masai people in Kenya wait in line to view a USIA exhibit on agriculture in 1957. (National Archives)

The USIA outreach techniques in rural areas included bookmobiles such as this one in Rangoon, Burma, 1953. (National Archives)

many other organs of U.S. propaganda, including the embassy-based United States Information Service (USIS) offices (which gave their name to all USIA operations overseas). The USIA never had control of Radio Free Europe/Radio Liberty (RFE/RL). During the administration of President Jimmy Carter (1924–) the agency carried the alternative name United States International Communications Agency (USICA). Owing to the legislative restrictions of the Smith-Mundt Act of 1948, the USIA was never able to conduct propaganda within the United States or even to show its films without a special act of Congress; hence the agency's work was not well known by the American people. The fortunes of the USIA were frequently linked to that of its director and, in turn, that person's relationship to the president. Although the USIA director was not a statutory member of the National

Security Council (NSC), some presidents—such as Eisenhower and Ronald Reagan (1911–)—made a point of allowing the USIA director to sit in on these meetings and participate in its deliberations, while others—such as Richard Nixon (1913–1994)—kept the USIA director at arm's length.

The USIA facilitated the worldwide distribution of magazines, books, films, radio programs, press releases, and photographs that simply would not have been circulated based on commercial demand alone. Activities included touring exhibitions, World's Fair pavilions, language teaching, and educational exchanges. In the 1960s the agency produced highly effective documentary films dealing with such issues as civil rights (*The March,* 1964), the life of President Kennedy (*John F. Kennedy: Years of Lightning, Day of Drums,* 1964) and the Soviet invasion of Czechoslovakia

(*Czechoslovakia, 1968;* made in 1969). Two (including the latter) won Academy Awards in the "best documentary short" category.

The following have served as directors of the agency: Theodore Streibert (1953–1956), Arthur Larson (1956–1957), George V. Allen (1957–1960), Edward R. Murrow (1961–1964), Carl T. Rowan (1964–1965), Leonard Marks (1965–1968), Frank Shakespeare (1969–1973), James Keogh (1973–1976), John Reinhardt (1977–1981), Charles Z. Wick (1981–1989), Bruce Gelb (1989–1991), Henry Catto (1991–1993), Joseph Duffey (1993–1999). Of these, Murrow brought with him considerable prestige as a well-known broadcaster and did much to raise the national profile of the agency. Carl Rowan and Leonard Marks found themselves struggling to explain U.S. policy in Vietnam to the world while also attempting to administer much of the media war on the ground. John Reinhardt used the agency to revitalize America's image in the aftermath of Vietnam and Watergate by promoting a new human rights agenda. Charles Z. Wick, who benefited from being a close friend of Ronald Reagan, mobi-lized the agency for the second Cold War, introducing such new initiatives as the Worldnet satellite TV channel and the Radio Martí radio station for Cuba. The USIA may have become a victim of its own success. Following the end of the Cold War—hastened by the flow of agency and other media material into the Eastern bloc—the USIA seemed unnecessary. Congress needed a "peace dividend," and in 1999 its main functions returned to the State Department under an undersecretary of state for public diplomacy.

Nicholas J. Cull

See also Cold War; Cold War in the Middle East; Cultural Propaganda; Exhibitions and World's Fairs; Kennedy, John F.; Latin America; Murrow, Edward R.; Public Diplomacy; Reagan, Ronald; Satellite Communications; Suez Crisis; United States; Vietnam War; VOA; Wick, Charles Z.

References: Hixson, Walter L. *Parting the Curtain: Propaganda, Culture and the Cold War, 1945–1961.* New York: St. Martin's, 1997; Sorenson, Thomas C. *The Word War: The Story of American Propaganda.* New York: Harper and Row, 1968; Tuch, Hans N. *Communicating with the World: U.S. Public Diplomacy Overseas.* New York: St. Martin's, 1990.

V

Vietnam

Vietnam has been both a target for and a practitioner of propaganda during a long history of conflict with foreign and domestic forces. The Vietnamese have repeatedly demonstrated the importance of a strong national identity in times of foreign threat. In the twentieth century Vietnamese nationalist feelings and Communism combined to produce a potent mixture. The Vietnamese proved masters of what they called "armed propaganda" in their wars with the French and the Americans.

Vietnam entered the sixteenth century under the Le dynasty, which ruled according to Confucian ideology borrowed from China. In 1516 the first Portuguese traders arrived, but it was not until 1615 and the coming of Jesuit missionaries that Western ideas began to make significant inroads into Vietnam. In 1627 the work of the missionaries was made easier thanks to Jesuit priest Alexandre de Rhodes (1591–1660), who invented *quoc ngu* (national language), a method of transcribing the Vietnamese language into roman script. As the Le dynasty declined, effective power passed to two warring families, who divided Vietnam into North and South after a bitter civil war. In 1771 the Tayson peasant rebellion challenged the domination of the families and

sent the Le dynasty scurrying to China for aid. The link between the Le and China opened a rich vein for Tayson propaganda, for Vietnam had two thousand years' worth of songs, poems, and stories dealing with resistance to China. The Tayson also mobilized the tradition of the *chinh nghia* (just cause) and of mass involvement in a common struggle. In 1788 the Le dynasty fell and the rebel Nguyen Hue (1752–1792) took the throne as the emperor Quang-Trung (r. 1788–1792).

At this point the Vietnamese received their first lesson in the power of the Western media. The child heir apparent to the throne of South Vietnam and a French priest named Pierre Pigneau de Behaine (1741–1799) traveled to Paris and begged Louis XVI (1754–1793) for aid. The exotic appeal of the child was immediately apparent and "Cochin China" became a cause célèbre in the French press. French volunteers set sail for Vietnam, and by 1802 they had assisted in establishing the Nguyen dynasty, which lasted until 1945. The new dynasty proceeded to resist—at times violently—any French influence.

The nineteenth century saw the creeping advance of French military and economic power in the region. In 1887 France declared the Indo-Chinese Union between present-day Vietnam, Laos, Cambodia, and the

Qinzhouwan region of China. Different parts of Indo-China were ruled in various ways. French cultural power was strongest in South Vietnam (Cochin China), which was officially part of France under the policy of assimilation. France was given a central place in the educational system, as though Cochin China were as French as Paris. Resistance to the French was expressed in songs and poetry. By the turn of the century propaganda included such intellectual arguments for nationalism as those advanced by Phan Boi Chau (1867–1940). Phan was a founder of the Vietnam Quang Phuc Hoi (Vietnam Restoration Society), which established links with nationalists struggling elsewhere in the east Asian region. Although this effort marked a beginning, mass propaganda would only come with the arrival of the Communists.

Vietnamese Communism is inseparable from the career of the man born Nguyen Tat Thanh but better known by his nom de guerre Ho Chi Minh (1890–1969), which means bringer of enlightenment and can therefore be considered propaganda in its own right. Ho traveled to France during World War I and became a founding member of the French Communist Party in 1920. He studied in Moscow at a Soviet university called the University of the Toilers of the East, which was dedicated to the propagation of Communism. Moving to Canton, he founded the Vietnamese Revolutionary Youth League in 1925 and the Vietnamese Communist Party in 1930. In his writings Ho developed an eloquent critique of French imperialism and understood the need for such ideas to reach as many people as possible. In 1935 the Communist Party of Vietnam held its first conference in Macao, China. It founded a military wing called the Military Self-Defense Group. From the beginning propaganda was inherent in the Communist plan. The Communists conceptualized the soldier's role to be one of "armed propaganda," meaning that they would carry ideas as well as guns. Meanwhile, other nationalistic movements sprang up across Vietnam. Their prop-

aganda methods ranged from speeches and pamphlets to a sustained intellectual movement. The Know the New Group was founded in 1941 to rediscover the heroes of Vietnamese history.

Ho Chi Minh returned to Vietnam in 1941, announcing his agenda to merge all non-Communist activists into a single resistance movement. Anti-French opposition groups combined to form the League for the Independence of Vietnam, or Viet Minh. The Viet Minh aimed to defeat both the French administration (now a branch of the pro-Nazi Vichy government) and their Japanese allies, whose forces occupied the country. Ho understood the importance of propaganda for the revolutionary struggle. He knew that the Viet Minh would be judged both by their words and deeds and hence brought education and famine relief with them into the areas they "liberated." In 1944 the Communist Party established its own Peoples Army of Vietnam (PAVN) under a former history teacher named Vo Nguyen Giap (1912–). Giap held to the Communist Party's concept of armed propaganda, with PAVN's motto being: "Propaganda is more important than fighting." Giap saw political education as the "soul of the army" and the fighting as a means to the end of indoctrination and a way of making commitment to the cause tangible to the masses. By 1945 a sizable guerrilla insurrection with a revolutionary Communist propaganda campaign at its core had taken hold in Vietnam.

Ho Chi Minh hoped that at the end of World War II the United States would champion Vietnamese independence. As propaganda to achieve this end, Ho borrowed language from the U.S. Declaration of Independence for Vietnam's own declaration of independence. President Harry Truman (1884–1972) remained unmoved, with the U.S. government preferring to sponsor the French claim to Vietnam. Between 1947 and 1954 the French fought a bitter guerrilla war to reestablish control over Vietnam. They failed, and in 1954 the country was divided between the Communist North and the pro-

Western South, on the understanding that elections would be held in due course to agree to a united government. In place of elections the United States sponsored South Vietnam as a showcase for the American way in Asia and a bastion of anti-Communism. North Vietnam became a part of the Communist bloc. In 1960 the North Vietnamese oversaw the creation of the National Liberation Front (NLF), representing a new coalition of South Vietnamese opposition groups with Communist leadership. U.S. psychological warfare advisers contemptuously nicknamed the enemy "Viet Cong" (roughly equivalent to "Vietnamese Commies") but later abandoned the name since its "Viet" component emphasized the nationalistic claim of the movement. During the Kennedy and Johnson administrations the U.S. government gradually increased its military aid to South Vietnam, with large numbers of combat troops arriving in 1965. The Vietnam War had begun.

Propaganda lay at the heart of the North Vietnamese system and was an integral part of life in the NLF. Each soldier kept a diary to record his personal role in the war and to stress that the individual had value in the collective struggle. Units included a political officer with responsibility for the ideological well-being of the troops. Once infiltrated into South Vietnam, NLF propaganda followed the pattern of "armed propaganda" established in World War II. Military force was seen as a means to gain access to the peasants and persuade them to support the Communists and reject the South Vietnamese government. The infiltrators were usually originally from the region and were returning from exile. But the concept of armed propaganda also required ruthless violence against the Saigon government's regional power structure. The NLF left a trail of assassinated mayors, schoolteachers, and village chiefs in its wake, which in turn figured in U.S. propaganda about the conflict.

The NLF also understood the importance of contact with the foreign media. Agents in

Saigon passed photographs of the war to Western journalists to fuel the growing peace movement in the West. Damage resulting from American bombing campaigns proved particularly potent. But all sides in the Vietnam conflict attempted to manipulate images. When the Buddhist monk Thich Quang Duc (1897–1963) set fire to himself in 1963 to protest the U.S.-backed regime in the South, his colleagues called a Western photographer to record the event. South Vietnamese propaganda, however, relied heavily on American advice, and soon the South Vietnamese regime spoke only with an American accent. This undermined any claim to nationalism that the rulers of South Vietnam might have possessed in the immediate aftermath of the French withdrawal.

The United States acknowledged the importance of propaganda in Vietnam, and it became commonplace for the planners of the war to speak of the need to win the "hearts and minds" of the Vietnamese peasants. This ubiquitous phrase was borrowed from British counterinsurgency experts, who in turn had appropriated it from St. Paul's letter to the Philippians, chapter 4, verse 7, via the *Book of Common Prayer* (1664). Despite successes in the "Chieu Hoi" (Open Arms) campaign to encourage desertion, the presence of the U.S. armed forces, their behavior, and the effect of America's economic power on the client state of South Vietnam carried its own message.

In January 1968 the North Vietnamese launched a coordinated series of uprisings all over South Vietnam to coincide with the Tet festival. The Tet offensive proved a military disaster but a political victory for the North Vietnamese. Americans at home were shaken by the television images of its armed forces in disarray during the early stages of the conflict and disturbed by the extreme violence of the U.S. counterattack. The NLF suffered heavy losses during the uprising, and from this point on the war was fought by the North Vietnamese PAVN rather than the returning southerners. With the war at a stalemate, in

1973 the United States withdrew its armed forced from South Vietnam. In 1975 North Vietnam conquered South Vietnam. Propaganda figured prominently in the daily life of the Democratic Republic of Vietnam (DRV) as the Communist government extended the rigidly ideological educational system of the North and used the usual techniques of propaganda to promote the supremacy of the party. Dissenters found themselves interned in reeducation camps and fed on a diet of party propaganda. In order to prevail in its war with the United States, the North Vietnamese regime had become exactly the sort of hard-line totalitarian dictatorship that the Americans had predicted. Economic development was hard won. The DRV used forced migration to move about 10 percent of its citizens into New Economic Zones.

Since 1988—and especially since the appointment of Do Muoi (1917–) as general secretary of the party in 1991—the regime has permitted some economic liberalization and trading links with other nations in east Asia. Although the Vietnamese resumed relations with the United States in 1995, the memory of the struggle against the Americans remains a key rallying cry for national cohesion and a frequent theme in DRV propaganda, as it was in March 2000, when the party organized massive celebrations to mark the twenty-fifth anniversary of the end of the war.

Nicholas J. Cull

See also China; Counterinsurgency; France; Japan; Southeast Asia; Vietnam War

References: Karnow, Stanley. *Vietnam: A History.* New York: Viking; 1983; Lê, Huu Tri. *Prisoner of the Word: A Memoir of the Vietnamese Reeducation Camps.* Seattle: Black Heron, 2001; Page, Tim. *Ten Years After: Vietnam Today.* New York: Knopf, 1987; Pike, Douglas. *Viet Cong: The Organization and Techniques of the National Liberation Front of South Vietnam.* Cambridge, MA: MIT Press, 1966.

Vietnam War (1954–1975)

The U.S. propaganda war in Vietnam lasted from the Geneva Accords in 1954—accord-

Propaganda leaflet distributed by the U.S. military as part of a psychological warfare operation. The pamphlet urged the defection of Viet Cong and North Vietnamese to the side of the Republic of Vietnam. (National Archives)

ing to which the powers involved agreed to a temporary division of the former French colony of Indo-China into Communist North Vietnam and Nationalist South Vietnam—to 1975, when the southern regime finally collapsed under a northern invasion. This propaganda war can be divided into two phases: pre-1965, when the United States used its psychological-warfare capabilities to assist the South Vietnamese government, and post-1965, when propaganda and psychological warfare was an adjunct to the substantial U.S. military commitment to South Vietnam. For their part, the North Vietnamese and indigenous South Vietnamese revolutionaries used propaganda to advance their campaign in the villages of the South and to champion their cause internationally. In this latter task they were greatly assisted by the global media network of the Communist bloc; Russian and Chinese support was more often of the propaganda variety than material aid. In the 1970s the respective contributions to the North Vietnamese cause (or lack thereof) became a major issue in the Sino-Soviet propaganda duel. The U.S. government attempted to justify its actions internationally through the resources of the United States Information Agency (USIA) and domestically through the Pentagon and White House press apparatus. Despite the battlefield successes of psychological warfare, the chief legacy of Vietnam remains the perceived failures of U.S. press management and the way in which uncensored journalistic—especially TV news—coverage undermined American public support for the war.

The early U.S. propaganda effort in Vietnam is inseparable from the career of one man: Col. Edward Lansdale (1908–1987), who served as chief of covert action in the U.S. Saigon Military Mission. As he had in the Philippines, Lansdale used psychological operations (PSYOPS) to undermine the North. His best-known campaign, "The Virgin Mary Has Gone South," sought to encourage the migration of North Vietnamese Catholics into South Vietnam by alleging that the North planned to persecute Christians. The USIA also assisted in the process of nation-building in the South, and reputedly had a hand in devising the name Viet Cong (a pejorative term roughly translated as Vietnamese Commie) to describe the enemy. This name had limited propaganda value since it affirmed the enemy's nationalistic credentials, but no alternative emerged. In 1960 the North Vietnamese launched the National Liberation Front (NLF), a formal structure responsible for the insurgency in the South, whose major focus was political propaganda.

The decision by President John F. Kennedy (1917–1963) to escalate the U.S. role in Vietnam was closely related to issues of propaganda. After the abortive Bay of Pigs invasion of 1961, the United States needed, in Kennedy's words to James Reston of the *New York Times,* "to prove the credibility of her power." Vietnam seemed the logical venue for this display. The Kennedy administration took an active role in supporting South Vietnamese psychological operations. Major initiatives included the "Chieu Hoi" (Open Arms) program. Launched by South Vietnamese president Ngo Dinh Diem (1901–1963) early in 1963 and conducted in cooperation with the United States throughout the war, this campaign sought to persuade NLF fighters to surrender. American planes dropped billions of safe conduct passes and appeals over NLF territory. The "Chieu Hoi" program also used airborne loudspeaker appeals featuring sad songs and testimony from defectors. Troops who rallied were used for propaganda work and, later in the war, deployed in special Kit Carson Scout units. Although the precise effectiveness of the "Chieu Hoi" program is hard to gauge since statistics sometimes include refugees and professional defectors seeking only the monetary bounties offered later in the war, it certainly worried the North Vietnamese.

The United States also attempted to advise the South Vietnamese on its news management, but, given the regime's lack of interest in issues involving image projection, it ran into frequent difficulties. As guests in South Vietnam, the Americans themselves could not censor coverage of the growing struggle and focused instead on "accentuating the positive" in briefings.

In 1964, in a propagandistic sleight of hand, President Lyndon B. Johnson (1908–1973) manipulated an alleged North Vietnamese attack on a U.S. destroyer in the Gulf of Tonkin to get the U.S. Congress to pass the Tonkin Gulf resolution, which amounted to legislative authority for the president to wage undeclared war in Vietnam. Justifications for U.S. military escalation included a State Department white paper published in February 1965 that presented evidence of North Vietnamese aggression (rather than any indigenous South Vietnamese basis for the conflict). This remained a major feature of U.S. propaganda for the rest of the conflict. Other tactics included an emphasis on Viet Cong atrocities. The Pentagon did its best to sell the war at home through the efforts of Arthur Sylvester (1901–1979), the assistant secretary of defense for public affairs and a former journalist.

In the spring of 1965 President Johnson deployed U.S. regular troops in Vietnam. This increased the degree to which U.S. credibility was at stake in Vietnam and created a logical path for further deployments. The Johnson administration also centralized all U.S. information and psychological operations under a single Joint United States

Public Affairs Office (JUSPAO) at the embassy, run by Barry Zorthian (1920–), formerly of the USIA. This office linked the USIA, military PSYOPS, and civilian development initiatives, in addition to providing a central location for press briefings. This structure did not last long, and in 1967 key functions fell under the jurisdiction of Civilian Operations and Revolutionary Development Support (CORDS). U.S. operations included all of the following: campaigns to support the 1967 elections in South Vietnam; humanitarian projects intended to "win hearts and minds"; the dropping of leaflets containing peace appeals over North Vietnam (which often stressed the Chinese role in North Vietnam's war); the dropping of miniature radios over the North (tuned to specific frequencies); the distribution of TV sets to villages around South Vietnam; and the creation of radio programs intended to demoralize the enemy and build up the image of the South Vietnamese government. Recurrent problems included the U.S. tendency to displace the indigenous South Vietnamese information apparatus, thereby ensuring that the South Vietnamese regime always spoke with an American accent. Increased American propaganda hence often became counterproductive.

The presence of the world press in South Vietnam played a crucial role in the propaganda surrounding the conflict. The NLF understood the value of the Western media and infiltrated such bastions as *Time* magazine's Saigon office. Opposition groups in South Vietnam made sure to invite the press and photographers to their protests, the most famous being the self-immolation of Buddhist monk Thich Quang Duc (1897–1963) on 11 June 1963, which was captured by Malcolm Browne (1931–) of the Associated Press. Since the press drew much of its information from the U.S. servicemen themselves, their increasing doubts about the conflict made press coverage from Vietnam appear increasingly negative. Stories that left an impact within the United States included the destruction of the village of Cam Ne by U.S. Marines in August 1966, which was filmed by the CBS network. Coverage of the Communist's Tet offensive in January 1968 proved particularly controversial, with senior officials in the U.S. military suggesting that the media effectively betrayed them by overemphasizing the scale of the defeat. Pictures and reportage from Vietnam in general and the Tet in particular certainly provided a check on the generally upbeat "light at the end of the tunnel" predictions of the White House and the Pentagon. The U.S. government faced a credibility gap between its claims and the evidence from the ground.

Although much of the North Vietnamese propaganda effort was directed at its own forces in the South, the North Vietnamese released photographic evidence of the effect of U.S. bombing and atrocities, which fueled the antiwar movement within the United States and Western Europe. The North Vietnamese also invited selected U.S. journalists to Hanoi to see for themselves, the most famous being Harrison Salisbury (1908–1993) of the *New York Times.* Reports from Hanoi disproved the U.S. claim that bombing was only targeting military installations. Members of the peace movement also visited North Vietnam, including a celebrated visit by actress Jane Fonda (1937–). The Americans worked hard to dismiss North Vietnamese claims of atrocities. Radio Hanoi carried news of the My Lai massacre within days of its occurrence, but it took the investigative skills of reporter Seymour Hersh (1937–) to break the story in the United States. President Richard Nixon (1913–1994) responded to the growing criticism of the U.S. role in Vietnam with an aggressive campaign of his own intended to demonize critics of the war as dangerous radicals. He effectively reduced student opposition to the war by exempting students from the draft. In the end he was able to transform the U.S. withdrawal in 1973 into a "triumph for diplomacy" rather than victory resulting from North Vietnamese tenacity.

The Vietnam War has been used to generate many propaganda lessons. Rightly or wrongly, it underscored the need on the part of Western nations to manage battlefield reporting. It also pointed up the limits of what a propaganda campaign was capable of achieving. The USIA failed to convince Western Europe that the Vietnam War was either moral or ethical. In the final analysis, the United States was ultimately the victim of its own propaganda apparatus in Vietnam. The upbeat reports from the field and the inflated body counts of enemy dead eroded the basis in fact essential for sound policy making.

Nicholas J. Cull

See also Counterinsurgency; Falklands/ Malvinas War; *The Green Berets;* Gulf War; Kennedy, John F.; Nixon, Richard; Peace and Antiwar Movements (1945–); Philippines; Prisoners of War; Psychological Warfare; Southeast Asia; Television; United States; USIA; Vietnam

References: Braestrup, Peter. *Big Story: How the American Press and Television Reported and Interpreted the Crisis of Tet 1968 in Vietnam and Washington.* Boulder, CO: Westview, 1978; Chandler, Robert W. *War of Ideas: The U.S. Propaganda Campaign in Vietnam.* Boulder, CO: Westview, 1981; Hallin, Daniel C. *"Uncensored War": The Media and Vietnam.* Oxford: Oxford University Press, 1986; Hammond, William M. *Reporting Vietnam: Media and Military at War.* Lawrence: University Press of Kansas, 1998.

Willis Conover (seen here in 1978), legendary jazz disc jockey for Voice of America radio. Conover's jazz broadcasts won VOA a keen following in the the Eastern bloc during the Cold War. (National Archives)

VOA (Voice of America)

The U.S. government's short-wave radio station, the Voice of America (VOA) began transmitting on 24 February 1942, under the auspices of the Foreign Information Service (FIS) and later under the Office of War Information (OWI). It began by carrying news in German and then in French to occupied Europe; by the end of the war the radio station had expanded to cover many more languages. In 1953 the VOA was the target of an inquiry by Sen. Joe McCarthy (1909–1957). In order to ensure tighter political control, it moved from New York to Washington, D.C., becoming part of the newly established United States Information Agency (USIA). The VOA became a major element in the propaganda war with the Soviet Union. Although the USSR spent millions of rubles to jam the VOA for significant portions of the Cold War, much was still heard. Programming included the sort of news that the Soviet government sought to suppress (including news of the Chernobyl nuclear accident in 1986), as well as examples of American culture. One of the best known VOA broadcasters was jazz disc jockey Willis Conover (1920–1996), who believed that jazz had political value as a metaphor for the democratic way of life. The VOA was also widely heard in the developing world, where its penetration was assisted thanks to the development of "Special English," an easily understood version of English with a 1,200-word vocabulary read at just 90 words per minute.

Graffiti painted on the Russian parliament building by a grateful listener in 1992 at the time of the attempted coup against the ailing government of Mikhail Gorbachev. It translates: "Thank you Voice of America for telling the truth." (Voice of America)

Life at the VOA was frequently turbulent. The journalists who provided news programming believed that it had a duty to report the news to the world whether or not it reflected favorably on the United States. Their political masters at the USIA wanted ideological content, and the State Department tried to prevent the VOA from criticizing sympathetic regimes. As a result of pressure from its journalists, in 1960 the VOA acquired a charter requiring balance and objectivity in news reportage. In 1976, following attempts to manipulate the VOA during the last days of the Vietnam War, this charter became law. The Reagan administration invested heavily in the VOA as part of its renewed campaign against the USSR, but the VOA was subject to cuts following the collapse of Communism in 1989. In 1994 the VOA was subsumed under the International Bureau of Broadcasting (IBB). With the breakup of the USIA in 1999, the IBB became an independent home for both the VOA and RFE/RL, albeit one now exposed to unprecedented political influence from the White House.

At the time of its sixtieth anniversary in 2002, the VOA was providing over 900 hours of weekly radio, television, and Internet programming in fifty-three languages, with an audience estimated at 91 million people. Serious political issues still remain. In the aftermath of the attacks against the United States on 11 September 2001, the VOA attracted criticism for carrying an interview with the Taliban leader on its Pashto service.

Nicholas J. Cull

See also Cold War; Poland; Radio (International); RFE/RL; Suez Crisis; Terrorism, War on; USIA

References: Alexandre, Laurien. *The Voice of America: From Detente to the Reagan Doctrine.* Norwood, NJ: Ablex, 1988; Nelson, Michael. *War of the Black Heavens: The Battles of Western Broadcasting in the Cold War.* London: Brassey's, 1997; Rawnsley, Gary D. *Radio Diplomacy and Propaganda: The BBC and VOA in International Politics, 1956–64.* New York: St. Martin's, 1996; Schulman, Holly Cowan. *The Voice of America: Propaganda and Democracy, 1941–1945.* Madison: University of Wisconsin Press, 1990.

The War Game (1965)

This film is both a classic of antiwar propaganda and an example of television censorship. In 1965 the British Broadcasting Corporation (BBC) commissioned then rising star Peter Watkins (1935–) to create a film showing the effects of an atomic bomb exploding over the southeast of England. Watkins used amateur actors and his trademark documentary film techniques to show its devastating aftermath in terms of disease, social anarchy, and the institution of martial law. The BBC decided that the end result was too violent and *The War Game* became a celebrated case of BBC self-censorship. Watkins next attempted to make a version of the film in Germany, but the TV company changed its mind and pulled out of the project. The film won an Academy Award in the documentary feature category in 1967 and was widely screened as propaganda by the Campaign for Nuclear Disarmament (CND). In 1983 an ABC-TV miniseries entitled *The Day After* (dir. Nicholas Meyer) showed the effects of a nuclear explosion over Kansas. In 1985 the BBC produced *Threads* (dir. Mick Jackson), an updated version of the same idea dealing with a nuclear strike against Sheffield. Watkins subsequently worked in Sweden and in the Baltic region, where his films have included a documentary about peace entitled *The Journey* (1983–1986).

Nicholas J. Cull

See also BBC; Censorship; Cold War; Film (Documentary); Peace and Antiwar Movements (1945–); Scandinavia

References: Cook, John, and Patrick Murphy. *Freethinker: The Life and Work of Peter Watkins.* Manchester, UK: Manchester University Press, 2003; Gomez, Joseph. *Peter Watkins.* Boston: Twayne, 1979.

White Propaganda

A widely held belief claims that propaganda is a process that camouflages its origin, its motive, or both, and that it is conducted for the purpose of obtaining a specific objective by manipulating its audience. Propaganda, however, may also be open and aboveboard. For example, when the Nazis came to power in 1933, one of the first government departments to be established was the Ministry for Popular Enlightenment and Propaganda. The National Socialists made no secret of the name or, indeed, the task that this ministry was to perform. Joseph Goebbels (1897–1945), the minister for propaganda, openly declared in one of his first speeches that the new ministry would be responsible for "the mobilization of mind and spirit in Germany." The source here is known, aims and intentions are identified, and the public knows that an attempt is being made to influence it.

The distinction between "white" and "black" propaganda was well understood. By the 1930s there was a growing recognition that it was important to distinguish between overt or information-based propaganda—output that represents the official policy of the government and therefore needs to be "truthful" (in the sense of being factually accurate) to maintain credibility—and covert propaganda—which seeks to achieve immediate results by any and all means and whose essential requirement (apart from effectiveness) is that it must not be traceable back to its source.

White propaganda is largely conducted by an identifiable government agency. The information in the message tends to be accurate (although not necessarily verifiable) since any suggestion that the message might be false would undermine the credibility of the source. The message is intended to convince an audience of the superiority and justness of a particular regime or ideology. Thus, while the message disseminated is largely truthful, it is slanted to favor the value system of the propagandist. During the Cold War the Voice of America (VOA) and Radio Moscow employed this type of white propaganda in order to establish credibility with an audience that might prove useful at some point in the future.

David Welch

See also Black Propaganda; Goebbels, Joseph; Gray Propaganda; RMVP; Russia; United States; VOA

References: Ellul, Jacques. *Propaganda: The Formation of Men's Attitudes.* New York: Vintage, 1973; Jowett, Garth, and Victoria O'Donnell. *Propaganda and Persuasion.* London: Sage, 1992.

lywood director of the era. The objective of the series was to explain the issues of the war to conscripted soldiers who had grown up in the era of the interwar peace movement. The films combined brilliantly edited clips of newsreel footage from around the world with dramatic music, animated maps, and a powerful commentary to tell the story of the rise of Fascism and the coming of the war. Titles in the series included *Prelude to War, The Nazis Strike, Divide and Conquer* (dealing with the fall of France), *The Battle of Britain, The Battle of Russia, The Battle of China,* and *War Comes to America* (dealing with the events leading up to the Japanese attack on Pearl Harbor). Among the highlights were animation by Walt Disney (1901–1966) and the reappropriation of clips from Leni Riefenstahl's documentary *Triumph of the Will* (1935) for Allied propaganda purposes. The impact of four of the films on their audience was studied systematically. Although results suggested that they did little to deepen love of country, respect for allies, or hatred of the enemy, at the very least soldiers had absorbed the factual information relating to the origins of the war. Two films were thought worthy of a civilian release and became influential examples of compilation documentary filmmaking technique.

Nicholas J. Cull

See also Capra, Frank; Film (Documentary); *Triumph of the Will;* United States; World War II (United States)

References: Alpers, Benjamin L. *Dictators, Democracy and American Popular Culture. Envisioning the Totalitarian Enemy, 1920s–1950s.* Chapel Hill: University of North Carolina Press, 2003; Capra, Frank. *The Name above the Title.* New York: Macmillan, 1971; Culbert, David, editor-in-chief. *Film and Propaganda in America: A Documentary History.* 5 vols. Westport, CT: Greenwood Press, 1990–1993.

Why We Fight (1942–1945)

A series of seven one-hour propaganda documentary films produced for the U.S. Army Signal Corps during World War II by Frank Capra (1897–1991), the most successful Hol-

Wick, Charles Z. (1917–)

Longest-serving director of the United States Information Agency (USIA) during the Reagan administration, Charles Wick was a Hollywood impresario and film pro-

Ronald Reagan celebrates the fortieth birthday of the Voice of America in 1982 with USIA director Charles Z. Wick (left). VOA broadcasts to Eastern Europe did much to win the Cold War for the United States. (National Archives)

ducer who became closely associated with Ronald Reagan's (1911–) 1980 presidential campaign. Wick distinguished himself as a fund-raiser and successfully organized inaugural festivities. Reagan recognized his po-

tential to revitalize the USIA. The agency had not fared well under the Carter administration, having been renamed the International Communications Agency (ICA). Now it became a hive of activity. Wick restored the old name and increased propaganda to a level recalling the heady days of the early Eisenhower administration. He built up the Voice of America (VOA) and established Radio Martí, a radio station aimed at Cuba. He also moved into TV propaganda with a satellite network called WorldNet, which linked U.S. embassies around the world and permitted interactive discussions between policymakers in Washington, D.C., and foreign journalists. In 1982 Wick organized a spectacular TV event called "Let Poland Be Poland" to support the Solidarity movement in Poland.

For some observers in the U.S. press, the downside of Wick's tenure at the USIA was his attitude toward the VOA. Believing that it should be an instrument of propaganda rather than a source of news, he insisted on inserting political editorials into the VOA's output. The administration of the USIA became overtly political, resulting in a number of prominent resignations in protest during the early Wick era. Wick also attracted criticism from the U.S. press for his practice of taping incoming phone calls and alleged nepotism in hiring practices. In the wider history of propaganda, his tenure at the USIA, like Brendan Bracken's (1901–1958) war service as Winston Churchill's (1874–1965) minister of information, shows the degree to which the fortunes of a propaganda agency can be enhanced through a closely cultivated relationship between its director and the president or prime minister. Many at the USIA believed that the key to their agency's success during the 1980s was the friendship between Wick and Reagan and—no less significant—Wick's wife, Mary-Jane Wick, and First Lady Nancy Reagan.

Nicholas J. Cull

See also Bracken, Brendan; Castro, Fidel; Cold War; Reagan, Ronald; Satellite Communications; United States; USIA; VOA

References: Snyder, Alvin. *Warriors of Disinformation: American Propaganda, Soviet Lies and the Winning of the Cold War.* New York: Arcade, 1995; Tuch, Hans N. *Communicating with the World: U.S. Public Diplomacy Overseas.* New York: St. Martin's, 1990.

Wilkes, John (1727–1797)

A British M.P. and publisher, Wilkes used political propaganda in an innovative manner by associating his cause with the tradition of English liberty, freedom of the press, and open elections, thereby becoming a symbol of opposition propaganda in Britain and America. Wilkes's contribution to the history of propaganda as a radical innovator is considerable.

Born into an urban dissenting family, Wilkes was educated in Leyden, Holland. He enhanced his social position through marriage but gained a reputation, thanks to his membership in the Hell Fire Club, as a brilliant conversationalist and London socialite, "a rake on the make." He was elected M.P. for Aylesbury in 1757 as a supporter of William Pitt (1708–1778). Following the resignation of the Grenville-Pitt ministry (1757–1761), Wilkes became the leading parliamentary critic of the Earl of Bute (1713–1793), George III's favorite minister. In 1762 Wilkes established *The North Briton,* a pro-Pittite newspaper, taking his unrelenting vituperative attack on Bute "out of doors" by successfully appealing to popular "Scottophobia" and anti-Catholicism.

Despite Bute's resignation, *The North Briton No. 45* of April 1763 attacked both Bute and the new ministry of George Grenville (1712–1770) by ridiculing the king. Wilkes was arrested under a general warrant charging the publishers and printers of *The North Briton* with seditious libel. His release on a writ of habeas corpus—on the grounds that parliamentary privilege prevented the imprisonment of M.P.s on charges other than treason—was greeted by cheering crowds chanting "Wilkes and liberty!" Parliament voted by a vote of 273 to 111 that the issue in question was "false, scandalous and seditious libel" and ordered a public burning for Wilkes. Although Parliament resolved that the press's privilege did not extend to publishing seditious libel, Wilkes's arrest under a general warrant was adjudged unconstitutional.

In 1764 Wilkes was charged with blasphemy as coauthor of the pornographic *Essay on Woman.* Expelled from the Commons and subject to arrest, Wilkes fled to France. He returned in 1768, but his appeal for clemency was ignored by the authorities until his election as M.P. for Middlesex. Unable to take his seat as an outlaw, Wilkes surrendered himself at King's Bench prison, where he remained incarcerated for twenty-two months. Daily rioting in London to protest his imprisonment was violently suppressed by a Scottish regiment at St. George's Field, leaving seven dead and thereby boosting the popular appeal of Wilkes as a symbol of English liberty against Hanoverian despotism. Wilkes succeeded in making his own struggles symptomatic of centuries of struggle for habeas corpus, trial by jury, and liberty of the press, using a rhetoric tied to the principles of the Glorious Revolution expounded in his popular *History of England* (1768).

In 1769 Middlesex voters elected Wilkes three times, but each time he was expelled from the Commons, which finally declared his opponent the winner despite fewer votes. Supporters, outraged by Parliament's presumption of the right to determine its membership, formed the Society for the Supporters of the Bill of Rights, organizing a nationwide petitioning campaign that was supported by nearly sixty thousand people. Wilkes himself inaugurated the commercial production of campaign artifacts—including plates, teapots and mugs, snuffboxes, medals, buttons, ribbons, badges, and candles—that featured such Wilkite symbols as the number *45,* which also appeared in fashions and as graffiti. Throughout England and the colonies, supporters sent gifts and money to Wilkes in celebration of his release in 1770. A pipe maker in Gateshead produced 45 pipes each measuring 45 inches long for a supporters' feast consisting of 45 pounds of mutton, 45 potatoes, and 45 quarts of ale, while in Charleston, South Carolina, the crowd lit their liberty tree with 45 lights, followed by a celebration involving 45 bowls of punch, 45 bottles of wine, and 92 glasses.

In 1771 Wilkes again became a champion of press freedom when he announced his support for printers who had been arrested for reporting parliamentary debates. As an alderman of London, Wilkes used the immunity granted by the City to shelter printer John Wheble from the jurisdiction of parliamentary punishment. In 1774 Wilkes became lord mayor of London and M.P. for Middlesex, but he failed to find support for parliamentary reform. He became a reliable supporter of William Pitt (1759–1806) and defended property during the Gordon Riots in 1780.

Though motivated by opportunistic careerism, in declaring himself "the personification of English liberty" Wilkes became a symbol of patriotic opposition, achieving unprecedented popularity and being of great service to reformers who might otherwise have despised his personal morality and sexual license. *The North Briton*'s populist satire drew public opinion into the realm of political influence and generated popular support for liberty of the press. The relinquishing of general warrants (which were declared illegal in 1766) and the establishment of legal parliamentary reporting contributed to the end of censorship.

Karen M. Ford

See also Britain (Eighteenth Century); Revolution, American, and War of Independence
References: Colley, Linda. *Britons Forging the Nation, 1707–1837.* New Haven, CT: Yale University Press, 1992; Dickinson, H. T. *The Politics of the People in Eighteenth-Century Britain.* London: Macmillan, 1994; Holmes, Geoffrey, and Daniel Szechi. *The Age of Oligarchy: Pre-Industrial Britain, 1722–1783.* London: Longman, 1993; Maier, Pauline. "John Wilkes and American Disillusionment with Britain." *William and Mary Quarterly,* 3d ser., 20, 3 (1963): 373–395.

Women's Movement: European (1860–)

The mid to late nineteenth and early twentieth century in Europe saw a flowering of women's activism and campaigning. Propaganda techniques included journalism and the publication of arguments in essay and novel form. Nationally constituted women's movements have formed a succession of international alliances for mutual inspiration and support.

Pioneers of nineteenth-century French feminism included Jeanne Deroin (c.1810–1894), a journalist and first female candidate for election to the National Assembly (1849); Maria Deraismes (1828–1894), cofounder of the first French feminist organization, the Société pour la Revendication des Droits de la Femme (Society for Demanding Women's Rights) in 1866; and Humbertine Auclert (1849–1914), prolific and radical journalist and campaigner for suffrage in France. Auclert reached out to a mass audience through the organization Droit de la Femme (Rights of the Woman), later known as Société de Suffrage des Femmes (Society of Women's Suffrage), and such books as *Le Droit Politique des Femmes* (Political Rights of Women, 1878). Eugénie Potonie-Pierre worked to coordinate French feminism, founding the Federation Française des Sociétés Feministes in 1892. More militant French campaigners included Madeleine Pelletier (1874–1939), whose tactics included appropriating items of male clothing such as the necktie and bowler hat. Arguably the most significant modern women's advocate in France was Simone de Beauvoir (1908–1986), the philosopher and journalist whose book *Le Deuxième Sexe* (The Second Sex) (1949) was a major inspiration to the women's movement internationally.

Italian activists included Anna Maria Mozzoni (1837–1920), who preached a *"Risorgimento delle donne"* (rebirth of women), and Sibilla Aleramo (pseudonym of Rina Faccio) (1876–1960), a journalist, poet, and writer, best known for her autobiographical novel *Una Donna* (A Woman) of 1906.

Pioneer feminists in Germany included Luise Otto-Peters (1819–1895), who demanded equal rights for women during the revolution of 1848; the prolific writer Hedwig Dohm (1813–1919), whose polemics included *Der Jesuitismus im Hausstande* (Jesuitism in the Household; 1873); and the socialist Lily Braun (1865–1916), author of *Die Frauenfrage* (The Women Question, 1901). More conservative pioneers included Auguste Schmidt (1833–1902), who argued for the value of marriage and women's duty of moral leadership. Anita Augspurg (1857–1943), Minna Cauer (1841–1922), and Lida Gustava Heymann (1868–1943) cofounded a succession of suffrage organizations, including the Deutscher Verband für Frauenstimmrecht (German Union for Women's Suffrage) in 1904, and also worked internationally.

Russia produced a "triumvirate" of social campaigners: Anna Filosofva (1837–1912), Mariya Trubnikova (1835–1897), and Nadezhda Stasova (1822–1895). Their activities included founding a Women's Publishing Cooperative, which both published campaigning literature and provided employment for destitute women.

Feminist Russian revolutionaries included Inessa Armand (1874–1920), the French-born founder of the Russian revolutionary journal *Rabotnista* (Women Workers), who later became the first director of the postrevolution Zhenotdel (Women's Bureau), and Alexandra Kollontai (1872–1952), the only woman to serve in the Bolshevik government (as commissar for public welfare). Kollontai wrote widely and developed radical notions of alternative family life, attacking the element of economic domination in marriage as akin to the relation between a prostitute and her client. It seemed for a while that the Russian revolution would present a new model of gender relations, but old inequalities soon reemerged.

Arguably the most successful national movements emerged in Scandinavia. Suffrage leaders included Gina Grog (1847–1916) in Norway, Ellen Hagan (1873–1958) in Sweden, Alexandra Van Grippenberg (1859–1913) in Finland, and the husband-and-wife team Fredrik Bajer (1837–1922) and Matilde

Bajer (1840–1934) in Denmark. These and other campaigners succeeded in delivering women's suffrage somewhat in advance of their European counterparts. Of the European nations Finland was the first to grant female suffrage, in 1906 (lagging behind New Zealand [1893] and Australia [1902]), followed by Norway (1913), Denmark and Iceland (1915), and Soviet Russia (1917); Austria, Germany, Netherlands, Poland, Sweden, Luxembourg, and Czechoslovakia followed in 1919. Women won the vote in the United States in 1920 and Britain in 1928 but had to wait until 1945 in France and Italy

International women's organizations included the International Association of Women, founded in 1868 by the Swiss writer and higher-education campaigner Marie Goegg (c.1826–1904). The group held a congress in 1870 but was suppressed in 1871 by governments fearing the association of the word "International" with the Paris Commune of that year. Subsequent attempts to unite the world women's movement included the International Council of Women, which convened in Washington, D.C., in 1888. In 1904 Augspurg, Cauer, and Heymann led the foundation of the International Woman Suffrage Alliance, renamed in 1918 the International Alliance for Suffrage and Equal Citizenship; this organization became somewhat dominated by its U.S. members and marked by divisions on fundamental questions such as whether the vote should go to all women or just the educated class. The German socialist Clara Zetkin (1854–1933) created a Socialist Women's International (1907) and campaigned successfully for 8 March to be celebrated as an international women's day. In 1938 the American suffrage campaigner Alice Paul (1885–1977) founded the World Women's Party in Geneva; its achievements include ensuring that the United Nations charter recognized the rights of women. Many European women's rights activists became involved in international peace campaigning. Prominent advocates included the leading Austrian suffrage campaigner Mari-

anne Hainisch (1839–1936) and novelist Bertha Von Suttner (1843–1914), who in 1905 became the first woman to win the Nobel Peace Prize; the German Helene Stöcker (1869–1943); and the Dutch campaigner Rosa Manus (1880–1942).

Nicholas J. Cull

See also Peace and Antiwar Movements (1500–1945); Women's Movement: Precursors; Women's Movement: First Wave/Suffrage; Women's Movement: Second Wave/Feminism

References: Evans, Richard J. *The Feminists: Women's Emancipation Movements in Europe, America and Australasia, 1840–1920.* London: Croom Helm, 1984; Morgan, Robin, ed. *Sisterhood Is Global.* New York: Anchor Books, 1984; Tuttle, Lisa. *Encyclopedia of Feminism.* London: Longman, 1986.

Women's Movement: Precursors (1404–1848)

Public advocacy for women's liberation can be traced back to Christine de Pizan's (ca. 1364–ca. 1431) *Book of the City of Ladies* (1404). Early-modern precursors of the women's movement focused on persuading men to allow women access to education. Among such prominent British writers was Margaret Fell (1614–1702), a Quaker organizer who defended a woman's right to preach and take an active role in religious affairs. In her "Essay to Revive the Ancient Education of Gentlewomen" (1673) Bathsua Makin (1600–ca. 1674), governess to the children of Charles I of England and well-known mathematician, proposed serious academic study for girls. Philosopher Mary Astell (1666–1731) advocated the establishment of a higher-education retreat for unmarried women. In 1694 she published "A Serious Proposal to the Ladies for the Advancement of their True and Great Interest by a lover of her sex," which argued that since spiritual understanding was dependent on the thinking self, women must be encouraged to develop their rational capacity. In "Some Reflections on Marriage" (1700) she presented the idea of a rational, compassionate marriage based on friendship that required female education to create more rational wives and mothers. Catherine Macauley (1731–1791), although justly famous for her work as a historian, also argued in "Letters on Education with Observations on Religious and Metaphysical Subjects" (1770) that girls and boys should be exposed to the same physical sports and academic studies.

Mary Wollstonecraft's (1759–1797) *A Vindication of the Rights of Woman* (1792) also focused on the education of women and the realization of their potential as useful mothers and citizens. While Wollstonecraft's book garnered much attention, it was overshadowed by her notoriety, having returned from revolutionary Paris as an unmarried mother. Her undeserved reputation as a wanton effectively discouraged the appropriation of her convincing rhetoric by such nineteenth-century women's rights campaigners as George Eliot (née Mary Ann Evans) (1819–1880). Many other well-known women writers of this period distanced themselves from such claims. So-called bluestockings Anna Laetitia Barbauld (1743–1825) and Hannah More (1745–1833) were engaged in political and moral pamphleteering but nevertheless argued against the education of women.

A number of male Enlightenment thinkers also backed the education of women, most notably Condorcet (1743–1794), who published a plan in his *Lettres d'un Bourgeois de Newhaven* (1787) demanding not only better education for women but also equal civil and political rights. He viewed female suffrage as the logical extension of the call for universal suffrage. This was followed by his essay "Sur l'admission des Femmes au droit de Cité" (1790), in which he asserted: "Either no member of the human race has real rights or else all have the same."

Karen M. Ford

See also Women's Movement: European; Women's Movement: First Wave/Suffrage; Women's Movement: Second Wave/Feminism
References: Bridenthal, Renate, Susan Mosher Stuard, and Merry E. Wiesner, eds. *Becoming Visible: Women in European History.* 3d ed. Boston: Houghton Mifflin, 1998; Landes, Joan B. *Women and the Public Sphere in the Age of the French Revolution.* Ithaca, NY: Cornell University Press, 1988; Okin, Susan M. *Women in Western Political Thought.* London: Virago, 1980; Pinney, Thomas, ed. *Essays of George Eliot.* London: Routledge and Kegan Paul, 1963; Rendall, Jane. *The Origins of Modern Feminism: Women in Britain, France and the United States.* Basingstoke, UK: Macmillan, 1985; Sapiro, Virginia. *A Vindication of Political Virtue: The Political Theory of Mary Wollstonecraft.* Chicago: University of Chicago Press, 1992; Wollstonecraft, Mary. *A Vindication of the Rights of Woman.* 1792. Reprint, London: Penguin, 1992.

Women's Movement: First Wave/Suffrage (1848–1928)

The women's movement was a campaign for the enfranchisement of women. Because suffrage activists in both the United States and Britain did not have the support of any of the main political parties, they experimented with a range of new tactics for attracting attention and support to their cause, which gave their campaign a distinctly modern feel. An organized women's movement developed first in the United States and then in Britain in the mid-nineteenth century. In both countries woman suffrage increasingly came to be seen as the key to achieving further reform. Woman suffrage supporters lectured, wrote, lobbied, marched, and, in some cases, used more militant tactics, such as the destruction of property. Although American suffragists were initially bolder in their approach, militancy developed first and was more prevalent in Britain, where there was a strong, enduring opposition to what many considered a radical change. In the United States female suffrage finally became law in 1920 as the Nineteenth Amendment to the Constitution. In Britain the vote was extended to some women in 1918, but women as a class were not fully enfranchised until 1928. There is an ongoing debate concerning the relative effectiveness of the two wings—the constitutional

Women at a women's suffrage booth in New York City, 1914. (Bettmann/Corbis)

and the radical—of the movement in achieving reform.

The women's movement in the United States developed in the north and was linked to other reform movements, such as the abolitionist movement. In 1848 the first of a series of women's conventions were held at Seneca Falls, New York, where a "Declaration of Sentiments" was drafted that pointedly made use of the framework of the Declaration of Independence. Leaders of the movement—such as Elizabeth Cady Stanton (1815–1902), Susan B. Anthony (1820–1906), Lucy Stone (1818–1893), and Sojourner Truth (ca. 1797–1883)—went on speaking tours around the country. The demand for women's enfranchisement grew after the Civil War, when the vote was extended to black men but not to women. The two national suffrage organizations amalgamated in 1890 to form the National Ameri-

can Women Suffrage Association (NAWSA). Hoping to win support in the South, many of NAWSA's leaders denied their traditional association with the rights of blacks and used increasingly racist techniques. Despite this, an increasing number of black women actively supported woman suffrage. States held a series of referenda on woman suffrage. The California campaign of 1896 was particularly significant in terms of propaganda. Alice Park (1861–1961), one of the campaign's leaders, was a major advocate of the use of modern advertising methods, promoting what she called "personal advertising" in the form of lapel buttons, suffrage stationery, and baggage stickers. The use of such clever and witty promotional techniques challenged the assumption that suffragists were old-fashioned and humorless. It may also have been less disturbing to voters than more conventional political techniques. Subsequent state referenda campaigns became much more inventive and eye-catching in their propaganda thanks to the success of the California campaign.

Pioneers of woman suffrage in Britain included John Stuart Mill (1806–1873), notably in his work entitled *The Subjugation of Women* (1869). Most British suffragists did not use the mass propaganda techniques of their U.S. counterparts. They were reluctant to address mixed audiences publicly and there were no women's conventions. Class rather than race issues caused divisions. There was disagreement over whether to campaign for woman suffrage with the property limitations then applied to men or to support socialist campaigns for universal adult suffrage. With the founding of the first feminist paper, *The English Woman's Journal,* in 1858, the tradition of great women writers was drawn upon. The first British woman suffrage committee was formed in London in 1867, with other local societies and national organizations soon following. The two most important of these were the National Union of Woman Suffrage Societies (NUWSS) and the Women's Social and Political Union (WSPU). Established in 1897, from 1900 onward the NUWSS was led by Millicent Garrett Fawcett (1847–1929). Its members used moderate constitutional tactics. The WSPU, established in 1903 and led by Emmeline Pankhurst (1857–1928), began to use more radical methods to attract publicity. In response to government inaction and police violence, in 1907 the WSPU shifted from nonviolent tactics to the destruction of property and other militant behavior. According to the press, militant suffragists cut telegraph wires, broke windows, committed arson, burned mailboxes, refused to pay taxes, and carried out hunger strikes to protest their repeated imprisonment.

From Seneca Falls onward, the women's movement faced media hostility, but it was woman suffrage that created the strongest and most organized opposition. In the United States special interests and machine politics played an important role. In particular, links between the women's movement and the temperance movement aroused much concern among brewers and distillers. They and others with vested interests largely operated behind the scenes, providing financial support to antisuffrage organizations. Although their activity was sporadic, antisuffragists in both countries increasingly used political activism. They organized petitions, testified at hearings, cultivated legislators, and published various types of propaganda literature. They also assembled statistics to support their argument that the majority of women did not want the vote. Antisuffragist propaganda defined the context within which the suffragists had to develop their arguments. In addition, the "antis" (as they were commonly known) questioned the femininity and sexuality of the leaders of the suffrage movement, creating a negative stereotype of feminists that has had a long-term impact.

In the United States a second generation of leaders provided new ideas and energy. Carrie Chapman Catt (1859–1947), who served as president of NAWSA from 1900 to 1904 and again from 1915 to 1920, was one of the most politically astute leaders. A skillful organizer, she recruited large numbers of socially prominent and politically influential women. Other leaders, such as Alice Paul (1885–1977) and Harriet E. Blatch (1856–1940), appealed to young people, radicals, and working-class women. Paul, as head of the National Women's Party (NWP), shifted it from an electoral strategy to civil disobedience. In January 1917 Paul and her followers picketed outside the White House—a new tactic at the time. When, four months later, Congress voted to enter the war, suffragists carried signs questioning whether the United States could truly lead a crusade for democracy if its own women remained disenfranchised. They publicly burned President Woodrow Wilson's (1856–1924) speeches and chained themselves to the White House fence. Crowds assaulted the protestors and almost three hundred women were arrested for civil disobedience. These tactics did not become widespread in the United States.

While U.S. women organized for suffrage during wartime, most of those involved in the British women's movement suspended their campaigns after Britain declared war on Germany in 1914. Emmeline and Christabel Pankhurst (1880–1958) turned their energies to supporting the war effort. Although it is generally agreed that World War I played a decisive role in enabling women to finally get the vote, the nature of its impact is still debated. Despite the fact that militant tactics attracted international publicity and gained long-lasting renown, revisionist historians have questioned their effectiveness. For example, even at its peak in 1914, the WSPU only had around 2,000 members, whereas the NUWSS had over 100,000. However, it has also been argued that the attention that militant tactics attracted was important in spurring the growth of the constitutional movement. Many women who did not want to be associated with militancy nonetheless became more aware of the issues and felt impelled to signify their support for woman suffrage by joining the more moderate movement. Despite the eventual success of the woman suffrage movement, the 1920s and 1930s saw a renewed emphasis on female domesticity, which ultimately led to the second wave of feminist activism beginning in the 1960s.

Elizabeth Tacey

See also Abolitionism/Antislavery Movement; Peace and Antiwar Movements (1500–1945); Women's Movement: European; Women's Movement: Second Wave/Feminism

References: Bartley, Patricia. *Votes for Women, 1860–1928*. London: Hodder and Stoughton, 1998. Bolt, Christine. *Feminist Ferment: The Woman Question in the U.S.A. and England, 1870–1940*. London: UCL, 1995; Camhi, Jane Jerome. *Women against Women: American Anti-Suffragism, 1880–1920*. Brooklyn, NY: Carlson, 1994; Marilley, Suzanne M. *Woman Suffrage and the Origins of Liberal Feminism*. Cambridge, MA: Harvard University Press, 1996.

Women's Movement: Second Wave/Feminism (1963–)

A new wave of feminist activism began in the 1960s with the aim of increasing women's opportunities and freedoms not just through legislation but also by challenging the social and cultural factors that combined to confine women to their traditional domestic role. Liberal, socialist, and radical wings worked together and separately on a wide range of issues. In addition to numerous locally based organizations and programs, including feminist writing in a variety of formats, national events such as debates, conferences, and marches were used to raise awareness. Despite its undeniable success, ideological divisions within the movement led to increased tension, leaving the feminist movement vulnerable to attack. A backlash of antifeminist propaganda from the media and right-wing politicians began in the 1980s, and was particularly effective in the United States. Attention continues to be focused on issues such as pay inequalities, childcare provision, and abortion rights, but liberal, individualistic politics have increasingly replaced collective activism and calls for radical change among feminists in Britain and the United States.

The feminist movement effectively began in the United States with the publication of Betty Friedan's (1921–) book *The Feminine Mystique* (1963), which argued that the ideal of the happy housewife and mother was a damaging propaganda myth. Friedan became a figurehead for liberal feminism in the United States as the leader of the National Organization for Women (NOW), which was formed in 1966 to lobby for women's civil rights. Since NOW's members were typically middle-class, middle-aged, and financially successful, an array of other mass-membership organizations geared to the needs of specific groups of women not represented by NOW were quickly formed. Although *The Feminine Mystique* became an international best-seller and manifesto for the movement, liberal feminism remained weaker in Britain. Although the movement that emerged in

Britain from 1968 to 1970 shared many of the same issues, aims, and key texts with the feminist movement in the United States, it was more closely linked to socialist and Marxist groups of the New Left. However, both liberal and socialist feminists used the same type of propaganda methods. Viewing debates, conferences, marches, and articles in journals as the most effective way to educate the public and influence politicians, feminists used these tactics to lobby for important legislation. In particular, they focused on employment and pay issues, childcare, and matters related to sex discrimination and childbearing. In the United States the campaign for state ratification of the Equal Rights Amendment (ERA) drew large numbers of women into political activism. In Britain the Sex Discrimination Act (1975) was preceded by much lobbying and pressure-group activity. Radical feminists' suspicions of male-dominated institutions inclined them to bypass the mainstream political system. Known as "women's liberation," radical feminism first developed in the United States and Britain in the 1960s among a group of young women involved in a series of protest movements that challenged social norms and traditional values. Women began forming their own organizations to address their role and status both within these movements and in society in general, applying the same tactics of social agitation. In the United States involvement in the civil rights movement was particularly important in raising women's awareness of individual rights.

Radical feminists viewed sexual relations as the main cause of inequality and advocated a broader rejection of conventional gender roles. In 1968 feminists in the United States protested at the Miss World pageant in Atlantic City, New Jersey, by "trashing" such accoutrements of femininity as girdles, bras, and mascara, which they deposited in a bin. The publicity this attracted gave women's liberation immediate renown. However, the media transformed the episode into a mythic "bra-burning" event that for years remained the dominant cultural signifier of feminism, perpetuating the representation of feminists as "unfeminine" and unattractive and making many women reluctant to call themselves feminists. There was selective picketing of sex shops and movie theaters showing pornographic films, as well as strikes by female workers in the United States. However, the tactics involving civil disobedience used by militant Edwardian feminists in their campaign for woman suffrage were far from typical of second-wave feminism. Small consciousness-raising groups, intentionally designed to avoid the formal hierarchical structures typical of male politics, became a hallmark of women's liberation. Sharing their experiences of sexism in these groups proved an effective way of increasing individual women's awareness of feminist issues. A variety of grassroots projects, such as establishing women's safe houses and health centers, also drew women into the movement. Radical feminists launched their own magazines for women, such as *Spare Rib* in Britain and *Ms.* in the United States, as an alternative to the male-dominated mainstream press. Women's writing—including journalism, polemics, fiction, and women's history—was one of the foremost vehicles for the women's movement. Significant works included *The Female Eunuch* (1970) by the Australian-born Germaine Greer (1939–).

Feminism became almost fashionable during the 1970s, with a number of government-backed propaganda initiatives, such as the International Woman's Year in 1975. In 1977 the largest convention of women was held in the United States in Houston, Texas, under government sponsorship. However, increased links with mainstream politics intensified the movement's ideological divisions and internal disputes, with the result that it became increasingly diversified and ultimately ceased to exist as a national movement. In the 1980s feminism was scapegoated by the media, as well as by the right-wing political parties that had been returned to power, as responsible for all kinds of negative social change and moral decay. The backlash was stronger and more effective in the United States, particularly in the anti-abortion movement. At the same time, however, women adopted an increasingly positive stance toward the political system and organized to increase their representation.

In the 1990s it was argued that we had entered a "postfeminist" age. Films and advertisements increasingly portrayed women as assertive and empowered, and women's studies courses were replaced by gender studies, encouraging a tendency to assume gender equality. A men's movement developed, with books by such male authors as Neil Lyndon's (1946–) *No More Sex War* (1992). Lyndon questioned the historical assumptions underpinning feminism; however his argument was reduced by critics into a crude claim that men had now become the victims. A number of pressure groups were formed to address men's lack of rights, especially in the area of child custody. Naomi Wolf's (1962–) book *The Beauty Myth* (1990) and Susan Faludi's (1959–) *Backlash* (1992) were particularly influential in documenting how the legal and social gains previously made by the women's movement were now being eroded. Wolf argued that beauty had replaced domesticity as patriarchy's latest propaganda weapon against women. Feminism had successfully convinced women that they were not obliged to adopt traditional roles, but women's time, money, and emotional energy were now being consumed by attempts to conform to the media ideals of beauty with which they were surrounded. Faludi pointed to continuing inequalities between the sexes, such as unequal pay and employment opportunities, that were not being addressed as a result of "antifeminist" trendy media stories. In recent years much of the discussion has moved beyond the issue of equal rights and into territory that remains controversial even among feminists. Increased attention has been focused on the dilemmas posed by women's entry into the labor market, in particular how best to combine independence with domesticity. By the end of the 1990s it had become fashionable to portray the women's movement as confused and uncertain as to its future direction. However, despite its decline as an organized national movement, individual women and specific campaigns continue to address feminist issues.

Elizabeth Tacey

See also Civil Rights Movement; Friedan, Betty; Peace and Antiwar Movements (1945–); Women's Movement: European; Women's Movement: First Wave / Suffrage

References: Bouchier, David. *The Feminist Challenge: The Movement for Women's Liberation in Britain and the USA.* London: Macmillan, 1983; Faludi, Susan. *Backlash: The Undeclared War against Women.* London: Vintage, 1992; Friedan, Betty. *The Feminine Mystique.* London: Gollancz, 1963; Rosen, Ruth. *The World Split Open.* London: Penguin, 2000; Whelehan, Imelda. *Modern Feminist Thought.* Edinburgh: Edinburgh University Press, 1995.

World War I (1914–1918)

Also known as the Great War, World War I introduced a new definition as well as new levels of propaganda to warfare. The war was fought by two evenly matched alliances: the Entente Powers, or Allies (chiefly Great Britain, France, Italy [after 1915], Russia [until 1917], and the United States [as an "Associated Power" thereafter]) versus the Central Powers (chiefly Germany, Austria-Hungary, and Ottoman Turkey). This was the first war in history where both the ideology and practical resources existed for governments to mobilize entire industrial societies for warfare. Propaganda was an essential part of this war effort, developing in all countries as the war progressed. Propaganda was directed toward the home population to support the war, toward neutral countries as a means of influence, and toward the enemy as a weapon.

The entry for "Propaganda" in the 1911 edition of the *Encyclopaedia Britannica* was based on its original religious meaning. As a direct consequence of World War I, in 1921 the German writer Edgar Stern-Rubarth redefined propaganda as a political activity used

The original sheet music cover for George M. Cohan's patriotic song "Over There," 1917, depicting sailor William J. Reilly of the USS Michigan. (Courtesy of David Culbert)

by states at war, which remains the dominant usage. Since World War I organized propaganda has been regarded as an essential part of any war effort, increasing in importance throughout the twentieth century.

The rival alliances that began the war expected a violent but short war. Instead, the approximate equality of the opposing forces produced a stalemate and resulted in a protracted war. In 1915 the British introduced the concept of the "Home Front," based on government intervention on a massive scale in order to restructure the country's economy and society for war, with corresponding sacrifices from the civilian population. The French equivalent was known as the Union Sacré (sacred union), an alliance between government, industry, and civilians. The German version, introduced in late 1916, was called the Hindenburg Program, after General Paul von Hindenburg (1847–1934). Both control of the mass media and propaganda were seen as essential in maintaining national support. Until almost the end of the war, civilians in the most developed and cohesive societies—Great Britain, France, and Germany—generally supported their respective countries' war efforts virtually independent of propaganda. Most armies also were inclined to treat enemy propaganda as a joke unless they were facing imminent defeat.

At the start of the war most countries had only embryonic propaganda organizations. Institutions developed piecemeal, beginning as local initiatives that were later centralized as the war progressed. Propaganda in the form of poster campaigns and slogans became commonplace. The most successful of the war's propagandists were the British, who forged an alliance between newspaper owners, civilian intellectuals, and the government; their system became a model for others. British propaganda was initially aimed chiefly at political and social elites, only developing populist traits by 1916 through the use of such popular mass media as film. British propaganda development met resist-ance from the military and naval authorities, who took more than a year to be convinced of the need for war reporters—and then only under the strictest controls. Resistance also came from established ministries, and a centralized propaganda organization, the Ministry of Information, was not created until early 1918. The basic British approach, known as "the propaganda of facts," was for official propaganda to present events as accurately as possible, but with an interpretation favorable to British policy. Only on rare occasions were stories of horrific enemy behavior released, usually over the objections of professional propagandists. Famous atrocity stories of the war, such as the "crucified Canadian," were frequently spontaneous or private initiatives. Upon entering the war in April 1917, the United States copied this British policy stressing facts by establishing its own Committee on Public Information (CPI), popularly known as the Creel Committee.

By comparison, the German approach to propaganda, which was largely controlled by the army, was unsophisticated and much less successful. German policy often played into the hands of Entente propagandists, as with their treatment of occupied Belgium, the bombing and shelling of British and French cities, and the adoption of unrestricted submarine warfare. Important propaganda work by the French and the Italians has been obscured by publicity given to British successes after the war. Austria-Hungary and Russia made little use of organized propaganda, in contrast to the Bolsheviks after 1917, who regarded it as an essential part of their war effort.

The chief neutral target of Entente propaganda was the United States until its entry into the war. The primarily British campaign was almost invisible, deliberately targeting American elite opinion, in contrast to the strident and public German campaign. The British were able to exploit their common language and their control of the transatlantic telegraph, having cut the German submarine cables at the war's start. The British campaign

Preparedness Day Parade in Baton Rouge, Louisiana, 1916, featuring a 300-foot-long American flag. Note the rigidly-segregated bystanders: whites on the left; blacks on the right. (Courtesy of David Culbert)

played a significant part in the decision by the United States to enter the war. Its scope and success caused a scandal among American isolationists when revealed after the war.

All sides targeted both enemy armies and civilian populations with propaganda. After the war, the British claimed considerable success in using propaganda against the German and Austro-Hungarian home fronts. This fitted in with the postwar German claim that its armies had not been defeated but "stabbed in the back." The belief in propaganda as a weapon of war heavily influenced Adolf Hitler. Subsequent research has shown that no major British propaganda campaign was mounted in either country (although Italian-led propaganda helped defeat Austria-

Hungary), whereas Allied propaganda leaflet campaigns did play a part in the collapse of the German and Austro-Hungarian armies at war's end.

This war was the first to target systematically produced government propaganda at the general public. It paved the way for developments in advertising and other aspects of twentieth-century mass society. The war also marked an important advance in film through newsreels, documentaries, and fictional films in Britain, France, and above all in the United States, laying the foundations for Hollywood's rise to respectability in the 1920s. Finally, the scale and success of mass propaganda led to intellectual disquiet about the consequences in terms of the relationship between government and society.

Stephen Badsey

See also *All Quiet on the Western Front;* Atrocity Propaganda; Australia; Austrian Empire; Beaverbrook, Max; The Big Lie; Black Propaganda; Britain; Bryce Report; Canada; Censorship; CPI; Creel, George; Fakes; Flagg, James Montgomery; France; Germany; Gray Propaganda; Intelligence; Italy; *Mein Kampf;* Memorials and Monuments; Morale; Netherlands, Belgium, and Luxembourg; New Zealand; Northcliffe, Lord; Ottoman Empire/Turkey; Peace and Antiwar Movements (1500–1945); Posters; Psychological Warfare; Raemakers, Louis; Russia; United States; Zimmermann Telegram

References: Cornwall, Mark. *The Undermining of Austria-Hungary.* London: Macmillan, 2000; Fussell, Paul. *The Great War and Modern Memory.* London: Oxford University Press, 1975; Messenger, Gary. *British Propaganda and the State.* Manchester, UK: Manchester University Press, 1992; Ross, Stewart Halsey. *Propaganda for War.* New York: McFarland, 1996; Taylor, Philip M. *Munitions of the Mind.* London: Patrick Stephens, 1990; Welch, David. *Germany, Propaganda and Total War, 1914–18.* New Brunswick, NJ: Rutgers University Press, 2000.

World War II (Britain)

The British approached propaganda in World War II with some trepidation, owing to the reaction against the perceived excesses of

British activity in World War I. Prewar planning proved chaotic, and the "dress rehearsal" in the form of the Munich Pact of 1938 showed that Britain had much to do to prepare for a full-scale war. Despite an acceleration of planning in 1939, the British began the war with an inefficient propaganda apparatus both at home and abroad, specifically the neutral nations. Britain adopted the strategy of conducting "propaganda with fact," basing key campaigns, including its approach to the neutral United States, on facilitating commercial news coverage of the war. This worked well, especially during the London Blitz.

Britain's principal propaganda structures were the Ministry of Information (MoI) for home, allied, and neutral territory, and the Political Warfare Executive (PWE) for enemy territory. The programs of the British Broadcasting Corporation (BBC) earned Britain a powerful reputation for credibility that proved an asset long after the war had ended. Britain also gained much from the rhetorical abilities of Winston Churchill (1874–1965), who served as prime minister from 1940 to 1945, broadcasters like J. B. Priestley (1894–1984), and documentary filmmakers like Humphrey Jennings (1906–1950). The British film industry supported the war effort under the leadership of producers like Michael Balcon (1896–1977) of Ealing Studios.

Britain was slow to specify its war aims and did so only when cornered by U.S. president Franklin Roosevelt (1882–1945). The result was the Atlantic Charter of August 1941, which prepared the way for the postwar United Nations. The charter played its part in convincing the American people that the war was a noble cause and not just a bid to save the British Empire. At home the propaganda apparatus during the war perpetuated the notion of a "people's war" and emphasized the possibility of postwar social change, which paved the way for the postwar Labour government. The war became a key point of reference in postwar British politics, and allusions to Britain's war experience were part of the political campaigns of Margaret Thatcher (1925–).

Nicholas J. Cull

See also BBC; Black Propaganda; Bracken, Brendan; Britain; Censorship; Churchill, Winston; Health; *London Can Take It;* Lord Haw-Haw; MoI; Morale; Netherlands, Belgium, and Luxembourg; Opinion Polls; Orwell, George; Psychological Warfare; PWE; Rumor; Scandinavia; Thatcher, Margaret

References: Aldgate, Anthony, and Jeffrey Richards. *Britain Can Take It: The British Cinema in the Second World War.* Edinburgh: Edinburgh University Press, 1994; Chapman, James. *The British at War: Cinema, State and Propaganda, 1939–1945.* London: I. B. Tauris, 1998; Cruickshank, Charles. *The Fourth Arm: Psychological Warfare, 1938–1945.* Oxford: Oxford University Press, 1981; Cull, Nicholas J. *Selling War: British Propaganda and American "Neutrality" in World War Two.* New York: Oxford University Press, 1995; McLaine, Ian. *Ministry of Morale: Home Front Morale and the Ministry of Information in World War II.* London: Unwin, 1979; Taylor, Philip M. *British Propaganda in the Twentieth Century: Selling Democracy.* Edinburgh: Edinburgh University Press, 1999.

World War II (Germany)

In September 1939 the Nazi regime faced the challenge for which it had been preparing since its takeover of power, namely, a major war. Much of Adolf Hitler's (1889–1945) popularity after he came to power rested on his achievements in foreign policy. A recurring theme in Nazi propaganda before 1939 was that Hitler was a man of peace, but that he was determined to recover German territories "lost" as a result of the Treaty of Versailles (1919). Providing foreign-policy propaganda could highlight the achievements of revisionism without German bloodshed. It was relatively easy then to build consensus that favored overturning the humiliating postwar peace settlements. Much of the responsibility for ensuring that this occurred lay with the Reichsministerium für Volksaufklärung und Propaganda (Reich Ministry for Popular Enlightenment and Propaganda

Enormous vertical red banners, at the time of a Nazi Party rally, Nuremberg, September 1934, seen in Leni Riefenstahl's propaganda film Triumph of the Will. *(Courtesy of David Culbert)*

[RMVP]), whose minister was Joseph Goebbels (1897–1945).

However, there was a basic contradiction between propaganda that presented Hitler as a "man of peace" and an ideology that was inexorably linked to struggle and war. Obsessed by territorial expansion in the east, in November 1937 Hitler confided to his military leaders at the Hossbach Conference that "Germany's problems could only be solved by means of force" (Welch 2001, 62). Accordingly, the RMVP began preparing the nation for war by claiming that the latter was unavoidable and was being forced upon Germany. Anticipating Germany's expansion as a major world power, the propaganda apparatus had to prepare the nation psychologically and to mobilize it into a "fighting community." An ominous slogan of the period proclaimed: "Today Germany, tomorrow the world."

To achieve these goals the propaganda machine was faced with two main tasks: to persuade the nation that the war needed to be fought and to convince the German people that the war could and would be won. The exigencies of war demanded of Goebbels a more intense concern with the tactics of propaganda and greater flexibility to respond to changing military situations. His directive entitled "Guidelines for the Execution of NSDAP Propaganda," issued at the outbreak of war, outlined the means he expected his staff to employ in disseminating propaganda. This included radio and newspapers, films, posters, mass meetings, illustrated lectures, and *Mundpropaganda* ("whisper" or word-of-mouth propaganda). During the course of the war four major propaganda campaigns emerged, all of which were dictated by changing military fortunes: (1) the Blitzkrieg, (2) the Russian campaign, (3) total war and the need for strengthening morale, and (4) promises of retaliation or revenge (*Vergeltung*).

Goebbels's immediate task, once war had been declared, was to counteract the negative opinions held by the population at home. From September 1939 to December 1941 this proved relatively easy in the wake of a succession of stunning German Blitzkrieg victories. Propaganda was able to advertise military victories and to create the expectation of new ones. Thus, during the period of lightning strikes in Poland, Scandinavia, the Low Countries, and France, German belief in an early termination of the war was strengthened by a concerted propaganda campaign, which was able to persuade the population that Germany's actions were a preemptive response to the aggressive intentions of her enemies.

Having decided to invade Russia on 22 June 1941, by the beginning of 1942 Hitler had begun to lose control of the military situation. Between 1942 and 1945, with Germany facing increasing setbacks, government propaganda emphasized the threat posed by the "subhuman" Bolshevik hordes from the

Nazi Party rally, Nuremberg, September 1934. (Courtesy of David Culbert)

East and presented the Reich as the defender of European civilization. A constant theme was "encirclement." Propaganda claimed that Germany was the victim of a conspiracy between a Bolshevik Russia and a plutocratic Britain, orchestrated by Jews who dominated both states. As the situation deteriorated, propaganda increasingly emphasized the terrible fate that would await the German people if the Bolsheviks proved successful.

Russian resistance proved tougher than the Nazis had expected. From 1942 onward Nazi propagandists were forced to shift their focus from the initial euphoria of the Blitzkrieg victories to account for a rapidly deteriorating military situation. The impact of the Nazi defeat at Stalingrad on the morale of the German people cannot be overestimated. It affected their attitude toward the war and created a crisis of confidence in the regime among broad sections of the population.

Goebbels adopted a stance of frankness and realism by proclaiming "total war," demanding the complete mobilization of Germany's human resources for the war effort. During the period 1943–1945, Nazi propaganda encouraged the population to believe that Germany was developing secret weapons capable of transforming the military situation.

In the final years of the war, the notion of retaliation or revenge by means of these "miracle" weapons played a crucial role in sustaining morale. The promise of revenge was widely seen as a panacea for all of Germany's troubles. However, dejection set in once it became apparent that the new weapons would not bring the war to an end. The concept of "total war" had attempted to mobilize the home front and elicit a fanaticism to fight to the death against Bolshevism. The promise of retaliation was the Nazis' last-ditch effort to guarantee future victory. It was a promise that could not be kept. Belief in retaliation and other propaganda clichés had worn thin for quite some time.

In the final year of the war, Goebbels attempted to resurrect the Führer cult by depicting Hitler as a latter-day Frederick the Great, ultimately triumphant in the face of adversity. In the face of the gathering Russian occupation of Germany, this absurd image represented an alarming flight from reality that no amount of propaganda could sustain. The "Hitler myth" could not survive the military reverses and was on the verge of extinction—as was the Third Reich.

David Welch

See also Film (Nazi Germany); Germany; Goebbels, Joseph; Hitler, Adolf; Lord Haw-Haw; Netherlands, Belgium, and Luxembourg; Radio (International); RMVP; Scandinavia

References: Herzstein, Robert. *The War That Hitler Won: The Most Infamous Propaganda Campaign in History.* London: Hamish Hamilton, 1979; Welch, David. *Hitler: Profile of a Dictator.* London: Routledge, 2001;———. *The Third Reich: Politics and Propaganda.* London: Routledge, 2002.

World War II (Italy)
See Fascism, Italian

World War II (Japan)
The roots of Japanese war propaganda date back to the Meiji government's programs to nationalize the population while instilling the idea that Japan was simultaneously attempting to modernize itself and protect Asia. In World War II Japanese propaganda operated on three main fronts: domestically; China and Southeast Asia; and the West.

Massive propaganda programs went well beyond mere military information campaigns. The government planned to popularize the notion that it was Japan's manifest destiny to expand into Asia and bring Asia itself into the modern era. Officially the Cabinet Board of Information, the Japanese government's attempt to copy what it felt was

Nazi Germany's proper course of action, with a centralized Ministry of Propaganda, managed nonmilitary propaganda. However, actual propaganda campaigns developed in a variety of areas. Privately owned entertainment companies such as film giants Toho and Shochiku and the entertainment company Yoshimoto sent platoons of entertainers to China to amuse the imperial troops. These brigades then returned to the home islands and publicized Japanese military success in China. Government-sponsored programs urged writers to reorganize into "voluntary" blocs and write about the effort to educate the civilian population during wartime. Semiprivate advertising companies, employed as subcontractors for the Imperial General Headquarters, designed and produced propaganda leaflets that blanketed villages and fields in China and Southeast Asia. The Japanese military itself often distributed these materials and kept records of how local areas responded.

On the home front, the police and their various special agencies maintained careful surveillance of the domestic population, tabulating rumor campaigns, arresting so-called spies, and censoring media deemed anti-imperial. The government and private business were also interested in boosting tourism as a means of instilling support for the war effort, as well as educating foreigners about Japan. Tourism campaigns were partially orchestrated by the Ministry for Foreign Affairs, as were later campaigns to encourage Asian students to travel to Japan to study.

Following the "China Incident" of 7 July 1937, which restarted war between Japan and China, the Japanese authorities increased censorship and social pressure to support Japanese military aims. As the war in China stagnated, newsreels became a prominent source of propaganda. The prime minister even called the heads of the newsreel companies to his residence and asked them to support the war effort.

After 1937 press controls were tightened even further by the passage of laws such as the Newspaper and Publication Control Ordinance in January 1941. Military press matters came under the direct supervision of the Daihonei Honbu, or Imperial General Headquarters Press Department. This section oversaw all press reports that dealt with any matter, however tangentially related to the military. Even weather reports were banned following the attack on Pearl Harbor on the assumption that such information could provide vital information to the enemy. Japanese newspapers continued to provide coverage—albeit biased—of the war. With few exceptions, a majority of writers and journalists avoided arrest even in the face of draconian laws and censorship regulations. As Japanese military triumphs mounted, domestic excitement created by the initial victories peaked. Editors and writers, along with the general population, believed in the justice of Japan's cause and its ability to defeat its enemies.

With the attack on Pearl Harbor in December 1941, Japan was faced with the daunting military task of fighting on two fronts simultaneously—in China and the Pacific. The Japanese government asked its people, already under duress since the mid-1930s, to endure further economic restrictions, recycle scarce materials, do with less, and live by wartime slogans such as "luxury is the enemy." During the many Pacific island battles, American troops found it difficult to take Japanese prisoners alive. A great number of both Japanese civilian and military personnel often chose suicide over capture. Intense domestic pressure and propaganda campaigns often left Japanese infantrymen little choice.

While Japanese propaganda generally failed in Asia, domestically the results were different. By the summer of 1945 the United States had to acknowledge that Japanese rule, with the emperor as head, must be left intact or a viable peace would not be obtainable. Following the Japanese capitulation on 15 August 1945, the U.S.-managed occupation was quick to install its own pro-Western propaganda institutions. However, the occu-

pation forces soon realized that they had neither the human resources nor the ability needed to "democratize" Japan single-handedly. Ironically, American occupation forces employed many of the same high-level Japanese special police and military propagandists who, only months earlier, had been fighting against the West.

Barak Kushner

See also Australia; China; Indonesia; Japan; Korea; Philippines; Radio (International); Southeast Asia; Tokyo Rose; World War II (United States)

References: Dower, John. *War without Mercy: Race and Power in the Pacific War.* New York: Pantheon, 1986;———. *Embracing Defeat: Japan in the Wake of World War II.* New York: Norton, 1999; Friend, Theodore. *The Blue-eyed Enemy.* Princeton, NJ: Princeton University Press, 1988; Garon, Sheldon. *Molding Japanese Minds.* Princeton, NJ: Princeton University Press, 1997; Ienaga, Saburo. *The Pacific War, 1931–1945.* New York: Random House, 1978; Lebra, Joyce C. *Jungle Alliance, Japan and the Indian National Army.* Singapore: Asia Pacific Press, 1971; Meo, L. D. *Japan's Radio War on Australia.* Melbourne: Melbourne University Press, 1968; Sato, Masaharu, and Barak, Kushner. "Negro Propaganda Operations: Japan's Short-wave Radio Broadcasts for World War II Black Americans." *Historical Journal of Film, Radio and Television* 19, 1 (1999): 5–26; Shillony, Ben-Ami. *Politics and Culture in Wartime Japan.* New York: Oxford University Press, 1981; Young, Louise. *Japan's Total Empire, Manchuria and the Culture of Wartime Imperialism.* Berkeley: University of California Press, 1998.

World War II (Russia)

Known in Russia as the "Great Patriotic War," World War II propaganda played a central role in rallying the Soviet population to resist the Nazi invasion. The German attack on the Soviet Union (Operation Barbarossa) found the regime of Joseph Stalin (1897–1953) ill prepared for battle. The Nazi forces nearly succeeded in breaking the Soviet Union in the months that followed. By November the German army had seized the Ukrainian Republic, besieged Leningrad (present-day Saint Petersburg, the USSR's second-largest city), and threatened Moscow itself. By the end of 1941, however, the German forces had lost their momentum. German movements were increasingly hampered by harsh winter weather, attacks by partisans, and difficulties in maintaining overextended supply lines. At the same time, the Red Army had recovered from the initial blow and began to strike back.

After the initial shock, including a rumored escape from the capital by Stalin himself, the formidable Soviet propaganda machine hit its stride almost immediately. Within two days of the invasion Vyacheslav Molotov (1890–1986), the commissar for foreign affairs, addressed the nation by radio in an angry and defiant tone. Newsreels captured the grim-faced determination of Soviet citizens while listening to his speech, images that were on Soviet screens within a week. Stalin was able to launch his call to arms at the start of July. He addressed his audience as "brothers and sisters" (not comrades) and called for a defense of the *rodina* (motherland).

One famous poster reminded viewers: "Higher vigilance in every unit—always remember the treachery and baseness of the enemy!" Another warned: "When on lookout duty, check the branches, too. Do not sleep—you are responsible for everyone." Finally, one poster showing fighters escorting bombers in formation over Red Square proclaimed "Long Live the Mighty Aviation of the Country of Socialism!" at a time when there was no Soviet airforce to speak of.

In the spring of 1942 the German army renewed its offensive, including an attempt to crush the city of Stalingrad (present-day Volgograd). Here, as elsewhere, Soviet forces put up fierce resistance even after the Germans had reduced the city to rubble. In such desperate moments the Soviet government had to rely on the support of the people. To increase popular enthusiasm for the war, Stalin reshaped his domestic policies to heighten the patriotic spirit. Nationalistic slogans replaced much of the Communist

rhetoric in official pronouncements and the mass media.

Cinema—that "most important of all the arts," according to Lenin—was called to arms. Esfir Shub (1894–1959) was able to make two full-length documentaries: *Fascism Will Be Destroyed* (1941) and *Homeland* (1942). Both films were able to make disastrous outcomes appear successful. The name of master filmmaker Dziga Vertov (1896–1954) was attached to three films during the war years: *Blood for Blood, Death for Death* (1941), *In the High Zone* (1941), and the five-reel *To You, Front!* (1942).

The cities of Leningrad and Stalingrad became physical embodiments of—and thus propaganda gifts to—the Soviet Union's moral right to victory. After several failed attempts to take Leningrad by storm, Nazi forces settled in for a 900-day siege (August 1941 to January 1944), which was publicized and eulogized as an example of unprecedented courage and heroism. With Leningrad straining for victory—with no electricity, heat, or running water, and very little food—how could a Soviet citizen falter in the struggle against Fascism? When news of the utter heroism and sacrifice displayed during the siege of Stalingrad filled the newspapers, death or victory became the only options. With the surrender of German commander Friedrich von Paulus (1890–1957) to the Soviet forces in January 1943, victory was a certainty.

After Stalingrad, the Soviet Union held the initiative for the rest of the war. By the end of 1943, the Red Army had broken through the German siege of Leningrad and recaptured much of the Ukrainian Republic. By the end of 1944, the front had moved beyond the 1939 Soviet frontiers into Eastern Europe. Filmmaker Aleksander Dovzhenko (1894–1956) made *The Battle for Our Soviet Ukraine* (1943)—released in the United States as *Ukraine in Flames* (1944)—and *Victory in the Eastern Ukraine* (1945). The political message of these films was that irrespective of the events of the recent past, the Ukraine was part of the Soviet Union. If the liberated Ukraine was "eastern," then parts of Poland would soon be part of the Ukraine too.

With a decisive superiority in troops and weaponry, Soviet forces drove into eastern Germany, capturing Berlin in May 1945. As victory seemed within reach, the need for a celebration became paramount. Yelizaveta Svilova (1900–1975) directed the film *Berlin,* representing a compilation of the work of army cameramen, which was released in June 1945 as part of the victory celebrations.

The end of World War II saw the Soviet Union emerge as one of the world's two greatest military powers. Its battle-tested forces occupied most of Eastern Europe. These achievements came at a high cost, including the deaths of an estimated 20 million Soviet soldiers and civilians. The loss itself was fruitful propaganda material during the war and for decades thereafter. The dramatic events of the war years left a deep impact on Soviet literature, which was soon utilized in a propagandizing capacity. A genre of patriotic essays blossomed, including *Volga-Stalingrad* (1942) by Vassilii Grossman (1905–1964), who declared: "Here it is, the Russian character at large! A person might seem so ordinary, but as disaster strikes, no matter whether big or small, out comes a great strength—personal beauty." In *A Man's Life Story* (1942) Mikhail Sholokov (1905–1984) wrote: "I hope that this man, a Russian man of iron will, will survive and raise a son strong enough to cope with any difficulties, overcome all kinds of hardship." Soviet literature of the period, like all popular culture, urged the population to take action and stressed their moral superiority. The horror stories unearthed by Soviet camera teams as the Red Army moved west only underscored this moral certainty. The victory celebrations in Red Square in the summer of 1945 ushered in a new period of conviction—repeated each year in the poignant celebrations on "Victory Day" (8 May).

Graham Roberts

See also Film (Documentary); International; Lenin, Vladimir Ilyich; Russia; Stalin, Joseph
References: Hosking, Geoffrey. *A History of the Soviet Union.* London: Fontana, 1992; Pipes, Richard. *Russia under the Soviet Regime.* London: Harper, 1994; Taylor, Richard. *Film Propaganda: Soviet Russia and Nazi Germany.* London: I. B. Tauris, 1998.

World War II (United States)

The story of U.S. propaganda during World War II can be divided into two phases: a period of neutrality from September 1939 to December 1941, during which a great debate raged among the population at large, and the period of U.S. involvement in the war, when the government mobilized a major propaganda effort through the Office of War Information (OWI). Both phases witnessed a key role being played by the commercial media.

Although Adolf Hitler (1889–1945) was never popular in the United States, the widespread feeling that the U.S. role in World War I had been a mistake cooled American reactions to the outbreak of war. President Franklin D. Roosevelt (1882–1945) refused to ask his people to be "neutral in spirit" and called for the revision of U.S. neutrality laws to at least allow war materials to be sold to the Allies. The great neutrality debate began in earnest following the fall of France in June 1940. The pro-Allies lobby consisted of the moderate Committee to Defend America by Aiding the Allies and an actively interventionist Century Group (later known as the Fight for Freedom Committee). The proneutrality position was represented by the America First Committee. The isolationist camp included newspapers—especially those owned by William Randolph Hearst (1863–1951), the influential *Chicago Tribune,* and such well-known individuals as Charles Lindbergh (1902–1974). Both sides used rallies, petitions, and demonstrations to advance their causes. In Hollywood the independent producer Walter Wanger (1894–1968) and the Warner Bros. studio released a number of films with a political message, including *For-*

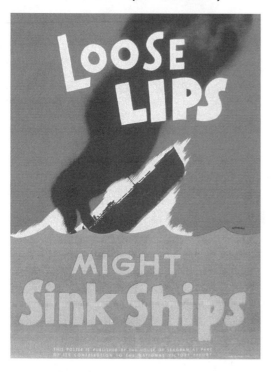

World War II U.S. poster. Every combatant made similar appeals for discretion. (National Archives)

eign Correspondent (1940) and *Confessions of a Nazi Spy* (1939). Isolationists in the Senate denounced such ventures as propaganda on behalf of Jewish and pro-British vested interests.

President Roosevelt initially took a backseat in the debate because of the impending presidential election. In December 1940 he demonstrated more active leadership by advancing his "Lend Lease" aid policy through a "fireside chat" over the radio. The Lend-Lease Act, promising "all aid short of war," passed Congress on March 15, 1941. As part of its policy of rearmament, the Roosevelt administration established a number of propaganda and information organizations, including the Rockefeller Bureau to rally opinion in Latin America (1940); the Office of Government Reports (1939) and Office of Facts and Figures (1940) to present information at home; and the Office of the Coordinator of Information, a new covert intelligence agency that included a propaganda branch. In August 1941 Roosevelt persuaded Churchill to sign

the Atlantic Charter, calling for a postwar United Nations and a policy of unconditional surrender. By the time of the Japanese attack on Pearl Harbor, December 7, 1941, the debate over U.S. foreign policy had been all but settled.

In the summer of 1942 the U.S. government regrouped it various propaganda agencies into a single Office of War Information (OWI), although some psychological operations remained under the new Office of Strategic Services (OSS). OWI tactical campaigns included massive leaflet drops to support the invasion of North Africa in 1942, and special air-dropped newspapers for occupied countries and eventually even enemy territory. Psychological warfare teams advanced alongside U.S. military forces and had considerable success in appealing to the enemy to surrender. At home campaigns conceived in collaboration with the commercial media included an effort to engage women in heavy-duty war work. During this campaign *Saturday Evening Post* artist Norman Rockwell (1894–1978) created the character of Rosie the Riveter. Some of the most important ideological initiatives came from outside the OWI. In January 1941 Henry Luce (1898–1967), the editor of *Time,* wrote an editorial proclaiming the "American Century." The idea that the time had come for American global leadership gained wide acceptance during the war. Internationalism received a boost from lawyer and Republican presidential candidate Wendell Willkie (1892–1944) and his book *One World* (1943). Roosevelt also contributed to the nation's morale, especially in his definition of Allied war aims. The notion of the Four Freedoms, dating from January 1941 (freedom of speech and of worship, freedom from fear and from want) proved particularly potent both in the United States and around the world. For a highly successful war bond drive Rockwell produced a series of paintings illustrating each of these freedoms.

The United States used propaganda to orient troops (most famously in the U.S. Army

Recruiting poster for women during World War II. (National Archives)

Signal Corps film series Why We Fight) and to motivate its civilian population. The approach varied between the European and Pacific theaters. Whereas in Europe the United States depicted the enemy as an evil regime, in Asia the enemy was depicted as an entire race. U.S. war bond posters variously pictured the Japanese as ratlike or simian monsters. U.S. newspaper cartoons took up the theme without official prompting, with the result that the fanatical Japanese soldier became a familiar and enduring stereotype. Parallel Japanese ideas about the West led to a war of mutual extermination on the island battlefields of the Pacific. Propaganda laid the foundation for U.S. use of the atomic bomb against Japan in August 1945.

During the war the U.S. government carefully controlled its use of atrocity stories, a tactic that had been much discredited following World War I. The American public seemed reluctant to believe the first news of Nazi genocide (which came from Jewish and Polish sources), and the U.S. government made little attempt to further publicize the story. The government often released news of Japanese atrocities in a very controlled way—often several months after the events became known—though not in the case of the notorious Bataan Death March, in which thousands of Allied soldiers died on their way to Japanese prisoner-of-war camps.

The extraordinary level of government and commercial propaganda in the United States during the war created a number of myths that crumbled in the postwar period. Joseph Stalin proved to be something less than the avuncular nationalist of U.S. wartime propaganda, nor did Chiang Kai-shek in China live up to his image as the democratic strongman of Asia. In Republican propaganda the apologies for Stalin were seen as evidence of left-wing domination of the Roosevelt administration, and the "loss" of China became evidence that Chiang had been betrayed by an American enemy within. Such claims set the stage for McCarthyism. The apparatus of U.S. wartime propaganda, such as the Voice of America (VOA) radio station, survived the war to become the core of the U.S. propaganda effort in the Cold War. On the battlefield Gen. Dwight D. Eisenhower (1890–1969) became convinced of the power of the "P" (psychological factor) in warfare and championed the use of propaganda during his presidency.

Nicholas J. Cull.

See also Capra, Frank; *Casablanca;* Censorship; Intelligence; OWI; Peace and Antiwar Movements (1500–1945); Psychological Warfare; Radio (International); Roosevelt, Franklin D.; United States; VOA; Why We Fight; World War II (Britain); World War II (Germany); World War II (Japan)

References: Blum, John M. *V Was for Victory: Politics and American Culture during World War II.* New York: Harcourt Brace Jovanovich, 1976; Casey, Steven. *Cautious Crusade: Franklin D. Roosevelt, American Public Opinion and the War against Nazi Germany.* New York: Oxford University Press, 2001; Dower, John. *War without Mercy: Race and Power in the Pacific War.* New York: Pantheon, 1986; Roeder, George H. *The Censored War: American Visual Experience during World War Two.* New Haven, CT: Yale University Press, 1993; Steele, Richard W. *Propaganda in an Open Society: The Roosevelt Administration and the Media, 1933–1941.* Westport, CT: Greenwood, 1985; Winkler, Allan M. *The Politics of Propaganda: The Office of War Information, 1942–1945.* New Haven, CT: Yale University Press, 1978.

World Wide Web

See Internet

Yugoslavia
See Balkans

Z

Zimmermann Telegram (1917)

This secret German telegram, which was leaked to the U.S. press by British intelligence, did much to bring the United States into World War I. It stands as a perfect example of intelligence and propaganda working hand in hand. In January 1917 British naval intelligence intercepted and decoded a telegram from Arthur Zimmermann (1864–1940), head of the German foreign office, to his ambassador in Mexico City, instructing him to offer Mexico the states of Texas, Arizona, and New Mexico if it would join Germany in any future war against the United States. The British, eager to draw the United States into the war, passed the telegram to the U.S. government, and on 1 March its contents became public. Americans were outraged, including those living in the traditionally isolationist regions of the West and Midwest. Coupled with unrestricted German submarine attacks against U.S. vessels, the telegram suggested that Germany now directly threatened the United States. It helped to unite public opinion behind the decision of President Woodrow Wilson (1856–1924) to ask Congress for a declaration of war, which he obtained on 6 April 1917.

Nicholas J. Cull

See also Britain; Intelligence; Mexico; United States; World War I

References: Beesley, Patrick. *Room 40: British Naval Intelligence, 1914–1918.* Oxford: Oxford University Press, 1984; Sanders, Michael, and Philip M. Taylor. *British Propaganda during the First World War.* London: Macmillan, 1982; Tuchman, Barbara. *The Zimmermann Telegram.* New York: Simon and Schuster, 1956.

Zinoviev Letter (1924)

Considered by some to be a fake used for propaganda purposes, this letter, like the Zimmerman telegram of 1917, is an example of the role that intelligence services can play in the area of propaganda. The letter purported to come from Grigori Zinoviev (1883–1940), chairman of the Comintern, a Soviet organization dedicated to extending the revolution. In it Zinoviev urged the British Communist Party to ferment dissent within the British army. The letter appeared in the conservative *Daily Mail* newspaper on 25 October 1924—a politically sensitive moment—just a few days before Britain's first Labour government faced a general election. Relations with the Soviet Union had been an issue ever since Ramsey Macdonald (1866–1937), the Labour prime minister, had concluded a trade treaty with Russia. Now the

Labour Party's opponents hammered home the "Red Letter" story, smearing the entire left by associating it with the Communist Party. On the eve of the election newsstands carried posters showing the Soviet and British flags and the caption: "Under which flag?" By some accounts—especially those of Labour politicians seeking to explain their defeat—it helped the Conservative Party to win by scaring Liberal voters into voting Conservative.

The exact origin of the letter remains uncertain. If genuine, as some have claimed, its capture represents a formidable intelligence coup. If fake, possible culprits include Polish intelligence agents and/or White Russian exiles eager to promote anti-Soviet feeling. The letter was originally passed along to the British government, where Prime Minister Macdonald resolved to lodge a formal protest at the Soviet embassy, but before this could be done someone leaked the letter to the *Daily Mail*. Plausible candidates for the leak include Joseph Ball (1885–1961), an officer in MI5 (British intelligence) who later joined the Conservative Party's Central Office where he worked as a propagandist and deployed techniques that included espionage and black propaganda.

Nicholas J. Cull

See also Elections (Britain); Fakes; Intelligence; Zimmermann Telegram

References: Chester, Lewis, Stephen Fray, and Hugo Young. *The Zinoviev Letter.* London: Heinemann, 1967; Ferris, John, and Uri Bar-Joseph. "Getting Marlow to Hold His Tongue: The Conservative Party, the Intelligence Services and the Zinoviev Letter." *Intelligence and National Security* 8, 4 (October 1993): 100–137.

Zionism

This political movement has as its goal the empowerment of the Jews through a return of the Jewish people to their ancestral homeland. The name of the movement is derived from the word "Zion," which refers to a mountain near Jerusalem. The official beginnings of Zionism can be traced back to the nationalistic stirrings of nineteenth-century Europe, coupled with the rise of modern anti-Semitism, which resulted in increasing persecution of the Jews of Europe as the century progressed. Theodor Herzl (1860–1904), the founder of political Zionism, was a journalist, playwright, and essayist from an assimilated Austrian Jewish family. The founding of the movement was heralded both by the publication of his most famous work, *Der Judenstaat* (The Jewish State), in 1896 and the convening of the First Zionist Congress in Basel, Switzerland, in 1897.

Taking its cue from Herzl, who was keenly aware of the importance of publicity, the Zionist movement initiated a number of political, cultural, and educational campaigns. Intent on regaining the ancestral homeland of the Jews, Herzl sought to unify European Jewry through a distinct secular nationalistic vision, namely, that of a "New Jewish Man" returning to the soil as a farmer and bringing about the uplifting of Palestine through the revival of the Hebrew language and Hebrew culture. Zionism benefited from the communications revolution of the late nineteenth and early twentieth century, which witnessed the proliferation of inexpensive printing methods and, later, the appearance of film and radio to convey its message to a worldwide Jewish audience. Ironically, Zionist propaganda—which, prior to 1933, had emphasized an agrarian future for the Jewish people—was directed at and achieved its greatest following among an urban, assimilated, middle-class Jewish audience.

Herzl himself was presented as the archetype of the "New Jew" that Zionism sought to create through art and literature. Herzl and the Zionists were pioneers in the use of visual images. Indeed, Herzl believed that it was crucial for people to "think in images," which provided the primary motivation for action. As a journalist Herzl recognized the powerful symbolic impact of music, as well as other cultural activities, on an educated middle class. The earliest publicity material of Herzlian Zionism consisted of a series of postcards and delegates' cards produced in conjunction with the First Zionist Congress. Although crude by later standards, these items helped introduce the pantheon of Zionist heroes to a wide audience, notably Herzl and Max Nordau (1849–1923), who formed the mainstay of Zionist imagery through World War I. After 1918 a new set of iconic figures emerged in the persons of Chaim Weizmann (1874–1952) and Albert Einstein (1879–1955), among others. The latter, in particular, became one of the most popular speakers at Zionist rallies.

In addition to championing these heroes, Zionism promoted the development of the "Muscular Jew." Taking its cue from the late-nineteenth-century mania for physical prowess and its perceived link to moral fitness, Zionist organizations promoted Jewish gymnasiums. In the wake of the creation of the modern Olympics in 1896, the World Zionist Organization (WZO) established the Maccabiah Games, named after the heroic figures of the biblical story of the Maccabees. These games were seen as a means of promoting physical development to meet the challenges of rebuilding a Jewish homeland. Maccabean organizations were established throughout Europe and the United States. The Maccabiah Games are still held every four years in Israel.

In 1901 Keren Kayemeth Leisrael (Jewish National Fund, or JNF) was established to finance the purchase of land in Palestine and to sponsor the redevelopment of the area. The JNF sold shares, issued stamps, and created souvenirs (such as tin boxes to collect money) using a variety of agrarian images as backdrops. The most successful and enduring of these campaigns—which continues to this day—is the reforestation of land through the sale of trees as memorials. A poster campaign begun in the aftermath of World War I showed the growth of Palestine (Israel after 1948) by emphasizing the collective agricultural movement known as the kibbutz.

Zionist organizations were slow to develop film as a propaganda medium, in part because of a shortage of funds. The most prominent example of pre–World War II Zionist film propaganda was *Land of Promise,* commissioned by the JNF and the Palestine Foundation Fund and premiered in Europe and the United States in 1935. Although not the first Zionist film, it was unique for its length (nearly an hour) and its imagery, which presented Palestine not merely as an agrarian center but a developing country where industry and intellectual life flourished. Shown in Nazi Germany the same year the infamous Nuremberg Laws were promulgated, the film reflected the new image of Palestine as a refuge for Jews facing the rising tide of Fascism. The film also reflected a relatively new campaign by Zionist organizations, namely, the promotion of tourism to Palestine. Through posters, postcards, and other ready-made souvenirs, it was marketed as a "must see" destination for assimilated Western Jews who had little or no intention of settling there. Although interrupted by World War II, the tourism industry became a mainstay of the emerging Israeli economy.

In the aftermath of World War II, Zionist propaganda continued to emphasize Palestine/Israel as a place of refuge for persecuted Jews. Although following 1948 the most prominent publicity has been that of the JNF, in the 1960s and 1970s many Zionist and pro-Zionist organizations became involved in the Movement for Soviet Jewry. The message "Never Again," a reference to the Holocaust, became a prominent part of the movement and appeared on posters, leaflets, and in a number of films. No longer emphasizing the agrarian vision of a "New Jew," the post-1945 Zionist message focused on Israel as a place where Jews are empowered by statehood. Zionist publicity achieved remarkable success in the aftermath of the Six-Day War (June 1967), when immigration to Israel (known as *Aliyah* in Hebrew) increased dramatically.

Frederic Krome

See also Herzl, Theodor; Israel

References: Berkowitz, Michael. *Zionist Culture and West European Jewry before the First World War.* New York: Cambridge University Press, 1993; ———. *Western Jewry and the Zionist Project,* *1914–1933.* New York: Cambridge University Press, 1997; Raider, Mark A. *The Emergence of American Zionism.* New York: New York University Press, 1998.

INDEX

ABOUT THE EDITORS

David Culbert is professor of history, Louisiana State University, Baton Rouge, and editor of the *Historical Journal of Film, Radio and Television.* He is the coauthor of *World War II, Film and History* (1996) and editor-in-chief of *Film and Propaganda in America: A Documentary History,* 5 vols. plus microfiche (1990–1993).

Nicholas J. Cull is professor of American studies and director of the Centre for American Studies at the University of Leicester, UK. He has written widely on the history of propaganda, including his 1995 book *Selling War: British Propaganda and American "Neutrality" in the Second World War.* He is currently completing a history of U.S. propaganda overseas since 1945.

David Welch is professor of modern history and director of the Centre for the Study of Propaganda at the University of Kent at Canterbury, UK. His books include *The Third Reich: Politics and Propaganda,* 2d edition (2002), *Hitler: Profile of a Dictator* (2001); *Propaganda and the German Cinema 1933–45* (2001), and *Germany, Propaganda and Total War, 1914–1918* (2001). He is currently writing a history of propaganda in the twentieth century.